# Absolute
## returns

Founded in 1807, John Wiley & Sons is the oldest independent publishing company in the United States. With offices in North America, Europe, Australia, and Asia, Wiley is globally committed to developing and marketing print and electronic products and services for our customers' professional and personal knowledge and understanding.

The Wiley Finance series contains books written specifically for finance and investment professionals as well as sophisticated individual investors and their financial advisors. Book topics range from portfolio management to e-commerce, risk management, financial engineering, valuation and financial instrument analysis, as well as much more.

For a list of available titles, please visit our Web site at www.WileyFinance.com.

# Absolute
# returns

*The Risk and Opportunities
of Hedge Fund Investing*

# ALEXANDER M. INEICHEN

John Wiley & Sons, Inc.

Published by John Wiley & Sons, Inc., Hoboken, New Jersey.
Published simultaneously in Canada.

The documents "In Search of Alpha—Investing in Hedge Funds" © 2000 and "The Search for Alpha Continues—Do Hedge Funds Managers Add Value?" © 2001 are © UBS AG, and extracts from these documents are used with the permission of UBS AG.

For general information on our other products and services, or technical support, please contact our Customer Care Department within the United States at 800-762-2974, outside the United States at 317-572-3993 or fax 317-572-4002.

Wiley also publishes its books in a variety of electronic formats. Some content that appears in print may not be available in electronic books.

*Library of Congress Cataloging-in-Publication Data:*

Ineichen, Alexander.
    Absolute returns : the risk and opportunities of Hedge Fund investing
  / Alexander Ineichen.
        p.   cm.—(Wiley finance series)
    Includes bibliographical references and index.
      ISBN 0-471-25120-8 (cloth : alk. paper)
    1. Hedge funds.   I. Title: Risk and opportunities of Hedge Fund
investing.   II. Title.   III. Series.
      HG4530 .I446   2002
      332.64'5—dc21                                        2002010014

Printed in the United States of America.

10   9   8   7   6   5   4

*To Claudia, Natasha, and Thomas*

# contents

# acknowledgments

I owe thanks to so many people that it is difficult to come up with a complete list. A lot of credit for my written research as an analyst and as an author of this book has to be attributed to experienced and prudent investment professionals in the hedge fund industry as well as colleagues in research, prime brokerage, trading, and related areas. I would like to thank Keith Ackerman, Paddy Dear, Arun Gowda, Jens Johansen, William Kennedy, Rob Kirkwood, Scott Mixon, Simon Phillips, and Alan Scowcroft from UBS Warburg; Daniel Edelman and Mike Welch from UBS O'Connor; and David Smith from GAM, Michael J. Sacks from Grosvenor Capital Management, Donald J. Halldin, William H. Lawrence, and John L. Sica from Meridian Capital Partners for their invaluable feedback and generous assistance. A special gratitude I owe the team of the Quellos Group, namely Phillip Vitale and Bryan White, for helping me define and clarify my thoughts and for sharing information without which I would be without an edge. A special thanks to my wife, Claudia, and my children, Natasha and Thomas, who have nearly always been there with their support, understanding, and love.

Once upon a time investors took a holistic approach to their investments. Whether individuals or institutions, they would seek to generate returns by balancing stocks, bonds, and cash in a single portfolio. This was the first investment management paradigm. This approach was primarily implemented by the trust department of the neighborhood bank. This paradigm suffered two great weaknesses: mediocre returns and lack of accountability.

These weaknesses were the seeds that enabled a whole new investment management industry and a shift to the second paradigm: the relative performance game. Evaluating the success of a manager with the holistic approach was tricky. With the relative return approach, in contrast, clearly measurable passive market indexes provided the benchmark against which performance could be measured and investment managers held accountable. The second paradigm fits nicely with modern portfolio theory (MPT) and seminal academic work on performance evaluation. With a final push from regulatory changes, the ERISA Act of 1974 in particular, the second paradigm firmly established its roots in the United States and elsewhere.

However, the introduction of clear and meaningful performance evaluation highlighted one of active management's greatest weaknesses: poor performance. "Beating the benchmark" became the focus of a negative-sum game where only a small minority of managers outperforms the benchmark on a consistent basis. The introduction of a market benchmark introduced further negative phenomena such as an incentive to focus on asset growth (as opposed to performance), to execute trend following strategies (as opposed to contrarian strategies), and to seek mediocrity (as opposed to meritocracy). Throughout the 1990s it became clear that in the relative return paradigm one cannot win Charles Ellis' "loser's game," that there are more investment strategies than buy-and-hold, that increased market liquidity allowed efficient replication of major market benchmarks through passive strategies, and that any alpha, once isolated, could be transported onto any liquid market benchmark. As a result, interests between investors and managers had become misaligned.

Absolute return strategies are increasingly being embraced by individuals and institutional investors as the third investment paradigm. The absolute return approach seeks to solve some of the issues of the relative return approach. Investors introduce an absolute yardstick against which managers get measured. This avoids some of the pitfalls of the relative return approach, namely peer-group hugging, search for mediocrity, and misalignment of interests between manager and investor. However, the absolute return approach introduces new issues to be resolved. First, the loose mandate of absolute return managers (i.e., the lack of tracking error constraints) results in a wide dispersion between managers. This means that the costs and risks of manager selection as well as potential benefits are higher with the absolute return approach than with the relative return approach. Second, a paradigm shift (i.e., the introduction of something new) reduces transparency and increases costs. This is an advantage for early adapters picking up a risk premium, but a disadvantage for latecomers.

Active asset managers are hired and paid to exploit investment opportunities. Any investment opportunity, to state the obvious, involves risk. Absolute return managers manage money similarly to relative return managers, with the risk-free rate being the benchmark instead of a market index. However, absolute return managers do not hold positions that are passively replicable at low cost. Absolute return managers define risk as *total* risk, whereas in the relative return paradigm risk is defined relative to a benchmark; that is, risk is defined as *active* risk. Unlike with relative return managers, the paramount objectives of absolute return managers are avoiding absolute financial losses, preserving principal, as well as actively managing portfolio volatility. Defining risk as active risk means that it is the market that determines the investor's risk, and not the manager.

A further difference between the relative return and absolute return approach lies in the opportunity set. Putting it crudely: The absolute manager invests in the full range of investment opportunities whereas the relative return manager does not. An absolute return manager, for example, can hedge unwanted risk, can change risk profile by levering and delevering according to changes in opportunity set, can exploit inefficiencies on the short side, or can explore valuation differences among equal or similar financial instruments. For a skilled asset manager, a greater pool of investment opportunities leads to greater performance. There are also differences in terms of the magnitude of the investment opportunities in addition to differences in the opportunity set. If a relative return manager has a large cap U.S. equity market index as investment benchmark, he or she is forced to exploit inefficiencies in one of the most efficient financial markets in the world. The magnitude of mispricing is unlikely to be large and the cost of finding the inefficiency prohibitively high.

All investors define risk as total risk, that is, as destruction of principal or wealth and not being able to meet liabilities. Total risk is like an iceberg (similar to the one shown on the dust jacket of this book)—partly measurable (visible) and partly not. Ignoring the invisible portion of an iceberg because of its invisibility is not necessarily a wise risk management decision. Any definition of risk that does not include risk in its entirety is like only worrying about the layout of deck chairs on the *Titanic*.

ALEXANDER M. INEICHEN, CFA

*London, April 22, 2002*

# The Hedge Fund Industry

# Introducing Absolute Returns

*During the French Revolution such speculators were known as
agitateurs, and they were beheaded.*

—Michel Sapin*

## HISTORY OF THE ABSOLUTE RETURN APPROACH

### Prologue to the Twentieth Century

Most market observers put down 1949 as the starting date for so-called absolute return managers, that is, the hedge fund industry. However, if we loosen the definition of hedge funds and define hedge funds as individuals or partners pursuing absolute return strategies by utilizing traditional as well as nontraditional instruments and methods, leverage, and optionality, then the starting date for absolute return strategies dates further back than 1949.

One early reference to a trade involving nontraditional instruments and optionality appears in the Bible. Apparently, Joseph wished to marry Rachel, the youngest daughter of Leban. According to Frauenfelder (1987), Leban, the father, sold a (European style call) option with a maturity of seven years on his daughter (considered the underlying asset). Joseph paid the price of the option through his own labor. Unfortunately, at expiration Leban gave Joseph the older daughter, Leah, as wife, after which Joseph bought another option on Rachel (same maturity). Calling Joseph the first absolute manager would be a stretch. (Today absolute return managers care about settlement risk.) However, the trade involved nontraditional instruments and optionality, and risk and reward were evaluated in absolute return space.

Gastineau (1988) quotes Aristotle's writings as the starting point for

---

*Michel Sapin, former French Finance Minister, on speculative attacks on the franc.
From Bekier (1996).

options. One could argue that Aristotle told the story of the first directional macro trade: Thales, a poor philosopher of Miletus, developed a "financial device, which involves a principle of universal application."* People reproved Thales, saying that his lack of wealth was proof that philosophy was a useless occupation and of no practical value. But Thales knew what he was doing and made plans to prove to others his wisdom and intellect. Thales had great skill in forecasting and predicted that the olive harvest would be exceptionally good the next autumn. Confident in his prediction, he made agreements with area olive-press owners to deposit what little money he had with them to guarantee him exclusive use of their olive presses when the harvest was ready. Thales successfully negotiated low prices because the harvest was in the future and no one knew whether the harvest would be plentiful or pathetic and because the olive-press owners were willing to hedge against the possibility of a poor yield. Aristotle's story about Thales ends as one might guess: When the harvesttime came and many presses were wanted all at once, Thales sold high and made a fortune.

Thus he showed the world that philosophers can easily be rich if they like, but that their ambition is of another sort. So Thales exercised the first known options trade some 2,500 years ago. He was not obliged to exercise the options. If the olive harvest had not been good, Thales could have let the option contracts expire unused and limited his loss to the original price paid for the options. But as it turned out, a bumper crop came in, so Thales exercised the options and sold his claims on the olive presses at a high profit. The story is an indication that a contrarian approach (trading against the crowd) might have some merit.

## Lemmings and Pioneers

One could argue that in any market there are trend followers (lemmings) and pioneers or very early adopters. The latter category is by definition a minority. In the early 1990s, some people were running around with mobile phones the size of a shoe. Having a private conversation in a public place did not seem to be more than a short-term phenomenon. At the time, the author of this book thought they were in need of professional help, and therefore did not buy Nokia shares in the early 1990s so—unfortunately—cannot claim being a pioneer or having superior foresight. It turned out that those egomaniacs were really the pioneers, and it is us—the lemmings—who have adopted their approaches and processes.

In asset management there is a similar phenomenon. The pension and

---

*Note that George Soros, according to his own assessment, failed as philosopher but succeeded as an investor. From Soros (1987).

endowment funds loading up exposure to hedge funds during the bull market of the 1990s were the exception. They belong to a small minority of investors. The majority of institutional as well as private investors took for granted what was written in the press and steered away from hedge funds. However, economic logic would suggest that it is this minority, the pioneers, that have captured an economic rent for the risk they took by moving away from the comfort of the consensus. As the hedge fund industry matures, becomes institutionalized and mainstream, and eventually converges with the traditional asset management industry, this rent will be gone. The lemmings will not share (or will share to a much smaller extent) the economic rent the pioneers captured.

As Humphrey Neill (2001), author of *The Art of Contrary Thinking*, puts it:

> *A common fallacy is the idea that the majority sets the pattern and the trends of social, economic, and religious life. History reveals quite the opposite: the majority copies, or imitates, the minority and this establishes the long-run developments and socioeconomic evolutions.*

Note that trend following is not irrational. In a market where there is uncertainty and where information is not disseminated efficiently, the cheapest strategy is to follow a leader, a market participant who seems to have an information edge. This, however, increases liquidity risk in the marketplace. Persaud (2001) discusses herd behavior in connection with risk in the financial system and regulation. He makes the point that turnover is not synonymous with liquidity. Liquidity means that there is a market when you want to buy as well as when you want to sell. For this two-way market, diversity is key and not high turnover. Shiller (1990) and others explain herding as taking comfort in high numbers, somewhat related to the IBM effect: "No one ever got sacked for buying IBM." In the banking industry, for example, lemming-like herding is a risk to the system. If one bank makes a mistake, it goes under. If all banks make the same mistake, the regulators will bail them out in order to preserve the financial system.[1] Lemming-like herding, therefore, is a rational choice.

In Warren Buffett's opinion, the term "institutional investor" is becoming an oxymoron: Referring to money managers as investors is, he says, like calling a person who engages in one-night stands romantic.[2] Buffett is not at par with modern portfolio theory. He does not run mean-variance efficient portfolios. Critics argue that, because of the standard practices of diversification, money managers behave more conservatively than Buffett. According to Hagstrom (1994) Buffett does not subscribe to this point of view. He does admit that money managers invest their money in a more conventional manner. However, he argues that conventionality is not synonymous with conservatism; rather, conservative actions derive from facts and reasoning.

Some argue that history has a tendency to repeat itself. The question therefore is whether we already have witnessed a phenomenon such as the current paradigm shift (as outlined in the Preface) in the financial industry. A point can be made that we have: In the 1940s anyone investing in equities was a pioneer. Back then there was no consensus that a conservative portfolio included equities at all. Pension fund managers loading up equity exposure were the mavericks of the time.

The pioneers who were buying into hedge funds during the 1990s were primarily uncomfortable with where equity valuations were heading. A price-earnings (P/E) ratio of 38 for the Standard & Poor's 500 index (S&P 500) (as was the case when this was written) is not really the same as a P/E of 8 (as for example in 1982). Whether the long-term expected mean return of U.S. equities is the same is open to debate and depends on some definitions and assumptions. However, there should be no debate that the opportunity set of a market trading at 38 times prospective (i.e., uncertain) earnings is the same as the opportunity set of a market trading at eight times prospective earnings.

Some pension funds (pioneers perhaps) have moved into inflation-indexed bond portfolios and are thereby matching assets with liabilities, that is, locking in any fund surplus rescued from the 2000–2002 bear market. What if this is a trend? What if there is a lemming-like effect whereby the majority of investors take risk off the table at the same time? If the incremental equity buyer dies or stops buying there is only one way equity valuations will head and equity prices will go.

## The First Hedge Funds

The official (most often quoted) starting point for hedge funds was 1949 when Alfred Winslow Jones opened an equity fund that was organized as a general partnership to provide maximum latitude and flexibility in constructing a portfolio. The fund was converted to a limited partnership in 1952. Jones took both long and short positions in securities to increase returns while reducing net market exposure and used leverage to further enhance the performance. Today the term "hedge fund" takes on a much broader context, as different funds are exposed to different kinds of risks.

Other incentive-based partnerships were set up in the mid-1950s, including Warren Buffett's Omaha-based Buffett Partners and Walter Schloss's WJS Partners, but their funds were styled with a long bias after Benjamin Graham's partnership (Graham-Newman). Under today's broadened definition, these funds would also be considered hedge funds, but regularly shorting shares to hedge market risk was not central to their investment strategies.[3]

Alfred W. Jones was a sociologist. He received his Ph.D. in sociology from Columbia University in 1938. During the 1940s Jones worked for *Fortune* and *Time* and wrote articles on nonfinancial subjects such as Atlantic convoys, farm cooperatives, and boys' prep schools. In March 1949 he wrote a freelance article for *Fortune* called "Fashions in Forecasting," which reported on various technical approaches to the stock market. His research for this story convinced him that he could make a living in the stock market, and early in 1949 he and four friends formed A. W. Jones & Co. as a general partnership. Their initial capital was $100,000, of which Jones himself put up $40,000. In its first year the partnership's gain on its capital came to a satisfactory 17.3 percent.

Jones generated very strong returns while managing to avoid significant attention from the general financial community until 1966, when an article in *Fortune* led to increased interest in hedge funds (impact of the 1966 article is discussed in the next section). The second hedge fund after A. W. Jones was City Associates founded by Carl Jones (not related to A. W. Jones) in 1964 after working for A. W. Jones.[4] A further notable entrant to the industry was Barton Biggs. Mr. Biggs formed the third hedge fund, Fairfield Partners, with Dick Radcliffe in 1965.[5] Unlike in the 2000–2002 downturn, many funds perished during the market downturns of 1969–1970 and 1973–1974, having been unable to resist the temptation to be net long and leveraged during the prior bull run. Hedge funds lost their prior popularity, and did not recover it again until the mid-1980s. Fairfield Partners was among the victims as it suffered from an early market call of the top, selling short the Nifty Fifty leading stocks because their valuation multiples had climbed to what should have been an unsustainable level. The call was right, but too early. "We got killed," Mr. Biggs said. "The experience scared the hell out of me."[6] Morgan Stanley hired him away from Fairfield Partners in 1973. Note that around three decades later some hedge funds also folded for calling the market too early; that is, they were selling growth stocks and buying value stocks too early.

Jones merged two investment tools—short sales and leverage. Short selling was employed to take advantage of opportunities of stocks trading too expensively relative to fair value. Jones used leverage to obtain profits, but employed short selling through baskets of stocks to control risk. Jones' model was devised from the premise that performance depends more on stock selection than market direction. He believed that during a rising market, good stock selection will identify stocks that rise more than the market, while good short stock selection will identify stocks that rise less than the market. However, in a declining market, good long selections will fall less than the market, and good short stock selection will fall more than the market, yielding a net profit in all markets. To those investors who regarded short selling with suspicion, Jones would simply say that he was using "speculative techniques for conservative ends."[7]

Jones kept all of his own money in the fund, realizing early that he could not expect his investors to take risks with their money that he would not be willing to assume with his own capital. Curiously, Jones became uncomfortable with his own ability to pick stocks and, as a result, employed stock pickers to supplement his own stock-picking ability. Soon he had as many as eight stock pickers autonomously managing portions of the fund. In 1954, he had converted his partnership into the first multimanager hedge fund by bringing in Dick Radcliffe to run a portion of the portfolio.[8] By 1984, at the age of 82, he had created a fund of funds by amending his partnership agreement to reflect a formal fund of funds structure.

Caldwell (1995) points out that the motivational dynamics of Alfred Jones' original hedge fund model run straight to the core of capitalistic instinct in managers and investors. The critical motives for a manager are high incentives for superior performance, coupled with significant personal risk of loss. The balance between risk seeking and risk hedging is elementary in the hedge fund industry today. A manager who has nothing to lose has a strong incentive to "risk the bank."

## The 1950s and 1960s

In April 1966, Carol Loomis wrote the aforementioned article, called "The Jones Nobody Keeps Up With." Published in *Fortune*, Loomis' article shocked the investment community by describing something called a "hedge fund" run by an unknown sociologist named Alfred Jones.[9] Jones' fund was outperforming the best mutual funds even after a 20 percent incentive fee. Over the prior five years, the best mutual fund was the Fidelity Trend Fund; yet Jones outperformed it by 44 percent, after all fees and expenses. Over 10 years, the best mutual fund was the Dreyfus Fund; yet Jones outperformed it by 87 percent. The news of Jones' performance created excitement, and by 1968 approximately 200 hedge funds were in existence.

During the 1960s bull market, many of the new hedge fund managers found that selling short impaired absolute performance, while leveraging the long positions created exceptional returns. The so-called hedgers were, in fact, long, leveraged and totally exposed as they went into the bear market of the early 1970s. And during this time many of the new hedge fund managers were put out of business. Few managers have the ability to short the market, since most equity managers have a long-only mentality.

Caldwell (1995) argues that the combination of incentive fee and leverage in a bull market seduced most of the new hedge fund managers into using high margin with little hedging, if any at all. These unhedged managers were "swimming naked."[10] Between 1968 and 1974 there were two downturns, 1969–1970 and 1973–1974. The first was more damaging to the young hedge fund industry, because most of the new managers were swimming naked (i.e., were unhedged). For the 28 largest hedge funds in the Securities and Exchange Commission (SEC) survey at year-end 1968, assets under management declined 70 percent (from losses as well as withdrawals) by year-end 1970, and five of them were shut down. From the spring of 1966 through the end of 1974, the hedge fund industry ballooned and burst, but a number of well-managed funds survived and quietly carried on. Among the managers who endured were Alfred Jones, George Soros, and Michael Steinhardt.[11]

## Hedge Funds—The Warren Buffett Way

An interesting aspect about the hedge funds industry is the involvement of Warren Buffett, which is not very well documented as Buffett is primarily associated with bottom-up company evaluation and great stock selection. He is often referred to as the best investor ever and an antithesis to the efficient market hypothesis (EMH). According to Hagstrom (1994), Warren Buffett started a partnership in 1956 with seven limited partners. The limited partners contributed $105,000 to the partnership. Buffett, then 25 years old, was the general partner and, apparently, started with $100. The fee structure was such that Buffett earned 25 percent of the profits above a 6 percent hurdle rate whereas the limited partners received 6 percent annually plus 75 percent of the profits above the hurdle rate. Between 1956 and 1969 Buffett compounded money at an annual rate of 29.5 percent despite the market falling in five out of 13 years. The fee arrangement and focus on absolute returns even when the stock market falls look very much like what absolute return managers set as their objective today. There are more similarities:

- Buffett mentioned early on that his approach was the contrarian/value-investor approach and that the preservation of principal was one of the major goals of the partnership.[12] Today, capital preservation is one of the main investment goals of all hedge fund managers who have a large portion of their own net wealth tied to that of their investors. Warren Buffett's partnership had a long bias after Benjamin Graham's partnership. Selling short was not central to the investment strategy.
- Buffett's stellar performance attracted new money. More partnerships were founded. In 1962 Buffett consolidated all partnerships into a single partnership (and moved the partnership office to Kiewit Plaza in Omaha). The fact that stellar performance attracts capital is not new. Superior performance attracts capital in retail mutual funds as well as hedge funds. However, with some absolute return strategies there is limited capacity. In addition, there are manager-specific capacity constraints next to strategy-specific capacity constraints. Skilled managers are flooded with capital and eventually close their funds to new money.
- As the Nifty Fifty stocks like Avon, IBM, Polaroid, and Xerox were trading at 50 to 100 times earnings Buffett had difficulties finding value. He

ended his partnership in 1969. Buffett mailed a letter to his partners confessing that he was out of step with the current market environment:

> *On one point, however, I am clear. I will not abandon a previous approach whose logic I understand, although I find it difficult to apply, even though it may mean foregoing large and apparently easy profits to embrace an approach which I don't fully understand, have not practiced successfully and which possibly could lead to substantial permanent loss of capital.*[13]

These notions sound like an absolute return investment philosophy. There are two nice anecdotes with this notion: First, in recent years some market observers were claiming that Warren Buffett finally "lost it" as he refused to invest in the technology stocks of the 1990s as he had refused to invest in the Nifty Fifty stocks three decades earlier. The lesson to be learned is that absolute return managers do not pay 100 times prospective earnings, whereas relative return managers do.* Warren Buffett's quotation looks very similar to quotes by Julian Robertson. Julian Robertson wrote to investors in March 2000 to announce the closure of the Tiger funds (after losses and withdrawals). Robertson was returning money to investors, as did Warren Buffett in 1969. Robertson said that since August 1999 investors had withdrawn $7.7 billion in funds. He blamed the irrational market for Tiger's poor performance, declaring that "earnings and price considerations take a back seat to mouse clicks and momentum."[14] Robertson described the strength of technology stocks as "a Ponzi pyramid destined for collapse." Robertson's spokesman said that he did not feel capable of figuring out investment in technology stocks and no longer wanted the burden of investing other people's money.

There are also some similarities between Buffett and Soros: Both Warren Buffett and George Soros are contrarians.† There is a possibility that successful investors are contrarians by definition.‡ Hagstrom (1994) quotes Buffett: "We simply attempt to be fearful when others are greedy and to be greedy

---

*Assuming the stock is in the benchmark portfolio and the contribution to active risk is not negligible.

†Most investors believe they are contrarians—which, by definition, is not possible. Contrarian principles are nothing new. Jean-Jacques Rousseau was quoted saying: "Follow the course opposite to custom and you will almost always do well."

‡Lakonishok et al. (1994) found that because the market overreacts to past growth, it is surprised when earnings growth mean reverts. As a result, poor past performers have high future returns, and strong past performers have low future returns. Contrarians buy low (poor past performance) and sell high (strong past performance).

only when others are fearful."\* This sounds (in terms of content, not phraseology) very much like what George Soros has to say:[†] "I had very low regard for the sagacity of professional investors and the more influential their position the less I considered them capable of making the right decisions. My partner and I took a malicious pleasure in making money by selling short stocks that were institutional favorites."[15] Buffett compares investing with a game: "As far as I am concerned the stock market doesn't exist. It is there only as a reference to see if anybody is offering to do anything foolish. It's like poker. If you have been in the game for a while and don't know who the patsy is, you're the patsy." There are some similarities with how George Soros sees investing: "I did not play the financial markets according to a particular set of rules; I was always more interested in understanding the changes that occur in the rules of the game."[16]

Shareholders of Berkshire Hathaway were also exposed to various forms of arbitrage, namely risk arbitrage and fixed income arbitrage. Over the past decades, Warren Buffett created the image of being a grandfatherly, down-to-earth, long-term, long-only investor, repeatedly saying he invested only in opportunities he understood and implying a lack of sophistication for more complex trading strategies and financial instruments. However, there is no lack of sophistication at all. According to Hagstrom (1994) Buffett was involved in risk arbitrage (aka merger arbitrage) in the early 1980s and left the scene in 1989 when the game became crowded and the arbitrage landscape was changing. In 1987 Berkshire Hathaway invested in $700 million of newly issued convertible preferred stocks of Salomon, Inc. Salomon was the most sophisticated and most profitable fixed income trading house of the time and the world's largest fixed income arbitrage operation. Note that Long Term Capital Management (LTCM) was founded and built on the remains of Salomon staff after the 1991 bond scandal.[‡] Warren Buffett became interim

---

\*One could argue that a relative return manager can execute a contrarian approach as well. However, there is a strong incentive not to, since many investors evaluate managers on a yearly (or maximum three-year) basis. This means that not participating in a bubble, which can take many years to unfold and then burst, is too risky. The relative return manager will be pushed out of business before he or she is proven right. This is one of the odd incentives that absolute return managers want to avoid.

[†]Warren Buffett and George Soros agree on many other fronts—for example, that stock prices are driven by sentiment (fear and greed) much more than by fundamentals (in the short term, that is). This was formalized by Shiller (1981, 1989) and is probably a consensus view today.

[‡]In August 1991, Salomon controlled 95 percent of the two-year Treasury notes market despite rules only permitting 35 percent of the total offering. Salomon had exceeded this limit by a wide margin and admitted to violating Treasury action rules. From Hagstrom (1994), p. 171.

chairman of Salomon after chairman John Gutfreund resigned. Hagstrom (1994) argues that "Buffett's presence and leadership during the investigation prevented Salomon from collapsing." Had the board, led by Warren Buffett, not persuaded U.S. attorneys that it was prepared to take draconian steps to make things right, it seems highly likely that the firm would have been indicted and followed Drexel Burnham to investment banking's burial ground.[17]

Warren Buffett's Berkshire Hathaway was invested in Bermuda-based West End Capital during the turbulence caused by the Russian default crisis in 1998. Berkshire contributed 90 percent of the capital raised in July 1998 to West End Capital, which attempts to profit through bond convergence investing and uses less leverage (around 10 to 15 times) than comparable boutiques. However, the investment is not sizable when compared to long-only positions. In August 1998 John Meriwether approached Buffett about investing in LTCM. Buffett declined.[18] Later Buffett offered to bail out LTCM, an offer that was ultimately declined by LTCM.*

Throughout his extremely successful career, Warren Buffett has had some kind of involvement in what today is called the hedge fund industry, that is, money managers seeking absolute returns for their partners and themselves while controlling unwanted risk. Figure 1.1 shows what great money managers have in common: a focus on absolute returns.

One of the great ironies in the annals of finance is that George Soros is probably the most misunderstood and controversial figure in the money management scene. However, based on realized performance, he is probably the greatest investor the world has ever seen. This is ironic because George Soros' sterling conversion trade in 1992 is considered as symptomatic of pure speculation. Soros compounded at an annual rate of 31.6 percent (after fees) in the 33 years from 1969 to 2001. This compares with around 26.0 percent in the case of Warren Buffett in the 44 years ending 2001 and with around 22.4 percent for Julian Robertson in the 22 years ending 2001. Note that compounding $1 at 31.6 percent, 26.0 percent, 22.4 percent and 7.9 percent (S&P 500) over a 25-year period results in terminal values of $958, $323, $157, and $6.7 respectively. This, albeit anecdotal, can be considered a big difference.

Who is the greatest money manager of all time? Most people would probably agree that it is either George Soros or Warren Buffett. Figure 1.1 would suggest the former, Figure 1.2 the latter. Figure 1.2 shows annualized returns in relation to the standard deviations of these annual returns, that is, so-called risk-adjusted returns (implying that the standard deviation of returns is a sound proxy for risk). The sizes of the bubbles (and the numbers next to the

---

*Warren Buffett is the ultimate value investor. Acquiring LTCM's positions at a discount would have been a great trade, since most positions turned profitable after the "100-year flood" had settled.

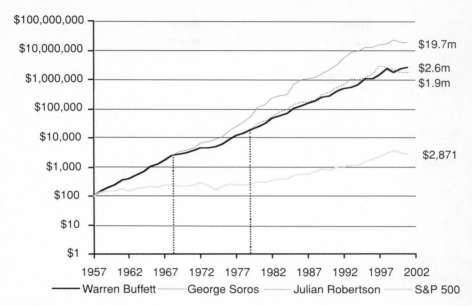

**FIGURE 1.1** Performance of Greatest Long-Term Money Managers
*Source:* Hagstrom (1994), Peltz (2001), Datastream, TASS, Managed Account Reports.

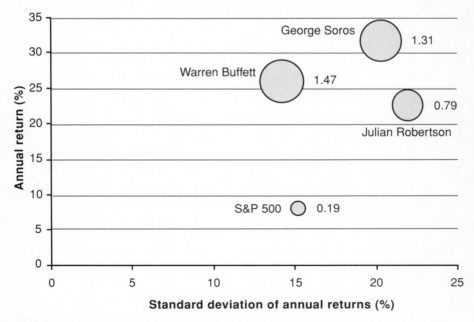

**FIGURE 1.2** Risk-Adjusted Returns of World's Greatest Money Managers
*Source:* Hagstrom (1994), Peltz (2001), Datastream, TASS, Managed Account Reports.

bubbles) measure the Sharpe ratios assuming a constant risk-free rate of 5 percent. Note that the risk-adjusted returns were calculated over different time periods.

Figure 1.1 and Figure 1.2 also reveal another interesting aspect of business life. According to Hagstrom (1994) Warren Buffett started with $100 in 1957. Figure 1.1 implies that his initial investment of $100 would have grown to only $2.6 million by the end of 2001. However, Warren Buffett is a multibillionaire and one of the wealthiest individuals on the planet.* The difference between $2.6 million and his X-billion wealth is attributed to entrepreneurism and not investment skill (albeit there is strong correlation between the two). This should serve as a reminder to day traders and other financial comedians: Unambiguous greatness and sustainable value creation are achieved through successfully setting up and running businesses and not through having a go at the stock market.

## The 1970s

Richard Elden (2001), founder and chairman of Chicago-based fund of (hedge) funds operator Grosvenor Partners, estimates that by 1971 there were no more than 30 hedge funds in existence, the largest having $50 million under management. The aggregate capital of all hedge funds combined was probably less than $300 million. The first fund of hedge funds, Leveraged Capital Holdings, was created by Georges Karlweis in 1969 in Geneva.[19] This was followed by the first fund of funds in the United States, Grosvenor Partners in 1971.

In the years following the 1974 market bottom, hedge funds returned to operating in relative obscurity, as they had prior to 1966. The investment community largely forgot about them. Hedge funds of the 1970s were different from the institutions of today. They were small and lean. Typically, each fund consisted of two or three general partners, a secretary, and no analysts or back-office staff.[20] The main characteristic was that every hedge fund specialized in one strategy. (This, too, is different from today.) Most managers focused on the Alfred Jones model, long/short equity. Because hedge funds represented such a small part of the asset management industry they went un-

---

*According to hereisthefinancialnews.com, based on *Forbes*' "World's Richest People" list, Warren Buffett is the second wealthiest man in the world after Bill Gates: "To give you some idea of what this means, consider the following anecdote: 'A man gave his wife $1 million to spend at a rate of $1,000 a day. In three years she returned for more. So he gave her $1 billion and she didn't come back for 3,000 years.' Warren Buffett's wife could go on a spending spree for 90,000 years." From hereisthefinancialnews.com, March 6, 2002.

noticed. This resulted in relatively little competition for investment opportunities and exploitable market inefficiencies. In the early 1970s there were probably more than 100 hedge funds. However, conditions eliminated most.

## The 1980s

Only a modest number of hedge funds were established during the 1980s. Most of these funds had raised assets to manage on a word-of-mouth basis from wealthy individuals. Julian Robertson's Jaguar fund, George Soros' Quantum Fund, Jack Nash from Odyssey, and Michael Steinhardt Partners were compounding at 40 percent levels. Not only were they outperforming in bull markets, but they outperformed in bear markets as well. In 1990, for example, Quantum was up 30 percent and Jaguar was up 20 percent, while the S&P 500 was down 3 percent and the Morgan Stanley Capital International (MSCI) World index was down 16 percent. The press began to write articles and profiles drawing attention to these remarkable funds and their extraordinary managers.

Figure 1.3 shows an estimate of number of hedge funds in existence through the 1980s. Duplicate share classes, funds of funds, managed futures, and currency speculators were not included in the graph.

During the 1980s, most of the hedge fund managers in the United States were not registered with the SEC. Because of this, they were prohibited from

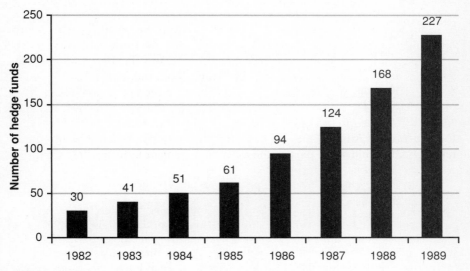

**FIGURE 1.3**  Number of Hedge Funds in the 1980s
*Source:* Quellos Group.

advertising, and instead relied on word-of-mouth references to grow their assets. (See Table 1.1.) The majority of funds were organized as limited partnerships, allowing only 99 investors. The hedge fund managers, therefore, required high minimum investments. European investors were quick to see the advantages of this new breed of managers, which fueled the development of the more tax-efficient offshore funds.

Caldwell (1995) puts the date where hedge funds reentered the investment community at May 1986, when *Institutional Investor* ran a story about Julian Robertson.[21] The article, by Julie Rohrer, reported that Robertson's Tiger Fund had been compounding at 43 percent during its first six years, net of expenses and incentive fees. This compared to 18.7 percent for the S&P 500 during the same period. The article established Robertson as an investor, not a trader, and said that he always hedged his portfolio with short sales. One of the successful trades the article mentioned was a bet on a falling U.S. dollar against other major currencies in 1985. Robertson had bought an option, limiting downside risk by putting only a fraction of the fund's capital at risk. Rohrer showed the difference between a well-managed hedge fund and traditional equity management.

Another fund worth mentioning was Princeton/Newport Trading Partners. Princeton/Newport was a little-known but very successful (convertible) arbitrage fund with offices in Princeton, New Jersey, and Newport Beach, California. Some practitioners credit the firm with having the first proper option pricing model and making money by arbitraging securities; this included optionality that other market participants were not able to price properly. For

**Table 1.1**  Hedge Fund Assets under Management in the 1980s ($ millions)

| Category | 1980 | 1985 | 1990 |
|---|---|---|---|
| Global | $193 | $517 | $1,288 |
| Macro | 0 | 0 | 4,700 |
| Market-neutral | 0 | 78 | 638 |
| Event-driven | 0 | 29 | 379 |
| Sector | 0 | 0 | 2 |
| Short selling | 0 | 0 | 187 |
| Long-only | 0 | 0 | 0 |
| Fund of funds | 0 | 190 | 1,339 |
| | | | |
| **Total (excluding fund of funds)** | $193 | $624 | $7,194 |
| **Total (including fund of funds)** | 193 | 814 | 8,533 |

*Source:* Eichengreen and Mathieson (1998), Table 2.2, p. 8, based on MAR/Hedge data.

two decades up to 1988, Princeton/Newport had achieved a remarkable track record with returns in the high teens and extremely few negative months. Unfortunately, Princeton/Newport was hit by overzealous government action that led to an abrupt cessation of operations in 1988.*

## The 1990s

During the 1990s, the flight of money managers from large institutions accelerated, with a resulting surge in the number of hedge funds. Their operations were funded primarily by the new wealth that had been created by the unprecedented bull run in the equity markets. The managers' objectives were not purely financial. Many established their own businesses for lifestyle and control reasons. Almost all hedge fund managers invested a substantial portion of their own net worth in the fund alongside their investors.

One of the characteristics of the 1990s was that the hedge fund industry became extremely heterogeneous. In 1990, two-thirds of hedge fund managers were macro managers, that is, absolute return managers with a rather loose mandate. Throughout the decade, more strategies became available for investors to invest in. Some of the strategies were new; most of them were not. By the end of 2001, more than 50 percent of the assets under management were somehow related to a variant of the Jones model, long/short equity. However, even the subgroup of long/short equity became heterogeneous. Figure 1.4 compares some alternative investment strategies with the traditional long-only strategy with respect to the variation in net market exposure. The horizontal lines show rough approximations of the ranges in which the different managers are expected to operate. It will become clear in later chapters that the superiority of the long/short approach is derived from widening the set of opportunities (and the magnitude of opportunities) from which the manager can extract value. The graph highlights a further aspect of hedge fund investing: Not all equity absolute return managers have the same investment approach. This diversity results in low correlation among different managers, despite the managers trading the same asset class. Low correlation among portfolio constituents then allows construction of low-risk portfolios.

---

*In 2002, a similar vendetta was unfolding. New York State Attorney General Eliot Spitzer was moving in on established Wall Street firms. Glassman (2002) makes the obvious point that every bear market requires a scapegoat, and this time the chosen victims are stock analysts. According to the *Wall Street Journal* (2002), Mr. Spitzer was bidding to be the next Ferdinand Pecora, the Congressional aide whose flaying of Wall Street gave birth to the Depression-era regulatory establishment that still hangs around today and which did nothing to prevent Enron or false market calls. As Warren Buffett puts it: "It's only when the tide goes out that you see who has been swimming with their trunks off."

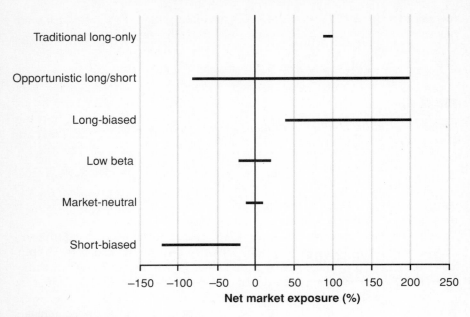

**FIGURE 1.4**  Different Strategies in Equities
*Source:* Quellos Group.

The 1990s saw another interesting phenomenon. A number of the established money managers stopped accepting new money to manage. Some even returned money to their investors. Limiting assets in many investment styles is one of the most basic tenets of hedge fund investing if the performance expectations are going to continue to be met. This reflects the fact that managers make much more money from performance fees and investment income than they do from management fees. Due to increasing investor demand in the 1990s, many funds established higher minimum investment levels ($50 million in some cases) and set long lock-up periods (three to five years).

Both Julian Robertson's Tiger Management and George Soros' Soros Fund Management reached $22 billion in assets in 1998, setting a record for funds under management.[22] Both organizations subsequently shrunk in size, and Tiger ultimately was liquidated. Today, there are dozens of organizations managing more than $1 billion. Based on data from Hedge Fund Research, Inc. (HFRI) the hedge fund industry grew in terms of unleveraged assets under management of $38.9 billion in 1990 to $456.4 billion in 1999 and $536.9 billion at the end of 2001.

## Conclusion

Some investors in the hedge fund industry argue that the pursuit of absolute returns is much older than the pursuit of relative returns (i.e., beating a benchmark). This view can be justified if we allow for a loose interpretation of historical deals. One could conclude that the way hedge funds manage assets is going back to the roots of investing. What Charles Ellis (1998) calls trying to win the loser's game, therefore, could be viewed as only a short blip in the evolution of investment management. Put differently, both the first and third paradigm of investment management were about absolute returns.

Irrespective of the history of hedge funds or whether hedge funds are leading or lagging the establishment, the pursuit of absolute returns is probably as old as civilization and trade itself. However, so is lemming-like trend following.

# INVESTMENT PHILOSOPHY OF ABSOLUTE RETURN MANAGERS

## Introduction

An absolute return manager is essentially an asset manager without a benchmark or with a benchmark that is the return on the risk-free asset. Benchmarking can be viewed as a method of restricting investment managers so as to limit the potential for surprises, either positive or negative. By defining a market benchmark and a tracking error band, the plan sponsor gives the manager a risk budget in which the manager is expected to operate. Recent legal action in the United Kingdom by a pension plan sponsor probably will mean that the relative return industry will be even more "benchmark-aware" than it already was.*

Separating skill from luck is one of the major goals of analyzing the performance of a particular manager, regardless of whether he is running long-only or absolute return money. In any sample of managers, a small percentage is bound to have exceptional performance (both positive and negative). Managers with exceptional positive performance will attribute the excess return to skill. Those who perform exceptionally poorly are unlikely to blame lack of skill but rather bad luck as the cause of their performance. Grinold and Kahn (2000a) categorize managers according to luck and skill. The

---

*A pension fund sued a large asset management firm for negligence resulting in 10 percent underperformance against the benchmark. The case was settled out of court. It was estimated that the asset manager paid around £70 million ($107 million) compensation.

lucky and skilled are "blessed." The lucky and unskilled are "insufferable." The unlucky but skilled are "forlorn," whereas the unlucky and unskilled are "doomed."

Grinold and Kahn argue that "nearly half of all roulette players achieve positive returns on each spin of the wheel." This means that the wheel most often stops on red or black (as opposed to 0 or 00). Even the existence of very large returns (such as when the ball stops on a single number bet like 7) does not prove skill. However, the expected return of the roulette gambler is negative. Over the long term, they all lose. The casino, however, has positive expected returns and wins (as long as it has enough cash or credit lines to live through a bad evening).*

The practical issue arising from performance analysis is that it requires a certain amount of data points before any conclusions can be drawn with a reasonable degree of confidence. For example, to analyze yearly returns, 16 years of observations are needed to judge whether a manager is top quartile (has an information ratio of 0.5) with 95 percent confidence. As the normal life span of an asset manager is less than 16 years, a 16-year monitoring period seems rather impractical. Assessing qualitative aspects (investment philosophy, trading savvy, risk management experience, infrastructure, incentive structure, etc.)—that is, bottom-up fundamental research and due diligence—is the only way around this issue.

## A Car without Brakes

The most comparable strategy to long-only equity is long/short equity. The HFRI Equity Hedge Index (equity long/short managers) outperformed most equity market indexes on an absolute as well as risk-adjusted basis by a wide margin. However, most long/short managers should underperform long-only managers in momentum-driven bull markets where all stocks increase rapidly.† The long/short manager should underperform because the short positions are a drag on performance (for example, in liquidity-driven momentum markets as in the late 1990s). However, when markets have only slightly positive or negative returns, long/short managers have outperformed the

---

*Running a casino, an insurance company, or the national lottery is a business called statistical arbitrage. The operators win as long as they can survive statistical outliers, that is, large but few occasional outflows or losses. Statistical arbitrage is one strategy executed by absolute return managers. The irony is that the public perceives absolute return managers to be like gamblers, whereas they are actually more like someone running a casino. Their expected return is positive.

†Note that this is a generalization and that generalizations are actually inappropriate in an industry as heterogeneous as the hedge fund industry or long/short equity subindustry. However, occasionally a generalization helps to put across a point.

long-only managers, at least in the past. In other words, long/short hedge funds underperform in strong bull markets and outperform in bear markets. This means that if the returns of the benchmark index are fairly normally distributed, the return profile of absolute return managers is nonlinear, that is, asymmetrical to the market. Figure 1.5 shows the symmetrical returns of an equity index and compares it with the asymmetrical return profile of a hedge fund index. The figure shows the average quarterly returns of the HFRI Equity Hedge Index when the MSCI World was positive and negative respectively. The average of the 34 positive quarterly returns between 1990 and 2001 was 5.8 percent. The corresponding return for the HFRI Equity Hedge Index was 6.6 percent. The averages of the 14 negative quarters were –7.3 percent and 0.9 percent respectively.

The main reason why traditional funds do more poorly in downside markets is that they usually need to have a certain weight in equities according to their mandate, and therefore are often compared to a car without brakes. The freedom of operation is limited with traditional asset managers and more flexible with absolute return managers. Another reason why hedge fund managers may do better in down markets is that they often have a large portion of their personal wealth at risk in their funds. Arguably, their interests are more aligned with those of their investors. This alignment, together with the lack of

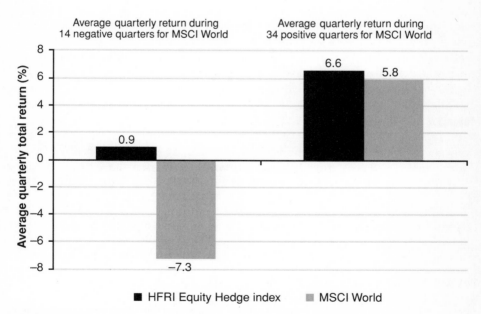

**FIGURE 1.5** Asymmetrical versus Symmetrical Return Profile, 1990–2001
*Source:* Hedge Fund Research, Datastream, UBS Warburg (2000).

a relative measure for risk, increases the incentive to preserve wealth and avoid losses.

## Avoiding Negative Compounding

Downside protection is closely related to avoiding negative compounding. A simple example may help illustrate the importance of wealth preservation: If one loses 50 percent, as various markets and stocks did during 2000–2001, one needs a 100 percent return just to get back to breakeven. That is, the positive return must be double the negative return. We argue that downside protection from the investors' point of view and avoidance of negative returns from the managers' point of view are different sides of the same coin.

Table 1.2 is an attempt to explain the investment philosophy of absolute return managers. Both absolute and relative return managers would argue that they were not hired by investors to lose money. The fundamental difference between the two investment philosophies lies in the aversion to absolute financial losses and the definition of risk. Absolute return managers define risk as *total risk* whereas relative return managers define risk as *active risk*.

Orthodox financial theory suggests that investors should focus on the long term. It also suggests that investors will generate satisfactory returns if they have a long enough time horizon when they buy equities. This may or may not be true. The problem faced by absolute return managers is that they might not live long enough to experience the long term. Absolute return managers do not care if the probability of equities underperforming bonds over a 25-year period is low. Moreover, absolute return managers are interested in

**Table 1.2**   Different Approaches to Creating Value

|  | Long-Only Buy-and-Hold | | | | Alternative Strategies | | | |
|---|---|---|---|---|---|---|---|---|
|  | MSCI World | S&P 500 | Nasdaq Composite | Nikkei 225 | Equity Market-Neutral | Equity Hedge | Macro | Fund of Funds |
| Dec. 1998 | $100 | $100 | $100 | $100 | $100 | $100 | $100 | $100 |
| Dec. 1999 | 125 | 121 | 186 | 137 | 107 | 144 | 118 | 126 |
| Dec. 2000 | 109 | 110 | 113 | 100 | 123 | 157 | 120 | 132 |
| Dec. 2001 | 91 | 97 | 89 | 76 | 131 | 158 | 129 | 135 |
| Return 1999 | 25% | 21% | 86% | 37% | 7% | 44% | 18% | 26% |
| Return 2000–2001 | −27 | −20 | −52 | −44 | 22 | 9 | 10 | 7 |
| Dec. 2001 vs. peak | −28 | −23 | −58 | −73 | 0 | −4 | 0 | 0 |
| Breakeven return[a] | 39 | 30 | 141 | 269 | 0 | 4 | 0 | 0 |

[a]Return required to break even from previous peak.
*Source:* Hedge Fund Research, Datastream.

how they get there; that is, they are interested in *end-of-period* wealth as well as *during-the-period* variance.

Table 1.2 summarizes what we mean by "avoiding negative compounding." It shows four long-only buy-and-hold portfolios as well as four alternative absolute return strategies. The absolute return manager could argue that the first four columns have nothing to do with asset management or risk management. Absolute return managers want to make profits not only when the wind is at their backs but also when it changes and becomes a headwind. Absolute return managers will therefore use risk management and hedging techniques—this is where the asymmetrical return profile discussed earlier comes from. From the point of view of absolute return managers, relative return managers do not use risk management,* and do not manage assets as they follow benchmarks. They are trend followers by definition.

In other words, the relative return manager is long; hence the term long-only. The relative return manager, again from the point of view of the absolute return manager, has no incentive, no provisions to avoid losses.† This does not make sense to many absolute return managers and is the reason why some absolute return managers believe relative return managers face obsolescence.

Table 1.2 shows that an investment in the four equity indexes in December 1998 would have ended in losses by December 2001, despite the phenomenal performance of equities in 1999.‡ The second row from the bottom measures the percentage from the peak in local currencies. The high losses in the Nikkei 225 make it clear why some Japanese investors are not as averse to hedge fund exposure as are, for example, U.K. pension fund trustees. (Demand for hedge fund products is larger from Japanese institutional investors than it is from U.K. institutional investors.) It also illustrates one of the incentives of absolute return managers. Absolute return managers would try to keep this figure at zero, because first they have their own money in the fund and do not want to lose it, and second, most hedge fund managers have a high-water mark. This

---

*Note that, for example, Lo (2001) expresses a diametrically opposing view, arguing that "risk management is not central to the success of hedge funds" whereas "risk management and transparency are essential" for the traditional manager.

†This is not entirely correct: A relative return manager has an incentive to grow funds under management (i.e., avoid funds under management falling) because fee income is determined based on the absolute level of funds under management.

‡It is interesting to note that some fund of hedge funds managers regard themselves as being boring. They do not offer the excitement of the swings as shown in Table 1.2. They simply want to offer financial wealth-increasing vehicles with low volatility. The ultimate irony, as mentioned several times in this book, is that hedge fund exposure is still regarded as more risky than long-only equity exposure by a majority of financial professionals and regulators and an even larger majority of the general public.

means that they can charge an incentive fee only from new profits; that is, the fund has to make up for any losses before it can charge its performance fee. For example, a fund falling to 80 from 100 and then rising back to 100 will not charge a performance fee on the 25 percent profit from 80 to 100.

Figure 1.6 shows two hypothetical saving schemes of a Japanese employee, assuming deposits are made at the end of each calendar year over a 20-year period and that deposits grew 2 percent per annum due to salary increases. The two series contrast a local stock market savings scheme (as measured by the Nikkei 225) and a fixed-rate scheme of 5 percent. Figure 1.6 should serve as a reminder that it is true that equity markets go up in the long term but: (1) Differences between markets are huge. Taking the S&P 500 as a proxy for equity investing over the past 10, 20, 50, or even 100 years is inappropriate because the U.S. stock market is the mother of all stock markets, that is, the winner of a large group of survivors. (2) An investor might not live long enough to experience the long term.

Nearly all analysis in the asset management industry is based on *time-weighted* rates of return. However, the most relevant metric from an investor's perspective is *dollar-weighted* rates of return or their internal rate of return (IRR). For example, Manager A earns 20 percent, 20 percent and –10 percent in years one to three, while Manager B earns –10 percent, 20 percent, and 20 percent. In both cases, the time-weighted return is the same (9 percent average

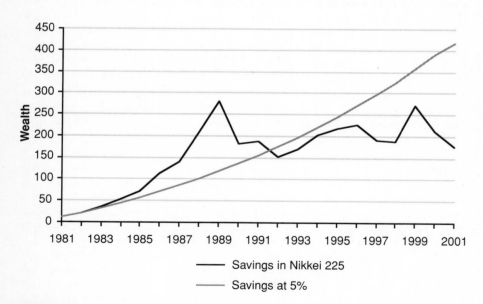

**FIGURE 1.6** Low Volatility Savings Plan Compared with Equity Investment
*Source:* Datastream.

annual compound growth). However, the dollar-weighted rate of return between the two managers will likely be vastly different for nearly all investors.
The only exception is investors that neither invest nor withdraw assets. These
investors would have earned the same IRR by investing with either manager. An
investor who was a saver, contributing $100 per year, would earn $120, $264,
and $328 with Manager A by the end of years one to three, respectively, but
$90, $228, and $394 with Manager B. The increase in wealth produced by
each fund ($328 versus $394) is dramatically different even though the time-
weighted return is the same. This effect is more pronounced the greater the degree of variation in returns. Earning 9 percent per year results in $357 at the
end of period three, that is, is in between the two other outcomes. Accumula-
tion of wealth is much more reliable (less risky) the lower the total risk.

Assume that the dark line in Figure 1.6 is the retirement plan of a 45-year-
old employee who started working 20 years ago and has been investing money
in the stock market every year, starting with $10 in year one. The employee's
wealth would have been $241 at the end of 2001. Invested at 5 percent, this
would have ended in wealth of $416 (assuming contribution increases at a rate
of 2 percent in both cases). In other words, the stock market has not been that
great for a Japanese saver over the past 20 years, despite the fact that the 1980s
was one of the greatest bull markets ever in the country's financial history (as
were the 1990s in the United States and Europe).* If the hypothetical Japanese
equity saver continues to get a salary increase of 2 percent per year and invests
it in the Nikkei 225, the annual growth rate of the Nikkei 225 over the next 20
years has to be around 9.6 percent to equal the fixed-rate investment over the
full 40-year period. If this growth rate materializes, the Japanese investor would
be as well positioned at retirement age 65 as if he or she had invested at 5 percent. The Japanese equity market might perform at a rate of 9.6 percent per
year over the next 20 years; however, and this is the whole point, it might not.†

The Nikkei 225 is an extreme example that was chosen on purpose. The
choice is based on the fact that the high volatility in equity markets can have a
large impact on end-of-period wealth as well as variance during the investment period. An investment strategy that does not manage both end-of-period

---

*For this not to happen to savers in the United States and Europe there is an urgent
need of incremental buyers, that is, buyers who consider valuations in the high thirties
or low forties—based on aggregate market earnings per share (EPS)—as cheap. Continental European pension funds have been announcing throughout the late 1990s that
they will increase their allocations to equities. Most investors and financial professionals hope that they do not change their minds. For a market to go up, there is a need for
(incremental) buyers. No buyers—no asset price inflation.
†At a rate of 9.6 percent per year, the Nikkei 225 would break through its all-time high
of around 40,000 during the year 2016 and close at 66,161 on December 31, 2021.

wealth as well as during-the-period variance is not an active but rather a passive investment strategy.

## Return Illusion

To the casual observer, the return of 86 percent on the Nasdaq index in Table 1.2 may look high even if it is followed by a retreat of *only* 52 percent. However, if $100 had been passively invested in the Nasdaq Composite index at the beginning of 1999 and transaction costs were zero, the portfolio would have declined to $89 by the end of December 2001 (an $86 gain in 1999 followed by a $97 loss in 2000–2001). This compares with $131 for a portfolio of equity market-neutral absolute return managers, $135 for the average fund of hedge funds, or $129 for a diversified exposure to global macro managers.* High returns as observed on the Nasdaq are good for headlines and selling financial magazines. However, these returns are an illusion in a long-term context. A volatile market-based strategy with returns such as 89 percent per year is an indication that the return figure might reverse in a linear fashion.

The figures in Table 1.2 are only moderately conclusive because the analysis has starting- and end-point bias. However, a point worth making is that investing in absolute return funds or adding alternative asset classes and strategies to traditional asset classes and strategies is a conservative undertaking. Diversifying into assets with low correlation to one's existing assets or combining assets with low correlation reduces total risk. Diversification and hedging unwanted risks are laudable concepts—despite the popular belief that, apparently, (still) suggests otherwise: In the United States, 401(k) plans allow a 100 percent allocation to one stock. In the United Kingdom, some pension funds recently had a larger allocation to one domestic stock than to the whole U.S. stock market due to benchmark considerations. It is unlikely that these examples of suboptimal allocation of risk will persist forever.

## Perception of Risk

Misunderstanding about absolute return managers is derived from the observation that relative and absolute return managers do not speak the same

---

*The irony here is that macro hedge funds are considered as the most speculative investment vehicles, since the managers are the most extravagant and their investment process is the least transparent. However, what is often overlooked is that the different personalities and loose investment mandate result in huge diversity among macro managers. This diversity means that the returns from different macro managers have a low correlation with one another because their performance is attributed to different factors, opportunities, and investment approaches. The low correlation among macro hedge funds allows an investor to substantially reduce portfolio volatility by combining different macro managers.

language. Terminologies and perceptions can be as different as the strategies. One perception has to do with risk. When a relative return manager speaks of risk he or she normally means *active risk*. When an absolute return manager speaks of risk he or she usually means *total risk*, that is, the probability of losing everything and being forced to work for a large organization again.

Traditional long-only managers whose benchmark is, for example, the S&P 500 see a "riskless" position as holding all 500 stocks in exact proportion as the index. Shifting 10 percent out of high-beta stocks into cash is perceived as an increase in risk. Absolute return managers would view such a shift as decreasing risk. In other words, absolute return managers have a different perspective.

This does not mean that a relative return manager perceives true financial risk as active risk. Losing money is obviously worse than making money. However, it is active risk that is linked to their remuneration and future career prospects. Their incentive and mandate is to manage active risk, not total risk. The investment consulting boom beginning in the late 1960s and the paper on asset allocation by Gary Brinson et al. (1986) were probably the key moments in the bifurcation of the second paradigm of asset allocation, that is, the migration from an absolute return to a relative return perspective. Institutional investors, academics, and consultants were the drivers pushing money managers to assimilate the relative perspective toward risk and return—whether long-only managers liked it or not. The third paradigm in asset management mentioned in the Preface is steering away from the odd incentives derived from a relative return approach.

## Risk Illusion from Time Diversification

An often-debated phenomenon in equity markets is the benefit of time diversification. Some argue that equities are safe in the long term.* The argument goes as follows: Equities have a 60 percent probability of outperforming government

---

*Swank et al. (2002), for example, recommend pension plans to be 100 percent invested in equities (i.e., they recommend portfolio concentration as opposed to portfolio diversification): "While an appropriate investment strategy depends on a number of factors, many of them plan-specific, in many cases we believe it is in the best interest of both the pension plan's sponsor and its participants to invest the plan's assets entirely in equities. Certainly plans must maintain the liquidity necessary to make annual contributions and benefit payments, but many plans have the financial stability and liquidity to handle a downturn in the market even if invested 100 percent in equities. For these plans, any amount not invested in equities simply reduces the long-term growth of assets with no offsetting benefit." It is unlikely that the authors would have drawn the same conclusions had the analysis been done with Nikkei 225 or MSCI Europe index returns instead of S&P 500 returns.

bonds over a one-year period and a 95 percent outperformance probability over 25 years. In addition, long-term volatility is normally lower than short-term volatility. The apparent conclusion, therefore, is that investing in equities is foolproof as long as one has a long time horizon. The debate surrounding whether time reduces risk is often referred to as the time diversification controversy. Another school of thought argues that time diversification is an illusion and a longer time horizon does not reduce risk.

The illusion (or misconception) of time reducing risk arises from a misunderstanding of risk. It is true that the annual average rate of return has a smaller standard deviation for a longer time horizon. However, it is also true that the uncertainty compounds over a greater number of years. Unfortunately, this latter effect dominates in the sense that the total return becomes more uncertain the longer the investment horizon. Had a long-term investor with a 100-year investment horizon decided to put money into the U.S. stock market in 1900, the investment would have compounded at a reasonable rate. However, other choices were other large markets such as Argentina, Imperial Russia, or Japan. The 100-year return of these markets was materially different than the U.S. experience.

An eye-opener is the difference between the probability of suffering a loss at the *end of* the investment period and the probability of suffering a loss *during* the investment period. The former is very small and the latter large by comparison. The practical significance is that large absolute losses are very uncomfortable for most investors, private as well as institutional. The difference between 15 percent and 18 percent rates of return seems relatively small. The impact on ending wealth is considerably larger ($3,292 versus $6,267 compounded over 25 years for a $100 initial investment). Thus the variation or risk in end-of-period wealth does not decrease with time. Further, this analysis specifies no utility function for the investor. If an investor had uncertainty as to when he or she would withdraw money, the variability in ending wealth would further diminish the value of the risky investment over the safer investment. *End of the period* and *during the period* lose significance if the end of the investment period is not known with 100 percent certainty.

The financial industry has not yet paid a lot of attention to risk-adjusted returns. Pure returns or, in some cases, active returns are the main focus point when performance is presented to investors and/or prospects. With Table 1.3 we try to make the point that two portfolios with the same return are not necessarily the same.

Table 1.3 shows the difference of achieving an 8.1 percent annual return over a 10-year period with volatile returns and with stable returns. The volatile returns are annual total returns in U.S. dollars for an investment in the MSCI World index for the 10-year period ending in 2001 (in reverse order). The stable returns were calculated for volatility to equal 1.58 percent, that is, one-tenth of MSCI World return volatility. Note that

**Table 1.3**   Volatile versus Stable Returns

| Year | Volatile Returns | Year-End Wealth | Stable Returns | Year-End Wealth |
|------|------------------|-----------------|----------------|-----------------|
|      |                  | $100            |                | $100            |
| 1    | −17%             | 83              | 9.6%           | 110             |
| 2    | −13              | 72              | 6.6            | 117             |
| 3    | 25               | 90              | 9.6            | 128             |
| 4    | 24               | 112             | 6.6            | 137             |
| 5    | 16               | 130             | 9.6            | 150             |
| 6    | 13               | 147             | 6.6            | 159             |
| 7    | 21               | 178             | 9.6            | 175             |
| 8    | 5                | 186             | 6.6            | 186             |
| 9    | 23               | 229             | 9.6            | 204             |
| 10   | −5               | 218             | 6.6            | 218             |
| Average return per year   |  | 9.2% |  | 8.1% |
| Compound return per year  |  | 8.1  |  | 8.1  |
| Volatility                |  | 15.8 |  | 1.58 |
| Sharpe ratio (5%)         |  | 0.20 |  | 1.96 |

the 10-year period covered a large part of the 1990s, which is generally considered to be one of the greatest decades for equity investors in the history of financial markets.

The view of an absolute return manager is that many investors underestimate the impact of negative years on overall wealth creation. The first strategy in Table 1.3 looks superior because the average of the simple returns is 9.2 percent whereas it is only 8.1 percent for the second strategy. However, once the compound annual return of 8.1 percent is put into context with the variance of the returns, the investment with the stable returns does not appear to be inferior. As a matter of fact, if end-of-period wealth as well as during-the-period variance matter, the investment with the more stable returns is superior.*

Many absolute return managers probably subscribe to Benjamin Graham's rule of investing:

---

*For the stable-return investment to result in a volatility of 15.8 percent the investor could use leverage of around 7:1. The compound annual return would increase to 24.5 percent. This is a further indication that a low-volatility investment is superior to a high-volatility investment when the expected return is the same.

*The first rule of investment is don't lose. And the second rule of invest-
ment is don't forget the first rule. And that's all the rules there are.*

Today this is considered Wall Street wit and regularly used for entertainment purposes. However, the notion has probably more than just entertainment value. It is the reason why absolute return managers are more than just
relative return managers with cash as their benchmark. It is also the reason
why many investors regard investing to be at least as much alchemy (Soros,
1987) or art (Yale Endowment, 2001) as it is pure science. Figure 1.7 shows
that portfolio volatility matters.

Figure 1.7 shows two 10-year investments that double over a 10-year period. The dark line is a $100 investment growing at 7.2 percent over the 10-
year period. The lighter line experiences a loss of 30 percent in the first year.
The growth rate to match the 7.2 percent growth rate in the remaining nine
years is 12.4 percent. If the second investment grew from 70 after the first
year at a rate of 7.2 percent, the end-of-period wealth would accumulate to
only $131. The annualized return would result in a compounded annual
growth rate of only 2.7 percent. To an absolute return manager, an investment vehicle where there is no provision to manage volatility is, to use the politically correct term, suboptimal. Note that in many continental European

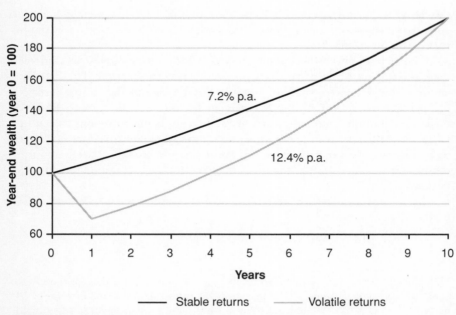

**FIGURE 1.7**   Different Ways of Doubling an Initial Investment of $100

countries the equity culture began in the late 1990s. It is not unreasonable to assume that for some investors the 2000–2002 bear market was the first experience with equities as an asset class.

## Managing Volatility

Putting it crudely: Absolute return managers have an incentive to manage volatility, whereas long-only managers do not. The portfolios of most long-only managers closely track the benchmark. When the benchmark has a volatility of around 10 percent (as some developed equity markets had around 1995), then the portfolio of the long-only manager will have a volatility of 10 percent. When the volatility of the benchmark increases to 25 percent (as in most developed markets in the period 1997 to 2000), then the portfolio of the long-only manager will have a volatility of around 25 percent. This makes sense because it is in line with the mandate (i.e., mimicking the benchmark market index). Whether this makes sense on a more general level is, for the time being, in the eye of the beholder.

Table 1.4 shows five different ways of managing equity risk. The first is the traditional long-only way where there is no incentive to hedge market risk. The MSCI World index was used as a proxy for a long-only portfolio.

**Table 1.4**   Long-Only Compared with Market-Neutral and Long/Short Equity

| Year | Long-Only MSCI World (Total Return) Index | Alternative Strategies HFRI Equity Market-Neutral Index | HFRI Statistical Arbitrage Index | HFRI Equity Hedge Index | HFRI Equity Non-Hedge Index |
|------|---------|---------|---------|---------|---------|
| 1990 | −16.5% | 15.5% | 11.2% | 14.4% | −7.0 |
| 1991 | 19.0 | 15.6 | 17.8 | 40.1 | 57.1 |
| 1992 | −4.7 | 8.7 | 10.8 | 21.3 | 22.8 |
| 1993 | 23.1 | 11.1 | 12.6 | 27.9 | 27.4 |
| 1994 | 5.6 | 2.7 | 4.7 | 2.6 | 5.1 |
| 1995 | 21.3 | 16.3 | 14.2 | 31.0 | 34.8 |
| 1996 | 14.0 | 14.2 | 19.6 | 21.8 | 25.5 |
| 1997 | 16.2 | 13.6 | 19.4 | 23.4 | 17.6 |
| 1998 | 24.8 | 8.3 | 10.1 | 16.0 | 9.8 |
| 1999 | 25.3 | 10.8 | −1.3 | 46.1 | 41.8 |
| 2000 | −12.9 | 14.6 | 8.9 | 9.1 | −9.0 |
| 2001 | −16.5 | 6.4 | 1.2 | 0.4 | 0.7 |
| | | | | | |
| Annual return | 6.99% | 11.09% | 10.68% | 20.32% | 17.33% |
| Volatility | 14.59 | 3.28 | 3.87 | 9.26 | 14.91 |
| Sharpe ratio (5%) | 0.14 | 1.86 | 1.47 | 1.65 | 0.83 |
| Return for 1.86 Sharpe ratio | 32.13 | 11.09 | 12.20 | 22.23 | 32.72 |

*Source:* Hedge Fund Research, Datastream.

The four other equity strategies involve managing downside market risk to different degrees. The HFRI Equity Market-Neutral and HFRI Statistical Arbitrage indexes are both relative value strategies where market risk is fully hedged at all times. The other two strategies are long/short strategies. In equity hedge managers have a small long bias, and in equity nonhedge there is a large long bias. Of these five investments, the market-neutral one has the highest risk-adjusted returns whereas the MSCI World index has the lowest. Assume an investor has a risk budget for equitylike risk, which one of the five investments is superior over the other four?

As shown in Figure 1.8, the five (capital market) lines originate at the risk-free rate, which is most often assumed to have zero risk.* Each line is drawn through the risk/return point in the graph. The steepest line is considered the best. It is not important where the dot is. The reason why the position of the dot is irrelevant is because of the use of leverage. If an investor has a risk budget (risk appetite) of 9.26 percent as the second best investment in Figure 1.8, he could borrow money and invest in the best investment. Assum-

---

*An investment at the risk-free rate is considered risk free. However, volatility is not zero. The ambiguity derives from the fact that in financial theory volatility (annualized standard deviation of returns) is used as a proxy for risk.

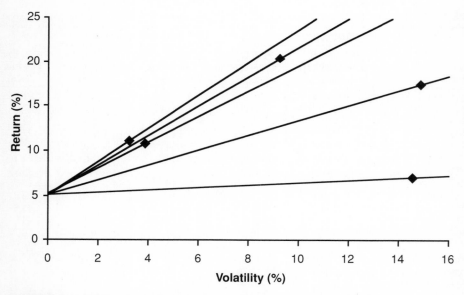

**FIGURE 1.8** Risk/Return Trade-off of Five Equity Investment Styles
*Source:* Hedge Fund Research, Datastream.

ing the investor borrows money at the risk-free rate, invests in the best investment, and accepts a volatility of 9.2 percent, the resultant return would be around 22.2 percent, that is, approximately 190 basis points higher than the second best investment with the same volatility. If the investor is ready to accept the volatility of the most volatile investment (which also happens to be the worst investment of the five), that is, a volatility of 14.59 percent, he or she can lever up and invest in the best investment. The return of using leverage and investment in the best investment would result in an annual return of around 32.1 percent. This seems to represent a big difference from the 7.0 percent in the MSCI World.

Where does this analysis fail? There must be something wrong. First, hedge fund data is inflated for various reasons discussed in later chapters. In addition, volatilities are most likely too low; that is, Sharpe ratios too high. However, these measurement imperfections are unlikely to explain the 2,471 basis points between the best investment in Figure 1.8 and the worst. Second, there is a capacity issue. The worst investment in Figure 1.8 has a market capitalization in excess of $25 trillion whereas the best investment is probably around $50 billion.* What would happen if the investors holding the $25 trillion were to rebalance their portfolio by moving funds from the worst investment to the best investment? The capital market lines would move. Putting it crudely: The suppliers of the $50 billion can deliver Sharpe ratios of 1.86 only if the holders of the $25 trillion do not mind having a Sharpe ratio of 0.14. If the holders of $25 trillion decide tomorrow that a Sharpe ratio of 1.86 is more appealing than a Sharpe ratio of 0.14, then the suppliers of a Sharpe ratio of 1.86 will get flooded with funds. In other words, once all investors start requesting higher Sharpe ratios, the capital market lines in Figure 1.8 will converge. The suppliers of a Sharpe ratio of 1.86 for $50 billion will, by definition, not be able to deliver a Sharpe ratio of 1.86 for $25 trillion. The pioneers of absolute return strategies were enjoying an economic rent that cannot be supported if $25 trillion was managed in this format. Superior risk-adjusted returns—that is, superior performance—attracts capital. Assuming alpha is finite, the alpha will be spread over more investors going forward.† This means that unlocking the alpha in the hedge fund industry is becoming more difficult over time.

---

*Assuming around 10 percent of the hedge funds universe is market-neutral (or is delivering a Sharpe ratio of 1.86 on a consistent and sustainable basis).
†Unless the regulator intervenes, that is. If regulators only allow certain investors to invest at a Sharpe ratio in excess of 1.5 (which most of them currently do), then the regulator will be determining the winners and losers of the game.

## Conclusion

The investment philosophy of absolute return managers differs from that of relative return managers. Absolute return managers care not only about the long-term compounded returns on their investments but also how their wealth changes during the investment period. In other words, an absolute return manager tries to increase wealth by balancing opportunities with risk, and run portfolios that are diversified and/or hedged against strong fluctuations. To the absolute return manager these objectives are considered conservative.

## DEFINING THE HEDGE FUND INDUSTRY

### Definition

There are nearly as many definitions of hedge funds as there are hedge funds. We define a hedge fund as follows: A hedge fund constitutes an investment program whereby the managers or partners seek absolute returns by exploiting investment opportunities while protecting principal from potential financial loss. With this definition we capture the balancing act of the absolute return manager. On one hand, the absolute return manager tries to make money by exploiting investment opportunities. However, the profit opportunity is always put into context with the potential loss of principal. (Note that this definition does not apply for the relative return manager where the goal is to beat a benchmark.) Crerend (1995) defines hedge funds as follows:

> Hedge funds are private partnerships wherein the manager or general partner has a significant personal stake in the fund and is free to operate in a variety of markets and to utilize investments and strategies with variable long/short exposures and degrees of leverage.

Unfortunately, not all hedge fund managers have "a significant personal stake" in the fund. Nonetheless, beyond the basic characteristics embodied in this definition, hedge funds commonly share a variety of other structural traits. They are typically organized as limited partnerships or limited liability companies. They are often domiciled offshore, for tax and regulatory reasons. And, unlike traditional funds, they are not as much burdened by regulation. Less regulation means less protection for the investor and more flexibility for the hedge fund manager. Less protection means higher risk for the investor, for which the investor seeks compensation.

As elaborated on in the appendix to Chapter 2, the reputation of hedge funds is not particularly good. The term "hedge fund" suffers from a similar fate as "derivatives" due to a mixture of myth, misrepresentation, negative press, and high-profile casualties. Hedge fund strategies are occasionally also referred to as skill-based strategies or absolute return strategies, which, from a marketing perspective, avoids the negative bias attached to the misleading term "hedge fund." Skill-based strategies differ from traditional (market-based) strategies. The former yields a particular return associated with the skill of a manager whereas the latter primarily captures the asset class premium of a market.

## Categorization of Hedge Funds

There are three ways to categorize hedge funds: (1) as a separate, alternative asset class; (2) as asset management firms executing alternative investment strategies within a traditional asset class; and (3) as financial services companies. The consensus view is that hedge funds are a separate asset class because return, volatility, and correlation characteristics differ from those of other asset classes such as equities, bonds, commodities and natural resources, real estate, and private equity. In addition, it allows separation between liquid asset classes (e.g., equities and bonds) and less liquid asset classes (e.g., real estate, private equity, and hedge funds). Treating hedge funds as a separate asset class also allows the showing of efficiency improvements gained by including hedge funds in traditional portfolios in mean variance space. One of the practical issues with this classification is that there is limited data availability. Most databases show between 6 and 14 years of data, whereas asset/liability studies are normally based on longer time series.

Viewing hedge funds as an investment style within the asset management industry is an alternative way of categorizing the hedge fund industry. Looking at absolute return managers as part of the asset management industry makes sense because absolute return managers are asset managers who define return and risk objectives differently but manage money by investing in traditional asset classes—equities, bonds, currencies, commodities, or derivatives thereof. They recruit staff from the same pool of talent as do other money managers and offer their products to the same client base. This view finds further support in the fact that more and more traditional asset management firms are offering nontraditional (i.e., alternative) strategies to their investors. The benefits to them are twofold: First, they add a high-margin product to their low-margin long-only product. Second, revenues from alternative products are not necessarily correlated with fee income from traditional products. As the revenues of traditional products are a percentage of funds under management, revenues decline when markets fall. As demand for hedge funds is probably negatively correlated with the direction of the stock market, falling revenues from the traditional product can be, to some extent, balanced with products in the alternative investment segment.

The third way of looking at hedge funds—viewing a hedge fund as a financial services company—is not very common. However, sooner or later there will be hedge fund organizations going public. The price of the entity will be determined—as with other financial services or asset management companies—based on discounted value of future cash flows or assets under management or whatever valuation tool is in fashion at the time. The main benefit of viewing a hedge fund as a company is to understand all the risk components of a hedge fund as an organization. Any investor selecting hedge fund managers will conduct a bottom-up analysis, similar to the work any equity or credit analyst does on quoted companies. The categorization of financial risk in Figure 1.9 might be helpful to understanding the diversity and complexity of the task of the hedge fund analysis and due diligence.

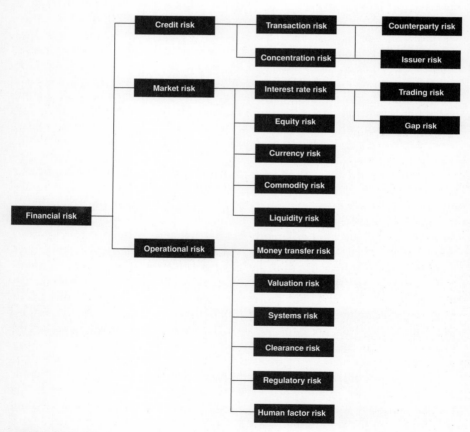

**FIGURE 1.9**   Categorization of Risk
*Source:* Estenne (2000).

Normally financial risks are grouped into market risk, credit risk, and operational risk. By viewing hedge funds as a separate asset class or as alternative investment strategies, one might have a tendency to underestimate operational risk. (Note that operational risk is idiosyncratic risk; that is, it can be immunized through diversification.) These operational risks are not reflected through the standard deviation of historical return series but through bottom-up fundamental analysis and due diligence. Figure 1.9 essentially says that the evaluation of companies in general or hedge funds in particular is more complex than can be summarized by one number, for example, the volatility of returns. As with any quoted company there are risks associated to the operation of the business (i.e., process risks, legal risks, human risks, etc.). Note that there are many more operational risks than are shown in Figure 1.9. We shall revisit operational risks with hedge funds in Part III of this book, which will examine the fund of (hedge) funds industry.

Figure 1.10 summarizes the categorization of hedge funds. In any portfolio optimization process there is some merit in viewing hedge funds as a separate asset class, because the performance characteristics differ from those of traditional assets. However—for example, in a core-satellite approach where the core of the portfolio is invested passively in domestic equity and bonds and smaller mandates are outsourced to active specialist managers—there is also some merit in viewing hedge funds as a niche specialist (i.e., one of the satellites). In evaluating hedge funds there are many risk aspects where the only reasonable approach is bottom-up fundamental company research and due diligence.

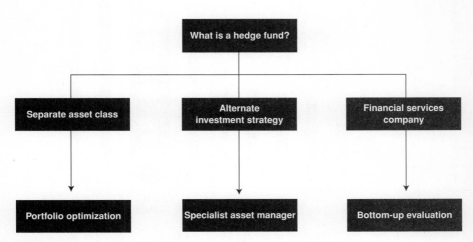

**FIGURE 1.10**   Categorization of Hedge Funds

## Main Characteristics of the Hedge Fund Industry

**Industry Size and Growth**    The hedge fund industry is still in its infancy; it is still a niche industry. Estimates of the size of the hedge fund industry are scarce and fluctuate substantially. The estimates for the number of funds range between 2,500 and 6,000, and assets under management between $500 billion and $600 billion globally. Compared with global pension funds or U.S. financial institutions, the estimated $500 to $600 billion in assets under management remains relatively small. Global pension fund assets grew from $4.6 trillion in 1990 to $15.9 trillion in 1999.[23] (At the same time the equity holdings of pension funds increased from $1.6 trillion to $8.0 trillion—or from 35 percent to 51 percent of total assets.) At the end of the third quarter of 2001, U.S. commercial banks had $4.9 trillion in total assets, mutual funds had assets of approximately $3.7 trillion (compared to $4.9 trillion a year and a half earlier), private pension funds had $4.0 trillion, state and local government employee retirement funds had $2.1 trillion, and life insurance companies had assets of $3.1 trillion.[24]

Figure 1.11 shows one estimate in terms of growth and industry size. Based on data from Hedge Fund Research, Inc., the assets under management

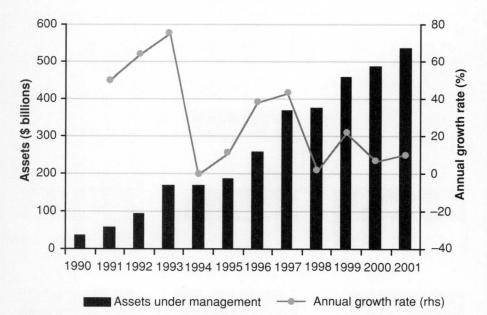

**FIGURE 1.11**    Estimated Growth of Hedge Fund Assets
*Source:* Hedge Fund Research, Inc.

grew from $38.9 billion in 1990 to $536.9 billion at the end of 2001.* The average annual growth rate was 29.3 percent, and the compounded annual growth rate was 26.9 percent. The year 1997 saw accelerated growth. These funds went to a large extent into fixed income arbitrage. Annual growth for 2000 and 2001 were 6.8 percent and 10.1 percent, respectively. Main beneficiaries were risk arbitrage (in 2000), convertible arbitrage, and long/short equity. These two growth rates compare with returns for the HFRI Hedge Fund Composite index of 5.0 percent and 4.8 percent, respectively. In other words, asset growth was partially due to performance and partially due to funds inflow. Figure 1.12 shows growth and size in terms of number of funds.

Based on estimates from Hedge Fund Research, Inc., there were around 4,191 hedge funds in operation as of the third quarter of 2001. The average annual growth rate was 19.7 percent. The annual growth rate has been falling throughout the 1990s. To some extent this falling growth rate would be expected as the industry matures. However, intuitively one would not have

---

*Hennessee Group LLC estimates 2001 net inflow at $144 billion and total assets under management at $563 billion at year-end 2001. From Bloomberg News (2002b).

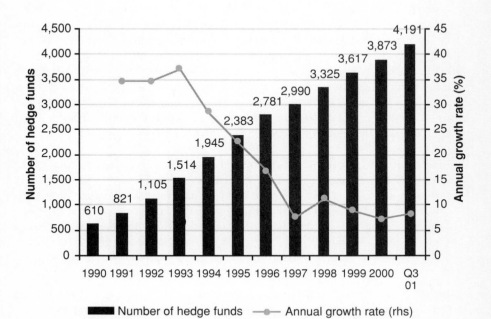

**FIGURE 1.12** Estimated Growth of Hedge Funds
*Source:* Hedge Fund Research, Inc.

thought that the growth rate would decline to 8.2 percent by 2001, since the barriers to entry have vanished, giving an incentive to start a hedge fund. Note that the attrition rate is high and that there could be measurement problems with respect to the number of funds in the industry.

The $150 billion California Public Employees' Retirement System (CalPERS) dropped a bombshell on the hedge fund industry on August 31, 1999, when it released a statement saying it would invest as much as $11 billion into "hybrid investments," including hedge funds.* Coming just one year after the collapse of LTCM, it was seen as a vote of confidence in an asset class that had been largely off-limits to public pension funds. While many other large and sophisticated institutional investors have been investing in the alternative investment strategies (AIS) sectors for years, the announcement by CalPERS (the largest pension system in the world) further legitimized AIS investments for the broad base of institutions seeking viable alternatives to their reliance on rising stock markets.

Historically hedge funds were targeted at private investors. In recent years the participation of institutional investors has risen. University foundations and endowments are among the most aggressive institutional investors. It is commonly known that prestigious schools such as Duke, Chicago, Stanford, and Princeton have large allocations to hedge funds. On the corporate side, large conservative firms such as IBM have been investing in hedge funds for years. Pension funds, under pressure to constantly look for new ways to diversify their holdings, are also starting to allocate capital to hedge funds. In addition, overfunded pension funds seek to preserve wealth by lowering risk. However, according to Hennessee Group, individuals remained the largest source of capital for hedge funds in 2001, contributing 48 percent ($270 billion) of total assets.[25] The share of assets under management is down, though, from 80 percent of total assets in 1994. Further findings from the *Eighth Annual Hennessee Hedge Fund Manager Survey* included:

■ Funds of funds were the second largest source of capital, contributing 20 percent of total assets according to Hennessee Group.
■ In addition, 37 percent of hedge fund managers indicated that high net worth individuals and family offices were the fastest growing source of capital, while 25 percent specified corporations, 10 percent pension

---

*CalPERS eventually approved a target for hedge fund allocation of just $1 billion. As of April 2002, it had made five $10 million allocations to five hedge funds with the option to increase four investments to $50 million and the other to $40 million. In other words, the excitement from the $11 billion headline somewhat cooled off in the months and years after the announcement.

funds, 9 percent both endowments/foundations and funds of funds, and 11 percent other sources of capital.

■ Due to the increased number of banks and insurance companies offering hedge fund products, 54 percent of hedge fund managers were Registered Investment Advisers in 2001, up from 47 percent in 2000.

Increased institutional participation portends a fundamental shift in the quality of hedge fund programs. In the past, the establishment of hedge funds has been largely supply-driven. Successful investors, often the heads of proprietary trading desks, decided to forgo their lucrative seven- and eight-figure Wall Street remuneration packages to establish boutique organizations as the primary vehicle for managing their own personal assets. Earning a return on their own assets (versus the collection of fees from outside investors) was the primary motivator for early hedge fund entrants. Entry costs were high, as the dealer community set lofty standards for those to which it would lend money/stock and establish credit lines.

Increasing participation from institutions is beginning to shift the expansion from being supply-driven to being demand-driven. This motivates a vast group of aspirants to enter the competition for these new investors. At the same time, the barriers to entry have been torn down. There have been hedge funds launched by 20-year-olds with little or no resources or investment experience.

As a result, the differentiation between quality and substandard managers is becoming more pronounced. Quality hedge fund managers should benefit from a proliferation of ill-managed funds, while investors need to stay alert to this potential degradation in the quality of hedge fund management. This proliferation and the high costs associated with actively selecting hedge funds are among the main reasons for accelerated growth in the funds of funds industry. We will take a closer look at funds of hedge funds in Part III.

The following two sections examine the distribution of dollars invested in hedge funds, by fund size and by fund investment style.

**Breakdown by Size**  Figure 1.13 shows estimates for the distribution of hedge funds by size. As of 1999 as well as 2000, around 83 percent of all funds under management were allocated to funds below $100 million and around 53 percent to funds smaller than $25 million. According to Peltz (1995) the breakdown in 1994 was that 72 percent of managers had $50 million or less, 9 percent between $50 million and $100 million, 14 percent between $100 million and $1 billion, and around 5 percent above $1 billion. The average size of hedge funds is decreasing. Based on the 1,305 hedge funds in the MAR/Hedge database (not shown in graph), the average fund size in October 1999 was $93 million compared with $135 million a year earlier.

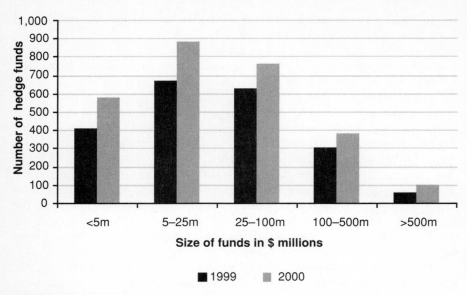

**FIGURE 1.13** Size Distribution of Hedge Funds
*Source:* Van Hedge Fund Advisors.

**Breakdown by Style**   Table 1.5 shows an estimate of assets under management by style as of the third quarter of 2001. We have assumed a total of $500 billion assets under management for the whole industry for this analysis, and applied the percentages from Tremont Advisors (2002).

■ Long/short equity is the largest style with a market share of around 45 percent based on assets under management.
■ Other estimates for managed futures indicate that around $50 billion is managed by those managers on an unleveraged basis.
■ In Table 1.6 note that equity nonhedge and equity hedge are what others define as long/short equity. The market share of long/short equity, therefore, was around 30 percent at the end of 1999 (not shown) and around 43 percent in 2001 according to estimates from Hedge Fund Research, Inc. Since 1990, long/short equity has grown at the expense of macro. All equity-related strategies in Table 1.6 have a share of 56.8 percent of total assets under management in 2001. This compares with 18.0 percent in 1990. The increase in equity-related strategies is primarily a function of the 1990s bull market.

**Table 1.5**  Estimated Allocation by Investment Style (Third Quarter, 2001)

| Category | Assets under Management ($ billions) | Percentage of Total Assets |
|---|---|---|
| Equity long/short | $228.3 | 45.65% |
| Event-driven | 108.4 | 21.67 |
| Global macro | 40.0 | 7.99 |
| Convertible arbitrage | 38.6 | 7.71 |
| Equity market-neutral | 34.9 | 6.97 |
| Fixed income arbitrage | 20.5 | 4.09 |
| Emerging markets | 17.3 | 3.46 |
| Managed futures | 9.9 | 1.98 |
| Short selling | 1.2 | 0.24 |
| Other | 1.2 | 0.24 |
| Total | $500.0 | 100.00% |

*Source:* Percentages in righthand column from Tremont Advisors (2002); center column, author's own calculations assuming total assets under management of $500 billion.

**Table 1.6**  Strategy Composition by Assets, 1990 versus 2001

| Category | 1990 | 2001 |
|---|---|---|
| Equity hedge | 5.28% | 30.83% |
| Macro | 71.04 | 13.48 |
| Equity nonhedge | 0.60 | 11.69 |
| Event-driven | 3.84 | 9.30 |
| Fixed income (total) | 3.24 | 8.24 |
| Equity market neutral | 1.68 | 5.59 |
| Sector (total) | 0.24 | 4.50 |
| Relative value | 10.08 | 4.12 |
| Convertible arbitrage | 0.48 | 3.89 |
| Emerging markets | 0.36 | 3.25 |
| Distressed securities | 2.40 | 2.58 |
| Merger arbitrage | 0.60 | 2.44 |
| Short selling | 0.12 | 0.11 |

*Source:* Hedge Fund Research.

■ Note that there are huge differences between style allocation estimates from Tremont Advisors and Hedge Fund Research. Tremont Advisors has a much higher estimate for convertible arbitrage and a lower estimate for global macro when compared with Hedge Fund Research. This is an indication of quantitative analysis in the hedge fund industry being as much art as science.

**Breakdown by Investor Type** Table 1.7 shows an estimated breakdown by investor type for U.S. and non-U.S. investors as well as the combined investor base. The investor breakdown estimates (last two columns) are from Hedge Fund Research, Inc. These estimates in combination with an estimate for total assets under management in the industry plus an assumption for the geographic breakdown allow the estimation of investor breakdown in absolute U.S. dollar terms. Our assumption for a geographic breakdown in terms of assets under management between U.S. and non-U.S. was 40 percent by U.S. investors and 60 percent by non-U.S. investors. Note that the figures in Table 1.7 are estimates and not necessarily consistent with all available surveys. U.S. figures are based on 160 responses representing $4.09 billion in hedge fund assets. Non-U.S. figures are based on 169 responses representing $4.55 billion in hedge fund assets.

The main difference between U.S. and non-U.S. investors has to do with the involvement of banks in the industry. U.S. banks hold only around 2.0 percent of hedge fund assets whereas rest of world (RoW) banks hold around 23.3 percent. The fund of funds allocation is also larger outside the United

**Table 1.7** Estimated Breakdown by Investor Types ($ billions)

| Category | All Investors | U.S. Investors | Non-U.S. Investors | All Investors | U.S. Investors | Non-U.S. Investors |
|---|---|---|---|---|---|---|
| Individuals | $129.5 | $80.0 | $49.5 | 25.9% | 40.0% | 16.5% |
| Fund of funds | 100.3 | 23.0 | 77.3 | 20.1 | 11.5 | 25.8 |
| Banks | 73.8 | 4.0 | 69.8 | 14.8 | 2.0 | 23.3 |
| Pension plans | 36.0 | 21.0 | 15.0 | 7.2 | 10.5 | 5.0 |
| Family offices | 27.2 | 10.7 | 16.5 | 5.4 | 5.4 | 5.5 |
| Corporate accounts | 24.5 | 14.0 | 10.5 | 4.9 | 7.0 | 3.5 |
| Foundations | 16.5 | 6.7 | 9.8 | 3.3 | 3.4 | 3.3 |
| Endowments | 15.0 | 15.0 | NA | 3.0 | 7.5 | NA |
| Insurance | 14.0 | 4.2 | 9.8 | 2.8 | 2.1 | 3.3 |
| General partners | 12.6 | 2.5 | 10.1 | 2.5 | 1.3 | 3.4 |
| Trust | 4.5 | 4.5 | NA | 0.9 | 2.3 | NA |
| Mutual funds | 2.0 | 2.0 | NA | 0.4 | 1.0 | NA |
| Other | 44.4 | 12.4 | 32.0 | 8.9 | 6.2 | 10.7 |
| Total | $500.0 | $200.0 | $300.0 | 100.0% | 100.0% | 100.0% |

*Source:* Hedge Fund Research, author's own estimates.

States. Assuming hedge fund assets are $500 billion globally, then funds of funds, banks, and pension plans hold $100 billion, $74 billion, and $36 billion respectively. However, the largest investor group is individuals, who hold around $130 billion (26 percent) of unleveraged hedge fund assets.

Table 1.7 is not consistent with a survey Greenwich Associates conducted in 2001. The survey found 1,445 of the 2,500 largest U.S. pension funds and endowments held a total of $35 billion in hedge fund investments (compared to $36 billion in Table 1.7). The survey notes that corporate and public pension funds in the United States together account for just $10 billion of the total (compared to $21 billion in Table 1.7). Our estimates in Table 1.7 are also different from a survey conducted by Barra Strategic Consulting Group (2001). According to this survey, hedge fund assets under management were $450 billion as of July 2001, of which $350 billion (78 percent) were held by U.S. investors, $78 billion (17 percent) by European investors, and $22 billion (5 percent) by Asian investors. This extreme bias toward U.S. buyers probably is, in our opinion, more appropriate for sellers (i.e., hedge fund managers) where the United States is still the dominant marketplace by a wide margin. Around 85 percent of managers are based in the United States.

**Use of Leverage**   Leverage is an important issue to most investors when investing in hedge funds. Institutionally, leverage is defined in accounting or balance sheet terms as the ratio of total assets to equity capital (net worth). Alternatively, leverage can be defined in terms of risk, in which case it is a measure of economic risk relative to capital.

Hedge funds vary greatly in their use of leverage. Nevertheless, compared with other trading institutions, hedge funds' use of leverage, combined with any structured or illiquid positions whose full value cannot be realized in a quick sale, can potentially make them somewhat fragile institutions that are vulnerable to liquidity shocks. While trading desks of investment banks may take positions similar to hedge funds, these organizations and their parent firms often have both liquidity sources and independent streams of income from other activities that can offset the riskiness of their positions.

Table 1.8 shows estimates of how different hedge fund managers are typically leveraged. Based on a report from Van Money Manager Research, around 72 percent of hedge funds used leverage as of December 1999. However, only around 20 percent have balance-sheet leverage ratios of more than 2:1. Fixed income arbitrageurs operate with the smallest margins and therefore gear up heavily to meet their return targets. However, Table 1.8 shows leverage pre-LTCM. Leverage in fixed income arbitrage in the post-LTCM era is closer to 10 to 15 times equity. Hedge funds that operate in emerging markets use little leverage primarily because derivatives markets and securities lending are not developed.

Note that there was massive delevering in hedge funds as brokers tightened credit lines as a direct result of the near collapse of LTCM in 1998. Equity

**Table 1.8**  Estimated Use of Balance Sheet Leverage

| (%) | Balance-Sheet Leverage |
| --- | --- |
| Fixed income arbitrage | 20-30 |
| Convertible arbitrage | 2-10 |
| Risk arbitrage | 2-5 |
| Equity market-neutral | 1-5 |
| Equity long/short | 1-2 |
| Distressed securities | 1-2 |
| Emerging markets | 1-1.5 |
| Short selling | 1-1.5 |

*Source:* UBS Warburg (2000).

long/short managers delevered quite substantially during the 2000–2001 market decline. By 2002, cash levels in long/short equity were at an all-time high. As of 2001 there was very little leverage in the system when compared to summer 1998. This is probably the main reason why hedge funds, in general, could preserve wealth so successfully during the difficult market environment that was 2001 (and first half of 2002).

Not all hedge fund managers use leverage. Table 1.9 shows that around 31.6 percent do not use leverage and a further 44.8 percent use less leverage than 2:1. As of 1999, 28.5 percent claimed not to use leverage, 52.1 percent were using leverage less than 2:1, and 19.4 percent more than 2:1. In other words, hedge funds claiming not to use leverage rose from 28.5 percent in 1999 to 31.6 percent in 2000.

High leverage is the exception rather than the rule. Hedge funds lever the capital they invest by buying securities on margin and engaging in collateralized borrowing. Better-known funds can buy structured derivative products without first putting up capital, but must make a succession of premium payments when the market in those securities trades up or down. Pre-LTCM, some hedge funds negotiated secured credit lines with their banks, and some relative value funds even obtained unsecured credit lines.

**Characteristics of the "Average" Hedge Fund**    The hedge fund industry is heterogeneous. This means that a typical hedge fund may not be representative of its brethren. One of the industry's main characteristics is heterogeneity and not homogeneity. However, Table 1.10 lists some average characteristics from the Van Hedge hedge fund universe for 1999 and 2000. Table 1.11 lists some further

**Table 1.9** Use of Leverage as of 2000 (%)

| | Don't Use Leverage | Use Leverage | | |
|---|---|---|---|---|
| | | Low (<2:1) | High (>2:1) | Total |
| Total sample | 31.6 | 44.8 | 23.6 | 68.4 |
| Aggressive growth | 29.3 | 56.3 | 14.4 | 70.7 |
| Distressed securities | 50.9 | 45.6 | 3.5 | 49.1 |
| Emerging markets | 36.5 | 49.2 | 14.4 | 63.6 |
| Fund of funds | 35.6 | 47.9 | 16.5 | 64.4 |
| Income | 49.2 | 28.6 | 22.2 | 50.8 |
| Macro | 10.0 | 48.0 | 42.0 | 90.0 |
| Market neutral — arbitrage | 20.7 | 22.0 | 57.3 | 79.3 |
| Market neutral — securities hedging | 35.5 | 25.6 | 38.8 | 64.4 |
| Market timing | 42.1 | 22.4 | 35.5 | 57.9 |
| Opportunistic | 27.3 | 44.9 | 27.8 | 72.7 |
| Several strategies | 34.9 | 36.5 | 28.6 | 65.1 |
| Short selling | 30.3 | 45.5 | 24.2 | 69.7 |
| Special situations | 28.2 | 55.6 | 16.1 | 71.7 |
| Value | 31.6 | 55.5 | 12.9 | 68.4 |

*Source:* Van Money Manager Research.

characteristics. Note: The *mean* measures the arithmetical average. The *median* measures the point on either side of which lies 50 percent of the distribution. A median is often preferred over the mean as a measure of central tendency because the arithmetic average can be misleading if extreme values are present.

The main change between 1999 and 2000 is in fund age. The median fund age declined from 5.3 years in 1999 to 3.9 years in 2000. The main reason for this continuous decline in longevity is that the barriers to entry have been falling. The lower the barriers to entry, the cheaper is the call-option-like incentive for a new entrant to set up a hedge fund. The falling barriers to entry are causing a dilution of the talent pool within the hedge fund industry. The practical implication is that manager selection is becoming more difficult and more laborious.

The number of funds using a high-water mark has been increasing from 64 percent in 1995 to 87 percent in 2000. Hurdle rates are not very common with single hedge funds but are more common with funds of hedge funds. Some of the characteristics in Table 1.11 will be highlighted when comparing hedge funds with mutual funds in Chapter 3. The following section discusses

**Table 1.10**   Characteristics of Typical Hedge Fund

| Characteristic | 1999 | | 2000 | |
|---|---|---|---|---|
| | Mean | Median | Mean | Median |
| Fund size ($ millions) | 87 | 22 | 90 | 22 |
| Fund age (years) | 5.9 | 5.3 | 5.0 | 3.9 |
| Minimum investment ($) | 695,000 | 250,000 | 630,729 | 250,000 |
| Management fee (%) | 1.7 | 1.0 | 1.3 | 1.0 |
| Performance-related fee (%) | 15.9 | 20.0 | 16.7 | 20.0 |
| Manager's experience (years) | | | | |
| In securities industry | 17 | 15 | 17 | 15 |
| In portfolio management | 11 | 10 | 12 | 10 |

*Source:* Van Money Manager Research.


**Table 1.11**   Trends in Descriptive Statistics between 1995 and 2000

| Characteristic | 1995 | 1999 | 2000 |
|---|---|---|---|
| Manager is U.S.-registered investment adviser | 54% | 45% | 68% |
| Fund has hurdle rate | 17 | 17 | 18 |
| Fund has high-water mark | 64 | 75 | 87 |
| Fund has audited financial statements or audited performance | 97 | 98 | 96 |
| Manager has $500,000 of own money in fund | 78 | 75 | 79 |
| Fund can handle "hot issues" | 25 | 53 | 54 |
| Fund is diversified | 57 | 57 | 52 |
| Fund can short sell | 76 | 84 | 84 |
| Fund can use leverage | 72 | 72 | 72 |
| Fund uses derivatives for hedging only, or not at all | 77 | 71 | 71 |

*Source:* Van Money Manager Research.


the developments in Europe, which many regard as a growth area for raising capital for absolute return strategies.

### Situation in Europe

Based on estimates from the trade publication *EuroHedge*, the size of European hedge fund assets under management is about $64 billion.[26] (See Figure 1.14.) This represents around 11 percent of the total assets under management of $500 billion to $600 billion.* The growth rates as estimated by *Eu-*

---

*Note that the 11 percent is an estimate of assets *managed* by European hedge funds. The allocation of European investors *investing* in hedge funds is probably around 45 to 50 percent.

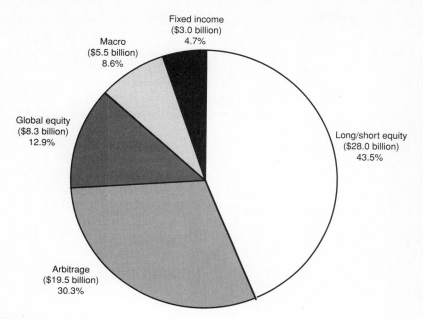

**FIGURE 1.14** Assets under Management by European Hedge Funds
*Source:* Wall Street Journal Online (2002), based on *EuroHedge* estimates.

*ro*Hedge for 1999, 2000, and 2001 were 80 percent, 65 percent, and 40 percent respectively. Most of the growth in Europe came from private investors as opposed to institutional investors.

In March 2000, based on the Ludgate Communications (2000) survey, investing in hedge funds was not something widely considered by all German institutional investors. One CIO was quoted in the survey as saying:

> No, we don't [currently invest in hedge funds]! It is completely obvious that hedge funds don't work. We are not a casino.*

---

*This quote is not representative for Europe. The amusing part of this quote is that running a casino can be a profitable, low-risk business. The casino running a roulette wheel is, as mentioned earlier, in the business of statistical arbitrage (as are insurance companies and the national lottery). It is the gambler who speculates—not the casino. The ultimate business of statistical arbitrage is what Adam Smith refers to as tax "on all the fools in creation": the national lottery. Ask yourself the following question: Would you sell $1 lottery tickets where every 11th ticket allows the buyer to claim $10 from you? If your answer is no, you might consider not investing in hedge funds. However, if your answer is yes, you are ahead of at least one CIO.

Note that the survey was conducted at the chief investment officer (CIO) level. Another investor was quoted arguing that investing in hedge funds is against the respondent's philosophy and that hedge funds still have a stigma attached to them. It is interesting that there are many investors who are willing and legally permitted to invest in a business model attempting to corner the global market for dog food via the Internet, but are unwilling to invest in some of the most talented investment professionals in the financial industry.

In 2001, Golin/Harris Ludgate (2001) commissioned Fulcrum Research to carry out a survey of European investing institutions regarding their sentiment toward institutional investment in hedge funds. The total sample of respondent institutions accounted for $9.6 trillion (£6.7 trillion) of assets under management, equivalent to approximately 67.6 percent of total European assets under management. The interviews took place in January 2001. Figure 1.15 shows institutional investors invested in hedge funds by 2001 and by 2000. Figure 1.16 shows respondents planning to invest in hedge funds. Note: Ireland was not part of the 2000 survey. The allocation of Italy in 2000 was 0 percent.

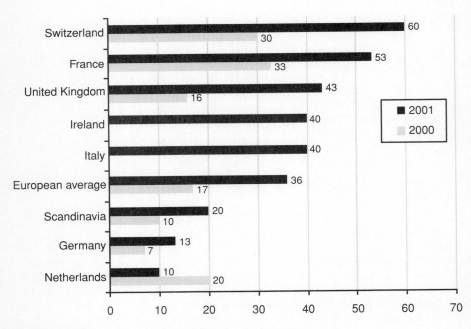

**FIGURE 1.15**  Currently Invested in Hedge Funds (%)
*Source:* Golin/Harris Ludgate (2001), Ludgate Communications (2000).

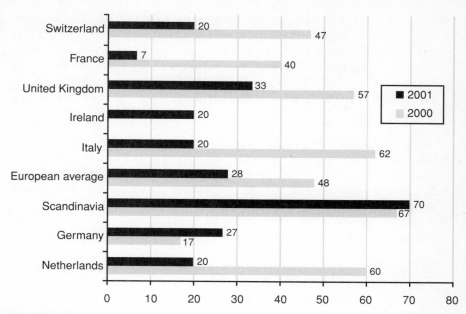

**FIGURE 1.16** Planning to Invest in Hedge Funds (%)
*Source:* Golin/Harris Ludgate (2001), Ludgate Communications (2000).

■ In January 2001 36 percent of European institutions surveyed confirmed that they were investing institutional money in hedge funds. This has more than doubled from the year before when only 17 percent confirmed that they were doing so. Only institutional investors in the Netherlands, according to the survey, invested less than in the previous year. (This is not consistent with the press coverage of Dutch institutions investing in hedge funds.) The reasons for Dutch investors not investing in hedge funds were quoted as conservatism (hence preference for long-only), uncertainty with respect to sustainable source of return, and view of hedge funds as "too risky."*

---

*To some extent the Dutch responses in the survey are contradictory. When asked whether their views on institutional investments in hedge funds had changed over the past 12 months, three of the sample of 10 answered that they were more positive whereas seven respondents thought their views were unchanged. All European respondents either became more positive or were unchanged in their views. From Golin/Harris Ludgate (2001), p. 42. Note that the number of respondents was very small relative to the whole market. The 2001 survey was based on only 100 investors, of which 10 were in the Netherlands. The survey therefore is indicative rather than representative.

■ Also, 28 percent of the European institutions surveyed were intending to invest in hedge funds before 2005, with the vast majority (39 percent) of these planning this for 2001 or 2002. There were fewer institutions planning to invest in hedge funds in the 2001 findings. This was largely due to the increase of actual investors, illustrating the growing acceptance of the hedge fund industry by institutional investors.

■ Swiss institutions had the highest allocation to hedge funds.

■ The U.K., French, and Italian market best demonstrated the move from intending to invest last year to actually investing this year.

■ The German market best illustrates the shift from previously not considering hedge funds to aiming to invest in them in the next few years.

■ Scandinavia—which had a high proportion of institutions with hedge funds on their agendas last year—still had a high proportion in 2001.

■ The most often quoted reason to invest in hedge funds was falling stock prices. Efficiency gains through diversification were also mentioned.

Table 1.12 records the responses to the question "Has your view on institutional investments in hedge funds changed over the past 12 months?" Of 98 investors who answered the question, 43 were more positive and 55 had not changed their (positive or negative) views. No one seemed more negative in 2001 when compared with 2000. With regard to another question, 77 out of 86 (89.5 percent) of the responding investors saw growth continuing. In France, all 15 companies surveyed responded to this question, with six predicting a favorable future for hedge funds in the institutional market due to the diversification benefits and good returns that they offer. Two also saw increasing demand from clients as a significant factor in the likely growth of the hedge fund mar-

**Table 1.12**   Change in Sentiment from 2000 to 2001

| Country | Total Respondents | More Positive | More Negative | Unchanged | Main Reason |
|---|---|---|---|---|---|
| Germany | 15 | 5 | 0 | 10 | Weak equity market |
| France | 15 | 4 | 0 | 11 | Diversification |
| United Kingdom | 28 | 25 | 0 | 13 | Diversification |
| Switzerland | 10 | 4 | 0 | 6 | Diversification |
| Netherlands | 10 | 3 | 0 | 7 | Weak equity market |
| Scandinavia | 10 | 7 | 0 | 3 | Diversification |
| Ireland | 5 | 2 | 0 | 3 | Weak equity market |
| Italy | 5 | 3 | 0 | 2 | Change in regulation |
| Total | 98 | 43 | 0 | 55 | |

*Source:* Golin/Harris Ludgate (2001), pp. 42–45.

ket, while another saw asset allocation to hedge funds increasing. However, five respondents expressed concern regarding the risk posed to institutions if allocations to hedge funds were too heavily weighted in the event of a market crash. Two others thought the risk posed by hedge funds was too excessive, while one company believed that there would be less investment in hedge funds in the future. Two French investors were quoted:

> *What we see is just a fashion favoring hedge funds, but it will not continue very much longer.*
>
> *Hedge funds are not really viable for large institutions, even if they use the low-risk market-neutral strategy. They are too big a risk because hedge funds use leverage usually, which influences the volatility of the asset and the investment house risks losing its entire investment. It's also hard to find a good hedge fund manager, which adds to the unpredictability that large institutions are keen to avoid.*

An Irish investor took the diametrically opposite view by arguing:

> *Yes, institutions will diversify. This is partly due to the idiocy of having index-driven benchmarking. Hedge funds use absolute return benchmarking and are consequently more attractive.*

One U.K. investor increased the entertainment value of the survey by saying:

> *Having been deeply conservative over equities, the continentals\* are hardly likely to suddenly leap to the other end of the spectrum.*

**The European Pension Fund Puzzle**   The generally low allocation to hedge funds by non-Swiss pension funds in Europe is puzzling. Relative performance and benchmarks may enable traditional managers to look at their competitive positions relative to their peer groups. But consistent long-term returns—independent of market movements—make a compelling reason for embracing the world of absolute return for all investors, including pension funds. Concepts such as the core-satellite approach and the portable alpha

---

\*Short for continental Europeans. Note that some Brits think of continental Europeans about as highly as a football hooligan appreciates porcelain art from the Ming dynasty (1368–1644).

approach* to investing large amounts of money strongly favor hedge fund investing for the active mandate in these approaches.

An interesting aspect of a survey by Indocam/Watson Wyatt (2000) was the selection criteria for alternative investment managers. Table 1.13 shows the most important alternative investment manager selection criteria analyzed geographically for those pension funds that are currently outsourcing these types of mandates. Interviewees were asked to rate each criterion on a scale from one to four, with one representing the least important and four representing the most important. The table shows respondents from only three countries for presentation purposes.

Generally, the selection criteria do not differ substantially from those exhibited for more conventional asset mandates. There is a considerable amount of uniformity relating to what respondents regarded as the most important of alternative investment manager selection criteria. These criteria generally relate to mandate suitability, investment performance, investment philosophy, staff continuity, caliber of investment professionals, and quality of client servicing.

The least important of the alternative investment manager selection criteria were remarkably similar when analyzed geographically. Respondents generally believed the softer factors to be less important as selection criteria, namely brand comfort, culture of organization, and prior knowledge of organization. Additionally, fees were not deemed to be of particular importance for selection. Generally, the more operational selection criteria, particularly quality of reporting and administration, were regarded as being of moderate importance by respondents.

When asked for their rationales for investing in alternative investment strategies (AIS), the respondents collectively chose average low correlation as

---

*The core-satellite approach is an alternative to the all-inclusive balanced asset allocation approach. In a core-satellite strategy, a money manager will invest typically 70 to 80 percent of assets in an index tracking fund. Specialist fund managers are hired around this "passive core" as "satellites" to invest in sectors where index-tracking techniques are difficult to apply, for example, alternative investment strategies, smaller companies, or emerging markets. With the portable alpha approach, the alpha of a manager (or group of managers) or a strategy is transported to a target index. For example, a pension fund allocates its fund to a bond manager who generates an alpha of 200 basis points yearly without an increase in credit risk. In addition, it swaps total returns of an equity index with the risk-free rate. The end result is the total index return plus 200 basis points. This approach can be used quite broadly. Alpha can be generated in many different areas and transported into virtually any index. The limiting factor is the availability of derivatives to carry out the alpha transfer. One of the disadvantages is the cost of the transfer. However, if the target index is an index with a liquid futures contract, the costs are usually less than 100 basis points per year.

**Table 1.13** Alternative Investment Manager Selection Criteria

|  | Switzerland | Netherlands | Sweden | Average |
|---|---|---|---|---|
| Mandate suitability | 3.7 | 3.5 | 3.8 | 3.67 |
| Investment performance | 3.6 | 3.6 | 3.6 | 3.60 |
| Investment philosophy | 3.6 | 3.6 | 3.5 | 3.57 |
| Staff continuity | 3.4 | 3.4 | 3.5 | 3.43 |
| Investment professionals | 3.0 | 3.5 | 3.4 | 3.30 |
| Quality of client servicing | 3.1 | 3.3 | 3.1 | 3.17 |
| Financial strength | 3.0 | 3.4 | 3.0 | 3.13 |
| Quality of reporting | 2.9 | 2.9 | 2.9 | 2.90 |
| Quality of administration | 2.9 | 3.1 | 2.6 | 2.87 |
| Rapport at presentation | 2.8 | 2.8 | 3.0 | 2.87 |
| Culture | 2.6 | 2.6 | 2.9 | 2.70 |
| Brand comfort | 2.8 | 2.6 | 2.4 | 2.60 |
| Prior knowledge | 2.5 | 2.5 | 2.6 | 2.53 |
| Fees | 2.5 | 2.2 | 2.6 | 2.43 |

Rating Scale: 1—least important; 4—most important.
*Source:* Indocam/Watson Wyatt (2000).

the most important aspect followed by outperformance against equity, outperformance against fixed income, and hedge against inflation.

According to Indocam/Watson Wyatt (2000), of the 196 continental European pension funds surveyed, some 30 percent outsource to hedge funds or other alternative investment managers. Another 8 percent believe they will be doing so within three years. Indocam/Watson Wyatt anticipates a rise of the allocation to alternative investments by respondents who already invest in AIS as well as those who are about to invest in these asset classes. The allocation from European pension funds could rise from less than €1 billion to in excess of €12 billion. Since many Swiss respondents did not respond to the survey for three years, this figure is probably understated. The most considerable growth is expected to come from the Dutch, Swedish, and Swiss pension funds. Elsewhere there is expected to be at least some appetite expressed, which is consistent with the findings from the Ludgate Communications survey.

*EuroHedge* ran a story in 2000 examining why U.K. investors have a small allocation to hedge funds. The headline read:

*No hedge funds, please, we're British*[27]

It seems U.K. investors are following John Maynard Keynes' maxim that "worldly wisdom teaches us that it is better for reputation to fail conventionally than to succeed unconventionally." To some extent investing in a third-party fund is abdicating their responsibility to manage the assets. Other deterrents are trustees who do not have the knowledge or resources to understand the benefits of "new" investment vehicles such as derivatives and hedge funds. In addition, the U.K. pension fund market is driven by consultants who have only recently started to look at the subject.

While fees are of limited concern to pension fund managers on the European continent (as surveys suggest), fees are a big stumbling block in the United Kingdom, according to *EuroHedge*. To the trustees of the average U.K. fund, which pays about 30 basis points for asset management, hedge fund charges of 1 percent or 2 percent (management) and 20 percent (performance) appear astronomical. Unless they are convinced that the value added is worth the charges, trustees are even less likely to pay an extra layer of fees for a fund of funds. Another problem is that large U.K. pension funds aim for a target equity market exposure, and will likely either under- or overweight their guidelines if their hedge fund managers' betas are constantly changing—as they will, especially if the managers use leverage. This, in turn, makes it difficult for pension funds to track active risk against their benchmarks.

However, the fact that these problems are being discussed is evidence of changing attitudes. Pension consultants are warming to the concept of hedge funds—though with great caution, so as not to alienate clients.

## APPENDIX: Risk Illusion

> *Question: What is the definition of a stock that fell by 90 percent?*
> *Answer: A stock that fell by 80 percent and then halved.*
> —Hedge fund investor humor*

Try to count the black dots in Figure 1.17.

There are none. All dots are white. The human brain is tricked.

Which one of the three investments in Figure 1.18 has the highest risk?

Most people would intuitively view investment A as the most risky. Is this a trick? To some extent it is. Figure 1.18 compares the worst 12-month drawdown between January 1990 and December 2001 with a qualitative estimate

---

*Note that for the traditional hedge fund investor, being long a portfolio of stocks is regarded as of much higher risk than being long a portfolio of hedge funds. Low correlation among hedge fund managers allows construction of portfolios with a portfolio volatility of 5 percent or lower. This is not possible with long-only equities. When equities start falling, correlation normally increases substantially.

**FIGURE 1.17** Optical Illusion
*Source:* www.eyetricks.com.

for the balance-sheet leverage of three investments where idiosyncratic risk
has been diversified.

Investments A and B seem of high risk, as maximum drawdown is high.
No one would expect investment C to be the most risky. Only when we reveal
the nature of investment C to the press or the local regulator does investment
C become the most risky investment. Investment C is a proxy for a portfolio
of equity market-neutral strategies as measured by the HFRI Equity Market-
Neutral index. Investment A is the S&P 500 Banks index, and investment B is
the S&P 500 Composite index. All indexes are total returns and in U.S. dollars. Note that the observation period includes war and the oil price shock
(1990–1991), sharp Federal Reserve tightening (1994), the peso crisis
(1994–1995), the Asian crisis (1997), the Russian debt crisis (1998), the burst
of the Internet bubble (2000), and the World Trade Center attack (2001).

We acknowledge the fact that something unfamiliar or unknown is
more risky than something familiar, simply because risk is—at the most
general level—a synonym for uncertainty. However, a point can be made
that investment C is as much the most risky investment as there are black
dots in Figure 1.17.

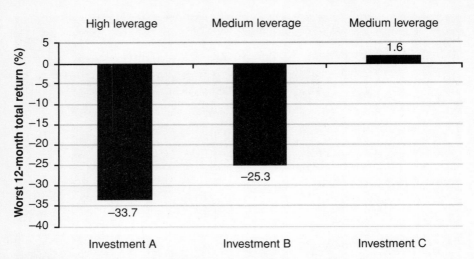

**FIGURE 1.18**   Worst 12-Month Return Compared with Leverage
*Source:* Hedge Fund Research, Datastream.

## Correlation Is Not Directly Visible—
## Stocks Are Highly Correlated

One reason why this risk illusion might exist is the lack of visibility of correlation between securities or between asset classes. Correlation is not visible to the human eye. By reading the newspaper or sitting in front of a Bloomberg screen, we observe return and volatility on a daily or weekly basis. Both variables are easily observable. Correlation, however, is not.

Investment C comprises constituents with extremely low correlation with each other whereas investments A and B contain assets with high correlation with each other. If we analyze the constituents of investment C in isolation, we might conclude that they are of high risk (high risk to a single manager blowing up). However, in portfolio construction, the expected correlation between the constituents is a key variable; that is, idiosyncratic risk should be immunized through diversification.

# CHAPTER 2

# Myths and Misconceptions

*Hedge fund managers can be tough to like, but it is difficult not to admire the great confidence and faith that they have in themselves, demonstrated by the willingness to risk their future on their skills.*
—William Crerend

## INTRODUCTION

Are hedge funds the fireflies ahead of the storm sweeping over the asset management industry? Given the strong language (paradigm shift) used in the Preface of this book, one would think so. However, apart from the term "paradigm shift" being overused, for a paradigm shift to unfold there are some barriers to be torn down first. In this chapter we address some of the barriers that present themselves as myths and misconceptions. The popular press and to some extent the financial press still portray hedge funds as gunslingers. Since the United States has evolved pretty well post Boston Tea Party and Little Big Horn, there is hope for hedge funds taking a similar path to greatness, once the cowboys grow up.

Hedge funds generally suffer from negative press. (Some thoughts on press coverage have been added in the appendix of this chapter.) The headlines since 1998 have not always been favorable for the industry. Prior to autumn 1998, there was little press coverage on hedge funds. Similarities can be drawn between the hedge fund industry and the airline or the derivatives industry where only disasters get coverage. Given the negatively biased press coverage of hedge funds, the evolution of hedge funds will take a route similar to that of derivatives to full acceptance as investment instruments to manage portfolio risk. Since hedge funds have gained the public's interest, the negative press on derivatives has come to a full standstill.*

## HEDGE FUND LOSSES AND DISASTERS

Louis Moore Bacon from Moore Capital presented an intuitive way of classifying hedge fund disasters at the 2000 Hedge Fund Symposium in London in April 2000. More precisely, he presented five warning signs for investors to look out for when investing in hedge funds. These are:

1. Size
2. Leverage
3. Transparency
4. Funding
5. Hubris

### Size

There is a capacity constraint for every hedge fund style and most likely for every single hedge fund. Recent history has proven that once a fund reaches enormous proportions the value added diminishes or, even worse, turns negative.

Mr. Bacon used Julian Robertson's Tiger funds as an example. In Bacon's view a hedge fund should deleverage or return capital to its investors and partners once it reaches a certain size. A hedge fund manager should control size according to the fund's capacity to implement its investment strategy. According to Bacon, Robertson kept on raising money despite respectable organic growth.

### Leverage

Leverage and liquidity are interconnected. Both occasionally turn the laws of economics upside down, because lower prices bring out less demand and more selling. George Soros, in *The Alchemy of Finance* (1987), talks about

---

*Note that the Barings scandal in 1995 to a large extent was blamed on derivatives whereas the Allied Irish Bank (AIB) scandal of 2002 was not blamed on derivatives although derivatives were involved. Convictions and prejudices *do* change.

"reflexivity." Blind adherence to economic orthodoxy, plus leverage, he says, lead to boom-bust mania.*

Excess leverage is bad.† Most examples of financial disasters involved an excess use of leverage. A sound risk management system relates open positions with liquidity. In other words, analyzing a hedge fund's risk control systems and risk management skill is extremely important—much more important than with other money managers who are restricted and/or regulated by internal and/or external regulatory bodies.

Managing hedge funds has at least as much to do with risk management as with picking stocks or following a market. According to Ian Wace from Marshall Wace Asset Management, the average correlation of the average European hedge fund to the market is 0.89, while the average net market exposure is 85 percent. He noted that since the returns are derived mainly from market moves, these funds are "beta merchants, not hedge funds."[1]

## Transparency

Transparency is the third warning sign. The purpose of transparency is to monitor risk without damaging the manager. Full transparency of current positions is commercially unwise. This is true for hedge funds and proprietary trading desks as well as other money managers of large size. The reason why it is more important for hedge funds is because they involve short positions much more frequently than traditional funds. In many regions, traditional money managers are restricted from selling short.

Short positions require more sensitive treatment than long positions. Many equity hedge funds are involved in illiquid markets, as the inefficiencies are higher in illiquid markets than in liquid and efficient markets.‡ The results of being squeezed out of a short position in an illiquid market can be disastrous to overall portfolio performance. One way of controlling this risk is by not unveiling one's positions to the market.

Bacon used the examples of the Hunt brothers and their silver speculation. In 1979 and 1980 the brothers tried to corner the silver market and took

---

*Reflexivity is discussed in the appendix to Chapter 4.

†Note that leverage is strategy-dependent. A balance-sheet leverage for a macro manager of 5:1 would be considered high. However, for fixed income arbitrage the same leverage would be considered low.

‡Grossman (1976) argues that perfectly informationally efficient markets are an impossibility, for if markets are perfectly efficient, the return to gathering information is nil, in which case there would be little reason to trade and markets would eventually collapse. There must be sufficient inefficiencies to compensate investors for the costs of trading and information gathering.

managed accounts and charged spectacular fees. They were leveraged 20 to 1, with only 5 percent margin down. According to Bacon, traders on the trading floor (Bacon at the time was on the floor as well) apparently used to wait until the Hunts' broker entered the elevator that brought him into the trading pit. The runners alerted the traders in the pit that the broker was on his way. The traders knew that he was going to buy silver, so they bought silver beforehand, front-running the Hunts' broker until the commodity was limit up and trading halted. But when the day came to sell, the price collapsed.

## Funding

The fourth of Bacon's warning signs is a mismatch between assets and liabilities, or the terms of funding. One example used by Bacon was Julian Robertson's Tiger Management. Apparently Julian Robertson was constantly growing by accepting new capital. The funds grew fast without reducing leverage or returning capital to investors. In Bacon's opinion, a hedge fund should keep its capital base stable once it reaches an optimal size, either by closing the fund to new investors, returning accumulated gains to investors, or reducing leverage.

The capital invested in a hedge fund should be stable. Both the debt from the prime broker as well as the equity from the investors should be stable. Hedge funds are long-term investments. Hence, hedge funds have long redemption periods. If the capital base is not secure there is a chance that capital is withdrawn at exactly that moment when it is most needed. Note that many of Long Term Capital Management (LTCM)'s strategies would have worked if it could have held onto its assets for some months longer (and some broker/dealers had not traded against them). Measures that indicate the stability of capital are the redemption periods or the portion of the fund that belongs to the managers. Stable debt is an even bigger issue. Avoiding forced deleveraging through margin calls from counterparties is immensely important. The higher the leverage, the more important are secure credit lines. In addition, higher volatility in capital markets increases the need for secure financing.

The most extreme case of secure financing is perpetual financing. Credit lines can to some extent be secured by the spreading financing relationships across the Street, negotiating different and independent financing terms with different liquidity providers. Equity financing can be secured through high lockups. For example, a hedge fund can implement a three-year lockup period where no more than 5 percent of the equity can be redeemed every calendar quarter. In this example, an investor redeeming for liquidity purposes can redeem 100 percent of his or her allocation as long as the total calendar redemption (this redemption and the redemptions of other investors) does not exceed the 5 percent threshold. If the total redemption is 10 percent, 5 percent can be redeemed this quarter and the rest at the end of the following quarter. If all investors want to redeem at the same time, they, in total, can redeem only 5 percent. In other words, if all investors want to redeem at the same time, it takes 20 quarters (five years) until all investors receive all their funds. In hedge fund time, five years is perpetuity. If the threshold is 2 percent, it takes 50 quarters (12.5 years). Hedge fund managers, therefore, hedge themselves against a mass exodus by having secure financing lines. To some extent this feature is like an option written by the investor for which he or she needs compensation.

## Hubris

The last point of Louis Bacon's warning signs is the sin of hubris, or arrogance and pride. According to Bacon, hubris can make a manager embrace leverage and size, and care less about transparency and the stability of capital. Hubris can also make a manager reluctant to embrace change. Bacon quotes John Maynard Keynes: "When circumstances change, I change my view. What do you do?"

With respect to hubris, consider the following exchange between Myron Scholes, LTCM partner and Nobel laureate, and Andrew Chow, vice president in charge of derivatives for potential investor Conseco Capital. Chow was quoted in the *Wall Street Journal* (November 16, 1998) as saying to Scholes: "I don't think there are many pure anomalies that can occur." Scholes responded: "As long as there continue to be people like you, we'll make money."

This excerpt highlights two aspects: First, it was not necessarily lack of self-confidence that brought down LTCM. Secondly, Myron Scholes alludes to the fact that traditional money managers to a large extent focus on relative returns whereas hedge funds focus on making money, that is, absolute returns. The focus on relative returns together with internal as well as external regulatory boundaries has some negative side effects, including market inefficiencies. An example of inefficiency in the equity arena is additions and deletions of index constituents. Traditional money managers often have to buy stock or subscribe to a large initial public offering (IPO) regardless of their fundamental evaluation of the stock. Taking into account an increasing trend toward herd behavior of traditional money managers opens a large range of opportunities for nontraditional (i.e., alternative investment) managers.* In essence, Myron Scholes had a good point.

---

*Tracking error between a portfolio and its benchmark is a function of volatility and correlation. If volatility increases, the tracking error increases as a result. The rise of volatility over the past four years has resulted in active managers reducing their active bets, that is, moving closer to their benchmark. Hence the expression "index huggers" (active managers who are not index fund managers but invest close to the index to avoid being caught on the wrong side of the market). Over the 2000–2001 period there have been celebrated money managers who stuck to their guns (bias toward value stocks) and went out of business as a result. Hence, hugging an index is as much about financial risk as about business risk. Market inefficiencies are the result.

Hubris is a risk factor when investing in hedge fund managers. The risk of hubris, to some extent, is understandable. Hedge fund managers are often compared to successful athletes in terms of energy, commitment, drive, and financial compensation. Most often the manager's character profile resembles that of an entrepreneur as opposed to the profile of an administrator. A further parallel is that the most successful managers become seriously wealthy at a young age. For some absolute return managers in their thirties or early forties a net wealth of $100+ million does not have a material impact on their energy, commitment, and drive. For others it does.

## BACON'S GAME THEORY

Bacon expressed the view that money management is like a game. There are no rules about the game except that it will change. But, most importantly, one should avoid becoming the game. Paraphrasing John Kenneth Galbraith, who was quoted as saying: "We have two classes of forecasters: Those who don't know—and those who don't know they don't know," Bacon distinguished between three types of hedge fund managers:

1. There are those who know they are in the game.
2. There are those who don't know they are in the game.
3. There are those who don't know they are in the game and have become the game.

The first group is attractive to investors. For example, a former convertibles arbitrage desk of an investment bank leaves the bank, opens a hedge fund, has a sound track record, understands the market, has the discipline to focus on the edge (i.e., avoid speculation), and has the skill, staff, and technology to manage risk.

The second group should be avoided. Often these hedge fund managers are long-only managers camouflaged as hedge funds. Fundamental research of the individual hedge fund enables the investor to distinguish between those who just were able to raise money from those who are in the game because they have an edge and experience in controlling risk. Analysis of investment philosophy and risk management systems should help distinguish the first from the second group.

In Bacon's opinion, the third category is the worst. One does not want to be invested in funds that, in Bacon's terminology, "have become the game." These funds are funds that have exhibited all of the five warning signs. Bacon stated three examples of fund managers who became the game and where investors lost money: the Hunt brothers, LTCM, and Julian Robertson's Tiger funds. LTCM, for example, had all of Bacon's warning signs:

*Size:* LTCM, with total assets of about $125 billion at year-end 1997, was significantly larger than any other reporting hedge fund family at the time, according to a report of the President's Working Group on Financial Markets (1999). The fund had 60,000 trades on its books. LTCM had stress loss predictions that it could lose $2.3 billion in a worst-case scenario. In fact, it lost $4.4 billion during 1998. Jorion (2000) argues that it not only underestimated risk but also failed to appreciate that its very size made it impossible to maneuver once it had lost $2.3 billion.

*Leverage:* The aim was a profit of 20 to 30 basis points on each position and an annual return for the fund of 30 percent net of fees,* which is achievable only through high leverage. The notional amount of LTCM's total over-the-counter (OTC) derivatives position was $1.3 trillion at the end of 1997 and $1.5 trillion at year-end 1998. As of December 1997, total swap positions amounted to $697 billion, futures to $471 billion, with options and other over-the-counter (OTC) derivatives accounting for the rest. The Bank for International Settlements (BIS) reported the total swap market to be around $29 trillion at the same date. Hence, LTCM's swap positions accounted for 2.4 percent of the $29 trillion swap market, and its futures positions for 6 percent of the $7.8 trillion futures markets.[2] Only six banks had a notional derivatives amount above $1 trillion at the time. The equity capital was around $5 billion at the end of 1997.†

*Transparency:* LTCM's fate got considerably worse once the market knew its positions and how it was going to trade to unwind positions. The fallout from the liquidation was far greater than it might have been. LTCM claimed that the selling of securities was made worse by brokers front-running the LTCM portfolio.‡ It is hard to verify these claims. Jorion (2000) brings it to the point: "The firm had badly underestimated its risk and did not have enough long-term capital to ride out the turbulence of 1998."

*Funding:* LTCM was able to leverage its balance sheet through sale-repurchase agreements (repos) with commercial and investment banks. Under these repo agreements, the fund sold some of its assets in exchange for cash and a promise to repurchase them back at a fixed price on some future date.

---

*Given the 2+20 fee structure (2 percent management fee plus 20 percent performance fee), this implies a 40 percent target gross return.

†LTCM returned $2.7 billion of capital to investors in 1997 while keeping total assets at $130 billion, explaining that "investment opportunities were not large and attractive enough." By shrinking the capital base to $4.7 billion, the leverage ratio went from 18 to 28, amplifying returns to investors that remained in the fund. Some investors who were forced out were reported to be upset that the partners did not reduce their own equity. From Jorion (2000).

‡Goldman Sachs later dismissed this argument as "absurd." From Jorion (2000).

Normally, brokers and lenders require collateral that is worth slightly more than the cash loaned, by an amount known as a "haircut," designed to provide a buffer against decreases in the collateral value. LTCM, however, was able to obtain unusually good financing conditions, with next-to-zero haircuts, as it was widely viewed as safe by its lenders. This must have been due to the fact that no counterparty had a complete picture of the extent of LTCM's operations.[3]

*Hubris:* According to Bacon it was the "height of hubris" that after the debacle LTCM claimed that market conditions had been a "one-off" or the "perfect storm."[*] But it failed to realize that LTCM itself had been the perfect storm. It had become the game.

### Epilogue

On September 23, 1998, the New York Federal Reserve Bank organized a bailout of LTCM, encouraging 14 banks to invest $3.6 billion in return for a 90 percent stake in the firm. LTCM unwound its position under the control of the 14-member consortium, formally known as Oversight Partners I LLC. By the end of 1999, all of the money had been paid back to investors and John Meriwether had started a new hedge fund. Of the $4.4 billion lost, $1.9 billion belonged to the partners, $700 million to a large bank in Switzerland, and $1.8 billion to other investors.

## DEMYSTIFYING HEDGE FUNDS

Occasionally hedge funds are considered secretive. This is actually not a myth but true. The hedge funds industry—to some extent—*is* secretive. Why any manager worth his salt will not reveal his short book will be discussed later. One of the reasons for this secrecy is that there are no talking heads of the industry who appear on CNBC or CNN on a regular basis. Information started to flow more efficiently only in the year 1998. The reason for the absence of talking heads or regular hedge fund manager forums is to some extent obvious. Hedge fund managers have different incentives than Wall Street talking heads where self-promotion is a key to success. If you have a trading strategy

---

[*]On August 21, 1998, the portfolio lost $550 million. By August 31, the portfolio had lost $1,710 million in one month only. Using the historical standard deviation of $206 million, the loss translated into an 8.3 sigma event. Assuming a normal distribution, such an event would occur once every 800 trillion years, or 40,000 times the age of the universe. From Jorion (2000).

or investment process with superior risk/reward trade-off in absolute return space, why do you want to tell it to the world for free?

## General Myths

### Myth: Investing in Hedge Funds Is Unethical
According to the myth, investing in hedge funds is speculative and therefore unethical.* We would like to turn the argument around and postulate that for a fiduciary not considering investing in alternative investment strategies (AIS) in a portfolio context in general or absolute return strategies in particular is, if anything, unethical. The empirical evidence from absolute return managers exploiting inefficiencies and producing high risk-adjusted returns is overwhelming, and academia is in the process of confirming that market inefficiencies exist (i.e., migrating to a very weak form of market efficiency).†

Views and definitions of ethics vary across countries and cultures. Any view, therefore, is subjective and has a strong home or cultural bias. The following view is based on the Prudent Expert Rule from the Employee Retirement Income Security Act (ERISA) and the Code of Ethics from the Association of Investment Management and Research (AIMR).‡ According to the AIMR Code of Ethics (AIMR 1999) members shall:

1. Act with integrity, competence, dignity, and in an ethical manner when dealing with the public, clients, prospects, employers, employees, and fellow members.
2. Practice and encourage others to practice in a professional and ethical manner that will reflect credit on members and their profession.
3. Strive to maintain and improve their competence and the competence of others in the profession.
4. Use reasonable care and exercise independent professional judgment.

Under ERISA, fiduciaries must discharge their duties with respect to the plan:[4]

---

*For example, *Barron's* from January 7, 2002, page 3: ". . . . out of the goodness of their hearts (it's the first concrete indication they possessed that organ), [hedge] fund managers. . . ."
†There are hardly any investment professionals who experienced the 1987 crash *and* believe in the efficient market hypothesis.
‡The AIMR is a global nonprofit organization of more than 41,000 investment professionals from more than 90 countries worldwide. Its mission is to advance the interests of the global investment community by establishing and maintaining the highest standards of professional excellence and integrity.

1. Solely in the interest of plan participants and beneficiaries.
2. For the exclusive purpose of providing benefits to participants and their beneficiaries and defraying reasonable plan expenses.
3. With the care, skill, prudence, and diligence under the circumstances then prevailing that a prudent person acting in like capacity and familiar with such matters would use in the conduct of an enterprise of a like character and with like aims (the Prudent Expert Rule).
4. By diversifying the investments of the plan so as to minimize the risk of large losses, unless doing so is clearly not prudent under the circumstances.
5. In accordance with the governing plan documents, as long as they are consistent with ERISA.

Assuming ERISA's Prudent Expert Rule is some indication of how a fiduciary should act and AIMR's Code of Ethics is a reference for ethical conduct and integrity of a financial professional, investing in hedge funds cannot be categorized as unethical. Taking this argument one step further, one could argue that, if anything, ignoring absolute return strategies and the benefits of its inclusion to a portfolio might be unethical.* The fourth of ERISA's points listed states that a fiduciary should diversify and reduce risk of large losses. In a portfolio context, risk is reduced by increasing the allocation to less volatile assets or introducing assets with low or negative correlation to the core of the portfolio. The strategies by relative value managers exploiting inefficiencies have proven to be conceptually sound as well as empirically characterized by high risk-adjusted returns and low correlation to traditional assets.† In addition, once risk to single hedge funds is diversified (idiosyncratic risk), large losses hardly occur especially when compared with traditional investments that are essentially long the asset class outright. Some U.S. and U.K. pension funds (mostly long-only investors) have gone from overfunded to underfunded (liabilities exceeding assets) in only two years after the equity market peaked in 2000.

In the United Kingdom a precedent from 1883 dictates that the unpaid laymen who make up the majority of most trustee boards must take all the care "an ordinary prudent man of business would take in managing similar

---

*Amin and Kat (2001), for example, stress that it is important to view hedge funds in a portfolio context and not in isolation.
†The fact that nondirectional absolute return strategies have return distributions that do not match a normal distribution does not automatically mean that the strategies are conceptually unsound. Returns from equities or cash flows from insurance companies are not normally distributed, either.

affairs of his own."* In the first quarter of 2002 the Department for Work and Pensions issued three consultation papers, one of which is aimed at raising the quality of investment decisions taken by pension fund trustees. In the United Kingdom it is often noted that the average pension fund trustee spends around 12 hours per year[†] thinking about themes related to investment management. This fact introduces a lemming-like peer group driven investment process and a "tabloid bias." Putting it crudely: Equities and bonds are good, and derivatives and hedge funds are bad. The thought that the combination of (noncorrelated) risky assets can result in a conservative portfolio is intellectually out of reach for the average U.K. pension fund trustee. This is why "conservative" is defined as having a 70 to 80 percent allocation to equities with the majority invested in the domestic market.[‡] This is probably the reason why the U.K. institutional involvement (on the demand side) in absolute returns is one of the lowest in Europe. However, there is a trend to the better. First, the government is aware of the issues arising from the world moving from defined benefit to defined contribution pension schemes. Second, the

---

*A common market for pensions in Europe is a long-sought goal within the European Union (EU). The European Commission (EC) proposed to base pension regulation on the "prudent person" principle in October 2000. The United Kingdom, Ireland, Sweden, and the Netherlands backed the EC proposals whereas most of the remaining member states, led by France and Germany, have expressed some doubts. This despite the EC stressing that funds in member states where the prudent person principle has been applied—namely the United Kingdom and the Netherlands—have achieved returns over the past 15 years that were twice as high as those subject to quantitative restrictions. The Spanish delegation came up with the idea to create a "prudent person plus" principle. This new principle would combine the basic principle with some fortified quantitative restrictions.

[†]Occasionally a figure of 20 hours per year is quoted as the average time spent on financial matters by the average U.K. pension fund trustee. Given the complexity of asset/liability management and solvency issues it is unlikely that 12 or even 20 hours per year are sufficient.

[‡]Note that during the technology, media, and telecommunications (TMT) expansion, some U.K. pension funds had a larger allocation to a single U.K.-domiciled company than to the whole of the U.S. stock market. Fortunately the stock lost "only" around 80 percent of its value from peak to trough—outperforming its peer group on the European continent, which fell between 92 percent and 96 percent. Therefore, hardly anyone asked questions. However, an allocation of more than 5 to 10 percent to a single stock is definitely in breach of modern portfolio principles, which state that idiosyncratic risk should be immunized through diversification. It is probably also in violation of point four of AIMR's Code of Ethics and certainly in violation of ERISA's Prudent Expert Rule. In other words, running strongly concentrated portfolios and avoiding hedge funds because the local tabloids suggest they are dangerous is certainly not the result of a prudent expert thinking about risk.

Myners Report* suggests, among other issues, that U.K. pension funds should move away from finding comfort in the peer-group consensus and seek idiosyncratic solutions to their financial requirements, that is, become a little bit more open-minded with respect to the financial innovations of the past 30 years.

The relationship between institutional funds and the agents engaged to manage the portfolio assets has always provided a fertile breeding ground for conflicts of interest. Yale endowment fund manager David Swensen puts it as follows:

> *Institutions seek high risk-adjusted returns, while outside investment advisers pursue substantial, stable flows of fee income. Conflicts arise since the most attractive investment opportunities fail to provide returns in a steady, predictable fashion. To create more secure cash flows, investment firms frequently gather excessive amounts of assets, follow benchmark-hugging portfolio strategies, and dilute management efforts across a broad range of product offerings. While fiduciaries attempt to reduce conflicts with investment advisers by crafting appropriate compensation arrangements, interests of fund managers diverge from interests of capital providers even with the most carefully considered deal structures.[5]*

**Myth: Fee Structure Gives Incentive to Speculate**   Every investment is based on a forecast of some sort, that is, on some assumption of the future. A return (the result of investing) is, therefore, uncertain by definition. The term "speculation" is ill-chosen. Investors do not speculate; they balance their odds. A gambler at the roulette wheel, on the contrary, speculates. There is no intellectual balancing process between losing scarce funds and gaining potential rewards at the roulette table. Buying a lottery ticket is speculation, too. However, buying a mispriced convertible bond and hedging associated risks to benefit from a market inefficiency is not.

## Myths with Respect to Risk

**Myth: Hedge Funds Are Risky**   Hedge funds, examined in isolation, are risky—as are technology stocks, or energy trading companies, or airline stocks. However, most investors do not hold single-stock portfolios. They diversify

---

*The government sponsored Paul Myners (executive chairman of Gartmore Investment Management in the United Kingdom from 1987 to 2001) for an independent review of the United Kingdom pension fund industry. Myners is promoting the so-called Myners code of best investment practice, which fund management houses are supposed to sign up to by March 2003.

stock-specific risk (idiosyncratic or nonsystematic risk) by investing in a range of stocks with different characteristics. To most investors, it is regarded as unwise not to diversify idiosyncratic risk. It should be similarly unwise not to diversify risk to a single hedge fund. Note that many critics of hedge funds do not distinguish between systematic and nonsystematic risk when demonizing hedge funds.

Schneeweis and Spurgin (1998) and many others have shown that hedge funds offer an attractive opportunity to diversify an investor's portfolio of stocks and bonds. This is true even if the returns earned by hedge funds in the future are merely on a par with those of stocks and bonds. There is no need to see risk-adjusted returns as high as they have been to justify diversification benefits into hedge funds. Any investment with a positive expected return, low volatility, and low correlation to the rest of the portfolio will have a great chance of reducing portfolio volatility.

**Myth: Hedge Funds Are Speculative**   Hedge funds are risky (as is any other investment when compared to U.S. government bonds) but they are not speculative. The misunderstanding of hedge funds being speculative comes from the myopic conclusion that an investor using speculative instruments must automatically be running speculative portfolios. Many hedge funds use speculative financial instruments or techniques to manage conservative portfolios. Not everyone understands this. Popular belief is that an investor using, for example, leveraged default derivatives (a financial instrument combining the most cursed three words in finance) must be a speculator. The reason why this is a misconception is that the speculative instrument is most often used as a hedge, that is, as an offsetting position. The incentive to use such an instrument or technique (for example, selling stock short) is to reduce portfolio risk—not to increase it.

This is the reason why most absolute return managers regard themselves as more conservative than their relative return colleagues. The decision of an absolute return manager to hedge is derived from whether or not principal is at risk. To absolute return managers, preserving wealth is conservative. The protection of principal is not a primary issue for relative return managers, as their mandate is outlined and risk defined differently. It is the absolute return manager who will think about all the risks and judge whether to hedge or not to hedge. In other words, it is actually the relative return manager who speculates on many variables that are not the subject of the benchmark. In addition, relative return managers, more often than not, manage OPM (other people's money). So do hedge funds. However, hedge fund managers, more often than not, have their own wealth in their funds; that is, their capital, incentives, and interests are aligned with those of their investors. Most people care about the risk of loss of principal—especially when it is their own. As Yale endowment fund manager David Swensen (2000) puts it:

*While any level of co-investment encourages fund managers to act like principals, the larger the personal commitment of funds, the greater the focus on generating superior investment returns. . . . The idea that a fund manager believes strongly enough in the investment product to put a substantial personal stake in the fund suggests that the manager shares the investor's orientation.*[6]

**Myth: Hedge Funds Generate Strong Returns in All Market Conditions** Generally speaking, the correlation between hedge fund returns and the equity market is not zero. However, one cannot generalize across all hedge fund styles and managers. Some hedge funds do better than others during bear markets. The hedge fund industry is extremely heterogeneous. There is great diversity among different trading and investment styles and strategies.*

Figure 2.1 shows the seven worst quarters for the S&P 500 index during the period from January 1990 to December 2001. The bars measure the total return (i.e., including dividends) in U.S. dollars for the calendar quarters. Seven quarters were chosen in order to include the first quarter of 1994, which was a particularly bad quarter for macro managers. One quarter stands out: the third quarter of 1998 when Russia defaulted on its ruble-denominated debt and which caused the investment public to realize the sensitivity of spread risk† in a flight-to-quality scenario and a drying up of liquidity. Most hedge fund style indexes were in negative territory in that particular quarter. In most other quarters where equity markets fell, the different hedge fund strategies behaved more or less in a different fashion. Note that, for example, the equity market-neutral index was in positive territory all the time except in the third quarter of 1998. In that quarter the HFRI Equity Market-Neutral index fell by 1.14 percent. (Detailed performance analysis will be covered in Part II of this book.) This illustrates a second point: the

---

*The industry is becoming even more diverse. Up until recently there was no "genderal" diversification. This has changed. A new group called "100 Women in Hedge Funds" was created. The group hopes to fill a void in a community where, according to Reuters (2002), women have long complained about being excluded from the so-called old-boy networks that still provide introductions to jobs and investors. Diversity is, indubitably, a laudable concept.

†Most hedge funds, especially nondirectional hedge funds, are long one financial instrument and short a related instrument. In other words, the fund is exposed to many different spreads, here called "spread risk." Spread risk has a nonsystematic as well as systematic risk element; that is, it cannot be perfectly immunized through diversification. The main characteristic of spread risk is that it causes the fat tails in the fund's return distribution. In rare occasions, in a flight-to-quality scenario, spreads have a tendency to widen all at the same time (as in the third quarter of 1998).

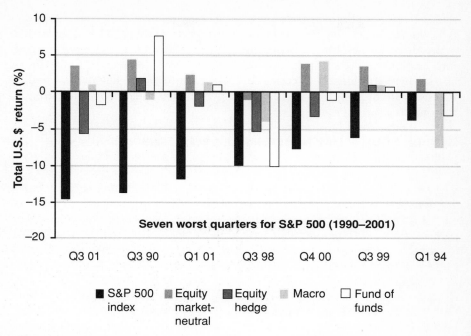

**FIGURE 2.1** Performance in Worst Quarters for U.S. Stock Market
*Source:* Hedge Fund Research, Datastream.

magnitude of loss. When balanced hedge funds portfolios fall they do not fall by the same magnitude due to the low-volatility characteristics of the portfolio. The HFRI Equity Hedge index (equity long/short funds with small long bias), for example, was in negative territory five out of the seven worst quarters for the S&P 500. At first sight correlation looks high, but the magnitude of loss is a different story. All five returns were not as negative as the corresponding S&P 500 returns.

Most long/short managers regard being long-only as extremely speculative because the assets under management are fully exposed to the whims of the stock market. To them, having the same exposure to equities when equity volatility is 10 percent (as, for example, in the United States and United Kingdom in 1995) or 20 to 70 percent (as in most years since 1995) is a strange way of managing money. Figure 2.1 is an indication of what this translates to in periods of stress.

The hedge funds from the 1960s did extremely poorly during the bear market of the 1970s (as discussed in Chapter 1). Many managers went out of business, essentially because they were long, leveraged, and totally exposed to the market. However, the degree of sophistication of hedge funds relative value investment strategies has increased since the 1960s. Anecdotal evidence from the bear market starting in spring 2000 indicates that many directionally biased hedge funds had deleveraged and were moving into cash as markets fell. In the first half of 2002, long/short equity managers where still largely in cash. This fact introduces the debate of whether investors should pay a 1 percent management fee to someone investing in the risk-free rate.

**Myth: The Lesson of LTCM Is Not to Invest in Hedge Funds**   Thomas Schneeweis (1998b) wrote:

> *There are many lessons to be learned from LTCM: (1) diversify, (2) high-return investments are also potential low-return investments, (3) trading in illiquid secondary markets is potentially disastrous in extreme market conditions, (4) an asset that returns in excess of 30% per year, as LTCM did, is a very risky investment. These are, of course, lessons that are true for all investments, and have nothing to do with the fact that LTCM was a hedge fund.*

A hedge fund is a business. Businesses, unfortunately, occasionally fail and go bankrupt for various reasons. This is one of the main reasons why investors diversify across businesses (i.e., diversify idiosyncratic risk). Although a repeat of a disaster such as LTCM is regarded as unlikely,* some hedge funds are likely to go bankrupt in the future; they potentially could destroy wealth under management. However, a point can be made that entrepreneurs should have exposure to idiosyncratic risk whereas investors should diversify idiosyncratic risk, that is, be exposed to (and get compensated for) systematic risk. In other words, investors should hold portfolios of hedge funds as opposed to a handful of hedge funds.

Table 2.1 shows a list of some of the more recent casualties. There are only a few cases, if any, where markets are to be blamed. The losses or defaults are a function of organizational malpractice (i.e., business risk). It is business risk if:

- Key staff leave the firm and the firm's edge walks out the door.
- A fund is inappropriately funded with respect to its market risk.
- The hedge does not work.
- A hedge fund manager departs from field of expertise without telling investors.

---

*A flight-to-quality scenario, however, is very likely to occur at one stage in the future.

**Table 2.1**  Hedge Fund Disasters and Large Losses

| Case | Strategy | Date | Loss (US$m) | What Went Wrong? | Risk |
|---|---|---|---|---|---|
| **Askin Capital Management** | Fixed income arbitrage (mortgage-backed securities) | 1994 | 420 | Hedge did not work. Liquidity squeeze. Could not meet margin calls. Did not inform investors. | Market |
| **Argonaut Capital Management** | Macro | 1994 | 110 | Market losses. Departure of general partner. | Market/ business |
| **Vairocana Limited** | Fixed income arbitrage | 1994 | 700 | Change of strategy from duration-neutral to punt on falling interest rates. Could not calculate proper net asset value(NAV) figures. Investors lost confidence. | Market/ business |
| **Fenchurch Capital Management** | Fixed income arbitrage | 1995 | NA | Change of strategy from U.S. bond basis trading and U.S. yield curve arbitrage to European bonds and equities despite being unacquainted with markets. | Market |
| **Global Systems Fund (Victor Niederhoffer)** | Macro | 1997 | NA | Market losses. Short puts in market correction. Failed margin calls. | Market |
| **Long Term Capital Management (LTCM)**[a] | Fixed income arbitrage | 1998 | 4,400 | Market losses. Excess leverage. Margin calls. | Market/ business |
| **Manhattan Investment Fund (Michael Berger)** | Long/short equity (short bias) | 1999 | 400 | Market losses. Fictitious statements sent by manager. | Fraud |
| **Princeton Economics International (Martin Armstrong)** | Macro | 1999 | 950 | Market losses. Fraudulent sale of notes and misrepresentation of assets. | Fraud |
| **Tiger Management**[b] **(Julian Robertson)** | Macro | 2000 | 2,600 | Concentrated portfolio, style drift, redemptions, "mouse clicks and momentum" | Market/ business |
| **Soros Fund**[c] **(George Soros)** | Macro | 2000 | NA | Departure of key personnel, lack of opportunity. | Market/ business |
| **Ballybunion Capital Partners (Michael Higgins)** | Long/short equity | 2000 | 4.6 | Reporting of false performance figures. Wrong information on Web. | Fraud |
| **Maricopa Investment Corp. (David M. Mobley)** | Long/short equity (quantitative) | 2000 | 59 | Market losses. Reporting of false performance figures. Fraudulent misrepresentation of assets. Ponzi scheme, paying distributions with new investor assets. | Fraud |
| **Cambridge Partners, LLC (John C. Natale)** | Long/short equity | 2000 | 45 | False audits, tax documents, and monthly statements. Overstatement of performance. Pleaded guilty to securities fraud, theft, and misappropriation of property. | Fraud |
| **HL Gestion/Volter Fund (Imad Lahoud)** | Managed futures | 2000 | 40 | French regulators closed down the money manager because the firm's capital had fallen below the minimum level of 50 million euros required to operate in France. | Market |

*(Continued)*

**75**

**Table 2.1** *(Continued)*

| Case | Strategy | Date | Loss (US$m) | What Went Wrong? | Risk |
|---|---|---|---|---|---|
| Ashbury Capital Partners (Mark Yagalla) | Long/short equity | 2001 | 50 | Reporting of false performance figures and accused of running a pyramid scheme. Used investors' funds to finance lavish lifestyle. | Fraud |
| ETJ Partners (E. Thomas Jung) | Relative value | 2001 | 21 | Market losses. Reporting of false performance figures. Fraudulent misrepresentation of assets. | Fraud |
| Nidra Capital (Richard Roon) | "Knowledge advantage" | 2001 | 2.6 | Market losses. Reporting of false performance figures. | Fraud |
| Sagam Capital (Yehuda Shiv) | Mortgage-backed securities (MBO) leveraged | 2001 | NA | Market losses. Reporting of false performance finance figures. Fraudulent misrepresentation of assets. | Fraud |
| Lipper & Co. | Convertible bond | 2002 | NA | Wrong valuation of assets. | Business |

[a]According to Lowenstein (2000), initial investors compounded at 18% as LTCM returned funds in 1997.
[b]There were $7.65 billion withdrawals between August 1998 and April 2000. Tiger assets went from $22.8 billion in October 1998 to $6 billion in March 2000. However, Tiger Management compounded at 24.8% between 1980 and 2000.
[c]Quantum fund compounded at 32.1% between 1969 and 2000. $3 billion were redeemed when Stanley Druckenmiller announced his departure.
*Source:* Cottier (1997), Peltz (2001), Bloomberg News, UBS Warburg (2000).

- A hedge fund manager selling Internet stocks reports high positive returns while stocks skyrocket and nobody harbors suspicions.
- Even fraud is not atypical for the hedge fund industry, but it is a risk of corporate life (otherwise firms could allocate funds spent for legal advice to productive projects).*

There are many ironies surrounding the collapse of LTCM. One is that the brightest academics in finance together with the most trading-savvy investment professionals on Wall Street could not avert one of the largest disas-

---

*In 1992 Robert Maxwell raided the U.K. *Mirror* newspaper group's pension fund. In 1996, rogue fund manager Peter Young caused Deutsche Morgan Grenfell Asset Management in the United Kingdom some awkward headlines (next to financial losses). In 1998, rogue futures trader Nick Leeson brought down Barings Bank due to fraudulent trading. In 2002, currency trader John Rusnak caused damage to Allied Irish Bank (AIB) through rogue trading. What does this mean? If the popular press would apply the same economic logic and diligence in their coverage of the hedge fund industry as for the rest of the business world (i.e., draw conclusions from anecdotal evidence), it would mean: "Don't do business with the people from the British Isles. They neglect risk management and are famous for fraudulent business practice. All financial scandals have their roots in the British Isles."

ters in financial history. Another interesting aspect is that LTCM is the hedge fund that is most commonly known. The irony is that LTCM was a very atypical hedge fund. Its trading strategies were more in line with those of a capital market intermediary. When investors or issuers needed to change their positions or risk exposures, they would go to an investment bank or dealer to buy or sell securities or structured products. In turn, the dealer would utilize the capital markets to cover this exposure. LTCM was often on the other end of these transactions, in some sense wholesaling risk to the intermediary who was working directly with clients. LTCM viewed its main competitors as the trading desks at large Wall Street firms rather than traditional hedge funds.

### Myth: The Failure of a Single Hedge Fund Is Cause for Concern   Thomas Schneeweis (1998b) wrote:

> *Many hedge funds failed before LTCM, and many could fail in the future. Some failed quietly, returning some investor capital after liquidating positions. Others, like LTCM, failed in a more spectacular fashion. The failure of a single firm or investment product is always of concern to the investors as well as those who invest in similar ventures. However, modern investment theory points out that no person should have a sizeable portion of their wealth invested in any single investment product.*

Schneeweis, as have many academics and financial professionals before him, stresses the point that unless one has a perfect forecast of the future, diversification is a laudable concept when dealing with uncertainty.*

> *The stock market has survived the bankruptcy of many companies. This does not mean that stocks are bad investments. It does not even mean that the investors in a company that loses money ex-post initially made the wrong choice. The most notable aspect of the LTCM collapse is not in its collapse, but in the fact that many highly sophisticated investors held a single large portion of their personal wealth in the fund, which is completely contrary to modern investment principles.*[7]

The failure of LTCM to some extent is similar to the failure of Enron. Table 2.2 shows commonalties as well as differences. Both events caused headlines as well as headaches. Interventionists called for more regulation and government supervision immediately after the event in both

---

*Peter Bernstein's *Against the Gods* and William Sherden's *Fortune Sellers* are well-researched, educational, as well as entertaining to read. Anyone who has spent a large part of his or her professional life on a trading floor will also enjoy some of the amusing anecdotes in Taleb's *Fooled by Randomness*.

**Table 2.2**  LTCM and Enron Collapse Compared

|  | LTCM | Enron |
|---|---|---|
| **For the history books: largest . . .** | Hedge fund failure | Bankruptcy |
| **Investors lost around . . .** | $4.4 billion | $64 billion[a] |
| | | |
| **Commonality 1** | Cry for government action after event | |
| **Commonality 2** | Showcase for investors' portfolio concentration | |
| **Commonality 3** | "Bad press day" for derivatives | |
| | | |
| **Nominal annual return for initial investors** | 18%[b] | 1.8%[c] |
| **Number of small investors hurt** | None | Thousands |

[a]Loss to investors from all-time high.
[b]Note that LTCM returned equity before collapse. Reinvestment was not an option.
[c]From January 1972 to December 2001 and assuming dividends and other payouts were reinvested in stock.
*Source:* Lowenstein (2000), Bloomberg News.

instances.* Both collapses showed that many investors held extremely inefficient portfolios; they were exposed to nonsystematic risk that could have been immunized through diversification. Derivatives did not necessarily benefit from favorable press coverage.†

There were also differences. In terms of absolute wealth destruction LTCM was a minor glitch when compared with the collapse of Enron or some of the other corporate governance failures in 2002. Figure 2.2 compares the market capitalization of Enron with two other blue-chip stocks. The nominal annual return for the initial investor was around 18 percent[8] in the case of LTCM but much lower for Enron. Most retail investors did not hold the stock from its launch in 1972. Most investors had close to a total loss rather than a 1.8 percent nominal annual return as suggested by Table 2.2. A further difference is that small investors lost substantial parts of their accumulated wealth whereas this was not the case with LTCM. The unfortunate irony, of course,

---

*Albeit for different reasons. In 1998 it was the fragility of the financial system that grabbed attention and caused concern. The collapse of Enron triggered discussion with respect to diversification characteristics and risk tolerance (allowance for large percentage being in one stock) of 401(k) and other retirement systems. Questionable business practice of auditors also raised an eyebrow or two.
†It is worth pointing out that derivatives had not been on the radar screen of the popular press for some years prior to the Enron collapse. Since LTCM, the popular press has had hedge funds to blame for any excess volatility or havoc in financial markets.

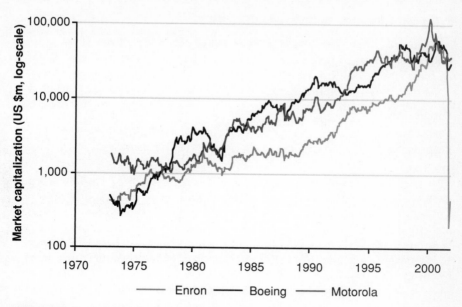

**FIGURE 2.2** Enron Compared with Other U.S. Blue-Chip Stocks
*Source:* Datastream.

is that many jurisdictions allow small investors to buy stock but not hedge funds. To the seasoned hedge fund investor this is not necessarily logical since a diversified portfolio of absolute return funds is considered to be of lower risk than outright exposure to a diversified portfolio of stocks.

With respect to press coverage there were commonalities as well as differences. One commonality was the cry of government intervention. After all, the government is the last resort of responsibility. The difference in coverage had more to do with the magnitude of required governmental action. In the case of LTCM, the coverage was very much anti hedge fund industry. This was not the case with the bankruptcy of a stock. A bankruptcy of a stock is, sort of, okay. No one suggested limiting access to the stock market or even shutting down the industry (as was the case in 1998 for the hedge fund industry). It is generally understood that this is one of the slightly negative aspects of free markets and capitalism itself. Bankruptcies are understood to be a cleansing process in the economic evolution (survival of the fittest, reallocation of scarce resources, etc.). The same logic should apply to hedge funds. At the end of the day, hedge funds are organizations that try to yield a financial return to their founders, partners, and shareholders or investors. Occasionally an organization folds. This is true for hedge funds as well as other organizations in an economy.

## Myths with Respect to Investment Strategy

### Myth: Hedge Funds Are Always Hedged Hence the Name Hedge Funds   Some
funds that are called hedge funds do not actually hedge market risk. Because
the term is applied to a wide range of alternative funds, it also encompasses
funds that may use high-risk strategies without hedging against market risk.
For example, a global macro strategy may bet on changes in countries' economic policies that impact interest rates, which impact all financial instruments, while using high degrees of leverage. The returns can be high, but so
can the losses, as the leveraged directional investments (which are not hedged)
tend to make the largest impact on performance.

Many hedge funds, however, do seek to hedge against various types of
market risk in one way or another, making consistency and stability of return,
rather than magnitude, their key priorities. Thus, some hedge funds are generally able to deliver consistent returns with lower risk of loss. Long/short equity funds, while dependent on the direction of markets, hedge out some of
this market risk through short positions that provide profits in a market
downturn to offset losses made by the long positions. Equity market-neutral
funds that invest equally in long and short equity portfolios, generally in the
same styles of the market, are not correlated to market movements. That does
not mean there is no directional risk. It only means there is no directional
*market* risk.

### Myth: Selling Short Is the Opposite of Going Long   Mutual funds are normally
restricted from selling short. The regulatory environment, however, is only
one issue with respect to short selling. Selling short is not the opposite of going long. Most equity investors have a long-only mentality and are less familiar with hedging, managing risk, and the dynamics of short positions.

Short positions behave differently from long positions. The portfolio consequences of adverse price movements require greater diversification of short
positions. If a stock moves against a short seller by increasing in price, the position and portfolio weight increases. To take advantage of the now more at-
tractively priced short-sale opportunity (more attractive because the price is
even higher than when the stock initially was sold), the short seller faces the
uncomfortable prospect of further increasing the position. Starting with a
modest allocation to a particular short idea allows an increase in position size
without creating an uncomfortable concentration in a single stock. Contrast
the dynamics of a losing short position with the behavior of a losing long position. As the long position's price declines, it becomes a smaller portion of
the portfolio, reducing its impact on returns and facilitating new purchases at
the newly discounted, relatively more attractive price levels.

There also is a technical difference between buying and selling short. To
execute a short sale, the investor has to borrow securities to deliver to the

buyer on the other side of the trade. If the lender recalls the shares, the short seller has to cover, that is, buy back and deliver the stock. When the market for borrowing a particular security becomes tight, short sellers face a short squeeze. Security borrowers tend to have the most trouble with small, less liquid companies, which are exactly the type of security most likely to present interesting short-sale opportunities.

Short selling is also considered a typical strategy of a contrarian. Most investors either buy, consider whether to buy, or eventually do not buy stocks. However, a short seller is nearly a contrarian by definition. The short sale (as opposed to selling a long position) is a fraction of all executed trades. The most aggressive piece of Wall Street wit appears in *Confessions of a Wall Street Insider* by the self-named C. C. Hazard:

> *The stock market is built on necessary foundation of error. You make money on the market mainly by living off the error of other players. You become a predator, in fact, a carnivore, a beast of prey. Others must die that you might live . . . The stock market requires an endless supply of losers.*[9]

This quote is not necessarily the pinnacle of political correctness. However, it underlines the fact that the quest for alpha is a zero-sum game before transaction costs and a negative-sum game on an after-fee basis and that the earlier quoted "contrarian wit" from Rousseau, Buffett, and Soros might contain an element of truth.

**Myth: Hedge Funds Are Unique in Their Investment Strategies**   As outlined in Chapter 1, investors focusing on absolute returns while trying to preserve principal have been around for some time. It is actually the relative return approach (i.e., the second paradigm in asset management) that is new by comparison. What was referred to as the third paradigm in the Preface is actually a combination of the absolute return focus of the first paradigm (absolute returns but holistic approach) with the high degree of specialization of the second paradigm (specialized relative return approach).

Not even the strategies hedge funds execute are new. As Schneeweis (1998b) puts it:

> *Some hedge funds can be viewed as the privatization of the trading floors of investment banks. New technology has permitted investment professionals to leave investment banks and trade externally what formerly was conducted only internally. The strategies are not new. Insurance companies, endowments, and other institutional investors have invested in alternative investments such as private debt, private equity, and derivative strategies for years. When these large, diversified investors took losses in*

*a particular product, it often was hidden by their gains in other areas. What is new is that for a single hedge fund, the lack of product diversification heightens its risk. This does not necessarily increase the risk of its investors, though, as they should be well diversified across a number of hedge funds and a number of asset classes.*

## Myths with Respect to Economic Logic

**Myth: Short Selling Is Bad**   There are many myths with respect to short selling. One of the more recent occasions of misconception came from Hans Eichel, the German finance minister, who wrote an article for the "Personal View" column of the *Financial Times*.[10] According to the article, the German government has included in its draft of a fourth Financial Market Promotion Act a clause enabling short selling of shares to be temporarily banned in Germany. In the article the finance minister warns that in a largely integrated international financial system, distortions in national financial markets and financial institutions can pose a threat to global financial stability. Mr. Eichel points to the two main factors, which are weak banking supervision in offshore financial centers and insufficient monitoring of risk positions of hedge funds. Hans Eichel uses LTCM and short selling after September 11 to demonize hedge funds.

The U.S. Securities and Exchange Commission (SEC) has a slightly different view on the economics of short selling than has the German finance ministry:

> *Short selling provides the market with two important benefits: market liquidity and pricing efficiency. Substantial market liquidity is provided through short selling by market professionals, such as market makers, block positioners, and specialists, who facilitate the operation of the markets by offsetting temporary imbalances in the supply and demand for securities. To the extent that short sales are effected in the market by securities professionals, such short sale activities, in effect, add to the trading supply of stock available to purchasers and reduce the risk that the price paid by investors is artificially high because of a temporary contraction of supply.*[11]

The second benefit of short selling after increasing market liquidity is an increase in pricing efficiency. Efficient markets should price both positive as well as negative information, that is, require that prices fully reflect all buy and sell interest. The short sale of a short seller is the mirror image of another person's buy transaction. The former forecasts that the price will fall (or uses the short sale to offset other risk factors in the portfolio) while the latter bets on prices to rise. Both the purchaser and the short seller hope to buy low and sell high, that is, make money by buying the stock at one price and selling at a higher price. The distinguishing factor is that the strategies differ in the sequence of the transactions. Equity managers who believe a stock is overvalued sell the stock short in an attempt to profit from a perceived divergence of prices from true economic values. Pricing efficiency is increased because the market is informed about the short seller's negative evaluation of the future stock price performance. This evaluation is reflected in the resulting market price of the security.

One of the main ingredients of any marketplace therefore is the presence of buyers as well as sellers. In other words, a marketplace needs heterogeneity, not homogeneity. One of the phenomena of financial bubbles (as the recent Internet bubble showed) is that it is difficult for short sellers to borrow stocks and sell them short. A bubble is a departure of prices from their intrinsic value and is caused by an imbalance between buyers and sellers. In addition, in a collapse long-only investors are more likely to start selling in a panic. The short seller is more likely to buy to close out the short position.

The most significant error made with respect to short selling is to describe hedge funds as a homogenous mass of like-minded investors. In practice there is a multitude of different types of hedge funds, each with different investment criteria and different risk/reward objectives. However, in general, the majority of those investing in equities fall into two categories: arbitrage and long/short. The arbitrage hedge funds will be short a security as a hedge against a commensurate long in a closely connected security (say a convertible bond, a warrant, or a company being bid for where there is a share-for-share deal). Thus their activity may involve large transactions, but is neutral to the direction of the overall entity or market. The long/short investors are investing on the fundamentals of the companies, and in addition to holding short positions in overvalued companies they will hold long positions in undervalued companies. Thus, again, their activities may involve large transactions but are close to net neutral from a market perspective. There are some funds that are more directionally oriented: macro funds and short sale funds. However, these are actually a very small proportion of the hedge fund universe. Even accounting for leverage, the actual amount of net shorts run by hedge funds is negligible in the overall scheme of markets.

The banning of short selling increases market inefficiencies: One of the characteristics of an efficient market is that new information is disseminated quickly and enters the price rapidly. Bad news (normally) decreases the price whereas good news increases the price of a security or an asset. This mechanism causes the price to reflect the available news at all times. Banning short selling causes good news to enter the price mechanism quickly, whereas it limits the price mechanism to adjust for the bad news. In other words, the price mechanism (i.e., the interaction of buyers and sellers) becomes dysfunctional, and market efficiency decreases.

Miller (1987) suggests an amendment to the efficient market hypothesis (EMH) by arguing that "prices are bounded by limits set by the buying and short-selling of informed investors." Short sellers who will stop the ascent of the price if the potential return is great enough to augment the costs of being short set the upper limits of securities prices. The short seller's ability to sell becomes the critical variable in the upper price boundary. Because there are many restrictions on short selling (regulatory ban, institutional prohibitions, prohibitive transaction costs, limited universe of borrowable shares, etc.), stocks trade not at one efficient price but within a band of prices.[12] Miller advises portfolio managers to search for mispriced stocks to sell because more overpriced than underpriced stocks can be identified.

Diamond and Verrechia (1987) model effects of short-sale constraints on the speed of adjustment to private information of security prices. The four empirical implications of the study:

1. Reducing the cost of short selling (for example, by introducing option trading) increases the speed of adjustment to private information, especially to bad news.
2. Reducing the cost of short selling makes the distribution of excess returns on public information announcement days less skewed to the left-hand side of the distribution's mean and makes the excess returns smaller in absolute value.
3. An unexpected increase in the announced short interest in a stock is bad news.*
4. Periods with an absence of trading are bad news because they indicate an increased chance of informed traders with bad news who are constrained from selling short. This implies that a recent period of inactive trading imparts a downward bias to measured excess returns because the previous transaction price is an upward biased measure of the stock's value.

Asquith and Meulbroek (1996) examine short interest as an indicator of future stock performance. The traditional view is that high short interest is a bullish signal, because it is an indicator of future demand; all short positions must eventually be covered by purchasing shares. A more recent appraisal of short interest is that it represents negative information about a firm's future prospects. Asquith and Meulbroek investigated the information content of short interest by examining whether firms that are heavily shorted subsequently experience negative returns. Using data on monthly short interest po-

---

*Today, this point is open to debate. The years 2001 and 2002 saw a massive increase in short selling activity. With the increase in hedge funds, equity markets have become more efficient with respect to bad news entering the pricing mechanism.

sitions for all New York Stock Exchange (NYSE) and American Stock Exchange (AMEX) stocks from 1976 to 1993, they detect a strong negative relation between short interest and subsequent returns, both during the time the stocks are heavily shorted and over the following two years. This relationship persists over the entire 18-year period, and the abnormal returns are even more negative for firms that are heavily shorted for more than one month. The results indicate that short interest does indeed convey negative information. They also provide a foundation for the view that stock prices reflect positive information more efficiently than negative information.

According to Staley (1997), sell-side analysts are not fully independent. They have, apparently, a positive bias. Staley finds that most brokerage stock recommendations range from buy to hold, with few analysts willing to rank stocks as sells. This bias causes the risk/reward trade-off for short selling to be more favorable, as the potential for negative surprises causing large swings in price is greater than positive surprises (as all the good news is already in the price). According to Staley, short sellers often disagree with Wall Street analysts. The conflict of interest inherent in the job description of analysts apparently strikes short sellers as a consistent reason for flawed information.

New research indicates that analysts in the United States moved from being too optimistic to too pessimistic. In an international study of trends between 1976 and 1999, Bird and McKinnon (2001) suggest a change in the behavior of earnings surprises. In the U.S. market, analysts have become quite pessimistic in their earnings forecasts, and an increasing number of U.S. firms have announced small positive earnings surprises; the findings in Japan are exactly the opposite. A major driving force behind differences in behavior has been the relative state of the two economies, and in the United States growth in the use of stock options has caused management to be more interested in boosting the short-term share price.

As with any other economic activity there are always individuals who do not play the game according to its rules. Short selling is no different. The main offense (and perhaps the one most practiced) is spreading rumors. Some short sellers will spread news with a negative content, hoping the market will react to the news and put pressure on the price. Another offense is spreading good news, such as a rumor of a merger just around the corner. Internet chat rooms have in the past sometimes been used as platforms for dissemination of false information. A further strategy could involve "talking down" the price of a stock ahead of a hostile takeover. The takeover company circulates negative information that is either false or grossly exaggerated. Because it is inherently difficult for companies to combat bad news, this simple strategy can serve to drive down the share price of the target company to levels that allow the takeover company to accumulate cheap shares before the target company can correct its position in the market. Another example of manipulation is the "bear raid" where a stock is sold short in an effort to drive down the price by creating an imbalance of selling pressure.

After the terrorist atrocities of September 2001, many articles appeared in the press about hedge funds exploiting the tragic events and how short selling has been driving markets lower. This has led to criticism of the stock loan market itself. Much of what has been said is at best ill-informed speculation and at worst arrant nonsense. It may well be human nature to look to blame someone when markets gap down, but blaming hedge funds and short selling is not only missing the point but also creating a danger of upsetting some of the better workings of the marketplace. Stock loans are needed in many areas of market activity: Any trader providing liquidity to a buyer needs to be able to borrow the stock in order to deliver on the sale; stock loans are required in order to ease the settlement process to prevent trades failing; anyone trading derivatives needs to be able to borrow stock to hedge positions. In addition, the majority of the professional stock loan market surrounds dividends and is traded between investors with different tax liabilities. And yes, stock loans are also used by hedge funds, when they want to sell short. If stock loans disappeared, the effects would be a dramatic drying up of liquidity, a vast reduction in the amount of derivatives available, and an increased friction cost in transactions due to delayed settlement.

Staley (1997) quotes Bernard Baruch on the first page of her book. This quote summarizes the issues surrounding short selling and brings it to a point:

> *Bears can make money only if the bulls push up stocks to where they are overpriced and unsound.*
>
> *Bulls always have been more popular than bears in this country [U.S.] because optimism is so strong a part of our heritage. Still, over-optimism is capable of doing more damage than pessimism since caution tends to be thrown aside.*
>
> *To enjoy the advantages of a free market, one must have both buyers and sellers, both bulls and bears. A market without bears would be like a nation without a free press. There would be no one to criticize and restrain the false optimism that always leads to disaster.*

**Myth: Hedge Funds Are Responsible for Worldwide Financial Crisis**   Hedge funds are often blamed when government or central bank policy goes wrong. However, there is an increasing amount of evidence that the truth differs from the immediate headlines after an event. Several research studies have shown that hedge funds were not the cause of the Asian crisis or other major world economic collapses. Brown, Goetzmann, and Park (2000), for example, tested the hypothesis whether hedge funds in the currency markets caused the crash in the Malaysian ringgit as suggested by the Malaysian prime minister Mohamad Mahathir. While not alone in holding currency fund operators like

George Soros responsible for the currency crisis, Mohamad Mahathir was clearly the most outspoken. The authors' empirical analysis of the dynamics of hedge funds and Asian currencies suggested little evidence that hedge fund managers as a group caused the crash. In particular, it is difficult to believe, the authors conclude, that George Soros was responsible for a bear raid on the ringgit when the performances of three of his funds were less than stellar. If anything, it appears that the top 10 hedge funds were buying into the ringgit as it fell in the late summer and early fall of 1997. The authors draw the same conclusion for other Asian currencies.

In today's markets, capital reacts quickly to new information. When something goes wrong, markets react and process the new information in the pricing mechanism quickly and, sometimes, erratically. Funds today move quicker than they moved one or two decades ago, simply because the financial system has become more efficient with respect to processing information. Erratic capital flight might have its own associated problems. However, the alternative to free flows of capital is almost always worse. If investors are afraid of an inability to retrieve capital, it simply will never go there in the first place. CalPERS' decision in February 2002 to remove Thailand, Malaysia, Indonesia, and the Philippines from the list of emerging markets it is allowed to invest in might indicate that this is true.

Fung and Hsieh (2000a) analyzed the role of hedge funds during some macro turbulence in the 1990s. Many episodes were attributed to action by hedge funds, resulting in a negative bias in the industry's reputation. The authors concluded:

- Hedge fund activities were prominent and probably exerted market impact during several episodes.
- There was no evidence that hedge funds used positive feedback trading in any of these episodes.
- Hedge funds did not act as a single group.
- There was no evidence that hedge funds deliberately herded other investors into doing the same thing.

The evidence indicates that, by themselves, hedge funds were not likely to have caused the market turmoil analyzed in the paper. Rather, the evidence indicates that some highly leveraged trades, practiced by hedge funds as well as other market participants, can lead to market disruptions when they are subsequently unwound. The unwinding of the leveraged "carry trades" (borrowing funds at a lower rate and lending at a higher rate) led to the 1994 Mexican peso crisis, in which hedge funds had no discernible role. The unwinding of the leveraged "carry trades" also resulted in the 1992 ERM (European Rate Mechanism) crisis and the 1997 Asian currency crisis, in which hedge funds had a significant role alongside other much larger market participants. However, hedge funds were not the cause for the unwinding of the carry trades.

Table 2.3 outlines the true causes of some financial disasters where hedge funds were blamed for causing the havoc.

In a surprise reversal of the time-honored tradition of vilifying hedge funds as perpetrators of global market calamities, the Monetary Authority of Singapore in January 1999 announced its intent to attract hedge funds. In a statement reported by Bloomberg News (1999), Ms. Teo Swee Lian stated:

> *There are proprietary trading departments of perfectly respectable banks that punt the market. They are more damaging than hedge funds. Do we say "no" to the banks then?*[13]

The recognition of similarities between proprietary trading desks and hedge funds by regulators is positive.* This recognition could reduce the risk that arbitrary and capricious legislation will be enacted to restrict the activities of hedge funds.

The stance toward hedge funds is also changing in Hong Kong. In August 1998, Hong Kong spent about $21 billion buying stocks to protect the local currency's peg to the U.S. dollar from an attack that then Financial Secretary Donald Tsang blamed on hedge funds, calling for them to be curbed. The Hong Kong Securities and Futures Commission called for public comment on the introduction of hedge funds in December 2001. Hong Kong's new Financial Secretary, Antony Leung, grappling with a HK$65.6 billion budget deficit, was quoted saying that the city would like to set itself up as a regional center for hedge funds.[14]

**Myth: Hedge Funds Offer No Economic Value**    There is a myth with respect to hedge funds being about as valuable to the health of the financial system as U.S. corporate creative accounting is to the health of a 401(k) plan. The myth is based on a misunderstanding of the efficient allocation of scarce resources. Schneeweis (1998b) brings it to the point:

> *Hedge funds invest in a wide variety of investment arenas, including private equity, private debt, merger and acquisitions, and emerging markets.*

---

*Note that there are also differences between running proprietary money for an investment bank and managing hedge fund money. First, funding of the former is normally cheaper. Second, there is a difference between being given a credit line to trade and operating with a finite equity base. The performance measure for the former is a dollar profit or loss, whereas performance for the latter is measured in return on equity.

**Table 2.3**  Cause and Effect of Financial Disasters Where Hedge Funds Were Blamed

| Effect | Cause |
|---|---|
| **1992 European Rate Mechanism (ERM) crisis** | It is beyond doubt that macro hedge funds had a significant short position in sterling in 1992 that impacted the market. It is, however, difficult to determine whether this position caused the Sterling devaluation, because it coincided with net capital outflows from the United Kingdom. The prologue to the 1992 ERM crisis was the conversion play, estimated to be around $300 billion, by the International Monetary Fund (IMF). Altogether, European Central Bank interventions amounted to roughly $100 billion. The $11.7 billion in hedge fund positions coincided with at least another $90 billion of sales in European currencies.<br><br>Fung and Hsieh find neither herding nor positive feedback trading. |
| **1994 Mexican peso crisis** | General capital outflow of $5.1 billion from the Mexican debt market in Q4 94 followed by $11.5 billion in the next nine months. The IMF concluded that Mexican residents, not foreign investors, played the leading role in the 1994 crisis. |
| **1997 Asian currency crisis** | Macro hedge funds had sizeable gains in July 1997, when the Thai baht devalued 23%. Stanley Druckenmiller, who headed the daily operations of the Quantum fund, confirmed the existence of short positions in the Thai baht and Malaysian ringgit in a *Wall Street Journal* interview. The position sizes were not disclosed. The popular press assumed that the short position was large and profitable. It turned out that the monthly returns of large macro hedge funds were more correlated with the U.S. equity market than with Asian currencies. The Asian crisis was reminiscent of the ERM crisis of 1992. Substantial amounts of "carrytrades" were involved in the buildup of both crises. These carry trades allowed Thai corporations and banks to borrow in foreign currencies, which had lower interest rates than the domestic currency. As long as the domestic currency did not depreciate, the foreign currency loans represented a cheap source of funding. In the end, the carry trades led to an unsustainable equilibrium. By fixing the exchange rate, the Thai Central Bank was indirectly paying a risk premium to foreign investors to support domestic funding needs. However, when these foreign"lenders" are themselves highly leveraged institutions such as proprietary desks from investment banks (and occasionally leveraged domestic corporations), the resultant equilibrium is at best tenuous.<br><br>In July 1997, for whatever reason, some foreign lenders decided to unwind their carry trades in Thailand. They sold baht and bought dollars in the spot market, putting tremendous pressure on the baht.<br><br>Fung and Hsieh draw the same conclusions as the IMF: (1) Hedge fund positions were relatively modest at the beginning of the crisis. (2) Hedge funds did not utilize positive feedback trading to destabilize the Asian markets. If anything, they displayed some contrarian trading in being long the Indonesian rupiah while it was still falling. (3) Hedge funds cannot be blamed for other investors doing the same trade. The underlying economic fundamentals were ripe for an accident to happen. |

*Source:* Fung and Hsieh (2000a), Eichengreen and Mathieson (1999).

*Without their participation, many worthwhile projects could not find the necessary financing. In addition, hedge funds trade in financial products, offering liquidity to other investors in these assets. The primary use of derivative products is to offer a mechanism for firms to reduce or manage their own risk. Financial innovations such as mortgage-backed bonds provide a means for individuals and institutions to raise capital more efficiently. Recent innovations are much more exotic but have the same objective: to allow one to effectively raise capital and manage risk. In many cases, hedge funds are a primary purchaser of these new securities, both in the primary market and in the secondary market. Without hedge funds, financial markets could have fewer risk management choices and, for some projects, a higher cost of capital.*

**Myth: The Financial Marketplace Must Be Controlled**   Chances are that the problems a regulation is designed to curb are solved, but the inefficiencies introduced through the new rule outweigh the benefits two to one. Regulation, probably by definition, is reactive as opposed to proactive. It is always possible, in hindsight, to see the mistakes that lead to chaos, havoc, or collapse. It is often easy, ex post, to see where a simple rule or regulation might have prevented a catastrophe. Improving one's risk control and analysis is always laudable. However, all possible losses cannot be prevented or ironed out—especially not through regulation. If no risk is taken in an economic system, most projects or products would remain unfunded. Growth requires investment in risky ventures. Risky ventures imply the possibility of loss. Dan Quayle on risk: "If we don't succeed, we run the risk of failure."

In 1994, George Soros was invited to deliver testimony to the U.S. Congress on the stability of the financial markets, particularly with regard to hedge fund and derivatives activity.[15] Soros believed that the banking committee was right to be concerned about the stability of markets, saying: "Financial markets do have the potential to become unstable and require constant and vigilant supervision to prevent serious dislocations."

However, he felt that hedge funds did not cause the instability. He blamed institutional investors, who measure their performance relative to their peer group and not by an absolute yardstick: "This makes them trend-followers by definition."

Persaud (2001) argues that regulatory and risk management systems do not prevent or warn from disasters such as the default of Argentina or Enron—that the regulatory mantras of common standards and market-based risk management encourage the herd mentality that characterizes investment flows and increases the correlation between events that spread instability through financial markets.[16] He uses the term "liquidity black hole" for situations where there is liquidity when you buy but no liquidity when you want to sell. One obvious conclusion is that turnover is not synonymous with liquidity. Technology stocks had high turnover during the bull run. However, when the time came to sell, there were no buyers, only sellers—or, put differently, the buyers all turned into sellers (otherwise the price would not have collapsed 80 to 100 percent). Persaud rightly notes that it is market diversity that increases liquidity in markets, and not turnover. In other words, a marketplace needs contrarians next to the traditional market participants who find comfort in high numbers, that is, the consensus. Market participants acting countercyclically (e.g., derivatives trading unit of investment bank, absolute return managers) should not be ruled out of existence by regulation.

## CONCLUSION: HEDGE FUNDS— THE FIREFLIES AHEAD OF THE STORM?

There is still a lot of mythology with respect to hedge funds; much of it is built on anecdotal evidence, oversimplification, myopia, or simply a misrepresentation of facts. Although hedge funds are often branded as a separate asset class, a point can be made that hedge fund managers are simply asset managers utilizing other strategies than those used by relative return long-only managers. The major difference between the two is the definition of their return objective: Hedge funds aim for absolute returns by balancing investment opportunities and risk of financial loss. Long-only managers, by contrast, define their return objective in relative terms. Long-only managers aim to win what Charles Ellis (1993) calls the loser's game, that is, to beat the market.

Ellis calls the pursuit of beating a benchmark the loser's game. In a winner's game, the outcome is determined by the winning actions of the winner. In a loser's game, the outcome is determined by the losing behavior of the loser. Ellis makes reference to a book by Simon Ramo: *Extraordinary Tennis for the Ordinary Tennis Player* (New York: Crown Publishers, 1977). Dr. Ramo observed that tennis was not one game, but two: one played by professionals and a very few gifted amateurs; the other played by all the rest of us. Professionals win points; the rest lose points. In expert tennis, the ultimate outcome is determined by the actions of the winner. In amateur tennis, the outcome is determined by unforced errors (i.e., the activities of the loser—who defeats himself or herself).

The future path of an economy or stock market is not predictable with any reasonable degree of confidence. Having a year-end target for the S&P 500 in January is similar to having a view in July as to what the weather will be on Christmas Eve. Both systems (weather as well as the economy) are complex as opposed to determinable.* Any argument to the contrary must derive from a model with an R-squared of 1.00 (Bernstein 1999). However, there is no such thing. Decision making with respect to the future will always involve uncertainty regardless of the approach used. What we know for sure about equity markets and their volatility is uncertainty itself. There will always be uncertainty.

The preceding statement is not as fatuous as it may sound. It raises the question of what a money manager should focus on in the long term: expected return or risk. Looking at the world from the view of a risk manager it is obvious: risk. A risk manager would argue that one cannot manage expected return, but one can manage risk. Return is the by-product of taking risk. Banks today do not manage portfolios; they manage risk. Their long-term investment strategy is to define the risk they want to be exposed to and manage that exposure accordingly. This implies that banks have an absolute return focus as opposed to a relative return focus. Potentially, asset management could be in the process of moving in the direction of banks—and hedge funds (i.e., defining risk in absolute terms rather than relative terms). In other words, the asset management industry might be in the process from moving from the second to the third paradigm, as outlined in the Preface of this book. One could also argue that the asset management industry is moving back to an absolute return orientation (first and third paradigm) and that the passion with market benchmarks (second paradigm) was only a brief blip in the industry's evolution, driven perhaps by an increasing involvement of consultants and trustees. In other words, what we call hedge funds today could simply be the fireflies ahead of the storm about to be sweeping over the asset management industry.

---

*Until a couple of decades ago, scientists viewed the world as an orderly place governed by immutable laws of nature. Once uncovered, it was believed, these laws would enable scientists to determine the future by extrapolating from historical patterns and cycles. This approach worked well for Sir Isaac Newton. Once he discovered the mathematics of gravity, he was able to predict the motions of our planets. This line of thinking, called determinism, is based on the belief that future events unfold following rules and patterns that determine their course. Current science is proving this deterministic view of the world to be naive. The theories of chaos and complexity are revealing the future as fundamentally unpredictable. This applies to our economy, the stock market, commodity prices, the weather, animal populations, and many other phenomena. Sherden (1998) analyzed 16 different types of forecasting. He found that from the 16, only two—one-day-ahead weather forecasts and the aging of the population—can be counted on; the rest are about as reliable as the 50–50 odds of flipping a coin. An interesting view is that only one of the 16—short-term weather forecasts—has any scientific foundation. The rest are typically based on conjecture, unproved theory, and the mere extrapolation of past trends, "something no more sophisticated than what a child could do with a ruler (or perhaps a protractor)."

# APPENDIX: Press Coverage of Hedge Funds

*Convictions are more dangerous foes of truth than lies.*
—Friedrich Wilhelm Nietzsche

*Nonsense is good only because common sense is so limited.*
—George Santayana, philosopher, 1863–1952

The headlines since 1998 have not always been favorable for the hedge fund industry. Some countries have an extremely negative bias (e.g., Germany), and others have a neutral or even somewhat positive bias (e.g., Sweden). The reason for the negative press is surprising. The writing guild should feel happy that intelligent and hardworking investment professionals can achieve substantial wealth by taking risks. Envy should not stand between truth and a good story.

To participants in the hedge fund industry the press coverage of hedge funds is cause for disbelief as well as, occasionally, for outright bursts of laughter. "They don't get it" summarizes the comments on most coverage. In this respect, the coverage of hedge funds is similar to the coverage of derivatives in the 1990s. Since hedge funds entered public discussion (probably since 1998), the derivatives industry has attracted hardly any negative press coverage. Now hedge funds seem to capture all the imagination and creativity of the writing guild.

At the most general level, the reason for the negatively biased coverage is as follows: Hedge funds often use speculative instruments to manage conservative portfolios. The reason for the misunderstanding is: "How can a speculative financial instrument be part of a conservative investment approach?" The "logic" is that an investment style employing "speculative" instruments must result in an overall "speculative" portfolio. The purchase of a call option, for example, is, when viewed in isolation, speculative.* The "logical"

---

*Note that to a derivatives user even the purchase of a call option is conservative. The reason is that the derivatives user will compare the call purchase with buying, for example, stock exposure (delta) through cash instruments (i.e., buying stock directly). As a call option is synthetically the stock plus a put option (insurance), buying a call option is essentially buying stock with an insurance against a falling stock price. In other words, the derivatives user would argue that buying stock for $100 is more speculative than buying a call option for $10 and putting $90 into an interest-bearing account. If the underlying asset falls by $50, the stock investor loses $50 while the call buyer loses only $10. The latter strategy is more conservative (less speculative) despite the fact that it involves derivatives as well as leverage. Unfortunately, in the real world conservatism is often defined as what the majority of other people think as opposed to what could cause high financial losses.

consequence is, therefore, that anyone buying call options must be running a speculative portfolio. The possibility that the call purchase is part of mone-tizing an equity stake (taking profits by selling stock and retaining some up-side potential [but limited downside] through the purchase of a call) or the possibility that the call purchase is part of an arbitrage trade where the call is sold synthetically at the same time either is not understood or does not seem to be taken into consideration.

## Example

A hedge fund manager buys Internet stock A and sells Internet stock B against it. Selling short viewed in isolation is a risky strategy. The loss poten-tial is unlimited in the case where the stock price rises to infinity.* The riski-ness is amplified if the hedge fund manager uses all his (or her) capital to enter long stock positions and uses leverage (debt) to enter short positions. If, for example, his equity is 100, he buys stocks for 100, borrows stocks and sells other stocks short for 100, his leverage would be twice his capital. He would be leveraged 2:1. To many market observers, this does look risky.† The fact that banks are leveraged 15:1 is obviously overlooked for the sake of argument. The motto often seems to be: "Don't put anything between me and a good story!"

Figure 2.3 shows the risk/reward payoff between some of the more "risky" hedge fund strategies compared with some equity indexes. The size of the bubble in the graph measures the maximum 12-month loss over the 12-year period. The HFRI Equity Non-Hedge index (essentially an equity long/short manager with a long bias), for example, has had a higher annual total return (dividends reinvested) than the S&P 500 (17.3 percent com-pared with 12.9 percent for the S&P 500), slightly higher volatility (14.9 percent compared with 14.5 percent for the S&P 500) combined with

---

*A long stock position can only go to zero but no further; that is, the maximum loss is limited to the capital tied to the investment.
†Equity market-neutral managers balance their longs with their shorts often using leverage. A portfolio of equity market-neutral managers (i.e., a portfolio where idio-syncratic risk has been diversified) had a volatility of around 3.3 percent over the past 12 years to 2001. A portfolio of global stocks, by comparison (i.e., a portfolio where idiosyncratic risk also has been diversified), had a volatility of around 14.6 percent. This book will try to get across the point that a portfolio with a volatility of 3.3 per-cent is more conservative than a portfolio with a volatility of 14.6 percent.

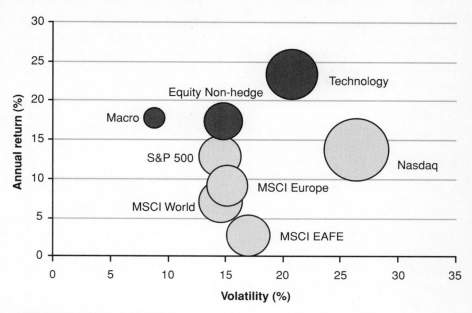

**FIGURE 2.3**   Risk/Reward Trade-Off
*Note:* Based on total U.S. dollar returns January 1990 to December 2001; HFRI Technology index since January 1991.
*Source:* Hedge Fund Research, Datastream.

lower maximum loss (21.7 percent compared with 26.6 percent for the S&P 500).*

Figure 2.3 reveals another interesting aspect: The general public considers macro managers as extremely speculative (risky). Given their loose investment mandate, this is probably true although the macro subgroup has become very heterogeneous, meaning that generalizations are actually inappropriate. Nevertheless, from a press coverage point of view, macro managers are the source of great stories. What is regularly overlooked is the fact that a diversified portfolio of macro managers can result in a conservative

---

*Note that the HFRI Equity Non-Hedge index is inferior to the HFRI Equity Hedge index. The latter consists of true equity long/short managers—managers who want to make money by picking stocks as opposed to timing the market (Alfred Jones model). Annual return, volatility, and maximum 12-month drawdown for the HFRI Equity Hedge index were 20.3 percent, 9.3 percent, and 8.2 percent respectively.

portfolio. The macro index in Figure 2.3 has lower volatility and lower maximum drawdown and higher returns than all equity indexes. If low volatility and low maximum loss potential* are not measures for conservative portfolios we do not know what is.† The reason for low portfolio volatility and low maximum drawdown is low correlation between the portfolio constituents, the single macro managers.

There is a further aspect worth pointing out with respect to press coverage and macro managers. Often there is no distinction between systematic risk and nonsystematic (i.e., idiosyncratic) risk. Modern portfolio principles suggest that investors will not be compensated for being exposed to nonsystematic risk. Nonsystematic risk (for example, stock-specific risk or single hedge fund risk) can be immunized through diversification. Systematic risk can be reduced only by hedging. The difference between diversifying nonsystematic risk and hedging systematic risk is that the former is for free whereas the latter is not. Diversifying risk to Enron or LTCM (nonsystematic risk) can be eliminated by holding 100 other stocks or funds. One could even go one step further by stating that most press coverage of hedge funds is probably not relevant because the press coverage makes a story out of a failure of a single hedge fund. Most often a failing fund (or a bankrupt company) might uncover interesting information (the story) but is not representative for the whole system and, therefore, has little (statistical) significance. Drawing conclusions from unrepresentative anecdotes, to some, is considered unwise. For an investor, headline-catching events are only noise and are hardly relevant because idiosyncratic risk can be reduced through diversification. It is the systematic risk of the hedge fund industry or the common risk factors within the hedge fund industry that are relevant.

## Summary

The reason why some people don't get it is that they might be misled to some extent because of what was referred to as "risk illusion" in the appendix to Chapter 1: namely, the fact that stocks have high correlation when markets

---

*Note that this is slightly simplified. An investment strategy could experience low volatility and low maximum drawdown for a long time and still blow up in the end. If returns are not normally distributed, low volatility could lead to myopic loss perception, that is, an underestimation of the true risk.
†Note that, obviously, low volatility and low maximum drawdown have to be put into the context of the return. The Sharpe ratio (which is one way of looking at risk-adjusted returns) for the macro portfolio in Figure 2.3 was 1.44. This compares with 0.54 for the S&P 500 index, 0.33 for the Nasdaq index, and 0.14 for the MSCI World index.

fall (i.e., volatility and maximum drawdown are relatively high).* With portfolios of absolute return managers this is not necessarily the case. Correlation among constituents is lower. Portfolios of absolute return managers are neither identical nor even similar. There is no benchmark portfolio to adopt. The lower correlation reduces volatility and also the maximum drawdown. Some practitioners go even as far as arguing that the non-normal return distribution of hedge funds does not matter to long-term investors. The reason is the excess kurtosis (fat tails) of monthly returns disappears when annual returns are analyzed.[17] In addition to this, a five-sigma outlier return of a portfolio with a volatility of 5 percent is not half as bad as a two-sigma return of a portfolio of 30 percent volatility—in absolute return space, that is.

---

*The 1987 stock market crash caused many market participants to think about whether there are any better ways of managing money than through long-only strategies.

# CHAPTER 3

# Difference between Long-Only and Absolute Return Funds

*If hedge funds were allowed to advertise performance figures, the mutual fund industry would be history.*

—Donald J. Halldin*

## INTRODUCTION

There are many differences between long-only and absolute return managers. This chapter discusses some of the differences. However, there are many commonalities as well. All active asset managers seek to add value. The active long-only relative return manager aims for alpha,[†] that is, achieving a higher return than would be possible with a passive alternative. The absolute return manager does not have a formal benchmark; hence the term "alpha" is not appropriate. The value added is defined in compounding capital at a stable rate with little downside volatility. Further commonalities are that all managers seek talent from the same pool and aspire for the best service from the Street.

---

*President and cofounder of Meridian Capital Partners, Inc., a fund of (hedge) funds operator.
[†]Alpha measures the portion of a manager's performance that is attributable to skill, while beta measures the exposure to the market.

## PERFORMANCE

One of the main differences is performance. There are essentially two main reasons to invest in hedge funds: superior performance and diversification. The former reason is occasionally referred to as the "alpha argument" and the latter as the "diversification argument."

### The Alpha Argument

Simply put, alpha is honest pay for a hard day's work. Buying large-cap stocks is easier than evaluating the probability of a merger being completed and trading the spread during the merger period. The latter requires investments in technology and a diverse set of talents, the former to a lesser extent. If hard work would not yield high returns, no one would bother. As the work gets easier, the returns go down.

The alpha argument does not go down very well with (sophisticated) institutional investors: If there was a market inefficiency, someone else would already have exploited it. There are probably many reasons for this observation. One is that most institutional investors have more or less the same educational background with respect to economics and financial theory. One of the main pillars of financial theory is the efficient market hypothesis (EMH),[*] or random walk hypothesis. Given the observation that a large portion of active large-cap equity managers in the developed equity markets constantly underperform the benchmark on an after-fee basis, one could assume that these markets are information efficient or the costs of exploiting the inefficiencies are too high. Disciples of the EMH will not invest in hedge funds, as hedge funds are active managers trying to exploit market inefficiencies. However, there are two recent (past 10 to 15 years) trends in consensus thinking with respect to financial markets that affect the demand side of hedge fund investing:

1. It is probably fair to say that the consensus view with respect to EMH is moving toward the belief that financial markets are not as efficient as was the consensus view 10 or 15 years ago.
2. A further consensus seems to be that excess returns or superior performance is strongly associated with some sort of a competitive advantage on the part of the active manager.[†]

---

[*]Norton (1996) on EMH: "The efficient market paradigm is so riddled with anomalies that the only people who espouse the hypothesis are people vending index funds."
[†]This view can be derived from combining the work done by Campbell, Lo, and MacKinlay (1997) and Lo and MacKinlay (1999) with that done by Richard Grinold and Ronald Kahn [i.e., Grinold (1989) and Grinold and Kahn (2000 a,b)].

Putting these two lines of thinking together forms the consensus with respect to active management. If skill is zero, the ex ante alpha is zero by definition. Any excess return above a benchmark is a function of chance. In other words, an active manager should have an edge of some sort that can be identified by a prospective investor in advance, that is, before investing. Only an active manager with an edge has the opportunity to win the negative-sum game that is active asset management.

A further, rather weak, reason why the alpha argument does not always work is because of something called the "investment paradox."* The investment paradox asks, "If you are so skilled, why do you want to invest someone else's money?" Putting it crudely: If someone has investment skill, he or she will lever his or her own funds and buy call or put options on anything that moves. As a matter of fact, there are many absolute return managers that manage their own money only. However, the paradox does not always apply, mainly because of economies of scale (allocations from primary market, service from the Street, execution costs, diversification benefits, etc.). In other words, there is an incentive to reach critical mass.†

One could argue that the difference between the relative return approach and the absolute return approach is becoming less important as the possibility of portable alpha (transporting the alpha of one manager to a passive benchmark) increases. Once alpha is separated from all systematic risks, the alpha of a manager can be ported to any liquid market benchmark. Duen-Li Kao (2002) from General Motors Asset Management discusses the battle for alpha between hedge funds and long-only managers. The study examined whether the alphas of hedge funds and those of long-only portfolios present different distributions and are derived from different risk factors. One of the main conclusions of the study is that when adjusted for return volatility differences, hedge funds seem to offer more consistent alphas for potential alpha transfer to either equity or bond asset classes than do long-only portfolios—even under extreme market conditions. Potential explanations for the findings include lack of data reliability and differences between hedge funds and actively managed long-only funds in compensation, investment constraints, and structures. Factors related to market index returns do not adequately detect hedge funds' risk postures beyond a fund's exposure to the market-directional risk of standard asset classes. Risk factors derived from asset prices in financial markets

---

*Bernstein (1992) argues that market advice for a fee is a paradox: "Anybody who really knew just wouldn't share his knowledge. Why should he? In five years, he could be the richest man in the world. Why pass the word on?"
†Note that there are hedge funds as well as funds of funds that do not take foreign capital. Some successful managers close their funds after a couple of years to run their own money.

do provide timely and systematic descriptions of the risks underlying trading strategies used by hedge funds.

## The Diversification Argument

The diversification argument is stronger than the alpha argument when dealing with institutional investors. The benefits of diversification are rooted within the origins of modern portfolio theory. One cannot disagree that combining independent return distributions does not reduce risk. Institutional investors who either have invested in absolute return managers in the past or are in the process of investing in hedge funds know that a vehicle with positive expected return, low volatility, and low correlation does add value to the portfolio in the form of efficiency gains. The task, therefore, does not become determining whether hedge funds are a good thing. The focus of attention is on whether the return, volatility, and correlation characteristics of the past are an indication for the future. This evaluation in combination with the fact (or observation) that we (the global economy) might have entered a new real interest rate regime* caused a demand for more efficiently balanced portfolios with a bias to taking risk off the table (as opposed to rising expected returns with the same amount of risk). This demand or risk aversion is the primary driver for institutional involvement in the hedge funds arena. It is probably a question of time until the last chief investment officer, plan sponsor (plan trustee), or board member has bought into the diversification argument.[†]

Future alternative investment strategies will gain momentum based on these principles. Timber, for example, is an asset class where the return to the investor is partly due to the weather and the growth of the trees. In other words, the ex ante correlation is lower than 1.0 because the weather is not

---

*Every book probably has a "period bias," that is, some bias with respect to the period in which it was written. Most of this book was written between July 2000 and April 2002, when equity markets were falling. In this period, an observer got the impression that the probability distribution for future equity returns was leaning (or moving) to the left. Increasing awareness of rising liabilities of pension funds (due to longevity and falling interest rates [but high and frozen actuarial rates]) in combination with an increasing effect on corporate balance sheets as well as an increasing risk awareness (as well as aversion) by private investors toward equities was not necessarily the rosiest of outlooks. "Goldilocks" (economic growth without inflation) and the tailwind from disinflation seemed a distant memory.

[†]Those who currently compare hedge funds with a casino and those who still believe that a balanced hedge fund portfolio is more risky than a balanced equity portfolio are likely to be the last to do so.

correlated with the stock market.* The same is true for weather risk itself. The ex ante return distribution is certainly not normal (as it is not for relative value managers in the hedge fund industry). However, the expected return is positive (assuming the insurer or reinsurer gets the statistical arbitrage part right) and the ex ante correlation is low.

## Differences in Performance

Hedge funds outperform mutual funds in most market conditions, but not all.† The academic literature supports the notion that hedge funds offer more attractive risk-adjusted returns than mutual funds. McCarthy and Spurgin (1998a), for example, find that over the time period analyzed (1990–1997) hedge funds offered risk-adjusted returns greater than traditional stock and bond investments. However, results also demonstrate that there are considerable differences in the relative performance of these hedge fund indexes. These differences are sizable enough that investors must realize that the use of seemingly similar benchmark hedge fund indexes may result in different asset allocation decisions.

Goldman Sachs and Financial Risk Management (1999) examine the performances of hedge funds in terms of the fund objectives and suggested that institutional investors might improve their risk-adjusted returns by adding hedge funds to their portfolios. The study indicates that hedge funds performed well in terms of lower volatilities, lower downside deviations, and higher Sharpe ratios than benchmarks, and such measures were particularly good for the market-neutral and event-driven funds. In addition, all four fund categories studied exhibited low correlation of returns with the benchmarks. During periods of market decline when the equity market declined by 3 percentage points, all the hedge funds categories outperformed the S&P 500 by at least 270 basis points.

Schneeweis and Spurgin (1999) argue that the ability to obtain alpha (i.e., return above the risk-free rate) is not indicative of managerial ability. In fact,

---

*Two caveats: (1) Ex post correlation analysis of timber with marketable securities is a little bit of a joke because the monthly or quarterly values are based on appraisals. (2) There is "research" (which we came across but have disposed of and therefore cannot quote) suggesting that weather actually does have an influence on stock markets. Demand seems to be stronger on sunny days. Also, lunar constellations, apparently, can have an influence on market participants and drive their market activity. If this research proves to be correct, there could be correlation between stock market returns and the photosynthesis in timber forests.
†Chapter 5 looks at hedge fund performance in more detail. Chapters 6 through 8 examine single hedge fund strategies as well as their performance and risk characteristics.

any strategy that has volatility should use a benchmark return above the risk-free rate. The authors discuss various forms of alpha determination. Moreover, the article emphasizes the problem of using Sharpe ratios to compare return/risk performance of two dissimilar strategies, especially when these strategies would be added to a predetermined portfolio. The authors also distinguish between "marketing" alpha and relative performance alpha. If the manager can choose asset positions with a higher return than (but the same ex ante risk as) some comparable naive investment position, then that person can be said to achieve a positive alpha. Managers may say that investors never care about relative returns, but only absolute returns.* But performance alpha is all about properly measured relative return. Schneeweis and Spurgin therefore argue that one needs a benchmark to define alpha. They also believe that using the risk-free rate is probably not appropriate, as every investment decision involves some risk.

Active funds underperform passive funds because active money management is more costly than passive money management. Bogle (1998), for example, compares the performance and risk characteristics of 741 mutual funds with peer groups and index funds that have similar average returns, and they have very different standard deviations. Within a style group, however, funds having different returns have nearly the same risk. Expense ratios, rather than risk, show cross-sectional variation in performance within a style group. Index funds appear to have significantly better risk-adjusted returns than the average funds within the same style, suggesting that low-cost funds and index funds represent attractive investment opportunities for those seeking specific style representation. Bogle (1991) reports that in the decade ending in 1979, about 47 percent of equity fund managers outperformed the S&P 500, compared with 37 percent in the 1980s. Elton, Gruber, and Blake (1996) find that the average mutual fund underperforms passive market indexes by about 65 basis points per year from 1985 to 1994. Results from a study by Daniel, Grinblatt, Titman, and Wermers (1997) in the *Journal of Finance* also indicate that performance based on selectivity and timing is not statistically greater than the difference between active and passive expenses.

Mutual funds as a group most often underperform their benchmarks, but not always. Ikenberry, Shockley, and Womack (1998), for example, argue that provided they lack superior information/skills, active fund managers as a group should consistently underperform the S&P 500 index over time, given research, trading, and investor servicing costs. However, data does not show such consistency. In some years, managers as a group have outperformed the S&P 500, sometimes by a substantial amount. The authors concluded that

---

*Someone once said: "You cannot eat relative returns."

size premium and the skewness of long-run stock returns are important determinants of this inconsistent performance.

The current state of research suggests that institutional money managers might not consistently beat their benchmarks (after all, they are playing the loser's game) but do better than private investors. Barber and Odean (1999) conducted a study using a data set of 10,000 private accounts to test for excessive trading and the disposition effect (selling winners too early and holding losers too long). One of the conclusions was that the proportion of gains realized was consistently above losses realized. Not only have the examined private accounts not covered trading costs, but the stocks bought underperformed on average the stocks sold. A study by Chen, Jegadeesh, and Wermers (2000) reestablished the value proposition of the professional active long-only asset management industry. Today this study is one of the (few) tools of the active mutual fund lobby in its battle with low-margin producers such as index funds. Chen et al. investigated the value of active mutual fund management by examining the stock holdings and trades of mutual funds. Their data covered all U.S. mutual funds between 1975 and 1995. The authors found that stocks widely held by funds do not outperform other stocks. However, the stocks that funds actively bought had significantly higher returns than the stocks that were actively sold. In other words, active long-only managers actually do have stock-selection ability.

It is fair to state that the amounts by which traditional fund managers as a group beat or are beaten by the market fall within the margin of statistical uncertainty. As David F. Swensen (2000), Yale's chief investment officer, puts it:

> In spite of the daunting obstacles to active management success, the overwhelming majority of market participants choose to play the loser's game. Like the residents of Lake Wobegon, who all believe their children to be above average, all investors believe their active strategies will produce superior results. The harsh reality of the negative-sum game dictates that in aggregate, active managers lose to the market by the amount it costs to play, in the form of management fees, trading commissions, and dealer spread. Wall Street's share of the pie defines the amount of performance drag experienced by the would-be market beaters.

## HEDGE FUND PERFORMANCE COMPARED WITH MUTUAL FUND PERFORMANCE

Chapter 5 will summarize hedge fund performance by investment strategy, and in Chapters 6 to 8 risk and return will be examined in more detail. Table 3.1 compares annual returns of traditional indexes with nontraditional indexes.

**Table 3.1** Hedge Fund Returns Compared with Mutual Fund and Index Returns

| | Traditional | | | Nontraditional | | |
|---|---|---|---|---|---|---|
| | MSCI World Total Return Index | S&P 500 Total Return Index | Morningstar Average Equity Mutual Fund | Van Global Hedge Fund | HFRI Fund Weighted Composite Index | CSFB/ Tremont Hedge Fund Index |
| 1988 | 24.0% | 16.6% | 14.9% | 25.0% | NA | NA |
| 1989 | 17.2 | 31.7 | 25.5 | 24.9 | NA | NA |
| 1990 | −16.5 | −3.1 | −7.1 | 7.2 | 5.8% | NA |
| 1991 | 19.0 | 30.5 | 31.9 | 29.4 | 32.2 | NA |
| 1992 | −4.7 | 7.7 | 6.5 | 17.0 | 21.2 | NA |
| 1993 | 23.1 | 9.8 | 19.3 | 29.0 | 30.9 | NA |
| 1994 | 5.6 | 1.5 | −2.3 | 0.4 | 4.1 | −4.4% |
| 1995 | 21.3 | 37.6 | 25.0 | 18.1 | 21.5 | 21.7 |
| 1996 | 14.0 | 22.9 | 17.5 | 18.6 | 21.1 | 22.2 |
| 1997 | 16.2 | 33.4 | 17.0 | 15.6 | 16.8 | 25.9 |
| 1998 | 24.8 | 28.6 | 10.1 | 6.0 | 2.6 | -0.4 |
| 1999 | 25.3 | 21.0 | 29.5 | 39.5 | 31.3 | 23.4 |
| 2000 | −12.9 | −9.1 | −6.1 | 8.1 | 5.0 | 4.8 |
| 2001 | −16.5 | −11.9 | −12.5 | 6.1 | 4.8 | 4.4 |
| Average | 10.0 | 15.5 | 12.1 | 17.5 | 16.4 | 12.2 |
| Median | 16.7 | 18.8 | 16.0 | 17.6 | 18.9 | 13.3 |
| High | 25.3 | 37.6 | 31.9 | 39.5 | 32.2 | 25.9 |
| Low | −16.5 | −11.9 | −12.5 | 0.4 | 2.6 | −4.4 |

*Note:* Based on total U.S. dollar returns. Hedge fund returns are net of fees.
*Source:* Van Money Manager Research, Hedge Fund Research, CSFB/Tremont, Datastream.

Table 3.1 speaks more or less for itself. Average, median, and highest returns are quite similar for both traditional and nontraditional (in this case hedge funds) investment vehicles. The big difference between traditional and hedge funds is shown in the last row of Table 3.1: Diversified hedge fund portfolios, in the past, lost a fraction of traditional long-only portfolio losses. This is why it is an absolute mystery to many investment professionals in the alternative investments universe as to why hedge funds are branded (and regulated) as a high-risk asset class. How can an investment vehicle where its managers' main goal is to avoid financial losses be considered a high-risk product?

Figure 3.1 shows the performance of absolute return managers relative to the MSCI World index, a proxy for relative return managers. To an absolute return manager this comparison does not add anything because relative performance is not part of the absolute return objective. However, the comparison might be useful to make the following point: Hedge funds underperform the stock market only when the latter is strong, that is, when the stock market yields a positive annual return. The years when global hedge

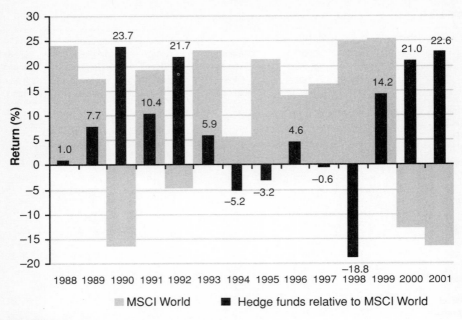

**FIGURE 3.1**   Relative Performance of Hedge Funds
*Source:* Van Money Manager Research, Datastream.

funds (here measured by the Van Global Hedge Fund index) underperformed
global long-only equities were 1994, 1995, 1997, and 1998. In all those four
occasions, equity investors had an absolute profit on their equity exposure.
In all those four occasions, hedge fund investors also had a positive absolute
return.* However, the return from a diversified hedge fund portfolio was less
than from a diversified equity portfolio. The years when hedge funds outperformed long-only equities by a wide margin were the years when the equity
market declined. Over the 14 years shown in Figure 3.1 those years were
1990, 1992, 2000, and 2001. Those were the years when there was a big difference whether one is in equities or in hedge funds: On those four occasions
equity investors suffered an absolute loss and hedge fund investors did not.
Why is this important?

---

*This is true based on composite indexes from Van Money Manager Research and
Hedge Fund Research. However, the HFRI Fund of Funds index measured a negative
return of –3.5 percent in 1994 and –5.1 percent in 1998.

The obvious relevance of this observation, to put it crudely, is that not losing money is better than losing money. However, apart from this rather simplistic comment, there is another aspect shown in Figure 3.1: Most investors have higher negative utility from falling prices than positive utility from rising prices. In other words, the expected marginal utility benefit from a $1 profit is less than the expected marginal utility cost from a $1 loss. However, standard expected utility theory is too simplistic in the real world, because investors consider many periods in making their portfolio decisions[1] and it ignores the financial status quo of the investor. Given the shortcomings* of standard expected utility models, Kahneman and Tversky (1979) and Tversky and Kahneman (1992) formulated a psychological model: prospect theory.[†] Prospect theory is a mathematically formulated alternative to the theory of expected utility maximization and justifies the existence of the status quo bias. Samuelson and Zeckhauser (1988) define the status quo bias as the tendency for decision makers to do nothing or maintain their current or previous decision. Loss aversion,[‡] which states that losses loom larger than gains,

---

*Allais (1953), for example, reported examples showing that in choosing between certain lotteries, people systematically violate the fundamentals behind expected utility theory. He formulated the "certainty effect" where preferences for certain identical outcomes are given.

†One of the shortcomings is the notion that people behave rationally, or accurately maximize expected utility, and are able to process all available information. Shiller (1997): "Prospect theory is very influential despite the fact that it is still viewed by much of the economics profession as of far less importance than expected utility theory. . . . Despite the attractiveness of expected utility theory, it has long been known that the theory has systematically mispredicted human behavior, at least in certain circumstances." Behavioral finance and market efficiency is discussed in the appendix of Chapter 4 entitled "On Market Efficiency and Unorthodox Economics."

‡Tversky (1995): "Loss aversion—the greater impact of the down-side than the up-side—is a fundamental characteristic of the human pleasure machine." The failures to accept many bets when one considers them individually have been called "myopic loss aversion" by Benartzi and Thaler (1995), who argue that, under estimated values for the magnitude of the kink in the value function, the "equity premium puzzle" can be resolved. They show that if people use one-year horizons to evaluate investments in the stock market, then the high equity premium is explained by myopic loss aversion. Benartzi and Thaler (1999) demonstrated experimentally that when subjects are asked to allocate their defined contribution pension plans between stocks and bonds, their responses differed sharply depending on how historical returns where presented to them. If they were shown 30 one-year returns, their median allocation to stocks was 40 percent, but if they were shown 30-year returns, their median allocation to stocks was 90 percent.

provides support for this decision making bias.* Prospect theory actually resembles expected utility theory in that individuals are represented as maximizing a weighted sum of "utilities," although the weights are not the same as
probabilities and the "utilities" are determined by what is called a "value
function" rather than a utility function.[2] The difference between the value
function (of wealth or payout) in prospect theory and the utility function in
expected utility theory is that the former has a "kink" at a "reference point."
The reference point is the individual's point of comparison, the "status quo"
against which alternative scenarios are compared. In the field of investment
management the reference point is the current amount of wealth.

Table 3.1 and Figure 3.1 to some extent illustrate what absolute return
investing is all about: The downside has a different weight than has the upside; that is, the cost of losing $1 is larger than the benefit of a $1 profit. The
cost of absolute losses weighs much stronger than the benefit of profits. Figure
3.1 shows that absolute return managers do not always do better than relative
return managers (i.e., the stock market). However, two things are different
between the two. (1) With absolute return managers risk is defined as total
risk (i.e., as "losing money") whereas the relative return manager defines risk
as active risk (i.e., as "underperforming the benchmark").[†] (2) The underperformance of hedge fund portfolios occurs in rising markets, still resulting in a
positive absolute return for the investor. If investing in hedge funds is no free
lunch, then the protection from negative absolute returns is acquired through
giving up some potential upside. In other words, the potential price of the
protective put is an opportunity cost in absolute return space. These two factors align investor utility with the S-shaped value function in prospect theory.

In Figure 3.2 we compare the MSCI World total return index and the
HFRI Equity Hedge index with the "Super MSCI World." The Super MSCI

---

*An extreme example of loss aversion and status quo bias was about the proposed use
of ground troops in the Kosovo conflict during the Clinton administration: Key U.S.
officials insisted on not using ground troops. When it comes to the loss of life, most
people are prone to forget even the most ostentatious of humanitarian goals and focus
on the prospect of casualties. Riskier propositions beget greater loss aversion. Polls indicated that Americans did not accept the risk involved with the introduction of
ground troops, even if such a strategy had a better chance of meeting NATO's objectives than the executed policy of bombing. The result was the maintenance of the status quo, as the disadvantages of pursuing a course other than bombing were weighted
larger than the potential advantages.
†Throughout this book it is argued that absolute return managers are driven by total
risk, that is, a P&L, whereby relative return managers focus on active risk, that is, a
market benchmark. The term *total risk* is not entirely unambiguous, as relative return
managers also use the term for the overall portfolio risk.

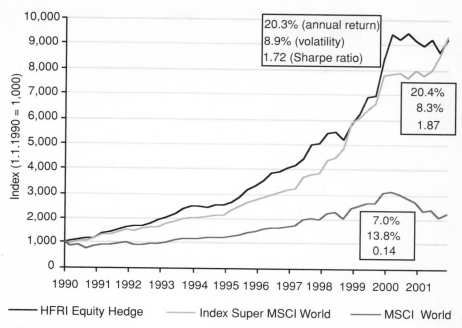

**FIGURE 3.2**    Hedge Funds versus Super MSCI World
*Source:* Hedge Fund Research, Datastream.

World is a fictitious time series. For the sake of argument we have assumed perfect foresight: At the beginning of every calendar quarter an absolute return manager invests in either the MSCI World total return index or in the JPM Global Government Bond total return index. The selection is dependent on the future quarterly performance of these two instruments. In other words, the Super MSCI World shows the performance of an investor who manages to be invested in the better-performing vehicle in all calendar quarters—that is, who has perfect foresight of quarterly returns. The Super MSCI World matches the performance of a diversified portfolio of long/short equity managers rather neatly. Risk-adjusted returns (here measured with the Sharpe ratio assuming a constant risk-free rate of 5 percent) of the Super MSCI World are slightly higher than for the hedge funds index. What is amazing (or at least should entail some entertainment value) is that the hedge funds index is a closer match to the artificial Super MSCI World than is the real MSCI World index.

Comparing performance indexes has its limitations. Table 3.2 compares certain segments of hedge funds and mutual funds based on five-year net compound annual returns. Previous observations and conclusions remain

**Table 3.2** Comparison of the Best and Worst Performing Hedge Funds and Mutual Funds

|  | 1995–1999 | | 1996–2000 | |
|---|---|---|---|---|
|  | Hedge Funds | Mutual Funds | Hedge Funds | Mutual Funds |
| Top 10 | 62.2% | 51.5% | 53.6% | 36.0% |
| Top 10% | 46.3 | 27.2 | 37.5 | 21.9 |
| Top 25% | 36.3 | 20.3 | 29.9 | 18.5 |
| Bottom 25% | 6.4 | 5.6 | 4.0 | 2.4 |
| Bottom 10% | 0.7 | 4.0 | −1.5 | −0.5 |
| Bottom 20 | −4.4 | −16.1 | −7.7 | −19.8 |

*Source:* Van Money Manager Research.

unchallenged. In addition to the average hedge fund outperforming the average mutual fund, the highest-returning hedge funds significantly outperformed the highest-returning mutual funds. This is, to some extent, attributable to leverage. However, the worst 20 hedge funds lost less than the worst 20 mutual funds despite the former operating with leverage. This is an indication of the focus on absolute returns versus relative returns. Note, however, that the bottom 10 percent of mutual funds actually outperformed the bottom 10 percent of hedge funds.

## A Word on Survivorship Bias

Mutual fund as well as hedge fund returns data suffer from survivorship bias. Grinblatt and Titman (1989); Brown, Goetzmann, Ibbotson, and Ross (1992); Malkiel (1995); and Elton, Gruber, and Blake (1996) found that survivorship biased mutual fund returns upward by between 0.5 and 1.4 percent a year. Survivorship bias occurs when data samples exclude markets or investment funds or individual securities that disappeared. The data sample of survivors describes an environment that overstates the real-world return and understates the real-world risk.* For hedge funds, it is unclear by how much

---

*A classic example of survivorship bias is the paradigm that equities do well in the long run since market studies primarily focus only on returns for securities in the United States, United Kingdom, Switzerland, or Sweden (surviving markets). Early in the twentieth century active stock markets existed in Russia, France, Germany, Japan, and Argentina, all of which have been interrupted for a variety of reasons, including political turmoil, war, nationalization, and hyperinflation. We will revisit this bias in Chapter 12.

survivorship bias inflates returns of hedge fund indexes. Poorly performing hedge funds, as well as those with stellar performances, exit the database. Inferior hedge funds exit because of poor performance. Stellar hedge funds can close to new partners and, as a result of good performance, stop reporting returns to the data vendor. Some hedge funds do not enter the database at all. Hedge funds report their performance on a voluntary basis. This self-selection bias may partially offset the survivorship bias caused by the disappearance of poorly performing funds.

A small, well-performing fund attracts assets. Unlike mutual funds, many absolute return strategies have limited capacity. This means that, over any given time period, performance may well decline when a fund's size gets too large. If it subsequently experiences poor performance, assets begin to flow out. In some cases, the fund can return to some equilibrium level of assets under management and the fund survives. However, there will be other cases where assets shrink so much that it is no longer economical to cover the fund's fixed overhead; the manager closes it down, and the fund exits. This can occur even if the returns during the latter stage are above the surviving funds' average, but compare poorly to its peers in the same trading style. In other words, funds exiting the sample can easily have returns higher than the population average of the survivors.[3]

In addition, a successful hedge fund that has reached its perceived capacity and has stopped accepting new investments has no incentive to market the fund and distribute returns information to third-party data vendors. In other words, a successful hedge fund with above-average returns might decide to close the fund to new money and choose not to report its performance to data vendors.

Liang (1999) found survivorship bias in hedge fund returns data from January 1992 through December 1996. However, Liang concluded that on a risk-adjusted basis the average hedge fund outperformed the average mutual fund and that the outperformance cannot be explained by survivorship bias. Brown, Goetzmann, and Ibbotson (1999) and Fung and Hsieh (2000b) both estimated survivorship bias in hedge fund indexes to be around 3.0 percent per year.

## DOWNSIDE PROTECTION

A further differentiation between mutual funds and hedge funds is with respect to downside protection or with the incentive to avoid financial losses. This distinction is, obviously, related to the previously discussed issue of performance. Mutual funds are not able to protect portfolios effectively against declining markets other than by going into cash or by shorting a limited amount of stock index futures. Hedge funds, however, are often able to protect against declining markets by utilizing various hedging strategies. The strategies used vary tremendously depending on the investment style and type of hedge fund. But as a result of these hedging strategies, certain types of hedge funds are able to generate positive returns even in declining markets. In addition, the starting point for a relative return manager is the market benchmark, that is, a long-only portfolio. The starting point for an absolute return manager is a white piece of paper. Positions (long as well as short) will be driven by investment opportunity and the active call of the risk/return trade-off by the manager.

International diversification is often questioned because correlation between developed markets approaches one when markets fall due to a global crisis (oil shock, Gulf War, Asian crisis, etc.). In other words, the concept of diversification breaks down when it is most needed to preserve wealth. Table 3.3 speaks for itself. The table shows that as an asset group, hedge funds do not decline in line with the market. The low correlation of hedge funds with equities remains low, even when markets fall. High correlation (third quarter 1998) is the exception, not the rule. When the S&P 500 falls or is flat during a quarter, the average mutual fund falls as well. The sum of the negative quarters in the 12-year period to 2001 was −84.0 percent in the case of mutual funds, compared with −3.3 percent for the average hedge funds portfolio. Assuming hedge fund data is inflated by 75 basis points per quarter (300 basic points per year) does not change the conclusions drawn from Table 3.3.

The main reason why traditional funds do more poorly in down markets is that they usually have to have a certain weight in equities according to their mandate and therefore are often compared with a car without brakes (see Chapter 1). The freedom of operation is limited with traditional money managers and more flexible with alternative managers. This is just one reason explaining why hedge funds do better in down markets. Another reason is the fact that hedge fund managers have a large portion of their personal wealth at risk in their funds and therefore their interests are aligned with those of their investors. This increases the incentive to preserve wealth. Driving a car without brakes is fine as long as it goes uphill. However, driving downhill, brakes are required to manage risk. Or as Jim Rogers (2000) puts it:

> One of the biggest mistakes most investors make is believing they've always got to be doing something, investing their idle cash. In fact, the worst thing that happens to many investors is to make big money on an investment. They are flushed, excited, and triumphant that they say to themselves, "Okay, now let me find another one!"
>
> They should simply put their money in the bank and wait patiently for the next sure thing, but they jump right back in. Hubris! The trick in investing is not to lose money. That's the most important thing. If you compound your money at 9 percent a year, you're better off than in-

**Table 3.3**  Performance Comparison in Negative S&P 500 Quarters

|  | S&P 500 Index | Morningstar Average Equity Mutual Fund | Van U.S. Hedge Fund Index | HFRI Fund of Funds Index |
|---|---|---|---|---|
| **Q1 90** | −3.0% | −2.8% | 2.2% | 3.51% |
| **Q3 90** | −13.7 | −15.4 | −3.7 | 7.72 |
| **Q2 91** | −0.2 | −0.9 | 2.3 | 1.11 |
| **Q1 92** | −2.5 | −0.6 | 5.0 | 3.32 |
| **Q1 94** | −3.8 | −3.2 | −0.8 | −3.32 |
| **Q4 94** | 0.0 | −2.6 | −1.2 | −2.43 |
| **Q3 98** | −9.9 | −15.0 | −6.1 | −10.02 |
| **Q3 99** | −6.2 | −3.2 | 2.1 | 0.72 |
| **Q2 00** | −2.7 | −3.6 | 0.3 | −2.21 |
| **Q3 00** | −1.0 | 0.6 | 3.0 | 0.60 |
| **Q4 00** | −7.8 | −7.8 | −2.4 | −1.19 |
| **Q1 01** | −12.1 | −12.6 | −1.6 | 0.73 |
| **Q3 01** | −15.0 | −16.9 | −3.8 | −1.83 |
| | | | | |
| **Cumulative** | −77.9 | −84.0 | −4.7 | −3.3 |

*Source:* Van Money Manager Research, Hedge Fund Research, Datastream.

*vestors whose results jump up and down, who have some great years and horrible losses in others. The losses will kill you. They ruin your compounding rate, and compounding is the magic of investing.*

Jim Rogers (apart from being a successful investor, he also taught finance at Columbia University) might or might not have had the institutional investor in mind when he was writing the above statement. Chances are that the investment philosophy needed rephrasing if the intention was to reach out to readers of the *Journal of Finance*. However, when a developed nation's pension fund industry has 80 percent in equities after the greatest bull market in its capital markets' history and only a very small minority has figured out that the concentration toward a common risk factor could be "a little risky," then it should accept all the advice it can get. Waiting until the approach of avoiding negative compounding is touted in financial textbooks and (with a lag) marketed by financial consultants might be about as wise and promising as King Canute's order for the ocean to roll back.

One of the overriding themes of this book is that great investors believe that losing money is not a very good idea for long-term financial success. The quotes by Soros, Buffett, Graham, and Rogers throughout this book sound strange in an institutional setup. Practitioners (or authors of books on new paradigms) using these entertaining quotes take the risk of being discredited, as humor is not considered by all as eligible to bring across a serious and important point of view. The reason why these quotes are humorous is because they sound obvious. Of course it is not a good idea to lose money, if prosperity or wealth preservation are major goals. However, if risk is not defined as total risk and the purpose of risk management is not to preserve wealth, then avoiding losses is not a paramount objective. Our anticipated and suggested third paradigm of absolute returns might not entirely be consistent with the way investors think about risk and uncertainty today. It does not fit as nicely with the assumptions behind modern portfolio theory and, admittedly, contemporary thinking in finance. However, if failure (destroying wealth) is not a paramount objective, meritocratic performance is out of reach to begin with. Investment performance will be mediocre by definition.

## PERFORMANCE MEASUREMENT

One of the major differences between mutual funds and hedge funds is how mutual funds measure performance and how hedge funds measure performance. Mutual funds are measured on relative performance. Their performance is compared to a relevant benchmark index or to comparable peer mutual funds in their style group. Most hedge funds focus on absolute returns. The idea behind an absolute return approach is the attempt to make profits under all circumstances, even when markets fall.

Occasionally, hedge funds are considered not as absolute return managers but as relative return managers where the benchmark is not an index but the risk-free rate plus, say, 500 basis points. The logic is that an absolute return of 10 percent is meaningless if one does not know whether the risk-free rate is 5 percent or 30 percent. However, absolute return strategies by definition do not have a classical benchmark (otherwise they would not be called *absolute* return strategies). In a nutshell, one can stress that one of the reasons why hedge funds (absolute return managers) exist is because a benchmark introduces incentives that, economically speaking, do not make sense. The incentives introduce concepts such as defining risk as *active risk* instead of *total risk* and an inducement to buy last year's winners with new money coming into the fund (as last year's winners often have the largest marginal contribution to active risk). Absolute return managers want to steer away from these odd incentives.

Another way of looking at performance measurement differences is as follows: Normally, risk-adjusted returns are measured by the Sharpe ratio. The Sharpe ratio is calculated by subtracting the return of the risk-free asset from the return of the portfolio and then dividing by the standard deviation of portfolio returns. For example, if a portfolio achieves a return of 15 percent, the risk-free rate is 5 percent, and the standard deviation of returns is 20 percent, the Sharpe ratio would be 0.5. The contribution of an active manager is measured with the information ratio. The information ratio is calculated by dividing the active return (excess return above the market benchmark) by the active risk; ex post this is the tracking error between the active portfolio and the benchmark. For example, if a manager outperformed the benchmark by 100 basis points with a tracking error of 200 basis points, the information ratio would amount to 0.5. An interesting observation is that an information ratio of 0.5 for an active manager is regarded as high, whereas a Sharpe ratio of 0.5 is not, or to a much lesser extent. This is not necessarily intuitive since the Sharpe ratio and the information ratio are related. The Sharpe ratio has beta plus alpha in the numerator and the standard deviation of beta plus alpha in the denominator. The information ratio has only alpha in the numerator and the standard deviation of alpha in the denominator. In other words, the information ratio is similar to a Sharpe ratio that was adjusted for beta. The practical implication is that an information ratio of 0.5 by a long-only manager is perceived as being large whereas a Sharpe ratio of 0.5 by a hedge fund manager is not perceived as large. The hedge fund manager has to deliver Sharpe ratios in excess of 1.0 for investors to start getting excited.

## BENCHMARK CONUNDRUM

There is a tendency (a force) not to move to the third paradigm but to include the absolute return approach in the second paradigm of relative returns. In other words, there is an attempt to transform hedge funds into mutual funds by introducing a benchmark. There are good reasons to introduce a benchmark. However, none of the reasons are based on economics.

A benchmark to measure performance is normally required by plan sponsors and fiduciaries in the traditional asset management industry. The author of this book, while giving an after-dinner speech in Sydney, Australia, was nearly thrown into the harbor when postulating that the typical benchmark approach does not work for hedge funds. The audience requested an answer on how to assess whether managers are doing their job if there is no benchmark other than cash.*

---

*Dessert was nearly refused after the remark that investors should focus on variables that can be assessed ex ante, such as experience, motivation, investment philosophy, and competitive advantage, instead of focusing on historical performance.

A benchmark index essentially fulfills two purposes: (1) display performance of a market in order to compare performance of an active manager relative to the market, and (2) enable instrumentation of passive investment strategies. The requirements of a typical benchmark in the traditional asset management industry focusing on liquid and marketable securities should have four main characteristics. The benchmark index should be:

1. Unambiguous.
2. Representative.
3. Measurable.
4. Replicable (i.e., an investable passive alternative to an active position).

Two trends are unfolding in the hedge fund and asset management industry. The first trend is that the hedge fund industry is becoming institutionalized; the allocation from institutional investors is growing at a faster rate than the allocation from private investors. The second trend is some sort of conversion between the traditional asset management industry and the alternative (i.e., hedge funds) industry. The benchmarking of hedge funds is an ongoing and open debate. However, it is doubtful that hedge fund benchmarks will meet the four aforementioned criteria anytime soon.

## Hedge Fund Classification Systems Are Ambiguous

Unambiguity would imply that the hedge fund universe is classifiable. However, classifying hedge funds is difficult. As will be outlined in Chapter 5, classifying hedge funds is an attempt to fit something into a box that does not, by any means, fit into a box. All classification systems of hedge funds are ambiguous. The different classification systems of data vendors are at least as heterogeneous as the hedge fund industry. Not only are the borders between the strategies and funds blurred, they are constantly changing. The industry is not only heterogeneous but also dynamic. This is different from the traditional asset management universe. The traditional asset long-only industry is homogeneous when compared with the diversity of strategies executed by hedge funds. A manager investing in global pulp and paper companies on a long-only basis can be compared with an index measuring the performance of all listed pulp and paper companies. A subgroup (sector) of the asset class (listed equities) is the benchmark. The number of investment opportunities (i.e., market inefficiencies) that can be exploited by someone with an information edge in the pulp and paper sector is not relevant.

## A Hedge Fund Index Cannot Be Representative or Measurable

Every existing database of hedge funds is incomplete. The universe of hedge funds is extremely broad, as the definition of a fund is unclear and there is no obligation to register a fund. Hedge funds are most often private, that is, not publicly listed. This is mainly because there is no requirement for a hedge fund to list or report performance data. (The universe of exchange-listed securities, by comparison, is easily determinable.) In other words, any attempt to measure the performance of a strategy would be not only ambiguous but also not representative.

## A Hedge Fund Index Is Not a Passive Alternative to an Actively Managed Hedge Fund Portfolio

Any market benchmark should be replicable. For example, a stock index used as a benchmark to measure the performance of a manager is a passive alternative to allocating funds to the manager. This is possible if the constituents are marketable, but is impossible if they are not. Hedge funds by definition are not marketable. Most hedge funds are not listed. There have been attempts to make them more marketable, but the success of these attempts is as yet uncertain. In addition, there is the issue of matching the liquidity of the index with those of the hedge funds.

## Conclusion

The use of a hedge fund benchmark has many inherent problems. First, there is no requirement that a hedge fund manager reports performance numbers to any organization. Therefore, representation is not a given. Second, most of the numbers submitted are unaudited and may be estimates that may change over time. There is no guarantee that the performance numbers submitted are correct.[4]

It is unlikely that all current (passive) hedge fund products in the market are an enrichment for the investment community. Not all hedge fund products are based on economic merit.

## Outlook

What is the alternative to a market or peer group benchmark? How will active managers be held accountable for performance under the paradigm of absolute returns? Is there an objective metric, that is, a metric that can be objectively measured and enforced? Is the measured alpha (value added) true alpha or disguised alpha? That is, has the manager potentially achieved superior returns through systematically selling some sort of tiny out-of-the-money put option? How is the problem of asymmetric information between manager and investor solved?

Unfortunately, we do not have the definite answers to these questions. The following remarks, as well as most of this book, are an attempt to help solve some of the suboptimal features of the way money is managed today. The current paradigm of measuring the value added by a manager quantitatively through a ratio is certainly appealing. Most often the ratio is some form of excess return over active risk relative to the passive alternative. The information ratio is probably the most often used.

One possible solution could be to combine objective quantitative assessment with qualitative judgment. The classical market benchmark could, for example, be replaced by a set of absolute investment objectives. The objectives are enforced through consent between manager and investor. The active manager will then be measured and held accountable against these objectives. A set of objectives could be:

1. Generate a positive return by exploiting inefficiencies in U.S. small- and mid-cap financial stocks.
2. Preserve capital over a 12-month period.
3. Provide consistent monthly returns resulting in annual returns of around 10 to 15 percent and portfolio volatility of around 8 to 12 percent.

From today's perspective, replacing a market benchmark with absolute objectives sounds futuristic. However, replacing a market benchmark with quantitative absolute investment objectives in combination with a qualitative overlay has some advantages:

1. An active manager has an incentive not to lose money; that is, the manager defines risk as total risk and uses hedging and risk management techniques to manage risk. This implies that the portfolio manager will have to aim for an asymmetrical return profile by design. The unattractive normal distribution is not part of the manager's objectives. The manager is paid to manage the (bell-shaped) curve from outright exposure to a market. This would be a material departure from the paradigm of relative returns.
2. Both target return as well as target portfolio volatility are defined and quantified in advance based on the investor's idiosyncratic objectives or risk budgets. Both manager and investor agree at what rate their wealth should compound, and, more importantly, at what cost (i.e., total risk). They would also need to agree that the objectives are realistic in the respective market.
3. The investor's weight in financials does not necessarily increase due to a fashion in the market. If all equity allocations are benchmarked long-only

allocations, then the sector weights of the portfolio are a function of fashion and fads. Good recent performers increase in weight, while poorly performing sectors decrease. The portfolio will be trend-following (as opposed to contrarian) by definition. In addition, core weightings can be obtained through passive vehicles more efficiently. If the investor wants beta instead of alpha, he or she can simply buy an index fund or enter a total return swap. Both passive strategies are probably more efficient than the hybrid approach of what today is referred to as active management, that is, trying to actively add value by managing money with the same tools a passive manager uses to manage (active) risk.

4. If something goes wrong, there is nowhere to hide. The manager is held accountable against an absolute yardstick.

The qualitative overlay is important, although, potentially, it introduces subjectivity, or worse, ambiguity. During the last phases of the technology bubble some conservative active managers lost mandates or were sent into exile because of continuous underperformance relative to their benchmarks. ("Continuous" in the asset management industry is defined as two to three years.) The problem with this course of action is that the investor did not understand the fundamentals behind the underperformance. The reason for the manager's underperformance was risk awareness in absolute return space. The reason for underperformance was a conservative stance to changes in total risk, that is, a reluctance to buy multiples of one or two hundred times earnings, or buy companies with no earnings (and little prospect of success), or accept the consensus wisdom of the time, namely that revenues relative to enterprise value is an intelligent way of evaluating future prospects of a business without earnings. The relative return approach has created incentives for the "active" manager that are entirely misaligned with those of the investor. This is one of the reasons why the paradigm of relative returns needs replacement or, if not replacement, a serious overhaul.

In hedge fund space relative comparisons are also done. For example, a convertible arbitrage manager is compared to one or two convertible arbitrage indexes or to a subselection of managers with similar risk appetite, geographical focus, and investment process. There is nothing wrong with this. However, what do you do if the index is up by 15 percent and your manager is up by only 10 percent? Answer: Under the paradigm of relative returns you sack your manager—if not today, then certainly if it happens again.*

---

*Strong or colloquial language is occasionally used to bring across a point clearly. There are more similarities between absolute return and relative return managers than is, at times, implied by the author.

Potentially, this is the wrong answer. There could be a good reason for the "underperformance." The return has to be put into context with total risk. Risk is most often measured quantitatively through the volatility of returns (albeit imperfectly) and qualitatively through a thorough understanding of the strategy's fundamental characteristics. For example, the aforementioned convertible arbitrage manager might have used less leverage than the peer group because he felt that the market was getting overcrowded and therefore taking risk off the table was the right thing to do (after all, it is his money in the fund as well, not only other people's money). Another example could be that he paid for hedging certain risk he felt uncomfortable with while the peer group took that particular risk. This form of risk control will not necessarily show by measuring risk quantitatively. Without understanding the fundamentals of the underperformance, the investor will not be able to assess whether the manager is worth keeping.

What does this mean for the future of asset management? It depends. If this book proves to be an unimaginative collection of intellectually disturbed thinking and incomplete research, or the ideas herein prove completely wrong and the industry continues to be stuck in the suboptimal second paradigm of relative returns, then nothing happens. The two industries will not converge, and the performance difference not melt. However, if there is a paradigm shift, the two groups eventually will converge. What today is called absolute return or hedge fund will be considered active—that is, the managers driven by balancing P&L (achieving "P" while trying to avoid "L")—and what today is referred to as active (benchmarked long-only) will be passive—that is, the managers driven by a market benchmark.* Judging the institutional asset management industry by fees for hedge fund exposure (alpha) and index funds and other long-only vehicles (beta), the paradigm shift, sort of, has actually already happened.

---

*Note that passive investing is not synonymous with indexing (or index tracking). Indexing, like total return swaps, is an extreme form of passive investing where an index is replicated through either full replication or a tracking basket of stocks. Passive investing, on the other hand, also encompasses strategies such as enhanced indexing, where the core is indexed but the manager has a risk budget to exploit certain investment opportunities actively. Under the paradigm of absolute returns, the approach of benchmarked long-only managers would be classified as enhanced indexing (i.e., passive investing), as a large core is normally held to manage active risk whereby investment opportunities are exploited around that core.

## SOURCE OF RETURN

A further difference between long-only and alternative money managers is the source of return. The primary source of return in investing in an asset class comes from earning the economic risk premium. In equities this is the equity risk premium. These strategies are also called market-based strategies because their return is derived from a market (such as, for example, the equity market). Absolute return strategies are referred to as skill-based because their return is based on the manager's ability to turn an investment opportunity into a profit. At the most general level, a long-only equity fund delivers the risk-free rate plus beta plus alpha, whereas a market-neutral fund delivers the risk-free rate plus alpha, forgoing beta altogether.

Figure 3.3 and Figure 3.4 compare returns from a typical equity mutual fund with returns from a typical relative value hedge fund.

Through a long-only fund the investor essentially gets exposure to beta. Figure 3.3 shows that the returns from the equity mutual fund are generated essentially by being long the underlying stock market. This is intuitive since this is what the managers are paid to do. A point can be made that plain-vanilla exposure to a liquid and developed market can be more cheaply

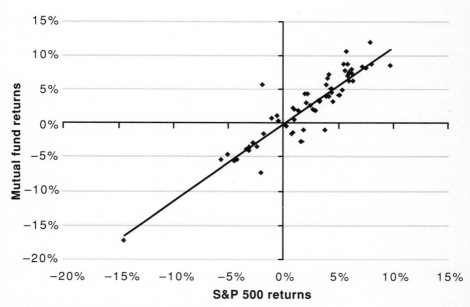

**FIGURE 3.3**    Typical Equity Mutual Fund
*Source:* UBS Warburg (2000).

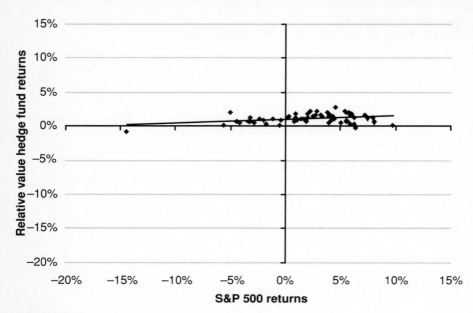

**FIGURE 3.4** Typical Relative Value Absolute Return Fund
*Source:* UBS Warburg (2000).

gained through indexation or swaps. Note that the intercept of the regression line is zero.

Figure 3.4 compares returns of a typical relative value hedge fund manager with returns in the underlying stock market. The main difference between Figure 3.3 and Figure 3.4 is that the returns in Figure 3.4 are generated with almost no exposure to the market. In other words, the source of return is something other than beta, in this case the S&P 500 index. Someone marketing hedge funds will argue that the portion not explained by beta is attributable to skill (i.e., alpha). Someone selling indexed hedge funds vehicles will argue that the portion not explained by stock market beta is explained by other factors, some of which are dynamic and include optionality. The truth is most likely somewhere in between the two extremes.

## REGULATION

Mutual funds differ from hedge funds with respect to regulation. Some refer to the continued high performance of hedge funds as "regulatory arbitrage." Mutual funds are highly regulated, in many occasions restricting the use of short selling and/or derivatives; that is, they are restricted to manage risk properly. From the managers' point of view, these regulations serve as handcuffs, making it more difficult to outperform the market or to protect the assets of the fund in a downturn (assuming that even under the paradigm of relative returns the managers prefer making money over losing it). Playing the piano with one arm tied behind your back does not sound that great, even if you are a maestro.

From the investors' point of view, regulation is like being long a put option, that is, some sort of an insurance. The historical underperformance of long-only managers relative to long/short managers and other absolute return managers, therefore, could be viewed as the premium outlay for the put option (insurance premium) the investors are either willing or forced to pay. Hedge funds are less regulated and therefore less restricted. They allow for short selling and other strategies designed to accelerate performance or reduce risk. However, an informal restriction is generally imposed on all hedge fund managers by professional investors who understand the different strategies and typically invest in a particular fund because of the manager's expertise in a particular investment strategy. These investors require and expect the hedge fund to stay within its area of specialization and competence. Hence, one of the defining characteristics of hedge funds is that they tend to be specialized funds, operating within a given niche, specialty, or industry that requires a particular expertise. A high degree of specialization is what the third paradigm in asset management has in common with the paradigm about to be replaced, that is, the second paradigm of relative returns.

At a conference hosted by the Securities and Exchange Commission (SEC), the (at the time) vice chairman of Fidelity Management and Research Company, Robert Pozen, was quoted saying that the lack of federal hedge fund regulation is a "total abdication" of regulatory responsibility.[5] He added that this is a "class issue":

> *Middle class investors are being harmed because many of the sharpest fund managers are forgoing mutual funds (which are open to any investor) to run hedge funds (which are open only to the rich).*[6]

Mr. Pozon's solution?

> *More SEC regulation of hedge funds and the requirement of symmetrical performance fees for hedge fund managers—in other words, make hedge funds like mutual funds.*[7]

## Damocles' Sword of the Hedge Fund Industry

The regulatory environment with respect to hedge funds could be perceived as a threat to the hedge fund industry. Regulation is probably the most important factor when assessing the sustainability of the attractive risk/return character-istics of some of the hedge fund strategies. It is a pending issue with most regu-lators. In the first quarter of 2002, it seemed that some regulators were warming up toward hedge funds.

Hedge funds are not free from all regulation. Hedge funds are not ex-empt from regulations designed to monitor and safeguard the integrity of markets. The U.S. Treasury, for example, requires traders to report large positions in selected foreign currencies and Treasury securities. The Securi-ties and Exchange Commission requires traders to report positions that ex-ceed 5 percent of the shares of a publicly traded firm. The Federal Reserve has margin requirements for stock purchases that apply to all market par-ticipants. The Commodity Futures Trading Commission (CFTC) requires traders with large futures positions to file daily reports. In addition, the CFTC and the futures exchanges set futures margins and position limits on futures contracts. These regulations apply to all market participants, in-cluding hedge funds.

Hedge funds in the United States are not allowed to advertise their offer-ings. In February 2002 the Managed Funds Association, which represents the hedge fund industry, proposed a rule change in a letter to the SEC signed by group president John Gaine.[8] Under the association's plan, hedge funds could publish advertisements similar to the "tombstone" advertisements that public companies run in newspapers during public securities offerings. Such adver-tisements could state the name of the fund, the types of securities involved, and the telephone number and web site of the seller. The advertisements would have to be accompanied by a legend stating that the shares could be sold only to "accredited investors."*

The mutual fund lobby has an obvious interest that the ban on advertise-ments does not change as the introduction of a market benchmark results in a bias to mediocrity by definition. John Collins, a spokesperson for the Invest-ment Company Institute, which represents the $7 trillion U.S. mutual fund in-dustry, was quoted saying:

> *We strongly oppose advertising by hedge funds. They can be highly risky. Granting this would eventually lead to mass advertising of risky pools that are unsuitable for average investors.*[9]

---

*According to U.S. federal law, an accredited investor is someone whose income ex-ceeded $200,000 each of the prior two years and is likely to do so in the coming year—or someone whose net worth is more than $1 million. Banks, securities firms, and other financial institutions also are considered accredited investors.

A lot is wrong with this statement. First, hedge funds are only for accredited investors and not for "average investors." Second, hedge funds are indeed highly risky, but viewing them in isolation misses the point. Stocks on the Nasdaq or stocks of Texas oil trading companies are also highly risky when viewed in isolation. "Average investors" are still allowed to put their savings into these investments. However, what is relevant to investors when comparing financial vehicles is the systematic risk of financial instruments, since nonsystematic risk should be immunized through diversification in the first place. Occasionally fraud is used as an argument for tighter regulation of hedge funds. However, as of mid-2002, this argument seems ludicrous. Investors lost a couple of million dollars due to hedge fund fraud. This is peanuts when compared with the hundreds of billions of dollars of value destroyed by U.S. corporates due to fraudulent accounting.

Figure 3.5 shows two different investment vehicles where idiosyncratic risk has been diversified. The graph measures the index level as a percentage of the previous all-time high. The HFRI Composite index is a proxy for exposure to hedge funds where single manager risk has been diversified. We leave it to the humble reader to judge which investment is "unsuitable for average investors."

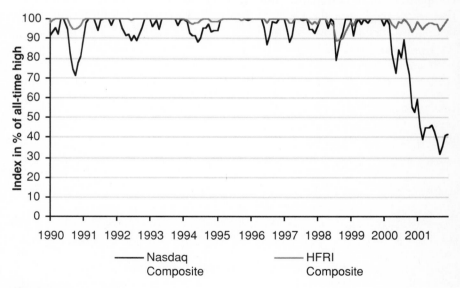

**FIGURE 3.5**  Assets Underwater
*Source:* Hedge Fund Research, Datastream.

## INCENTIVES

Incentives are different between a long-only mutual fund manager and a hedge fund manager. Most often the former is an employee of a large organization, whereas the latter is an entrepreneur. Putting it simply: An entrepreneur normally has more skin in the game than an employee; hedge fund managers usually have a substantial portion of their net wealth invested alongside their investors' wealth or investments. Mutual funds generally remunerate management based on a percentage of assets under management. Hedge funds always remunerate managers with performance-related incentive fees as well as, more often than not, a fixed fee. George Soros calls this type of fund "performance funds." Warren Buffett's first investment vehicle also was a performance fund, as defined by Soros (1995). Not surprisingly, the incentive-based performance fees tend to attract the most talented investment managers to the hedge fund industry.

### Aligning Goals of Principal and Agent

There is a conflict of interest between manager and investor. The former normally seeks short-term gratification whereas the goals of the latter are quite often long-term in nature. David Swensen (2000) wrote:

> *Individuals desire immediate gratification, leading to overemphasis on policies expected to pay off in a relatively short time frame. At the same time, fund fiduciaries hope to retain power by avoiding controversy, pursuing only conventional investment ideas. By operating in the institutional mainstream of short horizon, and uncontroversial opportunities, committee members and staff ensure unspectacular results, while missing potentially rewarding longer-term contrarian plays.*

Aligning incentives between the manager and the investor reduces the principal/agent conflict and may lead to greater care in the management of funds. The investment managers' levels of commitment are meaningfully higher when substantial portions of their liquid personal assets are invested in the strategies and when their remuneration is linked to investment performance.

The attractive incentives in the hedge fund industry are regarded as one of the main drivers of high returns of hedge funds since they attract managers who have superior skill (as well as, unfortunately, those who do not). Hedge fund managers may just be better than other active fund managers. It is not, after all, unreasonable to think that the attractive fee structure used by hedge funds may succeed in enticing money managers with the greatest skill to the hedge fund industry. The remarks cited earlier by Robert Pozen, who was head of the largest mutual fund complex, might be taken as evidence that this is in fact happening. Peltz (2001) shows a table of mutual fund managers who left their employer between 1996 and 2000 to start hedge funds.[10] Nine out of 17 were from Fidelity, of which Jeffrey Vinik was probably the most prominent. Robert Pozen, after all, was certainly in a position to know whether he was losing his best fund managers.

## Optionlike Incentives Are a Hot Potato

Most hedge fund managers have high-water marks and (less often) hurdle rates, which add optionality to the incentive structure. Optionlike incentives are scarce in the mutual fund industry and pension fund management industry, but are prevalent in the real estate sector, the venture capital sector, and the hedge fund sector. U.S. mutual fund performance-based fees must satisfy the fulcrum rule. That is, gains and losses must have a symmetric effect, in the sense that the same amount of over- and underperformance relative to a benchmark must result in the same amount of positive and negative incentive fees for a mutual fund manager. Hedge fund managers are not subject to the fulcrum rule, or, for that matter, any rules other than what the investors would bear (some managers have a 50 percent performance fee). This embedded put option remains a highly debated issue on hedge fund managers' compensation.

Anson (2001a) argues that hedge fund incentive fees can be considered a call option on a portion of the profits that the hedge fund manager earns for investors. In the case of a profit, an incentive fee is paid (call option ends in-the-money). In the case of no profit, no incentive fee is paid (call option ends out-of-the-money). The hypothesis is whether this call option is free, that is, whether hedge fund investors are selling a call option (which has time and probability value) without receiving the option's premium. Potentially there is a conflict of interest: The hedge fund *investors* own the underlying partnership and receive payoffs offered by the entire distribution of return outcomes. In contrast, the hedge fund *manager* is the holder of a contingent claim on the value of the underlying partnership. The hedge fund manager, as the owner of the option, receives payoffs only from the tails of the hedge fund return distribution. Anson concludes that the contingent claim nature of the incentive fee call option makes higher variance desirable to the hedge fund managers. Anson finds it ironic that "investors in the hedge fund actually provide the incentive to the hedge fund manager to increase the volatility of the return distribution for the hedge fund."

There is also a diametrically opposed view, namely that the performance fee in reality is an option premium paid by the investor to the manager to keep the fund small and returns high. If there is no performance fee but only a flat fee, the manager has an incentive to take an infinite amount of money, irrespective of capacity. Funds under management are maximized, not optimized. Maximizing funds under management is not in the interest of the hedge fund investor. The introduction of a performance fee provides an incentive to reach an optimal size for the fund. The optimal size is where profit for the manager (capital appreciation of own stake plus fee income) and returns for the investor (capital appreciation minus fees) are maximized. Exceeding a certain fund size (which varies between manager and strategy) eats into the performance of both.

There are other options to be considered. Most hedge fund managers are experienced investment professionals who were successful during the 1980s and/or the 1990s. This means that they do not belong to the population's lowest decile in terms of net wealth. Rookie MBAs and PhDs from business schools normally do not start as hedge fund managers. They start as either analysts, long-only portfolio managers, or traders. If they are unsuccessful they seek employment elsewhere. It is unlikely (but not impossible) that graduates start their own hedge fund. Hedge fund manager is often a career choice one makes during or at the end of a successful career in finance, not at the beginning (although there are exceptions). The relevance of this is that hedge fund managers become entrepreneurs where they bring their wealth into the companies (the hedge funds). The ideal case is where a hedge fund manager has 100 percent of his or her net wealth in the fund. The fact that the manager has his or her own money in the fund means that the incentive to take risk (the free call option mentioned earlier) is neutralized.

To go one step further, the hedge fund manager has negative utility from losing money. Prospect theory and common sense suggest that the incentive to preserve capital (i.e., not to lose money) is stronger than the incentive to take risk and make money through the incentive fee—the aforementioned free call option moving in-the-money. Only in the extreme case where the hedge fund manager has none or very little of his or her own money in the firm does he or she have a free call option. In other words, the case analyzed in Anson (2001a) is probably the exception, not the rule. The rule is most likely that the investor implicitly buys a put option (as opposed to granting a free call option to the manager). All hedge fund data in this book indicates that wealth preservation is the common denominator in the hedge fund world, that is, an incentive to balance investment opportunity with risk where risk is defined as total risk.

One can even go further: The investor is probably long not only an at-the-money put option but also an out-of-the-money put option with a strike price of around 75 percent of notional. The reason for this is as follows. A hedge fund manager who loses more than 25 percent of capital is in trouble. Most staff will leave the organization because the prospect of not receiving a bonus for two years until the fund is at the high-water mark is not encouraging to hedge fund analysts and managers. In addition, the reputation is ruined and the hedge fund career terminated.* The experiences of George Soros and Julian Robertson in 2000 (losses, redemptions, staff exodus) are a risk for a hedge fund operator. All investors lose money occasionally. However, a hedge fund manager has a strong incentive to avoid losses in general and large, erratic losses in particular, that is, to stay away from the aforementioned (albeit arbitrary) 75 percent strike. This incentive—to avoid losses and keep portfolio volatility low—is, obviously, also in the interest of the investor.

## RISK MANAGEMENT

Risk control and capital preservation are among the main areas where the best hedge funds consistently excel. Many hedge funds grew out of a risk management environment, and many hedge fund managers focus entirely on their edge of exploiting investment opportunities while managing total risk. As highlighted in Chapter 1, the main difference between risk management in a relative return setup versus an absolute return setup is that the term "risk" is defined differently. In relative return space risk is defined as *active risk*, which is the possibility of a deviation from the benchmark. Oversimplified, this means that an 18 percent return when the benchmark is up 20 percent is bad, whereas a 20 percent loss is okay as long as the benchmark is down 20 percent, too. The absolute return manager defines risk as *total risk*. Simply put, this means that an 18 percent return is good whereas a 20 percent loss of capital is bad.

Given the leverage used by some hedge funds, the odds of large losses are much larger than with traditional investment vehicles. Risk management is therefore more important for investors, lenders, and counterparties. Regulators are concerned with systemic risk. They seek to avert systemic threats to the financial system by limiting imprudent extensions of credit. These regulations include margin requirements, collateral requirements, and limits on the exposure of financial intermediaries to individual customers. All of them affect hedge funds' business with banks, brokers, and other intermediaries.

---

*This is not entirely true. There are exceptions. John Meriwether, for example, was fined by the SEC after the 1991 Salomon bond scandal but still was able to raise money for LTCM and, after LTCM failed, was still able to raise money for a new fixed income arbitrage fund.

## SHORT SELLING

Hedge funds are not restricted from selling short. There are reasons to believe that greater inefficiencies may exist on the short side of the market than on the long side. As we have highlighted in Chapter 2, when short selling is restricted and investor opinion is diverse, market prices are no longer efficient, and the capital asset pricing model (CAPM) and arbitrage pricing theory (APT) do not hold. When investors have diverse opinions, some tend to be more pessimistic than others. Without complete freedom to sell short, the pessimism of these investors will not be fully represented in security prices, and some stocks will tend to be overpriced.

Security overpricing may be supported by fads or bubbles. Overpricing may also be supported by corporate publicity, which tends to favor good news over bad. Good news tends to be publicized in a timely manner, whereas bad news is subject to delay, window dressing, and actual fraud. The reason lies with the incentives of the main providers of information. The company itself from CEO downward has an incentive to publish positive news first. After all, it is the positive news that drives the stock price up, which then increases the value of the share options of the compensation plan. Given the lavish compensation plans for CEOs and senior management in the more recent U.S. corporate history, there was a strong incentive to bias the news flow in a positive manner.

These positive biases cause positive information to be priced in quickly and negative news to be priced with a time lag. For a short seller or long/short equity manager, asymmetric dissemination of information is an opportunity. This behavioral pattern causes an information inefficiency in equity markets. Managers can extract value from this inefficiency by conducting their own research to find stocks that are too expensive relative to fundamentals as opposed to stocks that seem too cheap relative to their fundamental values.

## DEAD WEIGHT

White (1995) argues that hedge fund managers minimize "dead weight." Dead weight in a portfolio results from securities owned that the manager has no insight into. For example, in a long equity portfolio, the manager may maintain a market weighting in one sector in order to control tracking error within an acceptable range, even when the manager has no insight into the sector. The proportion of the portfolio that is held to control residual volatility (volatility relative to the benchmark) is the proportion that will not add value.

In a hedge fund, in general, only positions about which the manager has conviction will be held or sold short. Portfolio volatility and higher-moment* and residual risks are controlled with risk management instruments or other hedging techniques, most of which require less capital than holding dead weight positions in the cash market. Consequently, a higher proportion of the hedge fund manager's capital is invested in positions about which the manager has conviction. Hedge fund managers therefore should be able to add more value, since relative outperformance against a benchmark is not the primary objective.

## INDUSTRY CHARACTERISTICS

There are also differences on an industry level. For the sake of argument, it has been assumed here that there are two separate industries although it could easily be argued that there is only one asset management industry. Due to the fact that hedge funds are less regulated, the industry is extremely heterogeneous, whereas the mutual fund industry is homogeneous in comparison. Heterogeneity means low correlation, and results in diversification opportunities. Fung and Hsieh (1997a) and many others have found that hedge fund returns were substantially different from those of mutual funds and standard asset classes. Mutual funds are essentially long the asset class, whereas hedge funds can, putting it simply, more or less invest in anything. Some hedge funds have very strict predefined and disciplined investment processes, whereas others have full flexibility.

Institutional investors tend to favor hedge funds that stick to their niches or areas of expertise. There have been cases where hedge fund managers have left their areas of expertise and gone into areas where they have no edge—for example, a fixed-income arbitrageur executing volatility or pair trades in the equity market. Institutional investors want to isolate the edge (skill) and diversify the different exposures. In this context, hedge fund managers departing from their fields of expertise (called style drift) represent an idiosyncratic risk to the investor.

## CONCLUSION

There are many differences between relative return long-only funds and absolute return funds. Stellar past returns of the latter relative to the former is

---

*The mean return and the variance around the mean return are referred to as the first two moments of a return distribution. Skewness and kurtosis are called the third and fourth moments of the distribution.

one characteristic. However, past returns are not necessarily a good indication for future returns. This chapter highlighted also (more importantly) conceptual differences. One example of a conceptual difference refers to the way managers are compensated. It is difficult not to acknowledge the fact that interests between manager and investor are more closely aligned when they share both profits and losses. The flexibility of the absolute return manager to take risk off the table when the opportunity set changes is one of the pillars of our hypothesis of absolute returns being the future for active management, that is, the third paradigm. A further conceptual difference refers to the efficiency of processing information and managing money.

## Appendix: Guatemalan Dentist

> *The only hope to produce a superior record is to do something different. If you buy the same securities as other people, you will have the same results as other people.*
>
> —John Templeton

Where would the reader rather visit a dentist for a serious tooth operation: in the suburbs of Quezaltenango* or Switzerland?

While Switzerland would be the more rational choice, there are still voices opting for Quezaltenango. It seems that some would prefer Quezaltenango relative to Switzerland. This despite Swiss dentists operating with modern technology and high-end dental equipment, and with likely higher dental standards than in the suburbs of Quezaltenango.

Akin to Swiss dentists, hedge funds use more advanced techniques and instruments for hedging, enhancing returns and financing. Traditional fund managers do to a much lesser degree. The reasons are manifold. The two main reasons are that they might be restricted to using certain instruments or that they do not understand how to utilize the instruments to their advantage.

A money manager who does not consider using derivatives and short selling is similar to the aforementioned Guatemalan dentist. Both do not use the technology and equipment (techniques) that are available to them. Both, to some extent, have missed out on capitalizing on the developments of the past three decades.

---

*Quezaltenango is a city in southwestern Guatemala, 7,656 feet (2,334 meters) above sea level, near the foot of the Santa María Volcano; population (1989 est.), 88,769 (*source:* www.britannica.com).

The author, regrettably, is not particularly familiar with the developments of dental techniques and equipment over the past three decades. However, the developments over the past three decades in finance and portfolio construction are about risk and the measurement and control thereof. As a result of these developments, there is a risk management, derivatives, and financial engineering industry. Ignoring and/or avoiding derivative strategies, cash equivalents and alternatives, and financial engineering techniques cannot be the most efficient way of managing money.

Most people cannot choose the locations of their dentists. They have no option. In addition, someone with a tooth problem visiting Quezaltenango will most likely see a local dentist.

Some investors cannot choose between relative return managers and absolute return managers; they have no option. To all others, the author recommends revisiting the value of the option to invest with absolute return managers—if they have not already done so.

# CHAPTER 4

# Advantages and Disadvantages of Investing in Hedge Funds

*Capitalism is the astounding belief that the most wickedest of men will do the most wickedest of things for the greatest good of everyone.*

—John Maynard Keynes

## ADVANTAGES

Common sense and financial theory prescribe three primary factors upon which any investment should be evaluated: prospective return, risk, and correlation to other investments. The main advantages of investing in absolute return managers from an investor's point of view are high risk-adjusted returns and diversification benefits, which are not achievable with traditional assets. A 1994 survey by *Institutional Investor* asking U.S., U.K., and Swiss institutional investors to rank their reasons for investing in hedge funds resulted in the list in Table 4.1.

The Goldman Sachs and Frank Russell Company (2001) survey examined allocations and expectations for tax-exempt institutional investors in North America, Europe, Australia, and Japan. The average strategic allocation to hedge funds in North America was 6.0 percent of total fund assets. This simple average included funds that have committed to hedge funds but have made no formal allocation. Most of these respondents included hedge

**Table 4.1** Reasons for Investing in Hedge Funds

| Rank | Reason |
| --- | --- |
| 1 | Superior performance |
| 2 | Diversification/hedging |
| 3 | Access to modern techniques and markets |
| 4 | Little regulation/high flexibility |

*Source:* Bekier (1996).

funds in their public equity allocation. Excluding those hedge fund investors with a 0 percent strategic allocation, the simple average rose to 8.8 percent of total fund assets. Market-neutral was the most popular strategy among respondents. Figure 4.1 shows the preferences of U.S. tax-exempt institutional investors.

According to the survey, the most popular strategies for tax-exempt institutional investors in Europe were market-neutral, distressed securities, merger arbitrage, and convertible arbitrage. In the United Kingdom as well as in continental Europe the Myners Report has caused pension funds to reconsider their conservative stance toward alternative investment strategies.* The Myners Report has resulted in the recommendation of a voluntary code of best practices. A formal review process will take place at the end of March 2003 to monitor compliance with the principles. Specifically included in the investment principles is the requirement that pension funds consider all asset classes. The average strategic allocation among European hedge fund investors according to the Goldman Sachs and Frank Russell survey was 1.7 percent of fund assets; it is expected to double to 3.4 percent by 2003. Though the number of hedge fund investors is modest, at only 15 percent of respondents, a further 11 percent expect to invest by 2003. The preference of European institutions looks similar to the preference of U.S. institutions (Figure 4.1). The main difference is a lower allocation by European institutions in distressed securities (25 percent

---

*U.K. pension fund managers have a slightly different definition of "conservative" than, for example, fund of hedge funds managers. Conservative for a U.K. pension fund manager means a 75 to 80 percent allocation to equities with a strong home bias, that is, *portfolio concentration.* Conservative to the fund of funds manager means spreading risk across different managers and factors, that is, *portfolio diversification.* One possible explanation for the confusion could be addressed by distinguishing between *intellectual* and *financial conservatism.* Financial conservatism refers to portfolios with low risk. Intellectual conservatism means to stick with old ideas—the we-always-did-it-like-this-around-here effect.

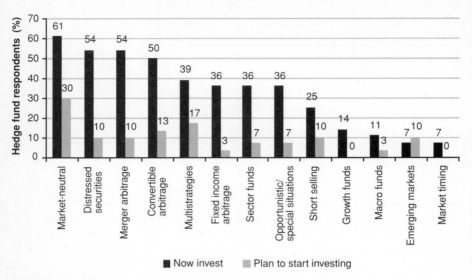

**FIGURE 4.1** Strategy Preference by U.S. Institutional Investors
*Source:* Goldman Sachs and Frank Russell (2001), p. 32.

versus 54 percent in the United States), convertible arbitrage (33 percent versus 50 percent) and opportunistic/special situation strategies (8 percent versus 36 percent). Europeans had larger allocations in multistrategy (50 percent versus 39 percent), emerging markets (17 percent versus 10 percent), and market timing (17 percent versus 0 percent).

## Sustainable Good Performance

The past performance of most hedge fund categories was stunning once single-manager risk was diversified. Some investors argue that past performance is too good to be true, implying hedge funds are paranormal or a mystery. Hopefully, this book sheds some light on the past performance and sustainability of such high risk-adjusted returns. CAPM does not explain the hedge fund phenomenon nor does imperfect hedge fund return data.

One of the main risk factors that could affect all hedge funds is change in regulation. As noted earlier, the high flexibility of hedge fund managers is certainly a factor that contributes to the attractive performance characteristics. However, a second case similar to LTCM would most certainly be negative for the whole industry. It is doubtful whether a second case of such proportions would develop so smoothly, and it is questionable whether the industry would recover as quickly as it did after LTCM. The pressure on regulators could increase manyfold.

There is a consensus opinion on capacity constraints endangering the sustainability of high risk-adjusted returns of absolute return strategies. With some relative-value strategies there is a natural capacity constraint determined by the number of opportunities in the market and the amount of capital chasing the deals. However, investment banks are lowering their exposure to proprietary trading to increase the quality of earnings (i.e., reduce the volatility associated with earnings from trading). Further consolidation in the investment banking industry could mean that proprietary trading units are merged. This means there are more deals available to be exploited by hedge funds, which themselves are often ex-trading franchises from investment banks scaling down their risks to trading activity.

Figure 4.2 shows supply and demand in capital markets. Table 4.2 shows a potential capacity limit for some absolute return strategies. Note that different absolute return strategies have different capacity limits.

In equity strategies, capacity is determined by market capitalization, turnover, and volatility. If the market shrinks, so does the pool of opportunities. Turnover is relevant because liquidity risk of existing positions is often based on average daily volume or number of days to unwind the positions, which itself is based on average daily volume. Volatility is a measure for the opportunity set. If markets do not move, there is no opportunity to generate absolute returns. In the period from mid-2000 to early 2002 many equity long/short managers deleveraged and moved into cash as a result of a diminishing investment opportunity set. In other words, leverage is an instrument to increase risk when there are many opportunities and decrease risk when the opportunity set declines.

Figure 4.3 shows global equity market capitalization compared with equity volatility. We used year-end short-term implied volatility of OEX (S&P 100) options as a proxy for equity volatility. Equity turnover is somewhat correlated with market capitalization, that is, it had been increasing until

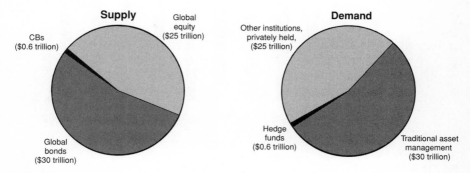

**FIGURE 4.2**  Supply and Demand
*Source:* Adapted from Morgan Stanley Dean Witter (2001), author's own estimates.

**Table 4.2**   Capacity Limit for a Selection of Absolute Return
Strategies

| Strategy | Capacity Limit | Capacity ($ trillions) |
| --- | --- | --- |
| Convertible bond arbitrage | Issuance | 0.6[a] |
| Merger arbitrage | M&A activity | 1.643[a] |
| Fixed income arbitrage[b] | Global bond markets | 30 |
| Equity market-neutral | Global equity markets | 25 |
| Equity hedge | Global equity markets | 25 |
| Equity nonhedge | Global equity markets | 25 |
| Macro | Global capital markets[c] | NA[c] |

[a]Estimated market size in 2001. Convertible bond issuance in 2001 was around $166 billion.
[b]Excluding mortgage-backed and asset-backed securities.
[c]Sizable: $55 trillion equities and bonds plus foreign exchange, commodities, money markets, private markets, and everything else that moves.

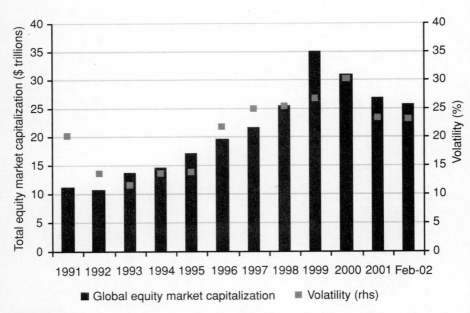

■ Global equity market capitalization     ■ Volatility (rhs)

**FIGURE 4.3**   Global Equity Market Capitalization and Equity Volatility
*Source:* World Federation of Exchanges, Datastream.

2000. Based on data from the World Federation of Exchanges, equity trading volume in 2000, in 2001, and in January and February 2002 was $232 billion, $167 billion, and $148 billion per trading day, respectively. This compares with around $1.2 trillion in the foreign exchange market and $600 billion per day in global bonds.

Charles Ellis (1998) calls the quest for alpha a loser's game. In theory (i.e., in frictionless markets and with no transaction costs), the quest for alpha would be a zero-sum game. All benchmarks put together comprise the overall market. If there are market participants who beat the benchmark, there must be losers—investors who underperform the benchmark. However, reality is worse than that. In the real world, the quest for alpha is a loser's game because of transaction costs. All the alpha of the game does not add up to zero; it adds up to zero minus the cost of playing the game. The broker/dealers are (or have been during the 1980s and 1990s) playing a winner's game. They earn commissions and the bid/ask spread on most trades. This is nothing new. One of the most ancient stories on Wall Street is the one of the customers' yachts:

> *Once in the dear dead days beyond recall, an out-of-town visitor was being shown the wonders of the New York financial district. When the party arrived at the Battery, one of his guides indicated some handsome ships riding at anchor. He said, "Look, those are the bankers' and brokers' yachts."*
> *"Where are the customers' yachts?" asked the naïve visitor.*[1]

The problem for hedge funds sustaining their superior performance is that more and more investors are copying the strategies that are resulting in superior performance. This is what economic intuition would imply. If there is an economic rent of some sort, there is a tendency that the rent is eroded through competition. The speed of the rent disappearing is dependent on the barriers to entry. In the pharmaceutical industry there are artificial barriers protecting innovative products. In the financial industry there are no patents for intellectual capital—just reputation and brand.

Over the past five years, the barriers to entry to the hedge fund industry have been falling. In the mid-1990s, it was difficult to set up a hedge fund and raise money. A hedge fund manager walking through the door of an institution and suggesting 10 to 15 percent absolute returns with low volatility was kicked out. After all, the stock market was compounding at 15 to 20 percent. To many investors, the proposition of stable returns in the low teens was not very attractive. However, by 2000 and 2001 the landscape had changed. The role of the prime broker expanded to helping setting up hedge funds and raising capital. In other words, the barriers to entry have fallen rapidly. In addition, with equity markets in free fall, the proposition of stable returns in the low teens has changed and has suddenly become attractive.

## Diversification

Correlation between alternative investment strategies and traditional assets is typically low. This is in fact one of the most important advantages of nontraditional products. For investors it is important to know how their prospective nontraditional investments correlate to the rest of their portfolios. A high-volatility hedge fund with a low correlation to one's overall portfolio might in fact be a less risky investment than a low-risk but highly correlated hedge fund. Correlation, however, is not stable over time. Correlation often rises in certain market situations when many funds start investing in the same opportunities.

Figure 4.4 shows how adding hedge funds to traditional asset classes increases the efficiency of a portfolio. This is probably the second most often shown graph at any hedge fund conference.*

Not only are alternative assets weakly correlated with traditional assets, they are weakly correlated with each other. The past few years have been characterized by both high volatility and high correlation among developed

---

*The most often shown graph is the historical return versus the historical volatility of hedge funds in a two-dimensional grid.

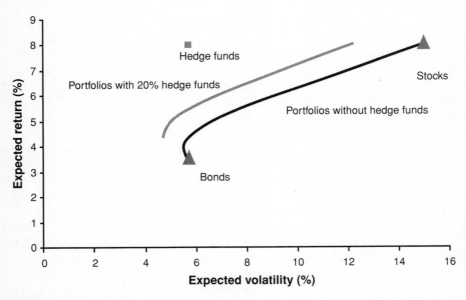

**FIGURE 4.4** Efficiency Gains in Mean-Variance Space
*Source:* UBS Warburg (2000).

traditional capital markets. For an investor investing in alternative investment strategies, this means that combining different (uncorrelated) alternative investment strategies in the portfolio can further reduce portfolio risk.

Figure 4.5 shows two portfolios derived from combinations of nine different hedge fund strategies. One portfolio is equally weighted, whereas the other portfolio is optimized for high risk-adjusted return, that is, highest Sharpe ratio.*

---

*When UBS Warburg (2000) was published with data starting in January 1990 and ending March 2000 instead of December 2001 as in this book, the highest Sharpe ratio portfolio had 62 percent equity market-neutral (versus new 41 percent), 35 percent risk arbitrage (13 percent), 3 percent distressed securities (0 percent) with zero weight in convertible arbitrage (33 percent), equity hedge (1 percent), and non-hedge and emerging markets. This is an indication that the portfolio construction process involves more work than just optimizing historical time series. Merely entering historical data into an optimizer is never robust nor sufficient. In any case, Sharpe ratios work best with symmetrical distributions—which is what all hedge funds attempt to avoid by design.

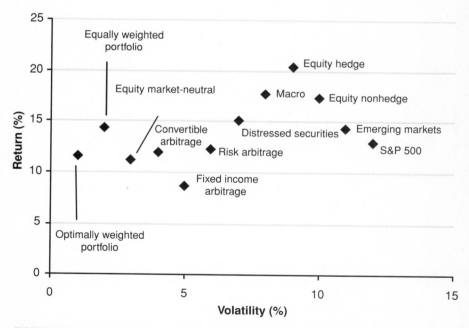

**FIGURE 4.5** Expected Risk and Return for Different Hedge Fund Combinations
*Note:* Sharpe ratio maximized portfolio: 41% equity market-neutral, 33% convertible arbitrage, 13% risk arbitrage, 9% fixed income arbitrage, 3% macro, and 1% equity hedge with zero weight in distressed securities, equity nonhedge, and emerging markets.
*Source:* UBS Warburg (2000), based on data from Hedge Fund Research.

The optimized portfolio resulted in a portfolio with a strong weight in equity market-neutral due to its historically high Sharpe ratio of 1.9 and its low correlation with other strategies. The optimizer resulted in a Sharpe ratio of 2.7 (expected return of 11.6 percent with volatility of 2.4 percent). The S&P 500 has been added in Figure 4.5 to show how these hedge fund portfolios compare with a long-only equity investment in one of the best-performing indexes during one of the best periods for equity long-only investment in the history of capital markets.

**Caveat Emptor**   There is a caveat to this sort of analysis: It applies risk/return characteristics in a mean-variance optimized fashion as suggested by modern portfolio theory.* However, hedge fund returns are derived from skill exploiting market inefficiencies whereas in a CAPM framework there is no such thing as skill. Markets are assumed to be efficient. Increasing one's return, therefore, is possible only by increasing risk.[†]

The comparison in Figure 4.5 has further shortcomings. Very often the value of alternative investments is based on appraisals and not on market prices. In other words, we are not comparing like for like. As soon as a fund of funds product is listed on an exchange and attracts some liquidity, the volatility exceeds the volatility of the net asset value (NAV) by far. In other words, comparing marketable securities with nonmarketable securities has its limitations. As Shiller (1981, 1989) pointed out, most of the volatility of marketable equities is nonfundamental—that is, attributable to fear and greed. Estimating volatility of unlisted hedge fund products leaves out the "fear and greed" factor. However, it is extremely unlikely that the superiority exemplified in Figure 4.5 can be explained away by excess market volatility, model, and valuation imperfections.

**Yale Endowment Fund**   An institution widely followed by the establishment is the endowment fund of Yale University, especially after publication of *Pioneering Portfolio Management—An Unconventional Approach to Institu-*

---

*Any mean-variance optimization using historical data is a quantitative exercise for illustration purposes only. Michaud (1989) calls mean-variance optimizers "error maximizers" when using historical data. The optimizer will overweight assets with high recent average returns. Note that, as Jorion (2000) points out, one of the main failures of LTCM was that it was using the same covariance matrix to measure risk and to optimize positions. This inevitably led to biases in the measurement of risk.

[†]Some might argue that the increase in risk comes from high manager risk. This argument is not valid. Manager risk is nonsystematic risk and therefore can be immunized through diversification. Corporate bankruptcy as well as hedge funds failure are nonsystematic risk.

*tional Investment*, written by its manager, David Swensen. Yale's investment policy is as follows:

> *Yale's portfolio is structured using a combination of academic theory and informed market judgment. The theoretical framework relies on mean-variance analysis, an approach developed by Nobel laureate Harry Markowitz while he was at Yale's Cowles Foundation. Using statistical techniques to combine expected returns, variances, and correlations of investment assets, the analysis estimates expected risk and return profiles of various asset allocation alternatives and tests the sensitivity of the results to changes in input assumptions.*
>
> *Because investment management involves as much art as science, qualitative considerations play an extremely important role in portfolio decisions. The definition of an asset class is quite subjective, requiring precise distinctions where none exist. Returns, risks, and correlations are difficult to forecast. Historical data provide a guide, but must be modified to recognize structural changes and compensate for anomalous periods. Finally, quantitative measures have difficulty incorporating factors such as market liquidity or the influence of significant, low-probability events.[2]*

Table 4.3 shows the asset allocation of the Yale Endowment Fund and its targets as of June 2001. The asset allocation is compared with the mean of U.S. educational institutions and an estimate for the average asset allocation of U.K. pension funds.

Critics of this book will note that it does not give advice on the optimal allocation of absolute return strategies. The reason for the absence of a definite answer is because we agree with Yale's (and George Soros') assessment of investment management being as much art (or alchemy) as science. There is

**Table 4.3**   Asset Allocation

| Asset Class | Yale University | | Educational Institutional Mean | Average U.K. Pension Fund[a] |
| | June 2001 | Current Target | | |
| --- | --- | --- | --- | --- |
| Domestic equity | 15.5 | 15.0 | 43.3 | 50.0 |
| Foreign equity | 10.6 | 10.0 | 12.4 | 25.0 |
| Fixed income | 9.8 | 10.0 | 23.1 | 20.0 |
| Absolute return | 22.9 | 22.5 | 9.1 | 0.0 |
| Private equity | 18.2 | 25.0 | 6.1 | 1.0 |
| Real assets | 16.8 | 17.5 | 2.8 | 1.0 |
| Cash | 6.2 | 0.0 | 3.2 | 3.0 |

[a]Author's own estimates.
*Note:* Data as of June 30, 2001.
*Source:* Yale Endowment (2001).

no objective allocation to absolute return strategies. A pension fund in Reykjavik might have different resources, return objectives, risk appetite, regulatory and investment policy constraints, and liquidity requirements compared with those of an endowment fund in New Haven. Mean-variance considerations are a starting point. Put another way: The objective part of Markowitz's approach is that portfolio diversification is better than the opposite, portfolio concentration. Table 4.3 suggests that Yale University aims for portfolio diversification whereas U.K. pension funds aim for portfolio concentration. As of June 2001, Yale University had around 26 percent concentrated in marketable equities whereas the allocation for U.K. pension funds has been traditionally between 70 percent and 80 percent.

One of the reasons for running concentrated portfolios is that many market participants place extraordinary value on liquidity.

> *Players seek the ability to trade out of yesterday's loser and acquire today's hot prospect, to sell during a market panic and buy into a bull market. Managers responsible for large sums of money focus on heavily traded securities, allowing movement in and out of positions with minimal market impact. However, in pursuing more-liquid securities investors miss out on the opportunity to establish positions at meaningful discounts to fair value in less frequently traded assets.*[3]

However, with respect to liquidity Yale Endowment (2001) deviates from the consensus view. Table 4.4 shows the asset allocation in Table 4.3 broken down in terms of underlying liquidity of the asset classes. Equities, bonds, and cash are *liquid assets*, absolute return strategies are *quasi-liquid assets*; and private equity and real estate are *illiquid assets*.

It is probably fair to state that the Yale Endowment Fund is picking up a premium for liquidity. Not being able to turn the portfolio into cash within 24 hours is a disadvantage to investors for which they seek compensation. However, there are three issues with this point of view. First, long-

**Table 4.4**   Liquidity

|  | Yale Endowment Liquidity | Average Endowment Liquidity | Average U.K. Pension Fund Liquidity[a] |
|---|---|---|---|
| Liquid assets | 42.1% | 82.0% | 98.0% |
| Quasi-liquid assets | 22.9 | 9.1 | 0.0 |
| Illiquid assets | 35.0 | 8.9 | 2.0 |

[a]Author's own estimates.
*Note:* Data as of June 30, 2001.
*Source:* Yale Endowment (2001).

term investors (pension funds, endowment funds, insurance companies, etc.) do not need to turn 80 percent of their holdings into cash within 24 hours. Second, liquidity evaporates when most needed. In the crash of October 1987, market makers possessed neither the resources nor the willingness to absorb the extraordinary volume of selling demand that materialized. The liquidity premium that investors paid to hold "liquid" assets evaporated in the panic selling, just when the ability to make an immediate sale might have had value. Third, opportunities for active money management are negatively related to market efficiency and, hence, liquidity. The widespread availability of information in highly efficient and liquid markets (e.g., large capitalization stocks in developed economies) makes it difficult and costly to obtain an analytical edge.

## DISADVANTAGES

Table 4.5 shows the results of two surveys with respect to why investors do not invest in hedge funds.

Risk was the key concern of investors, followed by a perceived lack of fit with their investment strategies and concerns regarding the transparency of what the funds were really doing. Bekier (1996) assumed that the cost factor

**Table 4.5** Reasons for Not Investing in Hedge Funds

| Rank | Bekier (1996) | Goldman Sachs/Frank Russell (2001)[a] |
|---|---|---|
| 1 | Risk | Risk/return profile not consistent with investment objectives |
| 2 | Not a fit with strategy | Prohibited (legally or by investment policy) |
| 3 | Lack of understanding/transparency | Lack of disclosure and transparency |
| 4 | Not allowed | Lack of understanding at board level preventing in-debt consideration |
| 5 | Use of leverage | |
| 6 | Cost | |
| 7 | Lack of regulation/liquidity | |

*Source:* Bekier (1996). Goldman Sachs/Frank Russell (2001).
[a]North American respondents.

was underestimated by the survey. However, with respect to cost, the survey is consistent with a hedge funds survey by Indocam/Watson Wyatt (2000). European institutional investors in the Goldman Sachs and Frank Russell (2001) survey mentioned the following reasons for not investing in hedge funds:

- Unclear supervisory guidelines.
- Lack of information, transparency, and control.
- High fees.
- Insufficient data and track records to judge risk/return profile.

Some hedge fund professionals argue that track record (or the lack thereof) is irrelevant and that institutional investors new to the game put too much faith in past performance. Most often track records are ambiguous as they cover a period when there are substantial differences with respect to funds under management, changes in strategy, and managers running the portfolio. On some occasions the return figures are pro forma and/or unaudited.

This section will discuss some disadvantages of investing in hedge funds:

- Excessive fees.
- Excessive leverage.
- Lack of transparency.
- Low liquidity.
- Capacity constraints.
- Similarity to being short a disaster put option.

## Excessive Fees

**Excessive Fee Hypothesis**   According to Indocam/Watson Wyatt (2000), fees are not an issue when investing in hedge funds; fees were ranked last by the investors surveyed. This seems counterintuitive as well as inconsistent with our experience in the field. Perhaps for existing hedge fund investors fees are a small issue, whereas they are likely to be a big issue for potential investors currently evaluating future commitments to the hedge fund industry. Some investors, or more precisely potential investors, regard the fee structure of hedge funds as excessive. There are two counterarguments that can challenge the view that hedge fund fees are excessive:

1. Net returns matter.
2. Fees are small relative to alpha.

**Net Returns Matter**   A point could be made that net returns matter more than gross returns. Utility is derived from net returns, not from gross returns. What matters even more are net risk-adjusted returns. Risk-adjusted performance compensation could be a possible solution to some of the pending fee-related issues.[4] Two points seem important with regard to fees:

1. *Alignment of investors' risk and return preferences with managers' incentives.* Where an investor is risk averse, the standard fee does not align the manager's incentives with investor preferences since the standard fee rewards higher returns with no reference to volatility or risk.
2. *Asymmetry.* The fee is positive only and can create an optionlike transfer of expected value from the investor to the manager. The asymmetry may provide an incentive for the manager to add to the risk of the fund by applying or increasing leverage to the underlying positions. This asymmetry is similar to risk control issues of investment banks where traders have an incentive to increase risk—large personal upside with little downside risk. This asymmetry is often referred to as a free call option.*

**Fees Are Small Relative to Alpha**     A further counterargument to the excessive fee hypothesis is that hedge fund fees might be high in absolute terms but low relative to alpha. Which of the following managers, A or B, has the more attractive fee structure?

■ A, on average, generates a pre-fee alpha of 20 basis points and requires a fee of 20 basis points of assets under management.
■ B, on average, generates a pre-fee alpha of 10 percent and requires a flat fee of 1 percent of assets under management plus 20 percent of alpha with a high-water mark.†

---

*Cottier (1997) suggests that this call option could be an incentive for a manager to take more risk to increase profits, potentially "making him rich." This might be true for the 20-year-old "manager" raising funds for his "trading strategy," but not for the experienced ex-head of trading who invests his eight-figure fortune in his own fund. This person already is rich, and does not join the game entirely for the fees, but for a combination of capital gains, entrepreneurial and competitive kick, and, most often, freedom from the political and administrative hassle from working for a large organization. See also Anson (2001a).

†Example is simplified to make a point. It is not the case that long-only managers generate alpha of 0 percent and hedge fund managers alpha of 10 percent. The term "alpha" does not apply very well to absolute return strategies, as to calculate alpha one needs a benchmark. Absolute return managers have no benchmark. Hence, the calculation of alpha is different to relative return managers. However, to the extent that absolute return managers outperform the London Inter-Bank Offered Rate (LIBOR) they can transfer this to the S&P 500 or any other tradable market benchmark. In other words, to some extent alpha in relative return space and alpha in absolute return space can be compared.

It is neither absurd nor excessive when an active manager gets paid for alpha. Mutual funds, on average, generate an alpha of zero on a net basis.* There is empirical evidence to suggest that if an active manager on average is able to generate alpha it is usually only on a gross basis. On a net basis active management in large developed markets does not generate alpha. Put another way, the fee an investor actually pays for active management is 100 percent of the alpha generated. This compares with only 20 percent of alpha for manager B. Manager A charges for beta whereas the large portion of manager B's fees are based on alpha.† This is interesting and relevant because nowadays—with high liquidity in risk management instruments such as swaps and futures—beta in a developed market can be "bought" at very low cost and/or alpha ported on nearly any liquid market benchmark.

The risk-free rate is the compensation to the owner of capital for deferring its use—the time value of money. The asset class premium represents the incremental return over the risk-free rate earned by an investor passively investing in an asset class. This premium compensates the investor for the risk of holding that type of asset. For traditional strategies, the significant source of excess return (return above the risk-free rate) is earned by accepting the asset class risk and thereby earning the asset class premium. Excess return from these managers is attributable to the active management premium, that is, the risk and reward of actively managing a portfolio.

With hedge funds the total return is not attributed to any asset class. The return is attributed to the risk-free rate, other factors and variables, and alpha (or excess return or the part of the return that is purely attributable to skill). In Figure 4.6 we called the other factors "unaccounted for." In Chapters 6 to 8 these factors will be accounted for for all major absolute return strategies. Only for systematic risk factors are relevant, as the nonsystematic risk factors can be immunized through diversification. The systematic factors vary across the different alternative investment strategies. This is one reason why the hedge fund industry is heterogeneous. It is also the reason why George Soros calls the long-only industry "trend-followers by definition."[5] All managers are doing the same thing, and their returns are derived from the same factor—the asset class. This, he concludes, is a larger risk to the financial system because

---

*Kao (2002) finds that the general perception is that, as a group, hedge fund managers produce just enough active return to earn their overall fees whereas long-only managers fail to do so.

†In defense of manager A one could argue that the investor does not pay for beta but for ex ante alpha. A fee arrangement between an investor and manager A could be specified as a fixed 20 basis points where the ex ante alpha is estimated to be 100 basis points. In this case the fee arrangement of managers A and B would actually be quite similar.

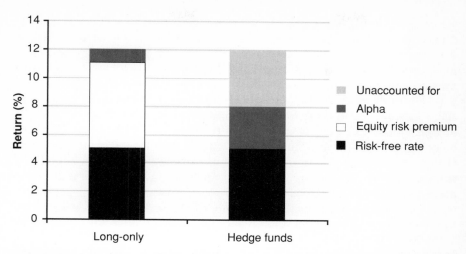

**FIGURE 4.6** Elements of Returns for Traditional and Alternative Asset Manager

it is a concentration of risk. If all investors buy at the same time or sell at the same time (driven by benchmark considerations), the stability of the system is at risk.* Only when managers are measured against an absolute yardstick is there less concentration (i.e., less systemic risk).

A further fact often overlooked is that hedge funds regularly have a high-water mark and a hurdle rate. A high-water mark assures that a fund only takes performance-related fees on the value added to the investor. If a fund moves from 100 to 80, it has to move back to 100 before performance fees can be charged. This increases the fiduciary's incentive not to destroy the wealth in mandate. A manager with a high-water mark who experiences a large loss has an incentive to return capital to investors if it looks as though it will take too long to regain the losses. Goetzmann, Ingersoll, and Ross (2001) note that the high-water mark feature can represent a large transfer of expected value from investor to manager. The transfer occurs because the manager is motivated to take more risk when below the high-water mark so as to maximize the likelihood of exceeding the mark and earning a performance

---

*Persaud (2001) argues that the lack of diversity increases systemic risk as it introduces "liquidity black holes." Jorion (2000) makes the point that the blind acceptance of value at risk (VAR) increases systemic risk. If a majority of market players use the same risk system with the same input variables, all those market participants will get the same output. This is a concentration of risk, as all these market participants will want to rebalance their (usually already similar) positions at the same time, thus increasing systemic risk.

fee. Such a motivation to take extra risk is costly only to the investor. The authors conclude that hedge funds "may be priced about right" where investors are rational and expect a large positive risk-adjusted return in compensation for higher fees. Liang (1999) found that hedge funds with high-water marks provide significantly better returns than funds without them.

The hurdle rate is a further mechanism that aligns the hedge fund manager's incentives with those of the investors. A hurdle rate is a predefined rate of return that has to be achieved before the incentive fee kicks in. However, most hedge funds have a hurdle rate of zero. Based on research by Liang (1999), unlike the high-water mark, a hurdle rate is not critical for fund performance. Note that the hurdle rate and the high-water mark serve different purposes. The hurdle rate is used for collecting incentive fees, whereas the purpose of a high-water mark is to assure that past losses are recovered before the manager gets paid a performance fee.

**Conclusion**    There is a strong case against the excessive fee hypothesis. First, net returns should matter and not the difference between gross and net returns. Second, alternative investment strategies base their fees on the value added and not the risk premium of the asset class. However, lucrative fee structures are an incentive for managers to become fee-oriented as opposed to result-oriented. The current institutionalization of the hedge fund industry is transforming the industry from a capital gain business to a fee business. This emphasizes the importance and costs of due diligence in actively selecting hedge funds. In the funds of hedge funds approach, the selection of hedge funds is transferred to industry specialists who have the knowledge, skill, and experience to avoid hedge funds with investor-unfriendly fee structures.

A case could be made that when institutional investors move into alternative investments, they could push hedge funds to lower their fees. With trillions of dollars in assets, there was the perception that institutional investors had the power to combat high fees. So far (April 2002), the opposite seems to be taking shape.

Not only are hedge fund managers sticking to their traditional 1 percent management and 20 percent performance fees, but many of the more popular funds are even raising their fees by a few percentage points due to high demand from institutional clients. The justification for raising fees is the additional risks of managing a larger fund in a relatively illiquid market. In other words, capacity constraints could, in the future, result in lower net returns for the investor because of a higher fee structure (and diminishing investment opportunities).

To some extent, institutional investors have been able to bargain down fees when dealing with new entrants in the hedge fund arena. This trend could mean that the more persistent institutional investors will end up with the least talented managers. It is doubtful that the most talented in the hedge fund industry will undersell their services and skill.

## Excessive Leverage

There also is an excessive leverage hypothesis postulating that exposure to hedge funds is not attractive because of the use of high leverage. To some extent this is a valid concern. Most financial disasters in history in one way or another are associated with excess leverage or, more precisely, the misuse of leverage. However, five points can be made in again trying to debunk the hypothesis:

1. Leverage of hedge funds is relatively low.
2. The risk to single hedge funds can be eliminated and exposure to leverage reduced through diversification.
3. There is a misunderstanding with respect to what leverage is.
4. Balance sheet leverage is not an adequate measure for risk.
5. The LTCM effect is misleading.

**Relatively Low Leverage of Hedge Funds**   Average hedge fund leverage is low when compared with other financial institutions. According to Van Money Manager Research, around 72 percent of analyzed hedge funds used leverage. Only around 24 percent use balance sheet leverage in excess of 2 to 1. The report of the President's Working Group on Financial Markets (1999) also acknowledges that a "significant majority" of hedge funds have balance sheet leverage ratios of less than 2 to 1. In comparison, the balance sheets of banks are leveraged around 10 or 15 to 1. Residential real estate is typically levered 5 to 1 (a 20 percent down payment is common, with 80 percent borrowed). In other words, leverage in the hedge fund industry is comparably low (at least based on these simplistic measures of balance sheet leverage). In addition, in the period 2000–2001 many hedge fund managers deleveraged due to vanishing opportunities in their fields of expertise. By the end of 2001, increased levels of cash were much more a characteristic of the hedge fund industry, as opposed to excess levels of debt (i.e., leverage). In summer 2002, cash levels of hedge funds were at or close to an all-time high.

The management of leverage is one of the key risk control instruments for the absolute return manager. The level of leverage depends on the opportunity set. If there are few opportunities, leverage is low (as for example in 2001). If there are many opportunities, leverage is high (as for example in 1998). An exogenous shock to the system, therefore, is more likely to result in heavy losses when it occurs in times where leverage is high, such as during the Russian default crisis in the third quarter of 1998. An exogenous shock does not cause as much damage if it occurs in times where leverage is low, such as during the September 2001 atrocities in New York and Washington, D.C. The leverage in the system in September 2001 was low; hence there was little negative financial impact on hedge funds.

### Less Exposure to Leverage and Single-Manager Risk through Diversification

Some practitioners recommend one should view hedge funds like a call option: Downside is limited to principal, whereas there is unlimited upside through leveraged participation in the underlying of whatever the hedge fund is dealing in. The author does not subscribe to this view as it does not distinguish between the various strategies and implies high risk. Some relative-value strategies are very low-risk since beta is kept at zero and leverage is used to hedge as opposed to increase exposure.

Another view is to look at a hedge fund as a company and the risk associated with a single manager as company-specific, that is, idiosyncratic risk. In this sense, the use of operational and financial leverage is company-specific. The risk of a company or a hedge fund manager misusing leverage is idiosyncratic (nonsystematic) risk to the investor. Investors should eliminate idiosyncratic risk through diversification. Occasionally, listed companies fold because of the misuse of leverage. When this happens investors normally do not question capitalism as a system itself. The same logic should be applied with hedge funds.

**Misunderstanding of Leverage**   When investors borrow funds to increase the amount that they have invested in a particular position, they use leverage. Investors use leverage when they believe that the return from the position will exceed the cost of the borrowed funds. Sometimes managers use leverage to enable them to put on new positions without having to take off other positions prematurely. Managers who target very small price discrepancies or spreads will often use leverage to magnify the returns from these discrepancies. Leveraging can magnify the risk of the strategy as well as creating risk by giving the lender power over the disposition of the investment portfolio. This may occur in the form of increased margin requirements or adverse market shifts forcing a partial or complete liquidation of the portfolio.

Institutionally, leverage is defined in accounting or balance-sheet terms as the ratio of total assets to equity capital (net worth). Alternatively, leverage can be defined in terms of risk, in which case it is a measure of economic risk relative to capital.

Hedge funds obtain economic leverage in various ways, such as through the use of repurchase agreements, short positions, and derivatives contracts. At times, the choice of investment is influenced by the availability of leverage. Beyond a trading institution's risk appetite, both balance-sheet and economic leverage may be constrained in some cases by initial margin and collateral at the transaction level, and also by trading and credit limits imposed by trading counterparties. For some types of financial institutions, regulatory capital requirements may constrain leverage, although this limitation does not apply to hedge funds. Hedge funds are limited in their use of leverage only by the willingness of their creditors and counterparties to provide such leverage.

**Balance Sheet Leverage Not an Adequate Measure for Risk**  The hedge fund whose schematic balance sheet is shown in Table 4.6 is leveraged 6:1. If instead of purchasing the Treasury bonds financed at a floating rate—the repo (repurchase agreement) rate—the fund enters into a swap* to receive fixed and pay floating on a notional of 500, which is an economically equivalent position in terms of interest rate exposure, the fund would have only cash and equity on its balance sheet and its leverage would be 1:1. Finally, if the fund were to enter into an additional but offsetting position in which it sells short a comparable maturity Treasury bond that it borrows through a reverse repo transaction, its balance sheet would be as shown in Table 4.7. The leverage increases to 11:1, even though the offsetting short position in Treasury bonds vastly reduces the risk of the portfolio. Balance sheet leverage by itself is an inadequate and sometimes misleading measure of risk. For any given leverage ratio, the fragility of a portfolio depends on the market, credit, and liquidity risk in the portfolio. In addition, a high capital requirement based on balance-sheet concepts alone might induce fund managers to shift their risk-taking activities

---

*The traditional interest rate swap is an exchange of fixed interest payments for floating rate payments.

**Table 4.6**  Balance Sheet A

| 10-year U.S. Treasury bonds | 500 | Collateralized financing (repurchase agreement) | 500 |
|---|---|---|---|
| Cash | 100 | Equity | 100 |
| Total  assets | 600 | Total  liabilities | 600 |

*Source:* HBS (1999).

**Table 4.7**  Balance Sheet B

| 10-year U.S. Treasury bonds | 500 | Collateralized financing (repurchase agreement) | 500 |
|---|---|---|---|
| Collateralized financing (reverse repo agreement) | 500 | Short Treasury bonds | 500 |
| Cash | 100 | Equity | 100 |
| Total assets | 1,100 | Total liabilities | 1,100 |

*Source:* HBS (1999).

to more speculative trading strategies as they seek to meet rate-of-return targets on the required capital.[6] It could also induce managers to move to off-balance-sheet risk-taking strategies such as the use of derivatives.

The report of the President's Working Group on Financial Markets (1999) recognizes that placing direct constraints on leverage presents certain difficulties. Given investors' diverse exposures to risk and differences in their links to other market participants, requiring a uniform degree of balance sheet leverage for all investors does not seem reasonable.

An alternative measure to balance sheet leverage is the ratio of potential gains and losses to net worth, such as value at risk relative to net worth. An advantage of such a statistical measure is its ability to produce a more meaningful description of leverage in terms of risk. A disadvantage is the potential pitfalls in measuring value at risk, such as through faulty or incomplete modeling assumptions or narrow time horizons. These issues suggest that enforcing a meaningful regulatory capital requirement or leverage ratio for a wide and diverse range of investment funds would be a difficult undertaking.

The report of the President's Working Group on Financial Markets (1999) also highlights credit-risk management as an alternative tool for indirectly influencing excessive leverage. Credit-risk management can help to constrain the leverage employed by significant market participants, including hedge funds, thereby reducing systemic risk. The diversity of the credit risk and liquidity profiles of borrowers had led creditors to use a variety of tools to control credit risk. The President's Working Group suggested that public policy initiatives relating to hedge funds should build upon those practices that have worked well, and should encourage their use and improvements in their implementation.

**LTCM Effect**    Investors in LTCM lost around $4.4 billion; $1.9 billion belonged to the partners and $2.5 billion to other investors. According to Jorion (2000), out of the $4.4 billion lost, around $3 billion came from the two main types of bets, interest rate swaps and equity volatility. LTCM is the only hedge fund known to the general public. The excess use of leverage of LTCM is generalized and assumed to be the case for all hedge funds.

Hedge funds leverage the capital they invest by buying securities on margin and engaging in collateralized borrowing. Better-known funds can buy structured derivative products without putting up capital initially, but must make a succession of premium payments when the market in those securities trades up or down. In addition, some hedge funds negotiate secured credit lines with their banks, and some relative-value funds may even obtain unsecured credit lines. Credit lines are expensive, however, and most managers use them mainly to finance calls for additional margin when the market moves against them. These practices may allow a few hedge funds, like

LTCM (prior to its reorganization), to achieve very high leverage ratios. This practice is exceptional.

At the end of August 1997, LTCM had a balance sheet leverage of 19:1, which was at the lower end of the historical range of 19:1 to 31:1 since it had reached global scale in 1995.[7] However, in August 1997 the gross notional size of the fund's off-balance sheet positions, including swaps, options, and other derivatives, was approximately $1.25 trillion.[8] This figure, handed around broadly by the popular press, was practically meaningless. It simply summed the absolute values of the notional amounts of the contractual agreements and futures, even when their risks where offsetting. What mattered was the total risk of the fund.

## Lack of Transparency

**Transparency Is a Double-Edged Sword**    According to a survey conducted by Barra Strategic Consulting Group (2001) the lack of transparency is the greatest concern for institutional investors. Full transparency of current positions is commercially unwise. This is true for hedge funds and proprietary trading desks as well as other money managers of large size. The reason why it is more important for hedge funds, as already outlined in Chapter 2, is because hedge funds involve short positions much more frequently than, for example, pension funds and mutual funds do.

Hedge fund investors are in a similar relationship to the hedge funds as are stockholders to the company. The shareholder does not have full access to all the information of the company, such as future projects or contracts with suppliers. The same applies for hedge fund investors with respect to the hedge fund. The hedge fund manager will hold back confidential information, especially current positions. In a game of poker it is considered unwise to show your cards. Hedge fund managers disguise their positions to the market, just like car manufacturers disguise their new models during test drives.

Transparency in the hedge fund industry is increasing at a fast pace. This is primarily due to the increasing involvement of institutional investors, who require a much higher degree of transparency than private investors do. In the future institutional money will play a more important role in the hedge fund industry, which means requirements will be higher.

## Low Liquidity

Low liquidity (i.e., high redemption periods) is often brought up as an argument against investing in hedge funds. This is understandable for a treasurer managing the company's cash and requiring a high degree of liquidity. It is less intuitive, however, why a high-duration pension fund has a problem with high redemption periods. Generally speaking, long-term investors get compensated for holding less liquid assets; they pick up a liquidity premium.

Some investors might find comfort in the fact that most hedge fund managers have a large portion of their net wealth tied to the fund and thus have the same high redemption periods as other investors. A more pragmatic argument for low liquidity is the fact that hedge funds exploit inefficiencies and therefore are by definition in markets that are less liquid than the bluest of blue chips. Exploiting inefficiencies by its nature involves some degree of illiquidity.

Many hedge funds pursuing strategies such as investing in distressed securities and emerging markets or mortgage-backed securities arbitrage are holding a large part of their assets in rather illiquid positions. These strategies would be difficult to play if investors had the option to withdraw funds at any time without notice. In general, scarce subscription and redemption possibilities result in lower cash reserves held and less administrative work due to fewer deposits and withdrawals. Ceteris paribus, the performance should increase as less liquidity is offered to the investors. The following analysis uses the frequency of redemptions as a proxy for liquidity, the assumption being that subscription and redemption frequency are similar.

The advantages of long redemption periods are manifest in performance statistics. Cottier (1997) found that the possibility that long redemption frequency has a positive effect on performance is in fact very strong. (See Table 4.8.) Note that the volatility increases for funds providing only semiannual and annual redemptions.

## Capacity Constraints

**The Size Factor**   Size is often seen as a risk rather than a performance-enhancing factor, particularly when assets grow too rapidly (Cottier 1997).

**Table 4.8**   Impact of Redemption Frequency on Performance (January 1990 to June 1996)

| Redemption Period | Annual Return | Volatility | Sharpe Ratio | Maximum Number of Funds | Minimum Number of Funds |
|---|---|---|---|---|---|
| Daily | 13.0% | 5.9% | 1.35 | 19 | 5 |
| Weekly | 11.4 | 6.6 | 0.97 | 30 | 9 |
| Monthly | 14.2 | 5.0 | 1.85 | 155 | 17 |
| Quarterly | 19.6 | 5.9 | 2.46 | 97 | 12 |
| Semiannually | 22.0 | 13.1 | 1.30 | 11 | 3 |
| Annually | 25.4 | 11.2 | 1.82 | 16 | 4 |

*Source:* Cottier (1997), based on TASS database.

Niches become too small; it becomes difficult and costly to move quickly in and out of positions and to execute trades. In addition, the top trader of a large fund is distracted by administrative duties and personnel management instead of being devoted entirely to trading. There are also arguments in favor of size, such as administrative and legal economies of scale, lower brokerage commissions, more research spending, and possible influence and manipulation of markets. Furthermore, there may be a survival bias. Large funds have often existed for many years; they had to survive in many market situations, leading to more managerial experience.

The empirical evidence is inconclusive. Table 4.9, for example, shows that funds larger than $500 million have returns nearly double those with assets of $1 million to $5 million. However, Peltz (1995) found the opposite. In 81 percent of a sample of approximately 400 hedge funds in the MAR/Hedge database, Peltz found that performance deteriorated as assets grew.

## Short a Disaster Put Option

As Part II will discuss at length, investing in some of the absolute return strategies, to some extent, is similar to selling disaster put options. Some absolute return strategies are more prone to losses in disasters than others. However, most return distributions in the real world are not normal. This is true for equities and especially some relative-value absolute return strategies. This does not mean that these strategies are unattractive per se. It means, however, that investing in hedge funds is not a free lunch. There are costs associated with the superior performance. One of the costs, one could argue, is the possibility of a large loss in a disaster scenario. Note, however, that hedge funds outperformed equities in all disasters over the past 12 years except in the Russian debt crisis. In the third quarter of 1998 most hedge funds had a

**Table 4.9**  Impact of Size on Performance (July 1994 to June 1996)

| Assets under Management (US$m) | Annual Return | Volatility | Sharpe Ratio |
|---|---|---|---|
| 1–5 | 10.7% | 4.8% | 1.18 |
| 5–10 | 15.4 | 7.4 | 1.41 |
| 10–20 | 14.4 | 5.3 | 1.79 |
| 20–50 | 12.1 | 3.7 | 1.91 |
| 50–100 | 15.6 | 4.3 | 2.45 |
| 100–500 | 13.2 | 4.6 | 1.78 |
| >= 500 | 20.9 | 8.1 | 1.95 |

*Source:* Cottier (1997).

difficult time. At the most general level, it was a combination of four factors that led to mark-to-market losses and blowups: (1) rapidly widening credit spreads and lack of liquidity due to flight-to-quality scenario, (2) a lot of leverage in the (hedge fund) system, (3) forced deleveraging due to prime brokers tightening credit lines, and (4) deleveraging due to fear of investors' redemptions (which did not materialize).

One of the ironies in the hedge fund industry with respect to selling disaster put options is an anecdote involving Victor Niederhoffer's trading style. Niederhoffer was considered eccentric and brilliant. He was a legend of the hedge fund business. Indeed he had compiled an outstanding track record—a 32 percent compound annual return since 1982.[9] Niederhoffer sold naked out-of-the-money index put options,* believing that the market would never drop by more than 5 percent in a single day. When the stock market dislocated by 7 percent on October 27, 1997, he was unable to meet margin calls for some $50 million. His brokers liquidated the positions, wiping out his funds. Like most other active money managers, he refuted some of the axiomatic theories that are taught at business schools around the world. Victor Niederhoffer:

> *I am not a great believer in efficient markets, random walks, or rational expectations. My own trading especially refutes these. I trade strictly based on statistical "anomalies," the analysis of multivariate time series, and the quantifications of persistent psychological biases. . . .*
>
> *In statistical terms, I figure I have traded about 2 million contracts in my life thus far, with an average profit of $70 per contract (after slippage of perhaps $20). This average profit is approximately 700 standard deviations away from randomness, a departure that would occur by chance alone about as frequently as the spare parts in an automotive salvage lot might spontaneously assemble themselves into a McDonald's restaurant.*[10]

The irony comes from a friend of Victor Niederhoffer after reading an early draft of Niederhoffer's *The Education of a Speculator*. Niederhoffer quotes the friend in the Preface of the book, which was dated November 1996. The book hit the bookstore shelves during 1997, and the fund blew up in October 1997. The friend commented:

---

*Note that the term "naked" does not refer to the dress code of a trader but to the trade position. A naked put sale refers to a short put position that was not covered (either by margin or by a corresponding short position in the underlying cash market).

*It's obvious that it's only a question of time until you go under. Why in the world would I ever risk money in the futures market and, if I ever gave in to such folly, why should it be with Niederhoffer!? I know that must come across harshly, but I thought it better to put it that way rather than sugarcoat it.*[11]

## SUMMARY

Investing in hedge funds has some disadvantages. However, high fees per se are not an argument against investing in hedge funds. Fees have to be put in the context of the value added. Leverage is also not a disadvantage because most hedge funds have low leverage, and exposure to hedge funds with high leverage can be diversified through holding different strategies and different hedge funds. The lack of transparency is a disadvantage. However, the trend is for more transparency as institutional money plays a larger role. The lack of liquidity, which is occasionally quoted as a disadvantage, is actually an advantage: Long-term investors are able to pick up a liquidity premium.

## APPENDIX: On Market Efficiency and Unorthodox Economics

*There is an impressive and growing body of evidence demonstrating that investors and speculators don't necessarily learn from experience. Emotion overrides logic time after time.*
—David Dreman

### Efficiency of Markets

Hedge fund managers, especially in the relative-value arena, make money by exploiting objective market inefficiencies. The high risk-adjusted returns are in stark contrast with what is still taught at business schools and what some distinguished academics and practitioners rely on: the paradigm that capital markets are efficient or close to efficient. The migration to indexation and core-satellite structures are the result of this paradigm. However, the pendulum is swinging back. Today, there is a group of academics as well as practitioners who believe that with a competitive advantage there is the possibility to gain excess returns that can be explained by manager skill. The balance between EMH disciples and heretics is probably shifting toward that latter.

The efficient market hypothesis and its close relative the random walk hypothesis are among the most controversial and hotly contested ideas in all the social sciences. They are disarmingly simple to state, have far-reaching consequences for academic pursuits and business practices, and yet are surprisingly resistant to empirical proof or refutation. Even after three decades of research and literally thousands of journal articles, economists have not yet reached a consensus about whether capital markets are efficient.

The first serious application of the random walk hypothesis to financial markets can be traced to Paul Samuelson (1965a).*

*In an information-efficient market—not to be confused with an allocation- or Pareto-efficient market—price changes must be unforecastable if they are properly anticipated, i.e., if they fully incorporate the expectations and information of all market participants.*[12]

Lo and MacKinlay (1999) add:

*Unlike the many applications of the random walk hypothesis in the natural and physical sciences in which randomness is assumed almost by default, because of the absence of any natural alternatives, Samuelson believed that randomness is achieved through the active participation of many investors seeking greater wealth. Unable to curtail their greed, an army of investors aggressively pounce on even the smallest informational advantages at their disposal, and in doing so, they incorporate their information into market prices and quickly eliminate the profit opportunities that gave rise to their aggression. If this occurs instantaneously, which it must in an idealized world of "frictionless" markets and costless trading, then prices must always fully reflect all available information and no profits can be garnered from information-based trading (because such profits have already been captured).*

---

*We could go back as far as the early nineteenth century when the English physicist Robert Brown discovered a phenomenon where molecules randomly collide with one another as they move in space (Brownian motion). Louis Bachelier, a French mathematician, found in 1900 that if stock prices vary according to the square root of time, they bear remarkable resemblance to a Brownian motion. In finance, the Brownian motion came to be called the random walk, which someone once described as the path a drunk might follow at night in the light of a lamppost (Bernstein 1992). Others would put the start date at 1933 when the founder of *Econometrica*, Alfred Cowles III, answered the question "Can Stock Market Forecasters Forecast?" with a three-word abstract: "It is doubtful" (Cowles 1933). His analysis concluded that the performance of the stocks analyzed as a whole were negative relative to the performance of the market as a whole. The results could have been achieved through a purely random selection of stocks.

Fama (1970) argued that "prices fully reflect all available information." Eugene Fama gained a reputation preaching the EMH. According to Fama (1998), market efficiency survives the challenge from the literature on long-term return anomalies. Consistent with the market efficiency hypothesis that the anomalies are chance results, apparent overreaction to information is about as common as underreaction, and post-event continuation of pre-event abnormal returns is about as frequent as post-event reversal. Most important, consistent with the market efficiency prediction that apparent anomalies can be due to methodology, most long-term return anomalies tend to disappear with reasonable changes in technique.

**There Is No Free Lunch Plan**   Three and a half decades after the previously quoted statement from Paul Samuelson, Lo and MacKinlay (1999) express the view:

> *Financial markets are predictable to some degree, but far from being a symptom of inefficiency or irrationality. Predictability is the oil that lubricates the gears of capitalism.*[13]

Campbell, Lo, and MacKinlay (1997) and Lo and MacKinlay (1999) argue that the EMH is some sort of benchmark against which market efficiency can be compared. In this sense, full market efficiency is a theoretical concept and markets are compared to 100 percent efficiency. The authors make the point that if one wants to exploit these occasional excess profit opportunities one has to have a competitive advantage of some sort. This could be in the form of information gathering (in combination with focus on underresearched small caps or potential short sale candidates), superior technology, or financial innovation. An active manager therefore has to develop some sort of area of competency or competitive advantage. If this is not the case, the ex ante alpha is zero (or negative). Any realized excess return, therefore, is not a function of skill but of chance (or a function of the wrong benchmark against which the excess return is measured). Lo and MacKinlay (1999) argue:

> *In this version of the Efficient Markets Hypothesis, an occasional free lunch is permitted, but free lunch plans are ruled out.*[14]

**Market Timing**   Probably one of the most pleasurable activities for academics in finance is to make fun of erring financial forecasters or financial professionals underperforming a passive benchmark. Some Schadenfreude is probably derived from the fact that most often (but not always) money managers, analysts, and strategists earned much more than academics during the excesses of the 1982–2000 bull market. There is a possibility that there will always be forecasters in financial markets as there have been seers, prophets, and fortune-tellers throughout the 5,000 years of the documented history of civilization.* The inability to forecast market direction in a consistent manner is often used as an argument for market efficiency. A lot of the entertainment value is derived from the fact that market timers and forecasters view the world as deterministic (as in Newton's view of orbits) as opposed to chaotic (like, for example, the weather). Forecasters trying to assess a complex system will fail by definition because the set of variables and links between these variables is only a small subset of the total dynamic system. Assessing all variables and links in an unbiased fashion is not possible. What is often overlooked, however, is that the only alternative to an intelligent assessment of the future is an unintelligent one. Most investors opt for the former. Wall Street economists and market wizards and gurus will probably get paid a multiple of their former tutors at university for some time to come.[†]

The problem of expert failure can be traced to man's capabilities as an information processor. Every human organism lives in an environment that generates millions of new bits of information every second, but the bottleneck of the perceptual apparatus does not admit more than 1,000 bits per second. We react consciously to only a fraction of the information that is given to us. Then it is up to relative levels of skill, which also vary.

Dozens of studies discrediting experts have made it clear that expert failure extends far beyond the investment scene. And the problems often reside in man's information processing capabilities. Current work indicates that the expert is a serial or sequential processor of data who can handle information reliably in a linear manner—that is, can move from one point to the next in a logical sequence. However, a solution to a complex problem can require configural (or interactive) reasoning. In a configural problem, the forecaster's in-

---

*Sherden's *Fortune Sellers* (1998) summarizes some aspects of forecasting quite profoundly.

[†]Note that strategists actually *do* add value to some investors. The value is in the assessment of the market (i.e., the complex system) even if their forecast (which, as a group, does not deviate significantly from randomness) is wrong, as with most strategists in 2001. Lateral thinking adds value, even (or perhaps especially) in a complex system. The value added is comparable with a mathematics exam in primary school where one used to get points for the solution process as opposed to the end result itself. Nevertheless, at the most general level, it is probably fair to say that the stronger the investors' bias toward financial econometrics, the less seriously a guru's view is taken. To a Bayesian econometrician, a strategist is an entertainer at best. (Thomas Bayes, 1702–1761, was an English clergyman and mathematician. His pioneering work, "Essay Towards Solving a Problem in the Doctrine of Chances" [1763], attempted to establish that the rule for determining the probability of an event is the same whether or not anything is known antecedently to any trials or observations concerning the event.)

terpretation of any single piece of information changes depending on how the individual evaluates many other inputs. The configural relationships of a company or the market place itself are extremely complex. In addition, research in configural processing has shown that experts not only can analyze information incorrectly, they can also find relationships that are not there—a phenomenon called "illusionary correlation."

The complexity of the marketplace naturally leads to an attempt to simplify and rationalize what seems at times to be reality. Often investors notice things that are simply coincidental, and then come to believe that correlations exist when none are actually present. And if they are rewarded by the stock going up, the false validity of the practice is further ingrained. The market thus provides an excellent field for illusionary correlation.

If experts err so badly and are wrong so consistently, will the experts be relieved of their duty to forecast?* Probably not. When dealing with volatility and uncertainty, an expert's view is likely to be considered in the decision-making process. Consulting an expert is better than the next best alternative. What is the next best alternative? Alternatives to an expert's view are the fortune-teller's or the chartist's view (i.e., the nonexpert's view).[†] Those might not be considered an alternative at all.

**Some Hedge Fund Managers Have a Competitive Advantage**  The consistently high risk-adjusted returns of hedge funds when compared with traditional managers support the views expressed by Lo and MacKinlay (1999). Good hedge fund managers narrowly define their area of competency. The first hedge fund by Alfred Jones was about narrowing down the competitive advantage (stock picking skill) and hedging away residual risk (especially market risk). Today this is not different. Most hedge fund managers start operating in an area of financial markets where they have (and/or believe to have) a competitive advantage.[‡] Their starting point is a white piece of paper as opposed to a portfolio benchmark—that is, positions where the manager is

---

*Sherden (1998) on forecasting: "Remember the First Law of Economics: For every economist, there is an equal and opposite economist—so for every bullish economist, there is a bearish one. The Second Law of Economics: They are both likely to be wrong."

†Robert N. Veres on forecasting: "Personally, I think everybody who predicts the future with a straight face should be required (by federal law) to change out of the business suit, wrap him/herself in a gypsy shawl, wear one of those pointed wizard's hats with a picture of a crescent moon on it, and make conjuring sounds over a crystal ball. That way, everybody would know exactly what's going on and how much credibility to give the answer."

‡The successful hedge funds will scale (and by doing so, diversify some risk) their business by expanding into competencies where there are synergies to their core competency. Most multistrategy funds evolved over time to become multistrategy from a single strategy foundation.

unlikely to have full insight. There might be different degrees of risk management sophistication in the hedge fund industry. However, a nearly universal characteristic is that the hedge fund managers know their strengths (e.g., extracting value from a mispriced bond) and weaknesses (e.g., predicting the unpredictable). From an investors' point of view this means that the evaluation of the manager or managers has paramount importance. Hedge fund investors do not invest in a seemingly randomly changing and volatile investment vehicle (e.g., the equity market). They invest in the skill of experienced and (ideally) prudent investment professionals who put their edge at work within a predefined and, ideally, disciplined investment process in whatever it is the managers define as their area of expertise. This is why the hedge fund business is a "people's business" and not an "I-analyzed-some-time-series-and-found-that-hedge-funds-are-a-function-of-XYZ business."

## UNORTHODOX ECONOMICS

Next to the academic (scientific) discussion about market efficiency there is an alternative way of thinking about market mechanisms. These approaches are considered as nonscientific or unorthodox by the academic establishment. Here three of them will be discussed briefly: praxeology, reflexivity, and behavioral finance. Note that, over the past couple of years, behavioral finance has become, to some degree, an accepted niche of economics.

George Soros* argues that successful investing is at least as much alchemy as it is science. Departures from classical economics are nothing new and are available in different wrappings. Thomas Carlyle branded economics as "dismal science," and Karl Marx stigmatized the economists as "the sycophants of the bourgeoisie."[15] Others take pleasure in referring to economics as "orthodox" or "reactionary."

Praxeology, which does not get a lot of coverage these days, dates back to the early twentieth century. The intellectual founder of praxeology is Ludwig von Mises, a leading so-called "Austrian economist." The defining difference between mainstream and Austrian economics lies in their opposing philosophies toward learning truth. Reflexivity is George Soros' theory on economic affairs. Behavioral finance is a maverick splinter-niche of financial theory, evolved from the insight that some of the assumptions of classical economic theory might not be as axiomatic as initially thought.

---

*Charles Ellis (2001) on Soros: "Humility is as rare a commodity on Wall Street as customers' yachts. But then George Soros shares little with Wall Street—he's in it, but not *of* it. Soros ignores Street research and has antagonized the major block-trading houses with what many consider an abrasive and arrogant manner. Other observers, however, attribute such criticism to plain jealousy; they say that Soros, to date, has simply been able to outfox the most cunning Wall Street traders."

Why are these approaches mentioned in a book about pure active management, that is, absolute return strategies? Well, if unorthodox economics has only a small grain of truth and this small grain of truth is fully ignored by the investment establishment, then, by definition, market prices and markets will be biased and, by definition, there will be unorthodox ways for these inefficiencies to be exploited and value extracted.

## Praxeology

The Austrian school of economics is a very small group of libertarians who oppose mainstream economics. Many of the disciples reject even the scientific method that mainstream economists use, preferring to use instead a prescientific approach that ignores real-world data and scientific tests and is based purely on logical assumptions. It deduces truths from a priori knowledge. Von Mises (1996):

> *The a priori sciences—logic, mathematics, and praxeology—aim at a knowledge unconditionally valid for all beings endowed with the logical structure of the human mind. The natural sciences aim at a cognition valid for all those beings which are not only endowed with the faculty of human reason but with human senses.*[16]

It is obvious that this does not go down very well with the scientific approach, as it is the method that thousands of religions use when they argue their opposing beliefs and assert the logic of the existence of God (or Buddha, or Mohammed, or Gaia, etc.).\* The fact that the world has thousands of religions demonstrates the implausibility of this approach. Theories ungrounded in facts and data are easily spun into any belief a person wants. Initial assumptions and trains of logic may contain inaccuracies so small as to be undetectable, yet will yield entirely different conclusions. Academia has generally ignored the Austrian school of economics. It continues to exist because it is financed by wealthy business donors on the far right.† The movement does not exist on its own scholarly merits.

---

\*Soros on the scientific approach: "Scientific method is designed to deal with facts; but, as we have seen, events which have thinking participants do not consist of facts alone. The participant's thinking plays a causal role; yet it does not correspond to the facts for the simple reason that it does not relate to facts." From Soros (1987), p. 34.

†Ronald Reagan on von Mises: "Ludwig von Mises was one of the greatest economic thinkers in the history of Western Civilization. Through his seminal works, he rekindled the flames of liberty. As a wise and kindly mentor, he encourages all who sought to understand the meaning of freedom. We owe him an incalculable debt." (*Source:* http://philosophyquotes.com/board/messages/21.html)

Austrian economists accept the scientific method in principle, but argue that it is more appropriate for hard sciences like physics or chemistry, not soft sciences like sociology or economics. The problem is that humans, unlike electrons, have freedom of choice.* Humans are therefore vastly more unpredictable, even if placed in the same situation twice. Austrian economists favor a method called "apriorism." A priori knowledge is logic, or knowledge that exists in a person's mind prior to, and independent of, outer world experience. For example, the statement "two plus two equals four" is true whether or not a person goes out into the garden and verifies this by counting tomatoes. What this means is that Austrian economists reject the attempt to learn economic laws through experiment or real-world observation. The only true economic laws are those based on first principles, namely, logic.

To be a science, a school of thought must produce theories that are falsifiable, or verifiable. If a theory's correctness or falseness cannot be verified, then it is not science. Perhaps it's religion, or metaphysics, or an unsupported claim. Austrian economists make claims about the market (such as markets know better than governments), but then deny the tools for verifying those claims (such as statistics). Von Mises (1996):

> *Statistical figures referring to economic events are historical data. They tell us what happened in a nonrepeatable historical case. Physical events can be interpreted on the ground of our knowledge concerning constant relations established by experiments. Historical events are not open to such an interpretation.*[17]

The point of view that historical data is one of many probable outcomes is a view most investors will probably share. The view that the future is uncertain is not unorthodox at all. Most risk managers will use a probability distribution of some sort to assess potential future outcomes. In von Mises' (1996) words: "Every action refers to an unknown future. It is in this sense always a risky speculation."

The reason for discussing nonorthodox economics in a book on absolute returns and total risk is strange (or unorthodox) to say the least. The reason is that, and this is a hypothesis, orthodox economic thinking is not perfect and its evolution is far from finished. Too long, potentially, have some of the standard axioms and assumptions been unchallenged (or the challenges been ignored). The rise of behavioral economics in trying to explain some of the phenomena in financial markets, such as the interaction of buyers and sellers, is most likely a step in the right direction. The reason why we contrast behavioral finance with praxeology and reflexivity is that the common denominator

---

*A view shared by Soros (1987).

of the three areas of thought is pretty large. Von Mises, for example, argued that not connecting an economic theorem to the foundation of real human purposes and plans would be nothing more than a free-floating abstraction unconnected to the world we live in and thus irrelevant as a mental exercise. Disciples of reflexivity and behavioral finance probably would put their names behind that statement—with some conditions.

## Reflexivity

George Soros' reflexivity is not discussed in the academic financial literature. Financial academics ignore it because it is not based on the scientific approach but is based on "observation and partly on logic."[18] Reflexivity is discussed in detail in Soros' *The Alchemy of Finance: Reading the Mind of the Market*. To Louis Moore Bacon it is the best financial book ever written.[19] In the Preface, Soros argues that reflexivity was developed as an abstract philosophical concept before he entered the financial markets. "In other words, I failed as a philosophical speculator before I succeeded as a financial one." Soros also notes in the Preface (of the first reprint) that he probably went too far by claiming that economic theory is false and social science a false metaphor. "Since far-from-equilibrium conditions arise only intermittently, economic theory is only intermittently false."[20]

Soros argues that market participants are biased. Behavioral finance theorists make a living by running around at conferences and presenting these biases affecting human judgment and decision making. Soros goes one step further by arguing that not only are there biases but these biases can have an impact on so-called fundamentals. This recursive relationship renders the evolution of prices indeterminate and the so-called equilibrium price irrelevant. Money values do not simply mirror the state of affairs in the real world. Valuation is a positive act that makes an impact on the course of events. Monetary and real phenomena are connected in a reflexive fashion; that is, they influence each other mutually. The reflexive relationship manifests itself most clearly in the use and abuse of credit:

> *It is credit that matters, not money (in other words, monetarism is a false ideology), and the concept of a general equilibrium has no relevance to the real world (in other words, classical economics is an exercise in futility).*[21]

Soros argues that the generally accepted view is that markets are always right: that is, market prices tend to discount future developments accurately even when it is unclear what those developments are. Soros starts with the opposite point of view. He believes that market prices are always wrong in the sense that they present a biased view on the future. The participants' perceptions are inherently flawed, and there is a two-way connection between flawed perceptions and the actual course of events, which results in a lack of correspondence between the two. Soros calls this two-way connection "reflexivity." Soros also views financial markets as a laboratory for testing hypotheses, albeit not strictly scientific ones. "The truth is, successful investing is a kind of alchemy."[22]

Soros notes that he first fantasized that his work would be viewed on a par with Keynes' *General Theory of Employment, Interest and Money*, which explained the Great Depression of the 1930s. The general theory of reflexivity was supposed to explain the great bust of the 1980s. However, the bust did not occur and George Soros has no general theory.

> *What I have is an approach that can help to illuminate the present precarious state of our financial system. It cannot explain and predict the course of events in the manner to which we have become accustomed during our long love affair with natural science for the simple reason that reflexive processes cannot be explained and predicted in that manner.*[23]

Soros argues that equilibrium in markets is never reached and is the product of an axiomatic system. The possibility that equilibrium is never reached need not invalidate the logical construction, but when a hypothetical equilibrium is presented as a model of reality a significant distortion is introduced. The "crowning achievement" of the axiomatic approach according to Soros is the theory of perfect competition. The theory holds that under certain specified circumstances the unrestrained pursuit of self-interest leads to the optimum allocation of scarce resources. The equilibrium point is reached when each firm produces at a level where its marginal cost equals the market price and each consumer buys an amount whose marginal utility equals the market price. The equilibrium position maximizes the benefit of all participants, provided no individual buyer or seller can influence market prices. It is this line of thinking that results in the current belief in the "magic of the marketplace."

Soros notes that it is the assumptions behind the theory that are wrong. The main assumptions include perfect knowledge or perfect information, homogeneous and divisible products, and a large enough number of participants so that no single participant can influence the marketplace. However, it is a cardinal principle of scientific method that perfect knowledge is not attainable. Scientists work by constantly testing plausible hypotheses and propounding new ones. If they did not treat conclusions as provisional and subject to improvement, natural science could not have reached its present state of development and it could not progress any further.

Buy and sell decisions are based on expectations about future prices, and future prices, in turn, are contingent on present buy and sell decisions. Soros argues that to speak of supply and demand as if they were determined by forces that are independent of the market participants' expectations is misleading. The situation is not quite so clear-cut in the case of commodities, where supply is largely dependent on production and demand is dependent on consumption. But the price that determines the amounts produced and consumed is not necessarily the present price. On the contrary, market participants are more likely to be guided by future prices, either as expressed in futures markets or as anticipated by themselves. In either case, it is inappropriate to speak of independently given supply and demand curves because both curves incorporate the participants' expectations about future prices.[24]

In 1994, George Soros testified before Congress on the stability of the financial system and was also invited by Rudi Dornbusch to present "The Theory of Reflexivity" at the MIT Department of Economics World Economy Laboratory Conference in Washington, D.C., on April 26, 1994. Soros started by quoting the beginning of his testimony to Congress:

> *I must state at the outset that I am in fundamental disagreement with the prevailing wisdom. The generally accepted theory is that financial markets tend towards equilibrium, and on the whole, discount the future correctly. I operate using a different theory, according to which financial markets cannot possibly discount the future correctly because they do not merely discount the future; they help to shape it. In certain circumstances, financial markets can affect the so-called fundamentals which they are supposed to reflect. When that happens, markets enter into a state of dynamic disequilibrium and behave quite differently from what would be considered normal by the theory of efficient markets. Such boom/bust sequences do not arise very often, but when they do, they can be very disruptive, exactly because they affect the fundamentals of the economy.*

Soros went on to say he had not been able to expound his theory before Congress,

> *so I am taking advantage of my captive audience to do so now. My apologies for inflicting a very theoretical discussion on you.*[25]

## Behavioral Finance

Shefrin (2000) argues behavioral finance "is the application of psychology to financial behavior—the behavior of practitioners." Scott et al. (1999) group the universe of behavioral biases into two main categories: overconfidence and prospect theory. Behaviorists seek to replace the behaviorally incomplete theory of finance. They seek to understand and predict systematic financial market implications of psychological decision processes, while recognizing that the existing paradigm can be true within specified boundaries. Some suggest that the tenacity and the generality of many human decision attributes indicate that their roots lie in human evolution.[26]

> *Behavioral finance is part of science in that it starts from fundamental axioms and asks whether a theory built on these axioms can explain behavior in the financial marketplace. Contrary to some assertions, behavioral finance does not try to define rational behavior or label biased decision-making as biased or faulty; it seeks to understand and predict systematic financial market implications of psychological decision-making processes. In addition, behavioral finance is focused on the application of psychological and economic principles for the improvement of financial decision-making.[27]*

Olsen (1998) quoted the finding of Van Harlow that one's propensity to take risks can be known by measuring the level of a neurochemical called *monoamine oxidase* in one's blood. The due diligence of fund of funds managers does not yet include blood samples. Perhaps it should.

Behavioral finance is not as despised as praxeology or reflexivity. One could easily argue that behavioral finance is increasingly gaining acceptance and popularity. The author of *Irrational Exuberance*, Robert Shiller, is one of the leading figures in the field. Given the high degree of acceptance of Shiller's work, one could easily stipulate that behavioral finance is becoming an "orthodox unorthodox" economic discipline. The observation that excess volatility in the equity market is not based on fundamental uncertainty of future cash flows to investors, which was discussed by Shiller (1981, 1989), today is the consensus view by most investors and market observers.* Kahneman and Tversky's (1979) prospect theory is probably accepted by some economists. However, behavioral finance does not have a unified theory yet.

We have noted earlier George Soros' remarks with respect to his congressional testimony that hedge funds were actually stabilizing markets because they bet against trend-following (i.e., benchmarked) institutional investors. Economists used to think that idiosyncratic irrationality would not translate

---

*Behavioral finance appears to offer an explanation for what observers label excessive stock price volatility as discussed in Shiller (1981, 1989). Financial economists appear to agree that security price volatility and trading volume should vary directly with the divergence of opinion. At this point, standard finance is unable to explain a wide divergence of opinion except to invoke the concept of asymmetrical information. In public markets for widely traded securities, however, where asymmetries are likely to be small, it seems unlikely that differential information among investors could create the kind of divergence of opinion necessary to account for many instances of high stock-price volatility.

into market irrationality because it would take only a few rational investors to offset herd behavior. This economic view is in line with the EMH, which suggests that any irrational trading would soon be corrected through arbitrage and fast money. However, markets do not trade only on available news and rational responses. At times they reflect investors' irrational impulses. One personality factor influencing financial risk taking is "sensation-seeking."[28] Bernstein (1995) argues that human risk behavior has always been shaped by the environment of the period. Large parts of the 1990s were determined by a fun element—a personal factor influencing financial risk taking or, as Clements (1997) puts it: "People get pleasure from it [investing]. It's thrill-seeking behavior. People use investing the way other people go to concerts or to parties." The various investment infotainment programs on television, essentially discussing noise (statistically speaking), might be an indication that these views are not that far off.

Today's financial environment has become too complex to the extent that standard theories like the CAPM and the EMH are under attack. Bernstein (1995) pointed out that current classical capital ideas are "suspected of suffering from kurtosis, skewness, and other less familiar malignancies," and that they are under attack from the "nonlinear hypothesis" and "overwhelmed by fears of discontinuity rather than pricing volatilities and factors" and "frequently made irrelevant by exotic new financial instruments that come in unfamiliar shapes and hedge unfamiliar risks." Bernstein added, "As the mathematics that define these risks grow increasingly complex, the dimensions, contours and limits of risks are becoming correspondingly obscure." He concluded that the effort to abandon the beautiful and coherent logic of classical ideas does not mean that the classical ideas were in some sense "wrong," but rather it reflects on the changing environment in which we live today. In a world that is changing faster than we can grasp, risk seems more difficult to understand and control.[29] Paraphrasing John Maynard Keynes (again): "When circumstances change, I change my view. What do you do?"

**In Search of Mediocrity**   One of the interesting themes (among many) in behavioral finance is the discussion of overconfidence with market participants. Detecting overconfidence in combination with herding behavior and the resulting mean reversion process is probably one of the main goals of contrarians, value investors, and statistical arbitrageurs. It is difficult to believe that the bubble and burst of the technology sector in the 1960s as well as the 1990s is the function of a random walk.

The classic *In Search of Excellence: Lessons from America's Best Run Corporations* by Peters and Waterman (1982) is not necessarily a guide for investors. The book's authors (business consultants) took a list of companies regarded as innovative by a group of informed businesspeople, and screened them on the following six measures of long-run financial superiority:

1. Rate of growth in corporate assets.
2. Rate of growth in book value.
3. Average ratio of market price to book value.
4. Average return on corporate assets.
5. Average return on book value.
6. Average ratio of net income to sales.

The list of companies they came up with was regarded as fundamentally the best companies. In 1987 an article in the *Financial Analysts Journal* by Michelle Clayman was published in which the analyst tracked the performance of the stocks of these companies in a period following the ranking, 1981–1985. These firms had established strong records of performance prior to 1980. By 1980 they had become growth stocks. If the market overreacted and overpriced them, their performance after 1980 should have been poor as the market corrected and the prices of the stocks fell to more reasonable levels.

Clayman (1987) compares the performance of the "excellent" companies with another group she called "unexcellent." These were the 39 companies in the S&P 500 population that had the worst combination of the six characteristics as of the end of 1980. Between 1981 and the end of 1985 the excellent companies increased by 81.6 percent. However, the unexcellent group rose by 197.5 percent.

Clayman reveals that the stunning characteristics of the excellent companies quickly reverted toward the mean in the years that followed their 1980 screening. Rates of growth in assets and book value nearly halved. Significant reductions were experienced in the other four categories as well. The unexcellent companies also reverted toward the mean. They showed substantial improvement in their median values for all six categories. The market did not anticipate the mean reversion. In Clayman (1994) the author repeats the methodology of her previous work and finds that the "excellent" companies again outperformed as a group during 1988–1992, with a monthly alpha of 0.38 percent. Financial ratios of both "excellent" and "unexcellent" companies are again found to regress toward the mean. Other research has shown that this phenomenon also exists outside the U.S. stock market. Capaul, Rowley, and Sharpe (1993), for example, looked at annualized return differences between stocks in various international stock markets in the period from January 1982 to June 1992.

The *representativeness heuristic* and *overconfidence* can to some extent explain some stock market anomalies. Social scientists and behavioral finance theorists call the phenomenon representativeness heuristic, where most investors think that good stocks are the stocks of good companies, although the evidence indicates that the opposite is true. A further consequence of this heuristic is a tendency for people (e.g., chartists, astrologers) to see patterns in data that are truly random. The concept of representativeness heuristic is not new. It goes back to Tversky and Kahneman (1974), who introduced the term in the 1970s with respect to decision making under uncertainty.

Classical economic theory posits the notion of *rational expectation*: People are efficient information processors and act on that information. The classical theory does not assume that people know everything, but it does assume that they make good use of the information that is available to them and that their evaluation of the evidence is unbiased. Rational economic agents are supposed to make decisions in such a way as to maximize their utility. If the decision outcomes are uncertain, then utility is a random variable, so rational agents act to maximize their expected utility. Empirical evidence suggests, however, that people's judgments are often erroneous—and in a very predictable way. People are generally overconfident (Tversky 1995).

**Loss Aversion and Prospect Theory**   Tversky (1995) on loss aversion:

*Loss aversion—the greater impact of the downside than the upside—is a fundamental characteristic of the human pleasure machine.*

In 1738 Bernoulli suggested that, to evaluate risk, the weighted utility of wealth associated with each possible action is taken into consideration. *Expected utility theory* came a long way. However, because risk aversion does not hold in all cases, a different model from the classical model is called for. Today, *prospect theory* (as opposed to the standard model of expected utility) suggests that losses are weighted differently to gains. The S-shaped function of prospect theory has three features that distinguish it from the concave utility function of classical economic analysis:

1. It is defined in terms of gains and losses rather than in terms of asset position, or wealth. This approach reflects the observation that people think of outcomes in terms of gains and losses relative to some reference point, such as the status quo, rather than in terms of final asset position. Because people cannot lose what they do not have, classical economic theory does not address losses. The language of losses presupposes that people evaluate things relative to some reference point. The paradigm of relative returns fits nicely with expected utility theory. The paradigm of absolute returns fits nicely with prospect theory where avoiding losses matters disproportionately.
2. The second feature is that the value function is concave above the reference point and convex below it, which results in the characteristic S shape. This feature means that people are maximally sensitive to changes near the reference point. It also means that people are actually risk-seeking on the downside.

3. The third feature of the value function in prospect theory is that it is asymmetrical. The loss appears larger to most people than a gain of equal size. This characteristic is called loss aversion.

Kahneman and Tversky were not the first to challenge utility theory: Friedman and Savage (1948) proposed that the coexistence of the human tendency to gamble and risk avoidance might be explained by utility functions that become concave upward in extremely high range. Savage (1954) showed that the axioms from which expected utility theory is derived are undeniably sensible representations of basic requirements of rationality. Samuelson (1965a) explains the violation of expected utility theory. Although it proceded prospect theory, it illustrates the importance of the kink in the value function from Kahneman and Tversky.

For Shefrin (2000) there are two implications of investor overconfidence. First, investors take bad bets because they fail to realize that they are at an information disadvantage. Second, investors trade more frequently than is prudent, which leads to excessive trading volume.

**The Short Run and the Long Run**   In the long run there is mean reversion, as shown earlier. However, in the short run there is serial correlation.* Stocks with high returns over the past year tend to have high returns over the following three to six months. This phenomenon is called momentum effect, and a momentum strategy, as opposed to a contrarian strategy, buys the winners and sells the losers. Jegadeesh and Titman (1993) classified stocks as winners or losers, and then measured their subsequent relative performance for U.S. stocks for the period 1980–1989.

Winners were defined as the 10 percent of the stocks in their sample that had the best returns over the past six months, and losers were defined as the 10 percent with the worst returns. Apparently, the market was being pleasantly surprised by the earnings reports of the winners during these months and unpleasantly surprised by the losers. The market's surprises in the eight months that followed the trailing six reflect its failure to recognize that good reports foretell of a few more good ones to follow, and the bad reports foretell of bad ones to follow. The subsequent good or bad reports caught the market by surprise, and the winners outperformed the losers as they reported.

---

*Serial correlation is also referred to as autocorrelation and indicates a condition in which the random error terms in a sequence of observations are not independent (violation of serial independence).

## CONCLUSION

There is a case for active money management. Markets are unlikely to be fully efficient. The reason that most active large-cap equity managers underperform the benchmark does not mean that markets are efficient. It means that alpha is not symmetrically distributed among market participants searching for it. For example, it is unlikely that lemming effects, consensus hugging, and buying excellent companies (once everyone agrees they are excellent) lead to success. Market inefficiencies will likely be around for a while; and consequently so will sophisticated and trading-savvy market participants who exploit the inefficiencies by hedging unwanted risks.

# Risk and Opportunities of Absolute Return Strategies

# Classification and Performance of Hedge Funds

*If you think education is expensive, try ignorance.*
—Derek Bok (former Harvard President)

## DEFINING HEDGE FUND STYLES

One of the most important issues from an investor's perspective in terms of investing in hedge funds is knowledge about the different investment styles in the hedge fund industry. Equity investors are typically familiar with the fact that the equity market has different regions, sectors, and styles to invest in and that the different styles have different return, risk, and correlation characteristics. The same is true for alternative investment styles in general and for hedge funds in particular. Many absolute return strategies differ widely from the Alfred Jones model. Figure 5.1 shows one way of classifying the alternative investment (AI) universe.

One of the contemporary debates is whether hedge funds are a separate asset class. Viewing hedge funds as a separate asset class is probably the consensus view among institutional investors as of April 2002. However, Singer, Staub, and Terhaar (2001) make the point that the strategies executed by hedge funds are alternative strategies as opposed to an alternative asset class. Normally, investment vehicles with different risk, return, and correlation attributes are classified into different asset classes. This would suggest that

**179**

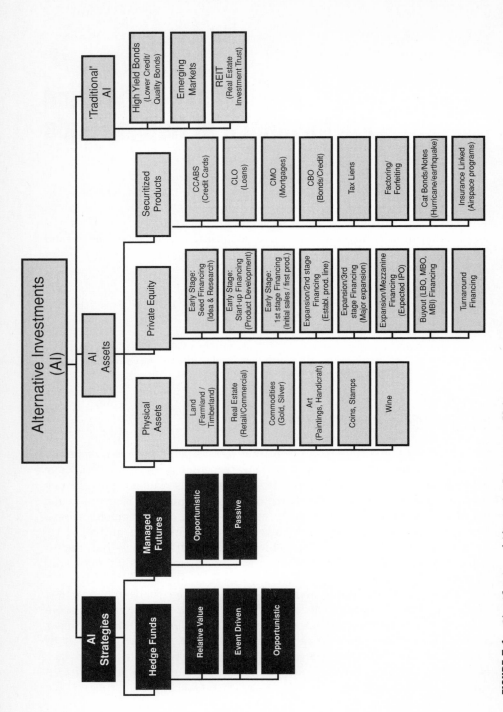

**FIGURE 5.1** Classification of Alternative Investments Universe
*Source: Partners Group*

hedge funds are a separate asset class, as their risk, return, and correlation attributes are different from those of equities and bonds. However, value and growth investing have different attributes but are not separate asset classes. One could argue that long-only, market-neutral, or long/short strategies are simply other investment styles (but not different asset classes), as are value, growth, and small-cap investing. The classification system in Figure 5.1 distinguishes between alternative investment strategies, alternative investment assets, and traditional alternative investments. This book is limited to the far left-hand side of Figure 5.1, hedge funds. Note that some investors classify managed futures as hedge funds as well.

Two of the main differences between hedge funds and other asset managers is, as mentioned earlier, their heterogeneity and the fact that hedge funds are less regulated. This means categorizing hedge funds is difficult and any classification is therefore subjective, inconsistent with some hedge fund data vendors, and incomplete. Any classification of hedge funds is an attempt at fitting something into a box that by its very nature does not fit into a box. However, classifying hedge funds is valuable despite the ambiguity and impreciseness. It allows ordering the investment universe and simplifies the construction of portfolios, and it means that any classification system must be used with knowledge of the imperfections.

In one respect hedge fund styles differ widely from styles and sectors in the equity arena. In equities, all sector and style indexes have a beta (exposure) to the market of around one. The betas of the different hedge fund styles vary from minus a multiple of one (short seller using leverage) to a multiple of plus one (long-biased fund using leverage). Figure 5.2 shows one way of segmenting the main hedge fund strategies into styles and substyles. This classification is the basis of Chapters 6 to 8.

Figure 5.2 first divides the universe in relative-value, event-driven, and opportunistic strategies. The logic behind this classification is that the directional bias increases from left to right. Note that the term "relative-value" is often used as synonym for "market-neutral." Strategies in this category are typically strategies that have very little or no exposure to the underlying equity or bond

| Relative-Value | Event-Driven | Opportunistic |
| --- | --- | --- |
| Convertible arbitrage | Risk arbitrage | Macro |
| Fixed income arbitrage | Distressed securities | Short selling |
| Equity market-neutral | | Long region, sector, or style |
|    Statistical arbitrage | | Emerging markets |
|    Fundamental arbitrage | | Long/short equity |

**FIGURE 5.2**  Classification System I
*Source:* UBS Warburg (2000).

market. The event-driven strategies in the middle section are essentially, as the name implies, strategies where the underlying investment opportunity and risk are associated with an event. In risk arbitrage (aka merger arbitrage*) this is normally an announced merger. In distressed securities this is a company in distress. The difference between the two is that the latter has a long bias whereas risk arbitrage does not.[†] The last category is called opportunistic. There are essentially all hedge fund styles that do not fit the narrower definitions of the other two categories. Macro and short selling, one would assume, have little in common. However, the distinguishing factors are that they do not fit in categories 1 or 2 and that most strategies under the category "opportunistic" have a directional bias.

An equity market-neutral fund is classified as relative-value. These fund managers are essentially averse to market risk. Any biases (especially market long bias but also to some extent sector or style tilts) are controlled—either hedged or actively monitored. The equity market-neutral category could be further divided into statistical arbitrage and fundamental arbitrage. The underlying theme of statistical arbitrage is mean reversion patterns in equity markets. The strategy is based on quantitative models for selecting specific stocks with equal dollar amounts comprising the long and short sides of the portfolio. Fundamental arbitrage seeks to profit by exploiting pricing inefficiencies between related equity securities where the active manager has a fundamental valuation view on the spread between two stocks. One example of this strategy is to build portfolios made up of long positions in the strongest companies in several industries while taking corresponding short positions in those showing signs of weakness. In Chapter 8 there is an attempt to shed some light on the confusion with respect to the difference between market-neutral and long/short.

The main bone of contention regarding the classification in Figure 5.2 is the labeling of long/short equity (aka equity hedge) as opportunistic. Long/short equity is arguably the oldest hedge fund strategy and also the largest style in terms of number of managers pursuing the strategy. However, the managers in this group are not homogeneous. Some have long biases, while others are market-neutral or short or vary over time. The managers in the long/short equity substyle who are close to market-neutral are effectively pursuing a relative-value strategy and therefore are closer to the equity market-neutral camp. For example, Schneeweis and Pescatore (1999) distinguish

---

*Some investors use the term "risk arbitrage" for what here is called "statistical arbitrage." What most market observers have in common is the misuse of the original term "arbitrage."

[†]However, Chapter 7 will show that the fat tails in risk arbitrage are highly correlated with dislocating markets, that is, fat tails in equity markets.

between five sectors (based on Evaluation Associates Capital Markets): relative value, event-driven, equity hedge, global asset allocators, and short selling. Long/short equity is a subsector of the relative-value sector. They define the equity hedge sector as long and short securities with varying degrees of exposure and leverage, such as domestic long equity (long undervalued U.S. equities, short selling is used sparingly), domestic opportunistic equity (long and short U.S. equities with ability to be net short overall), and global international (long undervalued global equities, short selling used opportunistically).

Figure 5.3 is another way of looking at the hedge funds universe. This classification represents some newer trends within the hedge fund industry. For example, there is a whole group dedicated to the asset class equities. This makes sense because throughout the 1990s there was an increase in the number of funds dedicated to equities. While in 1990 around 70 percent of funds under management were managed on a macro basis, at the end of 2001 long/short equity was the dominating factor with an allocation in this substrategy exceeding 50 percent of the $500 to $600 billion assets under management. The main reason for this expansion in long/short equity is the involvement of long-only managers in search of a professional career change. Long-only managers were launching long/short equity funds at an increasing rate as the markets started to tumble in mid-2000. These long/short equity funds were launched from within a traditional long-only shop* or by long-

---

*By some market participants disrespectfully dubbed "hedge fund lite."

| Arbitrage | Equities | Opportunistic |
|---|---|---|
| Relative-value | Style | Equities |
| Convertible arbitrage | Generalist vs. sector | Currencies |
| Statistical arbitrage | Value vs. growth | Commodities |
| Fixed income arbitrage | Market cap | Fixed income |
| Option volatility arbitrage | Geographic focus | Multistrategy/macro |
| Diversified relative-value | Market exposure | |
| Event-driven | Long (80% or more) | |
| Risk arbitrage | Long bias (20% to 80%) | |
| Distressed | Neutral (+/–40%) | |
| Diversified event-driven | Short bias (–20% to –60%) | |
| Multistrategy | Short (–60% or less) | |
| | Variable | |

**FIGURE 5.3**   Classification System II
*Source:* Grosvenor Capital Management.

only managers leaving firms and setting up shops themselves. The incentives to launch a long-only asset management firm are obvious: First, a hedge fund product is a high-margin product (typically 1 to 2 percent flat fee plus 15 to 25 percent incentive fee), while the traditional active long-only services are low-margin products by comparison (typically 15 to 50 basis points in the institutional arena). The second incentive was the observation that revenues from hedge fund fees are countercyclical to revenues from the long-only business: In a bull market, the latter increases; in a bear market (as was 2000–2001) there is an increase in revenues from the alternative investment products.

A further advantage of the classification in Figure 5.3 is the introduction of a subcategory for multistrategy funds for both the arbitrage category as well as the opportunistic category. This makes sense because these multistrategy funds have different volatility and correlation characteristics than do single-strategy funds. It also takes into account a recent trend in the industry where successful single hedge funds found themselves in the position of their business not being scalable. One way of exceeding the capacity of a fund is to expand into related areas. These are substrategies where a single strategy manager has synergies, that is, has the opportunity to obtain a competitive advantage at low cost.

A typical example is risk arbitrage and distressed securities. The research for both strategies has a strong legal/regulatory bias. In addition, both strategies to some extent are countercyclical. Risk arbitrage does well when the economy expands and the creativity of corporate financiers is at its peak (or the corporates' obligingness to buy into a good story is at a low). Distressed securities offer many investment opportunities when the economy contracts. The period 2000–2001 is a good example. The year 2000 was a record M&A year but 2001 was not (as a matter of fact quite the opposite). However, 2001 offered many investment opportunities on the distressed side. Bankruptcies soared.

A further combination is convertible arbitrage and risk arbitrage. The link between the two strategies lies not necessarily within similar fundamental drivers of the strategies. Synergies arise more from an incentive point of view: The worst-case scenario for a convertible bond (CB) arbitrage fund is a takeover situation where debt is put into the balance sheet of the acquiree. Since the traditional trade of CB arbitrage is long the bond and short the stock, the arbitrageur loses on both positions. On the one hand the stock, where the arbitrageur has a short position, of the company to be taken over increases, taking into account the premium paid by the predator. On the other hand, credit quality deteriorates, that is, credit spreads widen as a result of an increase in debt. Falling credit quality causes the CB to lose in value.*

---

*To some extent this might be balanced (in theory) or softened through an increase in implied volatility which increases the value of the bond. However, it is usually short-term implied volatility that spikes, while CBs are normally priced on medium-term implied volatility.

Schneeweis and Spurgin (2000) present an intuitive way of cataloging the hedge funds universe from the investors' perspective. (See Figure 5.4.) There are four main groups instead of only three as shown in Figure 5.2 and Figure 5.3. All four groups have different return, risk, and correlation characteristics. In addition, they serve different purposes. The first group are risk reducers—strategies with modest but stable returns that are regularly achieved without taking a lot of long-only (equities or duration) risk. This results in low correlation to equities and bonds. These characteristics have a risk-reducing effect on a portfolio comprised of equities and bonds. One negative aspect of this group is normally a high degree of excess kurtosis, that is, fat tails.*

---

*Note that a 5 percent loss of a convertible arbitrage manager with a 1 percent standard deviation of monthly returns is a six-sigma event (assuming mean return of 1 percent), that is, the frequency distribution of monthly returns will show the presence of negative outliers (excess kurtosis). Being exposed to six-sigma events on the downside often penalizes (relative-value) hedge fund managers. Little emphasis is put on the fact that the six-sigma event in convertible arbitrage is roughly a seven-hour move on a good day at the Nasdaq—in absolute return space, that is.

| Classification | Expected Return | Expected Volatility | Expected Correlation | Effect on Portfolio |
| --- | --- | --- | --- | --- |
| Relative-value | Low | Very low | Low | Risk reducer |
|    Equity market-neutral | Low | Very low | Low | Risk reducer |
|    Convertible hedge | Low | Very low | Low | Risk reducer |
|    Bond hedge | Low | Very low | Low | Risk reducer |
| Event-driven | Medium | Low | Low | Return enhancer |
|    Merger arbitrage | Medium | Low | Low | Return enhancer |
|    Bankruptcy | Medium | Low | Low | Return enhancer |
|    Multistrategy | Medium | Low | Low | Return enhancer |
| Equity hedge | High | Medium | Medium | Return enhancer |
|    Domestic long | High | Medium | High | Return enhancer |
|    Hedged equity | High | Medium | Medium | Return enhancer |
|    Global/international | High | Medium | High | Return enhancer |
| Global asset allocation | High | Medium | Medium | Total diversifier |
|    Discretionary | High | Medium | Medium | Total diversifier |
|    Systematic | High | Medium | Low | Total diversifier |
|    Short selling | Medium | Medium | Negative | Pure diversifier |

**FIGURE 5.4** Classification System III
*Source:* Adapted from Schneeweis and Spurgin (2000). The three middle columns are the author's own and not consistent with the text in Schneeweis and Spurgin.

Event-driven strategies and equity-related strategies are return enhancers. These strategies, according to Schneeweis and Spurgin (2000), have the purpose of enhancing the return of the portfolio (as opposed to reducing the volatility of the portfolio). Event-driven strategies in the past had lower returns, lower volatility, and lower correlation with equities than had equity-based non-neutral strategies such as long/short equity. Global asset allocations where considered as total diversifiers and short sellers as pure diversifiers, since their correlation with equities is most often negative (as opposed to just low).

The classification system in Figure 5.5 segments the universe of strategies into a matrix grid. The horizontal separation is by asset class and the vertical is subdivided into relative-value, directional, and hedge funds that use multiple strategies. As mentioned earlier, the separation between nondirectional (in Figure 5.5 referred to as relative-value) and directional is obvious, although the borderline might involve some gray areas. The separation between fixed income and equities also makes sense. In the future there is a possibility that in a risk-budgeting process institutional investors will substitute, for example, parts of their traditional (long-only) equity risk with nontraditional (long/short or market-neutral) equity risk. In the fixed income universe the same could happen: diversifying duration and credit risk with alternative fixed income strategies where the performance drivers are not only duration and credit. A further advantage of this classification system is that it creates a separate group for hedge funds that are involved in more than one single strategy.

Classifying event-driven strategies is difficult. In most classification systems event-driven strategies are shown as a separate group. The logic is that the risk is associated with an event (merger, company in distress, special situation, etc.). Another way of dicing the universe is by correlation characteristics and, therefore, diversification benefits to the investor. The classification system in Figure 5.5 does the latter. It classifies risk (merger) arbitrage and distressed securities in two separate boxes. This can be justified by the fact that distressed securities have a long bias whereas risk arbitrage has a long bias to a much smaller extent. However, not all strategies are easily categorized into traditional asset classes. Distressed securities, for example, are classified as fixed income but also are involved in the equity of a company. Convertible arbitrage is classified under equities but is essentially a hybrid between debt and equity, that is, a bond with an option on equity.

Figure 5.6 shows a classification system by index provider Morgan Stanley Capital International (MSCI) and hedge fund consultant Financial Risk Management (FRM). The indexes were officially launched in July 2002. It will be interesting to observe whether MSCI manages to introduce an industry standard once it starts flexing its muscle in the asset management industry. Currently there is no such thing as an industry standard. The reason for this is twofold: First, the industry throughout the 1990s was in an early stage of its industry maturity life

| | Fixed Income | Equities | Futures, Currencies, Commodities |
|---|---|---|---|
| **Relative-Value** | **Relative Value Fixed Income Strategies**<br>• Fixed income arbitrage<br>• Asset- and mortgage-backed securities | **Relative Value Equity Strategies**<br>• Convertible bond arbitrage<br>• Reg D private convertibles<br>• Index and options arbitrage<br>• Statistical arbitrage<br>• Market neutral long/short<br>• Equity arbitrage<br>• Merger arbitrage | **Relative Value Futures and Commodities Strategies**<br>• Commodities arbitrage |
| **Directional** | **Directional Fixed Income Strategies**<br>• Bank loans<br>• High yield bonds<br>• Distressed securities<br>• Emerging markets debt | **Directional Equity Strategies**<br>• Long/short U.S. equities<br>• Long/short European equities<br>• Long/short Japanese equities<br>• Long/short emerging markets<br>• Long/short sectors<br>• Short-biased equities<br>• Mutual fund timers | **Directional Managed Futures and Currency Strategies**<br>• Long-term systematic traders<br>• Short-term systematic traders<br>• Currency traders<br>• Discretionary managed futures |
| **Multiple** | | **Multiple Strategies:**<br>• Macro hedge funds<br>• Multistrategy funds<br>• Fund of funds | |

**FIGURE 5.5** Classification System IV
*Source:* Harcourt Investment Consulting AG (2002).

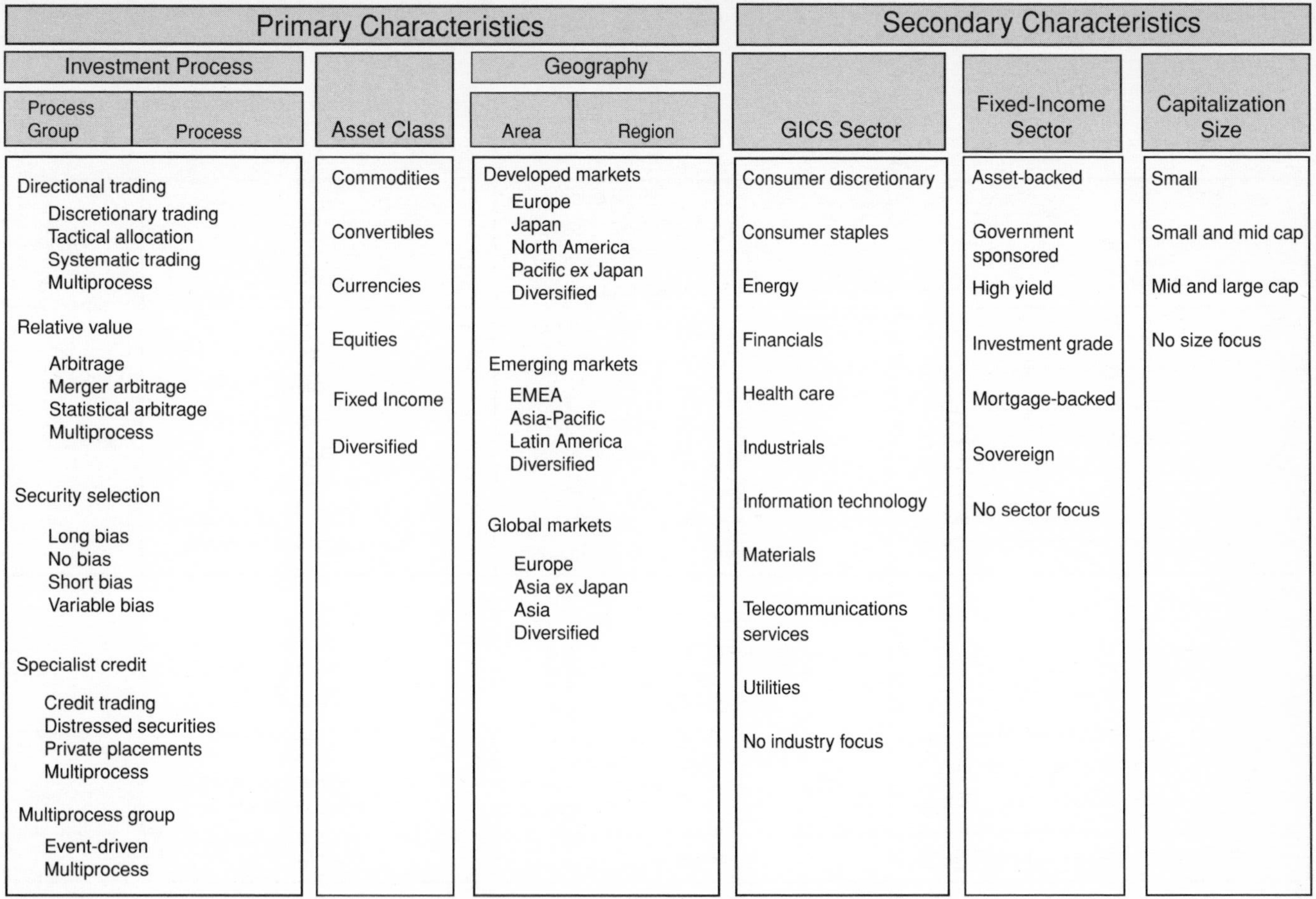

## Primary Characteristics

### Investment Process

| Process Group | Process |
|---|---|
| Directional trading | Discretionary trading |
| | Tactical allocation |
| | Systematic trading |
| | Multiprocess |
| Relative value | Arbitrage |
| | Merger arbitrage |
| | Statistical arbitrage |
| | Multiprocess |
| Security selection | Long bias |
| | No bias |
| | Short bias |
| | Variable bias |
| Specialist credit | Credit trading |
| | Distressed securities |
| | Private placements |
| | Multiprocess |
| Multiprocess group | Event-driven |
| | Multiprocess |

### Asset Class

- Commodities
- Convertibles
- Currencies
- Equities
- Fixed Income
- Diversified

### Geography

| Area | Region |
|---|---|
| Developed markets | Europe |
| | Japan |
| | North America |
| | Pacific ex Japan |
| | Diversified |
| Emerging markets | EMEA |
| | Asia-Pacific |
| | Latin America |
| | Diversified |
| Global markets | Europe |
| | Asia ex Japan |
| | Asia |
| | Diversified |

## Secondary Characteristics

### GICS Sector

- Consumer discretionary
- Consumer staples
- Energy
- Financials
- Health care
- Industrials
- Information technology
- Materials
- Telecommunications services
- Utilities
- No industry focus

### Fixed-Income Sector

- Asset-backed
- Government sponsored
- High yield
- Investment grade
- Mortgage-backed
- Sovereign
- No sector focus

### Capitalization Size

- Small
- Small and mid cap
- Mid and large cap
- No size focus

**FIGURE 5.6** MSCI Hedge Fund Classification System

*Source:* Morgan Stanley Capital International, Financial Risk Management.

cycle. This means that the evolution of the industry was too dynamic for one standard to gain acceptance. The second reason is that the process of institutionalization is fairly new. Throughout most of the 1990s only institutions that had pioneer status were involved in the hedge funds industry (see Chapter 1). Not until 2000–2001 was there a lemmings-like movement into hedge funds. Given that the hedge fund industry is moving along its evolutionary life cycle (maturing), the time for an industry standard could be just about right.

The first separation of the MSCI classification system is into primary and secondary characteristics. The secondary characteristics are adopted from the traditional investment equity and bond universe. The Global Index Classification System (GICS), currently in operation with MSCI and Standard & Poor's (S&P) indexes, is the first breakdown of stocks into sectors.

The main part of the classification system is by investment process where there are five main process groups. Most process groups have a multiprocess subgroup. This is in line with more recent changes in the industry. The basis for this distinction is that many older (and larger) hedge funds are using synergies and adding new strategies to their core strategies. This is true for directional as well as less directional or nondirectional hedge fund strategies. A further advantage of the classification is that it gives stock pickers its own group (security selection).

The remainder of Chapter 5 will summarize hedge fund performance by strategy. Chapters 6 to 8 will discuss risk and return by strategy in more detail.

## PERFORMANCE OF HEDGE FUNDS

Table 5.1 shows some annualized performance figures for a large sample of hedge funds strategies and substrategies. The first column measures the number of observation months ending December 2001, as some strategies have shorter histories. Most strategies, however, have 144 observation points for the 12-year period from January 1990 to December 2001. Those strategies can be compared with the top five rows that show performance characteristics of four equity indexes and one bond index. All monthly returns were total returns (including dividends) and in U.S. dollars.

Table 5.1 shows that it is pretty difficult to detect a hedge fund strategy with risk-adjusted returns inferior to the MSCI World index.* Only two indexes had a lower Sharpe ratio than the MSCI World. From the 33 strategies, 30 have higher Sharpe ratios than the S&P 500 index. Only nine strategies (from 33) have a lower maximal monthly drawdown than the 13.32 percent of the MSCI World. Eight strategies have a 12-month drawdown that is

---

*This statement is oversimplistic and will be corrected in Chapters 6 to 8.

**Table 5.1** Performance of HFRI Hedge Fund Universe

| | Number of Returns | Annual Return (%) | Volatility (%) | Sharpe Ratio (5%) | Highest 1M Loss (%) | Negative Months (%) | Worst 1Y Return (%) | Correlation with MSCI World | Correlation with JPM Bonds |
|---|---|---|---|---|---|---|---|---|---|
| S&P 500 (Total return) | 144 | 12.85 | 14.54 | 0.54 | −14.48 | 35 | −26.63 | 0.838 | 0.158 |
| MSCI World (Total return) | 144 | 6.99 | 14.59 | 0.14 | −13.32 | 40 | −27.87 | 1.000 | 0.295 |
| MSCI EAFE (Total return) | 144 | 2.70 | 17.03 | <0 | −13.91 | 43 | −28.27 | 0.936 | 0.351 |
| MSCI Europe (Total return) | 144 | 9.15 | 15.19 | 0.27 | −12.56 | 38 | −25.49 | 0.863 | 0.335 |
| JPM Global Bond Index (Total return) | 144 | 6.59 | 5.94 | 0.27 | −3.30 | 41 | −6.18 | 0.295 | 1.000 |
| HFRI Convertible Arbitrage Index | 144 | 11.88 | 3.41 | 2.02 | −3.19 | 13 | −3.84 | 0.301 | −0.015 |
| HFRI Distressed Securities Index | 144 | 15.21 | 6.41 | 1.59 | −8.50 | 19 | −6.41 | 0.342 | −0.157 |
| HFRI Emerging Markets (Total) Index | 144 | 14.34 | 16.31 | 0.57 | −21.02 | 35 | −42.52 | 0.614 | −0.063 |
| HFRI Emerging Markets: Asia Index | 144 | 8.54 | 14.21 | 0.25 | −12.07 | 40 | −30.85 | 0.592 | 0.007 |
| HFRI Emerging Markets: Eur/CIS Index | 92 | 17.99 | 36.32 | 0.36 | −38.59 | 40 | −69.45 | 0.427 | −0.235 |
| HFRI Emerging Markets: Global Index | 119 | 14.93 | 17.06 | 0.58 | −27.46 | 35 | −44.45 | 0.519 | −0.200 |
| HFRI Emerging Markets: Latin Am Index | 131 | 20.98 | 20.99 | 0.76 | −15.63 | 35 | −28.46 | 0.478 | −0.032 |
| HFRI Equity Hedge Index | 144 | 20.32 | 9.26 | 1.65 | −7.65 | 27 | −8.21 | 0.600 | 0.045 |
| HFRI Equity Non-Hedge Index | 144 | 17.33 | 14.91 | 0.83 | −13.34 | 34 | −21.66 | 0.698 | 0.032 |
| HFRI Equity Market-Neutral Index | 144 | 11.09 | 3.28 | 1.86 | −1.67 | 15 | 1.57 | 0.087 | 0.164 |
| HFRI Event-Driven Index | 144 | 20.58 | 9.33 | 1.67 | −7.65 | 26 | −4.76 | 0.591 | 0.067 |
| HFRI Fixed Income (Total) Index | 144 | 11.29 | 3.68 | 1.71 | −3.27 | 13 | −3.10 | 0.430 | −0.044 |
| HFRI Fixed Income: Arbitrage Index | 144 | 8.58 | 4.81 | 0.74 | −6.45 | 20 | −10.40 | 0.023 | −0.271 |
| HFRI Fixed Income: Convertible Bonds Index | 107 | 12.00 | 12.68 | 0.55 | −11.51 | 33 | −22.68 | 0.707 | −0.118 |
| HFRI Fixed Income: Diversified Index | 83 | 8.41 | 3.85 | 0.88 | −1.57 | 27 | −1.06 | 0.074 | 0.228 |
| HFRI Fixed Income: High Yield Index | 144 | 9.21 | 6.98 | 0.60 | −7.16 | 25 | −12.11 | 0.394 | −0.042 |
| HFRI Fixed Income: Mortgage-Backed Index | 107 | 10.57 | 4.79 | 1.16 | −9.24 | 11 | −9.84 | −0.035 | −0.140 |
| HFRI Macro Index | 144 | 17.76 | 8.87 | 1.44 | −6.40 | 31 | −7.10 | 0.443 | 0.085 |
| HFRI Market Timing Index | 144 | 14.72 | 6.91 | 1.41 | −3.28 | 33 | −3.26 | 0.649 | 0.098 |
| HFRI Merger Arbitrage Index | 144 | 12.18 | 4.56 | 1.58 | −6.46 | 10 | 0.44 | 0.381 | 0.049 |
| HFRI Regulation D Index | 71 | 19.27 | 7.28 | 1.96 | −3.97 | 21 | −11.24 | 0.116 | −0.147 |
| HFRI Relative Value Arbitrage Index | 144 | 13.72 | 3.88 | 2.24 | −5.80 | 12 | 1.13 | 0.338 | −0.074 |
| HFRI Sector (Total) | 144 | 22.51 | 14.32 | 1.22 | −13.00 | 26 | −24.63 | 0.533 | 0.028 |
| HFRI Sector: Energy Index | 84 | 28.51 | 21.93 | 1.07 | −11.75 | 37 | −37.08 | 0.313 | 0.158 |
| HFRI Sector: Financial Index | 120 | 21.92 | 12.64 | 1.34 | −18.66 | 25 | −17.68 | 0.418 | −0.043 |
| HFRI Sector: Health Care/Biotechnology Index | 108 | 22.18 | 23.95 | 0.72 | −17.73 | 39 | −18.33 | 0.291 | −0.047 |
| HFRI Sector: Miscellaneous | 132 | 18.45 | 10.60 | 1.27 | −7.57 | 30 | −12.61 | 0.132 | 0.062 |
| HFRI Sector: Real Estate Index | 94 | 10.98 | 6.56 | 0.91 | −2.50 | 37 | −0.81 | 0.046 | 0.032 |
| HFRI Sector: Technology Index | 132 | 23.35 | 20.72 | 0.89 | −15.16 | 37 | −37.50 | 0.611 | −0.007 |
| HFRI Short Selling Index | 144 | 1.99 | 23.22 | <0 | −21.21 | 50 | −38.01 | −0.642 | −0.030 |
| HFRI Statistical Arbitrage Index | 144 | 10.68 | 3.87 | 1.47 | −2.00 | 24 | −0.86 | 0.458 | 0.193 |
| HFRI Fund Weighted Composite Index | 144 | 15.91 | 7.32 | 1.49 | −8.70 | 26 | −6.41 | 0.661 | −0.009 |
| HFRI Fund of Funds Index | 144 | 11.14 | 6.07 | 1.01 | −7.47 | 25 | −6.63 | 0.421 | −0.083 |

*Source:* Hedge Fund Research, Datastream, author's own calculations.

worse than the drawdown of the MSCI World of 27.87 percent. Chapters 6 to 8 will go into more detail.

## Performance Attribution

Performance attribution is becoming more and more important to the fee-paying investor base. The distinction between performance attributable to beta and performance from alpha is, therefore also becoming increasingly important. Figure 5.7 shows the results of a study conducted by Fung and Hsieh (1997a) based on a sample of 3,327 U.S. mutual funds and 409 hedge funds/CTAs (commodity trading advisers). The authors compared the performance attribution of mutual funds with the performance attribution of hedge funds using nine asset classes: MSCI U.S. equity, MSCI non-U.S. equity, JPM U.S. government bonds, JPM government non-U.S. bonds, one-month eurodollar deposit, the U.S. dollar (Federal Reserve's Trade-Weighted Dollar Index), gold, IFC (International Finance Corporation) emerging markets, and high yield corporate bonds.

**Mutual Fund Performance Attribution and Style Analysis**  Fung and Hsieh ran style regressions for 3,327 open-ended mutual funds in the Morningstar database (updated through December 1995) that had at least 36 months of returns. Figure 5.7 summarizes the distribution of $R^2$s of the regressions. It shows that 47 percent of the mutual funds have $R^2$s above 75 percent, and 92 percent have $R^2$s higher than 50 percent. The two most statistically significant factors were U.S. equity and U.S. government bonds, as 87 percent of mutual funds were correlated to these two asset classes. In 99 percent of the funds,

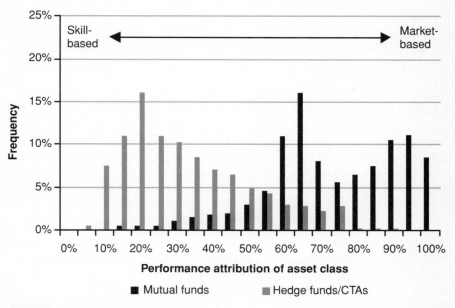

**FIGURE 5.7**  Performance Attribution
*Source:* Fung and Hsich (1997a). (Terms "skill-based" and "market-based" are not in original.)

the coefficients of the most significant asset class are positive. The authors note that the high correlation between mutual fund returns and standard asset class returns implies that choosing the style mix among mutual funds is similar to determining the asset mix in one's portfolio. The high level of correlation between mutual fund returns and asset classes indicates that mutual fund styles are basically buy-and-hold strategies utilizing various asset classes.

The regression was run on 406 hedge funds and CTA pools* that had at least 36 months of returns and at least $5 million in assets under management. While more than half the mutual funds have $R^2$s above 75 percent, nearly half (48 percent) of the hedge funds have $R^2$s below 25 percent. No single asset class is dominant in the regressions, unlike with mutual funds where U.S. equities and U.S. bonds are dominant. Unlike mutual funds, a substantial fraction (25 percent) of hedge funds are negatively correlated with the standard asset classes.

This is, obviously, not the full story. The flexibility comes at a cost. In addition, hedge fund returns are not normally distributed, adding an extra layer of complexity and calling for greater efforts in due diligence, portfolio construction, and risk monitoring.

The authors concluded that the evidence indicates that hedge funds are dramatically different from mutual funds. Mutual fund returns have high and positive correlation with asset class returns, which suggests that they behave as if deploying a buy-and-hold strategy. Hedge fund returns have low and sometimes negative correlation with asset class returns.

**Financial Literature on Performance and Performance Attribution**  Performance attribution is important for all investors. Understanding the links between investment styles and traditional asset classes is paramount in the way investment strategies are implemented and how they relate to overall portfolio efficiency. A lot of the academic work tries to find asset-based style factors to model hedge fund returns. Sharpe (1992) is most often the starting point. Sharpe's paper was intended to be an asset-class model that reduced the myriad mutual fund styles to a model involving only a limited number of major asset classes. The paper provides an explicit link between investment styles and traditional asset classes. Table 5.2 highlights some of the more recent research on hedge fund performance and performance attribution.

---

*Managed futures or CTA funds invest in listed financial and commodity futures markets and currency markets around the world. The managers are usually referred to as commodity trading advisers (CTAs). Trading disciplines are generally systematic or discretionary. Systematic traders tend to use price and market-specific information (often technical) to make trading decisions, while discretionary managers use a judgmental approach. Some market observers view CTAs as hedge funds, while others see them as a separate discipline.

**Table 5.2**  Selection of Papers on Hedge Fund Performance and Performance Attribution

| Authors | Title | Conclusions |
|---|---|---|
| **Schneeweis and Spurgin (1998)** | "Multi-Factor Analysis of Hedge Fund, Managed Futures, and Mutual Funds Return and Risk Characteristics" | In this study, a wide set of factors is used to describe return movement of both traditional stock and bond funds and managed futures and hedge fund investment. Results indicate that a different set of market factors explains returns of mutual funds, hedge funds, and managed futures investment, and that, correspondingly, each investment can contribute to a diversified portfolio. |
| **McCarthy and Spurgin (1998a)** | "A Comparison of Return Patterns in Traditional and Alternative Investments" | The authors find that over the time period analyzed (1990–1997), hedge funds offered risk-adjusted returns greater than traditional stock and bond investments. However, results also demonstrate that there are considerable differences in the relative performance of these hedge fund indexes. These differences are sizable enough that investors must realize that the use of seemingly similar benchmark hedge fund indexes may result in different asset allocation decisions. |
| **McCarthy and Spurgin (1998b)** | "A Review of Hedge Fund Performance Benchmarks" | The authors examine the benchmark composition and performance of three hedge fund indexes: Management Accounts reports, Hedge Fund Research, and Evaluation Associates Capital Management. Data from 1990 to 1997 indicates that these three indexes all have similar risk-adjusted returns but have significantly higher Sharpe ratios than selected equity and fixed income benchmarks. Furthermore, results indicate that correlation of hedge fund index returns with equity index returns is positive, depending on hedge fund strategy. |
| **Brown, Goetzmann, and Park (1999)** | "Conditions for Survival: Changing Risk and the Performance of Hedge Fund Managers and CTAs" | The authors investigated whether hedge fund and CTA return variance depends on whether the manager is doing well or poorly. Results show that managers whose performance is relatively poor increase the volatility of their funds, whereas managers whose performance is favorable decrease volatility. This is consistent with adverse incentives created by the existence of performance-based fee arrangements. A corollary of this theory is that managers whose performance contract is out-of-the-money should increase volatility most. The data simply does not support this further implication—managers whose returns are negative do not substantially increase volatility. In some years of the sample, the authors found that they even decrease the volatility of their funds' returns. Thus, while the data fits with certain conjectures derived from theory about investment manager compensation, it appears to contradict others.

The authors find that relative returns and volatility play a role in determining which funds survive. In addition, the longer a fund is in business, the less likely it is to fail. Since the managers' performance fee contracts die with the funds, it is perfectly reasonable that they should care about relative performance and avoid excess volatility. This is particularly true for young funds. Such funds are more likely to fail, other things being equal. |
| **Liang (1999)** | "On the Performance of Hedge Funds" | The author argues that empirical evidence indicates that hedge funds differ substantially from traditional investment vehicles, such as mutual funds. Hedge funds' special fee structures apparently align managers' incentives with fund performance. Funds with high-water marks significantly outperform those without. Hedge funds provide higher Sharpe ratios than mutual funds, and their performance in the period January 1992 through December 1996 reflects better manager skills, although hedge fund returns are more volatile. Average hedge fund returns are related positively to incentive fees, fund assets, and the lockup period.

The outperformance cannot be explained by survivorship bias. |

*(Continued)*

**Table 5.2**   *(Continued)*

| Authors | Title | Conclusions |
|---|---|---|
| **Agarwal and Naik (2000b)** | "Performance Evaluation of Hedge Funds with Option Based and Buy-and-Hold Strategies" | The authors examined the performance of hedge funds following different strategies using a generalized asset-class factor model consisting of excess returns on buy-and-hold strategies and passive option-based strategies. This model is able to explain a significant proportion of variation in hedge fund returns over time. The result of this study suggested that only 35% of the hedge funds have added significant value in excess of monthly survivorship bias of 0.30%. Performance varies over time; with 37% of the funds adding value in the early 1990s compared to 28% in the late 1990s. A comparison of averages and the distribution of alphas and information ratios of funds that use leverage with those that do not suggested that the two are statistically indistinguishable in a majority of cases. |
| **Mitchell and Pulvino (2001)** | "Characteristics of Risk and Return in Risk Arbitrage" | The authors studied a sample of 4,750 stock swap mergers, cash mergers and cash tender offers during 1963–1998 to determine the risk and reward characteristics associated with risk arbitrage. Furthermore, the authors examined the performance of a sample of active risk arbitrage hedge funds during 1990–1998. Results from both samples indicate that risk arbitrage returns are positively correlated with market returns in severely depreciating markets but uncorrelated with market returns in flat and appreciating markets. This risk arbitrage return profile is similar to those obtained from selling uncovered index put options. As such, risk arbitrage may be better evaluated using a contingent claims analysis rather than a linear asset pricing model such as the CAPM. Overall, results indicate that risk arbitrage generated excess annual returns of roughly 400 basis points. |
| **Amin and Kat (2001)** | "Hedge Fund Performance 1990–2000: Do the Money Machines Really Add Value?" | The authors analyzed the performance of 77 hedge funds and 13 hedge fund indexes over the period May 1990 to April 2000. Their results show that hedge funds do not offer a superior risk return profile as a stand-alone investment. Hedge funds score much better when seen as part of an investment portfolio. Due to their weak relationship with the index, 7 of the 12 hedge fund indexes and 58 or the 72 individual funds classified as inefficient on a stand-alone basis are capable of producing an efficient payoff profile when mixed with the S&P 500. The best results are obtained when 10 to 20% of the portfolio value is invested in hedge funds.<br><br>A sample of U.K. equity mutual funds studied shows levels of inefficiency that far exceed those of the hedge funds. Given that hedge funds charge higher fees and are unlikely to be better diversified or to incur lower transaction costs than mutual funds, this suggests that hedge fund managers tend to be more skilled than mutual fund managers. |
| **Fung and Hsieh (2001a)** | "Asset-Based Hedge Fund Styles and Portfolio Diversification" | The authors extend the Sharpe style model, which is intended to be an asset-class model that reduces the myriad mutual fund styles to a model involving only a limited number of major asset classes to account for return characteristics of hedge funds. Results showed that hedge fund strategies with a directional component could be modeled with long-only asset-based style factors in the form of conventional indexes. This methodology explained more than 50% of the observed variance in hedge fund returns. Due to the optionlike return characteristics of hedge funds, techniques incorporating nonlinear return and risk patterns are required to improve on the explanatory power of this model. |

**Table 5.2**  *(Continued)*

| Authors | Title | Conclusions |
|---|---|---|
| **Fung and Hsieh (2001b)** | "The Risk in Hedge Fund Strategies: Theory and Evidence from Trend Followers" | Due to the option like return distribution of hedge funds strategies, the explanatory power of linear factor models using benchmark asset indexes is limited at best. The authors show how to model hedge fund returns by focusing on the popular trend-following strategy. By using look-back straddles to model trend-following strategies, the authors show that look-back straddles can explain trend-following returns better than standard asset indexes. The first implication of this study is that trend-following funds do have systematic risk not observable with standard asset benchmarks. The second implication is that trend followers, or a portfolio of look-back straddles on foreign exchange, bonds, and commodities, can reduce the volatility of a typical stock and bond portfolio during extreme market downturns. The authors suggest that the model is useful in the design of performance benchmarks for trend-following funds. |
| **Edwards and Caglayan (2001)** | "Hedge Fund Performance and Manager Skill" | Using data on the monthly returns of hedge funds during the period 1990 to 1998, the authors estimate six-factor Jensen alphas for individual hedge funds employing eight different investment styles. Result shows that 25% of hedge funds earn positive excess returns, and the frequency and magnitude of funds' excess returns differ markedly by investment style. Performance persistence was found for both winners and losers. The excess return is partially attributable to the skill of hedge fund managers. |
| **Caglayan and Edwards (2001)** | "Hedge Fund and Commodity Fund Investment Styles in Bull and Bear Markets" | A primary motivation for investing in hedge funds and commodity funds is to diversify against falling stock prices. The authors evaluate the performance of 16 different such funds during rising and falling stock markets between 1990 and 1998 both as stand-alone assets and as portfolio assets. They use the Sharpe ratio and alternative safety-first criteria to evaluate performance. The conclusion is that commodity funds generally provide more downside protection than hedge funds. Commodity funds have higher returns in bear markets than hedge funds, and generally have an inverse correlation with stock returns in bear markets. Hedge funds typically exhibit a higher positive correlation with stock returns in bear markets than in bull markets. Three hedge fund styles—market-neutral, event-driven, and global macro—provide fairly good downside protection, with more attractive returns over all markets than commodity funds. |
| **Schneeweis and Martin (2001)** | "The Benefits of Hedge Funds: Asset Allocation for the Institutional Investor" | The authors argue that hedge funds offer unique opportunities to (1) reduce overall portfolio volatility; (2) enhance portfolio returns in economic environments in which traditional stock and bond investments offer limited opportunities and in which even other alternative investment vehicles do not provide similar returns; and (3) participate in a wide variety of new financial products and markets not available in traditional investor products. |
| **Brooks and Kat (2001)** | "The Statistical Properties of Hedge Fund Returns and Their Implications for Investors" | The authors find that the monthly return distribution of many hedge fund indexes exhibit highly unusual skewness and kurtosis properties as well as first-order serial correlation. Authors demonstrate that although hedge fund indexes are highly attractive in mean-variance terms, this is much less the case when skewness, kurtosis, and autocorrelation are taken into account. Sharpe ratios will substantially overestimate the true risk-return performance of (portfolios containing) hedge funds. Similarly, mean variance portfolio analysis will overallocate to hedge funds and overestimate the attainable benefits from including hedge funds in an investment portfolio. Authors also find huge differences between hedge fund indexes and argue that investors' perceptions of hedge fund performance and value added will therefore strongly depend on the indexes used. |

*(Continued)*

**Table 5.2** *(Continued)*

| Authors | Title | Conclusions |
|---------|-------|-------------|
| **Amin and Kat (2002a)** | "Portfolios of Hedge Funds: What Investors Really Invest In" | Using monthly returns data over the period June 1994 to May 2001, the authors investigate the performance of randomly selected baskets of hedge funds ranging in size from 1 to 20 funds. The analysis shows that increasing the number of funds can be expected to lead only to lower standard deviation but also, and less attractively, to lower skewness and increased correlation with the stock market. Holding more than 15 funds changes little. The population average appears to be a good approximation for the average basket of 15 or more funds. With 15 funds, however, there is still a substantial degree of variation in performance among baskets, which dissolves only slowly when the number of funds is increased. Based on efficiency tests the authors recommend one needs to combine only a small number of funds to obtain a substantially more efficient risk return profile than that offered by the average individual hedge fund. |
| **Amin and Kat (2002b)** | "Who Should Buy Hedge Funds? The Effects of Including Hedge Funds in Portfolios of Stocks and Bonds" | Using monthly returns data on 455 hedge funds over the period 1994–2001, the authors studied the diversification effects from introducing hedge funds into a traditional portfolio of stocks and bonds. The results indicate that although the inclusion of hedge funds may significantly improve a portfolio's mean variance characteristics, it can also be expected to lead to significantly lower skewness as well as higher kurtosis. The authors argue that this means that the case for hedge funds includes a trade-off between profit and loss potential and suggests that hedge funds might be more suitable for institutional than for private investors. The results also emphasize the fact that to have at least some impact on the overall portfolio, one has to make an allocation to hedge funds that exceeds the typical 1% to 3% that many institutions are currently considering. |
| **Fung and Hsieh (2002)** | "Benchmarks of Hedge Fund Performance: Information Content and Measurement Biases" | This paper revolves around the information content and potential measurement biases in hedge fund benchmarks. Hedge fund indexes built from a database of individual hedge funds will suffer from measurement biases. The authors argue that the most direct way of measuring hedge fund performance is to observe the investment experience of hedge fund investors themselves. In terms of measurement biases, returns of funds of hedge funds can deliver a better estimate of investment experience of hedge fund investors. In terms of risk characteristics, indexes of funds of funds are more indicative of the demand side dynamics driven by investor preference of hedge funds. The authors conclude that indexes of funds of hedge funds can provide additional valuable information to the assessment of the performance of the hedge fund industry. |
| **Brunel (2002)** | "Absolute Return Strategies Revisited: Does a Higher Observed Correlation Really Change the Case?" | The author notes that research on absolute return strategies is based on the bull market of the 1990s and examines whether the low-volatility and low correlation characteristics still hold after dismal equity years of 2000 and 2001. One of the conclusions is that the case for including absolute return strategies in diversified portfolios is still solid based on return and risk arguments, but not as strong as previously thought in terms of overall diversification potential. The author also notes that lower expected returns would be a natural consequence of rising capacity issues and higher manager failures. |

## Performance Persistence

The persistence of manager performance is important. In most countries the tobacco industry has to put a disclaimer on their advertisements and products, warning the buyer of side effects from smoking (e.g., lung cancer, premature death, etc.). Every advertisement and product term sheet in the financial services industry also includes a disclaimer.* The side effects are (most often) financial and not medical in nature. The most prominent part is the warning that "past performance is no guarantee for future performance." This is, as most investment professionals will agree, true. In the United States, the Association of Investment Management and Research (AIMR) suggests asset managers to adopt their Performance Presentation Standards (PPS) which give the buyer a certain comfort level that the publicized figures met certain predefined minimum criteria. In the United Kingdom the Financial Services Authority (FSA) even went as far as starting a debate whether financial services firms should continue to be allowed to publicize (meaningless) historical performance data.

**Financial Literature on Performance Persistence**　　Table 5.3 lists some papers on performance persistence. The research on mutual funds primarily finds mean reversion patterns (winners become losers and losers become winners). The research on hedge funds seems to be controversial. The research seems to have found a consensus with respect to the losers but not for winners. Both Agarwal and Naik (2000a,c) and Edwards and Caglayan (2001) found that losers had a tendency to remain losers. However, there is less evidence, it seems, that winners have a tendency to remain winners. Edwards and Caglayan argue that there is persistence with both winners and losers, whereas Agarwal and Naik argue that the persistence with winners is less clear than with losers. In one respect most (but not all) research is conclusive: Manager selection is important.

---

*Occasionally the length of a financial disclaimer is viewed as an indication of risk; the longer the disclaimer, the higher the risk. This is unlikely to be true. The length of the disclaimer is correlated with the complexity of the product (or, in the cynic's view, negatively correlated with the sophistication of the regulator), not with risk.

**Table 5.3**    Selection of Papers on Hedge Fund Performance Persistence

| Authors | Title | Conclusions |
|---|---|---|
| Schneeweis (1998c) | "Evidence of Superior Performance Persistence in Hedge Funds: An Empirical Comment" | The author notes that considerable research exists on performance persistence among traditional stock and bond fund managers. Unfortunately, little evidence exists on the ability of traditional managers to consistently outperform other managers of similar style. One may hope that alternative fund managers may do better. The author finds that for the sample of hedge fund managers analyzed, the ability of certain managers to show consistent superior performance is limited. If the results hold true for a wider set of analyses, then asset allocation becomes of increasing interest. |
| Agarwal and Naik (2000a) | "Multi-Period Performance Persistence Analysis of Hedge Funds" | The authors examined the extent of before-fee and after-fee performance persistence exhibited by hedge funds during 1982 to 1998 using the traditional two-period framework and contrasted the findings with those observed using a multiperiod framework. Given the significant lockup period with hedge funds, the authors also examined if persistence observed is sensitive to whether the returns are measured over quarters or over years. Results suggest that there exists a considerable amount of persistence at a quarterly horizon, which decreases as one moves to yearly returns, indicating that persistence among hedge fund managers is primarily short-term in nature. Whenever persistence is observed, it is mainly driven by losers continuing to be losers instead of winners continuing to be winners. The authors also find that persistence seems to be unrelated to the type of strategy followed by the fund. |
| Agarwal and Naik (2000c) | "On Taking the 'Alternative' Route: The Risks, Rewards, and Performance Persistence of Hedge Funds" | The risk-return characteristics, risk exposures, and performance persistence of various hedge fund strategies remains an area of interest to alternative asset investors. Using a database on hedge fund indexes and individual hedge fund managers in a mean-variance framework, the results show that a combination of alternative investments and passive indexing provides a significantly better risk return trade-off than passively investing in the different asset classes. Moreover, using parametric and nonparametric methods, a reasonable degree of persistence is found for hedge fund managers. This seems to be attributable more to the losers continuing to be losers instead of winners continuing to be winners, highlighting the importance of manager selection in case of hedge funds. |
| Brown and Goetzmann (2001) | "Hedge Funds with Style" | The authors studied the monthly return history of hedge funds during 1989 to 2000 and find that there are at least eight different distinct styles of management. Results show that the persistence of fund returns from year to year has a lot to do with the particular style of fund management and that 20% of the variability of fund returns can be explained solely by the style of management. The authors concluded that appropriate style analysis and style management are critical success factors for investors looking to invest in the hedge fund market. |
| Edwards and Caglayan (2001) | "Hedge Fund Performance and Manager Skill" | Performance persistence was found for both winners and losers. The excess return is partially attributable to the skill of hedge fund managers. |

# CHAPTER 6

# Relative-Value and Market-Neutral Strategies

*History may not repeat itself. But it will definitely rhyme.*
—Doug Case*

## INTRODUCTION

This class of investment strategy seeks to profit by capitalizing on the mispricings of related securities or financial instruments. Generally, relative-value and market-neutral strategies avoid taking a directional bias with regard to the price movement of a specific stock market. This investment style is most appealing for investors who are looking for moderate but stable returns accompanied by low correlation to the equity market (see Table 6.1).

Relative-value and market-neutral strategies rely on identifying mispricings in financial markets. A spread is applied when an instrument (equity, convertible bond, equity market, etc.) deviates from its fair value and/or historical norm. Relative-value strategies can be based on a formula, statistics, or fundamental analysis. These strategies are engineered to profit

---

*Chief investment officer of Advanced Investment Technology, on the firm's stock-picking method (Quote of the Week, *Alternative Investment News*, No. 32, September 2001).

**Table 6.1**   Summary Risk/Return Characteristics Based on Historical Performance

| Subsector | Returns | Volatility | Downside Risk | Sharpe Ratio | Correlation to Equities | Leverage | Investment Horizon |
|---|---|---|---|---|---|---|---|
| Convertibles arbitrage | Medium | Low | Low | High | Medium | High | Medium |
| Fixed income arbitrage | Low | Low | Medium | Low | Low | High | Medium |
| Equity market-neutral | Medium | Low | Low | High | Low | Medium | Medium |

*Source:* UBS Warburg (2000).

if and when a particular instrument or spread returns to its theoretical or fair value.

To concentrate on capturing these mispricings, these strategies often attempt to eliminate exposure to significant outside risks so that profits may be realized if and when the securities or instruments converge toward their theoretical or fair value. The ability to isolate a specific mispricing is possible because each strategy should typically include both long and short positions in related securities. In most cases, relative-value strategies will likely seek to hedge exposure to risks such as price movements of the underlying securities, market interest rates, foreign currencies, and the movement of broad market indexes.

Disciples of the efficient market hypothesis (EMH) argue that the constant higher risk-adjusted returns of some hedge fund managers are derived from a faulty methodology with respect to accounting for risk. In perfectly efficient capital markets, the active management premium will be zero because active managers will earn only enough incremental investment returns to offset the fees they charge. The appendix of Chapter 4 expressed what may be becoming the consensus—essentially that the EMH is a handy theoretical concept to explain to first-year graduates the principles of information flow and capital markets. Or as Lawrence Summers puts it:

*The efficient market hypothesis is the most remarkable error in the history of economic theory.*[1]

The basic idea behind relative-value or arbitrage investing is to make money by finding relationships between securities by combining skill, discipline, and a sound investment process. It is with the last-noted where some market observers have some difficulty. If one believes that markets are fully information efficient, any excess return must be a function of chance. There are two issues with this view. The first was discussed in the appendix to Chapter 4: that markets are probably not perfectly information efficient, but rather semiefficient. The second issue is with respect to investment professionals having an edge over academia and the rest of the market. Weinstein (1931) explained how to exploit market inefficiencies with convertible securities* long before Samuelson (1965b) discussed the theory behind warrant pricing† and Thorp and Kassouf (1967) made money by trading options long before Black and Scholes (1973) formalized the relationship between the cash and options markets.‡ Not to appear too cynical, but there is the possibility that there are market participants who uncover systematic investment opportunities that disappear once they are in the public domain or discussed in peer-refereed journals.

Another argument brought against some relative value strategies is that opportunities are limited; there is a capacity constraint. Hedge fund excess returns will diminish as soon as a discipline reaches a capacity limit. With respect to capacity constraints, here is a market comment from 1931:

> *The last few years have been marked by steadily increasing arbitrage opportunities and arbitrage profits. Between 1927 and 1930 alone over five billion dollars ($5,000,000,000.00) worth of equivalent securities§ were placed on the market. In the same years the profits to the arbitrageurs totaled many millions of dollars. The year 1929 was perhaps the most profitable year in arbitrage history, but each year has yielded its quota of profits. Even the year 1930, which was marked by steadily declining prices, yielded excellent profits.[2]*

This market comment highlights two aspects, or, conversely, two misconceptions of investing in hedge funds. These are:

1. Arbitrage is not a new concept.§§ Mispriced derivatives and the exploitation of market inefficiencies by risk managers have been features of the industry for centuries. Weinstein (1931) puts the start date for arbitrage at around four centuries before the Christian era. Arbitrage in money and bills of exchange probably had its origin when the crude coins of one nation were exchanged for those of another.

---

*In Thorp and Kassouf (1967) convertible securities were defined as securities that could be changed into other securities, such as convertible bonds, warrants, options, puts and calls, convertible preferreds, and rights.

†This is slightly unfair, as the work of Paul Samuelson goes further back than 1965.

‡Note that Edward Thorp was cofounder of Princeton/Newport (see Chapter 1) as well as a former math professor of Michael Milken. From Fischel (1995).

§Equivalent securities is a predecessor term for convertible securities.

§§The term "arbitrage" has lost its original meaning of a simultaneous purchase and sale of the same or equivalent securities, commodities, or foreign exchange in different markets to profit from unequal price. Today nearly anything that involves a spread is referred to as arbitrage. For example, what was called "pair trading" in the 1980s was called "statistical arbitrage" in the 1990s.

2. Relative-value strategies can do well in falling markets, too. One of the criticisms of hedge fund investing in the 1990s was that hedge fund investing was a child of the 1990s bull market and therefore a bubble about to burst. The 2000–2001 experience defused the criticism. Market panic is full of opportunities for the arbitrageur. The 1929–1930 period was the worst in U.S. stock market history and arbitrageurs made money. The reason is that panic results in market inefficiencies and creates investment opportunities for the sophisticated, rational, and disciplined absolute return investor. When the majority of the market participants panic, alternative money managers eventually make money. Correlation in down markets will be quantified later in the book.

Lo and MacKinlay (1999) argue, for example, that the early profits by statistical arbitrageurs are not necessarily derived from the fact that markets were inefficient. They make the point that profits in statistical arbitrage can be viewed as:

> *economic rents that accrued to their [statistical arbitrageurs'] innovation, creativity, perseverance, and appetite for risk. Now that others have begun to reverse engineer and mimic their technologies, profit margins are declining.*[3]

The highlighted issue is one of the problems of relative-value strategies. Once the market has moved up the learning curve, the opportunity is gone. A flood of capital erodes the opportunity. This means that the investor not only invests in a manager executing an existing trade, but also has to evaluate whether the manager has the skill and energy to find new opportunities in the manager's field of expertise. Schumpeter's "creative destruction" also applies for capital markets.

The following three sections analyze three relative-value strategies, namely convertible arbitrage, fixed income arbitrage, and equity market-neutral strategies.

## CONVERTIBLE ARBITRAGE

### Strategy

At the most general level, convertible arbitrage is about exploiting market inefficiencies in the convertibles market by hedging equity, duration, and credit risks. Convertible arbitrage is the trading of related securities whose future relationship can be reasonably predicted. Convertible securities are usually either convertible bonds, warrants, or convertible preferred shares, which are most often exchangeable into the common stock of the company issuing the convertible security. The managers in this investment category attempt to buy undervalued instruments that are convertible into equity and then hedge out the market risks. Fair value is based on the optionality in the convertible bond and the manager's assumption of the input variables, namely the future volatility of the stock. This strategy is distinguished by the relationship between two securities that specifies exactly how one security can be converted into the other. This formula-based relationship provides a theoretical limit on the price spread between these securities.

Hedge Fund Research, Inc. estimates that convertible arbitrage was around 3.89 percent of the $537 billion of assets under management at the end of 2001 (i.e., around $21 billion). This estimate is probably rather at the low end, as some of the larger convertible arbitrageurs are not covered by hedge fund data providers. In addition, proprietary trading books of investment banks execute the identical strategy with balance sheet money. The total convertible bond market at the end of 2001 was around $600 billion. One estimate for the split among hedge funds, proprietary trading, and long-only accounts is 20:20:60. This would mean that hedge funds hold around $120 billion of convertibles, which would imply a leverage of around 5.7 times capital. Note that proprietary accounts (trading "infinite" balance sheet money) can lever more strongly than can hedge funds.

Most managers view the discounted price of the convertible in terms of underpriced volatility, and use option-based models both to price the theoretical value of the instrument and to determine the appropriate delta hedge. The risk is that volatility will turn out lower than expected. Other managers analyze convertibles using cash flow based models, seeking to establish positive carry positions designed to achieve a minimum level of return over their expected lives. (See Table 6.2.)

Although convertible arbitrage is technical (its basis for putting on a trade is a mathematical formula) it involves experience and the skill of its managers. Interviewed in MAR/Hedge in February 1997, Gustaf Bradshaw, at the time director of research of the BAII Funds, said:

> *The art of the convertible arbitrageur . . . lies in the calculation of the amount of underlying equity that should be sold short against the local convertible position. This ratio can be adjusted depending on a manager's market view and so there is a large element of personal skill involved. This is an area where the skill and experience of the portfolio managers are vital because the computer systems are there to be overridden by the managers. Liquidity is one of the constraints in trading convertibles or warrants. You can often see great opportunities but no exit.*[4]

**Table 6.2**   Key Risk Factors in Convertible Arbitrage

| Risk | Position | Effect |
|------|----------|--------|
| **Interest rates** | Long convertible bond (long duration, long convexity) | Convertible bonds, like regular bonds, move inversely with changes in interest rates. To some extent the short equity position is a natural hedge against rising interest rates since equities generally also move inversely to interest rates. Arbitrageurs can use Treasury futures or interest rate swaps to manage interest rate risk. |
| **Equity** | Short stock (neutral delta, long vega, long gamma) | The delta of the convertible bond is normally hedged through selling stock short resulting in a delta neutral position. The strategy is long equity volatility (long vega) through the optionality in the convertible bond. The strategy is also, although less significantly, long gamma: The position delta increases when the stock rises and vice versa. Vega and gamma risk are difficult to hedge (since strike and often maturity are unknown) and therefore are most often left unhedged. |
| **Correlation** | Long bond-equity correlation | The strategy is long correlation: If interest rates rise, losses on the long bond are reduced through gains on the short equity. If interest rates fall, losses on short equity are reduced through gains on the bond. This natural hedge does not work when correlation is low, for example when interest and stocks rise and bonds fall. |
| **Credit** | Long convertible, short equity | Being debt or preferred instruments, convertible bonds have an advantage to the common stock in case of distress or bankruptcy (exchangeables have different credit risk characteristics than plain-vanilla convertibles). If the securities are debt, they have a termination value that must be paid at maturity, or bankruptcy may occur. If preferred, they have a liquidation value. There is less risk in holding the convertible because it has seniority in payment. |
| | | To some extent, convertible arbitrageurs sell economic disaster insurance because they usually are short the credit spread similar to fixed income arbitrageurs. In an economic disaster, credit spreads widen and investors short the spread lose money. Additionally, liquidity dries up, worsening the situation. The result is a few but high standard deviation negative returns. Today, convertible arbitrageurs hedge credit risk along with equity and duration risk. Convertible arbitrageurs can use asset swaps to strip out the credit risk from convertible bonds. |
| **Prospectus/legal risk** | Long convertible | There have been cases where it has paid to read the prospectus in great detail, for example with respect to the treatment of dividends (Daimler's special dividend 1998). In addition there is regulatory risk (Japan's Ministry of Finance [MOF] ruling in 1998). |
| **Liquidity** | Short equity, long convertible bond | Convertible arbitrage is exposed to liquidity risk in the form of potential short squeezes in equities, or bid/ask spread in convertible bonds widening, or borrowing cost of short equity increasing. |

*Source:* UBS Warburg (2000).

In theory, convertible arbitrage is a relative-value strategy. The concept of the classic trade is to exploit a market inefficiency (and/or benefit from cheap issuance). However, convertible arbitrageurs can hedge imperfectly and be long delta to express a view on the underlying market or stock. To some, the high risk-adjusted returns of convertible arbitrage are partially attributable to most convertible arbitrages having a positive delta in the bull market of the 1990s. However, this theory is blatantly contradicted by the record profit of convertible arbitrageurs during the 2000 and 2001 bear market.

The degree of leverage used in convertible arbitrage varies significantly with the composition of the long positions and the portfolio objectives, but generally ranges between 2 and 10 times equity. Interest rate risk can be hedged by selling government bond futures. In most recent years, credit risk was often hedged in the burgeoning credit default swap market. Typical strategies include:

- Long convertible bond and short the underlying stock.
- Dispersion trade by being long volatility through the convertible bond positions and short index volatility through index options.
- Convertible stripping to eliminate credit risk.
- Arbitraging price inefficiencies of complicated convertible bonds and convertible preferred stocks with various callable, putable, and conversion features (such as mandatory conversion, conversion factors based on future dividend payments, etc.).
- Buying distressed convertible bonds and hedging by selling short the underlying equity by hedging duration risk.

One of the primary issues in convertible arbitrage over the past three years has been credit risk. The primary tools used to hedge credit risk of a convertible bond are default swaps and callable asset swaps. These instruments are part of a large and growing market in credit derivatives. Growth in this market has been driven by several factors, but the main one is the use by banks to remove credit risk from their loan portfolios and improve capital funding ratios. Banks are natural sellers of credit risk (or buyers of credit protection). The ability to isolate the credit exposure of the issuer allows convertible arbitrage managers to focus on their areas of expertise. Some managers may have expertise in evaluating the company's fundamentals and can add value by identifying cheap credits as well as cheap volatility. Others may prefer to avoid credit risk and focus solely on identifying cheap volatility. By being able to hedge away credit risk, the managers can buy bonds of an issuer that a more credit-oriented manager would avoid.

With a default swap, a holder of a bond trading at par can buy protection from default by entering into a default swap whereby, in exchange for a premium, the bondholder will receive a payment that offsets losses on the underlying bond should the issuer default. Buying protection is similar to shorting a corporate bond, and, conversely, selling protection is equivalent to buying or taking on credit exposure. In the event of default, the payment made to the protection buyer is normally par minus the market price of the defaulted bond. The advantage of default swaps is their superior liquidity and ease of execution. The main disadvantage is that they do not perfectly hedge against credit spreads widening and, should the bond actually default, the manager now owns distressed debt that may continue to decline in value and for which a short stock position is no longer an effective hedge. Financing concerns can arise if the manager is leveraged and has to liquidate holdings to meet margin calls.

The main objective of asset swaps is to separate interest rate risk and credit risk. Asset swaps are similar to interest rate swaps; payments can be swapped from fixed to floating or vice versa, swapped to another currency, or swapped for returns from some index. A callable asset swap, as the name implies, is an asset swap that may be called away from the asset swap purchaser (e.g., an investor or dealer) by the asset swap seller (e.g., the hedge fund manager). The main disadvantage of callable asset swaps is liquidity and potentially punitive terms for recalling the underlying bond. The advantage lies in establishing an absolute floor on capital at risk in the bond component of the convertibles.

## Examples

An example of relative-value disparity could be found in the capital structure of Amazon.com. At the end of the second quarter of 1999, the Internet bookseller had, in addition to its equity capital, two tranches of long-term debt outstanding: a $530 million stepped-coupon senior debt issue of 2008 and a $1.25 billion convertible issue of 2009. After adjusting these securities' prices to reflect market values as of June 30, 1999, a picture of the company's capital structure emerged. (See Figure 6.1.)

Despite no past earnings and no projected earnings for the fiscal year, equity holders believed the company to be extraordinarily valuable. The market capitalization was $20.2 billion as of June 30, 1999. The straight debt holders were somewhat less optimistic about Amazon.com's prospects, as implied by the yield spread of these securities and their credit rating. The yield spread had averaged about 450 basis points over comparable Treasuries, implying a significant element of risk. With the junior (equity) security holders euphoric and the senior security holders suspicious about the prospects of the company, one might have expected the middle tranche of convertible security holders to be "cautiously upbeat." Surprisingly, they were the most pessimistic stakeholders of all. Assuming 100 percent implied volatility, the credit spread was over 1,500 basis points, portending Amazon's imminent demise. Viewed differently, with a normalized credit spread of 600 basis points, the convertible was trading at a very low level of implied stock volatility. Either

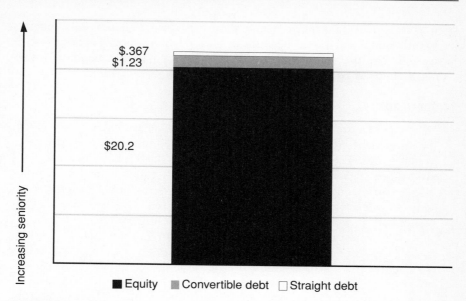

**FIGURE 6.1**   Capital Structure of Amazon.com ($ billions)
*Source:* UBS Warburg (2000).

the convertible was too cheap or equity was too expensively valued by the market. To exploit this inefficiency, convertible arbitrageurs sold expensive equity and bought the comparably cheap convertible bond.

Although this example seems to be a no-brainer example of convertible arbitrage, investors who put on the trade without hedging the credit risk have probably lost money. The convertible bond fell more or less in line with the stock. As Internet stocks fell in 2000, the markets' assessment of the credit ratings of these stocks fell as well. The companies were said to be burning cash. This resulted in the synthetic put of the convertible bond losing value. The value of the convertible bond became more a function of the straight debt value (bond floor) and less a function of the conversion value. The recent path of the Amazon.com arbitrage therefore not only is a good example of the mechanics of convertible arbitrage, it also highlights that convertibles can behave more as straight bonds after a dramatic fall of the share price, when the convertible bond becomes a function of credit risk as opposed to equity risk.

A profitable example of convertible arbitrage is the purchase of the Siemens Exchangeable 2005 (exchangeable into Infineon stock) and the sale of Infineon stock. Infineon is a technology spin-off from conglomerate Siemens. The attraction of exchangeables for spin-offs, such as Infineon by Siemens, is that the convertible bond carries the credit risk of the issuer (the blue-chip mother company), which in this case is Siemens, and allows the spin-off to finance itself more cheaply than if it issued a plain-vanilla convertible bond. Figure 6.2 shows the paths of both positions. Both financial instruments fell, but the stock underperformed the convertible bond. In other words, an initially delta-neutral position was profitable.

## Performance

■ As seen in Figure 6.3, the HFRI Convertible Arbitrage index performed in line with the MSCI World until the latter started to tumble. Volatility was much lower. The convertible arbitrage index underperformed the S&P 500 index slightly (as of December 2001) but outperformed most other major equity long-only benchmarks. As of July 2002, the Convertible Arbitrage index was up by 2.7 percent for the year which compares with −16.3 percent for the MSCI World total return index.

■ The smoothness of the wealth creation is worth pointing out. The wealth profile was flat on two occasions and slightly negative on one occasion. In 1990 convertible arbitrage added little value due to global recession and in 1994 due to U.S. interest rate rises. The fall in autumn 1998 resulted from widening of most arbitrage spreads and (some) redemptions from the industry due to LTCM.

■ As seen in Table 6.3, annual returns were around 11 to 12 percent achieved with a volatility of around 3.5 to 4.0 percent. The highest calendar year

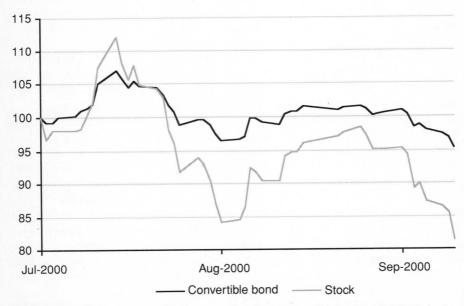

**FIGURE 6.2**  Infineon Share Price versus Siemens/Infineon Exchangeable 2005
*Source:* Bloomberg.

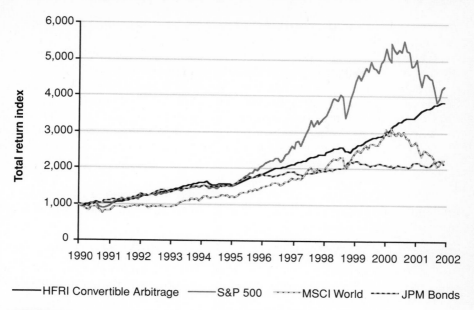

**FIGURE 6.3** Long-Term Performance of Convertible Arbitrage
*Source:* Hedge Fund Research, Datastream, UBS Warburg (2000).

**Table 6.3** Convertible Arbitrage Risk and Return Characteristics

| | # of Monthly Returns | Annual Return | Volatility | Sharpe Ratio (5%) | Worst 1-month Drawdown | Negative Months | Worst 12-month Drawdown | 12-month Drawdown Ended On | Highest 12-month Return |
|---|---|---|---|---|---|---|---|---|---|
| S&P 500 | 144 | 12.85% | 14.54% | 0.54 | −15.64 | 35.4% | −26.63% | Sep-01 | 52.10% |
| MSCI World | 144 | 6.99 | 14.59 | 0.14 | −14.30 | 39.6 | −27.87 | Sep-01 | 33.51 |
| MSCI EAFE | 144 | 2.70 | 17.03 | <0 | −14.97 | 43.1 | −28.27 | Sep-01 | 44.19 |
| MSCI Europe | 144 | 9.15 | 15.19 | 0.27 | −13.42 | 37.5 | −25.49 | Sep-01 | 45.93 |
| JPM Global Government Bonds | 144 | 6.59 | 5.94 | 0.27 | −3.40 | 41.0 | −6.18 | Jan-00 | 20.97 |
| JPM U.S. Government Bonds | 144 | 7.94 | 4.11 | 0.72 | −2.73 | 27.8 | −3.65 | Oct-94 | 17.34 |
| HFRI Convertible Arbitrage index | 144 | 11.88 | 3.41 | 2.02 | −3.19 | 12.5 | −3.84 | Jan-95 | 21.46 |
| Hennessee Hedge Fund Index—Convertible Arbitrage | 108 | 10.06 | 3.98 | 1.27 | −3.31 | 13.9 | −7.13 | Dec-94 | 22.30 |
| CSFB/Tremont Convertible Arbitrage | 96 | 11.03 | 4.84 | 1.24 | −4.68 | 15.6 | −8.97 | Jan-95 | 28.46 |

*Note:* All indexes are total return indexes and based in U.S. dollars. Data December 2001 inclusive.
*Source:* Hedge Fund Research, Hennessee, CSFB/Tremont, Datastream, Bloomberg, UBS Warburg (2000).

return of the HFRI Convertible Arbitrage index was in 1995 at 19.9 percent, and the lowest calendar year return was 1994 at –3.7 percent. Total returns in 2000 and 2001 were 14.5 percent and 13.5 percent respectively.

■ Convertible arbitrage has one of the lowest volatility averages of all strategies analyzed in this book. Annual volatility was around 3 to 4 percent. Only equity market-neutral strategies had a lower volatility.

■ Convertible arbitrage was among the top three strategies based on the worst monthly loss and number of negative months as a percentage of the total. It is midrange in terms of high Sharpe ratio, worst one-year cumulative return, and low correlation to equity markets.

Figure 6.4 shows the returns of various hedge fund indexes with some equity and bond indexes. Figure 6.5 compares monthly total MSCI World returns with HFRI Convertible Arbitrage index returns.

■ Figure 6.4 illustrates the attractiveness of convertible arbitrage. The returns are positive and more or less consistent across different data vendors and time periods. The volatility is lower than the volatility in bonds and

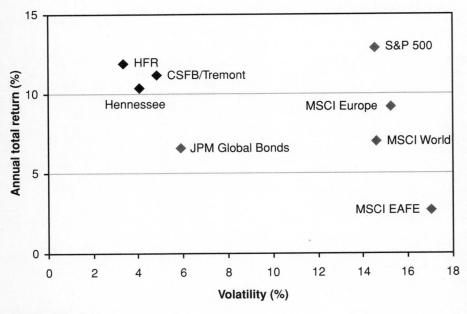

**FIGURE 6.4** Return versus Risk
*Source:* Hedge Fund Research, Hennessee, CSFB/Tremont, Datastream, UBS Warburg (2000).

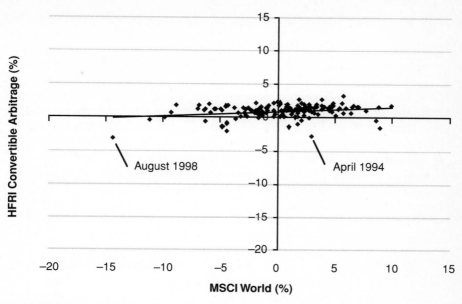

**FIGURE 6.5** MSCI World versus Convertible Arbitrage Returns
*Source:* Hedge Fund Research, Datastream, UBS Warburg (2000).

the returns average around 11 to 12 percent, which is higher than long-term equity returns. Note that all hedge fund indexes are net of fees. HFRI and Hennessee indexes are equally weighted, whereas CSFB/Tremont indexes are asset weighted.

■ Figure 6.5 shows that the returns are derived from convertible arbitrage and not by taking on equity market risk. The intercept (alpha) of the HFRI Convertible Arbitrage index to the MSCI World is 0.90. The slope (beta) measuring the exposure to the equity market is very low, around 0.07. Note that the largest negative months of the HFRI Convertible Arbitrage index occurred in both positive as well as negative equity markets.

■ Convertible arbitrage strategies can yield positive returns in equity bull markets despite their short stock positions. In the fourth quarter of 1999, for example, convertible arbitrage had positive returns despite world equity markets rising 17 percent during the quarter. Losses in short equity positions were balanced by an increase in equity volatility and because certain pockets, like investing in new issues and positive developments in a "busted" or low credit quality convertible, provided a source of returns.

Table 6.4 shows some further statistics of convertible arbitrage.

■ All convertible arbitrage indexes have positive alpha and extremely low beta against the MSCI World index. The low beta indicates that returns are generated without getting exposed to the equity market as a whole. In other words, the source of returns in convertible arbitrage is not derived from capturing the equity risk premium such as in long equity funds. The returns are derived to a large extent from exploiting market inefficiencies in the markets for convertible bonds.
■ The distribution of returns is slightly negatively skewed (to the left with a long tail to the left) and leptokurtic (narrow distribution with outliers). Later in the section Figure 6.8 will show that the negative outliers are small in absolute return space.
■ Correlation to equities was around 0.31 over the 12-year period ending 2001 and around 0.35 over the past six years. The correlation with bonds is negative, but statistically not significant. Intuitively we would have assumed a positive and statistically significant correlation to bonds, that is, a negative correlation to changes in interest rates. Convertible arbitrageurs are normally simultaneously long the convertible securities and short the underlying securities of the same issuer, thereby working the spread between the two types of securities. Returns result from the difference between cash flows collected through coupon payments and short interest rebates and cash paid out to cover dividend payments on the short equity positions. Returns also result from the convergence of valuations between the two securities. Positions are designed to generate profits from the fixed income security as well as the short sale of stock, while protecting principal from market moves. The worst-case scenario, therefore, is rising interest rates (losses on the bonds) and rising equity markets (losses on the short equity position), widening credit spreads (losses on the bonds), and falling stock implied volatility. The fact that correlation to bonds is not significant is an indication that the convertible arbitrageurs tend to hedge duration risk.

**Table 6.4**  Statistical Analysis of Convertible Arbitrage Returns

|  | Alpha to MSCI World | Beta to MSCI World | Skew | Excess Kurtosis | Correlation MSCI World | Correlation JPM Global Bonds |
|---|---|---|---|---|---|---|
| HFRI Convertible Arbitrage index | 0.90 | 0.07 | −1.44 | 3.56 | 0.31 | −0.01 |
| Hennessee Hedge Fund Index—Convertible Arbitrage | 0.76 | 0.07 | −0.66 | 3.10 | 0.24 | −0.13 |
| CSFB/Tremont Convertible Arbitrage | 0.85 | 0.03 | −1.79 | 5.07 | 0.10 | −0.23 |

*Source:* Hedge Fund Research, Hennessee, CSFB/Tremont, Datastream, Bloomberg, UBS Warburg (2000).

Figure 6.6 shows the three-month performance of convertible arbitrage in different market environments, and Figure 6.7 shows the average quarterly returns in down markets versus average quarterly returns in friendly markets.

■ Except for 1998, 1994 was the worst year based on the HFRI Convertible Arbitrage index, which was down by 3.7 percent during 1994. The year was characterized by rising U.S. interest rates. Convertible arbitrage showed a profit during the Asian crisis in 1997. All hedge fund strategies except short sellers suffered during the Russian crisis in 1998 partially due to the collapse of LTCM. However, convertible arbitrage, equity market-neutral, and risk arbitrage suffered least in absolute return space. Convertible arbitrage had positive returns during the Nasdaq fall and the World Trade Center attack. Falling equity prices and rising implied volatilities compensated rising credit spreads.

■ Theoretically, falling interest rates are good for convertible arbitrageurs because of the long position in the convertible, which reacts inversely to moves in interest rates due to its bond characteristics. However, declining interest rates in 1992, 1993, and 1995 encouraged many companies to call convertible issues and lower their cost of capital, thus adding to the

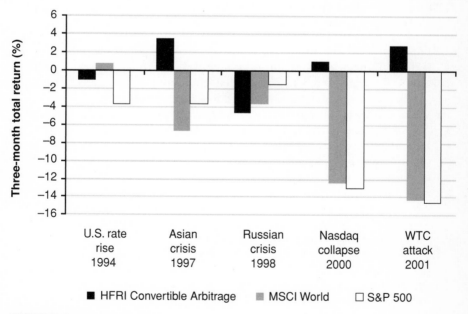

**FIGURE 6.6** Scenario Analysis
*Source:* Hedge Fund Research, Datastream, UBS Warburg (2000).
*Note:* US rate rise: Q1 94; Asian crisis: 8/1/97–10/31/97; Russian Crisis: 8/1/98–10/31/98; Nasdaq collapse: 9/1/90–11/30/90; WTC attack: 7/1/01–9/28/01.

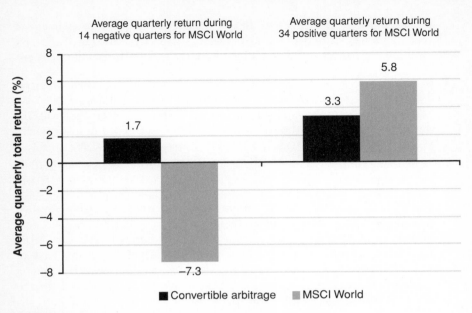

**FIGURE 6.7** Average Negative versus Average Positive Returns
*Source:* Hedge Fund Research, Datastream, UBS Warburg (2000).

hedging difficulties as investors prematurely lost their conversion premiums and accrued interest. The sudden rise in interest rates in 1994 caused additional problems as investment floors dropped dramatically.

■ When the Dow Jones Industrial Average dropped 554 points on October 27, 1997, and when similar volatility occurred later in the quarter in Japan, convertible arbitrage strategies performed well as the stock positions dropped more swiftly than the related convertible bonds. Thus, the managers earned more on their short stock positions than they lost on their long convertible positions. However, there were a few exceptions who lost money with Japanese resettables due to the lack of opportunity to sell short or because the instruments did not behave in the market as the pricing models suggested they would.

■ The fourth quarter of 1998 sent equity-linked markets in Japan into a tailspin due to the introduction of new short-selling rules. The uproar's inception was founded in the Ministry of Finance (MOF)'s initiative to curb "rumormongering" and other speculative attacks on Japanese stocks. The MOF promulgated securities legislation modeled after the U.S. regulation on short selling (the uptick rule). Unfortunately, it created mass confusion among custodians, stock lenders, and stock borrowers by not clearly stating under what conditions and to whom the rule's draconian penalties would apply. Large-scale and immediate retrenchment of stock lending activity resulted from the MOF's obfuscation of the new rules. Many convertible and warrant hedgers were forced to liquidate positions at distressed prices for fear of being caught naked-long without the offsetting short hedge. Ultimately, the MOF issued clarification of the rules the day they became effective, averting further deterioration in the market. Nonetheless, some losses were incurred. This example illustrates the exposure of the strategy to regulatory issues.

■ Convertible arbitrage also experienced difficulties during the LTCM collapse in autumn 1998. In the United States, the flight to quality and liquidity led investors to shun smaller and lower-credit quality convertible issues, leading to price deterioration and a significant widening in bid/ask spreads. Liquidations by hedge funds and proprietary trading desks in an already liquidity-hampered market further exacerbated the tone of the market.

■ 1999 was a difficult year for the convertible arbitrage industry, as the year was characterized by rising interest rates, mostly rising equity markets, and falling stock volatility (except for the last quarter). U.S. convertibles, which tend to be of lower credit quality, suffered when the Federal Reserve started to raise interest rates. There was even less activity than normal during summer from proprietary trading desks that did not want to take positions ahead of the enormous supply scheduled to the market in autumn. Potential illiquidity surrounding Y2K also discouraged participants. The main reason for the year ending profitably was the fact that issuance was extremely cheap making the arbitrage profitable despite rising rates and equities and falling volatilities.

■ The outperformance of convertible bond arbitrage in equity bear markets is worth pointing out. From January 1990 to December 2001 there were 14 quarters in which the MSCI World index reported a negative return (Figure 6.7). During these quarters convertible arbitrage showed an average return of 1.7 percent, compared with –7.3 percent in the case of the MSCI World. During the 34 quarters where MSCI World ended in positive territory, convertible arbitrage performed by 3.3 percent per quarter against 5.8 percent for the MSCI World index.

■ These examples illustrate that convertible arbitrage can perform well in bear markets, primarily due to short stock position in the arbitrage. Exposure to convertible arbitrage is attractive to bearish or neutral investors in search of instruments with positive expected return but low correlation to equities. In addition, due to its correlation and volatility characteristics it probably increases the efficiency (once idiosyncratic risk is diversified) of nearly any traditional portfolio.

Figure 6.8 shows how returns have been distributed in the past and compares the historic return distribution with a normal distribution of convertible

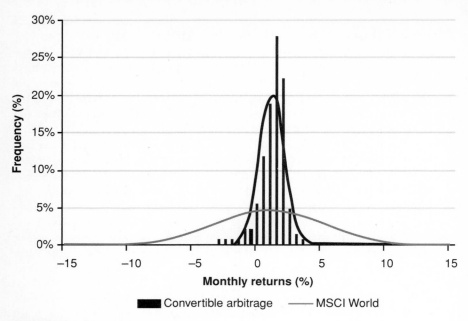

**FIGURE 6.8**    Return Distribution
*Source:* Hedge Fund Research, Datastream, UBS Warburg (2000).

arbitrage and a normal distribution of historical MSCI World returns, both based on historic mean return and standard deviation of returns. For Figure 6.9 we have sorted the convertible arbitrage returns and compared them with the corresponding market returns. This allows us to see in which market environment the extreme positive and negative returns were achieved.

- Figure 6.8 shows how narrowly around the mean the monthly returns were distributed, especially when compared with the equity market, here measured by the MSCI World index. The outliers were minor—especially in absolute return space. Seven returns were below the 95 percent range and one above. Three returns were outside the 99 percent range (all on the downside). Note that the standard deviation of monthly returns was only 0.98 percent. This means that the worst monthly drawdown of −3.19 percent is actually a 4.2-sigma event (as the mean of monthly return was 0.96 percent).
- Figure 6.9 shows that negative convertible arbitrage returns were not concentrated during equity market declines. The chart shows that convertible arbitrage returns tend to have low variability compared to equity returns and that there is little relation between the two sets of returns.

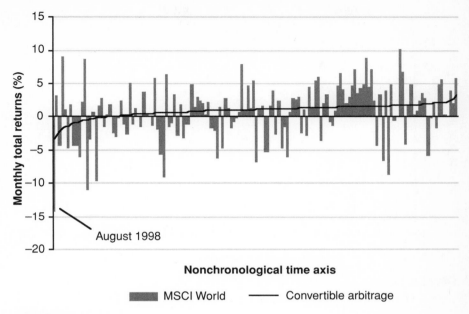

**FIGURE 6.9** Correlation
*Source:* Hedge Fund Research, Datastream, UBS Warburg (2000).

Figure 6.10 shows the magnitude of CB arbitrage trading below its previous peak level and the time to recover losses. A reading of 100 percent means that the index is trading at its all-time high, whereas a reading of 70 percent means that the index is trading 30 percent below the all-time high. Note that an index off 30 percent of its peak has to gain 43 percent (not 30 percent) to recover. This graph is called "underwater" because the aim of all investors as well as all swimmers is to stay at surface levels or reach surface levels again after diving. Figure 6.11 shows in which calendar quarters convertible bond arbitrage suffered its worst losses.

■ Figure 6.10 reveals that when a diversified portfolio of CB arbitrage hedge funds is underwater it was never under water by more than around 5 percent. In addition, the recovery period is similar to that of the equity market. Note that the magnitudes of losses are a fraction of those in equity long-only investments. If Figure 6.10 were to be shown to a regulator without revealing the nature of the two indexes, which index would the regulator (or pension fund trustee or any other person unfamiliar with the concept of risk and uncertainty) consider to be more risky?

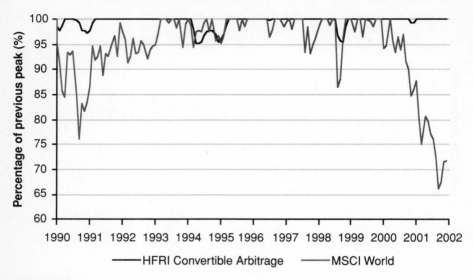

**FIGURE 6.10**   Underwater
*Source:* Hedge Fund Research, Datastream.

■ Figure 6.11 shows that there is little correlation with the worst quarters in CB arbitrage and equity markets; when CB arbitrage managers lose money, equity markets may be falling or may be rising. As with many other hedge funds strategies, the worst quarter was the third quarter of 1998.

Table 6.5 shows performance persistence over four three-year periods between 1990 and 2001.

■ Performance persistence was relatively high for the HFRI Convertible Arbitrage index when compared with some other absolute return strategies. Annual returns were between 10.0 percent and 14.1 percent over the four three-year periods.
■ The period 1999–2001 was superior in terms of risk-adjusted returns (i.e., high returns with comparably low volatility). It is unlikely that diversified portfolios of convertible arbitrage managers will continue to yield Sharpe ratios of 3.7 to infinity. The stellar recent performance of the strategy has led, to some degree, to saturation. Note that the worst 12-month return between 1999 and 2001 was a positive return of 6.6 percent, compared with a 27.9 percent loss in the case of the global equity market as measured by the MSCI World.

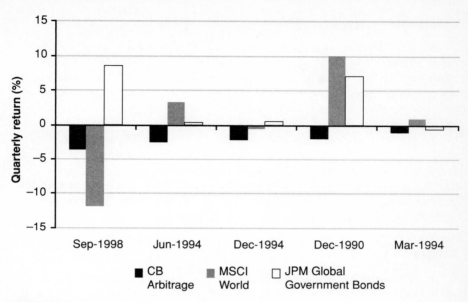

**FIGURE 6.11** Worst Quarters for Convertible Arbitrage
*Source:* Hedge Fund Research, Datastream.

**Table 6.5** Performance Persistence

|  | 1990–1992 | 1993–1995 | 1996–1998 | 1999–2001 |
|---|---|---|---|---|
| **MSCI World (Total Return)** | | | | |
| Annual return (%) | −1.80 | 16.40 | 18.25 | −3.05 |
| Volatility (%) | 16.70 | 10.29 | 14.47 | 15.73 |
| Average risk-free rate (%) | 5.61 | 4.37 | 5.07 | 4.64 |
| Sharpe ratio | <0 | 1.17 | 0.91 | <0 |
| Worst 1-month drawdown (%) | −11.12 | −5.81 | −14.30 | −9.21 |
| Worst 12-month drawdown (%) | −16.52 | −4.66 | 0.51 | −27.87 |
| **HFRI Convertible Arbitrage Index** | | | | |
| Annual return (%) | 11.81 | 9.95 | 11.65 | 14.14 |
| Volatility (%) | 3.27 | 3.89 | 3.64 | 2.60 |
| Sharpe ratio | 1.90 | 1.44 | 1.80 | 3.66 |
| Worst 1-month drawdown (%) | −1.57 | −2.83 | −3.24 | −0.71 |
| Worst 12-month drawdown (%) | 2.16 | −3.84 | 3.17 | 6.58 |

*Source:* Hedge Fund Research, Datastream.

## Conclusion

Convertible arbitrage has been an attractive hedge fund strategy. Stable returns of around 11 to 12 percent were achieved with very low volatility and low correlation to equities. The returns were achieved with little exposure to the equity market. Convertible arbitrages are not necessarily negative in equity market downturns. Downside risk is limited. No significant correlation to bonds suggests limited duration risk.

However, there are capacity constraints to convertible arbitrage. One of the main drivers of recent returns in convertible arbitrage is derived from initial public offerings (IPOs). Convertible arbitrageurs play a dominant role in the issuance of paper. Future performance is, therefore, to some extent dependent on future issuance. A further constraint is the ability to borrow stock and sell short. In other words, there is regulatory risk.

## Outlook

From a convertibles issuance perspective, the 1990s can be described as boom years. Convertible bonds became an asset class of their own. To some investors, convertibles are the best of both worlds: Convertible bonds pay income plus provide upside to equity. Bond investors bought convertible bonds because of the "equity kicker" in a low interest rates environment. Equity investors used convertible bonds to add some downside protection to ever-rising stock markets. Corporates like the "cheap" financing through low coupons, locking in low interest rates and reducing the costs of debt. Given the pending corporate restructuring in Europe and Asia, supply and demand for convertible bonds are expected to increase, and, the opportunities for convertible arbitrageurs should as well.

However, there are some Damocles' swords hanging over the convertible arbitrage industry. First, large portions of convertibles are in the hands of hedge funds. Estimates are widely dispersed. Assuming the CB market is around $600 billion, that CB arbitrage is around 3.9 percent of the total $537 billion of assets under management, and that the average leverage is 5.7:1, then hedge funds hold convertibles for around $120 billion. This would indicate a market share of around 20 percent of the total of $600 billion of outstanding convertibles. However, hedge funds have an 80 to 90 percent market share in trading in secondary markets.

The second danger is credit. Standard & Poor's (2002) announced in January 2002 that issuer defaults were at record levels. The CB arbitrage industry moved from a volatility play to a credit play. It is unlikely that all market participants will have capitalized this change to the same degree. In February 2002 one large CB fund caused news headlines for having some "difficulties" in pricing its convertible positions. Although credit is a known risk (since

1998), it can only be hedged imperfectly. Continuous deterioration of credit could be a risk for convertible arbitrageurs and investors. The dispersion of returns among different managers could increase dramatically.

A third issue could be the increasing complexity of convertible securities. If no one outside the arbitrage community is able to value the embedded option, the marketplace could become more concentrated than it already is.

# FIXED INCOME ARBITRAGE

## Strategy

Fixed income arbitrage managers seek to exploit pricing anomalies within and across global fixed income markets and their derivatives, using leverage to hedge as well as to enhance returns. In most cases, fixed income arbitrageurs take offsetting long and short positions in similar fixed income securities that are mathematically, fundamentally, or historically interrelated. The relationship can be temporarily distorted by market events, investor preferences, exogenous shocks to supply and demand, or structural features of the fixed income market. (See Table 6.6.) Hedge Fund Research, Inc. estimated that fixed income related strategies accounted for 3.2 percent of assets under management in 1990 and around 8.2 percent at the end of 2001. Assuming the total hedge funds universe is $537 billion, fixed income related strategies account for around $44 billion of assets under management. Assuming an average leverage of 15 times equity, fixed income hedge funds might control (long as well as short) a notional value of approximately $660 billion. In long-only space, this would amount to around 2.2 percent of the $30 trillion global bond market (including corporate and government bonds but excluding asset-backed and mortgage-backed securities). Fixed income arbitrage is only a small niche of the global bond market.

Often, opportunities for these relative value strategies are the result of temporary credit anomalies, and the returns are derived from capturing the credit anomaly and obtaining advantageous financing. These strategies can include:

- Arbitrage between physical securities and futures (basis trading).
- Arbitrage between similar bonds in the same capital structure.
- Arbitrage pricing inefficiencies of asset backed securities, swaptions, and other interest rate financial instruments.
- Arbitrage between on-the-run and off-the-run bonds (issuance-driven trade).
- Arbitrage between liquid mutual funds containing illiquid municipal bonds with Treasury bonds.

**Table 6.6**   Key Risk Factors in Fixed Income Arbitrage

| Risk | Position | Effect |
|------|----------|--------|
| Interest rates | Long and short (duration neutral) | By buying cheap fixed income instruments and selling short expensive securities, the fixed income arbitrageur usually hedges interest rate risk. The exposure to the yield curve is hedged by aiming for buying and selling instruments with similar duration. Yield curve arbitrage is exposed to the yield curve since the duration of the two positions is different. |
| Credit | Long and short default risk | The exposure to changes in credit risk depends on the strategy. The need to sell short limits arbitrageurs to markets where short selling is an option. Consequently, they tend to trade very liquid issues with high credit ratings that have low default risk and can easily be sold short. |
| Liquidity | Financing costs | Most strategies are contingent on low financing costs, borrowing being cheap relative to lending. Strategies depend on advantageous financing.<br><br>Often fixed income arbitrageurs are short liquidity. This means some trades involve a short position in a liquid instrument and the offsetting trade in a less liquid instrument. |
| Volatility | Short volatility | To some extent, fixed income arbitrageurs sell economic disaster insurance because they usually are short the credit spread. In an economic disaster, credit spreads widen and investors short the spread lose money. Additionally, liquidity dries up, worsening the situation. The result is few, but high standard deviation negative returns. |
| Legal/tax risk | Asset swaps | Asset swaps depend on stable relationship between low-risk bonds, such as Treasury or sovereign issues of a major developed nation, and the swaps. Changes in tax laws or a financial or political debacle in the issuing country can cause such relationships to change. |

*Source:* UBS Warburg (2000).

■ Yield curve arbitrage and yield curve spread trading.
■ Stripping bonds with multiple callable features or swaps with complicated cash flows into their components in order to arbitrage these stripped components.
■ Exploitation of intermarket anomalies (buying a TED [Treasury versus Eurodollar] spread by being long Treasury bill futures and short Eurodollar futures under the assumption that the spread will widen).

Because the prices of fixed income instruments are based on yield curves, volatility curves, expected cash flows, credit ratings, and special bond and option features, fixed income arbitrageurs must use sophisticated analytical models to identify pricing disparities and to manage their positions. Given the complexity of the instruments and the high degree of sophistication of the arbitrageurs, the fixed income arbitrageurs rely on investors less sophisticated than themselves to over- and undervalue securities by failing to value explicitly some feature on the instrument (for example, optionality) or the probability of a possible future occurrence (for example, a political event) that will likely affect the valuation of the instrument. The alpha of a fixed income hedge fund, therefore, is primarily derived from the skill needed to model, structure, execute, and manage fixed income instruments.

The spreads available tend to be very small, of the order of 3 to 20 basis points. Therefore, managers need to lever the position and expect to make money out of carry on the position and the spread reverting to its normal level. Despite the high leverage, the volatility of returns achieved by fixed income arbitrageurs is usually very low due to the market-neutral stance of most funds in this discipline. However, this strategy is more prone to "fat tail" return distributions, that is, a higher likelihood of large losses than would be predicted by a normal distribution.

In general, fixed income arbitrageurs aim to deliver steady returns with low volatility, due to the fact that the directional risk is mitigated by hedging against interest rate movements or by the use of spread trades. Managers differ in terms of the diligence with which interest rate risk, foreign exchange risk, intermarket spread risk, and credit risk is hedged.[5] Leverage depends on the types of positions in the portfolio. Simple, stable positions, such as basis trades, are leveraged much more highly than higher-risk trades that have yield curve exposure. Some managers take directional credit spread risk, which results in a violation with the "relative value" definition stated earlier. Some observers, due to large, unexpected losses in yield curve arbitrage in 1995, have also concluded that some trades with exposure to changes in the yield curve are not market-neutral.[6]

Basis trading is the most basic fixed income arbitrage strategy. A basis trade involves the purchase of a government bond and the simultaneous sale of futures contracts on that bond. Bond futures have a delivery option, which allows several different bonds to be delivered to satisfy the futures contract. Because it is not certain which bond is expected to become the cheapest to deliver at maturity, this uncertainty, along with shifts in supply and demand for the underlying bonds, may create profit opportunities.

**Example**   There were particularly attractive opportunities in this segment with the exodus of several proprietary trading desks and the downscaling of activities by other market participants such as LTCM. One situation in Brazilian fixed income instruments provides an interesting example of the inefficiencies in this area. The Brazilian sovereign market consists of many related securities, two of which are New Money Bonds and the Eligible Interest Bonds. Because New Money Bonds are somewhat less liquid then Eligible Interest Bonds they tend to react more slowly to changes in Brazilian fundamentals. During a rally in bonds in March 1999, for example, it was possible to purchase the lagging New Money Bonds at 55 and sell the Eligible Interest Bonds at 65, taking the 10-point credit differential, while picking up 125 basis points in yield. In either a bullish or bearish scenario, the trade was compelling: A deteriorating market would tend to cause the prices of both bonds to converge as a restructuring scenario unfolded, while (as it turned out) in a bullish market the money flows bid up the price of the New Money Bonds. Profits were taken as the prices converged to more normal levels.

## Performance

- Based on HFRI indexes, the fixed income arbitrage hedge fund style has outperformed the global as well as the U.S. government bond proxies with a similar degree of volatility. The events of 1998 (Russian ruble default, LTCM) stand out: Fixed income arbitrage suffered whereas (some) government bonds benefited (flight to quality). The HFRI Fixed Income Arbitrage index also has outperformed the MSCI World index over the 12-year period ending in December 2001. (See Figure 6.12.)
- Performance analysis would look more attractive if the second half of 1998 were excluded. From January 1990 to June 1998, the HFRI Fixed

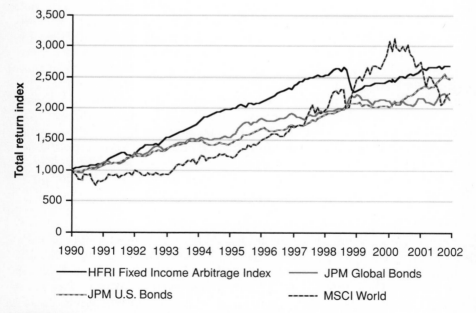

**FIGURE 6.12** Long-Term Performance of Fixed Income Arbitrage
*Source:* Hedge Fund Research, Datastream, UBS Warburg (2000).

Income Arbitrage index yielded 11.9 percent a year, compared with only 8.5 percent for the JPM Global Bonds index. The best year was 1992 when the HFRI Fixed Income Arbitrage index gained 22.1 percent. The worst year was 1998 where the hedge fund index fell by 9.9 percent. Returns in 2000 and 2001 were 4.8 percent and 4.5 percent, respectively. As of July 2002, the strategy was up by 6.9 percent.

■ The HFRI Fixed Income Arbitrage index has yielded a return of 8.6 percent with a volatility of 4.8 percent from 1990 to 2001. Returns were slightly higher than global bonds and volatility slightly lower. The risk-adjusted returns were comparable with a diversified portfolio of U.S. government bonds. (See Table 6.7.)

Figure 6.13 shows the returns of various hedge fund indexes with some equity and bond indexes. Figure 6.14 compares monthly total JPM Global Bond returns with the HFRI Fixed Income Arbitrage index.

■ Fixed income arbitrage had the second lowest returns of all 11 strategies analyzed in this book. Only short sellers did worse. When the 31 different single strategies of the HFRI universe are analyzed, fixed income arbitrage was ranked 28 in terms of returns and 23 in terms of Sharpe ratios.
■ Equity long/short is occasionally viewed as a substitute for long-only equity exposure. A similar logic could be applied to fixed income arbitrage; that is, an investment in fixed-income arbitrage could be viewed as similar to an investment in bonds without the duration risk. The two fixed income arbitrage indexes were not superior in terms of absolute returns

**Table 6.7**  Fixed Income Arbitrage Risk and Return Characteristics

| | # of Monthly Returns | Annual Return | Volatility | Sharpe Ratio (5%) | Worst 1-month Drawdown | Negative Months | Worst 12-month Drawdown | 12-month Drawdown Ended On | Highest 12-month Return |
|---|---|---|---|---|---|---|---|---|---|
| S&P 500 | 144 | 12.85% | 14.54% | 0.54 | −15.64% | 35.4% | −26.63% | Sep-01 | 52.10% |
| MSCI World | 144 | 6.99 | 14.59 | 0.14 | −14.30 | 39.6 | −27.87 | Sep-01 | 33.51 |
| MSCI EAFE | 144 | 2.70 | 17.03 | <0 | −14.97 | 43.1 | −28.27 | Sep-01 | 44.19 |
| MSCI Europe | 144 | 9.15 | 15.19 | 0.27 | −13.42 | 37.5 | −25.49 | Sep-01 | 45.93 |
| JPM Global Government Bonds | 144 | 6.59 | 5.94 | 0.27 | −3.40 | 41.0 | −6.18 | Jan-00 | 20.97 |
| JPM U.S. Government Bonds | 144 | 7.94 | 4.11 | 0.72 | −2.73 | 27.8 | −3.65 | Oct-94 | 17.34 |
| HFRI Fixed Income Arbitrage index CSFB/Tremont Fixed | 144 | 8.58 | 4.81 | 0.74 | −6.45 | 20.1 | −10.40 | May-99 | 22.11 |
| Income Arbitrage | 96 | 6.79 | 4.19 | 0.43 | −6.96 | 18.8 | −10.11 | Oct-98 | 16.04 |

*Note:* All indexes are total return indexes and based in U.S. dollars. Data December 2001 inclusive.
*Source:* Hedge Fund Research, CSFB/Tremont, Datastream, Bloomberg, UBS Warburg (2000).

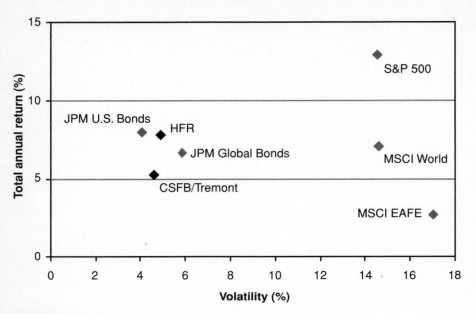

**FIGURE 6.13** Return versus Risk
*Source:* Hedge Fund Research, CSFB/Tremont, Datastream, UBS Warburg (2000).

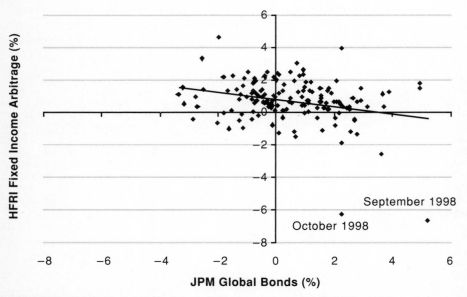

**FIGURE 6.14** JPM Global Bonds versus Fixed Income Arbitrage Returns
*Source:* Hedge Fund Research, Datastream, UBS Warburg (2000).

or risk-adjusted returns. The benefits arise from the fact that fixed income arbitrage managers use other strategies than just being long duration, hence the diversification benefits for any bond exposure in a traditional portfolio.

■ Figure 6.14 shows that the returns are derived from fixed income arbitrage and not by taking on interest rate risk. As a matter of fact, fixed income arbitrage is about exploiting market inefficiencies between related interest rate instruments and hedging away interest rate risk. The intercept (alpha) of the HFRI Fixed Income Arbitrage index to the JPM Global Bonds index was 0.80. The slope (beta) measuring the exposure to the bond market is negative and relatively low—in this case around –0.22.

■ Figure 6.14 shows the negative outliers in fixed income arbitrage located in the southeast corner of the diagram. The negative outliers occur when bonds rise, that is, when interest rates fall (unexpectedly). In other words, in fixed income arbitrage there is some exposure to Alan Greenspan providing liquidity by lowering interest rates. The two worst losses in the lower-right quadrant were from September and October 1998 where there was a flight to quality and liquidity was provided by the Fed.

Table 6.8 shows some further statistics of fixed income arbitrage. Note that it compares the fixed income arbitrage indexes with the JPM Global Government Bond Index.

■ The distribution of returns is slightly negatively skewed (to the left with a long tail to the left) and extremely leptokurtic (narrow distribution with outliers). Figure 6.18 later in the section shows that the negative outliers are relatively small in absolute terms but represent a strong deviation from normality of returns. The two (six-sigma) outliers occurred in September and October 1998—a period that will probably not go down in history as the happiest of times for fixed income arbitrageurs.

■ From an investor's perspective, fixed income arbitrageurs are short a disaster insurance policy because they usually are short the credit spread. In an economic disaster, credit spreads widen and investors short the spread

**Table 6.8** Statistical Analysis of Fixed Income Aribtrage Returns

| | Alpha to JPM Bonds | Beta to JPM Bonds | Skew | Excess Kurtosis | Correlation MSCI World | Correlation JPM Global Bonds |
|---|---|---|---|---|---|---|
| HFRI Fixed Income Arbitrage index | 0.80 | −0.22 | −1.78 | 9.13 | 0.02 | −0.27 |
| CSFB/Tremont Fixed Income Arbitrage | 0.64 | −0.26 | −3.28 | 15.19 | 0.07 | −0.25 |

*Source:* Hedge Fund Research, CSFB/Tremont, Datastream, UBS Warburg (2000).

lose money (or suffer book losses in mark-to-market space). Additionally, liquidity dries up, worsening the situation. The result is few, but high standard deviation negative returns. In other words, as with any other short put option position, the investor receives the premium in calm markets but has a cost in market turmoil, as the put option moves in-the-money. For long-term investors like insurance companies and pension funds, selling put options (insurance policies) can be attractive. In other words, the non-normality of the return distribution is not bad per se; it depends on whether the benefits from the puts (the put premium) exceed the costs in the long term.

■ Excluding these two outliers from 1998 results in a reduction of skew and an excess kurtosis to nearly zero. Figure 6.15 shows the rise in swap spreads due to the Russian default and the subsequent fall in fixed income arbitrage returns. An increase in swap spreads arises when there is a flight-to-quality situation. Such situations occur when a large number of investors seek the safety and stability of government securities to escape from turmoil in international stock and bond markets. The resultant buying of government securities generally causes the credit spread to widen.

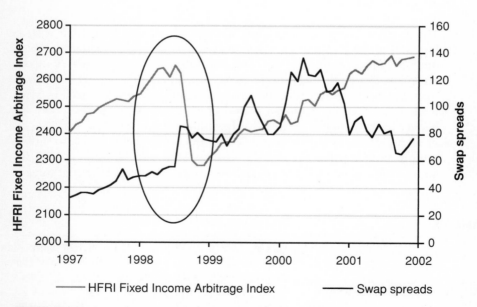

**FIGURE 6.15**   Fixed Income Arbitrage versus Swap Spreads
*Source:* Hedge Fund Research, Bloomberg.

Figure 6.16 and Figure 6.17 show the performance of the HFRI Fixed Income Arbitrage Index in different market environments and average quarterly returns in down markets versus average quarterly returns in friendly markets.

■ Figure 6.16 shows again where the outliers come from. Of all strategies analyzed in this book fixed income arbitrage had the second worst performance in autumn 1998. Only emerging markets (which, unlike fixed income arbitrage, have a strong directional bias) performed worse.

■ In October 1998, the bond markets went into a tailspin because a vast network of participants had essentially closed their trading doors, freezing the otherwise highly liquid and tightly traded bond markets. In a flight to quality and liquidity, all assets have been severely and negatively repriced. This included swaps, investment grade corporate bonds, high yield bonds, mortgage-backed securities, municipal bonds, and emerging-market bonds. The violence and velocity of these movements have been of historic proportions.*

---

*Throughout this book, the point is made that liquidity to some extent is a theoretical concept. Liquidity (defined as ability to close open positions) has a tendency to disappear when most needed by a majority of market participants. It is, sort of, like a claustrophobic sitting in the cinema and checking that the path to the exit is free of any obstacles in case fire breaks out. If fire breaks out, the carefully analyzed situation is likely to change.

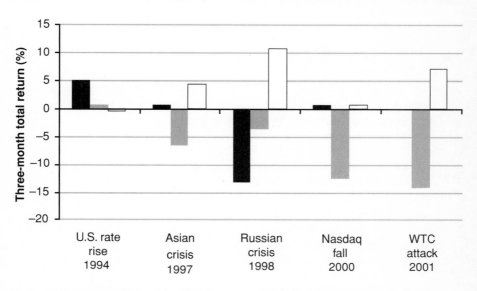

**FIGURE 6.16** Scenario Analysis
*Source:* Hedge Fund Research, Datastream, UBS Warburg (2000).

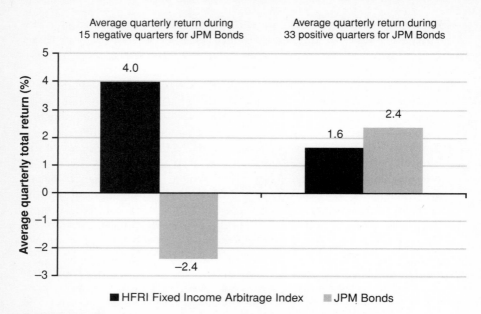

**FIGURE 6.17**  Average Negative versus Average Positive Returns
*Source:* Hedge Fund Research, Datastream, UBS Warburg (2000).

■ Fixed income arbitrage has been subject to negative press and regulatory scrutiny in the wake of LTCM 1998 catastrophe. Many investors departed from the strategy. Investors who acknowledged that the well-documented problems were not a result of an inherently flawed strategy, but were instead attributable to manager specific factors such as overleverage, investments outside of core competency, and too large a balance sheet were rewarded in 1999. The HFRI Fixed Income Arbitrage index increased by 7.4 percent in the year after LTCM despite swap spreads widening beyond the pre-LTCM levels.

■ Figure 6.17 shows in which market environments fixed income arbitrageurs make money. In the quarters where global bonds fell by an average of 2.4 percent fixed income arbitrage yielded 4.0 percent. In the quarters where global bonds increased by an average of 2.4 percent, that is, interest rates declined, fixed income arbitrage yielded only 1.6 percent.

Figure 6.18 shows how returns have been distributed in the past and compares the historic return distribution with a normal distribution of fixed income arbitrage and a normal distribution of historical JPM Global Government Bond returns both based on historic mean return and standard devia-

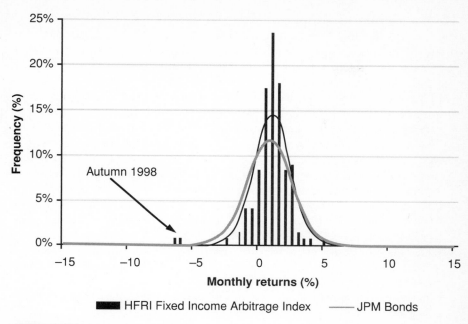

**FIGURE 6.18**   Return Distribution
*Source:* Hedge Fund Research, Datastream, UBS Warburg (2000).

tion of returns. For Figure 6.19, we have sorted the fixed income arbitrage returns and compared them to the corresponding market returns. This allows us to see in which market environment the extreme positive and negative returns were achieved.

- Figure 6.18 highlights the deviation of the historic return distribution from normality. There were four returns below the 95 percent range and none above this range. Two returns were below the 99 percent range. The experience in September and October 1998, where the HRFI Fixed Income Arbitrage index lost 6.5 percent and 6.1 percent respectively, was a six standard deviation event for this discipline. To put this into perspective, the largest monthly loss prior to autumn 1998 was only 2.6 percent.
- Fung and Hsieh (1999a) provide three explanations for why fixed income arbitrage provides equitylike returns with bondlike volatility:
  1. Fixed income arbitrage funds are capturing true mispricings.
  2. They are acting as market makers providing liquidity.
  3. They sell economic disaster insurance—where the low historical return volatility is consistent with a period over which the gathering of insurance premium has yet to be tested by a disaster payout.

The first two points are where the returns come from. The third point is where the risk comes from. The third point can explain the outliers since insurers are essentially short volatility. Fixed income arbitrage performs best in calm markets and worst in volatile markets.

■ Figure 6.19 shows that large negative returns in fixed income arbitrage are concentrated when bonds rise, that is, when liquidity is pumped into the system and interest rates fall. The most extreme positive returns from fixed income arbitrage occur both in rising and falling bond markets.
■ Figure 6.20 reveals the long recovery period of a diversified portfolio of fixed income arbitrage managers. After the losses in 1998, the fixed income arbitrage index did not reach its previous peak until April 2001.
■ The worst two quarters were, as mentioned before, the third and fourth in 1998. Figure 6.21 shows that the next three worst quarters were minor by comparison.
■ There is little consistency over the past 12 years. (See Table 6.9.) Fixed income arbitrage is a different strategy post-LTCM in terms of return, volatility, and correlation characteristics. However, a fully backward-looking approach in assessing an absolute return strategy is inappropriate.

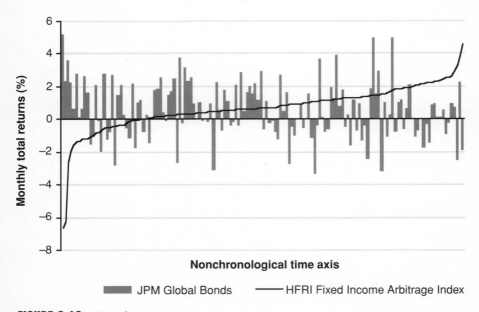

**Nonchronological time axis**

▓▓▓ JPM Global Bonds          ——— HFRI Fixed Income Arbitrage Index

**FIGURE 6.19** Correlation
*Source:* Hedge Fund Research, Datastream, UBS Warburg (2000).

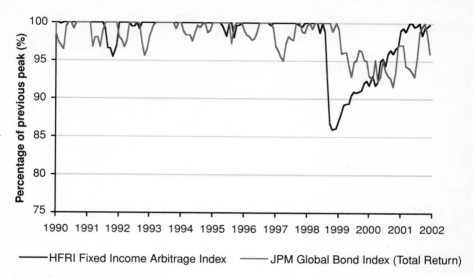

**FIGURE 6.20** Underwater
*Source:* Hedge Fund Research, Datastream.

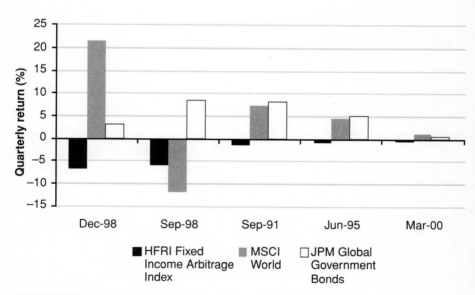

**FIGURE 6.21** Worst Quarters for Fixed Income Arbitrage
*Source:* Hedge Fund Research, Datastream.

**Table 6.9**   Performance Persistence

|                                         | 1990–1992 | 1993–1995 | 1996–1998 | 1999–2001 |
|-----------------------------------------|-----------|-----------|-----------|-----------|
| **JPM Global Bond Index (Total Return)** |           |           |           |           |
| Annual return (%)                       | 10.50     | 10.78     | 6.78      | −1.26     |
| Volatility (%)                          | 6.75      | 4.76      | 5.01      | 6.35      |
| Average risk-free rate (%)              | 5.61      | 4.37      | 5.07      | 4.64      |
| Sharpe ratio                            | 0.73      | 1.35      | 0.34      | <0        |
| Worst 1-month drawdown (%)              | −3.20     | −2.77     | −2.49     | −3.35     |
| Worst 12-month drawdown (%)             | 4.52      | 1.07      | 0.82      | −6.18     |
|                                         |           |           |           |           |
| **HFRI Fixed Income Arbitrage Index**   |           |           |           |           |
| Annual return (%)                       | 15.18     | 11.47     | 2.57      | 5.56      |
| Volatility (%)                          | 5.19      | 3.27      | 6.21      | 3.20      |
| Sharpe ratio                            | 1.84      | 2.17      | <0        | 0.29      |
| Worst 1-month drawdown (%)              | −2.61     | −1.91     | −6.67     | −1.55     |
| Worst 12-month drawdown (%)             | 9.11      | 4.70      | −9.89     | −10.40    |

*Source:* Hedge Fund Research, Datastream.

Many opportunities, as mentioned earlier, rose in the aftermath of the LTCM debacle.

■ The worst 12-month drawdown in the period 1996–1998 was due to the Russian default crisis, as of December 1998. The 12-month drawdown was 9.9 percent. The worst 12-month drawdown for the period 1999–2001 was for the same reason and was as of May 1999. The rolling 12-month return from June 1998 to May 1999 was a loss of 10.4 percent.

**Wolf in Sheep's Clothing**   Some describe LTCM as a "wolf in sheep's clothing." LTCM's traders, many formerly of Salomon Brothers, colorfully portrayed in Michael Lewis' *Liar's Poker* (1989), were notorious risk takers, although some well-known and respected academics and Fed officials were hired as well.

Jorion (2000) argues that LTCM failed because of its inability to measure, control, and manage its risk. This was due in no small part to the fact that LTCM's trades were rather undiversified. LTCM was reported to have lost about $1.5 billion from interest rate swaps and a similar amount from equity options. Table 6.10 describes the exposure of various reported trades to fundamental risk factors.

All the trades were exposed to increased market volatility. Most were exposed to liquidity risk, which itself is correlated with volatility. Many trades were exposed to default risk. Jorion points out that using the same covariance

**Table 6.10** Exposure of LTCM's Portfolio to Risk Factors

| Trade | Loss if Risk Factor Increases | | |
| --- | --- | --- | --- |
| | Volatility | Default | Illiquidity |
| Long interest rate swap | Yes | Yes | Yes |
| Short equity options | Yes | | |
| Long off-the-run/short on-the-run Treasuries | Yes | | Yes |
| Long mortgage-backed securities (hedged) | Yes | | Yes |
| Long sovereign debt | Yes | Yes | Yes |

*Source:* Jorion (2000).

matrix to measure risk and to optimize positions is not necessarily a good idea. This approach induces the strategy to take positions that appear to generate arbitrage profits based on recent history but also represent bets on extreme events, like selling options. LTCM is a good example of the biases in portfolio optimization. Only a few of the "convergence" trades could truly qualify as arbitrage trades. One example is the long position in the off-the-run bond offset by a short position in the on-the-run equivalent. In this case, the probability of default is identical, and eventually the two bonds will converge to the same value (in 30-some years). In the meantime, though, the spread could widen further, thus requiring the fund to carry enough capital (or secure credit lines) to absorb temporary losses. For most other trades, the portfolio was exposed to hidden risks. One of the hidden risks was liquidity risk, which causes losses when volatility increases. Traditional value at risk (VAR) methods assume that the fund is a price taker; that is, it is not large enough to affect prices. Risk managers now recognize that this assumption may not be appropriate for some users.

LTCM's interpretation of its failure was that the events of 1998 were "beyond the fund's capacity to anticipate."[7] That is missing the point. At the end of the day, LTCM's strategy exploited the intrinsic weaknesses of its risk management system. In fact, it had severely underestimated its risk. In addition, the payoff patterns of the investment strategy were akin to short positions in options. Even if it had measured its risk correctly, the firm failed to manage its risk properly. A *Wall Street Journal* article describing the experience of LTCM carries an interesting quote from Nobel laureate William Sharpe, a former Stanford colleague of Myron Scholes:

> *Most of academic finance is teaching that you can't earn 40 percent a year without some risk of losing a lot of money. In some sense, what happened is nicely consistent with what we teach.*[8]

## Conclusion and Outlook

The reputation of fixed income arbitrage as a relative-value strategy has suffered because of the LTCM debacle. However, LTCM is likely to go down in financial history as a mismanaged company where leverage was excessive. Most trades would have been profitable if funding had been managed appropriately and carried to the end. Note that some market observers (namely the popular press) occasionally put LTCM into the same category as Soros and Tiger (i.e., macro) due to its large size.

Inefficiencies in fixed income markets will continue to exist. The skill and the determination (read funding) for these inefficiencies to be exploited will not disappear because of LTCM. Fixed income arbitrage represents a sound alternative to allocating funds in bonds. This is especially the case in an environment of rising interest rates and inflation uncertainty, since fixed income arbitrage shows negative correlation with bond markets. Fixed income arbitrage, therefore, is best viewed as a diversifier to a long-only bond portfolio. The optionality in the so-called "nondirectional" strategies means that special care is required when measuring and managing risk.

## EQUITY MARKET-NEUTRAL

### Strategy

Equity market-neutral is designed to produce consistent returns with very low volatility and correlation in a variety of market environments. The investment strategy is designed to exploit equity market inefficiencies and opportunities and usually involves being simultaneously long and short matched equity portfolios of the same size. Market-neutral portfolios are designed to be either beta-neutral or currency-neutral or both. Equity market-neutral is best defined as either statistical arbitrage (previously known as "pair trading") or fundamental arbitrage (equity long/short with zero exposure to the market).* Based on estimates from Hedge Fund Research the allocation in equity market neutral was 1.7 percent in 1990 and 5.6 percent at the end of 2001.

---

*The distinction between fundamental arbitrage and statistical arbitrage is a tricky one. The former buys and sells shares based on a fundamental view, whereas the latter uses quantitative models to create long and short portfolios. The factors in the quantitative models of the statistical arbitrageur are fundamental variables as well. The overlying theme is most often mean reversion. Chapter 8 will revisit and elaborate in more detail in discussing long/short equity and the controversy as to what exactly is long/short and market-neutral.

Quantitative long/short funds apply statistical analysis to historical data (historical asset prices as well as fundamental or accounting data) to identify profitable trading opportunities. The traditional discipline entails hypothesizing the existence of a particular type of systematic opportunity for unusual returns, and then back-testing the hypothesis. Back-testing essentially entails gathering the historical data and performing the calculations on it necessary to determine whether the opportunity would have been profitable had it been pursued in the past. Simple hypotheses are preferred to complex hypotheses; the intricate trading rules favored by technicians and chartists are generally avoided. Normally, analysts hope to bolster their empirical findings with intuitive explanations for why the hypothesized opportunity should exist. Once a successful strategy is identified, it is normally implemented relatively mechanically. That is, the strategy is traded according to a limited set of clearly defined rules (the rules that were back-tested), which are only rarely overridden by the subjective judgment of the manager. "Quant" (quantitative) fund strategies are often closely related to work published by finance academics in peer-reviewed academic journals. In many cases, the fund managers come from academic backgrounds and, in some cases, created the academic research themselves. Quant fund managers are often very secretive, as their trading rules are potentially prone to theft. Mean reversion and earnings surprises have been the main drivers of this strategy.[9]

Users of quantitative strategies expect to identify small but statistically significant return opportunities, often across large numbers of stocks. Quantitative managers typically balance their longs and shorts carefully to eliminate most sources of risk except those that they expect will create returns. Since they are often trading long portfolio lists, they are able to reduce dramatically not only broad market risk, but also industry risk, and aggregate stock-specific risk. They appear less likely than fundamental managers to adopt substantial long or short biases.

One of the great advantages of equity market-neutral strategies is the doubling of alpha. A long-only manager who is restricted from selling short has the opportunity to generate alpha only by buying or not buying stocks. A manager of an equity market-neutral fund, however, can generate alpha by buying stock as well as selling stock short. Some market observers argue that this double alpha argument is faulty because an active long-only manager can over- and underweight securities, which means the manager is short relative to benchmark when underweight. However, there is a difference between selling short and being underweight against a benchmark. If a stock has a weight of 0.02 percent in the benchmark index, the possible opportunity to underweight is limited to 0.02 percent of the portfolio. Short selling is a risk management discipline of its own.

**Examples**    A typical example in this category would be a pair trade where one share category of the same economic entity is bought and the other is sold. The overriding theme is the law of one price. One example of such a pair trade is the unification of shares of Zurich Financial Services of Switzerland, which announced a merger with the financial services arm of BAT (British American Tobacco) Industries of the United Kingdom. This pair trade is typical for equity market-neutral managers because it does not involve market or sector risk. The two stocks are based on the same economic entity, which happen to deviate in price. Other typical pair trades involve trading voting rights, for example, buying Telcom Italia Mobile (TIM) savings shares and selling the ordinary shares.

For legal reasons two share categories were listed, Allied Zurich in the United Kingdom and Zurich Allied in Switzerland (see Figure 6.22). Each Allied Zurich share was entitled to receive 0.023 Zurich Allied shares. On April 17, Zurich Financial Services announced the unification of the two shares, sweetened with a 40 pence dividend for shareholders in Allied Zurich. The spread narrowed to zero by September 2000. The fact that Zurich Allied and Allied Zurich were not traded at the same price was a violation of the law of one price since both shares together made up Zurich Financial Services.

The mother of all pair trades is the spread between Royal Dutch and Shell. Royal Dutch Petroleum and Shell Transport and Trading jointly own the Royal Dutch/Shell entity. The corporate structure links the two companies

**FIGURE 6.22** Zurich Allied/Allied Zurich Spread
*Source:* Datastream, UBS Warburg (2000).

through dividing the joint cash flows at a certain ratio. The spread arises because Royal Dutch shares are traded in euros (before 1999 in Dutch guilders) on the Amsterdam exchange (Euronext) whereas Shell trades in sterling on the London Stock Exchange.* The dividend entitlements of the two companies are the same. However, the taxation of U.K. investors is not the same as for Dutch investors. Hence, the discounted value of after-tax dividends is not equal. However, this may account only for a spread of 2 percent. The fluctuation around this "fair value" is purely liquidity driven. Note that this Royal Dutch/Shell spread is often used by behaviorists to bring across the point of how inefficient markets are.

The spread (Royal Dutch normally trades at a premium) was in the news when LTCM put on the spread, and the trade went the wrong way. Figure 6.23 shows that in 1998 the spread (i.e., the premium of Royal Dutch) widened. There are some lessons learned from 1998 with respect to the law of one price. First, pair trades do not work all the time. The return distribution of pair trades is not normally distributed but leptokurtic—many small returns on the right-hand side of the mean and few larger negative returns on the left-hand side. Second, it might not necessarily be advisable to reveal your positions to the market when trading in size.

## Performance

■ As seen in Figure 6.24, the HFRI Equity Market-Neutral index outperformed most equity indexes but not the S&P 500 index. Returns in equity market-neutral have been around 11 percent in the past. Equity market-neutral can be characterized as having low volatility of around 3.3 percent, minimal drawdowns, and a high percentage of positive returns. (See Table 6.11.) On average, the annual returns in equity market-neutral were 630 basis points above U.S. short-term rates. At the end of 2001 and at the end of May 2002 the rolling 12-month returns were around 340 basis points above U.S. short-term rates, that is, slightly below their norm. Equity market-neutral indexes were flat in 1994 and showed some

---

*There are variations of the spread including stocks trading on the New York Stock Exchange. Royal Dutch, for example, was until July 19, 2002, in the S&P 500 index, and Shell is in the FTSE All Share index. Both stocks, therefore, have benefited from activity from passive mandates since both indexes are used for passive investment approaches. However, there is more passive money in the S&P 500 index than there is in the FTSE All Share index, causing further imbalances between the two entities. On July 11, 2002, Standard & Poor's has decided to exclude all foreign stocks from the S&P 500 effective July 19, 2002. After this announcement the spread narrowed as Royal Dutch was sold more heavily than Shell. Figure 6.23 shows the spread until July 12, 2002.

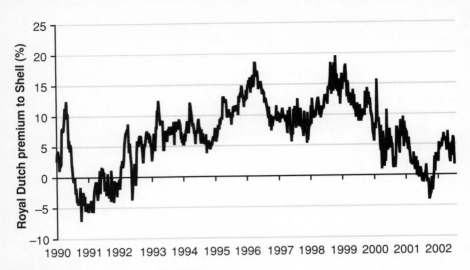

**FIGURE 6.23** Royal Dutch/Shell Spread
*Source:* Datastream.

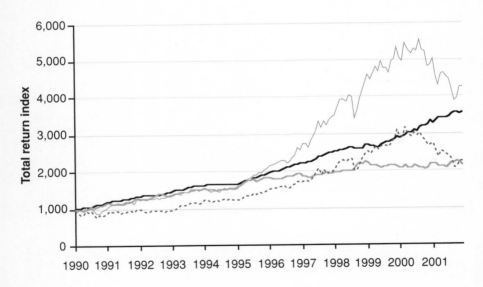

HFRI Equity Market Neutral Index    S&P 500  ····· MSCI World   JPM Bonds

**FIGURE 6.24** Equity Market Neutral Performance
*Source:* Hedge Fund Research, Datastream, UBS Warburg (2000).

**Table 6.11**   Equity Market-Neutral Risk and Return Characteristics

| | # of Monthly Returns | Annual Return | Volatility | Sharpe Ratio (5%) | Worst 1-month Drawdown | Negative Months | Worst 12-month Drawdown | 12-month Drawdown Ended On | Highest 12-month Return |
|---|---|---|---|---|---|---|---|---|---|
| S&P 500 | 144 | 12.85% | 14.54% | 0.54 | −15.64% | 35.4% | −26.63% | Sep-01 | 52.10% |
| MSCI World | 144 | 6.99 | 14.59 | 0.14 | −14.30 | 39.6 | −27.87 | Sep-01 | 33.51 |
| MSCI EAFE | 144 | 2.70 | 17.03 | <0 | −14.97 | 43.1 | −28.27 | Sep-01 | 44.19 |
| MSCI Europe | 144 | 9.15 | 15.19 | 0.27 | −13.42 | 37.5 | −25.49 | Sep-01 | 45.93 |
| JPM Global Government Bonds | 144 | 6.59 | 5.94 | 0.27 | −3.40 | 41.0 | −6.18 | Jan-00 | 20.97 |
| JPM U.S. Government Bonds | 144 | 7.94 | 4.11 | 0.72 | −2.73 | 27.8 | −3.65 | Oct-94 | 17.34 |
| HFRI Equity Market-Neutral Index | 144 | 11.09 | 3.28 | 1.86 | −1.67 | 15.3 | 1.57 | Oct-94 | 18.60 |
| CSFB/Tremont Equity Market-Neutral | 96 | 11.52 | 3.28 | 1.99 | −1.15 | 17.7 | −2.00 | Dec-94 | 21.28 |

*Source:* Hedge Fund Research, CSFB/Tremont, Datastream, Bloomberg, UBS Warburg (2000).

degree of volatility in 1998. As with other relative-value strategies, the smoothness of the wealth creation, as shown in Figure 6.24, is worth pointing out. Returns for 2000, 2001, and 2002 (July inclusive) were 14.6 percent, 6.7 percent, and 1.0 percent.

■ Figure 6.25 shows the returns of various hedge fund indexes along with some equity and bond indexes. This illustration highlights the attraction of exploiting opportunities as one activity while managing portfolio volatility as a second, but related, activity. Under the third paradigm of asset management, all active managers should be wanting to move northwestward in Figure 6.25. Currently this is not the case. Relative return managers are quite happy to move eastward, if that is where their benchmark is heading.

■ Figure 6.26 compares monthly total MSCI World returns with the HFRI Market-Neutral index returns. Figure 6.26 underlines the notion that the returns are achieved independently from market moves. Correlation is very low.

Given the strategy's "alpha purity," equity market-neutral strategies can by used within a portable alpha context; the alpha can be transported to more or less any benchmark. Consider the following (slightly simplified) example. An investor in 1990 swapped the risk-free rate plus 200 basis points with MSCI World total return and put down 15 percent of principal as collateral. The reminder (85 percent of principal) was then invested in a diversified portfolio of equity market-neutral managers (here measured with the HFRI Equity Market-Neutral index). Figure 6.27 compares the annual returns of such a venture with the total returns of the MSCI World index over the 12-year period.

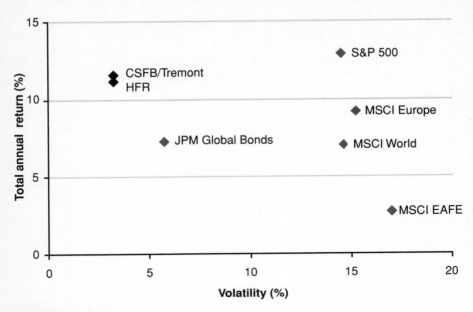

**FIGURE 6.25**  Risk and Return
*Source:* Hedge Fund Research, CSFB/Tremont, Datastream, UBS Warburg (2000).

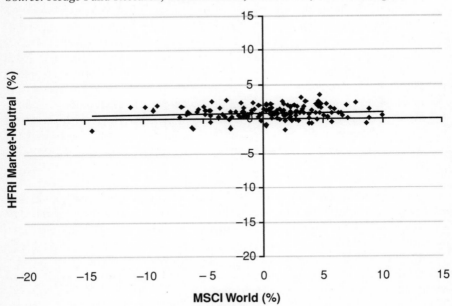

**FIGURE 6.26**  MSCI World versus Equity Market-Neutral Returns
*Source:* Hedge Fund Research, Datastream, UBS Warburg (2000).

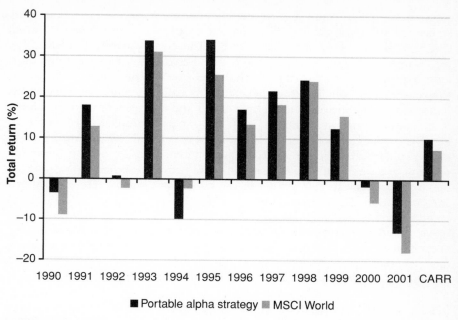

**FIGURE 6.27** Transporting Equity Market-Neutral Alphas to MSCI World Total Returns
*Source:* Hedge Fund Research, Datastream, UBS Warburg (2000).

■ The strategy would have outperformed rate of MSCI World in all years except 1994 and 1999. The compound annual return (CARR) of the portable alpha strategy and the MSCI World total return index were 10.0 percent and 7.0 percent, respectively. Note that swapping indexes in liquid and developed markets these days costs much less than the assumed 200 basis points.

The concept of portable alpha (or alpha transport) is ideally suitable in connection with hedge fund investing once risk to single hedge fund managers (i.e., nonsystematic risk) is diversified. Figure 6.27 shows the annual returns of such a strategy compared with MSCI World total returns. The (hypothetical) manager running such a strategy would have outperformed index funds most the time and the majority of active managed funds nearly all of the time.

One of the attractions of portable alpha is that nearly any alpha can be transported onto nearly any benchmark. The two main criteria are that the alpha can be isolated, that is, all betas hedged, and that the benchmark is passively replicable in an efficient manner. In a practitioners' article, Moller (2001) examined attractiveness of large-cap equity mutual funds, index funds, and transporting alpha from CTAs to index funds, and found evidence that active equity managers, especially those managing large-cap U.S. equity mutual funds, tended to underperform their benchmark during the 1991 to 1999 period. The fees charged to investors by these funds were based on asset balances, but averaged approximately 45 percent of the gross excess return generated. Moller showed that investors have the opportunity to achieve a more attractive excess return pattern by investing in an index fund and then generating their alphas from another source (e.g., from CTAs). The excess return generated by the selected CTAs had a much greater risk-adjusted return and a lower correlation to the benchmark than did the selected equity mutual funds as a group. The combination of an index fund and portable alpha proved to be superior to that of the average large-cap equity fund in the sample in terms of return, volatility, and correlation. The separation of beta (market-based) and alpha (skill-based) strategies will be one of the major themes in the years to come. There will be asset managers delivering beta (passive mandates at low cost) and active managers exploiting inefficiencies while managing total risk. Trying to do both at the same time is an inefficient way of utilizing scarce resources.

Table 6.12 shows some further statistics of equity market-neutral strategies.

■ As already mentioned, the alpha of the strategy is positive and the exposure to the equity market negligible. Apart from short sellers and fixed income arbitrage, equity market-neutral has the lowest correlation to the equity market among the strategies analyzed in this book

■ The return distribution is fairly normal; returns seem neither skewed nor kurtotic. This is a comforting observation, which, however, should not be overstated. Fixed income arbitrage was not very kurtotic, either, until "it" happened in 1998. The conservative investor should allow for some probability of a high-sigma event unfolding.

■ Correlation with equity markets is low, around 0.1 to 0.4. Note that the correlation coefficient between equity market-neutral and equities is high in a bull phase and negative in a bear market. The reason for this observation is that in a bull market there are many positive returns and fewer negative returns. Since market-neutral managers have positive returns in

**Table 6.12**    Statistical Analysis of Equity Market-Neutral Returns

|  | Alpha to MSCI World | Beta to MSCI World | Skew | Excess Kurtosis | Correlation MSCI World | Correlation JPM Global Bonds |
|---|---|---|---|---|---|---|
| HFRI Equity Market-Neutral Index | 0.87 | 0.02 | −0.11 | 0.30 | 0.09 | 0.16 |
| CSFB/Tremont Equity Market-Neutral | 0.84 | 0.10 | 0.01 | −0.07 | 0.44 | 0.04 |

*Source:* Hedge Fund Research, CSFB/Tremont, Datastream, UBS Warburg (2000).

most months, correlation is high. However, in a bear market such as 2000–2001 the correlation coefficients turn negative. In a bear market there are more negative returns and fewer positive returns. However, since market-neutral managers still have positive returns, the correlation coefficient becomes negative. Figure 6.29 illustrates this phenomenon.

Figure 6.28 shows the performance of the HFRI Equity Market-Neutral index in different market environments and Figure 6.29 shows average quarterly returns in down markets versus average quarterly returns in friendly markets.

■ The HFRI Equity Market-Neutral index was up both during the U.S. rate rise of 1994 as well as the Asian crisis in 1997. Since the Russian crisis coincided with the default of LTCM and the associated early redemptions, fear of early redemptions, and the (forced) reduction of leverage in difficult market conditions, even equity market-neutral funds reported, on average, small losses. The HFRI Equity Market-Neutral index was not negatively affected by the burst of the Internet bubble or the atrocities of September 2001 (financially speaking).

■ Since January 1990, there were 14 quarters where the MSCI World reported a negative return. (See Figure 6.29.) During these quarters, relative-

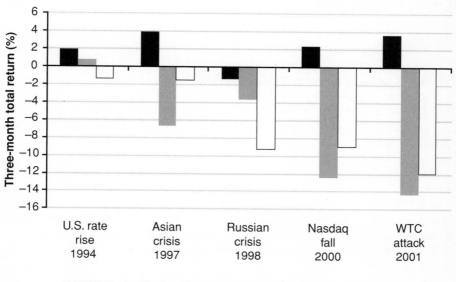

**FIGURE 6.28**  Scenario Analysis
*Source:* Hedge Fund Research, Datastream, UBS Warburg (2000).

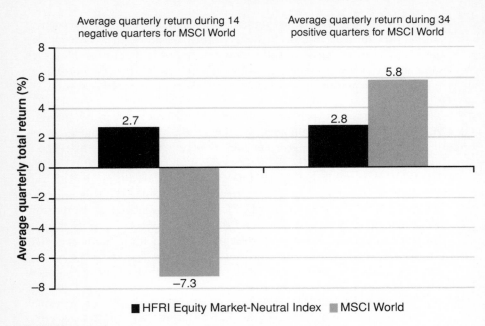

**FIGURE 6.29** Average Negative versus Average Positive Returns
*Source:* Hedge Fund Research, Datastream, UBS Warburg (2000).

value equity market-neutral showed an average return of 2.7 percent, compared with –7.3 percent in the case of the MSCI World total return index. During the 34 quarters where MSCI World ended in positive territory, the relative-value arbitrage index gained 2.8 percent per quarter against 5.8 percent for the MSCI World index. In other words, quarterly returns were (on average) around 2.75 percent regardless of equities going up or down.

Figure 6.30 shows how returns have been distributed in the past and compares the historic return distribution with a normal distribution of equity market-neutral and a normal distribution of historical MSCI World returns, both based on historic mean return and standard deviation of returns. For Figure 6.31, the equity market-neutral returns were sorted in ascending order and compared with the corresponding market returns. This allows seeing in which market environment the extreme positive and negative returns were achieved.

■ Figure 6.30 shows how narrowly around the mean the monthly returns were distributed, especially compared with the market. Four returns were below the 95 percent range and one return above. There were no returns

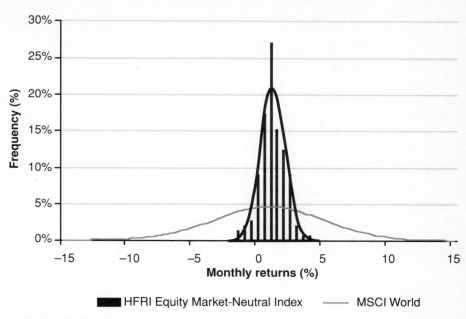

**FIGURE 6.30** Return Distribution
*Source:* Hedge Fund Research, Datastream, UBS Warburg (2000).

outside the 99 percent range, that is, three standard deviations from the mean. Only 22 of the 144 monthly returns were below zero. This compares with 51 and 57 for the S&P 500 the MSCI World, respectively. Note that the mean monthly return of the HFRI Equity Market-Neutral index was only 0.88 percent, while the standard deviation of monthly returns was 0.94 percent. In other words, a five-sigma event in equity-market neutral space would result in an absolute monthly loss of only around 3.8 percent (0.88% – 5 × 0.94%). Most investment professionals in the AIS industry are utterly amazed and puzzled that the narrow distribution in Figure 6.30 is what the press, large parts of the public, and still a majority of institutional investors (globally speaking) consider as the more risky of the two distributions. Not only has the MSCI World a much higher standard deviation of monthly returns than the HFRI Equity Market-Neutral index (4.23 percent versus 0.94 percent), it also has a lower mean monthly return (0.56 percent versus 0.88 percent). It is comparisons such as the one in Figure 6.30 that indicate that there might be better ways of dealing with uncertainty than just blindly accepting the whims of the market by being long and benchmarked. What we called the new or third paradigm in the asset management industry in the Preface of this book is essentially about balancing investment opportunities while managing the curve in Figure 6.30, that is, managing portfolio volatility in an absolute sense as opposed to being fully exposed to uncertainty. Managing uncertainty not only means smoothing monthly portfolio returns; it also means that existing intellectual paradigms under which we operate might potentially be outdated or be partly or outright false.

■ Figure 6.31 illustrates graphically what statistics already have revealed: low correlation with equities and that negative equity market-neutral returns were not concentrated during equity market declines.

■ As seen in Table 6.13, there is some variation in the three-year annual returns as well as variation in risk-adjusted returns. However, the variation is not correlated with the variation in equity returns.

■ Volatility has been increasing slightly over the 12-year period.

■ The bottom row in Table 6.13 shows that the worst 12-month periods all have resulted in positive absolute returns for the investor.

■ Figure 6.32 relates the worst losses for diversified market-neutral portfolios with swings in the stock market. Table 6.12 did show little excess kurtosis for equity market-neutral managers, while Figure 6.32 shows that the five worst quarterly losses were minor. This implies hardly any downside financial risk. The track record of market-neutral managers as a group

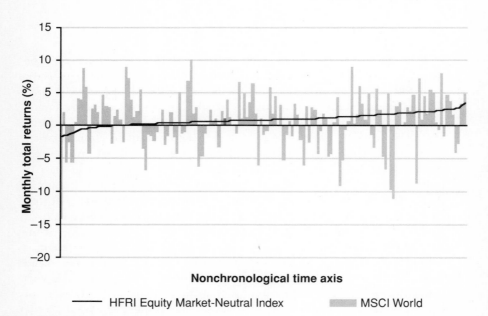

**FIGURE 6.31**  Correlation
*Source:* Hedge Fund Research, Datastream, UBS Warburg (2000).

**Table 6.13**  Performance Persistence

|  | 1990–1992 | 1993–1995 | 1996–1998 | 1999–2001 |
|---|---|---|---|---|
| **MSCI World (Total Return)** | | | | |
| Annual return (%) | −1.80 | 16.40 | 18.25 | −3.05 |
| Volatility (%) | 16.70 | 10.29 | 14.47 | 15.73 |
| Average risk-free rate (%) | 5.61 | 4.37 | 5.07 | 4.64 |
| Sharpe ratio | <0 | 1.17 | 0.91 | <0 |
| Worst 1-month drawdown (%) | −11.12 | −5.81 | −14.30 | −9.21 |
| Worst 12-month drawdown (%) | −16.52 | −4.66 | 0.51 | −27.87 |
| | | | | |
| **HFRI Equity Market-Neutral Index** | | | | |
| Annual return (%) | 13.23 | 9.88 | 12.01 | 9.29 |
| Volatility (%) | 2.65 | 3.09 | 3.10 | 4.29 |
| Sharpe ratio | 2.87 | 1.78 | 2.24 | 1.09 |
| Worst 1-month drawdown (%) | −0.35 | −1.46 | −1.68 | −1.58 |
| Worst 12-month drawdown (%) | 8.73 | 1.57 | 4.91 | 1.87 |

*Source:* Hedge Fund Research, Datastream.

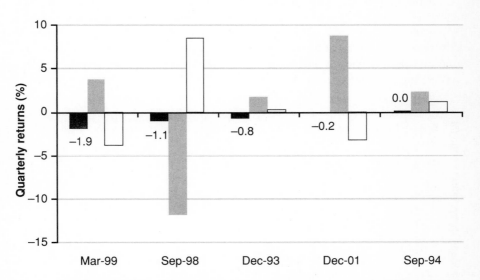

**FIGURE 6.32**  Worst Quarters for Equity Market-Neutral
*Source:* Hedge Fund Research, Datastream.

looks more than impressive. However, fixed income arbitrage pre-LTCM also showed little excess kurtosis while drawdowns were negligible. The conservative and diligent investor will not extrapolate the past performance record without judgment. Potentially (we do not yet know) the Armageddon for market-neutral managers lies somewhere in the future.

■ Figure 6.33 is an indication how foolish regulators look by banning retail investors from buying hedge fund exposure but allowing Nasdaq-like investments. One of the main objectives of market-neutral managers is to reduce volatility and to keep at "surface levels" (at 100 percent in Figure 6.33) at all times. Any falls below the surface were minor (in the past) and were recovered quickly. One wonders whether this (the aim of staying at the surface) may not become the future of active asset management.

## Conclusion and Outlook

Equity market-neutral is probably one of the most attractive absolute return strategies. The sector has proven that it's an alpha generator par excellence and not a beta merchant at all. The risk/return as well as the correlation characteristics of equity market-neutral strategies have been fairly stable. Capacity constraints are limited. The market capitalization of equity markets (around $25 trillion as of April 2002) is the capacity limit. There are some capacity constraints with respect to borrowing stock. However, as long as there are violations to the law of one price there will be market participants making money on the conversions.

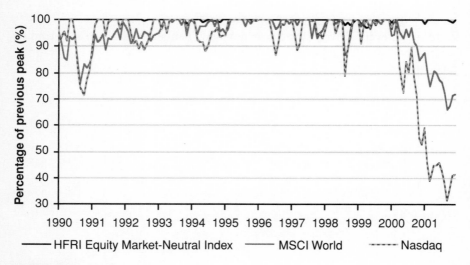

**FIGURE 6.33**   Underwater
*Source:* Hedge Fund Research, Datastream.

# CHAPTER 7

# Event-Driven Strategies

*We are ready for an unforeseen event that may or may not occur.*
—Dan Quayle

## INTRODUCTION

Event-driven strategies focus on identifying and analyzing securities that can benefit from the occurrence of extraordinary transactions. What we today refer to as an event-driven strategy is not new. Benjamin Graham was trading bonds of U.S. railroad companies in distress some decades ago. It is not entirely without irony that the father of conservative stock investment was also involved in what today is done by hedge fund managers.

Event-driven strategies concentrate on companies that are, or may be, subject to restructurings, takeovers, mergers, liquidations, bankruptcies, or other special situations. The securities prices of the companies involved in these events are typically influenced more by the dynamics of the particular event than by the general appreciation or depreciation of the debt and equity markets. For example, the result and timing of factors such as legal decisions, negotiating dynamics, collateralization requirements, or indexing issues are key elements in the success of any event-driven strategy. Based on estimates from Hedge Fund Research, the event-driven, distressed securities, and merger arbitrage allocations at the end of 2001 were 9.3 percent, 2.6 percent, and 2.4 percent, respectively, compared with 3.8 percent, 2.4 percent, and 0.6 percent in 1990. (See Table 7.1.)

**Table 7.1**    Summary of Risk/Return Characteristics Based on Historical Performance

| Subsector | Returns | Volatility | Downside Risk | Sharpe Ratio | Correlation to Equities | Leverage | Investment Horizon |
|-----------|---------|-----------|---------------|--------------|-------------------------|----------|--------------------|
| Risk arbitrage | Medium | Low | Medium | High | Medium | Medium | Medium |
| Distressed securities | High | Medium | High | High | Medium | Low | Long |

*Source:* UBS Warburg (2000).

Typically, these strategies rely on fundamental research that extends beyond the evaluation of the issues affecting a single company to include an assessment of the legal and structural issues surrounding the extraordinary event or transaction. In some cases, such as corporate reorganizations, the investment manager may actually take an active role in determining the event's outcome.

The goal of event-driven strategies is to profit when the price of a security changes to reflect more accurately the likelihood and potential impact of the occurrence, or nonoccurrence, of the extraordinary event. Because event-driven strategies are positioned to take advantage of the valuation disparities produced by corporate events, they are less dependent on overall stock market gains than are traditional equity investment approaches.

In times of financial crisis, the correlation between event-driven strategies and market activity can increase to uncomfortable levels. During the stock market crash in October 1987, for example, merger arbitrage positions fell in step with the general market, providing little protection in the short run against the dramatic market decline. As time passed, investors recognized that companies continued to meet contractual obligations, ultimately completing all merger deals previously announced. The return of confidence improved merger arbitrage results, providing handsome returns relative to the market.

## RISK ARBITRAGE

### Strategy

At the most general level, risk arbitrage (also known as merger arbitrage) involves a bet on a deal being accepted by regulators and shareholders. Risk arbitrage is an event-driven investment process. The specialists invest simultaneously in long and short positions in both companies involved in a merger or acquisition. In stock swap mergers, risk arbitrageurs are typically long the stock of the company being acquired and short the stock of the acquiring company. In the case of a cash tender offer, the risk arbitrageur is seeking to capture the difference between the tender price and the price at which the target company's stock is trading.

Moore (1999), author of *Risk Arbitrage*, defines risk arbitrage as follows:

> *The risk arbitrage investment process is the investment in securities involved in and affected by mergers, tender offers, liquidations, spin-offs, and corporate reorganizations. The securities involved in the risk arbitrage process can be common stocks, preferred stocks, bonds, or options. Once a transaction is announced, arbitrageurs try to assemble as much information as possible to help estimate each transaction's risk, reward, and probability of occurrence.*

During negotiations, the target company's stock can typically trade at a discount to its value after the merger is completed because all mergers involve some risk that the transaction will not occur. Profits are made by capturing the spread between the current market price of the target company's stock and the price to which it will appreciate when the deal is completed or the cash tender price. The risk to the arbitrageur is that the deal fails. Risk arbitrage positions are considered to be uncorrelated to overall market direction with the principal risk being "deal risk." Deal risk is nonsystematic risk. However, it will be highlighted later that deal risk includes a systematic component—risk that can not be immunized through diversification alone.

Former U.S. Secretary of the Treasury and Goldman Sachs partner Robert Rubin brought fame to the profession in the 1980s. Throughout the industry, Rubin was known as one of the best in the field.[1] His careful research and unemotional trading style were legendary. Rubin underlines the probabilistic nature of the strategy as follows:

> *If a deal goes through, what do you win? If it doesn't go through, what do you lose? It was a high-risk business, but I'll tell you, it did teach you to think of life in terms of probabilities instead of absolutes. You couldn't be in that business and not internalize that probabilistic approach of life. It was what you were doing all the time.[2]*

Risk arbitrageurs differ according to the degree to which they are willing to take on deal risk. Where antitrust issues are involved, this risk is often related to regulatory decisions. In other cases, as was predominant in the late 1980s, financing risk was the major concern to arbitrageurs. Most managers invest only in announced transactions, whereas a few are likely to enter positions with higher deal risk and wider spreads based on rumor or speculation. (See Table 7.2.)

Most managers use some form of "risk of loss" methodology to limit position size, but risk tolerance reflects each manager's own risk/return objectives.[3] Some managers simply maintain highly diversified portfolios containing a substantial portion of the transaction universe, typically using

**Table 7.2**    Key Risk Factors in Risk or Merger Arbitrage

| Risk | Position | Effect |
|------|----------|--------|
| Legal | Trust regulation | Risk arbitrage is primarily a bet on a deal being accepted by regulators and shareholders. If a deal is called off, the risk arbitrageur usually loses as the spread widens to preannouncement levels. |
| | | The risk/reward trade-off is extremely asymmetrical: There is normally a large probability of making a small amount (e.g., 20 cents per spread if the announced deal goes through smoothly) and a very small probability of losing a lot of money (e.g., $20 per spread if the deal breaks). |
| Equity | Short delta, long liquidity, and long volatility | One of the main performance variables is liquidity. Merger arbitrage returns depend on the overall volume of merger activity, which has historically been cyclical in nature. |
| | | In general, the strategy has exposure to deal risk and stock-specific risk, whereas market risk is often hedged by investing in 10 to 40 deals. Stock-specific risk has a large-cap bias since large caps are easier to sell short. |
| | | Most trades are transacted on a ratio basis as opposed to a cash-neutral basis assuming the spread converges. This leaves the arbitrageur with a small short delta position, as the cash outlay for long stock position is smaller than the proceeds from the short position. |

*Source:* UBS Warburg (2000).

leverage to enhance returns, whereas other managers maintain more concentrated portfolios (often unleveraged) and attempt to add value through the quality of their research and their ability to trade around the positions. Some managers are more rigorous than others at hedging residual market risk.

Given the high profile of risk arbitrage deals and their profitability to the arbitrageur, many long-only managers joined this discipline. However, there is a certain risk of this herd behavior backfiring. There is more to risk arbitrage than simply buying the stock of the company being acquired and selling the stock of the acquiring company. Risk arbitrage is not simply a binary event—will it work or fail? The deals are most often highly complex, and the management of unwanted risk requires knowledge, experience, and skill in all financial engineering and risk management disciplines. Here is just a selection of the tasks that are carried out by risk arbitrageurs entering a spread:

- Analysis of public information regarding the companies of the transaction and the markets in which they compete, including company documents, various industry and trade data sources, past Justice Department or Federal Trade Commission enforcement activities in the relevant product and geographic markets, and current antitrust agency enforcement policies.

■ Estimation of probabilities as to the likelihood of a government antitrust investigation and enforcement action, the likely outcome of such an action, and whether a remedial order can be negotiated eliminating the necessity for litigation.

■ Monitoring of litigation by the government and any private enforcement action and, in hostile transactions, analysis of the viability on antitrust and regulatory grounds of possible white knight candidates; analysis of the requirements and procedures of various federal and state regulatory approvals that may be required, depending on the nature of the acquired company's business operations.

■ Control of deal risk with respect to the acquirer walking away, deal delay, possibility of material adverse conditions, shareholder approval issues, tax implications, and financing conditions.

■ In hostile transactions, analysis of the viability of various antitakeover devices created by the target corporation in anticipation of or in the course of the unwanted takeover attempt and litigation arising from these defenses.

Moore (1999) puts all variables into a formula to calculate the risk-adjusted expected return on a transaction. The risk-adjusted return (RAR) is a function of the probability of a deal closing, the probability of a deal breaking, expected net profit, expected total loss, and the investment capital and (estimated) investment period. Warren Buffett has roughly the same formula: "How likely is it that the promised event will indeed occur? How long will your money be tied up? What chance is there that something better will transpire—a competing takeover bid for example? What will happen if the event does not take place because of antitrust action, financing glitches, etc.?"[4]

Table 7.3 shows various effects produced by changing the variables. One aspect of the recent past is that spreads have narrowed. This means that the return potential decreases for investment capital. Falling spreads has been a characteristic for a long time. After "arbitrage boutiques" dominated the game in the 1970s and 1980s, more participants (banks, hedge funds) entered the arena and put pressure on margins. Pension funds also play a role in risk arbitrage. A few decades ago, pension funds used to be sellers of target companies as they became subject to takeover attempts and mergers. Pension fund managers had been holding these securities as long-term investments. Once the deals were announced, pension managers usually cashed out. Arbitrageurs were generally the beneficiaries of these sales because they were able to purchase the target's securities at lower prices. Moore (1999) argues that now that some pension funds have hired arbitrageurs to take over the investment decisions on securities subject to takeover attempts, the supply of stock upon the deal's announcement has dwindled, causing further pressure on spreads and profits.

**Table 7.3** Risk-Adjusted Return of Risk Arbitrage Transaction

| | Return ($) | Risk ($) | Probability of Deal Closing | Probability of Deal Breaking | Estimated Investment Period (Days) | Initial Investment ($) | Risk Adjusted Return |
|---|---|---|---|---|---|---|---|
| Deal 1 | 8.00 | −20.00 | 99% | 1% | 100 | 100 | 28.18% |
| Deal 2 | 8.00 | −20.00 | 80 | 20 | 100 | 100 | 8.76 |
| Deal 3 | 8.00 | −20.00 | 99 | 1 | 50 | 100 | 56.36 |
| Deal 4 | 8.00 | −20.00 | 50 | 50 | 100 | 100 | −21.90 |
| Deal 5 | 2.00 | −20.00 | 99 | 1 | 100 | 100 | 6.50 |
| Deal 6 | 0.50 | −5.00 | 99 | 1 | 100 | 100 | 1.62 |
| Deal 7 | 0.50 | −2.00 | 99 | 1 | 100 | 100 | 1.73 |
| Deal 8 | 0.50 | −1.00 | 80 | 20 | 100 | 100 | 0.73 |

*Source:* Adapted from Moore (1999), with author's own examples.

Table 7.3 also shows the effect of the probability of a deal being accepted. Deals 1 and 2 have identical terms despite having different probabilities of closing. The higher the probability of a deal closing successfully, to state the obvious, the higher the expected risk-adjusted return. Deals 1 and 3 are identical apart from the expected investment period. The shorter the time period, the higher the expected risk-adjusted return. Deal 4 should be put on the other way around. This process is called "Chinesing."* Chinesing involves buying the acquirer (GE, Vodafone) and selling the target (Honeywell, Mannesmann) instead of the other (normal) way. The risk column of Table 7.3 becomes the potential return and the return column becomes negative. In deal 4 there is a 50–50 chance of closing or breaking but the profit potential from Chinesing is $20 whereas the potential loss is −$8 in case of the deal closing successfully. Few risk arbitrageurs bought Enron after the (friendly) takeover bid for Enron by Dynegy in November 2001. Some "Chinesed" the deal by selling Enron and buying Dynegy.

Risk arbitrage is not new. As a matter of fact, risk arbitrage has a long tradition. Two prominent arbitrageurs, Gus Levy and Cy Lewis, were instrumental in establishing Goldman Sachs and Bear Stearns as prominent Wall Street firms. Gus Levy invented risk arbitrage in the 1940s and Ivan Boesky

---

*Despite great effort, the author has not yet found out where the term "Chinesing" comes from. One market participant hypothesized it could be put in connection with "Chinese walls." Perhaps (this is pure speculation) risk arbitrageurs in investment banks in the 1980s put on the trade the other way around when they had superior information from the other side of the organization's "Chinese wall." Perhaps it is simply because China is on the other side of the planet or the writing is opposite of western style.

popularized it 40 years later.[5] In fact, the senior post at Goldman Sachs has traditionally been filled by the head of the "arb desk"—including former U.S. Secretary of the Treasury Bob Rubin. Risk arbitrage was Goldman Sachs' second most profitable department after mergers and acquisitions; it was regarded as a jewel in the firm's crown. Risk arbitrage received negative press coverage in the late 1980s when some well-known M&A specialists, such as Ivan Boesky and Martin Siegel, bought stock in companies before the merger announcements using inside information and Robert Freeman, chief of risk arbitrage, head of international equities, and trusted partner of Goldman Sachs, was forced to step down in ignominy.

In the 1980s, the most publicized domain of Wall Street activity was mergers and acquisitions (M&A) and the various forms of deals and trading opportunities they generated.[6] It was the time of Gordon Gekko's "greed is good"* and many Wall Street investment professionals running around in suspenders after seeing Michael Douglas in *Wall Street*.† Many of the merger deals were hostile takeover efforts resisted by both the management and employees of well-known corporations. Many of these deals also involved leveraged-buyout transactions in which the acquiring company would borrow as much as 90 percent of the purchase price, thereby exposing those with a long-term interest in the corporation to a substantial risk of bankruptcy. Some of these transactions were financed with junk bonds, high-yield corporate bonds of exceptionally low credit standing.‡ As Smith and Walter (1997) put it:

> *Most members of the financial and business community (and many business executives) believed that the aggressive roles played by investment bankers, commercial lenders, takeover lawyers, arbitrageurs, and junk-bond experts were appropriate and healthy. This competitive environment subjected all participants to the discipline of market forces. But many representatives of the besieged and often underperforming companies, as well as sympathizers in the media and in state and national politics, saw the 1980s as a time of lawlessness and greed that was running American industry, vastly overrewarding financial deal makers and corrupting the values of the young in the process.*§[7]

---

*A line taken from an Ivan Boesky speech.

†Michael Douglas' advertisement for suspenders potentially could be the second most successful product placement in film history, after Sean Connery's advertisement for Aston Martin's DB5.

‡After Michael Milken's exit from the bond market, the junk bond market has come to be known as the "high-yield" market.

§Given sentiment toward Wall Street and corporate boardrooms in June/July of 2002, one is inclined to believe that history has a tendency to repeat itself.

## Example

An illustrative and successful example of risk arbitrage activity is the completion of the acquisition of Mannesmann by Vodafone AirTouch. (See Figure 7.1.)

The deal was announced on Sunday, November 14, 1999, when Vodafone AirTouch bid 53.7 of its own shares for each Mannesmann share. At the close of the following Monday, the bid premium was 22.5 percent. On February 4, the Vodafone AirTouch board approved an increased bid of 58.9646 shares for each Mannesmann share. On February 10, the deal was declared wholly unconditional. The bid premium eventually melted to zero, resulting in a large profit for risk arbitrageurs, who sold stock of the acquirer and simultaneously bought stock of the target company.

## Performance

■ As shown in Figure 7.2, the HFRI Merger Arbitrage index has outperformed nearly all equity indexes over the past 12 years. This was the case when sentiment was friendly for equities and M&A activity was increasing. Risk arbitrage is another example of sustainable, smooth, stable, positive returns.
■ As shown in Table 7.4, absolute returns in risk arbitrage have been around 12 to 13 percent in the past with volatility of less than 5 percent

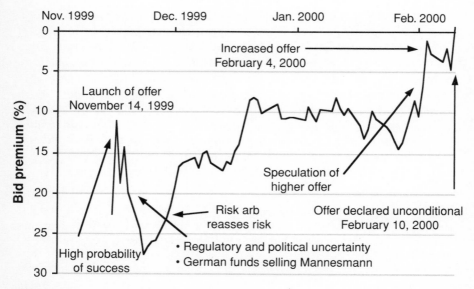

**FIGURE 7.1**   Vodafone/Mannesmann Spread
*Source:* Datastream, Bloomberg, UBS Warburg (2000).

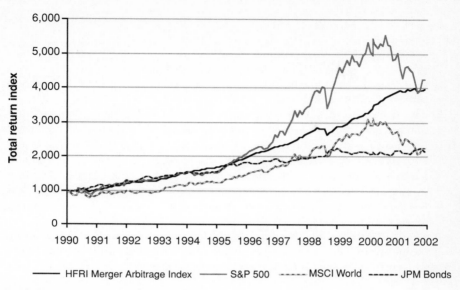

**FIGURE 7.2** Long-Term Performance of Risk Arbitrage
*Source:* Hedge Fund Research, Datastream, UBS Warburg (2000).

**Table 7.4** Risk Arbitrage Risk and Return Characteristics

| | # of Monthly Returns | Annual Return | Volatility | Sharpe Ratio (5%) | Worst 1-month Drawdown | Negative Months | Worst 12-month Drawdown | 12-month Drawdown Ended On | Highest 12-month Return |
|---|---|---|---|---|---|---|---|---|---|
| S&P 500 | 144 | 12.85% | 14.54% | 0.54 | −15.64% | 35.4% | −26.63% | Sep-01 | 52.10% |
| MSCI World | 144 | 6.99 | 14.59 | 0.14 | −14.30 | 39.6 | −27.87 | Sep-01 | 33.51 |
| MSCI EAFE | 144 | 2.70 | 17.03 | <0 | −14.97 | 43.1 | −28.27 | Sep-01 | 44.19 |
| MSCI Europe | 144 | 9.15 | 15.19 | 0.27 | −13.42 | 37.5 | −25.49 | Sep-01 | 45.93 |
| JPM Global Government Bonds | 144 | 6.59 | 5.94 | 0.27 | −3.40 | 41.0 | −6.18 | Jan-00 | 20.97 |
| JPM U.S. Government Bonds | 144 | 7.94 | 4.11 | 0.72 | −2.73 | 27.8 | −3.65 | Oct-94 | 17.34 |
| HFRI Merger Arbitrage index | 144 | 12.18 | 4.56 | 1.58 | −6.46 | 10.4 | 0.44 | Dec-90 | 20.81 |
| Zurich Hedge Event- Driven: Risk Arbitrage | 144 | 12.78 | 4.40 | 1.77 | −5.61 | 9.7 | −1.69 | Dec-90 | 26.94 |
| Hennessee Hedge Fund Index—Merger Arbitrage | 108 | 13.10 | 3.60 | 2.25 | −4.97 | 10.2 | 3.52 | Dec-01 | 23.39 |

*Source:* Hedge Fund Research, Zurich Capital Markets, Hennessee, Datastream, Bloomberg, UBS Warburg (2000).

resulting in a relatively high Sharpe ratio of around 1.6. After an above-average year in 2000, the years 2001 and 2002 (to July) were below average with respect to returns. The calendar return for 2001 was around 2.8 percent, while 2002 (July inclusive) was –2.8 percent. This is an indication that if the opportunities vanish, the arbitrageurs take risk off the table and preserve capital.

■ The worst monthly losses are higher than those of, for example, equity market-neutral. However, the worst annual return is around zero (neither an absolute profit nor a loss). The number of negative months is extremely low at around 10 percent. Most often deal risk is diversified; losses from breaking deals are balanced by profits from other deals. Only in rare circumstances (e.g., when equity markets dislocate or a large deal breaks) are losses experienced on a single fund as well as diversified level.

Figure 7.3 shows the returns of the various hedge fund indexes along with some equity and bond indexes. Figure 7.4 compares monthly total MSCI World returns with the HFRI Merger Arbitrage index.

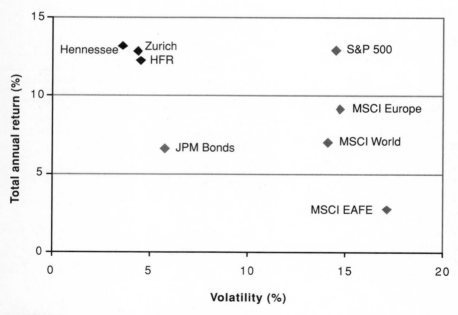

**FIGURE 7.3**   Return versus Risk
*Source:* Hedge Fund Research, Hennessee, Zurich Capital Markets, Datastream, UBS Warburg (2000).

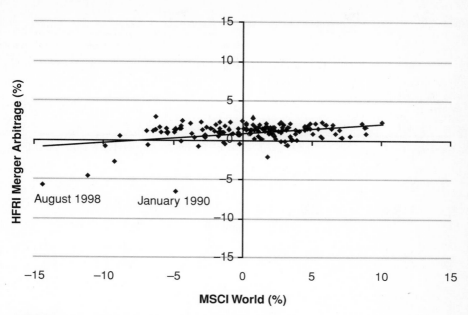

**FIGURE 7.4** MSCI World versus Risk Arbitrage Returns
*Source:* Hedge Fund Research, Datastream, UBS Warburg (2000).

■ Figure 7.3 puts the attractive risk/return characteristics described earlier into perspective. Risk arbitrage had high returns with volatility lower than that of global bonds. However, Figure 7.4 reveals some outliers in down markets.

Table 7.5 shows some further statistics of risk arbitrage.

■ The exposure to the market is higher than in equity market-neutral, but still very low at around 0.12.
■ The distribution of returns was negatively skewed and strongly leptokurtic, indicating the presence of outliers.
■ The correlation to the equity market was around 0.4 and statistically significant at the 99 percent level.

Figure 7.5 shows the performance of the HFRI Merger Arbitrage index in different market environments, and Figure 7.6 shows average quarterly returns in down markets versus average quarterly returns in friendly markets.

■ Neither the U.S. rate rise in 1994 nor the Asian crisis in 1997 negatively affected risk arbitrage. Normally, increases in downside volatility have no

**Table 7.5**  Statistical Analysis of Risk Arbitrage Returns

|  | Alpha to MSCI World | Beta to MSCI World | Skew | Excess Kurtosis | Correlation MSCI World | Correlation JPM Global Bonds |
|---|---|---|---|---|---|---|
| HFRI Arbitrage index | 0.89 | 0.12 | −3.19 | 14.27 | 0.38 | 0.05 |
| Zurich Hedge Event-Driven: Risk Arbitrage | 0.93 | 0.12 | −1.59 | 7.76 | 0.40 | −0.04 |
| Hennessee Hedge Fund Index— Merger Arbitrage | 1.01 | 0.02 | −2.26 | 11.49 | 0.46 | −0.04 |

*Source:* Hedge Fund Research, Zurich Capital Markets, Hennessee, Datastream, Bloomberg, UBS Warburg (2000).

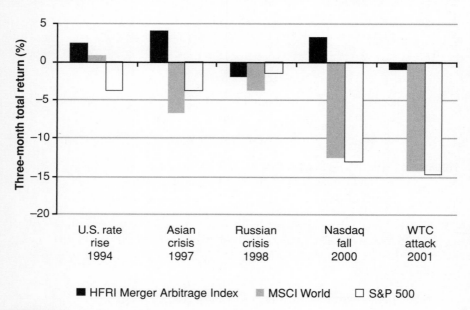

**FIGURE 7.5**  Scenario Analysis
*Source:* Hedge Fund Research, Datastream, UBS Warburg (2000).

impact on the long-term profitability of risk arbitrageurs, as the spreads eventually converge despite the markets' volatility. However, short-term volatility can have an impact on the spread of longer-duration deals. A market disruption can diminish the risk appetite for longer-duration deals of several months to completion. The spreads of the deals that are expected to be completed within a couple of weeks are normally not affected by short-term volatility.
■ The reason for the negative outliers in risk arbitrage is more micro than macro. There are only a limited number of transactions available to this

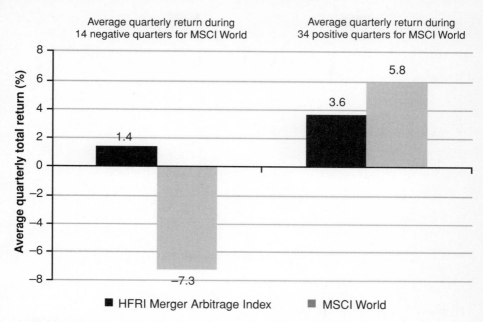

**FIGURE 7.6** Average Negative versus Average Positive Returns
*Source:* Hedge Fund Research, Datastream, UBS Warburg (2000).

category, and most managers employing this strategy have similar trades put on: long the stock of a company being acquired in a merger, leveraged buyout, or takeover and simultaneously short in the stock of the acquiring company. The opportunities are limited to deals where the acquiring company is a large, listed, and liquid traded stock where it is possible to borrow stock for shorting.

■ Risk arbitrage offers some degree of protection, although less than some relative-value strategies discussed earlier. To some extent, risk arbitrage is short equity market delta because a trade is normally transacted on a deal-ratio basis as opposed to a cash-neutral basis. Since January 1990, there were 14 quarters where the MSCI World index reported a negative return (Figure 7.6). During these quarters, risk arbitrage showed an average return of 1.4 percent, compared to –7.3 percent in the case of the MSCI World index. During the 34 quarters where MSCI World ended in positive territory, the risk arbitrage index gained 3.6 percent per quarter against 5.8 percent for the MSCI World.

Figure 7.7 shows how returns have been distributed in the past and compares the historic return distribution with a normal distribution of risk arbitrage

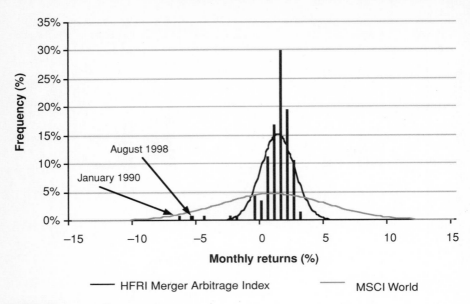

**FIGURE 7.7**  Return Distribution
*Source:* Hedge Fund Research, Datastream, UBS Warburg (2000).

and a normal distribution of historical MSCI World returns, both based on historic mean return and standard deviation of returns. For Figure 7.8, the risk arbitrage returns were sorted in ascending order (line) and compared to the corresponding market returns (bars). This allows seeing in which market environment the extreme positive and negative returns were achieved.

■ Figure 7.7 shows the leptokurtic features of the distribution very well. The historic return distribution has been narrow with more outliers than normality would suggest. Note that the outliers are on the downside and not on the upside. Four returns were outside the two-standard deviation range. This is what we would expect, because if a deal goes through the risk arbitrageur earns the gap between the two merging stocks—which in a semiefficient market is not huge (around 10 to 30 percent). However, if a deal goes wrong—for example, when a deal is canceled—the arbitrageur is left with a long stock position that collapses and a short position that rallies; there is a potential short squeeze since everyone in the market knows that there are many risk arbitrageurs who are being forced to unwind their positions. In other words, there are limited outliers on the upside, but outliers on the downside are in the nature of the strategy. It is fair to assume that the return distribution characteristics will remain similar going forward.

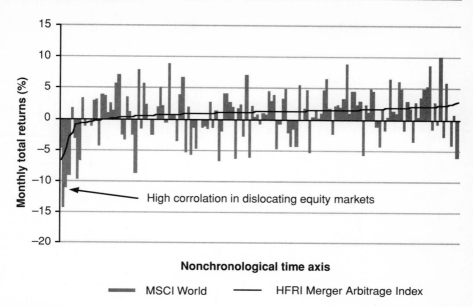

**FIGURE 7.8** Correlation
*Source:* Hedge Fund Research, Datastream, UBS Warburg (2000).

■ Figure 7.8 shows that most negative risk arbitrage returns occurred in down markets, whereas the extreme positive returns are not dependent on the direction of the market. This element of deal risk is systematic—it is not immunized through diversification in many deals.

■ Risk arbitrage occasionally faces some challenges with respect to antitrust issues. The Federal Trade Commission (FTC), one of the U.S. agencies charged with enforcing antitrust regulations, continues to rethink existing merger-review standards. This changing attitude stems from the FTC's view that a number of mergers that relied on negotiated divestitures have failed to protect competition. Thus, the FTC has taken the stance that it will simply give an opinion on whether the proposed merger would inhibit competition and thereby refrain from participating in more protracted settlement negotiations. When the FTC has communicated this position, a number of deals have experienced difficulties as evidenced by the break of Royal Ahold/Pathmark, the delayed approval of Exxon/Mobil, and the derailment of Abbott Labs/Alza.

■ In the case of the BP Amoco/ARCO acquisition, the FTC was effectively forced to take legal action if it had persisted in opposing the merger. As illustrated in Figure 7.9, the FTC's opposition and potential legal challenge to the BP Amoco/ARCO merger shook investors' confidence in the deal,

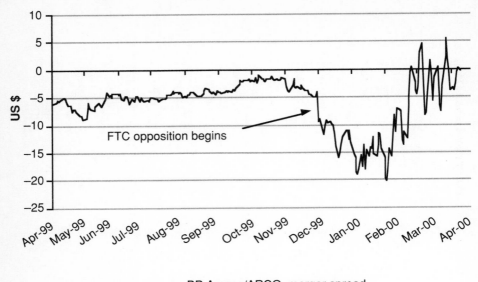

**FIGURE 7.9**   BP Amoco/ARCO Merger Spread
*Source:* Datastream, Bloomberg.

causing the spread to widen dramatically. Likewise, other merger deals with regulatory concerns have experienced similar effects. This is an example of regulatory issues driving the spread in risk arbitrage.

■ Figure 7.10 and Figure 7.11 reveal the increase in correlation in dislocating markets (i.e., losses when equity markets fall sharply). Figure 7.10 shows that the drawdowns in risk arbitrage are synchronous with the equity market falling sharply. Note that the recovery periods are brief. This is due to the fact that spreads narrow within weeks of the dislocations. The losses, therefore, are book losses due to mark-to-market position measurement. The small loss in June 2001 (Figure 7.10) is from the GE/Honeywell deal breaking.

■ Moore (1999) stresses the point that in most market environments the investment process of the risk arbitrageur is not dependent on the stock market rising; hence correlation is low in most market situations. However, he notes that there are periods where this nonrelationship breaks: For instance, during the crash of 1987 and the mini-crash of 1989, many announced merger transactions were reevaluated by the acquiring companies' boards of directors. Whenever the transactions were then terminated, the arbitrage community suffered losses. The reevaluations were generally done because of the large declines in stock

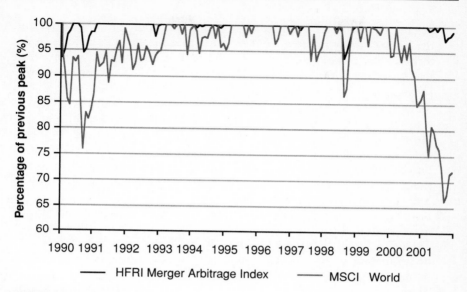

**FIGURE 7.10** Underwater
*Source:* Hedge Fund Research, Datastream.

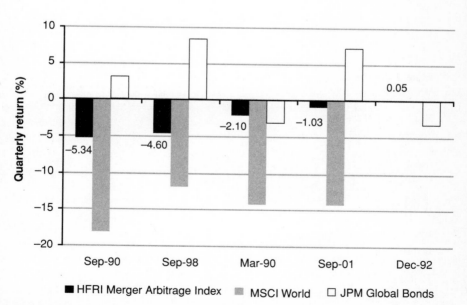

**FIGURE 7.11** Worst Quarters for Risk Arbitrage
*Source:* Hedge Fund Research, Datastream, UBS Warburg (2000).

prices. The transactions had been structured in an earlier period, and the higher equity prices at that time had been used as guidelines to determine the prices to be paid for particular companies. When stock prices declined dramatically, many board members felt they were overpaying for the assets they were trying to acquire. Furthermore, in this earlier period a tremendous number of transactions were driven by entrepreneurs who were trying to buy companies for the purpose of selling off the newly acquired assets in a short period of time. Many of these buyers were highly leveraged, and their strategies were dependent on the stock market's remaining healthy. When the market declined, their strategies were flawed and the sources of their financing began to pull their financing commitments.

■ If history were any guide for the future, then one could argue that losing money with risk arbitrage on a 12-month basis seems quite difficult. Table 7.6 shows that there was no 12-month period in which a diversified portfolio of risk arbitrage managers eroded principal (last row in Table 7.6).

■ There is less persistence of return and risk-adjusted returns in risk arbitrage than with other nondirectional absolute return strategies. This is a confirmation that there is some link to M&A activity, which itself is linked to overall economic activity and the stock market.

**Table 7.6**    Performance Persistence

|  | 1990–1992 | 1993–1995 | 1996–1998 | 1999–2001 |
|---|---|---|---|---|
| **MSCI World (Total Return)** |  |  |  |  |
| Annual return (%) | −1.80 | 16.40 | 18.25 | −3.05 |
| Volatility (%) | 16.70 | 10.29 | 14.47 | 15.73 |
| Average risk-free rate (%) | 5.61 | 4.37 | 5.07 | 4.64 |
| Sharpe ratio | <0 | 1.17 | 0.91 | <0 |
| Worst 1-month drawdown (%) | −11.12 | −5.81 | −14.30 | −9.21 |
| Worst 12-month drawdown (%) | −16.52 | −4.66 | 0.51 | −27.87 |
|  |  |  |  |  |
| **HFRI Merger Arbitrage Index** |  |  |  |  |
| Annual return (%) | 8.50 | 15.56 | 13.32 | 11.46 |
| Volatility (%) | 6.47 | 2.50 | 4.77 | 3.31 |
| Sharpe ratio | 0.45 | 4.48 | 1.73 | 2.06 |
| Worst 1-month drawdown (%) | −6.68 | −0.41 | −5.86 | −2.83 |
| Worst 12-month drawdown (%) | 0.44 | 7.89 | 5.51 | 2.61 |

*Source:* Hedge Fund Research, Datastream.

## Conclusion

Risk arbitrage is an attractive hedge fund strategy despite higher correlation to equity returns in dislocating markets. The risks to risk arbitrage are, to a large extent, of a legal/regulatory nature, so are uncorrelated to returns in capital markets in most market environments. Deal risk is primarily nonsystematic risk; it can by immunized through diversification. However, risk arbitrage has systematic risk in the form of spreads widening in dislocating markets.

## Outlook

Future profitability of risk arbitrage is determined by the number of announced deals and the amount of capital involved and to some extent is constrained by the ability to sell short.

On June 30, 2001, the Financial Accounting Standards Board (FASB) in the United States amended the regulations that govern mergers and acquisitions. The changes (especially FASB 142) are radical. The new rulings should result in increased merger activity. FASB 142 allows companies to realize merger expenses immediately rather than amortize them. Since goodwill is not amortized, future earnings look inflated. This could potentially put some companies in a different light. The elimination of goodwill pooling should also trigger more innovative deal structures, more aggressive types of acquisitions, and highly creative mixtures of acquisition currencies going forward.

The late 1990s have seen the beginnings of change in Europe manifested in the rise in size and number of cross-border corporate transactions. Despite the European Union (EU)'s sluggishness in forging uniform merger rules, it now appears imminent that the EU will adopt British-style takeover regulations.* Such rules would still have to be enacted at the national level; however, EU adoption coupled with market forces such as the Mannesmann/Vodafone transaction should pressure national governments to reform their laws. Additional impetus for change in Europe stems from Germany's tax reform approved by the Upper House on July 14, 2000. Tax-efficient portfolio reallocations from 2002 are expected to pave the way for in-market and cross-border mergers in the old economy sectors, and the realization of cost synergies through rationalization and economies of scale. Simultaneously, it will probably facilitate balance sheet optimization of financials and the reallocation of funds toward more profitable investment areas.

Through less concrete measures, Japan has also officially sanctioned the

---

*The European Commission (EC) Council of Ministers has agreed on a common position on takeovers in June 2000. The directive still needs to be approved by the European Parliament, but this is unlikely to present further difficulties.

unwinding of the cross holdings that have long been a feature of the *keiretsu* system. We are seeing the revitalization of the moribund equity-linked market as corporations issue exchangeable securities to monetize their cross holdings. The elimination of cross holdings would have the secondary effect of spurring corporate takeover activity as the barriers to corporate mergers are lowered. While Europe is further along in the process, the harmonization of takeover rules and elimination of tax barriers will likely provide a strong catalyst for change in Japan.

## DISTRESSED SECURITIES

### Strategy

At the most general level, distressed securities investing is about being long low investment grade credit. Distressed securities funds invest in the debt or equity of companies experiencing financial or operational difficulties or trade claims of companies that are in financial distress, typically in bankruptcy. These securities generally trade at substantial discounts to par value. Hedge fund managers can invest in a range of instruments from secured debt to common stock. The strategy exploits the fact that many investors are unable to hold securities that are below investment grade.

Distressed securities have a long tradition. The origins of these event-driven strategies probably go back to the 1890s when the main railway stocks were folding. Investors bought the cheap stocks, participated in the restructuring and issuance of new shares, and sold the shares at a profit. (See Table 7.7.)

Distressed securities often trade at large discounts since the sector is mainly a buyer's market.[8] Most private and institutional investors want to get securities of distressed companies off their books because they are not prepared to bear the risks and because of other issues, including noneconomic ones. Distressed companies are barely covered by analysts. Most banks do not get involved in the distressed securities business. Many distressed securities funds are long only.

Distressed securities specialists make investment returns on two kinds of mispricings. First, fundamental or intrinsic value is the actual value of the company that the bond interest represents. Second, relative value is the value of bonds relative to the value of other securities of the same company.[9] When the market price of a company's security is lower than its fundamental value due to temporary financial difficulties, distressed securities specialists will take core positions in these securities and hold them through the restructuring process. They believe that the security will approach its fair value after the restructuring is complete.

While a company is restructuring, the prices of its different financial in-

**Table 7.7**  Key Risk Factors in Distressed Securities

| Risk | Position | Effect |
|------|----------|--------|
| Credit | Long default risk | The nature of the strategy is to be long low investment grade credit. A widening of credit spreads is bad for the strategy. |
| Interest rates | Long duration | A rise in interest rates reduces the value of the strategy, which to a large extent contains long-duration instruments. |
| Equity | Long equity, short volatility | Event risk can be hedged by having long and short positions, but often the exposure and volatility of an instrument are accepted as risks that should not be managed. |
| | | Similar to in fixed income arbitrage, and to a lesser extent convertible arbitrage, investors invested in distressed securities are short a disaster put option. If disaster strikes, credit spreads widen, and distressed securities fund managers lose money. |
| Timing | Long patience | Strategies are usually long-term where the termination is not known in advance. Stable and long-term funding is important. |

*Source:* UBS Warburg (2000).

struments can become mispriced relative to one another. This is an opportunity for what is referred to as *intracapitalization* or *capital structure arbitrage*. The distressed securities specialists purchase the undervalued security and take short trading positions in the overpriced security to extract an arbitrage profit.

The main risks of distressed securities investing lie in the correct valuation of securities, debt, and collateral, as well as in the adequate assessment of the period during which the capital will be tied up (taking into account major lawsuits, etc.). Sometimes other asset classes are shorted in order to offset a part of the risks, and guarantees or collateral (such as brand names, receivables, inventories, real estate, equipment, patents, etc.) are used to hedge the risks. The diversification between securities, companies, and sectors is very important. Distressed funds have typically low leverage and low volatility. However, since positions are extremely difficult to value, investors have to bear mark-to-market risk. The volatility of the returns is therefore probably higher than published. The prices of distressed securities are particularly volatile during the bankruptcy process because useful information about the company becomes available during this period.

Investments in distressed securities are most often illiquid. Long redemption periods, therefore, are the norm. Frequent liquidity windows work against the nature of the strategy. A hedge fund manager will seek a long-term commitment from investors. It is essential that the manager has a large pool of committed capital so that liquidity is not a problem. The length of any particular bankruptcy proceeding is notoriously hard to forecast and the outcome is always uncertain, both of which make the duration of distressed securities strategies unpredictable. In addition, managers who participate on creditor and equity committees must freeze their holdings until an arrangement is reached.

Distressed securities investing has one of the highest gradations of all subgroups. It is difficult to find two managers with identical or even similar investment approaches; the subgroup is not a homogeneous but a heterogeneous group. However, at the most general level, one could classify distressed securites managers into active and passive managers. Active distressed managers get involved in the restructuring and refinancing process through active participation in creditor committees. In some cases, an investor may even actively reorganize the company. The passive manager simply buys equity and debt of distressed companies at a discount and holds onto it until it appreciates. Both approaches are very labor-intensive and require a lot of analytical work. The U.S. bankruptcy law is very detailed. Chapter 11 of the U.S. Bankruptcy Code provides relief from creditor claims for companies in financial distress. Large tax loss carryforwards, strict disclosure rules, and clear debt restructuring rules help in reorganizing distressed companies. The objective is to save distressed companies from total liquidation (Chapter 7). In Europe, however, bankruptcy is intended to end and not prolong the life of a company. U.S. distressed securities markets are therefore much more liquid than their European counterparts, which is why few distressed funds are active outside the United States.

## Typical Trades and Opportunities

- Entering into core positions in the debt and equity of a distressed company, accompanied by active participation in the creditor committees in order to influence the restructuring and refinancing process.
- Passive long-term core positions in distressed equity and debt as distressed securities can trade at substantial discounts.
- Short-term trading in anticipation of a specific event such as the outcome of a court rule or important negotiations.
- Partial hedging of the stock market and interest rate exposure by shorting other stocks of the same industry or by shorting Treasury bonds.
- Arbitraging different issues of the same distressed company (e.g., long mezzanine debt and short common stock).
- Vulture investing (derogatory term applied when a venture capitalist or a distressed securities investor gets an unfairly large equity stake).
- Providing buyout capital: equity or debt for privatizations, spin-offs, acquisitions, and takeovers (often by the firm's own management). Buyout capital may be leveraged.

- Purchase of distressed bonds (or any other obligation) that are secured by property or other assets.
- Collateralized debt obligations (CDOs): Opportunities arise from forced selling due to collateral deterioration.
- Debtor in possession (DIP) financings: Opportunities arise from lending on a first priority basis after a company has filed for bankruptcy, offering fees and relatively high pricing for the risk.

The number of opportunities in this category is positively related to the number of defaults. Figure 7.12 shows corporate defaults between 1982 and 2001. The number of opportunities, therefore, is somewhat countercyclical to economic growth (peaks in 1991 and 2001) and, as a result, countercyclical to M&A activity and therefore risk arbitrage. In 2000–2001, many established risk arbitrage funds departed from their field of expertise to become involved in distressed securities, where the opportunity set has been rising. Multistrategy absolute return managers have been lowering capital in risk arbitrage and increasing their allocations to distressed securities.

Corporate defaults soared in 2001, marking the third consecutive year that they have reached record levels. During 2001, 216 rated and formerly rated issuers defaulted on $116 billion of debt. Of these, 167 defaults took place in the United States, Argentina had 14, Canada 9, the United Kingdom

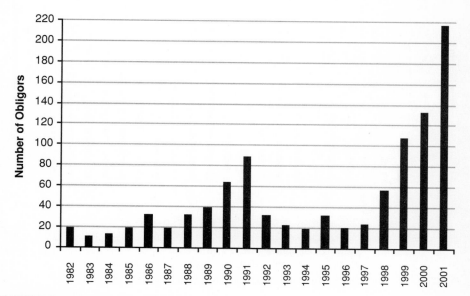

**FIGURE 7.12** Corporate Defaults, 1982–2001
*Source:* Standard & Poor's (2002).

6, Australia 4, Poland 3, Mexico 2. One default each took place in Bermuda, Germany, Greece, Indonesia, Korea, the Netherlands, Norway, the Philippines, Russia, Thailand, and Venezuela. Twenty-one of the defaulted companies in 2001 had originally been assigned an investment grade rating by Standard & Poor's. The rest were speculative grade. Eight companies that were investment grade at the beginning of 2001 defaulted during the year. The fall of investment grade Enron and the defaults by the California utilities caught many investors in investment grade companies off guard.

Telecommunications was the industry hardest hit in 2001, with 32 defaults affecting 10.77 percent of all rated issuers in that industry. The overall default ratio (number of defaults during the year divided by the number of rated issuers at the beginning of the year) for 2001 reached 4.09 percent, which exceeds the previous record of 4.01 percent set in 1991. The record number of defaults in 2001 resulted from the combination of a weak economy and an abundance of recently issued speculative grade debt. The late 1990s witnessed the entry of large numbers of speculative grade issuers onto the scene (Figure 7.13). These issuers—many of whom would have defaulted even

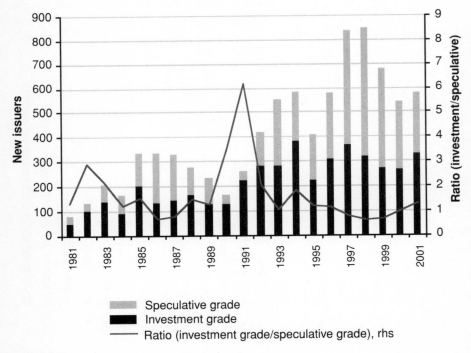

**FIGURE 7.13**  Rating Classification of New Issuers
*Source:* Standard & Poor's (2002).

in a strong economy—were subject to increased pressure as economies slid into recession. Standard & Poor's (2002) expects default rates to peak in 2002 and ease off by year-end as credit quality improves and the economy rebounds.

## Performance

■ Distressed securities, as Figure 7.14 implies, has been a star performer. It has beaten the mother of all indexes, the S&P 500 (total return) index with a fraction of the latter's volatility. The sustainability of high returns is one of the most attractive characteristics of this discipline. It seems that investing with a long-term horizon carries some sort of premium.

■ As seen in Table 7.8, distressed securities is a profitable hedge fund strategy, resulting in returns to the investor of around 15 percent a year. Returns in 2000 and 2001 were around 2.8 percent and 14.4 percent respectively. As of July 2002, the index was up by 1.0 percent (despite WorldCom). The worst yearly calendar return was −4.2 percent in 1998 and the best was 35.7 percent coming out of recession in 1991.

■ Volatility is slightly higher than with relative-value strategies or with bonds but substantially lower than with equities. The dispersion of

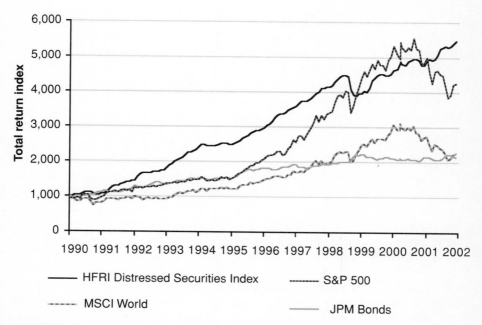

**FIGURE 7.14** Long-Term Performance of Distressed Securities
*Source:* Hedge Fund Research, Datastream, UBS Warburg (2000).

**Table 7.8** Distressed Securities Risk and Return Characteristics

| | # of Monthly Returns | Annual Return | Volatility | Sharpe Ratio (5%) | Worst 1-month Drawdown | Negative Months | Worst 12-month Drawdown | 12-month Drawdown Ended On | Highest 12-month Return |
|---|---|---|---|---|---|---|---|---|---|
| S&P 500 | 144 | 12.85% | 14.54% | 0.54 | −15.64% | 35.4% | −26.63% | Sep-01 | 52.10% |
| MSCI World | 144 | 6.99 | 14.59 | 0.14 | −14.30 | 39.6 | −27.87 | Sep-01 | 33.51 |
| MSCI EAFE | 144 | 2.70 | 17.03 | <0 | −14.97 | 43.1 | −28.27 | Sep-01 | 44.19 |
| MSCI Europe | 144 | 9.15 | 15.19 | 0.27 | −13.42 | 37.5 | −25.49 | Sep-01 | 45.93 |
| JPM Global Government Bonds | 144 | 6.59 | 5.94 | 0.27 | −3.40 | 41.0 | −6.18 | Jan-00 | 20.97 |
| JPM U.S. Government Bonds | 144 | 7.94 | 4.11 | 0.72 | −2.73 | 27.8 | −3.65 | Oct-94 | 17.34 |
| HFRI Distressed Securities index | 144 | 15.08 | 6.40 | 1.57 | −8.50 | 19.4 | −6.41 | Feb-99 | 44.18 |
| Zurich Hedge Event-Driven Distressed Securities | 144 | 14.42 | 7.18 | 1.31 | −9.22 | 22.2 | −7.57 | Mar-99 | 38.92 |
| Hennessee Hedge Fund Index— Distressed | 108 | 15.12 | 6.28 | 1.61 | −8.88 | 16.7 | −8.37 | Sep-98 | 34.39 |

*Source:* Hedge Fund Research, Zurich Capital Markets, Hennessee, Datastream, UBS Warburg (2000).

returns has also been higher with distressed securities than with other event-driven strategies such as risk arbitrage. Unlike risk arbitrage, distressed securities have a long bias. The annualized standard deviation has been around 7 percent. This results in a Sharpe ratio of approximately 1.5. Note, however, that the measured 7 percent volatility is probably an understatement.

■ Around 20 percent of the returns were negative. Distressed securities provide much less downside protection than some relative-value strategies discussed previously. However, the discipline is less erratic on the downside than equities. To some extent these smooth returns could be a function of the fact that some of the net asset values (NAVs) are based on appraisals, which introduces a smoothing effect to returns.

Figure 7.15 shows the returns of various hedge fund indexes along with some equity and bond indexes. Figure 7.16 compares monthly total MSCI World returns with the HFRI Distressed Securities Index.

■ The three distressed securities indexes are from three different sources covering two different time periods. The fact that they result in nearly the same risk/return profile is an indication that the characteristics are robust and could be stable going forward (at least the return component above the risk-free rate). However, there are some viable reservations regarding

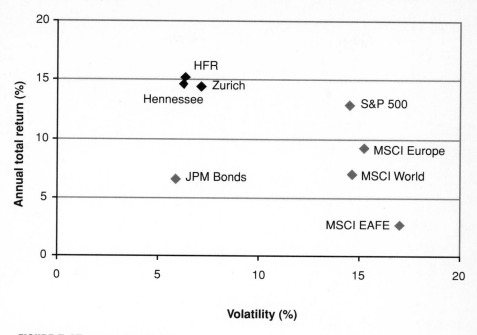

**FIGURE 7.15** Return versus Risk
*Source:* Hedge Fund Research, Zurich Capital Markets, Hennessee, Datastream, UBS Warburg (2000).

the quality of the data for distressed securities. Given the nature of the strategy, managers often hold illiquid positions for which there is no market, which makes calculating net asset values at the end of a month rather challenging.

■ Figure 7.16 points to some negative outliers that occur in both positive as well as negative markets.

Table 7.9 shows some further statistics of distressed securities.

■ The intercept between returns from distressed securities and MSCI World index is relatively high, indicating that there are returns not explained by CAPM.
■ The beta to the MSCI World index is around 0.2, which is slightly higher than with some relative-value strategies discussed in Chapter 6. In other words, there is a long bias in distressed securities.
■ Historical returns were slightly negatively skewed (to the left with a long tail to the left) and leptokurtic (narrow distribution with outliers).

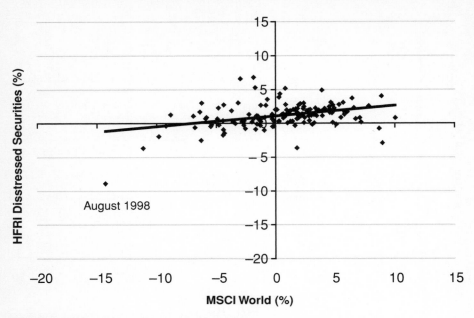

**FIGURE 7.16** MSCI World versus Distressed Securities Returns
*Source:* Hedge Fund Research, Datastream, UBS Warburg (2000).

**Table 7.9** Statistical Analysis of Distressed Securities Returns

| | Alpha to MSCI World | Beta to MSCI World | Skew | Excess Kurtosis | Correlation MSCI World | Correlation JPM Global Bonds |
|---|---|---|---|---|---|---|
| HFRI Distressed Securities index | 1.08 | 0.16 | −0.90 | 6.47 | 0.34 | −0.15 |
| Zurich Hedge Event-Driven: | | | | | | |
|   Distressed Securities | 1.00 | 0.21 | −1.04 | 4.72 | 0.43 | −0.03 |
| Hennessee Hedge Fund Index—Distressed | 1.05 | 0.15 | −1.70 | 10.26 | 0.33 | −0.20 |

*Source:* Hedge Fund Research, Zurich Capital Markets, Hennessee, Datastream, UBS Warburg (2000).

■ Correlation to equities was around 0.4, the same as for risk arbitrage, the other event-driven strategy discussed in this book. The correlation to bonds is not statistically significant. Note that relative-value strategies in equities have a correlation with the market of around 0.25 to 0.30 whereas event-driven strategies have a correlation coefficient of around 0.40.

Figure 7.17 shows the performance of the HFRI Distressed Securities Index in different market environments, and Figure 7.18 shows average

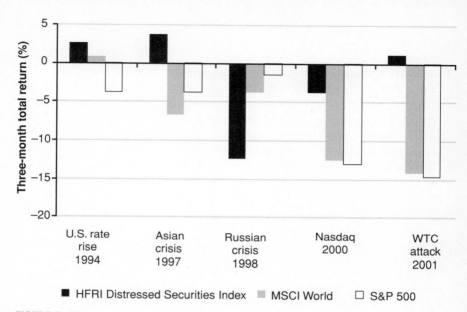

**FIGURE 7.17** Scenario Analysis
*Source:* Hedge Fund Research, Datastream, UBS Warburg (2000).

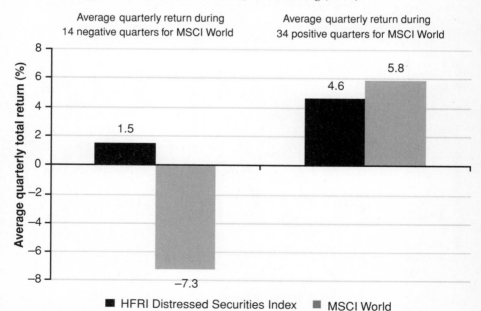

**FIGURE 7.18** Average Negative versus Average Positive Returns
*Source:* Hedge Fund Research, Datastream, UBS Warburg (2000).

quarterly returns in down markets versus average quarterly returns in friendly markets.

- Intuitively, we would not expect distressed securities to lose money during a global crisis since the positions in distressed securities are more micro than macro. Distressed securities showed nearly the same returns as risk arbitrage during the U.S. rate rise in 1994 and the Asian crisis in 1997. However, the strategy was one of the worst performers during the Russian crisis (or credit crisis) in 1998. Only emerging markets and fixed income arbitrage suffered larger losses during autumn 1998. The nature of the strategy is to be long low investment grade credit. A widening of credit spreads is bad for the strategy, as Figure 7.19 illustrates. The year 1998 was the worst year since 1990 when the HFRI Distressed Securities index lost 4.2 percent.
- Distressed securities strategies perform poorly in recessions. The years 1990 and 1994 saw returns of 6.4 percent and 3.8 percent, respectively. However, the recessions led to a number of well-established companies running into financial difficulties, which meant that there were good opportunities in this segment in the years that followed recession years. In the years 1991 and 1995, distressed securities yielded returns of 35.7 percent and 19.7 percent, respectively.

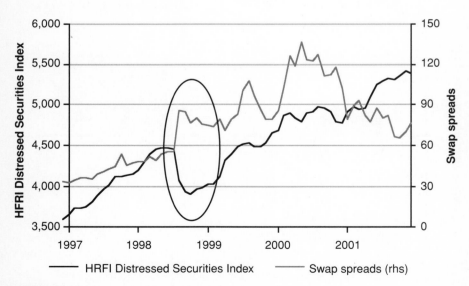

**FIGURE 7.19**   Distressed Securities versus Swap Spreads
*Source:* Hedge Fund Research, Bloomberg, UBS Warburg (2000).

■ The 1999 calendar year witnessed 144 publicly traded U.S. companies with total assets of $58.6 billion filing for Chapter 11 bankruptcy. This was the greatest number of defaults in any year since 1986 and the largest asset total in any year since 1992, when $64.2 billion went into Chapter 11. Calendar returns of the HRFI Distressed Securities index in 1992 and 1999 were 25.2 percent and 16.9 percent, respectively.

■ In average down quarters, distressed securities investing yields a positive absolute return, as Figure 7.18 shows. However, the strategy does better in equity-friendly markets. As fixed income arbitrage and, to a lesser extent, convertible arbitrage, investors invested in distressed securities are short a disaster put option. If disaster strikes, credit spreads widen, and distressed securities fund managers lose money.

Figure 7.20 shows how returns have been distributed in the past and compares the historic return distribution with a normal distribution of distressed securities and a normal distribution of historical MSCI World returns, both based on historic mean return and standard deviation of returns. In Figure 7.21 the distressed securities returns were sorted in ascending order and compared with the corresponding equity market returns. This allows one to

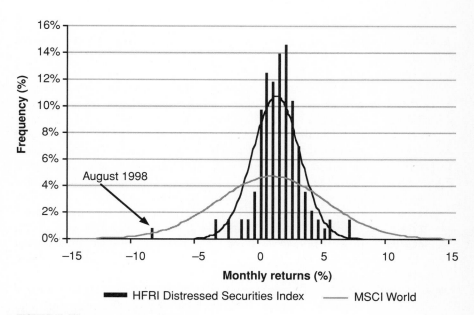

**FIGURE 7.20** Return Distribution
*Source:* Hedge Fund Research, Datastream, UBS Warburg (2000).

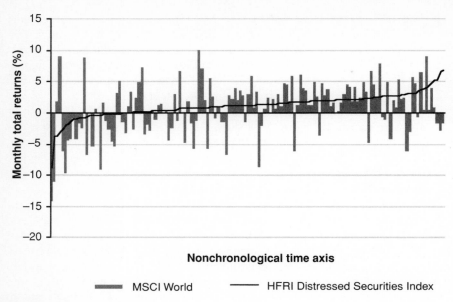

**Nonchronological time axis**

━━━ MSCI World          ──── HFRI Distressed Securities Index

**FIGURE 7.21**   Correlation
*Source:* Hedge Fund Research, Datastream, UBS Warburg (2000).

see in which market environment the extreme positive and negative returns
were achieved.

■ Figure 7.20 shows the excess kurtosis (narrow distribution with outliers)
  of the historical return distribution when compared with the normal distribution. Note that 28 from the 144 monthly returns were below zero,
  compared with 51 in the S&P 500 total return index and 57 in the case of
  the MSCI World total return index. There were nine observations outside
  the 95 percent range, five on the upside and four on the left-hand side of
  the mean return. The nature of the strategy dictates the presence of outliers going forward since, to some extent, investors in distressed securities
  are short a disaster put option. There were each one three-sigma returns
  on both sides of the mean. The worst monthly loss was a 5.4-sigma event.
■ Negative returns from distressed securities were moderately concentrated
  in down markets. Note that the highest returns were achieved in down
  markets, too (Figure 7.21).
■ As shown in Table 7.10, performance is not persistent. The first part of
  the 12-year observation period had much better risk-adjusted return and
  drawdown characteristics than had the second half of the observation pe-

**Table 7.10** Performance Persistence

|  | 1990–1992 | 1993–1995 | 1996–1998 | 1999–2001 |
|---|---|---|---|---|
| **MSCI World (Total Return)** | | | | |
| Annual return (%) | −1.80 | 16.40 | 18.25 | −3.05 |
| Volatility (%) | 16.70 | 10.29 | 14.47 | 15.73 |
| Average risk-free rate (%) | 5.61 | 4.37 | 5.07 | 4.64 |
| Sharpe ratio | <0 | 1.17 | 0.91 | <0 |
| Worst 1-month drawdown (%) | −11.12 | −5.81 | −14.30 | −9.21 |
| Worst 12-month drawdown (%) | −16.52 | −4.66 | 0.51 | −27.87 |
| | | | | |
| **HFRI Distressed Securities Index** | | | | |
| Annual return (%) | 21.83 | 18.12 | 10.10 | 11.19 |
| Volatility (%) | 7.73 | 4.58 | 7.07 | 5.30 |
| Sharpe ratio | 2.10 | 3.01 | 0.71 | 1.24 |
| Worst 1-month drawdown (%) | −3.65 | −1.72 | −8.88 | −2.52 |
| Worst 12-month drawdown (%) | 6.44 | −1.10 | −5.04 | −6.41 |

*Source:* Hedge Fund Research, Datastream.

riod. The 1990–1991 recession triggered much higher returns than were achieved during the reminder of the 1990s. The 1990–1992 period was the best for distressed securities and the worst for risk arbitrage (see Table 7.6). This shows some countercyclicality between the two event-driven strategies. In times when the economy is expanding there are many opportunities in M&A but fewer bankruptcies and companies in distress. However, if the economy moves into a recession there are fewer mergers and acquisitions but an increase in bankruptcies.

■ Figure 7.22 is an indication that the recovery period in distressed securities is not as fast as, for example, in risk arbitrage where spreads narrow within weeks or months after blowing up. However, when a diversified portfolio of distressed securities managers is compared to a diversified long-only stock portfolio, the former has to be considered as the more conservative.

■ Figure 7.23 shows the five worst quarters for distressed securities. Two of these five quarters were also among the five worst quarters for risk arbitrage: The third quarters of 1990 and 1998 were the worst and second worst quarters for risk arbitrage (Figure 7.11). To some extent, the opportunity set of distressed securities and risk arbitrage is countercyclical, as the former faces an increase in the opportunity set in a detracting economic environment which is the opposite of merger activity. However, the two event-driven strategies also share some elements of systematic risks.

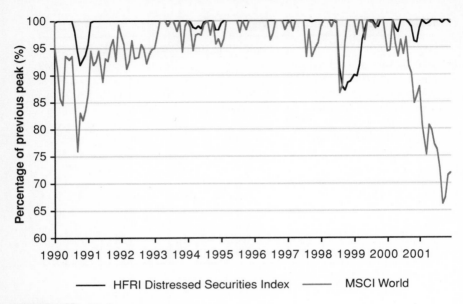

**FIGURE 7.22** Underwater
*Source:* Hedge Fund Research, Datastream.

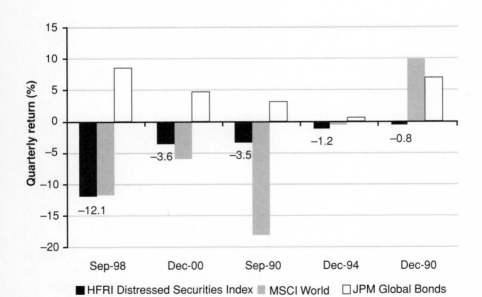

**FIGURE 7.23** Worst Quarters for Distressed Securities
*Source:* Hedge Fund Research, Datastream.

## Conclusion and Outlook

Given the involvement of Benjamin Graham in distressed securities, the strategy can best be described as the ultimate value strategy. Buying a security for 80 cents that is worth a dollar is an old strategy, has survived the test of time, and will be around for a long time. As long as companies blow up and/or creditors sell for noneconomic reasons, absolute managers of distressed securities are expected to make money. The strategy is a good example of regulatory arbitrage. Most investors must sell securities of troubled companies. Policy restrictions and regulatory constraints do not allow them to own securities with very low credit ratings. As a result, a pricing discount occurs that reflects both these structural anomalies as well as uncertainty about the outcome of the event. For the attractive risk/return combinations in distressed securities to disappear, investment policies and financial regulation would have to start making economic sense and change dramatically. This is unlikely to happen anytime soon.

# CHAPTER 8

# Opportunistic Absolute Return Strategies

*I did not play the financial markets according to a particular set of rules; I was always more interested in understanding the changes that occur in the rules of the game.*

—George Soros

## INTRODUCTION

The main section of this book is a detailed analysis of hedge fund historical risk and return characteristics. Despite having some reservations regarding to the quality of the hedge fund index return data, we analyzed time series to assess how these characteristics could be defined in the future. For this reason, we classified the hedge fund universe in three main groups—relative-value and non-relative-value plus a hybrid of the two. The key determinant for our classification is exposure to the market. An investor that understands where risk and returns in convertible arbitrage are generated should have the tools to judge the return, risk, and correlation characteristics in the future. The predictability of performance characteristics decreases as market exposure increases, i.e. predictability decreases if we move from left to right in Figure 8.1.

Figure 8.1 shows the dispersion of quarterly returns from Q1 90 to Q4 01. Every horizontal line represents a quarterly total return for the respective strategy. A short vertical line implies little dispersion of returns and a long

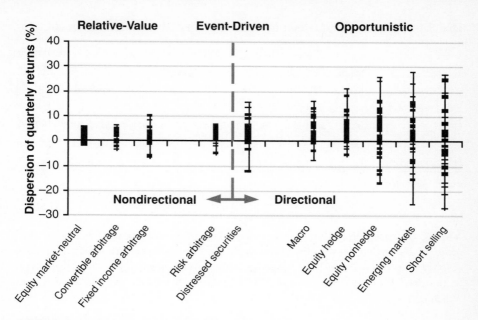

**FIGURE 8.1** Dispersion of Quarterly Total Returns
*Source:* Hedge Fund Research, UBS Warburg (2000).

vertical line implies that the dispersion of returns is large. Note that, for example, macro has its returns similarly distributed as distressed securities, just without the negative outlier (from Q3 98).

Other classification systems distinguish between directional and nondirectional at the first level instead of relative-value, event-driven, and opportunistic. (See Chapter 5 for a discussion of the ambiguities of classifying hedge funds.) With such a classification, risk arbitrage would be defined as nondirectional, whereas distressed securities is directional. Figure 8.1 would justify such a classification system as the dispersion of returns of risk arbitrage is much lower than for distressed securities which, as a group, have a strong directional bias.

The main difference between the four opportunistic strategies in Table 8.1 (sector specialists are here considered as long/short equity) and the previously discussed relative-value and event-driven strategies is volatility and the exposure to the market. The high volatility is primarily a function of beta, that is, a high exposure to the underlying asset class. As a result of higher volatility, risk-adjusted returns (as measured, for example, with the Sharpe ratio) are lower than with relative-value and event-driven strategies.

In the following sections we discuss the four different opportunistic absolute

**Table 8.1** Summary Risk/Return Characteristics Based on Historical Performance

| Subsector | Returns | Volatility | Downside Risk | Sharpe Ratio | Correlation to Equities | Leverage | Investment Horizon |
|---|---|---|---|---|---|---|---|
| Long/short equity | High | Medium | High | Medium | High | Medium | Short |
| Sector specialists | High | High | High | Low | High | Low | Medium |
| Macro | High | High | Medium | Medium | Medium | Medium | NA |
| Short selling | Low | High | High | Low | Negative | Medium | Medium |
| Emerging markets | High | High | High | Low | High | Low | Medium |

*Source:* UBS Warburg (2000).

return strategies. Note that macro was the largest strategy only 10 years ago. Today, long/short equity captures the largest slice of market share. In the appendix to this chapter we discuss the long/short controversy (essentially long/short managers marketing themselves as market-neutral). All returns are total returns (including dividends) and in U.S. dollars.

## LONG/SHORT EQUITY

### Strategy

At the most general level, long/short equity is about exploiting investment opportunities, and the freedom to use leverage, sell short, and hedge market risk. Long/short equity is by far the largest discipline in the hedge fund industry today. Based on estimates of Hedge Fund Research, long/short equity (equity hedge and equity nonhedge) was 5.9 percent of the total $39 billion assets under management in the hedge fund industry in 1990 and 42.5 percent of the $537 billion industry at the end of 2001. Including sector specialists, the allocation to long/short equity exceeds 50 percent of the overall $500 billion to $600 billion invested in hedge funds.

Long/short strategies combine both long as well as short equity positions. The short positions have three purposes, which can vary over time or by manager. First, the short positions are intended to generate alpha. This is one of the main differences when compared with traditional long-only managers. Stock selection skill can result in doubling the alpha (as well as, of course, the stock-specific risk). Second, the short positions can serve the purpose of hedging market risk. Third, the manager earns interest on the short while collecting the short rebate.

The long/short equity universe as a subgroup is heterogeneous. In other words, investment approaches by different managers differ. Some managers are more generalists while others are specialists. Some might have a growth bias others a value bias. Some managers are more trading oriented, and others more investment oriented. There is great variation in the net exposure between managers, as Figure 1.4 in Chapter 1 highlighted. There is also variation with respect to sector and geographic coverage. The investor who is equipped with the knowledge of all these differences will be in the position to construct conservative portfolios, as the correlation between managers is generally low.

Many long/short equity managers use position limits to control stock-specific risk and, more importantly, control liquidity. Some institutionalize daily P&L analysis similar to proprietary trading desks of investment banks. Selling short is not the opposite of going long. The ability to sell short allows the hedge fund managers to capitalize on opportunities unavailable to most traditional managers. One example (among thousands) of a successful short stock position done by equity long/short managers was a short position on Pediatrix Medical Group Inc., a provider of physician management services to hospital-based neonatal intensive care units. (See Figure 8.2.)

The company was *en vogue* on Wall Street in late 1998 and early 1999 due to the perceived high rate of growth in its revenues and profits. To some

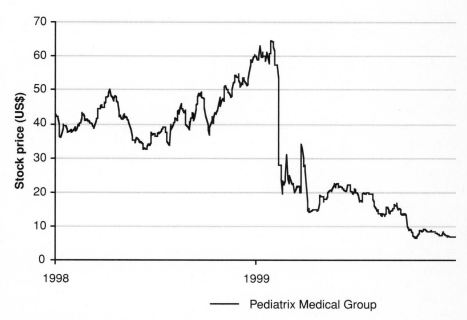

**FIGURE 8.2** Pediatrix Medical Group Share Price Performance
*Source:* Datastream, UBS Warburg (2000).

hedge fund managers, the stock was a potential short because the company's projected growth rate, attributed to the industry, far exceeded the rate at which babies were being born. Further research uncovered both aggressive accounting practices and inappropriate charges to insurance carriers. Hedge fund managers sold the stock short outright. Eventually, the company announced that earnings would be far below analysts' expectations and officials said they were investigating the company for possible insurance fraud.

Market-neutral and long/short equity are different absolute return strategies. Not everyone agrees. Some practitioners argue that market-neutral is the same as long/short equity.

## Market-Neutral versus Long/Short Equity

Traditionally, market-neutral investing has been the domain of arbitrageurs looking for small pricing discrepancies between financial instruments. The basic idea was to make a profit without being exposed to swings in the general market; that is, the overall portfolio is neither long nor short. The underlying philosophy is that the securities on each side of the transaction have a proven interrelationship. A profit is made when a trade is put on when there is a gap and the gap closes—when prices converge to what is perceived as fair value. It is trading pricing discrepancies ahead of this eventual convergence that offer the investment opportunity, independent of what the market may be doing. This does not mean there is no directional risk. It simply means there is no directional general market risk.

Some equity long/short managers have borrowed the market-neutral brand to describe a strategy of taking a long position in one stock against a short position of a similar size in another, whether or not they are in the same sector. This type of investing, while it may be implemented with every conceivable effort taken to minimize volatility, represents two separate strategies nonetheless. There is no prescribed convergence at some future date that will ensure that the stocks' values match one another. Indeed in this kind of trade the short could rise indefinitely, resulting in theoretically unlimited losses. The stocks could also exhibit different volatility characteristics. Both stocks could fall or rise significantly together, or indeed inversely but not in the desired direction, thus magnifying losses.

**Market Neutrality**    A market-neutral strategy is neutral at all times; notional value (or beta to the market) is kept close to zero and the performance is attributed to stock-specific risk and not market risk or market timing. The managers normally hold a large number of long equity positions and an equal, or close to equal, dollar amount of offsetting short positions, for a total net exposure close to zero. According to Nicholas (2000), a zero net exposure, referred to as "dollar neutrality," is a common characteristic of all equity market-neutral managers. Some, but not all, equity market-neutral managers extend the concept of neutrality to risk factors or characteristics such as beta, sector, investment style, and market capitalization. Their goal is to generate consistent moderate returns in both up and down markets. Within equity market-neutral one can distinguish between fundamental arbitrage and statistical arbitrage.

**Difference between Fundamental and Statistical Arbitrage**    Fundamental as well as statistical arbitrage are market-neutral strategies.* The former buys and sells shares based on a fundamental view, whereas the latter uses quantitative models to create long and short portfolios. The factors in the quantitative models of the statistical arbitrageur are fundamental variables as well. However, the overlying theme is most often an anticipated mean-reversion of one or a group of fundamental variables. Fundamental arbitrage is more judgmental, whereas statistical arbitrage is more quantitative in nature.

Statistical arbitrage involves creating groups of stocks that are fundamentally similar in some aspect, and then trying to exploit anomalous, statistical relationships between stocks within each group. Most common among these relationships is the tendency of the valuations of similar stocks to revert to the mean of the group. Stocks with valuations above the mean of the group are sold short, and stocks with valuations below the mean are held long. The expectation is that both sides will eventually converge on the mean of the group.

The basic assumption behind mean reversion strategies is that anomalies among stock valuations may occur in the short term, but, in the long term, these anomalies will correct themselves as the market processes information. The reason we like the term "statistical arbitrage" for this particular strategy is because the mean reversion does not always work but being done over and over again in a disciplined fashion it should work more often than not. Statistical arbitrage always has been the underlying theme for insurance companies, casinos, and, in the recent history of finance, financial trading houses and hedge funds. An insurance company selling life or car insurance will not make money on every policy. However, if it gets the statistics right, the proceeds from the profitable policies will exceed the losses from the loss-making accounts.† The same is true for a casino. It does not win with every spin of the

---

*The classification of hedge fund strategies is not entirely unambiguous—as highlighted in Chapter 5. Some call what here is referred to as "statistical arbitrage" as "risk arbitrage." In this book, the term risk arbitrage is used as a slightly broader classification for merger arbitrage that includes mergers as well as special (corporate) situations.
†At least in theory. Insurance companies have to some extent converted to becoming asset managers. In other words, the main source of profit is derived from managing assets as opposed to the core business of underwriting risk. The future source of return for insurance companies, if equities do not start compounding at 15 percent again, is anyone's guess.

wheel. However, most people familiar with statistics would prefer being in the position of the casino owner than in the position of the gambler.*

Nicholas (2000) finds many statistical arbitrageurs use a relative-value system to determine buy and sell decisions. Stocks sold short are usually added to the portfolio when their prices are sufficiently higher than the rest of the group. They are covered when their price drops back closer to the mean of the group. On the long side, stocks that are valued below a certain level are held long until they rise above the mean of the group. Other managers may have more absolute targets for stocks. How managers choose to set up their rules determines how much trading they do, how much turnover the portfolio experiences, and what their transaction costs are. Transaction costs and trade impact on market price are often included in mean reversion models, allowing managers to forgo trade opportunities when the cost of completing the transaction is greater than the potential gain.

A key to success for any active manager is control of transaction costs. This requirement often leads hedge fund managers to recognize that too much money run by the strategy will generate adverse market impact. Some funds close for new money others increase the fee level or lengthen the redemption period. The point is that the manager controls its size and growth. This is different to the traditional asset management industry where growth and size are maximized and not optimized for efficiency, that is, superior after-cost and risk-adjusted performance.

Nicholas (2000) points out that as markets are ever-changing, the factors that unified a group in the past may not always continue to do so in the future. Statistical arbitrage managers must determine when and if to drop stocks from their groups and/or add new ones. For example, in the flight-to-quality situation of Q3 98, market capitalization and credit quality became such powerful drivers in the market that they could confound formerly effective themes. If the goal is to create a model based on coherent groups with unifying themes, then keeping a model dynamic requires a certain level of vigilance. Deciding which factors are driving which groups, the essential component of model building, is a skill required of the individual manager.

One could argue that pair trading is an example of fundamental arbitrage.† A pair trade involves going long on a stock in a specific industry, and

---

*What comes to mind is the institutional investor (a CIO) quoted in the March 2000 Ludgate AIS survey (Ludgate Communications 2000) saying: "No, we don't [currently invest in hedge funds]! It is completely obvious that hedge funds don't work. We are not a casino." We have used this quote in this book before (Chapter 1) and apologize for duplication. However, this quote is, apart from being hilarious, the ultimate way of saying that one has no idea what absolute return strategies are all about.

†Note that Lo and MacKinlay (1999) use the term "pair trade" as a predecessor term to "statistical arbitrage."

pairing that trade specifically with an equal dollar-value short position in a stock in the same industry. Philosophically, the strategy tries to insulate the portfolio from systemic moves in industries by being long in one stock and short in another. Profit is derived from the difference in price change between the two stocks, rather than from the direction in which each stock moves. A trade between different share categories of the same stock would be an extreme pair trade as market, industry as well as most of the company-specific risk is immunized. The typical conversion play is an extreme form of a pair trade. Recent examples of such pair trades included options where a conversion of one category was conditioned on the share price of the other. Other managers (long/short, event-driven) also put on pair trades.*

A further distinction between statistical and fundamental arbitrage is the human discretion the managers allow in their investment process. While statistical arbitrage is to a large extent model-based with a judgmental overlay, the fundamental arbitrageur is essentially a stock picker who wants to be market-neutral when going home in the evening. In a sense, the fundamental arbitrageur shares the goal of market neutrality with the statistical arbitrageur and the enjoyment and thrill of stock picking with the equity long/short manager.

Table 8.2 compares annual total returns of equity long-only, equity market-neutral, and long/short hedge fund indexes. HFRI disaggregated its statistical arbitrage index from equity market-neutral in 1999 to more reflect the quantitative nature of this substrategy. The most extreme difference between the statistical arbitrage subgroup and equity market-neutral was in 1999 where mean-reversion did not work as valuations kept climbing. However, the long-term annual return and risk characteristics are similar.

The last row in Table 8.2 measures a hypothetical return when risk-adjusted returns (Sharpe ratio) are normalized. In other words, what is the return, given the volatility in Table 8.2 (third row from bottom) and a Sharpe ratio of 1.86 (as for the HFRI Equity Market-Neutral index)? The underlying assumption is that all strategies are on the same capital market line (as graphically shown in Figure 1.8 in Chapter 1) and that an investor can pick one strategy on the capital market line and leverage and deleverage according to his or her idiosyncratic risk appetite. Table 8.2 is identical to Table 1.4 in Chapter 1.

**Long/Short Is More Long Than Short**  Long/short equity has a variable beta; it can be neutral to the market, but also net long or net short. There is an element of market exposure. The mandate is more flexible, that is, more opportunistic.

---

*This is a further example of classifying hedge fund strategies being a challenge. There is overlap between strategies and managers.

**Table 8.2**   Yearly Returns of Market-Neutral and Long/Short Equity

| | Long-Only | Alternative | Strategies | | |
|---|---|---|---|---|---|
| | MSCI World (Total Return) Index | HFRI Equity Market Neutral Index | HFRI Statistical Arbitrage Index | HFRI Equity Hedge Index | HFRI Equity Non-Hedge Index |
| 1990 | −16.5% | 15.5% | 11.2% | 14.4% | −7.2% |
| 1991 | 19.0 | 15.6 | 17.8 | 40.1 | 57.1 |
| 1992 | −4.7 | 8.7 | 10.8 | 21.3 | 22.8 |
| 1993 | 23.1 | 11.1 | 12.6 | 27.9 | 27.4 |
| 1994 | 5.6 | 2.7 | 4.7 | 2.6 | 5.1 |
| 1995 | 21.3 | 16.3 | 14.2 | 31.0 | 34.8 |
| 1996 | 14.0 | 14.2 | 19.6 | 21.8 | 25.5 |
| 1997 | 16.2 | 13.6 | 19.4 | 23.4 | 17.6 |
| 1998 | 24.8 | 8.3 | 10.1 | 16.0 | 9.8 |
| 1999 | 25.3 | 10.8 | −1.3 | 46.1 | 41.8 |
| 2000 | −12.9 | 14.6 | 8.9 | 9.1 | −9.0 |
| 2001 | −16.5 | 6.4 | 1.2 | 0.4 | 0.7 |
| | | | | | |
| Return pa | 6.99 | 11.09 | 10.68 | 20.32 | 17.33 |
| Volatility | 14.59 | 3.28 | 3.87 | 9.26 | 14.91 |
| Sharpe (5%) | 0.14 | 1.86 | 1.47 | 1.65 | 0.83 |
| Return for 1.86 Sharpe ratio | 32.13 | 11.09 | 12.20 | 22.23 | 32.72 |

*Source:* Hedge Fund Research, Datastream.

However, the managers in long/short equity are not a homogeneous group. Some have long biases, others are close to market-neutral or short or vary over time. The managers in the long/short equity substyle who are close to market-neutral are effectively pursuing a relative-value strategy and therefore are closer to the equity market-neutral camp. Hedge Fund Research, as mentioned earlier, has two indexes for long/short equity. One category, called Equity Non-Hedge, has a long bias, and the second, called Equity Hedge, is closer to market neutrality. Equity Hedge has been chosen as a proxy for long/short equity in this chapter.

**Difference between Equity Hedge and Equity Nonhedge**   Of all the hedge fund strategies, equity hedge strategies have the longest name lineage (Nicholas 1999). They are the typical long/short strategies. They are direct descendants of A. W. Jones' original hedge fund. However, as was the case in the initial hedge fund rush of the late 1960s, during the bull market of the 1990s many practitioners have forgone the short exposure that was characteristic of the original funds. Thus, the long/short universe should be subdivided in two groups: equity hedge and equity nonhedge.

Equity hedge strategies combine core long holdings of equities with short sales of stock or stock index options. Their portfolios may be anywhere from net long to net short, depending on market conditions and the predefined opportunity set. The global equity market environment since March 2000 is a good showcase of how long/short managers vary their risk according to changes in the opportunity set. Many deleveraged and went partially into cash. It is in markets as these where long/short managers excel when compared with their long-only peer group.

One of the great advantages of spread-related strategies such as long/short equity or equity market neutral strategies is the doubling of alpha. Although not entirely uncontroversial, there is the argument that a long-only manager who is restricted from selling short only has the opportunity to generate alpha by buying or not buying stocks. A "not only long-only" manager, however, can generate alpha by buying stock as well as selling stock short. Some market observers argue that this "double alpha" argument is faulty because an active long-only manager can over- and underweight securities, which means he is short relative to benchmark when underweight. However, there is a difference between selling short and being underweight against a benchmark. Long/short strategies can capture more alpha per unit of risk. If a stock has a weight of 0.02 percent in the benchmark index, the possible opportunity to underweight is limited to 0.02 percent of the portfolio. One could even go as far as portraying short selling as a risk management discipline of its own.

## Performance of Long/Short Equity

- Long/short equity (equity hedge) was one of the most profitable hedge fund strategies in the past. (See Figure 8.3.) The HFRI Equity Hedge index, our proxy for this market segment, outperformed even the S&P 500 by a wide margin, and in traditional absolute return fashion did so with much lower volatility.

- By viewing Table 8.3 one needs to be reminded why to invest in long-only equities. In long/short equity, absolute returns, risk-adjusted returns, and maximum 12-month returns are higher whereas volatilities, drawdowns, and number of negative months are lower than with a long-only investment style. Many long/short managers view the long-only investment style as an investment style of high risk. To them, not having a volatility target seems unreasonable. Not having a volatility target for one's portfolio means having roughly the same volatility as the underlying market (i.e., the benchmark).* Most hedge fund as well as a fund of funds managers

---

*The relative return manager has some minor flexibility to manage market risk by changing the portfolio's beta to the benchmark or having a small allocation in cash.

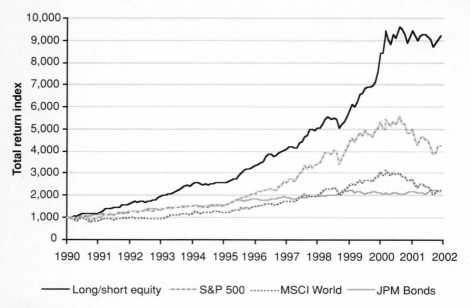

**FIGURE 8.3**   Long-Term Performance of Long/Short Equity
*Source:* Hedge Fund Research, Datastream, UBS Warburg (2000).

**Table 8.3**   Long/Short Equity Risk and Return Characteristics

| | # of Monthly Returns | Annual Return | Volatility | Sharpe Ratio (5%) | Worst 1-month Drawdown | Negative Months | Worst 12-month Drawdown | 12-month Drawdown Ended On | Highest 12-month Return |
|---|---|---|---|---|---|---|---|---|---|
| S&P 500 | 144 | 12.85% | 14.54% | 0.54 | −15.64% | 35.4% | −26.63% | Sep-01 | 52.10% |
| MSCI World | 144 | 6.99 | 14.59 | 0.14 | −14.30 | 39.6 | −27.87 | Sep-01 | 33.51 |
| MSCI EAFE | 144 | 2.70 | 17.03 | <0 | −14.97 | 43.1 | −28.27 | Sep-01 | 44.19 |
| MSCI Europe | 144 | 9.15 | 15.19 | 0.27 | −13.42 | 37.5 | −25.49 | Sep-01 | 45.93 |
| JPM Global Government Bonds | 144 | 6.59 | 5.94 | 0.27 | −3.40 | 41.0 | −6.18 | Jan-00 | 20.97 |
| JPM U.S. Government Bonds | 144 | 7.94 | 4.11 | 0.72 | −2.73 | 27.8 | −3.65 | Oct-94 | 17.34 |
| HFRI Equity Hedge index | 144 | 20.32 | 9.26 | 1.65 | −7.65 | 27.1 | −8.21 | Sep-01 | 55.24 |
| CSFB/Tremont Long/ Short Equity | 96 | 13.37 | 11.93 | 0.70 | −11.43 | 34.4 | −11.36 | Feb-01 | 61.79 |

*Source:* Hedge Fund Research, CSFB/Tremont, Datastream, Bloomberg, UBS Warburg (2000).

have a volatility target. They manage the portfolio accordingly. Managing volatility requires skill. This is the reason why absolute return strategies (seeking investment opportunities by controlling unwanted risk) occasionally are referred to as *skill-based* strategies whereas the long-only investment style is referred to as *market-based* investment strategy.

Figure 8.4 shows the returns of various hedge fund indexes with some equity and bond indexes. Figure 8.5 compares monthly total MSCI World returns with the HFRI Equity Hedge index.

■ Figure 8.4 makes one wonder whether long/short is a superior way of managing equity risk than is the long-only investment approach. Even when 300 basis points for survivorship bias is subtracted from reported returns and volatility is doubled due to illiquidity and other imperfections, the HFRI Equity Hedge index still beats most market indexes on a risk-adjusted return basis. Figure 8.4 also makes clear why the mutual fund lobby is trying to prevent hedge funds from advertising their performance figures. The result could potentially have a disastrous impact on the mutual

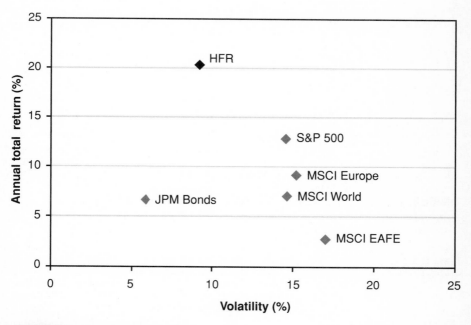

**FIGURE 8.4** Return versus Risk
*Source:* Hedge Fund Research, Datastream, UBS Warburg (2000).

funds' marketing strategy (which is essentially based on showing long-term compounded rates of return unadjusted for risk).

■ Figure 8.5 indicates where the outliers are: on the upside. Note the five observations were far north of the regression line.

■ As shown in Table 8.4, higher-moment risk, that is, skew and excess kurtosis of returns, is negligible.

■ The exposure to the market was high in general but varies strongly among different hedge funds. The long/short equity industry in itself is very heterogeneous.

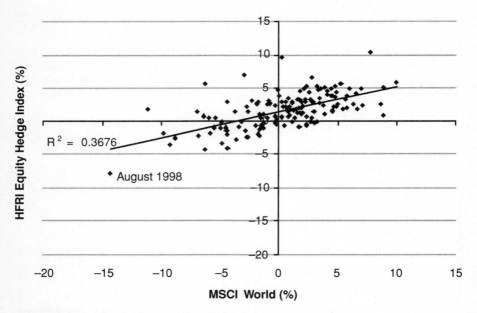

**FIGURE 8.5** MSCI World versus Long/Short Equity Returns
*Source:* Hedge Fund Research, Datastream, UBS Warburg (2000).

**Table 8.4** Statistical Analysis of Long/Short Equity Returns

|  | Alpha to MSCI World | Beta to MSCI World | Skew | Excess Kurtosis | Correlation MSCI World | Correlation JPM Global Bonds |
|---|---|---|---|---|---|---|
| **HFRI Equity Hedge Index** | 1.33 | 0.38 | −0.03 | 1.21 | 0.60 | 0.05 |
| **CSFB/Tremont Long/Short Equity** | 0.67 | 0.54 | −0.09 | 2.66 | 0.64 | 0.04 |

*Source:* Hedge Fund Research, CSFB/Tremont, Datastream, UBS Warburg (2000).

■ The correlation with the equity market was high. The strategy had the highest correlation with equities from the range analyzed in this book. Unlike equity market neutral, long/short equity has a long bias.

Figure 8.6 shows the performance of the HFRI Equity Hedge index in different market environments, and Figure 8.7 shows average quarterly returns in down markets versus average quarterly returns in friendly markets.

■ Figure 8.6 shows that long/short equity has outperformed equities (or has not significantly underperformed long-only indexes) in all major crises over the past 12 years.
■ Figure 8.7 shows that, on average, long/short equity outperforms equities both in down as well as up markets. Note that the outperformance in down quarters was 813 basis points, which compares to 73 basis points outperformance in up quarters. This suggests some sort of payoff, which is similar to that of a call option position (positive delta, long gamma): If markets rise, one has some leveraged return (as with a long call option) and the exposure to equities rises (as with a long gamma position). If the market falls, the value of the position falls as well, but to a smaller extent than the underlying market.

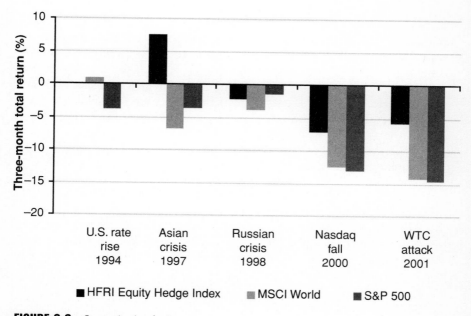

**FIGURE 8.6**  Scenario Analysis
*Source:* Hedge Fund Research, Datastream, UBS Warburg (2000).

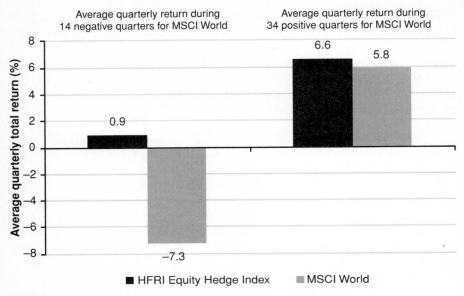

**FIGURE 8.7** Average Negative versus Average Positive Returns
*Source:* Hedge Fund Research, Datastream, UBS Warburg (2000).

■ Figure 8.7 brings up an issue with respect of leverage and total risk. In the public domain, hedge funds are considered risky because hedge fund managers use leverage. Assuming long/short managers use leverage to amplify returns and they outperform in positive quarters, shouldn't they underperform (as they use leverage) in down quarters? Shouldn't losses as well as returns be amplified if leverage was a measure of risk? The answer is that leverage is one of the most important tools for an absolute return manager to control risk. If opportunities are rich, leverage is high. If opportunities are poor, leverage is low. Managing risk according to changes in opportunity set is a tool that the long-only manager does not have. The American psychologist Abraham Maslow might have had a point: "To the man who only has a hammer in the toolkit, every problem looks like a nail." In long/short equity the opportunity set is somewhat correlated with the direction of the stock market. However, the notion that asset managers executing absolute return strategies are of high risk because of the use of leverage is at best incomplete and at worst utter nonsense.

Figure 8.8 shows how returns have been distributed in the past and compares the historic return distribution with a normal distribution of hedge funds in the long/short equity sector and a normal distribution of historical

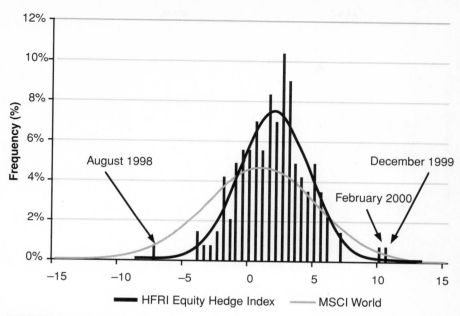

**FIGURE 8.8**   Return Distribution
*Source:* Hedge Fund Research, Datastream, UBS Warburg (2000).

MSCI World returns based on both historic mean returns and standard deviation of returns. For Figure 8.9 the hedge funds returns were sorted and compared to the corresponding market returns. This allows one to see in which market environment the extreme positive and negative returns were achieved.

■ Figure 8.8 shows that there is little difference between the normal distribution derived from historical returns and historical volatility and the frequency distribution in long/short equity. In other words, higher-moment return distribution characteristics played a minor role in the past. There were five returns outside the 95 percent range, three on the upside and two on the downside. There was one return on either side of the 99 percent range.

■ Figure 8.9 illustrates where the high correlation to the equity market is derived. The extreme negative returns are achieved during down markets whereas extreme positive returns were associated with positive market environments. However, Figure 8.9 also reveals that most of the outperformance comes from avoiding large losses. For example, the negative return in September 1990 is marked in Figure 8.9. Equity markets were falling due to uncertainties arising from Iraq invading Kuwait the month before.

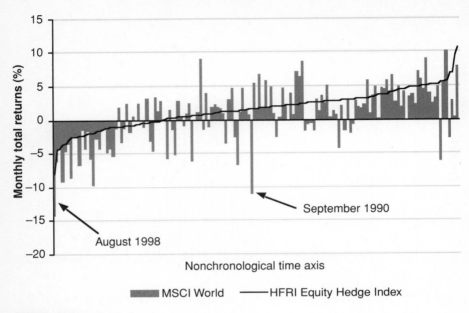

**FIGURE 8.9** Correlation
*Source:* Hedge Fund Research, Datastream, UBS Warburg (2000).

Long-only managers were hugging the benchmark, minimizing active risk, whereas long/short managers minimized total risk, that is, took risk off the table. This is a good example of why long-only managers are occasionally viewed as being in a car with no brakes: The risk regime has abruptly changed from one day to another and the long-only manager can do little other than drive into the collision ahead (i.e., lose money).

■ Figure 8.10 shows that long/short equity managers were underwater at the end of 2001. The magnitude of losses, however, was smaller than with broad market indexes such as the MSCI World and S&P 500.

■ Figure 8.11 shows that the correlation in down quarters is relatively high when compared to other absolute return strategies. The benefit to the investor is therefore not the direction but the magnitude of loss. In all the five worst quarters over the 1990–2001 period, a diversified portfolio of a long/short manager lost less in value than a globally diversified portfolio of stocks. A realistic assumption for future returns in long/short equity is that the correlation to equity markets will persist going forward. Long/short equity managers will most likely report positive absolute returns in bull markets and lose less than an outright long position when markets fall. If, going forward, superior long-term performance means

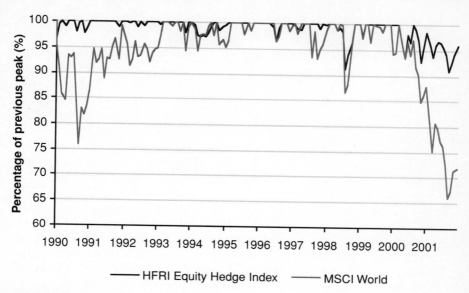

**FIGURE 8.10**  Underwater
*Source:* Hedge Fund Research, Datastream.

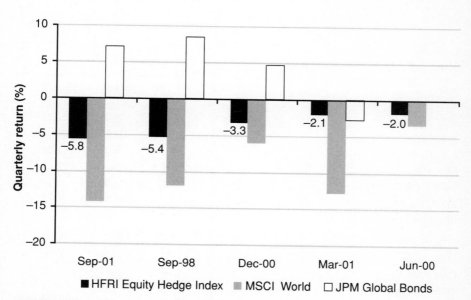

**FIGURE 8.11**  Worst Quarters for Long/Short Equity
*Source:* Hedge Fund Research, Datastream.

avoiding large losses, those managers who have an edge in managing risk will be the ones leading the performance tables.

■ Table 8.5 makes one wonder whether trigger-happy regulators one day will ban equity long-only exposure for retail investors instead of exposure to hedge funds. In all four periods, absolute returns as well as risk-adjusted returns were either higher or much higher when compared to the MSCI World index. The maximum monthly drawdowns in long/short equity were a fraction of those in long-only equity exposure. In three out of four observation periods the 12-month drawdown was a positive absolute return in the case of long/short whereas it was positive on only one occasion for the long-only investment style (by 51 basis points gross of fees).

■ The lack of persistence in terms of risk-adjusted returns could be viewed as a negative factor; long/short equity is not as pure an absolute return strategy as some other strategies discussed in Chapter 6 or 7. A high degree of correlation is clearly visible by viewing the last three three-year periods in Table 8.5. Absolute as well as risk-adjusted returns, volatilities, and drawdowns are correlated in the past three three-year periods. However, taking the risk of being repetitive, the large difference in magnitude of drawdowns between the long-only investment style and long/short when markets fall (last row in Table 8.5) is one of the raison d'être for the long/short approach to equity investing.

**Table 8.5**   Performance Persistence

|                                  | 1990–1992 | 1993–1995 | 1996–1998 | 1999–2001 |
|----------------------------------|-----------|-----------|-----------|-----------|
| **MSCI World (Total Return)**    |           |           |           |           |
| Annual return (%)                | −1.80     | 16.40     | 18.25     | −3.05     |
| Volatility (%)                   | 16.70     | 10.29     | 14.47     | 15.73     |
| Average risk-free rate (%)       | 5.61      | 4.37      | 5.07      | 4.64      |
| Sharpe ratio                     | <0        | 1.17      | 0.91      | <0        |
| Worst 1-month drawdown (%)       | −11.12    | −5.81     | −14.30    | −9.21     |
| Worst 12-month drawdown (%)      | −16.52    | −4.66     | 0.51      | −27.87    |
| **HFRI Equity Hedge Index**      |           |           |           |           |
| Annual return (%)                | 24.84     | 19.82     | 20.34     | 16.45     |
| Volatility (%)                   | 8.43      | 6.17      | 9.14      | 12.35     |
| Sharpe ratio                     | 2.28      | 2.51      | 1.67      | 0.96      |
| Worst 1-month drawdown (%)       | −3.40     | −2.10     | −7.96     | −4.40     |
| Worst 12-month drawdown (%)      | 14.43     | 0.55      | 4.33      | −8.21     |

*Source:* Hedge Fund Research, Datastream.

## Sector Specialists

Sector specialist hedge funds are a special type of long/short equity fund. At the most general level, they exploit opportunities in one sector only. The following section compares some sector hedge fund indexes with the sector indexes, that is, a proxy for the long-only investment style. We compare four sectors—technology, health care/biotechnology, financials, and energy—and compare the performance figures with U.S. indexes, since most sector hedge funds are based in the United States. Long/short equity hedge funds in Europe and Asia are in an earlier stage of their industry life cycle and have, generally speaking, broader defined mandates. Table 8.6 summarizes the main performance statistics for the four strategies. Note that the analysis was conducted over different time periods due to data availability. The number of observations in months will be listed in more detailed tables for all of the four strategies.

■ Absolute annual returns were between 22 percent and 29 percent. On a return as well as a risk-adjusted return basis, the absolute return strategies have outperformed long-only strategies by a wide margin. The substantial outperformance cannot be explained by survivorship bias or any other imperfections in the data collection process.
■ Volatility was lower in two strategies and higher in the other two strategies. In the energy sector a 17.5 percent outperformance was achieved with a 4.8 percentage points higher volatility.
■ The worst 12-month drawdowns were lower with technology and health care/biotechnology long/short strategies. However, drawdowns were slightly higher with long/short managers in financials and substantially higher in the energy sector when compared with the long-only investment style.

**Table 8.6**   Summary Statistics for Sector Specialists

| Sector Index | Annual Return | Annual Out-performance | Difference in Volatility (Percentage Points) | Sharpe Ratio Long/Short | Sharpe Ratio Long-Only | Worst 12-month Drawdown Long/Short | Worst 12-month Drawdown Long-Only |
|---|---|---|---|---|---|---|---|
| HFRI Sector: Technology | 23.4% | 7.2% | −6.3 | 0.89 | 0.42 | −37.5% | −59.8% |
| HFRI Sector: Health Care/ Biotechnology | 22.2 | 5.5 | 0.9 | 0.72 | 0.51 | −18.3 | −29.9 |
| HFRI Sector: Financial | 21.9 | 6.2 | −7.1 | 1.35 | 0.55 | −17.7 | −16.0 |
| HFRI Sector: Energy | 28.5 | 17.5 | 4.8 | 1.08 | 0.36 | −37.1 | −15.5 |

*Source:* Hedge Fund Research, Datastream.

## Technology

Table 8.7 compares the HFRI Technology index with the S&P 500 and two U.S. technology indexes, the S&P 500 Technology index and the Nasdaq Composite. The observation period for this analysis is over an 11-year period (132 months) from January 1991 to December 2001. All returns are in U.S. dollars.

■ Table 8.7 speaks for itself. The hedge funds index, a diversified exposure to a group of absolute return managers investing in technology stocks on a long/short basis, was superior in all aspects: Annual absolute as well as risk-adjusted return and maximum return were higher whereas all risk characteristics were lower. Correlation, for what it is worth, was high. The correlation coefficient between the hedge funds index and the S&P 500 Technology and the Nasdaq index was 0.78 and 0.90, respectively. The high correlation suggests that exposure to this type of investment is not a portfolio diversifier but a substitute for long-only exposure. The investor trades less liquidity and less regulatory protection for superior risk-adjusted performance.

Figure 8.12 is not self-explanatory (as all other graphs in this book should be). The figure compares the frequency distribution (5 percent increments) of the HFRI Technology index with the frequency distribution of the Nasdaq Composite index. A negative value shows that the hedge funds index has fewer observations than the long-only equity index in that particular bucket (dark bars). The light-gray bars show the frequency distribution of the 132 monthly returns of the hedge funds index.

■ The main focus point of Figure 8.12 is the left-hand side of the chart. The left-hand side of Figure 8.12 reveals where the superior performance comes from: by avoiding large losses. A diversified exposure to technology hedge funds has resulted in fewer occurrences of a monthly loss be-

**Table 8.7**   Long/Short versus Long-Only in the Technology Sector

| | # of Monthly Returns | Annual Return | Volatility | Sharpe Ratio (5%) | Worst 1-month Drawdown | Negative Months | Worst 12-month Drawdown | 12-month Drawdown Ended On | Highest 12-month Return |
|---|---|---|---|---|---|---|---|---|---|
| S&P 500 | 132 | 14.43% | 14.20% | 0.66 | −15.64% | 33.3% | −26.63% | Sep-01 | 52.10% |
| S&P 500 Technology | 132 | 16.68 | 28.32 | 0.41 | −31.40 | 40.2 | −61.62 | Sep-01 | 97.84 |
| Nasdaq Composite | 132 | 16.20 | 26.93 | 0.42 | −26.01 | 35.6 | −59.76 | Mar-01 | 105.27 |
| HFRI Sector: | | | | | | | | | |
| Technology index | 132 | 23.35 | 20.61 | 0.89 | −16.44 | 37.1 | −37.50 | Sep-01 | 169.05 |

*Source:* Hedge Fund Research, Datastream.

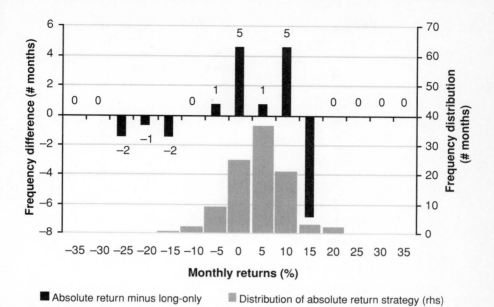

**FIGURE 8.12** Comparison of Return Frequency Distributions
*Source:* Hedge Fund Research, Datastream.

tween –10 percent and –25 percent. On the other side there are also fewer hedge fund returns in the 15 to 20 percent bucket. In other words, hedge funds avoid large swings on the downside but do not participate in large upswings (most often a rebound after a large decline) as a long-only strategy does. However, the long/short strategy has more months where the returns are in the 0 to 5 percent and 10 to 15 percent bucket.

■ All four indexes shown in Table 8.7 had an excess kurtosis of between 1.1 (hedge funds index) and 2.0 (Nasdaq) and skew of between –0.1 (hedge funds index) and –0.87 (Nasdaq). In other words, the non-normality of the hedge funds indexes is similar to those of the long-only benchmarks used for this analysis.

Table 8.8 is one for the regulator. It shows what avoiding large losses means to wealth creation (or preservation). The table shows the wealth of two investments starting at 100 in December 1996. The first investment is the long-only investment style, in this case the Nasdaq Composite. The second column is the long/short equity investment, the HFRI Technology index.

■ Table 8.8 shows that the long-only investment had a higher return in the first three years—a total return of 215 percent compared with the 208

**Table 8.8**  Comparison of Wealth Creation

|               | Nasdaq Composite | HFRI Technology |
|---------------|------------------|-----------------|
|               | 100              | 100             |
| Dec. 1997     | 122              | 107             |
| Dec. 1998     | 170              | 137             |
| Dec. 1999     | 315              | 308             |
| Dec. 2000     | 191              | 261             |
| Dec. 2001     | 151              | 228             |
| Return 1997–1999 | 215%          | 208%            |
| Return 2000–2001 | −52%          | −26%            |
| Underwater    | −52%             | −26%            |

*Source:* Hedge Fund Research, Datastream.

percent of the absolute return portfolio. However, the subsequent two-year period resulted in a loss of 52 percent for the former and a loss of 26 percent for the latter. This, we believe, is a big difference. At the end of July 2002, the two indices in Table 8.8 stood at 103 and 184 respectively.

■ The reason why Table 8.8 is "one for the regulator" is because it should initiate a debate regarding what kind of investment the retail investor needs protection from—outright exposure to volatile asset class (left column in Table 8.8) or hedged (or semihedged in this case) exposure to a volatile asset class. The fact that occasionally a hedge fund goes bankrupt (as do companies) does not matter in this debate, as single-manager or single-company risk is nonsystematic risk that can be immunized through diversification.

■ Correlation between the two proxies in Table 8.8 was close to one in the period from 1997 to 1999, during the bull market. The normalized long-only proxy fell from 315 to 151 in 2000–2001. The long/short proxy fell from 308 to 228. In other words, correlation is one on the way up and less than one on the way down. The losses of the long/short proxy in the bear market could be viewed as a call option premium outlay for a potential rebound in the Nasdaq. If the Nasdaq starts increasing again (which is a possibility), correlation is likely to move towards one.

Figure 8.13 shows average quarterly returns in down markets versus average quarterly returns in friendly markets.

Figure 8.13 reveals some interesting aspects of substituting long-only exposure with long/short exposure: The asset management industry is about alpha (at least from a marketing perspective). However, this might change.

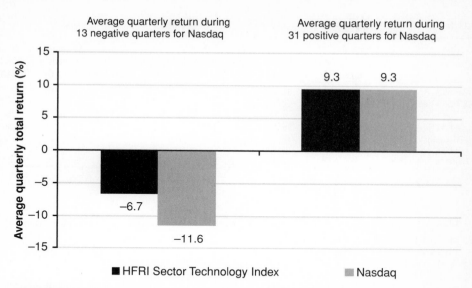

**FIGURE 8.13** Average Negative versus Average Positive Returns
*Source:* Hedge Fund Research, Datastream, UBS Warburg (2000).

Figure 8.13 shows that long-term superior returns derive from not losing your shirt (i.e., risk management) and not necessarily generating alpha. Or, assuming "not losing your shirt" is equal to generating alpha (an assumption one could make) then the key variable to investment success becomes risk management. The observation that the average positive quarterly return of technology hedge funds is equal to the average quarterly returns in the Nasdaq Composite index in Figure 8.13 is coincidence. However, what is not coincidence is that absolute return managers do not follow the benchmark down on a one-to-one basis. Long-term superiority is achieved from balancing investment opportunities with total risk. Investment long-only opportunities in equity markets might not be identical when the market trades at 8 times prospective earnings to when it trades at 38 times prospective earnings. The absolute return manager distinguishes between the two. The relative return manager, too, distinguishes between the two. The difference is that the relative return manager can do little about it because risk is defined as active risk and not as total risk.

## Health Care/Biotechnology

Table 8.9 compares the HFRI Sector Health Care/Biotechnology index with the S&P 500 and two related benchmark indexes, in this case the S&P 500

**Table 8.9**  Long/Short versus Long-Only in the Health Care/Biotechnology Sector

| | # of Monthly Returns | Annual Return | Volatility | Sharpe Ratio (5%) | Worst 1-month Drawdown | Negative Months | Worst 12-month Drawdown | 12-month Drawdown Ended On | Highest 12-month Return |
|---|---|---|---|---|---|---|---|---|---|
| S&P 500 | 108 | 13.53% | 14.66% | 0.58 | −15.64% | 34.3% | −26.63% | Sep-01 | 52.10% |
| S&P 500 Health Care Drugs | 108 | 16.72 | 22.84 | 0.51 | −17.45 | 35.2 | −28.88 | Feb-00 | 74.94 |
| S&P 500 Biotechnology | 108 | 22.55 | 39.27 | 0.45 | −53.66 | 38.9 | −29.91 | Dec-93 | 173.30 |
| HFRI Sector: Health Care/ Biotechnology index | 108 | 22.18 | 23.75 | 0.72 | −19.52 | 38.9 | −18.33 | Aug-98 | 144.63 |

*Source:* Hedge Fund Research, Datastream.

Health Care Drugs and the S&P 500 Biotechnology indexes. The observation period for this analysis is over a nine year period (108 months) from January 1993 to December 2001.

■ The long/short index has outperformed all benchmarks on a risk-adjusted return (here measured by Sharpe ratio) basis. However, the absolute return index has outperformed the S&P 500 Health Care Drugs index on an absolute return level but slightly underperformed the S&P 500 Biotechnology index. Note that the hedge funds index had roughly the same absolute return as the (high-beta) biotechnology subsector but with the volatility of the tamer health care sector.

■ The worst one-month drawdown for the hedge fund index was only a fraction of the biotechnology subsector and roughly in line with the health care sector. However, the absolute return managers clearly outperform long-only proxies in terms of the worst 12month drawdown.

■ As shown in Figure 8.14, the return distribution comparison is slightly different from the previously discussed technology sector. The superior performance does not derive only from avoiding negative outliers and having more moderate returns. The outperformance is derived from having more outliers on the upside. The reason for this observation is because we compare the absolute return index with the health care drugs sector and not with the biotechnology index. However, in terms of non-normally distributed returns the absolute return index shares the characteristics with the biotechnology index: The returns of the health care index have negligible excess kurtosis (−0.9) whereas the biotechnology index has 4.7 and the hedge funds index 5.6. However, there is a difference in skew. The distribution of the biotechnology index has negative skew of −0.9 whereas the hedge funds index has positive skew of 1.1. When the hedge funds index is compared with the biotechnology index (the former has roughly the same return but much lower volatility) the difference in

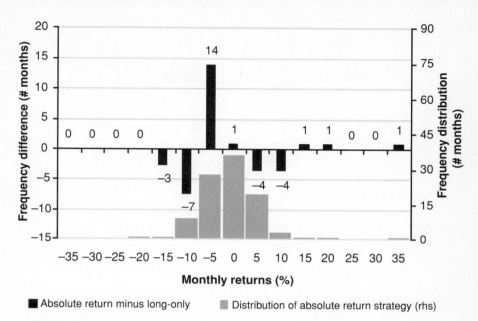

**FIGURE 8.14** Comparison of Return Frequency Distributions
*Source:* Hedge Fund Research, Datastream.

the return distributions is derived from avoiding some large negative losses and having a concentration in the two buckets between –5 percent and 5 percent.

■ Table 8.10 shows that the hedge funds index outperformed the long-only proxy in health care but not biotechnology in the five years ending in 2001.

■ An interesting characteristic is the fact that the three-year return from 1997 to 1999 is nearly identical to the return in the subsequent two-year period. This despite the fact that the underlying sectors (health care and biotechnology) have performed much better in the first period when compared with the second. The reason why this is interesting is because long/short managers list in their marketing material that they can make money in bull as well as bear markets. This is true, in theory. In practice this is not always the case, as the opportunity set is normally correlated with the performance of the market. Long/short has positive correlation with the underlying equity market. The superior performance is derived from, generally speaking, losing less when markets fall.

■ Figure 8.15 compares the hedge fund index with the S&P 500 Biotechnology index. The underperformance of the hedge fund index in rising

**Table 8.10** Comparison of Wealth Creation

|  | S&P 500 Health Care | S&P 500 Biotechnology | HFRI Health Care/ Biotechnology |
|---|---|---|---|
|  | 100 | 100 | 100 |
| Dec. 1997 | 157 | 100 | 101 |
| Dec. 1998 | 235 | 192 | 108 |
| Dec. 1999 | 191 | 442 | 159 |
| Dec. 2000 | 260 | 421 | 240 |
| Dec. 2001 | 198 | 405 | 253 |
| Return 1997–1999 | 91% | 342% | 59% |
| Return 2000–2001 | 4% | −8% | 59% |
| Underwater | −24% | −8% | 0% |

*Source:* Hedge Fund Research, Datastream.

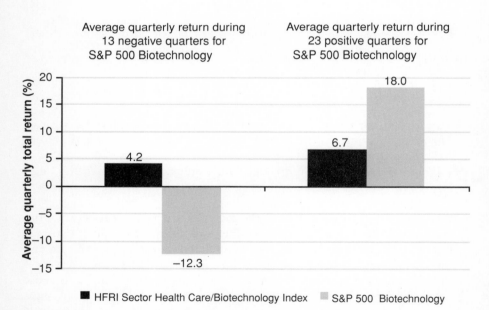

**FIGURE 8.15** Average Negative versus Average Positive Returns
*Source:* Hedge Fund Research, Datastream.

markets is 11.3 percent whereas the outperformance in falling markets is around 16.5 percent. In other words, the return profile is also asymmetrical—a phenomenon also found with most other long/short equity strategies.

## Financials

Table 8.11 compares the HFRI Sector Financials index with the S&P 500 Financials index. The observation period covers 10 years to December 2001.

■ The index of hedge funds focusing on investment opportunities in the financial sector outperformed the S&P 500 Financials index by a wide margin with substantially lower volatility. In other words, risk-adjusted returns were substantially higher than for the long-only investment proxy. The monthly drawdown was smaller for the hedge fund index (–20.7 percent versus –26.3 percent) but slightly higher over a 12-month period (–17.7 percent versus –16.0 percent). Note that the monthly drawdowns were higher (i.e., losses larger) than the 12-month drawdowns.
■ Figure 8.16 shows that the superior performance is derived from fewer monthly observations in the –10 to –5 percent bucket and more returns in the 0 to 5 percent bucket.
■ The frequency distribution of the hedge fund index has an extremely high excess kurtosis of 11, compared with 3.9 for the S&P 500 Financials and 1.6 for the S&P 500 index in the same time period. However, only two returns were outside the 95 percent range, one on each side of the mean. The monthly loss of 20.7 percent in August 1998 was a 5.7-sigma event resulting in the high excess kurtosis figure of 11.
■ Table 8.12 shows a somewhat unusual feature. The returns for the two periods (1997–1999 and 2000–2001) are not correlated. The returns for the S&P 500 Financials index were 63 percent for the period 1997 to 1999 and only 11 percent for the subsequent two years. The magnitudes

**Table 8.11** Long/Short versus Long-Only in the Financial Services Sector

| | # of Monthly Returns | Annual Return | Volatility | Sharpe Ratio (5%) | Worst 1-month Drawdown | Negative Months | Worst 12-month Drawdown | 12-month Drawdown Ended On | Highest 12-month Return |
|---|---|---|---|---|---|---|---|---|---|
| S&P 500 | 120 | 12.93% | 14.09% | 0.56 | –15.64% | 34.2% | –26.63% | Sep-01 | 52.10% |
| S&P 500 Financials | 120 | 15.76 | 19.62 | 0.55 | –26.33 | 35.8 | –15.99 | Oct-01 | 70.03 |
| HFRI Sector: Financial index | 120 | 21.92 | 12.55 | 1.35 | –20.65 | 25.0 | –17.68 | Mar-99 | 53.96 |

*Source:* Hedge Fund Research, Datastream.

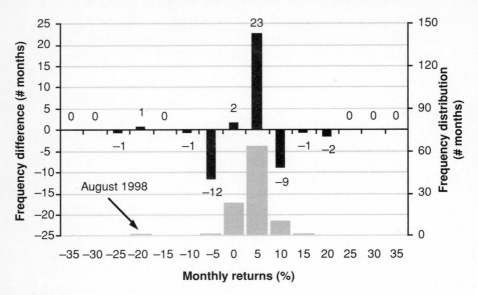

**FIGURE 8.16** Comparison of Return Frequency Distributions
*Source:* Hedge Fund Research, Datastream.

**Table 8.12** Comparison of Wealth Creation

|  | S&P 500 Financials | HFRI Financials |
|---|---|---|
|  | 100 | 100 |
| Dec. 1997 | 145 | 149 |
| Dec. 1998 | 159 | 131 |
| Dec. 1999 | 163 | 129 |
| Dec. 2000 | 202 | 176 |
| Dec. 2001 | 180 | 204 |
| Return 1997–1999 | 63% | 29% |
| Return 2000–2001 | 11% | 59% |
| Underwater | −11% | 0% |

*Source:* Hedge Fund Research, Datastream.

for the hedge fund proxy are the other way around. The HFRI Financials index had a return of 29 percent in the first period and a much higher return of 59 percent in the subsequent period. The reason for this difference in direction and magnitude is that the long-only proxy is purely dependent on the direction of the subgroup of the asset class (in this case the S&P 500 Financials index). The long/short proxy is a function of the investment opportunities *within* the subgroup of the asset class.

■ Figure 8.17 shows the familiar pattern for long/short equity: slight underperformance in positive quarters and huge outperformance in negative quarters. Long/short equity seems to follow the Wall Street wit according to which the best way of making money is not losing it.

## Energy

Table 8.13 compares the HFRI Sector Energy index with the S&P 500 Energy for the seven-year period (84 months) ending in December 2001.

■ Hedge funds operating in the energy sector, as a group, achieved an after-fee absolute return of 28.5 percent with a volatility of 21.7 percent, compared with a return of the S&P 500 Energy index, a proxy for a long-only

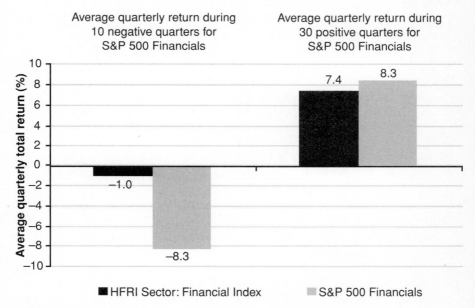

**FIGURE 8.17** Average Negative versus Average Positive Returns
*Source:* Hedge Fund Research, Datastream.

**Table 8.13**   Long/Short versus Long-Only in the Energy Sector

| | # of Monthly Returns | Annual Return | Volatility | Sharpe Ratio (5%) | Worst 1-month Drawdown | Negative Months | Worst 12-month Drawdown | 12-month Drawdown Ended On | Highest 12-month Return |
|---|---|---|---|---|---|---|---|---|---|
| S&P 500 | 84 | 15.91% | 15.98% | 0.68 | −15.64% | 33.3% | −26.63% | Sep-01 | 52.10% |
| S&P 500 Energy | 84 | 11.04 | 16.93 | 0.36 | −12.26 | 41.7 | −15.46 | Sep-01 | 45.31 |
| HFRI Sector: Energy index | 84 | 28.51 | 21.72 | 1.08 | −12.50 | 36.9 | −37.08 | Oct-98 | 115.08 |

*Source:* Hedge Fund Research, Datastream.

strategy, of 11.0 percent and a volatility of 16.9 percent. This results in outperformance on an absolute as well as a risk-adjusted level. One-month drawdowns were similar for both proxies. However, the absolute return strategy had a 12-month drawdown of 37 percent, which was more than double that of the long-only investment proxy. The energy sector is typically classified as low-beta (i.e., a defensive sector). Given that volatility and 12-month drawdown in the long/short proxy is higher, the long/short proxy does not share the defensive characteristics of the underlying benchmark.

■ Figure 8.18 shows that the superior performance of the long/short investment style was achieved by having fewer observations in the −5 to 0 percent and 0 to 5 percent buckets and more observations in the next three 5 percent buckets.

■ Figure 8.18 also shows that the frequency distribution (lower section of Figure 8.18) was very close to a normal distribution. As a matter of fact, excess kurtosis was 0.0 and skew was only 0.1. This compares with excess kurtosis and skew for the S&P 500 Energy index of 0.4 and 0.3, respectively. The correlation coefficient between the two proxies was 0.67. Note that the observation period was only seven years.

■ Table 8.14 shows a similar pattern as for financials. The second period showed a higher return than the first period. The energy sector had a volatility of 19.7 percent in the period from 1997 to 1999 and a volatility of 18.1 percent in the subsequent two years, so the opportunity set was not materially different between the two periods. This observation could be, potentially, just another nail in the coffin of traditional active long-only asset management.

■ Figure 8.19 is somewhat unusual. Normally, outperformance in long/short is achieved by having high correlation in positive market conditions and avoiding absolute losses. However, in the energy sector correlation on the downside seems higher where the outperformance is achieved in positive quarters. Note that there were only six negative quarters in the seven-year observation period.

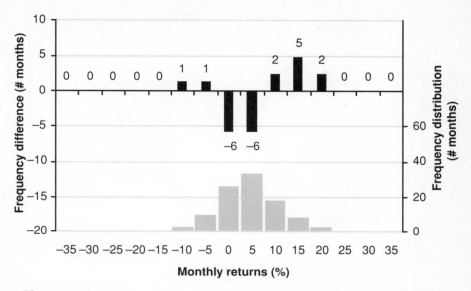

**FIGURE 8.18** Comparison of Return Frequency Distributions
*Source:* Hedge Fund Research, Datastream.

**Table 8.14** Comparison of Wealth Creation

|  | S&P 500 Energy | HFRI Energy |
|---|---|---|
|  | 100 | 100 |
| Dec. 1997 | 122 | 147 |
| Dec. 1998 | 119 | 114 |
| Dec. 1999 | 139 | 143 |
| Dec. 2000 | 155 | 227 |
| Dec. 2001 | 136 | 231 |
| Return 1997–1999 | 39% | 43% |
| Return 2000–2001 | –2% | 61% |
| Underwater | –12% | 0% |

*Source:* Hedge Fund Research, Datastream.

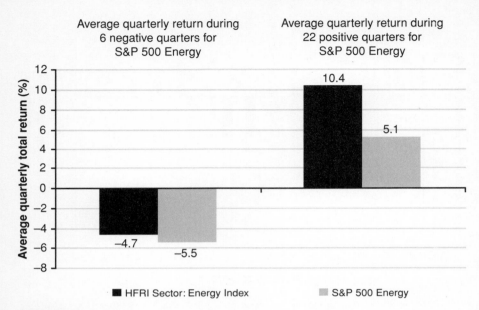

**FIGURE 8.19**   Average Negative versus Average Positive Returns
*Source:* Hedge Fund Research, Datastream.

## Conclusion

To some, long/short equity is the archetype of a hedge fund. Long/short equity, in the past, had high risk-adjusted returns, high volatility when compared with arbitrage strategies and low volatility when compared to long-only investment strategies and high correlation with equities. The dispersion between different long/short equity managers is wide and is not expected to narrow anytime soon.

## Outlook

A case could be drawn that outperformance will not be as high in the future as it was in the past. The average outperformance of the HFRI Equity Hedge index against the MSCI World total return index in the six-year period from 1990 to 1995 was 15.4 percent per year (22.3 percent versus 6.9 percent) but "only" 11.3 percent per year (18.4 percent versus 7.1 percent) in the six years to 2001.* Economic logic and common sense suggest that this trend

---

*The outperformance against the S&P 500 (total return) index was 9.3 percent in the first six-year period and 5.7 percent in the latter.

(decreasing outperformance) should continue. It is unlikely that a superior investment vehicle can maintain its superiority forever. Economic rents have a tendency to evaporate. Once all the lemmings have bought into the investment case for absolute return strategies the alpha will be gone (or spread over a much larger population of investors). The economic rent of the pioneers will have gone and the pioneers will have to find something new to deviate from the consensus. On a more positive note, the evaporation of alpha will not happen overnight. In mid-2002, close to 100 percent of U.K. pension funds were averse to hedge funds and around 70 percent in the United States. In Germany, hedge funds were still viewed as outlaws by government and press. In other words, the conversion of lemmings is a slow process and could unfold over a period of 10 years. By comparison, it took more than a decade for derivatives not to be viewed as the devil's instrument but as a tool for controlling risk.*

# MACRO

## Strategy

At the most general level, macro funds have the flexibility to move from opportunity to opportunity without restriction. Their investment process is the least restricted in the whole hedge funds industry. If a macro manager wanted to trade property on Mars, there is little that could stop him (assuming there is a market). There is primarily manager-specific risk associated with this subgroup, and little or no process or strategy risk. One advantage of full flexibility is the independence from deal or paper flow as in some of the arbitrage strategies such as convertible or risk arbitrage. The lack of a proper investment process is a disadvantage, that is, an insurmountable hurdle primarily for institutional investors. Based on estimates of Hedge Fund Research, macro hedge funds were 71.0 percent of the $38.9 billion hedge funds universe in 1990 and 13.5 percent of the $537 billion hedge funds universe at the end of 2001.

Macro hedge funds enjoy extraordinary flexibility regarding their investment opportunities and strategies. They are (or were) the big players of the hedge fund industry and the ones most often in the headlines. They are (or have been) regarded as the new trading and investment gurus.[1] Through their size and leverage, they are believed to influence and manipulate markets. Some macro hedge funds were accused of causing the fall in the pound ster-

---

*Although in the United Kingdom the general belief is still that it was derivatives (as opposed to mismanagement) that brought down one of the oldest banks in the country. As a result, asset managers on some occasions are still constrained from using derivatives in portfolios managed for pension funds.

ling in 1992,* resulting in its withdrawal from the European Monetary System. However, this allegation was brought into question by a study published by the International Monetary Fund (IMF).† Furthermore, it can be argued that since every move by one of the big macro players is amplified by many smaller copycats, they may not be entirely to blame for their large impact. For this reason, macro funds no longer disclose their positions, a move that has diminished the already low transparency of these funds.

Most often macro funds operate in very liquid and efficient markets such as fixed income, foreign exchange or equity index futures markets. However, there is a trade-off between liquidity and opportunity. Liquidity is correlated with efficiency. The more efficient a market, the higher the liquidity. High liquidity and high efficiency often mean close to perfect information and competition. Perfect information and perfect competition mean fewer opportunities to exploit inefficiencies. Macro funds, therefore, make their money by anticipating a price change early and not necessarily by exploiting market inefficiencies. Searching for imbalances in supply and demand might be considered the common denominator of macro managers.

Macro managers are a very heterogeneous subgroup. Generalizations as the one above are actually very imprecise. If there is a subgroup of managers who do not fit into a box, it is macro managers. Macro managers are as diverse as their mandate is loose. One generalization could be that they are, more often than not, contrarians. Jim Rogers, cofounder of George Soros' Quantum Fund and author of *Investment Biker*, describes his investment philosophy as follows:

> *In all my years in investing, there's one rule I've prized beyond every other: Always bet against central banks and with the real world. In the seventies, the central banks were defending the United States' artificially low price of gold. Central banks and governments always try to maintain artificial levels, high or low, whether of a currency, a metal, wool, whatever. When a central bank is defending something—whether it's gold at thirty-five dollars or the lira at eight hundred to the dollar—the smart in-*

---

*Or credited with keeping the British out of recession—depending on one's point of view.
†It is beyond doubt that macro hedge funds had a significant short position in sterling in 1992 that impacted the market. It is, however, difficult to determine whether this position "caused" the sterling devaluation, because it coincided with net capital outflows from the United Kingdom. The prologue to the 1992 ERM crisis was the conversion play, estimated to be around $300 billion by the International Money Fund. Altogether, European central bank interventions amounted to roughly $100 billion. The $11.7 billion in hedge fund positions coincided with at least another $90 billion of sales in European currencies.

*vestor always goes the other way. It may take a while, but I promise you you'll come out ahead. It's a golden rule of investing.[2]*

One of the ultimate ironies in capital markets today, and one that has been repeated several times in this book, is that a main goal of hedge fund managers is not to lose money. The reason why this is an irony is that one really needs to have an odd definition of risk to not agree with this notion being conservative. In addition, one also needs a rather strange view on what Amos Tversky (1995) in connection with loss aversion calls the human pleasure machine (see appendix to Chapter 4)—that is, how human psychology affects incentives and how incentives affect action and inaction. Jim Rogers on the issue of losing money:

*Don't lose money. If you don't know the facts, don't play. I just wait until there is money around the corner, and all I have to do is go over there and pick it up. I do nothing in the meantime.[3]*

This statement might or might not qualify for publication in the renowned *Journal of Finance*. Nevertheless, it more or less sums up what hedge funds do: balance investment opportunity with the risk of losing principal. If the active manager determines the risk to be in a disadvantageous probabilistic relationship with the investment opportunity, he or she does not trade. The move of active asset management from the second paradigm of relative returns to the third paradigm of absolute returns seems inevitable.

Returning to the subject of macro as a subgroup of directional hedge fund activity: Macro fund managers argue that most price fluctuations in financial markets fall within one standard deviation of the mean.[4] They consider this volatility to be the norm, which does not offer particularly good investment opportunities. However, when price fluctuations of particular instruments or markets push out more than two standard deviations from the mean into the tails of the bell curve, an extreme condition occurs that may only appear once every two or three decades. When market prices differ from the "real" value of an asset, there exists an investment opportunity. The macro investor makes profits by exploiting such extreme price/value valuations and, occasionally, pushing them back to normal levels.

Tremont (1999) distinguished two kinds of macro managers, those who come from a long/short equity background and those who come from a derivative trading background:

■ Macro funds run by companies like Tiger Investment Management and Soros Fund Management were originally invested primarily in U.S. equities. The success of these managers at stock picking resulted over time in substantial increases in assets under management. As the funds increased in size, it became increasingly difficult to take meaningful positions in smaller-capitalization stocks. Consequently, the funds started gravitating toward more liquid securities and markets in which bigger bets could be placed.

■ Funds run by Moore Capital, Caxton, and Tudor Investment developed from a futures trading discipline which, by its very nature, was both global and macroeconomic in scope. The freeing up of the global currency markets and the development of non-U.S. financial futures markets in the 1980s provided an increasing number of investment and trading opportunities not previously available to investment managers.

Tiger Management's large losses and George Soros' retreat were interpreted as a sign that the heyday of macro funds was over. At the end of April 2000, George Soros announced that he was cutting back on his Quantum Fund. Quantum had $8.5 billion in assets when Soros made the announcement that Stanley Druckenmiller, the manager of the fund, and his colleague Nicholas Roditi, who ran the $1.2 billion Quota Fund, were leaving the group. The Quantum Fund, which was renamed Quantum Endowment Fund, said then that it planned to stop making large, so-called macro bets on the direction of currencies and interest rates and expected to target an annual return of 15 percent, which was less than half the annual average posted since the fund's start in 1969. One month later, the Quantum fund was said to have 90 percent in cash according to Bloomberg News.

Trades of the magnitude of George Soros' sterling trade in 1992 might or might not belong to the past. However, the opportunistic hedge fund that has a mandate to invest in anything the general partners believe will yield a profit will continue to raise funds in the future. Whether an investor prefers the stable, highly predictable (albeit non-normally distributed) returns of relative-value strategies or the unpredictable, widely dispersed, and erratic returns generated by opportunistic funds is a matter of risk appetite and individual preference. Institutions have a bias toward the former where there is a balance between manager skill and a fundamental and disciplined investment process.

Institutional investors do not like the lack of a concrete investment process, the lack of transparency, and the extreme flexibility of the fund managers. Further reservations for macro funds derive from the belief that the superior macro managers can only be identified ex post but not ex ante. In 1969 it was difficult to foresee that a dollar given to Mr. Soros would grow to $8,668 by 2001.*

---

*A dollar given to Mr. Buffett in the beginning of 1969 would have grown to $973 in the same time period. A dollar invested in the S&P 500 index would have grown to $11 by the end of 2001 assuming dividends were taxed and then spent or to $32 had gross dividends been reinvested.

## Performance

■ Macro funds, as a group, have performed well in the past. Most macro indexes show higher returns than the S&P 500 with lower volatility (for diversified exposure to macro managers).

■ Figure 8.20 shows that macro managers as a group experienced some difficulties preserving capital at some of the economic turning points, namely 1994 (Fed rate hike) and beginning of 2000 (end of 1982–2000 bull market). Figure 8.20 implies steady growth because the macro index is not shown on a log scale. As Table 8.17 further on will reveal, the subgroup has experienced diminishing returns over time. The reason could be because of major currencies disappearing (due to the introduction of the euro) or central bankers becoming more aware about what is really going on in capital markets (although recent central bank history in Europe might suggest otherwise).

■ The differences between the macro indexes is an indication that, as mentioned before, macro as a subgroup is heterogeneous. Not all managers are chasing the same opportunities, as for example in risk arbitrage. The heterogeneity in the subgroup is good with respect to diversification; that is, the incremental benefits from adding different funds is high. The negative

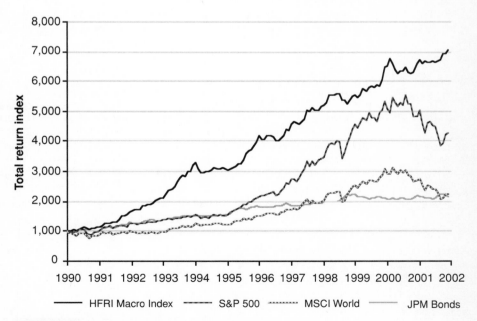

**FIGURE 8.20** Long-Term Performance of Macro
*Source:* Hedge Fund Research, Datastream, UBS Warburg (2000).

aspect of this heterogeneity is that charts such as Figure 8.20 do not really tell us a lot. The annual returns (albeit calculated over different time periods) shown in Table 8.15 range from 11.8 percent to 17.7 percent. The dispersion is even larger with respect to 12-month drawdown where the CSFB/Tremont Global Macro index measures a drawdown of 22.2 percent from August 1998 to July 1999. This could be due to the fact that CSFB/Tremont, unlike the other three data providers, weights its indexes on an asset-weighted basis as opposed to an equal-weighted basis. In macro the difference in methodology will result in large differences in performance figures, as the difference between the smallest and largest macro hedge fund is huge.

■ A further reason for the large differences in returns is that there is little overlap between the databases. Most hedge fund managers do not report their return figures to all data vendors but to only one or two. Since hedge fund managers do not follow a benchmark (as for example long-only managers) or have a standard investment process (as for example risk arbitrageurs) the correlation between managers is low. This low correlation allows the construction of low-volatility portfolios by combining different managers. However, it also means that there is a large selection bias with the collection of macro returns as shown in Table 8.16.

■ Risk-adjusted returns seem high when measured over the past 12 years. This is due to extraordinary high returns in the early 1990s. The average returns in the period from 1998 to 2001 are a fraction of those in the be-

**Table 8.15** Macro Risk and Return Characteristics

| | # of Monthly Returns | Annual Return | Volatility | Sharpe Ratio (5%) | Worst 1-month Drawdown | Negative Months | Worst 12-month Drawdown | 12-month Drawdown Ended On | Highest 12-month Return |
|---|---|---|---|---|---|---|---|---|---|
| S&P 500 | 144 | 12.85% | 14.54% | 0.54 | −15.64% | 35.4% | −26.63% | Sep-01 | 52.10% |
| MSCI World | 144 | 6.99 | 14.59 | 0.14 | −14.30 | 39.6 | −27.87 | Sep-01 | 33.51 |
| MSCI EAFE | 144 | 2.70 | 17.03 | <0 | −14.97 | 43.1 | −28.27 | Sep-01 | 44.19 |
| MSCI Europe | 144 | 9.15 | 15.19 | 0.27 | −13.42 | 37.5 | −25.49 | Sep-01 | 45.93 |
| JPM Global Goverment Bonds | 144 | 6.59 | 5.94 | 0.27 | −3.40 | 41.0 | −6.18 | Jan-00 | 20.97 |
| JPM U.S. Goverment Bonds | 144 | 7.94 | 4.11 | 0.72 | −2.73 | 27.8 | −3.65 | Oct-94 | 17.34 |
| HFRI Macro index | 144 | 17.68 | 8.84 | 1.43 | −6.40 | 30.6 | −7.10 | Jan-95 | 55.14 |
| Zurich Hedge Macro | 144 | 13.96 | 6.90 | 1.30 | −5.36 | 27.8 | −7.87 | Jan-95 | 49.73 |
| Hennessee Hedge Fund Index—Macro | 108 | 11.84 | 10.09 | 0.68 | −7.52 | 39.8 | −13.75 | Jan-95 | 40.02 |
| CSFB/Tremont Global Macro | 96 | 14.03 | 13.34 | 0.68 | −11.55 | 33.3 | −22.16 | Jul-99 | 50.74 |

*Source:* Hedge Fund Research, Zurich Capital Markets, Hennessee, CSFB/Tremont, Datastream, Bloomberg, UBS Warburg (2000).

**Table 8.16**  Annual Returns of Macro Indexes

| Year | HFRI Macro Index | Zurich Global Macro Median | Hennessee HF Index— Macro | CSFB/ Tremont Global Macro |
|------|------|------|------|------|
| 1990 | 12.6 | 11.3 | NA | NA |
| 1991 | 46.7 | 36.5 | NA | NA |
| 1992 | 27.2 | 22.4 | NA | NA |
| 1993 | 53.3 | 40.9 | 37.8 | NA |
| 1994 | −4.3 | −5.0 | −13.4 | −5.7 |
| 1995 | 29.3 | 11.2 | 18.3 | 30.7 |
| 1996 | 9.3 | 9.9 | 17.3 | 25.6 |
| 1997 | 18.8 | 16.0 | 17.2 | 37.1 |
| 1998 | 6.2 | 8.1 | 4.1 | −3.6 |
| 1999 | 17.6 | 8.5 | 27.1 | 5.8 |
| 2000 | 2.0 | 10.0 | −6.7 | 11.7 |
| 2001 | 7.0 | 5.6 | 14.3 | 18.4 |
| | | | | |
| 1990–1993 | 33.9 | 27.2 | NA | NA |
| 1994–1997 | 12.6 | 7.7 | 8.9 | 20.7 |
| 1998–2001 | 8.0 | 8.0 | 9.0 | 7.7 |

*Source:* Hedge Fund Research, Zurich Capital Markets, Hennessee, CSFB/Tremont.

ginning of the 1990s. In other words, performance persistence for macro as a subgroup of the hedge fund industry is low. Over the past 12 years, returns have been falling (albeit from a very high level).

■ All macro indexes show the worst performance in 1994. This is an indication that there are systematic risks in macro that cannot be diversified away. Despite the fact that macro as a strategy is a heterogeneous market as all managers pursue different strategies, there are certain risks to the strategy that are systematic as opposed to idiosyncratic. However, a recent trend in the subgroup is that the larger macro funds have mutated to multistrategy hedge fund groups. These multistrategy hedge funds pursue different strategies under one roof; that is, systematic strategy risks are to some extent reduced through diversification.

■ Table 8.17 shows how returns have been falling over the past 12 years. Volatilities have been constant as well as always below 10 percent over the four three-year periods. As mentioned earlier, low correlation among managers allows low-volatility exposure to this subcategory. Note that the maximum 12-month drawdown for macro is a positive return in two out of four three-year time periods. The maximum drawdowns are

**Table 8.17**   Performance Persistence

|                                  | 1990–1992 | 1993–1995 | 1996–1998 | 1999–2001 |
|----------------------------------|-----------|-----------|-----------|-----------|
| **MSCI World (Total Return)**    |           |           |           |           |
| Annual return (%)                | −1.80     | 16.40     | 18.25     | −3.05     |
| Volatility (%)                   | 16.70     | 10.29     | 14.47     | 15.73     |
| Average risk-free rate (%)       | 5.61      | 4.37      | 5.07      | 4.64      |
| Sharpe ratio                     | <0        | 1.17      | 0.91      | <0        |
| Worst 1-month drawdown (%)       | −11.12    | −5.81     | −14.30    | −9.21     |
| Worst 12-month drawdown (%)      | −16.52    | −4.66     | 0.51      | −27.87    |
| **HFRI Macro Index**             |           |           |           |           |
| Annual return (%)                | 28.05     | 23.80     | 11.30     | 8.99      |
| Volatility (%)                   | 9.19      | 9.63      | 8.45      | 7.24      |
| Sharpe ratio                     | 2.44      | 2.02      | 0.74      | 0.60      |
| Worst 1-month drawdown (%)       | −3.85     | −6.61     | −3.84     | −3.75     |
| Worst 12-month drawdown (%)      | 12.56     | −7.10     | 4.37      | −2.36     |

*Source:* Hedge Fund Research, Datastream.

smaller than with equities. In other words, despite macro's negative image in the public domain, not losing money is of paramount importance.

Figure 8.21 shows the returns of various hedge fund indexes along with some equity and bond indexes. Figure 8.22 compares monthly total MSCI World returns with the HFRI Macro index.

■ Figure 8.21 reveals that macro funds are difficult to review as a group. The group in itself is strongly heterogeneous. The dispersion among single fund returns is high. In addition, as pointed out earlier, hedge fund data in general is not perfect. Note that the four macro returns in Figure 8.21 were measured over three different time periods. However, the differences remain when only the past eight years to 2001 are measured. Over the past eight years, the annual returns range from 7.9 percent (Zurich Capital Markets) and 14.0 percent (CSFB/Tremont). Despite the imperfections of data, all indexes are above the U.S. as well as the global capital market line in CAPM space.
■ Figure 8.22 shows that there is correlation to equity markets.

Table 8.18 shows some further statistics on macro returns.

■ The distribution of historical returns is hardly skewed and shows only a minimal degree of excess kurtosis. Note that skew and excess kurtosis of

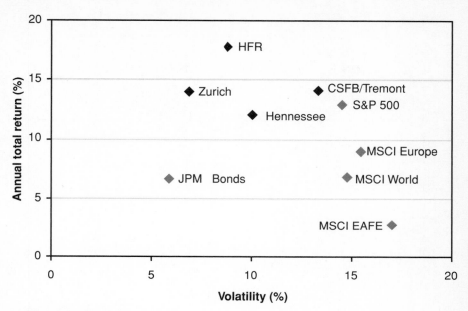

**FIGURE 8.21** Return versus Risk
*Source:* Hedge Fund Research, Zurich Capital Markets, Hennessee, CSFB/Tremont, Datastream, UBS Warburg (2000).

the S&P 500 index was −0.65 and 1.16, respectively, for the same time period. In other words, macro exposure is similar to equities with respect to higher-risk moments.

■ The correlation to equities ranges from 0.2 to 0.4.

Figure 8.23 shows the performance of the HFRI Macro index in different market environments, and Figure 8.24 shows average quarterly returns in down markets versus average quarterly returns in friendly markets.

■ Macro funds were hit hard during the U.S. rate rise in early 1994 and during the Russian credit crisis in 1998. In other words, there are some systematic risk factors despite the heterogeneity among the different managers. Macro funds, overall, were flat during the Asian crisis in 1997. They also preserved financial wealth during the bursting of the technology bubble and after the September 2001 atrocities. (See Figure 8.23.)
■ The Asian crisis was reminiscent of the ERM (European Rate Mechanism) crisis of 1992. Substantial amounts of carry trades were involved in the buildup of both crises. These carry trades allowed Thai corporations and

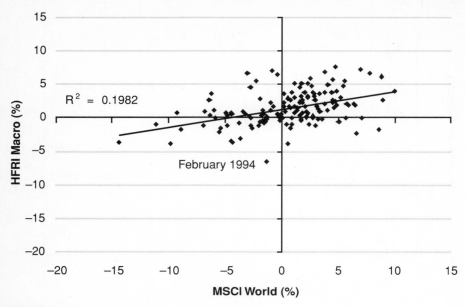

**FIGURE 8.22** MSCI World versus Macro Returns
*Source:* Hedge Fund Research, Datastream, UBS Warburg (2000).

**Table 8.18** Statistical Analysis of Macro Returns

| | Alpha to MSCI World | Beta to MSCI World | Skew | Excess Kurtosis | Correlation MSCI World | Correlation JPM Global Bonds |
|---|---|---|---|---|---|---|
| Zurich Hedge Macro | 1.20 | 0.27 | 0.15 | 0.24 | 0.44 | 0.09 |
| HFRI Macro Index | 0.98 | 0.19 | 0.79 | 2.23 | 0.39 | 0.05 |
| Hennessee Hedge Fund Index—Macro | 0.80 | 0.16 | −0.25 | 0.76 | 0.21 | −0.05 |
| CSFB/Tremont Global Macro | 0.95 | 0.21 | −0.20 | 1.29 | 0.22 | −0.17 |

*Source:* Hedge Fund Research, Zurich Capital Markets, Hennessee, CSFB/Tremont, Datastream, Bloomberg, UBS Warburg (2000).

banks to borrow in foreign currencies, which had a lower interest rate than the domestic currency. As long as the domestic currency did not depreciate, the foreign currency loans represented a cheap source of funding. In the end, the carry trade led to an unsustainable equilibrium. By fixing the exchange rate, the Thai central bank was indirectly paying a risk premium to foreign investors to support domestic funding needs. However, when these foreign "lenders" are themselves highly leveraged institutions

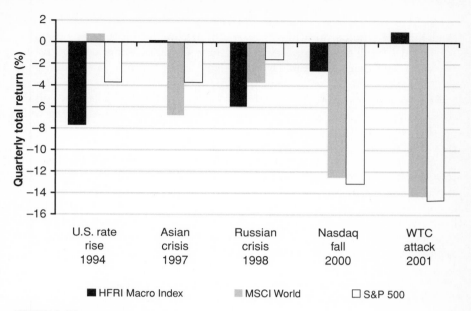

**FIGURE 8.23**   Scenario Analysis
*Source:* Hedge Fund Research, Datastream, UBS Warburg (2000).

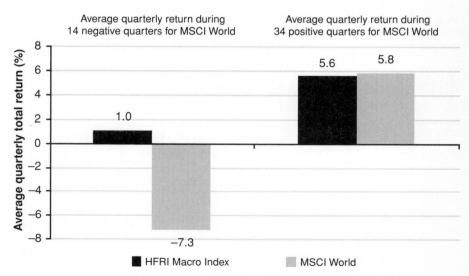

**FIGURE 8.24**   Average Negative versus Average Positive Returns
*Source:* Hedge Fund Research, Datastream, UBS Warburg (2000).

such as proprietary desks from investment banks (and occasionally leveraged domestic corporations), the resultant equilibrium is at best tenuous.
In July 1997, for whatever reason, some foreign lenders decided to unwind their carry trades in Thailand. They sold baht and bought dollars in
the spot market, putting tremendous pressure on the baht.

■ Figure 8.24 shows that the macro index is correlated with equities on the
upside. However, the correlation with negative equity returns seems to be
zero or even negative.

Figure 8.25 shows how returns have been distributed in the past and
compares the historic return distribution with a normal distribution of macro
and a normal distribution of historical MSCI World returns both based on
historic mean return and standard deviation of returns. For Figure 8.26 the
macro returns were sorted in ascending order and compared with the corresponding market returns. This allows one to see in which market environment the extreme positive and negative returns were achieved.

■ Figure 8.25 shows that the normal distribution of the macro index (a diversified portfolio of macro managers) is more narrow (returns less

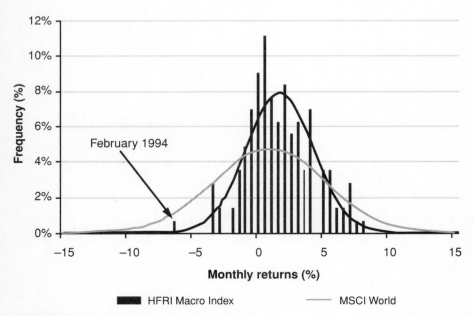

**FIGURE 8.25**  Return Distribution
*Source:* Hedge Fund Research, Datastream, UBS Warburg (2000).

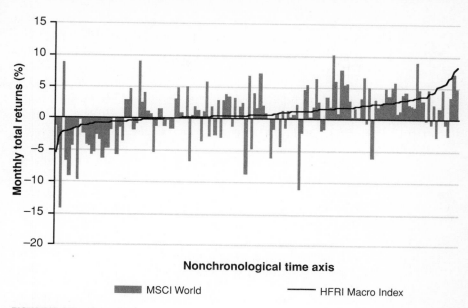

**FIGURE 8.26**   Correlation
*Source:* Hedge Fund Research, Datastream, UBS Warburg (2000).

volatile) than the normal distribution of the MSCI World. In addition, the mean of the macro index is further to the right (average returns are higher) than with the MSCI World index. To some extent this is ironic, as mentioned before, as macro is considered very risky by the public whereas investing long-only in the equity asset class is considered conservative.* In the frequency distribution, there were five outliers lower than two standard deviations from the mean and seven returns higher than

---

*Note that, for example, U.K. pension fund managers view themselves as conservative investors and, at the same time, have 70 to 80 percent of their assets in equities, that is, only one asset class. Some macro managers view U.K. pension funds as speculative because of this extreme portfolio concentration. The average macro manager has a more diversified portfolio than the average U.K. pension fund manager. There is some entertainment value in the observation of the use of the word "conservative." For the U.K. pension fund manager a large allocation in equities (i.e., portfolio concentration) is considered conservative. Most hedge fund managers also view themselves as conservative investors because they avoid portfolio concentration either through portfolio diversification or through using hedging techniques to reduce unwanted risk (most often directional market risk). Chances are that history is about to teach one of the two groups a lesson.

two standard deviations above the mean. The February 1994 return is outside the 99 percent range (3.1 standard deviations from the mean).

■ Figure 8.26 shows that the negative macro returns occurred in negative markets where as the extremely positive returns were primarily achieved during strong equity markets. This suggests that there is a high correlation to equities both in falling as well as in rising markets. However, it is worth pointing out that macro managers did not participate in all equity market downturns. Of the 14 occasions where the MSCI World showed a monthly loss in excess of −5 percent, the HFRI Macro index was in negative territory nine times, and only four of the nine negative monthly returns were larger than 1 percent.

■ Figure 8.27 shows the five worst calendar quarters for macro managers as a subgroup. The figure shows that bad quarterly returns from macro managers may or may not coincide with a falling equity market.

■ Figure 8.28 shows that the 1994 bond crisis was probably the most difficult period for macro managers. The magnitude of losses was larger and the recovery period longer than with a diversified equity portfolio. However, compared with the losses of diversified equity portfolios in 2000–2001 (recovery yet uncertain), the losses of diversified portfolios of macro managers seem negligible.

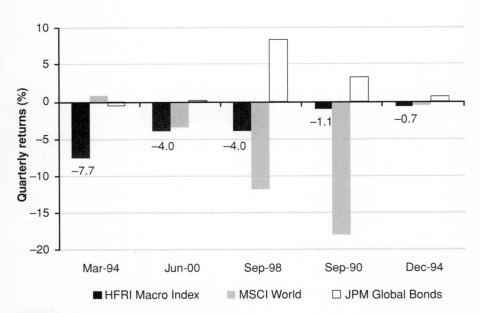

**FIGURE 8.27**    Worst Quarters for Macro
*Source:* Hedge Fund Research, Datastream.

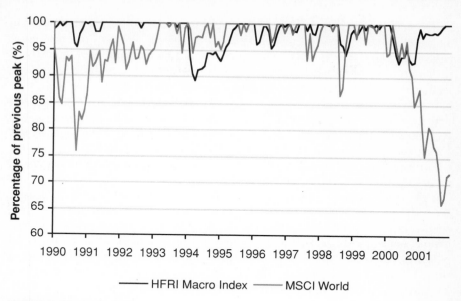

**FIGURE 8.28**   Underwater
*Source:* Hedge Fund Research, Datastream.

■ The period 2000–2001 seems to offer an interesting case study: Macro managers were to a large extent in equities during the last phases of the liquidity-driven bull market. However, as the wind started to change they changed their portfolios to take into account the change in the investment environment. This is unlike relative return equity investors who might have seen the change in wind but were unable to do anything about it because relative returns matter more than do absolute returns. Macro managers left equities and the recovery period was relatively brief. In 2001 macro managers reported positive returns, that is, started to make money even if equities were not going up. During 2001 macro managers even recovered from the negative press in 2000. The reason why this is a case study can be best explained by a quote from Lord Keynes: "When circumstances change, I change my view. What do you do?" The relative return manager stays long—the absolute return manager does not.

## Conclusion and Outlook

Given the heterogeneity in the subgroup it is probably unwise to give a general outlook for the whole category. However, in one aspect macro is a very pure form of absolute return asset management. It is the purest form of active money management and the diametrically opposite of an index fund. A macro manager is essentially an experienced investment professional investing his or her own money according to what he or she believes offers a good risk/reward investment opportunity. Money is raised to allow economies of scale and construct diversified portfolios. Some very successful opportunistic managers do not open for foreign money and continue to trade their own money in relative secrecy. There will always be investment professionals setting such organizations despite the aversion of institutional investors toward such investment houses. Investors in macro funds are neither bureaucrats nor lemmings. Single-manager risk is large. As Louis Moore Bacon put it: "At the end of the day, the overall viability of the . . . [macro] funds continues to rest on my abilities to call the markets and manage risk."[5]

The next opportunistic investment style to be discussed in this book is short selling. For a very brief moment in spring 2000, it looked like short sellers would experience a renaissance. Jeffrey Vinik, who ran Fidelity Investments' flagship Magellan Fund before starting his own firm, returned 25 percent after fees in the March–April 2000 period through judicious use of short sales and stock picking.* Although hedge funds with a pure short bias are rare, understanding the merits and dynamics of short selling is important with long/short equity funds.

## SHORT SELLING

### Strategy

At the most general level, short selling is about negative correlation to equities from the investors' point of view and about finding market inefficiencies on the short side from the managers' point of view. Schneeweis and Spurgin (2000) call short sellers "pure diversifiers." Kathryn Staley, author of *The Art of Short Selling*, calls short selling "a game of wits, with the odds in favor of the analysts who do hard work and think for themselves, who turn jaundiced eyes on what passes for Wall Street wisdom."[6] The short selling discipline has

---

*Jeffrey Vinik's name received notoriety with bad stock market calls a few years ago. As a star manager of the largest mutual fund, Fidelity Magellan, Vinik reckoned that stocks had peaked in 1995. So he invested in bonds—and balefully watched one of the strongest stock market rallies of the decade from the sidelines. The results were not pretty: Returns slumped, and investors withdrew money. To make matters worse, at the end of 1995 he came under SEC scrutiny for saying positive things about stocks he was selling. He was exonerated; but when he left Fidelity in June 1996, many believe he departed with a cloud over his head. The hedge fund he started after he left Fidelity doubled investors' money in 1997. The $800 million he raised when he started reached some $4 billion four years later.

an equity as well as a fixed income component. Short sellers seek to profit from a decline in the value of stocks. In addition, the short seller earns interest on the cash proceeds from the short sale of stock. Based on estimates of Hedge Fund Research, dedicated short sellers were 0.12 percent of the market in 1990 and 0.11 percent in 2001.

Short sellers are directional, information-based traders, that is, traders whose valuation studies show that a security is overpriced relative to their concept of fair value. Staley (1997) makes the point that short selling is not a new strategy but was practiced by the likes of Bernard Baruch, Joseph Kennedy, and other financial titans in the early decades of the twentieth century. However, before 1983 no dedicated short-only fund existed. Short selling was primarily the venue of hedge fund managers and sophisticated individuals.[7]

Asquith and Meulbroek (1996) provide evidence that short sellers, as a group, successfully identify securities that subsequently underperform the market. Dechow et al. (2001) identify the characteristics of the securities targeted by short sellers. The authors provide evidence that short sellers position themselves in stocks with low fundamentals-to-price ratios. The four ratios that were analyzed were: cash flow-to-price, earnings-to-price, book-to-market, and value-to-market. Given potential predictive ability of these ratios,[8] they provide a starting point for potential shorts. The authors further show how short sellers refine their trading strategies: First, short sellers concentrate on shorting stocks where the transaction costs associated with short selling are relatively low. Second, the authors showed that short sellers were able to distinguish between firms where the low fundamentals-to-price ratios were driven by temporarily high stock prices versus temporarily low fundamentals. (See also Table 8.19.)

Given the extensive 1990s equity bull market, short selling strategies have not done particularly well in absolute return space. Their performance is nearly a mirror image of equities in general. Figure 8.29 compares annualized returns of short sellers with the MSCI World index. Note that the mirror image is not symmetrical: When equity markets fall, short sellers are a leveraged bet on the market. However, when markets rise the loss is disproportionally smaller.

Short sellers borrow stock and sell it on the market with the intention of buying it back later at a lower price. By selling a stock short, the short seller creates a restricted cash asset (the proceeds from the sale) and a liability since the short seller must return the borrowed shares at some future date. Technically, a short sale does not require an investment, but it does require collateral. The proceeds from the short sale are held as a restricted credit by the brokerage firm that holds the account and the short seller earns interest on it—the short interest rebate.

One of the rationales of selling short, as discussed in Chapters 2 and 3, is

**Table 8.19**   Key Risk Factors in Short Selling

| Risk | Position | Effect |
|---|---|---|
| Equity | Short bias | Most often short delta, otherwise long/short fund. Usually short in large-capitalization stocks since larger-capitalized stocks can be borrowed to be sold short more efficiently. |
| | | Given the experience of the 1990s, one of the largest risks is momentum where overvalued stocks continue to outperform. A further risk is that the borrowed stock is recalled. |
| Interest rates | Short duration | If interest rates fall, the proceeds from the fixed income portion used as collateral as well as the rebate on the proceeds from the short sale are reduced. |

*Source:* UBS Warburg (2000).

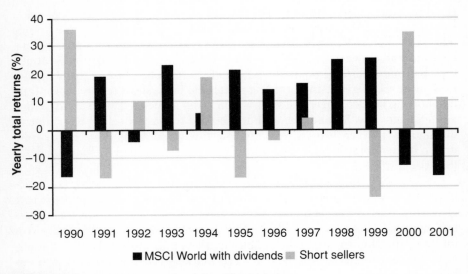

**FIGURE 8.29**   Short Sellers versus MSCI World Index
*Source:* Hedge Fund Research, Datastream, UBS Warburg (2000).

that there are more market inefficiencies with respect to the price mechanism incorporating bad news of companies. The basic idea is that information is positively biased and results in stocks being rather overpriced than undervalued. This is at the heart of the controversy of the investment banking industry and its objectiveness toward the corporate clients they serve. Short sellers' main toolkit, therefore, is fundamental company research and a rigid due diligence process to find an imbalance between positive information which is reflected in the stock price and negative information that is currently not reflected in the stock price but has the potential to destroy value once the information enters the price mechanism.

Security selection is the key driver of returns in the segment. A theme in 1999 that contributed to positive security selection on the short side was the exploitation of aggressive accounting by certain companies' managements.* These practices typically involve the acceleration of revenue recognition or the accounting of extraordinary items like mergers and acquisitions. Staley (1997) lists three broad categories for short-sale candidates:

1. Companies in which management lies to investors and obscures events that will affect earnings.
2. Companies that have tremendously inflated stock prices—prices that suggest a speculative bubble in company valuation.
3. Companies that will be affected in a significant way by changing external events.

The main weakness of professional short sellers, according to Staley (1997), is an inability to judge the timing of collapses. Short sellers are consistently too early when they sell stocks. Stockholders are always slow to sell even when the evidence is irrefutable and the future for profit bleak. The years of irrational price behavior in a deteriorating company provide stock owners with years to sell a problem stock.

Staley (1997) characterizes the typical short seller as follows:

*Short sellers are odd people. Most of them are ambitious, driven, antisocial, and single-minded. As individuals, they are not very likely to own a Rolex watch . . . or any other symbolic trapping of success; they are likely to have a wry, slightly twisted sense of humor. As a group, short sellers like to disagree, and they like to win against big odds. . . . As in the general population, some of them are cretins and some are not, but they are all smarter (most of them, in fact, are intellectual snobs) and more independent than most people. Contrary to popular wisdom, they do not form a cabal and bash stocks senseless. They normally are secretive and slightly paranoid. And they are frequently irreverent in their regard for business leaders and icons of Wall Street.*[9]

---

*Warren Buffett on accounting: "Managers thinking about accounting issues should never forget one of Abraham Lincoln's favorite riddles: *How many legs does a dog have if you call his tail a leg?* Answer: *Four, because calling a tail a leg does not make it a leg.*"

## Example

Tyco International, in its recording of large reserves on acquisitions in 1999, is an example of aggressive accounting practice. By taking large reserves, Tyco avoided future depreciation/amortization charges against profits and thereby showed increasing growth in earnings. While the company theoretically complied with GAAP, it was this methodology of aggressive accounting that had provided a source of short ideas.

Securities and Exchange Commission Chairman Arthur Levitt broached the role of Wall Street analysts in regard to the issue of aggressive accounting. In a speech in October 1999, he noted a "web of dysfunctional relationships" between Wall Street and corporate America that encourages analysts to rely too heavily on company guidance for earnings estimates and pushes companies to tailor results for the Street's consensus estimates. He continued, "Analysts all too often are falling off the tightrope on the side of protecting the business relationship at the cost of fair analysis." Many hedge funds managers argue that while Wall Street research is of limited value on the long side, it is of even less value on the short side due in large part to the conflicts mentioned by Mr. Levitt. This leaves hedge fund managers in the short discipline to uncover profitable short opportunities through their own research and security selection.

## Performance

■ As shown in Figure 8.30, given the long bull market, hedge funds dedicated to a short bias have not done extremely well in the past—on an absolute return level, that is. Most investment professionals do not consider short selling as a stand-alone investment strategy but as a investment tool for reducing portfolio risk. As a stand-alone strategy it has produced poor results. However, returns for 2000, 2001, and 2002 (July inclusive) were 34.6 percent, 9.0 percent, and 32.0 percent, respectively.

■ As shown in Table 8.20, all short selling indexes reported negative or very low annual returns over the 12-year period ending 2001. Volatility was substantially higher than with other hedge fund strategies. Only two out of 31 strategies from HFRI had a higher volatility than short sellers (HFRI Emerging Markets: Eur/CIS index and HFRI Sector: Health Care/Biotechnology index). Volatility of short sellers was even higher than in long-only equities. The worst one-month return varies between –9 percent and –21 percent, respectively. The worst one-year cumulative return varies between –28 percent and –38 percent, respectively.

■ Between 50 percent and 60 percent of the returns were below zero due to the extended length of the 1990s bull market. This makes it one of the few hedge fund strategies that has more negative months as a percentage of total than traditional long-only equity.

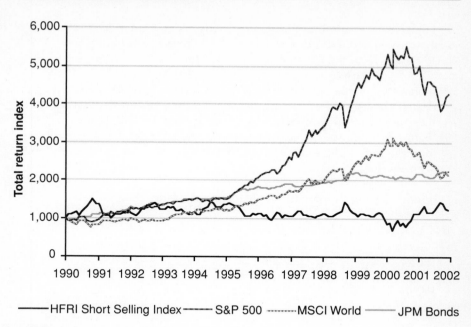

**FIGURE 8.30** Long-Term Performance of Short Sellers
*Source:* Hedge Fund Research, Datastream, UBS Warburg (2000).

**Table 8.20** Short Selling Risk and Return Characteristics

| | # of Monthly Returns | Annual Return | Volatility | Sharpe Ratio (5%) | Worst 1-month Drawdown | Negative Months | Worst 12-month Drawdown | 12-month Drawdown Ended on | Highest 12-month Return |
|---|---|---|---|---|---|---|---|---|---|
| S&P 500 | 144 | 12.85% | 14.54% | 0.54 | −15.64% | 35.4% | −26.63% | Sep-01 | 52.10% |
| MSCI World | 144 | 6.99 | 14.59 | 0.14 | −14.30 | 39.6 | −27.87 | Sep-01 | 33.51 |
| MSCI EAFE | 144 | 2.70 | 17.03 | <0 | −14.97 | 43.1 | −28.27 | Sep-01 | 44.19 |
| MSCI Europe | 144 | 9.15 | 15.19 | 0.27 | −13.42 | 37.5 | −25.49 | Sep-01 | 45.93 |
| JPM Global Government Bonds | 144 | 6.59 | 5.94 | 0.27 | −3.40 | 41.0 | −6.18 | Jan-00 | 20.97 |
| JPM U.S. Government Bonds | 144 | 7.94 | 4.11 | 0.72 | −2.73 | 27.8 | −3.65 | Oct-94 | 17.34 |
| HFRI Short Selling Index | 144 | 1.99 | 23.22 | <0 | −21.21 | 50.0 | −38.01 | Jan-95 | 55.14 |
| Zurich Hedge Short-Sellers | 144 | 1.43 | 18.16 | <0 | −12.12 | 47.9 | −27.79 | Oct-91 | 43.17 |
| Hennessee Hedge Fund Index—Short Only | 108 | −7.59 | 19.97 | <0 | −13.83 | 60.2 | −36.42 | Jan-95 | 40.02 |
| CSFB/Tremont Dedicated Short Bias | 96 | −1.18 | 18.36 | <0 | −8.69 | 53.1 | −28.03 | Aug-99 | 44.10 |

*Source:* Hedge Fund Research, Zurich Capital Markets, Hennessee, CSFB/Tremont, Datastream, Bloomberg, UBS Warburg (2000).

Figure 8.31 shows the returns of various hedge fund indexes along with some equity and bond indexes. Figure 8.32 compares monthly total MSCI World returns with the HFRI Short Selling index.

■ Figure 8.31 implies that there is little consistency between short selling indexes. The inconsistency is primarily a function of four risk/return ratios measured over three different time periods. (See Table 8.20.)
■ Figure 8.32 shows the negative correlation of short selling to equities. Short selling is the only strategy that has constant negative correlation with equities.

Table 8.21 shows some further statistics of short selling.

■ The exposure to the market as a whole is around –1.
■ Correlation to MSCI World is around –0.7 and statistically significant at the 99 percent level.

Figure 8.33 shows the performance of the HFRI Short Selling index in different market environments, and Figure 8.34 the average quarterly returns

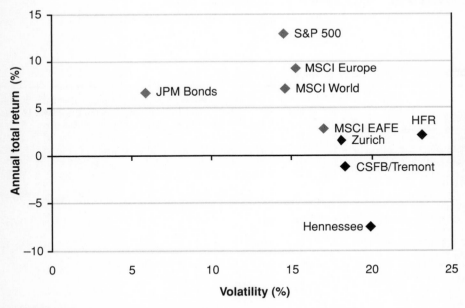

**FIGURE 8.31**   Return versus Risk
*Source:* Hedge Fund Research, Zurich Capital Markets, CSFB/Tremont, Hennessee, Datastream, UBS Warburg (2000).

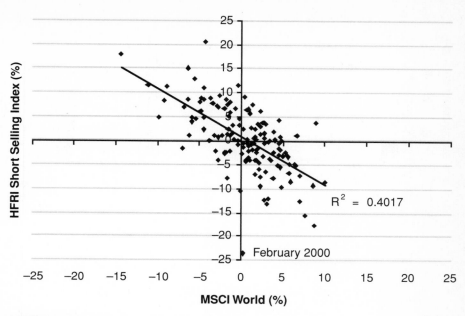

**FIGURE 8.32** MSCI World versus Short Selling Returns
*Source:* Hedge Fund Research, Datastream, UBS Warburg (2000).

**Table 8.21** Statistical Analysis of Short Selling Returns

| | Alpha to MSCI World | Beta to MSCI World | Skew | Excess Kurtosis | Correlation MSCI World | Correlation JPM Global Bonds |
|---|---|---|---|---|---|---|
| HFRI Short Selling Index | 0.73 | −1.00 | −0.19 | 1.19 | −0.64 | −0.03 |
| Zurich Hedge Short-Sellers | 0.56 | −0.77 | 0.21 | 1.31 | −0.65 | 0.00 |
| Hennessee Hedge Fund Index—Short Only | −0.11 | −0.68 | 0.80 | 4.71 | −0.48 | −0.10 |
| CSFB/Tremont Dedicated Short Bias | 0.57 | −0.97 | 0.71 | 1.32 | −0.75 | 0.03 |

*Source:* Hedge Fund Research, Zurich Capital Markets, Hennessee, CSFB/Tremont, Datastream, Bloomberg, UBS Warburg (2000).

in down markets versus average quarterly returns in friendly markets. Note that Figure 8.34 is slightly different than previous similar-looking figures in this book. For Figure 8.34 we have compared the *reverse* of the MSCI returns with the average returns in the dedicated short selling category. With this we compare like for like, because short sellers should be compared with a short position in equities and not with a buy-and-hold long position.*

---

*The cynic will argue that we are trying to make short sellers look good.

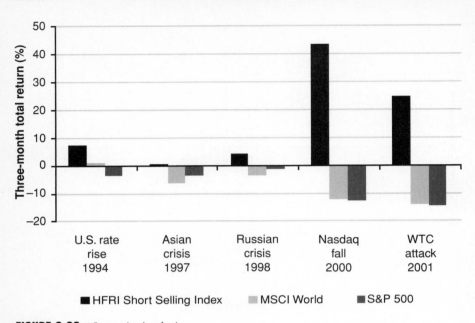

**FIGURE 8.33**   Scenario Analysis
*Source:* Hedge Fund Research, Datastream, UBS Warburg (2000).

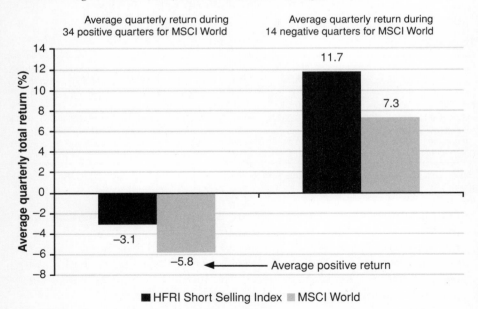

**FIGURE 8.34**   MSCI World versus Short Selling Returns
*Source:* Hedge Fund Research, Datastream, UBS Warburg (2000).

■ Figure 8.33 shows what dedicated short sellers should do to a balanced portfolio: provide negatively correlated and leveraged exposure to equities when markets fall. This is the reason for using dedicated short sellers in a portfolio context. Most other strategies have either a long bias or are short some sort of out-of-the-money disaster put option. By having some exposure to short sellers this risk can be partially balanced.

■ Short sellers were the only category reporting positive returns in autumn 1998. Short sellers outperformed the other strategies analyzed in this book in the first quarter of 1994 but not during the Asian crisis in 1997. Long/short equity performed best during the Asian crisis.

■ Figure 8.34 compares short sellers with a short position in the MSCI World index. When markets fall by $x$ percent, short sellers earn $1.60x$ on average. However, if markets rise by $x$ percent, short sellers lose around $0.53x$ on average. This asymmetry suggests that short sellers could perform well in flat or negative markets. The total return of the HFRI Short Selling index increased by 34.6 percent from the beginning of March 2000 to the end of July 2002. The total returns for the S&P 500 and the MSCI World indexes in the same time period were −31.2 percent and −35.6 percent respectively.

■ We described fixed income arbitrage and distressed securities being short a disaster put option because of its negative correlation with credit spreads and its erratic and negative returns when markets tumble. Short selling has some elements of a long disaster put option position. Returns are negatively correlated with equity markets. This negative correlation feature seems to hold during market crises; if history is any indication of the future, short sellers do well when nearly everyone else in the asset management industry does not.

Figure 8.35 shows how returns have been distributed in the past and compares the historic return distribution with a normal distribution of short sellers and a normal distribution of historical MSCI World returns, both based on historic mean return and standard deviation of returns. For Figure 8.36 the short sellers' returns have been sorted and compared to the corresponding market returns. This allows to seeing in which market environment the extreme positive and negative returns were achieved.

■ The frequency distribution of historical returns looks, statistically speaking, fairly normal with a few outliers. There were five outliers outside the 95 percent range, three on the downside and two on the upside. There were two outliers outside the three standard deviation range, one on each side of the mean. The most extreme positive return was achieved in April 2000 when technology, media, and telecommunications (TMT) went into reverse. The returns in calendar years 2000 and 2001 were 34.6 percent

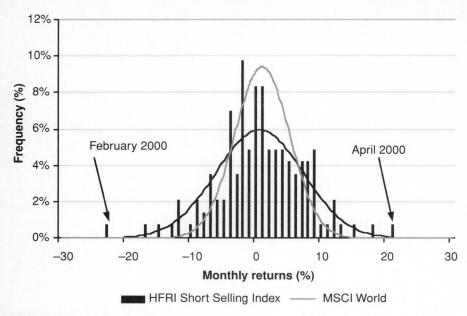

**FIGURE 8.35** Return Distribution
*Source:* Hedge Fund Research, Datastream, UBS Warburg (2000).

and 11.0 percent, respectively. Note that short selling is, as the two normal distributions in Figure 8.35 illustrate, one of the few hedge funds strategies that are more volatile than long-only equity portfolios.

▧ Figure 8.36 shows that most negative returns occur in positive markets (left-hand side of Figure 8.36) and most positive returns in falling markets. Note that the magnitude of the short sellers' returns is larger than those of the market.

Figure 8.37 shows the HFRI Short Selling index in all calendar quarters where the S&P 500 total return was in negative territory. The quarterly returns of the MSCI World have been added to give a feel for how high correlation of global equities really is when the U.S. stock market falls.

▧ Figure 8.37 shows the reverse relationship between market returns and returns from short selling. Note that the extreme returns from short selling are much more erratic than the corresponding market returns. This is due to profits from two different sources, the (leveraged) short equity position and the short interest rebate.

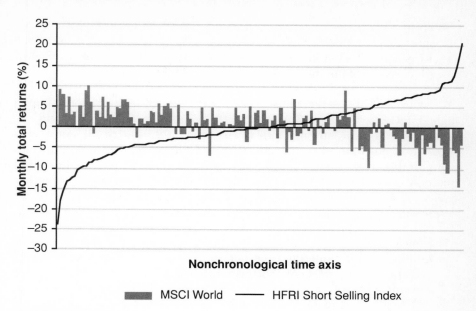

**Nonchronological time axis**

MSCI World ——— HFRI Short Selling Index

**FIGURE 8.36** Correlation
*Source:* Hedge Fund Research, Datastream, UBS Warburg (2000).

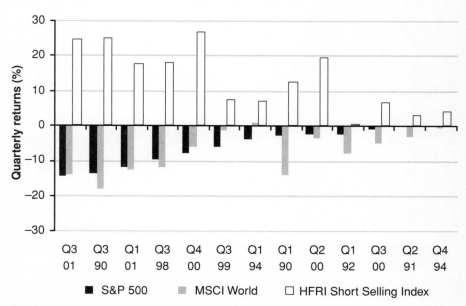

■ S&P 500   ■ MSCI World   □ HFRI Short Selling Index

**FIGURE 8.37** Short Sellers in Down Quarters
*Source:* Hedge Fund Research, Datastream, UBS Warburg (2000).

■ From 13 negative quarters in the S&P 500 (from Q1 90 until Q4 01), short sellers reported positive returns in all quarters. The average of the 13 negative S&P 500 returns was –6.0 percent, whereas the average of the corresponding short selling returns was +13.2 percent.

Figure 8.38 shows three indexes as a percentage of their previous all-time high: HFRI Short Selling index and MSCI World in U.S. dollars and the Nikkei 225 in local currency terms. The Nikkei 225 line in the graph also shows that portfolio diversification is a laudable concept whereas portfolio concentration (for example in domestic equities) is not. Failure to answer the question raised by some people quoted in this book "Why not 100 percent equities?" might not be the pinnacle of investment wisdom. A prudent investor will always allow for some margin of error.

■ Figure 8.38 shows that short selling has not recovered its previous peak from 1990 and underlines the notion that short selling is not suitable as a stand-alone strategy. However, this might not be true for Japanese investors. (As of July 2002 the three indices in Figure 8.38 were at 100%, 60.2% and 25.4% respectively.)
■ Short selling is more a portfolio construction tool than it is an investment strategy in its own right. One could argue that equity long-only is also

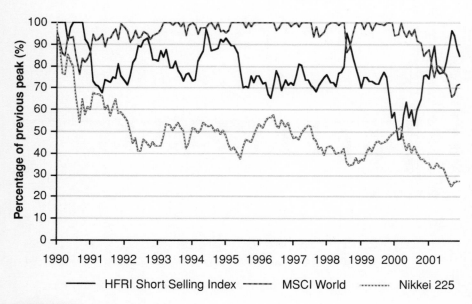

**FIGURE 8.38**    Underwater
*Source:* Hedge Fund Research, Datastream.

not an investment strategy in its own right. High equity volatility and increasing single stock correlation in falling markets indicate that beta to a particular market is also an unfinished part of a whole portfolio. One could argue that a manager managing different sources of risk (as for example a fund of hedge funds manager) is a complete asset management discipline whereas a manager managing only one source of risk (equity long-only or short-only) is only providing a building block to the investor.

■ As shown in Table 8.22, performance persistence is strongly negatively correlated with equity markets. In the two three-year periods where the annual return for equities was negative, short selling had a positive return that was higher than the reverse of the equity market return. However, the risk-adjusted returns when the strategy is viewed in isolation are around zero or negative.

■ There is some persistence with respect to the worst 12-month drawdowns: These drawdowns are always substantial. Table 8.22 shows that the worst losses from short selling occur—as one would expect—in rising equity markets.

■ Figure 8.39 shows that the worst calendar quarterly return for short sellers was in the fourth quarter of 1999, when there was a huge year-end (tech) rally. The second worst return was in the Desert Storm–induced bounce in global equity markets in the first quarter of 1991.

**Table 8.22**  Performance Persistence

|  | 1990–1992 | 1993–1995 | 1996–1998 | 1999–2001 |
|---|---|---|---|---|
| **MSCI World (Total Return)** | | | | |
| Annual return (%) | −1.80 | 16.40 | 18.25 | −3.05 |
| Volatility (%) | 16.70 | 10.29 | 14.47 | 15.73 |
| Average risk-free rate (%) | 5.61 | 4.37 | 5.07 | 4.64 |
| Sharpe ratio | <0 | 1.17 | 0.91 | <0 |
| Worst 1-month drawdown (%) | −11.12 | −5.81 | −14.30 | −9.21 |
| Worst 12-month drawdown (%) | −16.52 | −4.66 | 0.51 | −27.87 |
| | | | | |
| **HFRI Short Selling Index** | | | | |
| Annual return (%) | 7.57 | −3.15 | -0.28 | 4.15 |
| Volatility (%) | 21.04 | 17.48 | 19.66 | 31.95 |
| Sharpe ratio | 0.09 | <0 | <0 | <0 |
| Worst 1-month drawdown (%) | −17.72 | −10.49 | −9.40 | −23.84 |
| Worst 12-month drawdown (%) | −25.36 | −24.75 | −24.34 | −38.01 |

*Source:* Hedge Fund Research, Datastream.

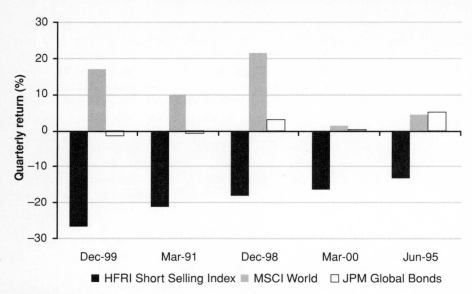

**FIGURE 8.39** Worst Quarters for Short Sellers
*Source:* Hedge Fund Research, Datastream.

## Conclusion and Outlook

The main advantage of short sellers is their negative correlation with equities. If the equity markets go down one can expect hedge funds with a short bias to make money. In a portfolio context, exposure to short sellers, therefore, can be seen as a partial hedge of equity market long-only risk.

Short sellers are only a very small part of the hedge funds industry. It is unlikely that this is to change significantly over time. However, the analyzable history of hedge funds has never witnessed an extensive bear market. It is possible that many long/short equity funds employ a short bias during a bear market. The experience from the 2000–2001 bear market was that a majority of long/short managers deleveraged and moved into cash, where a minority moved from long bias to short bias. Hennessee estimated the average hedge fund net market exposure in 2001 at 49 percent and attributes some of the superior performance versus long-only funds to the fact that hedge funds have the flexibility to move into cash. The average long exposure decreased by 8 percent to 83 percent according to Hennessee Group.[10] Whether this loss avoidance is market timing is probably open to debate. Hedge funds managers define risk as total risk and balance investment opportunities with total risk. If this balance moves against their favor, as it did during 2000 and 2001, they take risk off the table, that is, deleverage and move into cash. Balancing leverage with the opportunity set is not the same as market timing. This balancing act is not a key consideration for benchmarked long-only managers where risk is defined as active risk.

## EMERGING MARKETS

### Strategy

Emerging market hedge funds focus on equity or fixed income investing in emerging markets as opposed to developed markets. This style is usually more volatile not only because emerging markets are more volatile than developed markets, but because most emerging markets allow for only limited short selling and do not offer a viable futures contract to control risk. The lack of opportunities to control risk suggests that hedge funds in emerging markets have a strong long bias. Emerging market hedge funds are not regarded as a typical hedge fund strategy. Based on estimates from Hedge Fund Research, emerging market hedge funds held 0.36 percent of assets under management in 1990 and 3.25 percent in 2001. (See Table 8.23.)

A risk to the pessimist is an opportunity to the optimist. Investing in emerging markets therefore is full of risks or opportunities, depending on one's viewpoint. The risks include the difficulty of getting information, poor accounting, lack of proper legal systems, unsophisticated local investors, political and economic turmoil, and companies with less experienced managers. The opportunities are due to yet-to-be-exploited inefficiencies or undetected, undervalued, and underresearched securities.

**Table 8.23**  Key Risk Factors in Emerging Markets

| Risk | Position | Effect |
|---|---|---|
| Equity | Long bias | Usually long exposure to market risk. Stock-specific risk usually diversified. Limited opportunity to sell short or use derivatives. |
| | | One of the main differences between emerging markets and developed markets from a risk perspective is that correlation among stocks in an emerging market is much higher than in developed markets whereas the correlation among emerging markets themselves is lower than among developed markets. The country factor is the main variable. |
| Credit | Long default risk | Large exposure to the countries' credit ratings. |
| Currency | Neutral | Macro funds are famous for directional currency bets. Emerging market funds buy and sell undervalued financial instruments and hedge, when possible, residual risk such as currency. The focus is on exploiting inefficiencies as opposed to taking currency bets. |
| Liquidity | Long liquidity | Emerging market hedge funds are long inefficient markets and illiquid securities. They provide and enhance liquidity. |

*Source:* UBS Warburg (2000).

The 1994 Mexican peso crisis, when the Mexican peso devalued by more than 40 percent in December 1994, is an interesting example of the difference between a traditional emerging market fund and an alternative emerging market fund. (See Table 8.24.)

Emerging market hedge funds outperformed emerging market mutual funds. There were 18 hedge funds managing $1.8 billion specialized in Latin America from the HFRI database.[11] The average returns were –3.6 percent and –6.3 percent respectively. This compares with –15.0 percent and –11.0 percent respectively for the MSCI Latin America index. In comparison, Lipper Inc. (the data vendor, not the CB arb fund) reported that there were 19 U.S. equity mutual funds specializing in Latin America, with assets of $4.3 billion. These funds returned on average –17.4 percent in December 1994 and –14.0 percent in January 1995. This was more or less in line with the benchmark index.

One explanation for the specialty hedge funds outperforming the benchmark indexes and mutual funds was that they had earlier hedged their Latin American positions. Another explanation is that the specialty hedge funds were primarily betting on Brady bonds (which are denominated in U.S. dollars and therefore have no currency risk), as their returns were more in line with those of Brady bonds than Latin American equities. The point of this (anecdotal) comparison is that hedge funds hedge the risks they do not want to be exposed to. The comparison highlights two characteristics of investing in hedge funds:

1. By investing in a specialty hedge fund, one is not necessarily buying the beta of the local asset class, in this case emerging markets. The hedge fund manager might seek investment opportunities elsewhere (Brady bonds) and hedge unwanted risks (currency swings). This means that returns can be uncorrelated with traditional funds.
2. It also means that transparency is lower. If the plan sponsor is not in constant dialogue with the hedge fund manager, transparency is low. Even if

**Table 8.24**   Hedge Fund versus Mutual Fund Returns during Peso Crisis

|  | MSCI Latin American Index | Mutual Funds Specialized in Latin America | HFRI Emerging Markets Latin America Index |
|---|---|---|---|
| December 1994 | –15.0% | –17.4% | –3.6% |
| January 1995 | –11.0 | –14.0 | –6.3 |

*Source:* Returns from Fung and Hsieh (2000a).

there is a dialogue, the hedge fund manager might not want to reveal positions, especially not the short positions.

In his introduction on the risk management of hedge funds, Lo (2001), for example, argues when characterizing the typical hedge fund manager's perspective (among other things) that "risk management is not central to the success of a hedge fund." By contrast, he points out when characterizing relative return managers: "Risk management and risk transparency are essential." Further on, Lo (2001) argues with respect to hedge fund managers and risk management:

> *Perhaps because it is taken for granted that hedge funds are riskier, few hedge fund investors and even fewer hedge fund managers seem to devote much attention to active risk management. Hedge fund investors and managers often dismiss risk management as secondary, with "alpha" or performance the main objective.*
>
> *However, if there is one lasting insight that modern finance has given us, it is the inexorable trade-off between risk and expected return, hence one cannot be considered without reference to the other. Moreover, it is often overlooked that proper risk management can, by itself, be a source of alpha. This is summarized neatly in the old Street wisdom that "one of the best ways to make money is not to lose it."*

Most practitioners in the hedge fund industry will disagree with this view and point out that it is actually the other way around. Risk management is central to the success of absolute return managers. The source of confusion is not distinguishing between active risk and total risk. Some hedge funds practitioners would even go further and argue that the pursuit of absolute returns is nothing else but pure risk management. The reasoning of such an argument is that all the risks have to be balanced with the investment opportunity. The earlier example of the Mexican peso devaluation illustrates this investment philosophy. Disciples of such an "extreme" view would probably also consider the definition of risk in relative terms (active risk) as a perversion of the term "risk." Risk, to them, by definition is measured in absolute returns (total risk). Only the absolute return manager will consider hedging currency risk when investing in Mexico. A relative return manager will not consider hedging currency risk because he has no incentive or mandate to do so. Hedging currency risk reduces total risk but increases active risk. If Mexican beta is the benchmark of the relative return manager, Mexican beta is what the plan sponsor will get. This is the proposition of a passive manager. In other words, hedge fund investors pay the hedge fund manager to exploit opportunities in Mexico by actively balancing the opportunities with the risks involved. The mutual fund investor, in contrast, pays the mutual fund manager to buy beta in Mexico, irrespective of equity or currency valuation or whether Mexico is currently under attack by Martians.

## Performance

■ As seen in Figure 8.40, HFRI Emerging Markets has outperformed MSCI Emerging Markets Free (EMF) by a wide margin over the past 12 years.
■ Investing in emerging markets via hedge funds is not less volatile than investing in emerging markets through traditional investment vehicles. The HFRI Emerging Markets (Total) Index lost 33 percent in 1998 and rebounded 56 percent in 1999. Total returns for 2000 and 2001 were –10.7 percent and +10.8 percent, respectively, compared with the MSCI EMF index of –30.6 percent and –2.4 percent, respectively.
■ Over a 12-year period, hedge funds in emerging markets have performed around 13 to 14 percent annually, compared with 5.6 percent for the MSCI Emerging Markets Free index. (See Table 8.25.) Over shorter periods, emerging markets returns have been lower due to market turbulence essentially everywhere (Asia, South America, Russia). Note that the MSCI EMF moved a lot in the second half of the 1990s but ended the half-decade more or less unchanged.

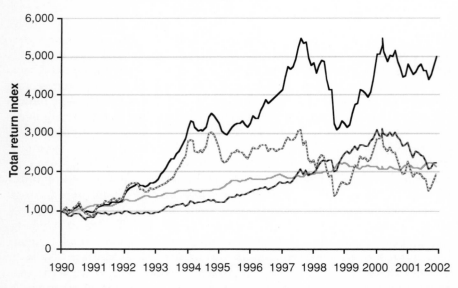

**FIGURE 8.40**   Long-Term Performance of Emerging Markets
*Source:* Hedge Fund Research, Datastream, UBS Warburg (2000).

**Table 8.25** Emerging Markets Risk and Return Characteristics

| | # of Monthly Returns | Annual Return | Volatility | Sharpe Ratio (5%) | Worst 1-month Drawdown | Negative Months | Worst 12-month Drawdown | 12-month Drawdown Ended on | Highest 12-month Return |
|---|---|---|---|---|---|---|---|---|---|
| S&P 500 | 144 | 12.85% | 14.54% | 0.54 | −15.64% | 35.4% | −26.63% | Sep-01 | 52.10% |
| MSCI World | 144 | 6.99 | 14.59 | 0.14 | −14.30 | 39.6 | −27.87 | Sep-01 | 33.51 |
| MSCI EAFE | 144 | 2.70 | 17.03 | <0 | −14.97 | 43.1 | −28.27 | Sep-01 | 44.19 |
| MSCI Europe | 144 | 9.15 | 15.19 | 0.27 | −13.42 | 37.5 | −25.49 | Sep-01 | 45.93 |
| MSCI EMF | 144 | 5.64 | 24.42 | 0.03 | −34.13 | 36.3 | −49.56 | Aug-98 | 77.16 |
| JPM Global Government Bonds | 144 | 6.59 | 5.94 | 0.27 | −3.40 | 41.0 | −6.18 | Jan-00 | 20.97 |
| JPM U.S. Government Bonds | 144 | 7.94 | 4.11 | 0.72 | −2.73 | 27.8 | −3.65 | Oct-94 | 17.34 |
| HFRI Emerging Markets (Total) index | 144 | 14.34 | 16.31 | 0.57 | −21.02 | 34.7 | −42.52 | Sep-98 | 82.04 |
| Zurich Hedge Global Emerging Markets | 144 | 13.05 | 16.96 | 0.47 | −26.65 | 31.3 | −45.13 | Sep-98 | 69.65 |
| Hennessee Hedge Fund Index—Emerging Markets | 108 | 8.99 | 14.73 | 0.27 | −20.10 | 39.8 | −39.89 | Sep-98 | 64.59 |
| CSFB/Tremont Emerging Markets | 96 | 4.64 | 19.82 | −0.02 | −23.03 | 44.8 | −44.25 | Sep-98 | 56.98 |

*Source:* Hedge Fund Research, Zurich Capital Markets, Hennessee, CSFB/Tremont, Datastream, UBS Warburg (2000).

■ Against an absolute yardstick, volatilities in emerging markets hedge funds are high. However, volatility was lower when compared with the MSCI EMF index. Volatility of emerging markets hedge fund returns was around 15 to 20 percent, compared with 24 percent in the case of the MSCI EMF. Hence, hedge funds in this segment as a group have produced superior risk-adjusted returns. The lower volatility from the four emerging markets hedge fund indexes is derived from the fact that the different hedge funds can run different strategies. Since these strategies are weakly correlated with each other, volatility of the hedge fund index or a portfolio containing different emerging markets hedge funds is low. Volatility is most likely lower than comparing a portfolio of traditional emerging markets funds, because traditional equity funds are simply long the asset class.

■ The worst monthly and worst annual drawdowns were slightly less severe in the case of the hedge funds than with the MSCI EMF index. This implies that the hedge fund industry invested in this segment has at least some ability to cut losses short or hedge. However, hedging in emerging markets is difficult or, in some cases, impossible because of market restrictions on selling short either directly or synthetically. Emerging markets, therefore, use lower leverage than hedge funds in developed markets. The lack of hedging possibilities and low use of leverage make emerging markets hedge funds look similar to traditional long-only funds. However, hedge funds have greater flexibility than traditional funds. They are not necessarily long the asset class; neither do they care about market benchmarks.

Figure 8.41 shows the returns of various hedge fund indexes with some equity and bond indexes. Figure 8.42 compares monthly total MSCI EMF returns with the HFRI Emerging Markets index.

■ Figure 8.41 shows that the two indexes with 12-year record are fairly consistent. The volatilities from political events, as occasionally unfold in emerging markets, filters through to the single hedge fund level.
■ Figure 8.42 shows that correlation between hedge fund returns and MSCI EMF index returns is high. The outliers are close to the slope.
■ As shown in Table 8.26, exposure to the region is the main explanatory factor of the emerging markets hedge fund returns. The beta and correlation are high at around 0.8.
■ Higher moment return distribution characteristics are similar to those of the MSCI EMF except excess kurtosis for the Zurich Hedge Global Emerging Markets index.

Figure 8.43 shows the performance of the HFRI Emerging Markets index in different market environments and Figure 8.44 compares average quarterly returns in down markets versus average quarterly returns in friendly markets.

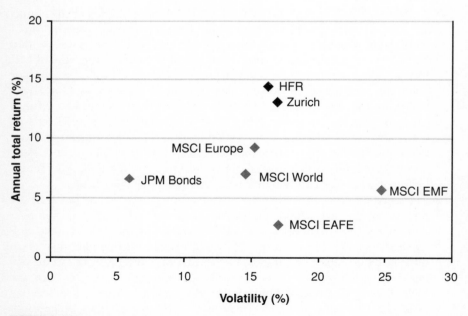

**FIGURE 8.41**   Return versus Risk
*Source:* Hedge Fund Research, Zurich Capital Markets, Datastream, UBS Warburg (2000).

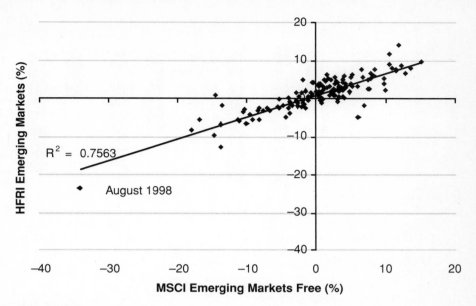

**FIGURE 8.42** MSCI EMF versus Emerging Markets Returns
*Source:* Hedge Fund Research, Datastream, UBS Warburg (2000).

**Table 8.26** Statistical Analysis of Emerging Markets Returns

| | Alpha to MSCI EMF | Beta to MSCI EMF | Skew | Excess Kurtosis | Correlation MSCI EMF | Correlation JPM Global Bonds |
|---|---|---|---|---|---|---|
| MSCI EMF (Total Return) | 0.00 | 1.00 | −1.08 | 3.23 | 1.00 | −0.04 |
| HFRI Emerging Markets (Total) Index | 0.86 | 0.57 | −1.12 | 4.91 | 0.87 | −0.06 |
| Zurich Hedge Global Emerging Markets | 0.79 | 0.52 | −1.84 | 12.97 | 0.75 | −0.05 |
| Hennessee Hedge Funds Index—Emerging Markets | 0.65 | 0.40 | −1.47 | 7.44 | 0.80 | −0.22 |
| CSFB/Tremont Emerging Markets | 0.61 | 0.62 | −0.87 | 4.11 | 0.68 | −0.24 |

*Source:* Hedge Fund Research, Zurich Capital Markets, Hennessee, CSFB/Tremont, Datastream, UBS Warburg (2000).

■ Hedge funds in emerging markets outperformed the MSCI EMF during most crises, but underperformed the index during the Russian credit crisis (see Figure 8.43). If history is any indication, outperformance in falling markets is the rule and underperformance in falling markets is the exception to the rule.

■ On average, however, hedge funds outperformed MSCI EMF by 5.7 percent during down quarters and underperformed the index by only 2.3 percent during up quarters (see Figure 8.44). This pattern lets us assume that hedge

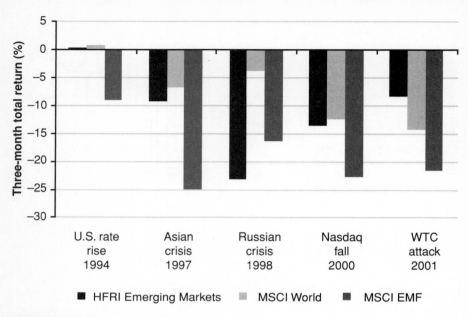

**FIGURE 8.43**   Scenario Analysis
*Source:* Hedge Fund Research, Datastream, UBS Warburg (2000).

    funds in this segment exploit other opportunities than long market beta or hedge market beta partially so they are not exposed to the full fall.

■ Figure 8.44 is a good example why some investors are using hedge funds as a substitute to get exposure to a particular market. The main reason is outperformance in falling markets. The outperformance comes at a cost in the form of some opportunity costs in rising markets (underperformance in up quarters), less liquidity (hedge funds are not as marketable as securities), and less transparency (the manager could or could not be in equities, or could or could not be hedging currency risk). The increasing allocations by institutional investors indicate that the advantage of superior returns in falling markets (an asymmetric return profile) outbalances the risks and disadvantages.

    Figure 8.45 shows how returns have been distributed in the past and compares the historic return distribution with a normal distribution of hedge funds in the emerging market sector and a normal distribution of historical MSCI EMF returns, both based on historic mean return and standard deviation of returns. For Figure 8.46 the hedge funds returns have been sorted and compared to the corresponding market returns. This allows one to see in which market environment the extreme positive and negative returns were achieved.

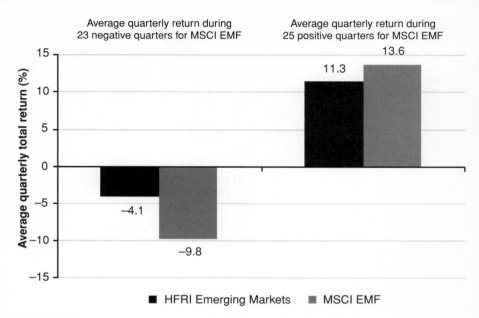

**FIGURE 8.44** Average Negative versus Average Positive Returns
*Source:* Hedge Fund Research, Datastream, UBS Warburg (2000).

■ The frequency distribution has some resemblance with a normal distribution. There were six returns outside the 95 percent range, two of them were positive. August 1998 was the only monthly return outside the 99 percent range. August 1998 was a 5.3-sigma event for the emerging markets hedge fund subgroup.

■ Figure 8.46 reveals that negative returns are concentrated in negative market environments and positive hedge fund returns in positive market environments. The graph also shows that hedge fund managers miss some but not all of the falls in the underlying market. This means hedge fund managers occasionally are hedged, that is, manage to avoid loss of principal. Missing only a few of the corrections increases the performance substantially. Hedge fund manager Ian Wace of Marshall Wace Asset Management thinks along these lines. Wace (2000) used the term "negative compounding":

*This business [hedge funds] has nothing to do with positive compounding; it has to do with avoiding negative compounding. . . . The P&L is the only moderator of hubris. You are not given money to lose it.*\*

---

\*Needless to say, neither are long-only managers hired to lose money. However, the absolute return focus puts more weight on preserving wealth in difficult market conditions such as in the 2000-2001 period. Managing volatility and avoiding losses subsequently results in superior long-term absolute as well as risk-adjusted performance.

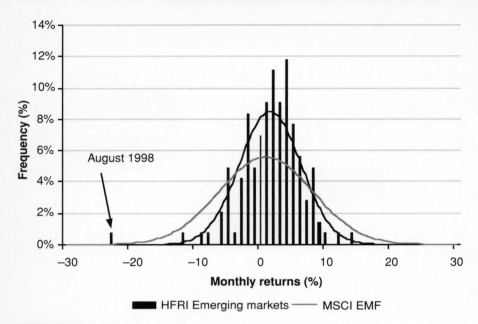

**FIGURE 8.45** Return Distribution
*Source:* Hedge Fund Research, Datastream, UBS Warburg (2000).

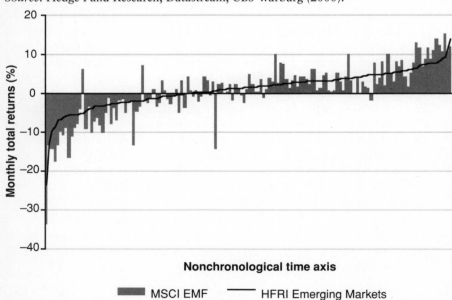

**FIGURE 8.46** Correlation
*Source:* Hedge Fund Research, Datastream, UBS Warburg (2000).

Ian Wace's view is diametrically opposing the aforementioned view by Lo (2001), that risk management is not essential for the success of a hedge fund. Pioneers agree with the former, lemmings with the latter. However, the consensus view is moving (albeit slowly) toward the former.

■ Figure 8.47 shows that the losses in the hedge funds index are of a smaller magnitude and that the losses were recovered quicker. The exception is the period of autumn 1998 where the losses were only marginally smaller and the recovery period roughly the same. However, note that at the end of 2001 the "wealth barometer" for the hedge funds index was at around 91 and at around 62 for the equity index. Note that the hedge fund index compounded at 14.3 percent while the MSCI EMF total return index compounded at 5.6 percent with higher volatility. (See Table 8.25.)
■ Figure 8.48 is a good example illustrating the investment philosophy of absolute return managers. Absolute return managers try to avoid losses. This does not mean they succeed all the time. Emerging market absolute return managers were unsuccessful in preserving wealth in the aftermath of Russia defaulting on its ruble-denominated debt. On most other occasions they were able to take risk off the table early enough to preserve

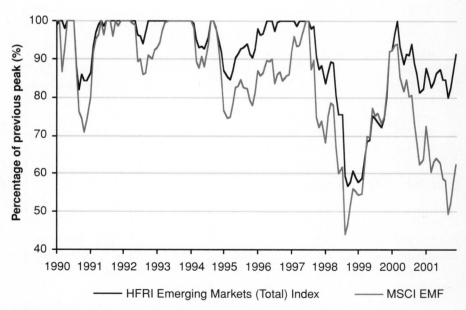

**FIGURE 8.47** Underwater
*Source:* Hedge Fund Research, Datastream.

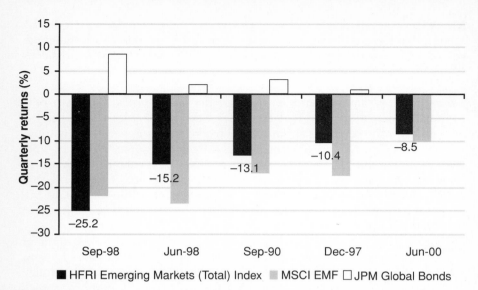

**FIGURE 8.48** Worst Quarters for Emerging Markets Hedge Funds
*Source:* Hedge Fund Research, Datastream.

wealth. Their former colleagues, who still work for large asset management firms running long-only money, had no incentive to reduce total risk. Hence the often-used analogy of a car without brakes in connection with relative return managers.

■ As shown in Table 8.27, annual returns have been higher in all four three-year periods for emerging hedge funds when compared to emerging markets long-only. The higher returns were achieved with lower volatilities even in the troublesome 1996–1998 period. The 1- and 12-month drawdowns were less severe for the absolute return investment style except for the 12-month drawdown in 1999 to 2001.

## Conclusion and Outlook

Emerging markets hedge funds have some appeal. Emerging markets are inefficient in many ways. The inefficiencies in these markets are full of opportunities for skill-based strategies apart from simply capturing the risk premium of the equity asset class. Exploiting inefficiencies by simultaneously controlling market risk in emerging markets is probably more profitable than in developed markets because there are more inefficiencies in less developed markets than there are in developed markets. This was true in the past and could easily hold in the future. However, if history is any guide, long-only as well as absolute return strategies in emerging markets are of high risk.

**Table 8.27** Performance Persistence

|                                      | 1990–1992 | 1993–1995 | 1996–1998 | 1999–2001 |
|--------------------------------------|-----------|-----------|-----------|-----------|
| **MSCI EMF (Total return)**          |           |           |           |           |
| Annual return (%)                    | 16.80     | 15.38     | −11.21    | 4.08      |
| Volatility (%)                       | 23.63     | 18.46     | 29.82     | 25.34     |
| Average risk-free rate (%)           | 5.61      | 4.37      | 5.07      | 4.64      |
| Sharpe ratio                         | 0.47      | 0.60      | <0        | −0.02     |
| Worst 1-month drawdown (%)           | −14.54    | −11.25    | −34.13    | −16.82    |
| Worst 12-month drawdown (%)          | −10.55    | −19.43    | −49.56    | −27.12    |
|                                      |           |           |           |           |
| **HFRI Emerging Markets (Total) Index** |        |           |           |           |
| Annual return (%)                    | 20.45     | 23.10     | −0.23     | 15.54     |
| Volatility (%)                       | 14.84     | 12.47     | 19.95     | 16.47     |
| Sharpe ratio                         | 1.00      | 1.50      | <0        | 0.66      |
| Worst 1-month drawdown (%)           | −12.86    | −5.66     | −23.60    | −6.82     |
| Worst 12-month drawdown (%)          | −3.35     | −8.74     | −42.52    | −33.00    |

*Source:* Hedge Fund Research, Datastream.

# APPENDIX: Long/Short Controversy

*No one wants advice—only corroboration.*

—John Steinbeck

## Introduction

There is a controversy whether long/short or market-neutral strategies are advantageous when compared with long-only strategies. The main bones of contention are whether there are more inefficiencies on the short side, whether there are diversification benefits, and whether there are efficiency gains. Table 8.28 summarizes a selection of the main papers on the subject. There is also a controversy as to whether long/short equity is the same as market-neutral.

## Performance Comparison

Although there are some reservations with respect to an upward bias of hedge fund indexes, Figure 8.49 compares two long-only strategies (S&P 500 and MSCI World) with four alternative investment styles.

■ One of the main differences between long/short equity and market-neutral strategies is performance. Long/short equity has outperformed all

**Table 8.28**    Chronology of Long/Short versus Long-Only Debate

| | |
|---|---|
| Grinold (1989) | Author shows that the information ratio depends on the strategy's information coefficient and its breadth where the information coefficient measures correlation between forecast and realization (essentially skill) and where breadth measures the number of independent bets per year. The author basically shows that strategies earn high information ratios by applying forecasting edge many times over. |
| Michaud (1993) | Short selling: Author observes that conventional active management involves de facto short selling, in the sense that the active strategy is short any assets that compose less of the portfolio than the benchmark. |
| | Alpha: Long/short strategies can capture more alpha per unit of residual risk, for portfolios with significant residual risk, than long-only strategies. Author makes the observation that, if the correlation between long-alpha and short-alpha approaches 1, a "long/short strategy may not substantially improve upon the investment characteristics of a long portfolio." |
| | Fixed costs and efficiency: Author cites the increased costs of long/short management as a serious impediment to successful long/short management. |
| | Suitability and correlation: "Given the current state of investment technology and implied levels of risk, the suitability of the strategy for long-term institutional investors is an open issue." |
| | Portable alpha: not limited to long/short strategies. |
| Arnott and Leinweber (1994) | Short selling: Authors note that the long-only manager can only be underweight by the weight of the stock in the benchmark. Thus, long-only managers can take on a significant short position in only the largest holdings of the benchmark. |
| | Alpha: Authors criticize Michaud for failing to point out that the correlation between the long portfolio and the short portfolio will always be less than 1, and consequently, a long/short strategy will always improve upon the investment characteristics of a long portfolio, albeit often only slightly, as long as the long and the short alphas are positive. |
| | Fixed costs and efficiency: Authors regard Michaud's argument as irrelevant because they would apply identically to long-only management. |
| | Suitability and correlation: Authors point out that the returns from long/short strategies are, unlike long-only strategies, not highly correlated with core assets (such as stocks and bonds). The contribution of even an extremely risky long/short strategy to total portfolio risk may be small or negligible. |
| | Portable alpha: Authors observed that alpha of long-only strategies is normally not ported. They regard this as probably the most significant unexploited opportunity in the institutional investment world to date. |
| Michaud (1994) | Short selling: "Surely, they do not believe that I intended to mislead by not explicitly citing such an obvious point." Author dismantles criticism by pointing to a footnote and unveiling a contradiction in Arnott and Leinweber (1994). |
| | Alpha: Author argues that the long/short portfolio will not always improve the investment characteristics of a long portfolio even when correlation is less than 1. Long/short strategy entails additional costs and risks. When these are considered, improvement of the after-cost active return-risk ratio with respect to the long-only portfolio may be minimal or negative. |
| | Fixed costs and efficiency: Author argues that the after-costs reward-to-residual-risk ratio is not superior for long/short strategies if one uses more realistic assumptions. |

**Table 8.28** *(Continued)*

| | |
|---|---|
| Michaud (1994) *(continued)* | Suitability and correlation: "Are they seriously claiming that long/short strategies are attractive because they have low correlation with stock and bond returns? Should institutional investors brace for a wave of managers touting lotteries, baseball cards, and postage stamps?"<br><br>Portable alpha: Author argues that the impact of alpha portability on the active risk-return trade-off is irrelevant because porting alpha does not alter the portfolio's relationship of active return to active risk. |
| Jacob and Levy (1995) | Short selling: Authors argue that Michaud's formal analysis ignores the added "flexibility" the long/short strategy offers over the long-only strategy. A properly constructed long/short portfolio can control risk by offsetting long and short positions; it does not have to hold neutral positions in order to control exposure to an arbitrary market index.<br><br>Alpha: The relaxation of index constraints in an integrated long/short portfolio provides added flexibility that translates into improved return and/or diminished risk vis-à-vis index-constrained long and short portfolios. Authors argue that Michaud (1993) concedes this by stating "a long/short strategy may be less 'index-constrained' than a long-only portfolio. . . . Consequently, a long/short portfolio may enhance the impact of forecast information."<br><br>Fixed costs and efficiency: Authors argue that whether the level of information the manager possesses is enough to justify the risks and costs of long/short investing, or active long investing, is an empirical question. While Michaud focuses on the many investors who do not possess sufficient information, the authors draw their attention to the few who do.<br><br>Suitability and correlation: Authors also raise some questions about Michaud's analytical framework, for example, integrated optimization. With integrated optimization, there are no separately measurable long and short alphas. And because long and short alphas are not separately measurable in an integrated long/short strategy, the correlation between long and short alphas is not a meaningful concept, hence cannot provide a meaningful gauge of the desirability of the strategy. What are meaningful are the extent and quality of the manager's information and the incremental costs associated with shorting. |
| Jacob and Levy (1996) | Authors demystify long/short investing by commenting on 20 myths. Some demystification is drawn from Jacobs and Levy (1995). Other examples include:<br><br>*Myth 16: Long/short management costs are high relative to long-only.* Authors argue that if one considers management fees per dollar of securities positions, rather than per dollar capital, there is not much difference between long/short and long-only fees. To the extent that a long-only manager's fee is based on the total investment rather than just the active element, the long-only fee per active dollar managed may be much higher than that of a long/short manager.<br><br>*Myth 18: Long short portfolios are not prudent investments.* The responsible use of long/short investment strategies is consistent with the prudence and diversification requirements of ERISA.<br><br>*Myth 19: Shorting is "un-American" and bad for the economy.* As Bill Sharpe noted in his 1990 Nobel laureate address, precluding short sales can result in "a diminution in the efficiency with which risk can be allocated in an economy . . . More fundamentally, overall welfare may be lower than it would be if the constraints on negative holdings could be reduced or removed." |
| Jacob and Levy (1997) | Authors calculate some practical examples of long/short strategies and filter in their justifying arguments for long/short strategies outlined in Jacobs and Levy (1996). |
| Brush (1997) | Abstract: Market-neutral long/short strategies get their returns from alphas and short rebates; long strategies get their returns from alpha and the market. Differing return and risk sources complicate their comparison, partly because of the strong market-referenced focus of conventional performance analysis. Compelling theoretical advantages of active return per unit of active risk suggests that long/short strategies are better able to deliver excess return than are conventional institutional long strategies. Long/short strategies, even with tiny positive alphas, are seen to improve investors' efficient frontiers when added to a traditional T-bill/long portfolio mix, mostly because their risk sources are uncorrelated. Surprisingly, the improvement occurs even if long/short strategies are Sharpe-ratio inferior to long strategies. These results provide theoretical support for including long/short strategies in most investors' mix of assets. |

*(Continued)*

**Table 8.28**   *(Continued)*

| Freeman (1997) | An active managed portfolio is essentially a "core" consisting of the benchmark index and an "active" portfolio consisting of the differences between the benchmark index and the subject portfolio. To the extent that active managers charge their fees for all assets under management, the index core can be thought of as "dead weight." |
|---|---|
| Jacob and Levy (1998) | Abstract: We consider the optimality of portfolios not subject to short-selling constraints and derive conditions that a universe of securities must satisfy for an optimal active portfolio to be dollar neutral or beta neutral. We find that following the common practice of constraining long-short portfolios to have zero net holdings or zero betas is generally suboptimal. Only under specific unlikely conditions will such constrained portfolios optimize an investor's utility function. We also derive precise formulas for optimally equitising and active long/short portfolio using exposure to a benchmark security. The relative sizes of the active and benchmark exposures depend on the investor's desired residual risk relative to the residual risk of a typical portfolio and on the expected risk-adjusted excess return of a minimum-variance active portfolio. We demonstrate that optimal portfolios demand the use of integrated optimizations. |
| Grinold and Kahn (2000) | Authors view short-side inefficiencies difficult to prove and highlight the issue of the high implementation costs. They view the diversification argument as misleading, or even incorrect. Authors focus on efficiency gain through loosening the long-only constraint. |
| | Abstract: We analyzed the efficiency gains of long/short investing, where we defined efficiency as the information ratio of the implemented strategy (the optimal portfolio) relative to the intrinsic information ratio of the alphas. The efficiency advantage of long/short investing arises from the loosening of the (surprisingly important) long-only constraint. Long/short and long-only managers need to understand the impact of this significant constraint. Long/short implementations offer the most improvement over long-only implementations when the universe of assets is large, asset volatility is low, and the strategy has high active risk. The long-only constraint induces biases (particularly toward small stocks), limits the manager's ability to act on upside information by not allowing short positions that could finance long positions, and reduces the efficiency of traditional (high-risk) long-only strategies relative to enhanced index (low-risk) long-only strategies. |

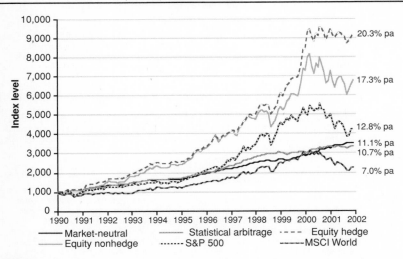

**FIGURE 8.49**   Performance Comparison of Long/Short Equity, Market-Neutral, and Long-Only
*Source:* Hedge Fund Research, Datastream.

major stock indexes. Investing in long/short equity is similar to investing in equities in general. Correlation with equity is high. The difference between long-only and long/short is that the long/short industry, in the past, did not give back profits to the market when the market declined. Long/short equity might have a long bias. However, the long bias seems to be significantly reduced when markets fall.

■ Equity market-neutral did not outperform the S&P 500 index, as the strategy is not designed to do so in one of financial history's most stupendous bull phases. However, it outperformed global equities with a fraction of the volatility. The main aim of market-neutral is generating positive returns in the low teens regardless of direction of the market. It has appeal to investors who want to preserve wealth more than to investors who want to create wealth by taking more risk.*

■ Figure 8.49 opens the question whether the difference of 13.3 percentage points between HFRI Equity Hedge (20.3 percent annual return between 1990 and 2001) and the MSCI World total return index (7.0 percent annual return) is sustainable over the next 12 years. It probably is not. However, it is unlikely that the 13.3 percentage points difference will melt to zero within a short period of a couple of years.

Table 8.29 shows difference between correlation with equity indexes and among the four hedge fund strategies.

■ Long/short equity has similar correlation coefficients as stock market indexes. In other words, correlation is high. Off-diagonal correlation of equity hedge and nonhedge is 0.60 and 0.64, respectively, compared with 0.63 for S&P 500, 0.57 for MSCI World, and 0.61 for the Nasdaq Composite.

Figure 8.50 is not an astronomical map of the Alpha Quadrant but shows the rolling two-year total return and two-year rolling volatility for market-neutral, equity hedge, and equity nonhedge. The size of the circle was fitted to encompass all readings per strategy. The chart makes it clear that market-neutral is a different strategy from long/short equity. The three lines in the graph show the chronological path of three hedge fund strategies in half-year increments. A reading in the lower right hand corner means high volatility and low returns.

---

*Although one could argue that if an investor's risk appetite exceeds the 3 to 4 percent volatility of equity market-neutral managers, he or she can lever up.

**Table 8.29**    Correlation Matrix

| | S&P 500 | MSCI World | Nasdaq Composite | Equity Market-Neutral | Statistical Arbitrage | Equity Hedge | Equity Non-hedge |
|---|---|---|---|---|---|---|---|
| S&P 500 | 1 | | | | | | |
| MSCI World | .84 | 1 | | | | | |
| Nasdaq Composite | .80 | .70 | 1 | | | | |
| Equity market-neutral | .11 | .09 | .10 | 1 | | | |
| Statistical arbitrage | .56 | .46 | .37 | .51 | 1 | | |
| Equity hedge | .65 | .61 | .81 | .31 | .31 | 1 | |
| Equity nonhedge | .78 | .71 | .91 | .16 | .38 | .89 | 1 |
| Off-diagonal average | 0.63 | 0.57 | 0.61 | 0.21 | 0.43 | 0.60 | 0.64 |

*Source:* Hedge Fund Research, Datastream, own illustration.

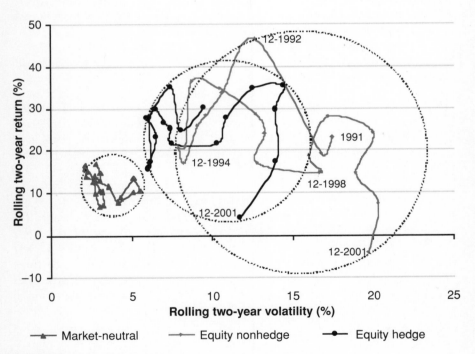

**FIGURE 8.50**    Equity Market-Neutral versus Long/Short Equity
*Source:* Hedge Fund Research, author's own illustration.

An interesting observation is that the last three data points (i.e., an 18-month period) for two-year returns of both long/short equity indexes are pointing downward whereas rolling two-year returns for market-neutral are not. This can not be explained by capacity constraints because new funds are flowing into both strategies. One explanatory factor could be correlation with equities in general: The longer the long bias the larger is the likelihood of falling rolling returns when markets fall. Another reason is the suspicion that quality of new long/short managers might be deteriorating as the barriers to entry have been torn down and institutional demand for hedge funds has started to materialize at an accelerating rate. The reason for quality deteriorating in long/short faster than in market-neutral could be (this is speculation) that market-neutral managers are more risk averse and probably have more experience with managing risk. The long/short equity universe has been flooded with long-only managers with no educational background in risk management and no experience in hedging or managing risk. However, since these managers are normally the best managers within a given organization (who set up hedge funds in-house or leave to set up their own),* one can expect these managers to move up the learning curve quickly. Figure 8.50 could be just an indication that they, as a group, are still in the process of learning by doing.

Many hedge fund strategies experience difficulties in dislocating markets as spreads widen and liquidity dries up. Figure 8.51 shows the three-month performance of the MSCI World and the three hedge fund strategies during the U.S. rate rise in 1994, the Asian crisis in 1997, the Russian default crisis in 1998, the Nasdaq implosion, and the atrocities of September 2001.

- There are differences between market-neutral and long/short equity when markets dislocate. Market-neutral is not necessarily affected when the market dislocates—as the strategy name "market-neutral" would suggest. Only in the Russian crisis does the strategy show a loss.
- Based on data from Hedge Fund Research, long/short equity with a long bias (equity nonhedge) seemed leveraged and long during three of the five stress periods shown in Figure 8.51. Equity hedge (Jones model) never lost more than the MSCI World except during the U.S. rate rise of 1994 where the index underperformed by 25 basis points.
- Note that equity hedge outperformed equity nonhedge in all five three-month periods of stress. The conclusion from this observation and the fact

---

*The worst managers are unlikely to leave to set up their own shops or be asked by their CIO to begin managing long/short money.

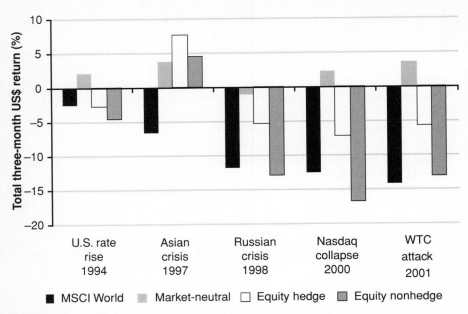

**FIGURE 8.51**   Market-Neutral and Long/Short Equity in Dislocating Markets
*Source:* Hedge Fund Research, Datastream.

that equity hedge shows far superior performance characteristics when compared with equity nonhedge suggests that the incentive and the skill to manage downside risk is paramount when selecting a long/short manager.

## Conclusion

Whether long/short is superior to long-only remains open to debate. However, market-neutral is not synonymous with long/short equity. From the managers' perspective, the primary risk factor in market-neutral strategies is stock-specific risk. Long/short equity involves stock-specific risk (nonsystematic risk) as well as market risk (systematic risk). However, the market exposure can be the result of a directional bet on the market or simply a portfolio tilt, a mismatch between long and short positions. From the investors' perspective, market-neutral strategies reduce the return volatility of any portfolio combinations due to their low volatility and correlation characteristics. Long/short equity, in the past, has enhanced portfolio returns. At the most general level, market-neutral strategies can be summarized as "portfolio volatility reducers" and long/short equity as "portfolio return enhancers."

# The Fund of Hedge Funds Industry

# CHAPTER 9

# Industry Overview

*Either you understand your risk or you don't play the game.*
—Arthur Ashe*

## INTRODUCTION TO FUND OF FUNDS

### Definition

At the most general level, a fund of hedge funds manager is—as the name implies—a fund manager who creates and manages portfolios of hedge funds. A fund of funds is a fund that mixes and matches hedge funds and other pooled investment vehicles, spreading investments among many different funds or investment vehicles. A fund of funds simplifies the process of choosing hedge funds, blending together funds to meet a range of investor risk/return objectives while generally spreading the risks over a variety of funds to diversify idiosyncratic risks. This blending of different strategies and asset classes aims to deliver a more consistent return than any of the individual funds.

A fund of hedge funds is a diversified portfolio of hedge funds. Most often the constituents are uncorrelated. However, a fund of funds can be widely diversified, as well as have a focus on a particular style, sector, or geographical region. The fund of funds approach has been the preferred investment form

---

*From Barra advertisement.

for many pension funds, endowment funds, insurance companies, private banks, family offices, and high-net-worth individuals.

Based on data from one data provider there were 444 funds of funds officially or unofficially reporting returns as of December 2000. According to more than one estimate, funds of hedge funds manage around 20 to 25 percent of the whole hedge funds universe of approximately $500 billion to $600 billion assets under management.

## A Fund of Funds Isn't That Simple

The operation of a fund of funds manager is complex and its process iterative. Table 9.1 is one way of looking at the tasks and risks of a fund of funds manager. Selecting and monitoring hedge fund managers and monitoring and managing hedge fund exposures is complex. Although conceptually simple, the implementation is difficult. The fund of funds operation involves quantitative as well as (and more importantly) qualitative processes and projections. In addition, it requires the knowledge, insight, and experience of getting a qualitative interpretation of the quantitative analysis. The whole process is iterative because there is no beginning or end to the process of manager selection, portfolio construction, risk monitoring, and portfolio rebalancing.

The heterogeneity of skill sets of a fund of funds operation might be a first, crude indication of its competitive strength. In assessing and selecting a fund of funds manager, the investor will have to judge whether the fund of funds manager has fundamental skill and, ideally, an edge in all variables. Obviously, there will be differences in fund of funds operations since every manager might have different objectives, strengths, and weaknesses. The point to highlight here is that a fund of funds operation is a business that includes huge diversity in individual skill sets.

## FUND OF FUNDS INDUSTRY CHARACTERISTICS

### Heterogeneous Marketplace

All hedge funds are not created equal. A poorly chosen portfolio of hedge funds can produce disappointing results. All fund of hedge funds managers are not created equal, either. A poor choice of fund of funds managers can yield disappointing results.

Not only is the hedge fund industry heterogeneous. The fund of hedge funds industry is heterogeneous as well. The diversity derives from the fact that not everyone is doing the same thing (as for example following a market benchmark). The long-only industry is, at least by comparison, homogeneous: Everyone executes a buy-and-hold (long-only) investment strategy. An

**Table 9.1**  Investment Risk Matrix

| Investment Activity | Potential Areas of Risk | | |
|---|---|---|---|
| Asset allocation (strategic/tactical) | Selection of asset classes/proxies | Market shocks | Underlying models |
| | Return/correlation projections | Market structures | Long term versus short term |
| | Sufficient diversification | Economic assumptions | Costs when changing policy |
| | Liquidity | Tax | Cash flows |
| | | | Liability projection |
| Benchmark determination | Selection— weight bias updates/changes | Costs | Rebalancing |
| Manager selection | Style—past, present, future | Guidelines | Concentration |
| | Misfit to benchmark | Trading instruments | Performance |
| | People | Philosophy | Process |
| | Compliance | Controls | Separation of functions (trading/back office) |
| Manager monitoring | Guidelines/controls | Models | Data |
| | Systems | | |
| Performance reporting | Calculation | Presentation | |
| Custody | Independence | Subcustodian | Capital |
| Accounting | Methodology | Separation of duties | |
| Valuation | Modeling risk | Process | Pricing source |
| | Size of position | Seasonality | |
| Operations | Business interruption | Staffing | Internal controls |
| | Recordkeeping | External relationships | Technology |
| | Insurance | Systems | Legal/regulatory |
| Business/event | Currency convertibility | Reputations | Legal/regulatory |
| | Credit rating shifts | Taxation | Disaster |
| | Market disruptions | | |

*Source:* Miller (2000), p. 55.

absolute return focus is, sort of, the opposite of a relative return investment philosophy.* To some absolute return managers the pure fact that everyone is doing the same thing is an opportunity to do the opposite (as pointed out in Chapter 1, hedge fund managers are quite often contrarians—not only in theory but also in their investment practice). If everyone is endlessly loading up telecommunications stocks it is not a question of *if* but *when* to put on the opposite trade. This diversity is the reason why correlation between managers and between strategies is low and, when compared to stocks, relatively stable. It is this diversity which allows to construct portfolios with volatilities of 5 percent and lower.

There are two levels of heterogeneity in the fund of funds industry. First, there is diversity with respect to the investment approach. Not all fund of funds organizations have the same investment objectives and strategy preferences. Competitive advantages also differ from fund to fund. Second, there is product diversity. For example, one single fund of funds manager might have a product where beta to the underlying equity market is held around zero and another that is long and leveraged. This diversity is one reason for the dispersion of returns among different managers that will be addressed shortly. It is also the reason why market or peer-group indexes do not work as a benchmark.

Figure 9.1 shows the dispersion of quarterly returns from a selection of funds of funds. At each point in time, the chart shows the range of outcomes that funds of funds experienced. This dispersion demonstrates the importance of evaluating individual fund of funds managers.

The dispersion of returns of funds of funds has increased—primarily on the downside. This could be function of a widening gap between talented and less talented fund of funds managers. It probably also is a function of an increased number of fund of funds managers having a bias toward investing in hedge funds with a long bias. In 1999 funds of funds suddenly appeared that invested solely in technology or Internet-related hedge funds. Some of these funds of funds shared a similar faith as did the Nasdaq. In other words, the increase in dispersion could be either a longer-term trend due to dilution of skill or an anomaly associated with the bursting of the Internet bubble—or a combination of both.

## Liquidity

Liquidity in fund of hedge fund vehicles is not as high as with marketable securities. Figure 9.2 shows the distribution of funds of funds by withdrawals

---

*One could argue, however, that an absolute return strategy is the same as a relative return strategy where the risk-free rate plus a couple of basis points is the benchmark.

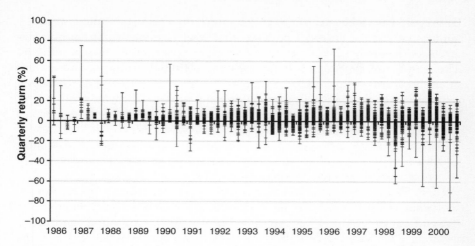

**FIGURE 9.1** Dispersion of Fund of Funds Returns (1986–2000, Quarterly Returns)
*Source:* Quellos Group, UBS Warburg (2001).

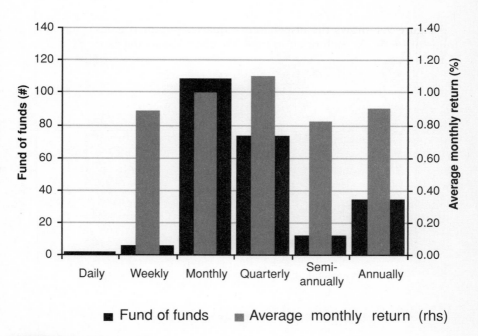

**FIGURE 9.2** Withdrawals
*Source:* Quellos Group, UBS Warburg (2001).

(left axis). The right axis of the graph shows the average monthly return by withdrawal for the 96 funds of funds that were in existence during January 1996 and December 2000. Figure 9.3 shows the distribution by contribution. The sample size for Figure 9.2 was 189 funds of funds products. The average monthly return was drawn from 78 funds of funds in existence over the five-year period ending in 2000. The overlapping sample size was 177 funds of funds (information on withdrawals as well as contributions).

■ As shown in the figures, 77 percent of the funds of funds had a withdrawal period of either monthly or quarterly (Figure 9.2), and 88 percent took monthly or quarterly contributions (Figure 9.3).
■ Of 177 funds of funds where information on withdrawals as well as contributions was available, 69 percent had a match between withdrawals and contributions; 17.5 percent took monthly contributions and had a longer withdrawal period; 28 percent had a longer withdrawal period than contribution period. No fund of funds had a shorter withdrawal period than contribution period.

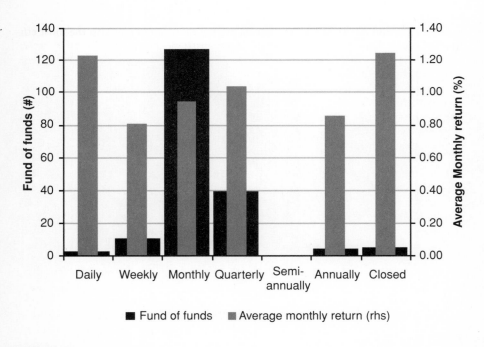

**FIGURE 9.3**   Contributions
*Source:* Quellos Group, UBS Warburg (2001).

**Relationship between Liquidity and Performance**   Whether there is correlation between liquidity and performance on a fund of funds level* and whether a fund of funds manager can have a duration mismatch between investors (liabilities) and investments in individual hedge funds (assets) is open to debate. In addition, liquidity on a single fund or fund of funds level is to some extent a theoretical issue. Most managers will have provisions to extend redemptions, either buried in the fine print of the offering memorandum or via some other legal recourse. In other words, liquidity is not necessarily as it appears at first sight.[†]

Liquidity terms of skillful hedge fund and fund of funds managers will probably get tougher. Since the hedge funds with the greatest skills will generate returns in less efficient markets, and demand going into hedge funds is expected to increase at a pace faster than new skilled managers can supply new capacity, skilled managers potentially will continue to be in the position to tighten (and dictate) liquidity terms. Thus we might expect more 2+20 fee structures for single hedge funds, tougher liquidity terms, and more lockup provisions. Potentially some managers may face a moral hazard of opening

---

*Liquidity on a single hedge fund level is a different matter. For example, currencies, interest rate, and equity index instruments are the most liquid and also the most efficiently priced. Thus, funds specializing in these instruments could easily offer weekly liquidity. Distressed and convertible bonds are relatively illiquid. Managers focusing here need quarterly redemptions if not longer. In general, the efficiency of an asset is highly correlated to its liquidity. Since we are trying for inefficient markets (as the potential for alpha is larger in inefficient markets), this necessitates less liquid investments. Interesting is the observation that if a hedge fund faces overwhelming investor demand the first thing it does is to extend the redemption period to withdraw money, thus making the capital base more stable. Increasing fees and/or closing the fund for new money usually follows as a second step.

†One could argue that liquidity in itself is a theoretical or at least ephemeral concept. Liquidity tends to evaporate when most needed. For example, there was no liquidity during the October 19, 1987, crash. According to the report of the Presidential Task Force on Market Mechanisms, market makers possessed neither the resources nor the willingness to absorb the extraordinary volume of selling demand that materialized. (From Swensen 2000, p. 93.) Just when investors most needed liquidity, it disappeared. Swensen quotes Keynes (1936) who argued that "of the maxims of orthodox finance none, surely, is more anti-social than the fetish of liquidity, the doctrine that it is a positive virtue on the part of investment institutions to concentrate their resources upon the holding of 'liquid' securities. It forgets that there is no such thing as liquidity of investment for the community as a whole." Swensen suggests that investors should purse success, not liquidity (i.e., fear failure, not illiquidity). If private, illiquid investments succeed, liquidity follows as investors gain interest. In public markets, as once-illiquid stocks perform well, liquidity increases as investors recognize progress. In contrast, if public, liquid investments fail, illiquidity follows as interest dries up.

their doors to new money once having closed. Nevertheless, one could argue that the truly skilled managers would not add capacity beyond what is optimal in their field of expertise and with their operational setup.

Liquidity has a tendency to disappear exactly when most demanded. Assuming that fund of funds managers must match the durations of their assets with their liabilities, they will have to tighten their liquidity terms as a result of expected trends. A counterargument to this view is that the fund of funds manager need only manage weighted average terms and probabilistic redemptions. This would be similar to a bank that needs only fractional reserves since a run on the banking industry is seen as unlikely. In addition, funds of funds, as banks or hedge funds themselves, in such catastrophic situations could refuse to pay redemptions. Nevertheless, in the long run, funds of funds will have to tighten their weighted average liquidity terms by either replacing old investors with new investors facing lockups or adding new vehicles with tougher terms.

Flight-to-quality scenarios such as in autumn 1998 do not happen often. A duration mismatch between assets and liabilities will not be a problem in most market situations. However, shocks to the system do happen. Sound funding and matching asset/liability duration are advisable.

## Fee Structure

This section examines the fee structures of some of the funds of hedge funds on which there was information available. One caveat of this analysis is that different investment styles are mixed. A fund of funds specializing in constant absolute returns will most likely have a different fee structure than a fund of funds shooting for the moon (i.e., with a strong directional bias). Information on kickbacks, trail fees, and retrocessions was not included in the data set.*

From the whole sample of funds of funds data available, there was information on base fee, hurdle rate, and performance fee for 118 funds. Figure 9.4 and Figure 9.5 (cumulative) show the distribution by flat fee.

---

*Kickback: Some funds of funds get a fee from the hedge fund's clearing broker (e.g., a fund of funds manager insisting that a hedge fund clears with a broker of its choosing and that broker then gives a percentage back to the fund of funds). Another kickback idea is for the hedge fund to give a percentage of its total fee income and a percentage of its hedge fund business for being an initial investor. Both of these things are rarely announced. A trail fee is usually payable on mutual funds and seen as a payment to an intermediary for ongoing client servicing and monitoring on the fund. Retrocession is a fee-sharing arrangement whereby a portion of the fees charged by the hedge fund or fund of funds is given back either to marketers or to other agents in consideration for their efforts in raising money for the product, or given back directly to the client as a form of compensation (mainly true of retail-distributed products).

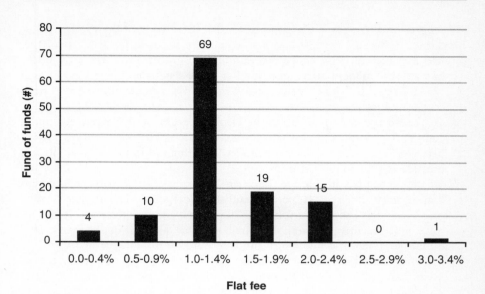

**FIGURE 9.4**   Distribution by Flat Fee
*Source:* Quellos Group, UBS Warburg (2001).

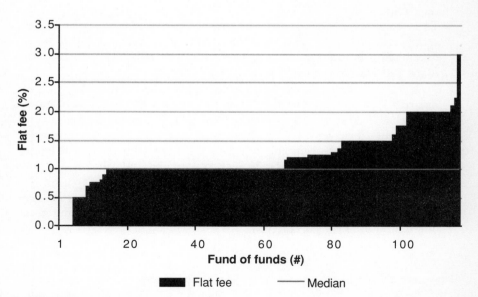

**FIGURE 9.5**   Flat Fee of Funds of Funds
*Source:* Quellos Group, UBS Warburg (2001).

■ As seen in Figure 9.4, 69 funds of funds (58 percent of the funds) had a flat fee between 1 percent and 1.4 percent; 88 funds of funds (75 percent) had a flat fee of between 1 percent and 1.9 percent. From the 118 funds of funds the median manager had a flat fee of 1 percent where the average was 1.2 percent. The range was between 0 percent (four funds) and 3 percent (one fund).

■ Of the 88 funds with a flat fee between 1 percent and 1.9 percent, only eight (9.1 percent) did not have an incentive fee. The incentive fee varied between 2 percent and 25 percent. Twenty funds of funds (22.7%) had a hurdle rate* of some sort in place.

■ Of the 88 funds with flat fees between 1 percent and 1.9 percent, the median incentive fee was 10 percent and the average 12 percent. The hurdle rate varied from 0 percent to S&P 500 returns. Figure 9.6 shows flat fee in relation to incentive fee from the whole universe of 118 funds of funds. The bubble size measures number of funds of funds with same fee structure.

■ The most common structure is a flat fee of 1 percent and incentive fee of 10 percent; 28 (21.5 percent) funds of funds had this structure. Of these 28, nine had a hurdle rate of 10 percent, six had no hurdle rate, and five had a hurdle rate associated with T-bills or other short-term interest rate benchmark. From the remaining eight funds of funds with a 1+10 structure, three had a hurdle rate of 8 percent, two of S&P 500 returns, and the remaining three had hurdle rates of 7 percent, 7.5 percent, and 8 percent, respectively.

■ The second most common structure was a 1 percent flat fee and a 15 percent incentive fee; 12 funds had this structure. However, all of these 12 funds had a hurdle rate ranging from T-bills to S&P 500 returns. Four funds had 1 percent plus 20 percent.

Figure 9.7 estimates the total fee from the universe of 118 funds of funds. The graph has been sorted by ascending total fees. We assumed a hedge fund gross return of 20 percent. For the benchmarked hurdle rate, we assumed a three-month rate of 6 percent and an equity return of 10 percent. The equity hurdle benchmark rate was either the S&P 500 or MSCI World.

■ For the total fee the median was 2.4 percent and the average was 2.7 percent. The range was from a total fee of 0.935 percent to 7.0 percent given our assumptions for gross return.

---

*The return above which a hedge fund manager begins taking incentive fees. For example, if a fund has a hurdle rate of 10 percent and the fund returns 25 percent for the year, the fund will take incentive fees on only the 15 percent return above the hurdle rate.

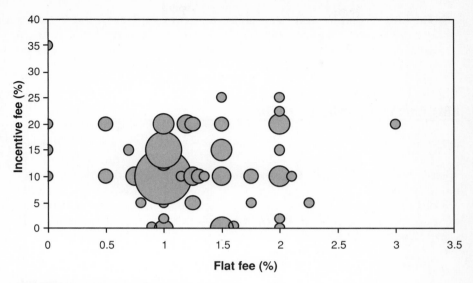

**FIGURE 9.6** Flat Fee versus Incentive Fee
*Source:* Quellos Group, UBS Warburg (2001).

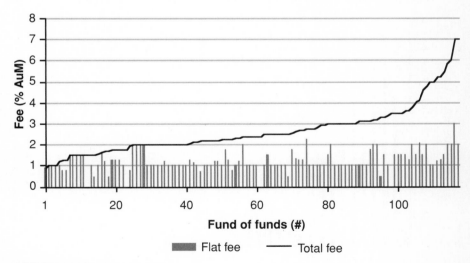

**FIGURE 9.7** Total Fee Structure
*Source:* Quellos Group, UBS Warburg (2001).

■ The lowest total fee was in a fund of funds with a flat fee of 0.9 percent and an incentive fee of 0.25 percent above a hurdle rate of two-year T-notes. The highest fee structure was 2 percent flat fee and 25 percent incentive fee with no hurdle rate.

## VOLATILITY OF FUNDS OF FUNDS

Different funds of funds have different objectives and, as a result, different portfolios with different volatilities. Figure 9.8 shows the dispersion of volatility for 475 funds of funds with at least 36 months of continuous monthly returns. A chart with only 286 funds of funds with at least 60 months of returns (not shown) looks nearly the same as Figure 9.8, although the two extreme outliers on the right-hand side of the volatility distribution were missing. This, in theory, could be a function of a smaller sample size.

■ It was found that 19.4 percent of funds of funds had volatilities that were 5 percent or lower, 34.1 percent were between 5 percent and 10 percent, 24.6 percent were between 10 percent and 15 percent, and 11.2 percent

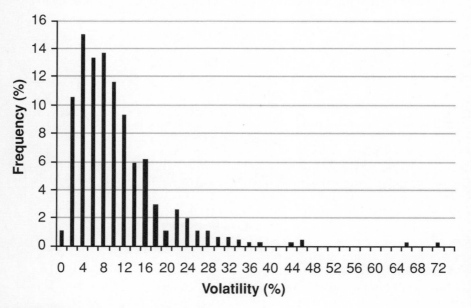

**FIGURE 9.8** Volatility of Funds of Funds
*Source:* Quellos Group, UBS Warburg (2001).

were between 15 percent and 20 percent; 10.7 percent of the funds of funds had annual volatilities higher than 20 percent.

■ Five funds of funds (1.1 percent of sample size) had a volatility lower than 2 percent. The lowest volatility was 1.17 percent (based on 48 monthly returns to December 2000).

■ Five funds of funds had volatilities above 45 percent. The two most volatile funds had volatilities of 72.7 percent and 66.3 percent (based on 36 and 48 monthly returns, respectively).

Figure 9.9 shows the most volatile compared with the least volatile funds of funds. Only funds with continuous monthly returns of five years or more were screened. The fund with the highest volatility had an annual standard deviation of monthly returns (volatility) equal to 47.6 percent (based on 180 returns to December 2000), whereas the lowest was 1.72 percent (based on 72 returns to December 2000).

The conclusion drawn from Figure 9.8 and Figure 9.9 is that the fund of hedge funds industry is probably as heterogeneous as is the hedge fund industry. The most volatile fund of funds in Figure 9.9 has a strong directional bias, hence the high volatility. The least volatile fund of funds in Figure 9.9 outperformed the most volatile fund of funds by 100 basis points per year in the five-year period ending 2001. The annual return of the most volatile was 8.9 percent while the least volatile fund of funds compounded at 9.9 percent.

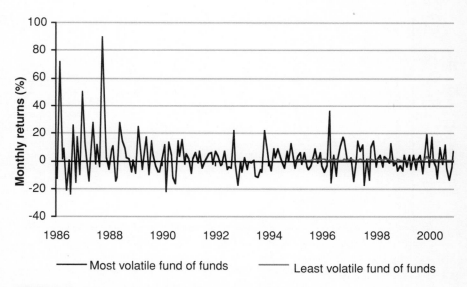

**FIGURE 9.9** Most and Least Volatile Funds of Funds
*Source:* Quellos Group, UBS Warburg (2001).

Figure 9.10 shows the cumulative performance of the two funds of funds. Although there is little statistical significance in comparing the two most extreme funds of funds in a sample, it nevertheless shows that the notion of higher risk resulting in higher return does not always hold. Figure 9.9 shows that there are funds of funds that are inefficient, that is, not properly diversified. The least volatile fund of funds is therefore closer to what we describe in the Preface as the third paradigm: exploiting investment opportunities while managing portfolio volatility in absolute return space.

## FUND OF FUNDS DOMICILE

Figure 9.11 looks at fund of funds domiciles. The chart is based on 130 funds of funds in operation in the two-year period from 1999 to 2000.

Sixty-three percent of the 130 funds of funds universe are in domiciles renowned as tax havens and boasting a fair amount of sunny days per year. Many funds of funds are registered in Delaware. There are some advantages to registering in Delaware:

■ No minimum capital is required to form a Delaware corporation.
■ There is no corporate income tax on companies formed in Delaware and not doing business in the state.

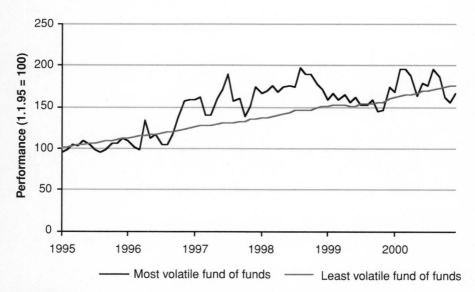

**FIGURE 9.10** Cumulative Return for Most and Least Volatile Funds of Funds
*Source:* Quellos Group, UBS Warburg (2001).

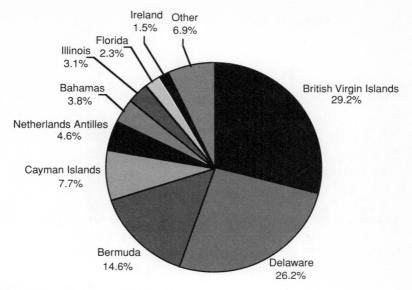

**FIGURE 9.11**   Fund of Funds Domiciles
*Other:* One fund each in British West Indies, California, Connecticut, Curaçao, Guernsey, Isle of Man, Luxembourg, Pennsylvania, and Texas.
*Source:* Quellos Group, UBS Warburg (2001).

■ Corporate records can be kept anywhere in the world.
■ No formal meetings are required, and shareholders need not be U.S. citizens.
■ Any legal business may be conducted in Delaware.
■ Ownership of a Delaware corporation is strictly confidential.
■ One person can act as the sole officer, director, and shareholder of a corporation.
■ It is inexpensive.

## MINIMUM INVESTMENT

Figures 9.12 and 9.13 show the distribution of fund of hedge funds by minimum investment requirement. The figures are based on minimum investment information of 395 fund of funds from a universe of 929 existing and distinct funds of funds.

The median fund of funds had a minimum requirement of $250,000. The

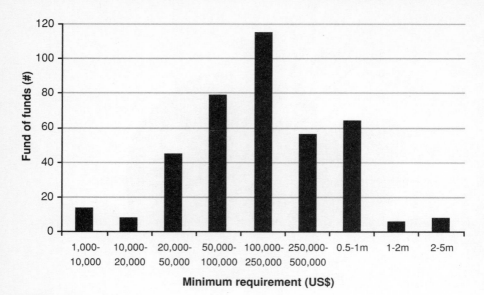

**FIGURE 9.12** Distribution by Minimum Investment
*Source:* Quellos Group, UBS Warburg (2001).

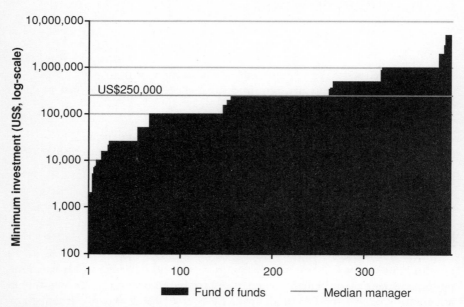

**FIGURE 9.13** Minimum Investment of Funds of Funds
*Source:* Quellos Group, UBS Warburg (2001).

range varies from $1,000 to $5 million. It was found that 66.1 percent of the funds of funds had a minimum investment requirement of $250,000 or less and 37.0 percent of $100,000 or less. Only 3.5 percent of the funds of funds had a requirement of more than $1 million. Figure 9.12 could have a slight bias to the left as some requirements of older funds of funds might not have been updated.

# PERFORMANCE

## Performance Data: Caveat Lector (Let the Reader Beware)

The performance herein and in UBS Warburg (2001) is based on proprietary data of Quellos Group LLC, a Seattle-based financial services and wealth management group. The advantage of being able to analyze a proprietary database is the size of the universe, which is a several times larger than any commercially available database in terms of number of data points and information. The disadvantage of such an analysis is that it is of little value for any academic pursuits because the data cannot be made available and, therefore, the findings cannot by verified or refuted by peers.

The total universe comprises 929 funds of funds products. The data includes terminated funds, different share classes of the same fund of funds, closed funds, as well as funds still in operation. It included performance data on 726 funds of hedge funds. Performance data of at least 12 consecutive months was available for 680 funds, of which 444 reported until December 2000. The data does not state why performance stopped (termination of fund or termination of reporting returns). The performance data starts in January 1986 and ends in December 2000.

## Analysis

Table 9.2 shows the annual returns of four fund of funds universes compared with some traditional indexes, a hedge fund composite index, and private equity. For the first Quellos universe we selected all 726 funds with performance data. For the second Quellos universe we took a selection comprising 258 funds of funds that had at least five years of monthly returns.

Note that there are some imperfections with this analysis. First, the average for 1986 is based on only 14 funds of funds. The number of funds of funds increased more or less linearly to 258 in 1996 and decreased to 202 at the end of December 2000. Second, we have calculated an average of funds of funds, not an average of fund of funds managers. A manager could have more than one fund of funds. Third, at no point in time would these returns have

**Table 9.2**   Fund of Hedge Funds Performance Compared with Traditional Indexes, Hedge Fund Composite Index, and Private Equity

| | Traditional Equities | | | | Bonds | HFR | Alternative Investment Strategies Fund of Hedge Funds | | | | Private Equity | | |
|---|---|---|---|---|---|---|---|---|---|---|---|---|---|
| (%) | MSCI World | S&P 500 | MSCI EAFE | MSCI Europe | JPM Global Gvt. Bonds | Comp. Index | Quellos (1) | Quellos (2) | HFR | Zurich/ MAR | All PE | Venture Capital | LB/ Mezz |
| 1975 | 34.5 | 31.5 | 37.1 | 43.9 | N/A | N/A | N/A | N/A | N/A | N/A | 3.8 | 4.2 | –13.2 |
| 1976 | 14.7 | 19.2 | 3.7 | –6.4 | N/A | N/A | N/A | N/A | N/A | N/A | 15.0 | 15.7 | –17.0 |
| 1977 | 2.0 | –11.5 | 19.4 | 23.9 | N/A | N/A | N/A | N/A | N/A | N/A | 18.7 | 18.8 | 10.7 |
| 1978 | 18.2 | 1.1 | 34.3 | 24.3 | N/A | N/A | N/A | N/A | N/A | N/A | 41.6 | 43.3 | –25.0 |
| 1979 | 12.7 | 12.3 | 6.2 | 14.7 | N/A | N/A | N/A | N/A | N/A | N/A | 22.7 | 22.9 | 45.8 |
| 1980 | 27.7 | 32.6 | 24.4 | 14.5 | N/A | N/A | N/A | N/A | N/A | N/A | 33.8 | 33.9 | 28.0 |
| 1981 | –3.3 | –4.9 | –1.0 | –10.4 | N/A | N/A | N/A | N/A | N/A | N/A | 16.9 | 18.8 | –1.9 |
| 1982 | 11.3 | 21.7 | –0.9 | 5.7 | N/A | N/A | N/A | N/A | N/A | N/A | 15.5 | 16.9 | 4.7 |
| 1983 | 23.3 | 22.5 | 24.6 | 22.4 | N/A | N/A | N/A | N/A | N/A | N/A | 34.7 | 38.6 | 9.3 |
| 1984 | 5.8 | 6.2 | 7.9 | 1.3 | N/A | N/A | N/A | N/A | N/A | N/A | 1.7 | 1.6 | 3.6 |
| 1985 | 41.8 | 31.8 | 56.7 | 79.8 | N/A | N/A | N/A | N/A | N/A | N/A | 11.6 | 4.6 | 35.8 |
| 1986 | 42.8 | 18.7 | 69.9 | 44.5 | 20.1 | N/A | 18.7 | 18.7 | N/A | N/A | 19.1 | 9.6 | 42.1 |
| 1987 | 16.8 | 5.2 | 24.9 | 4.1 | 13.8 | N/A | 35.9 | 35.9 | N/A | N/A | 16.7 | 12.3 | 24.1 |
| 1988 | 24.0 | 16.6 | 28.6 | 16.4 | 5.0 | N/A | 18.3 | 18.3 | N/A | N/A | 21.8 | 4.0 | 47.7 |
| 1989 | 17.2 | 31.7 | 10.8 | 29.1 | 6.8 | N/A | 19.7 | 19.7 | N/A | N/A | 16.8 | 5.2 | 29.3 |
| 1990 | –16.5 | –3.1 | –23.2 | –3.4 | 11.8 | 5.8 | 14.4 | 14.8 | 17.5 | 7.5 | 2.2 | 3.1 | 1.3 |
| 1991 | 19.0 | 30.5 | 12.5 | 13.7 | 15.4 | 32.2 | 12.2 | 11.5 | 14.5 | 11.3 | 12.7 | 16.9 | 11.8 |
| 1992 | –4.7 | 7.7 | –11.8 | –4.2 | 4.6 | 21.2 | 12.9 | 12.7 | 12.3 | 11.9 | 7.8 | 9.8 | 9.4 |
| 1993 | 23.1 | 10.1 | 32.9 | 29.8 | 12.3 | 30.9 | 24.6 | 24.9 | 26.3 | 24.2 | 23.4 | 19.0 | 27.8 |
| 1994 | 5.6 | 1.3 | 8.1 | 2.7 | 1.3 | 4.1 | –2.8 | –2.4 | –3.5 | –4.4 | 14.8 | 12.8 | 13.6 |
| 1995 | 21.3 | 37.6 | 11.6 | 22.1 | 19.3 | 21.5 | 12.4 | 12.8 | 11.1 | 12.3 | 20.8 | 39.7 | 12.6 |
| 1996 | 14.0 | 22.9 | 6.4 | 21.6 | 4.4 | 21.1 | 17.3 | 17.7 | 14.4 | 16.7 | 27.8 | 32.2 | 24.5 |
| 1997 | 16.2 | 33.4 | 2.1 | 24.2 | 1.4 | 16.8 | 17.1 | 18.0 | 16.2 | 17.2 | 22.5 | 28.9 | 19.9 |
| 1998 | 24.8 | 28.6 | 20.3 | 28.9 | 15.3 | 2.6 | 0.5 | –0.2 | –5.1 | 1.7 | 14.4 | 18.6 | 12.6 |
| 1999 | 25.3 | 21.0 | 27.3 | 16.2 | –5.1 | 31.3 | 27.1 | 24.3 | 26.5 | 16.2 | 57.6 | 142.8 | 26.1 |
| 2000 | –12.9 | –9.1 | –14.0 | –8.1 | 2.3 | 5.0 | 5.8 | 5.5 | 4.1 | 7.4 | 12.0 | 24.0 | 4.1 |
| 2001 | –7.5 | –4.4 | –10.8 | –13.7 | –3.6 | 3.0 | N/A | N/A | 2.3 | 3.0 | –4.5 | –8.0 | –3.1 |
| 1975–2000a | 15.6 | 16.0 | 16.1 | 17.3 | N/A | N/A | N/A | N/A | N/A | N/A | 19.5 | 23.0 | 14.9 |
| 1986–2000a | 14.4 | 16.9 | 13.8 | 15.8 | 8.6 | N/A | 15.6 | 15.5 | N/A | N/A | 19.4 | 25.2 | 20.5 |
| 1986–1995a | 14.9 | 15.6 | 16.4 | 15.5 | 11.0 | N/A | 16.6 | 16.7 | N/A | N/A | 15.6 | 13.2 | 22.0 |
| 1990–2000a | 10.5 | 16.4 | 6.6 | 13.0 | 7.5 | 17.5 | 12.7 | 12.7 | 12.2 | 11.1 | 19.6 | 31.6 | 14.9 |
| 1995–2000a | 14.8 | 22.4 | 8.9 | 17.5 | 6.3 | 16.4 | 12.6 | 13.0 | 11.2 | 11.9 | 25.8 | 47.7 | 16.6 |
| 1975–2000b | 14.7 | 14.5 | 20.7 | 19.7 | N/A | N/A | N/A | N/A | N/A | N/A | 12.3 | 27.2 | 18.3 |
| 1986–2000b | 15.7 | 14.4 | 22.6 | 15.0 | 7.4 | N/A | 9.8 | 9.7 | N/A | N/A | 12.4 | 34.2 | 13.1 |
| 1986–1995b | 16.5 | 13.9 | 25.5 | 16.0 | 6.4 | N/A | 9.9 | 9.9 | N/A | N/A | 6.6 | 10.7 | 14.9 |
| 1990–2000b | 15.3 | 15.9 | 17.4 | 14.0 | 7.6 | 11.5 | 9.6 | 8.9 | 10.3 | 7.9 | 14.6 | 38.3 | 8.7 |
| 1995–2000b | 14.3 | 16.6 | 14.5 | 13.2 | 9.2 | 10.9 | 11.9 | 9.0 | 10.8 | 6.2 | 16.5 | 47.1 | 8.4 |
| 1975–2000c | 0.72 | 0.76 | 0.54 | 0.63 | N/A | N/A | N/A | N/A | N/A | N/A | 1.18 | 0.66 | 0.54 |
| 1986–2000c | 0.60 | 0.83 | 0.39 | 0.72 | 0.48 | N/A | 1.08 | 1.08 | N/A | N/A | 1.16 | 0.59 | 1.18 |
| 1986–1995c | 0.60 | 0.77 | 0.45 | 0.65 | 0.94 | N/A | 1.17 | 1.18 | N/A | N/A | 1.61 | 0.77 | 1.14 |
| 1990–2000c | 0.36 | 0.72 | 0.09 | 0.58 | 0.33 | 1.09 | 0.80 | 0.87 | 0.70 | 0.77 | 1.00 | 0.69 | 1.13 |
| 1995–2000c | 0.68 | 1.05 | 0.27 | 0.95 | 0.14 | 1.05 | 0.64 | 0.89 | 0.57 | 1.11 | 1.26 | 0.91 | 1.39 |

*Note:* All annual returns are total returns in U.S. dollars. 2001 returns until June (except VE until March). Private equity (PE) returns are based on the pooled average method of calculating time weighted returns using periodic IRRs (internal rates of return).

[a]Arithmetic average of annual total returns.

[b]Standard deviation of annual returns.

[c]Sharpe ratio. Here calculated as arithmetic return—5% over standard deviation of arithmetic returns.

(1) Based on universe of 726 current and terminated funds of hedge funds. (2) Based on universe of 258 funds of funds with at least five years of consecutive monthly returns. (3) As of April 2001: 256 funds of funds with $22.2 billion assets under management. Abbreviations: HFR: Hedge Fund Research, Inc; VE: Venture Economics; LB: leveraged buyout; Mezz: mezzanine.

*Source:* Quellos Group, Hedge Fund Research, Zurich Capital Markets, Venture Economics, Datastream, UBS Warburg (2001).

been achievable by a passive investor. Fourth, an index is not constructed by averaging simple returns. In summary, therefore, these returns are—at best—only indicative of how the fund of hedge fund industry performed over time and how this performance compares with traditional investment strategies as well as private equity.

- Simple average annual returns of a large universe of funds of funds suggest that, at least in the past, fund of hedge funds managers have delivered what they promised: equitylike returns with bondlike volatility.
- When comparing the Quellos (1) universe of fund of funds in Table 9.2 with the MSCI World and S&P 500, one can see that the average fund of funds delivers superior risk-adjusted returns. Only for the period from 1995 to 2000 is the Sharpe ratio of 0.64 lower than the Sharpe ratio of MSCI World and S&P 500 of 0.68 and 1.05, respectively.
- The largest underperformance of funds of hedge funds relative to equities occurred in extremely bullish market environments such as 1986 and 1998. However, in strong equity years that follow a negative year (i.e., a "technical rebound year"), there is little underperformance. In 1988 and 1993, for example, when equities performed well after a difficult year, funds of funds did not underperform, or if so, by only a small amount.
- The largest outperformance of funds of funds relative to equities was in 1990. The HFRI Fund of Funds index outperformed the MSCI World total return index by 34.0 percentage points (17.5 percent profit versus 16.5 percent loss). Equities had to deal with war and a commodity inflation induced global recession while most capital markets were volatile. The second most extreme outperformance was in 2001. Calendar year return for the hedge fund index was 2.8 percent while the MSCI World declined by 16.5 percent. Note that volatility is a measure for risk but also a measure for the opportunity set for some absolute return managers.

Figure 9.14 shows a ranking process for the years 1986 to 2001. We have ranked 16 yearly returns for two traditional indexes (equities and bonds) and for two proxies for alternative investment strategies (hedge funds and private equity). Then the first column (MSCI World) was sorted by rank, with the best-performing year first and the worst last. The five best years for all proxies are marked light gray, and the worst five years are black. This ranking process is another way of assessing correlation between the investment vehicles.

The ranking process Figure 9.14 shows that whatever the correlation of alternative investment strategies (AIS) with equities and bonds, it is certainly not negative. The worst years for equities were not stellar years for bonds, or hedge funds, or private equity. In other words, it is not AIS or funds of funds in general that have low correlation to traditional assets. It is only a small

| Year | MSCI World | JPM Global Bonds | Hedge Funds | Private Equity |
|------|-----------|------------------|-------------|----------------|
| 1986 | 1 | 1 | 5 | 7 |
| 1999 | 2 | 16 | 2 | 1 |
| 1998 | 3 | 4 | 14 | 11 |
| 1988 | 4 | 9 | 6 | 5 |
| 1993 | 5 | 6 | 3 | 3 |
| 1995 | 6 | 2 | 11 | 6 |
| 1991 | 7 | 3 | 12 | 12 |
| 1989 | 8 | 8 | 4 | 8 |
| 1987 | 9 | 5 | 1 | 9 |
| 1997 | 10 | 14 | 8 | 4 |
| 1996 | 11 | 11 | 7 | 2 |
| 1994 | 12 | 15 | 16 | 10 |
| 1992 | 13 | 10 | 10 | 14 |
| 2000 | 14 | 13 | 13 | 13 |
| 1990 | 15 | 7 | 9 | 15 |
| 2001 | 16 | 12 | 15 | 16 |

**FIGURE 9.14** Ranking of Traditional Indexes and Alternative Investment Strategies
*Source:* Quellos Group, Venture Economics, Datastream, UBS Warburg (2001).

segment of the AIS universe which has consistent low correlation with traditional investment vehicles. The three worst years for the MSCI World were also the three worst years for private equity. Note that 2000 and 2001 were among the worst years in absolute return space.

## Fund of Hedge Funds Indexes

Figure 9.15 compares two fund of funds indexes with two equity indexes and one bond index. Note that it is debatable whether fund of funds indexes are of great value, given the heterogeneity (methodology as well as product specific) and huge return dispersion of fund of funds managers.

■ Funds of hedge funds outperformed the MSCI World but underperformed the S&P 500.
■ Using different indexes for funds of hedge funds results in slightly differing performance patterns. This indicates differences in fund of funds selection (most managers report figures to only one vendor) and methodology. In addition it supports our notion that the dispersion of returns among fund of funds managers is wide.
■ As shown in Table 9.3, both fund of funds indexes resulted in double-digit returns with volatility similar to that of bond indexes.

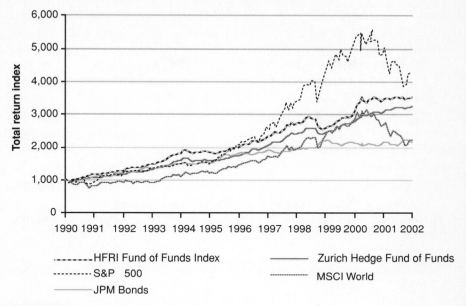

**FIGURE 9.15**  Fund of Hedge Funds Performance
*Source:* Hedge Fund Research, Zurich Capital Markets, Datastream, UBS Warburg (2001).

**Table 9.3**  Fund of Hedge Funds Risk and Return Characteristics

| | # of Monthly Returns | Annual Return | Volatility | Sharpe Ratio (5%) | Worst 1-month Drawdown | Negative Months | Worst 12-month Drawdown | 12-month Drawdown Ended On | Highest 12-month Return |
|---|---|---|---|---|---|---|---|---|---|
| S&P 500 | 144 | 12.85% | 14.54% | 0.54 | −15.64% | 35.4% | −26.63% | Sep-01 | 52.10% |
| MSCI World | 144 | 6.99 | 14.59 | 0.14 | −14.30 | 39.6 | −27.87 | Sep-01 | 33.51 |
| MSCI EAFE | 144 | 2.70 | 17.03 | <0 | −14.97 | 43.1 | −28.27 | Sep-01 | 44.19 |
| MSCI Europe | 144 | 9.15 | 15.19 | 0.27 | −13.42 | 37.5 | −25.49 | Sep-01 | 45.93 |
| JPM Global Government Bonds | 144 | 6.73 | 5.94 | 0.27 | −3.40 | 41.0 | −6.18 | Jan-00 | 20.97 |
| JPM U.S. Government Bonds | 144 | 7.94 | 4.11 | 0.72 | −2.73 | 27.8 | −3.65 | Oct-94 | 17.34 |
| HFRI Fund of Funds Index | 144 | 11.14 | 6.07 | 1.01 | −7.47 | 25.0 | −6.63 | Mar-99 | 33.52 |
| Zurich Hedge Fund of Funds | 144 | 10.34 | 4.56 | 1.17 | −6.40 | 18.8 | −6.21 | Jan-95 | 29.08 |

*Source:* Quellos Group, Hedge Fund Research, Zurich Capital Markets, Venture Economics, Datastream, UBS Warburg (2001).

■ On a Sharpe ratio basis, funds of funds appear superior to both equities and bonds. If we subtract 300 basis points off the return of the fund of hedge funds indexes to account for data imperfections, the Sharpe ratios fall in line with U.S. equity and bond indexes.

■ The worst 12-month return is comparable to developed-market government bonds and a fraction of the losses in equities.

Figure 9.16 shows the returns of two fund of hedge funds indexes along with some equity and bond indexes. Figure 9.17 compares monthly total MSCI World returns in U.S. dollars with the HFRI Fund of Funds index. Both graphs are based on returns from January 1990 to December 2001.*

■ Figure 9.16 is an indication that funds of hedge funds delivered what they promised in the past: equity returns with bond volatility.

■ Note that the correlation with equities is low, but not zero or negative (Figure 9.17).

---

*Compounded annual rate of return for the HFRI Fund of Funds index was 10.7% as of July 2002. This compares with 10.3% and 5.2% for the total return indexes of S&P 500 and MSCI World.

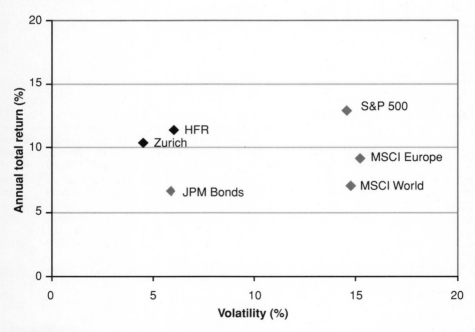

**FIGURE 9.16**   Return versus Volatility
*Source:* Hedge Fund Research, Zurich Capital Markets, Datastream, UBS Warburg (2001).

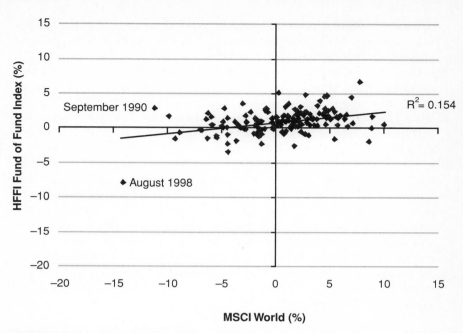

**FIGURE 9.17** MSCI World versus Funds of Hedge Funds
*Source:* Hedge Fund Research, Datastream, UBS Warburg (2001).

■ As shown in Table 9.4, both fund of funds indexes have positive alpha and low beta against the MSCI World. The low beta indicates that returns are generated without being exposed to the equity market as a whole. In other words, the source of returns in funds of hedge funds is not derived from capturing the equity risk premium, as in long-only equity funds.
■ The distribution of returns of both fund of funds indexes are slightly negatively skewed (to the left with a long tail to the left) and leptokurtic (narrow distribution with outliers).
■ Correlation to equities was around 0.45 over a longer period of time and around 0.55 over the five years to 2001. These correlation statistics indicate

**Table 9.4** Statistical Analysis of Fund of Hedge Funds Index Returns

|  | Alpha to JPM Bonds | Beta to JPM Bonds | Skew | Excess Kurtosis | Correlation MSCI World | Correlation JPM Global Bonds |
|---|---|---|---|---|---|---|
| HFRI Fund of Funds Index | 0.79 | 0.16 | −0.52 | 4.18 | 0.42 | −0.08 |
| Zurich Hedge Fund of Funds | 0.74 | 0.15 | −1.19 | 6.93 | 0.50 | −0.03 |

*Source:* Hedge Fund Research, Zurich Capital Markets, Datastream, UBS Warburg (2001).

that most funds of funds are a combination of directional as well as nondirectional hedge fund strategies. Funds of funds dedicated to nondirectional hedge fund strategies have lower correlation statistics.

- Autumn 1998 was a difficult period for most hedge funds. Funds of funds underperformed equities. In most other periods of equity market stress, funds of funds indexes outperformed equities. (See Figure 9.18.)
- Since January 1990 the total return index of MSCI World recorded 14 negative quarters of which the average fall was 7.3 percent. (See Figure 9.19.) This compares with 0.2 percent for the HFRI Fund of Funds index.
- In the positive quarters, funds of funds underperformed the MSCI World by 2.1 percent. In negative quarters, however, the MSCI World was beaten by 7.5 percent. Figure 9.19 reveals the same asymmetry as with most hedge fund strategies in this book: positive performance when the wind comes from behind while preserving capital when the wind changes and becomes a headwind. The definition of risk in absolute terms (total risk as opposed to active risk) by hedge funds and the consequent use of risk management techniques and instruments (to preserve capital as opposed to mimic a market index) are the reasons for the call-option-like asymmetric return pattern.

Figure 9.20 shows how returns have been distributed in the past and compares the historical return distribution with a normal distribution of the

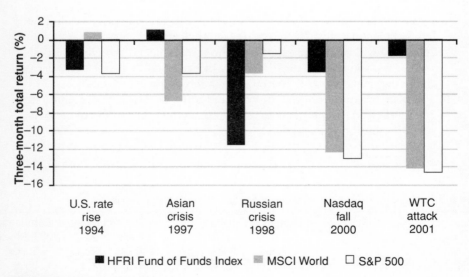

**FIGURE 9.18**  Scenario Analysis
*Source:* Hedge Fund Research, Datastream, UBS Warburg (2001).

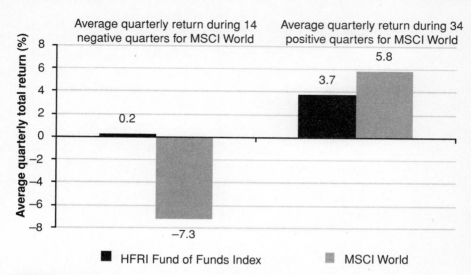

**FIGURE 9.19** Average Negative versus Average Positive Returns
*Source:* Hedge Fund Research, Datastream, UBS Warburg (2001).

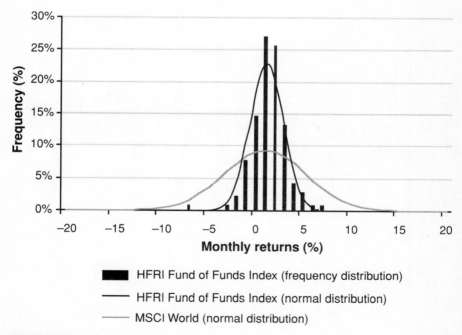

**FIGURE 9.20** Return Distribution
*Source:* Hedge Fund Research, Datastream, UBS Warburg (2001).

HFRI Fund of Funds index and a normal distribution of historical MSCI World returns. Both normal distributions are based on historical mean return and standard deviation of returns. For Figure 9.21 the fund of funds returns were sorted by magnitude in ascending order and compared with the corresponding market returns. This allows one to see in which market environment the extreme positive and negative returns were achieved.

■ Figure 9.20 shows how narrowly around the mean the monthly returns of funds of hedge funds were distributed, especially when compared with equities. There were eight outliers in the fund of funds series, six positive outliers above the 95 percent range and two below the mean of 0.82 percent. Only two outliers were outside the 99 percent range, one on the upside (December 1999) and one on the downside (August 1998).

■ Figure 9.21 shows that there is some concentration between negative returns of funds of funds and declining equity markets. This means that the average fund of funds loses money when equities fall. However, Figure 9.21 also illustrates that funds of hedge funds manage to avoid many

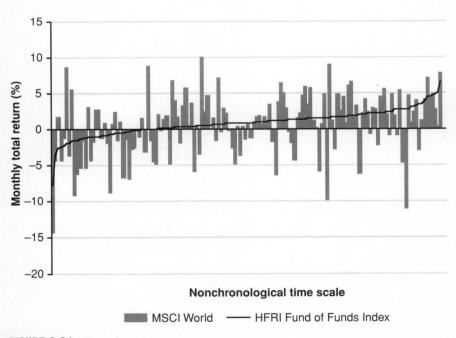

**FIGURE 9.21**  Correlation
*Source:* Hedge Fund Research, Datastream, UBS Warburg (2001).

down months in equities. The chart also shows that fund of funds returns tend to have low volatility compared to equity returns.

## Good Years versus Poor Hedge Fund Years

Table 9.5 shows annual returns for the MSCI World and a selection of hedge fund strategies between January 1990 and June 2001. The best and worst years for the 1990–2000 period are highlighted in black and light gray, respectively.

■ On an absolute basis, 2000 and 2001 belong to the worst years for equities as well as some equity-related hedge fund strategies. Merger arbitrage had one of its best years in 2000 (which is the main reason why the strategy was flooded with new capital). On the one hand this sounds counterintuitive, as 2000 was the year when hedge funds became broadly *en vogue*. On the other hand this could be an indication that some hedge fund strategies are niche strategies and suffer when swamped with capital.
■ The year 1999 was good for most directional hedge fund strategies, while 1998 (Russian default, LTCM) was bad for spread-related strategies. Note that there is a tendency for some years to be uniformly good and others uniformly poor.

## Directional versus Nondirectional Hedge Fund Exposure

As already pointed out in Chapter 5, the most relevant distinction of absolute return strategies is between directional and nondirectional. Unfortunately, the

**Table 9.5**  Annual Total Returns of MSCI World and Selected Hedge Fund Strategies (%)

| | 1990 | 1991 | 1992 | 1993 | 1994 | 1995 | 1996 | 1997 | 1998 | 1999 | 2000 | 2001 | 1990–2001 |
|---|---|---|---|---|---|---|---|---|---|---|---|---|---|
| MSCI World | −16.5 | 19.0 | −4.7 | 23.1 | 5.6 | 21.3 | 14.0 | 16.2 | 24.8 | 25.3 | −12.9 | −16.5 | 7.0 |
| Convertible arbitrage | 2.2 | 17.6 | 16.3 | 15.2 | −3.7 | 19.9 | 14.6 | 12.7 | 7.8 | 14.4 | 14.4 | 13.5 | 11.9 |
| Fixed income arbitrage | 10.8 | 12.9 | 22.1 | 16.6 | 11.9 | 6.1 | 11.9 | 7.0 | −10.3 | 7.4 | 4.8 | 4.5 | 8.6 |
| Equity market-neutral | 15.5 | 15.6 | 8.7 | 11.1 | 2.7 | 16.3 | 14.2 | 13.6 | 8.3 | 10.8 | 14.6 | 6.4 | 11.1 |
| Merger arbitrage | 0.4 | 17.9 | 7.9 | 20.2 | 8.9 | 17.9 | 16.6 | 16.4 | 7.2 | 14.3 | 18.0 | 2.6 | 12.2 |
| Distressed securities | 6.4 | 35.7 | 25.2 | 32.5 | 3.8 | 19.7 | 20.8 | 15.4 | −4.2 | 16.9 | 2.7 | 14.4 | 15.1 |
| Macro | 12.6 | 46.7 | 27.2 | 53.3 | −4.3 | 29.3 | 9.3 | 18.8 | 6.2 | 17.6 | 2.0 | 7.9 | 17.7 |
| Equity hedge | 14.4 | 40.1 | 21.3 | 27.9 | 2.6 | 31.0 | 21.8 | 23.4 | 16.0 | 46.1 | 9.1 | 0.4 | 20.3 |
| Equity nonhedge | −7.2 | 57.1 | 22.8 | 27.4 | 5.1 | 34.8 | 25.5 | 17.6 | 9.8 | 41.8 | −9.0 | 0.7 | 17.3 |
| Emerging markets | −3.4 | 45.4 | 24.4 | 79.2 | 3.4 | 0.7 | 27.1 | 16.6 | −33.0 | 55.9 | −10.7 | 10.8 | 14.3 |
| Managed futures[a] | N/A | N/A | N/A | N/A | 12.0 | −7.1 | 12.0 | 3.1 | 20.6 | −4.7 | 4.3 | 1.9 | 4.9 |

[a]From CSFB/Tremont.
*Source:* Hedge Fund Research, Zurich Capital Markets, Datastream, UBS Warburg (2001).

single fund of funds data did not allow for distinguishing between the two. We had to improvise and calculated two proxies for funds of funds, either biased to directional strategies or biased to nondirectional managers. The two portfolios in Figure 9.22 each comprise five directional and five nondirectional strategies. The portfolios were equally weighted with monthly rebalancing. The two hypothetical hedge fund portfolios were compared with two equity indexes and one global bond index.

In the past, the directional portfolio has compounded at 17.2 percent with 7.8 percent volatility, while the nondirectional portfolio has grown at a rate of 10.9 percent with 2.3 percent volatility. The main point of this illustration is that there are big differences in what a fund of funds manager tries to achieve. The three main distinctions are probably *cash plus*, *balanced*, and *growth*. Cash plus aims for extremely low volatility and, as a result, accepts a return that is only marginally higher (say 3–5 percent) than the risk-free rate. Balanced portfolios are the largest group. A typical return target was

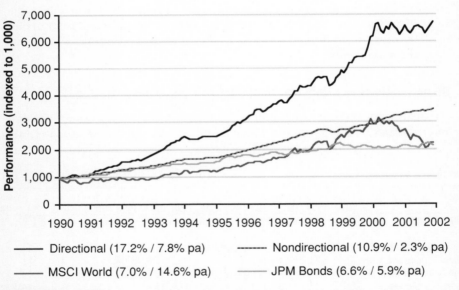

**FIGURE 9.22**   Performance of Hypothetical Directional versus Nondirectional Portfolio
*Note:* Hypothetical directional and nondirectional portfolios were equally weighted and rebalanced monthly. Nondirectional portfolio includes equity market-neutral, statistical arbitrage, CB arbitrage, fixed income arbitrage, and risk arbitrage. Directional portfolio includes equity hedge, equity nonhedge, macro, emerging markets, and market timing. Figures in parentheses show annual return and volatility, respectively.
*Source:* Hedge Fund Research, Datastream, UBS Warburg (2001).

around 12 to 15 percent return during the 1990s. In the low interest rate environment of 2002 this would equal a return target of around 9 to 12 percent above the risk-free rate. The volatility target is around 5 percent.* The third group is shooting for the moon, that is, maximizing returns. This means expected returns are around 20 percent. These fund of funds managers accept a higher volatility in their asset base of around 8 to 10 percent. Note that their target volatility is still far below the volatility of the stock markets in economically developed countries, which have a long-term (100+ years) average volatility of 15 percent and a medium-term (five years) average of 25 percent.†

Table 9.6 shows some detailed performance characteristics of the four time series shown in Figure 9.22. The two proxies for directional and nondirectional funds of funds could be viewed as benchmarks from the fund of funds manager's perspective. A fund of funds manager will compare active portfolio construction bets with a passive (naive) portfolio like those shown in Figure 9.22. By comparing a naive portfolio with the real portfolio, the fund of funds manager is able to assess whether he or she is adding value on a portfolio construction (asset allocation) basis.

## CLOSING REMARKS

It is worth mentioning that most fund of funds managers are averse to volatility and risk. They see themselves as asset managers who want their investors' as well as their own wealth to compound at a reasonable rate with little downside risk. Waking up one autumn morning in 1987 and seeing 30 percent of their wealth destroyed is not, to them, a very intelligent way of managing money. Being simply long any (passively replicable) asset class without an active assessment of total risk and without any downside risk provisions is regarded as a car with no brakes—a risky vehicle. Some would probably even go as far as calling the investment process of a long-only manager "Amish."

---

*The volatility of many long established fund of funds is inversely related with percentage of the proportion of nondirectional strategies available for selection. In 1990, nondirectional strategies were only a small part of the whole investment universe. This did not allow to constructing balanced portfolios with a volatility of less than 5 percent, which is possible today.

†Readers interested in financial anthropology and/or volatility in equity markets might find Jorion and Goetzmann (1999), Dimson et al. (2002), and Ineichen (2000a) of interest.

**Table 9.6**  Performance Comparison Directional, Nondirectional, and Traditional
Asset Classes

|  | Directional Portfolio (1) | Nondirectional Portfolio (2) | MSCI World (3) | JPM Government Bonds (4) |
|---|---|---|---|---|
| Annual return (%) | 17.21 | 10.95 | 6.99 | 6.59 |
| Volatility (%) | 7.84 | 2.34 | 14.59 | 5.94 |
| Sharpe ratio (5%) | 1.56 | 2.54 | 0.14 | 0.27 |
| Adjusted Sharpe ratio[a] | 0.85 | 0.55 | NA | NA |
|  |  |  |  |  |
| Worst 1-month drawdown (%) | −6.73 | −2.59 | −14.30 | −3.40 |
| Negative months (%) | 28.5 | 6.9 | 39.6 | 41.0 |
| Worst 12-month drawdown (%) | −5.74 | 1.23 | −27.87 | −6.18 |
| Best 12-month return (%) | 41.83 | 17.02 | 33.51 | 21.07 |
| Skew | −0.38 | −1.26 | −0.56 | 0.15 |
| Excess kurtosis | 0.48 | 4.39 | 0.65 | 0.00 |
|  |  |  |  |  |
| Correlation to (1) | 1.00 | 0.58 | 0.68 | 0.04 |
| Correlation to (2) | 0.58 | 1.00 | 0.43 | 0.01 |
| Correlation to (3) | 0.68 | 0.43 | 1.00 | 0.29 |

[a]Assuming annual returns are inflated by 300 basis points due to positive biases and volatility is 300 basis points
too low due to valuation drag factors and other data imperfections.
*Source:* Hedge Fund Research, Datastream.

# CHAPTER 10

# Advantages and Disadvantages of Investing in Funds of Hedge Funds

*To us who think in terms of practical use, the splitting of the atom means nothing.*
                                    —Lord Ritchie Calder, British science writer, 1932

## INTRODUCTION

Every business proposition or investment strategy has advantages and disadvantages; or as Alan Greenspan puts it: "Risk, to state the obvious, is inherent in all business and financial activity." The data on hedge fund performance from 1990 to 2001 shows superiority in most aspects, such as risk-adjusted returns and preservation of wealth. However, there is no free lunch, or, using Lo and MacKinlay's (1999) phraseology, there is no free lunch plan. In addition, it would be politically incorrect and inappropriate to agree with Walter Kerr, who was quoted saying: "Half the world is composed of idiots, the other half of people clever enough to take indecent advantage of them." Agreeing with Albert Einstein would be even considered rude: "Only two things are infinite, the universe and human stupidity, and I'm not sure about the former." Wisdom from Galileo Galilei would certainly be more appropriate in terms of political correctness: "I do not feel obliged to believe that the same God who has endowed us with sense, reason, and intellect has intended us to forgo their use."

The superior risk-adjusted performance comes at a cost that is not detected by standard models such as the CAPM. The disadvantages are mainly less regulation (less protection for the investor), less liquidity, and less transparency. Hedge fund investors, therefore, are trading these disadvantages with the advantages (i.e., superior financial performance).

## ADVANTAGES OF FUND OF FUNDS

### Value Added

One of the most important debates with respect to funds of funds is whether they add value. Do they outperform a randomly selected portfolio of, for example, 20 single hedge funds? Or do they outperform the (hypothetical) institutional investors who just recently bought into the case of absolute return investing? Does the fund of funds manager who might have been doing this for decades have a competitive advantage over this hypothetical investor—essentially a rookie—on an after-fee basis?

**Alpha Potential Is Inversely Related to Efficiency**   Chapter 3 defined alpha as "honest pay for a hard day's work." The potential to add value (i.e., generate alpha) is somewhat inversely proportional to the efficiency and/or liquidity of the underlying instruments. Note that there is at least one contradiction in this book: The term "alpha" is used too frequently. On the one hand we argue that hedge funds and funds of hedge funds capture alpha. On the other hand we argue that absolute return managers do not have benchmarks in a classical sense. However, without a benchmark, there is no way to determine alpha quantitatively. The value proposition of the fund of funds manager, therefore, has to be assessed qualitatively.

Figure 10.1 shows conceptually that the more inefficient a market, the larger the potential to add value. Note that one trend in asset management is to replace active mandates with passive mandates. These passive mandates are more cost efficient than active mandates. The more efficient a financial market, the less likely an active manager is going to add value beyond his or her fees and cost structure. That is the reason why passive money management is increasing in markets with a high degree of price efficiency and where there is a passive alternative to active long-only management. The greatest potential for adding value therefore is where information is not freely available, that is, in inefficient markets. There, the potential for active management is larger. Note that there is a difference between adding value in an informationally inefficient market through achieving an informational advantage or adding value by picking up a premium for liquidity

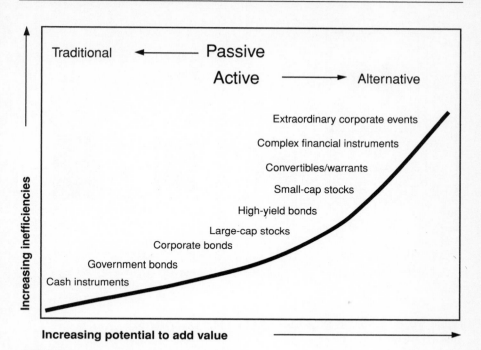

**FIGURE 10.1** Potential Alpha Generation
*Source:* Quellos Group.

in an informationally efficient market. Absolute return managers are involved in both.

**Hedge Fund Selection Is Value Added**    Given that the hedge fund industry is opaque (i.e., inefficient), the more experienced and skilled fund of funds managers should have an edge over the less experienced and skilled. Given the high dispersion of returns between managers (Figure 9.1 in the previous chapter), hedge fund selection is most likely a value-added proposition. Investing with the first quartile of hedge fund managers differs widely from investing with the lowest quartile. Figure 10.2 shows conceptually the expected dispersion of returns of active managers.

The dispersion of returns with alternative (skill-based) strategies is much higher than with market-based strategies where tracking error constraints drive the range of dispersion. The dispersion for passive bond funds, for example, with the same benchmark is probably minimal. Also,

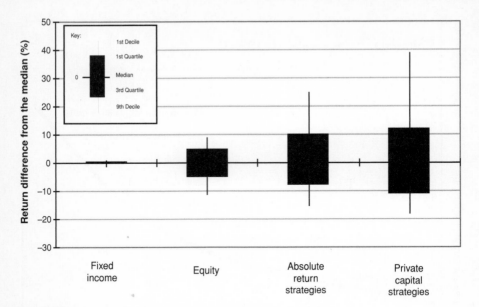

**FIGURE 10.2** Estimated Dispersion of Active Manager Returns
*Source:* Adapted from Quellos Group.

actively managed equity funds on, say, the FTSE All-Share index will have a relatively low dispersion.* A wide dispersion means that the lower quartile will do much worse than the upper quartile. To an investor with no edge this is a risk. To an active investor with a competitive advantage this is an opportunity to add value.

As the number of hedge funds increases, the number of fund of funds managers is also increasing as a result of increasing demand for exposure to

---

*The following is a hypothetical example: You are an equity manager with a bias to value stocks (but not necessarily a pure value manager). Your benchmark is a broad U.S. stock market index. All of a sudden, technology stocks start to rise uncontrollably (as did electronics stocks in the 1960s). The weight of these maverick stocks increases in weight in your benchmark. What do you do? You have two options. Match the weight in the benchmark or not match the weight in the benchmark (i.e., underweight). If you match the benchmark and buy overvalued companies you minimize your career risk as your tracking error will be small. If you do not match the benchmark and the craze continues, you will start losing business after around two or three years of underperformance. This is a conflict of interest: You have an incentive to not buy into the bubble but you also have an incentive to do so. Absolute return managers try to set up a business where such conflicts of interest are ruled out from day one.

hedge funds and falling barriers to entry. The lack of longevity of some of the newer funds of funds is a risk to the investor as is the low level of experience relative to fees by those fund of funds managers. The selection of a fund of hedge funds managers therefore will become more difficult and costly over time.

The accepted wisdom in the hedge fund industry is that it is a demand-led business. But quality hedge funds—those with superior business models, investment philosophies, and risk management capabilities—are actually driven by supply (capacity) rather than demand. There is an imbalance between the demand for hedge fund exposure in general (increasing fast) and the supply of quality hedge funds (increasing slowly).

Quality hedge fund managers are making their funds less attractive to new investors either by increasing fees, increasing redemption periods, or simply closing to new money. It seems that these hedge funds close at a continuously faster pace than normal hedge funds.*

One possible outcome of this supply and demand imbalance is that the quality of the median manager falls. If the current (2001–2002) acceleration of demand for hedge funds should quicken, the deterioration of quality could accelerate and those investors last to jump on the bandwagon will likely invest with the least talented hedge fund managers.† An experienced and established fund of funds manager, however, is probably more likely to invest with the most talented managers. This is a strong value proposition.

## Diversification

Portfolio diversification is probably the main reason why institutional investors invest in AIS in general and hedge funds in particular. The main reason for investing in a portfolio of hedge funds instead of a single hedge fund is diversification. Investing in a portfolio of hedge funds significantly reduces individual fund and manager risk, i.e., nonsystematic risk.

A fund of funds is normally not a random composition of hedge fund

---

*There is a distinction between hard and soft close. Hard close means that a fund is officially as well as unofficially temporarily not taking new funds from any investors. Soft close means that the fund is officially not open to new money. However, an allocation by a large long-term investor is still possible. Note that quality hedge funds are in a position to manage their client bases; not all investors are treated equally. Sophisticated long-term investors are preferred over unsophisticated short-term investors.
†One interesting aspect of the LTCM period is that initial investors had an 18 percent annual return over the life of the firm because LTCM returned more funds to investors in 1997 than it initially had invested. Investors who were paid out fully had an even higher return. However, investors who entered last (i.e., at the peak) lost money. See Lowenstein (2000), p. 224.

strategies. The fund of funds manager aims to deliver more stable returns under most market conditions through portfolio construction, combining the various absolute return strategies. Most often hedge fund portfolios are constructed in a way to reduce the volatility of traditional asset classes such as equities and bonds.

Figure 10.3 shows the efficiency improvements for a traditional portfolio including global equity and bonds by introducing alternative investment strategies or alternative assets. We will discuss portfolio construction in more detail in the next chapter. The traditional efficient frontier in Figure 10.3 looks flatter than in financial textbooks because we use historical data and the annual return of the MSCI World from January 1990 to December 2001 was only around 70 basis points higher than the annual return of the JPM Global Government Bond index.

Figure 10.3 was constructed using the two directional and nondirectional

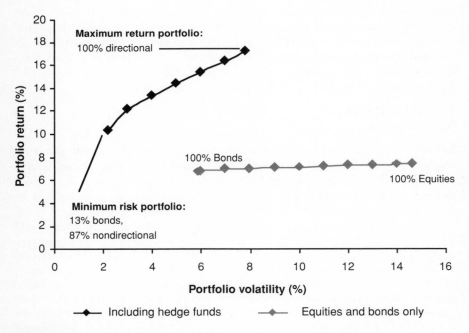

**FIGURE 10.3** Efficient Frontier Excluding and Including Hedge Funds
*Note:* Based on total U.S. dollar returns from January 1990 to December 2001. The new efficient frontier is based on the four portfolios in Figure 9.22 in the previous chapter—MSCI World Index, JPM Global Bond Index, a directional and a nondirectional hedge fund portfolio.
*Source:* Hedge Fund Research, Datastream.

portfolios in the previous chapter. (See Table 9.6.) These two portfolios are naive (passive) proxies for nondirectional and directional fund of hedge funds exposure where manager risk (most of the nonsystematic risk) is diversified. The graph illustrates why Lamm (1999) and other hedge fund marketers think loudly (and provocatively from a traditionalist's point of view) about "why not 100 percent in hedge funds?"\*

It is natural that some market participants get excited by historical performance (if this were not the case, financial marketers would face a stiff headwind under all market conditions). In other words, after a period of superior returns, articles and recommendations to invest 100 percent in the past outperforming asset class appear. See, for example, Thaler and Williamson (1994), and Swank et al. (2002). Both ask "why not 100 percent in equities?" Both papers suggest that it is probably a good idea for long-term investors to invest 100 percent in equities. After all, the U.S. stock market has outperformed U.S. bonds over the course of most of the twentieth century. Thaler and Williamson (1994), for example, argue that "sixty-nine years of history have shown the superiority of stocks." All papers suffer (apart from hindsight bias) from return illusion and the fallacy of time diversification (as discussed in Chapter 1).[†] If there is anything investors should have learned from history, it is that diversification is a laudable concept when dealing with uncertainty.

## Efficient Exposure

Analyzing hedge funds is laborious. Once the information is collected, which in itself is difficult, due diligence begins. What are the annual net returns of the fund? How consistent are the returns, year-on-year? Are audited returns available? What reputation does the principal have, and what objective references (investors, not friends) can the manager provide? How much of the

---

\*In Chapter 4 we argued that there is no objective optimal weight for AIS in general or hedge funds in particular, since investment management involves many qualitative aspects and, most likely, is as much art as science.

†Bierman (1998) responded to the Thaler and Williamson (1994) article: "Assume that the stock market in the years 1996–1999 attracts enormous amounts of new investment funds and that the level of the market has gone up far above 7,000 for the Dow Jones Index. The average P/E ratio is 30. . . . An inflated expectation of growth can lead to inflated stock prices, with the result that it is not desirable to buy stocks, given the opportunity to buy bonds that yield a higher return than the return to be earned on the stock. In theory, stocks can be so overpriced that an investment in stocks can never beat alternative investments." More recently, Arnott and Bernstein (2002a,b) make a strong point that extrapolating the 5 percent equity risk premium from the past is probably not the pinnacle of investment wisdom.

manager's money is at risk in the fund? Are any investor complaints on file with local or national authorities? Does the investing style make sense? Has the fund performed well in relative as well as absolute terms? What is the risk of losing the principal? How leveraged is the fund?

There are between 2,000 and 6,000 hedge funds available.* Certainly, many of them are closed or do not meet certain basic criteria.† However, picking hedge funds from a small, easily accessible universe is probably similar to building a diversified equity portfolio with pulp and paper stocks only.

There are two aspects with respect to staff analyzing and selecting hedge fund managers: finding and hiring. Since the hedge fund industry is relatively young, there is no oversupply of investment professionals who have the necessary skill set and experience to analyze the investment philosophy and quality of business franchise and management. Given the opaqueness of the industry, someone from within the industry will probably have a competitive advantage over someone from outside. Experience is an important variable in ex ante manager evaluation. Finding investment staff is not equal to hiring. Location matters. One could make the point that a plan sponsor located in the suburbs of Budapest will not appeal equally to all investment professionals with hedge fund manager selection experience. In other words, the costs of setting up one's own hedge fund selection process could exceed those charged by fund of funds managers.‡

A fund of funds allows easier administration of widely diversified investments across a large variety of hedge funds. Private and small institutional investors are not able to diversify properly by investing in single hedge funds. The fund of funds approach allows access to a broader spec-

---

*This is a pretty wide spread. The reason is that there is no consensus as to what a "fund" is. Some vendors, to exaggerate the size of their databases, list Class A shares (leverage 2:1) and Class B shares (leverage 3:1) as two separate funds. We would consider these two separate share classes. By this reckoning, the number of tranches joined by pari passu approaches (hot issues/no hot issues, onshore/offshore, leveraged/nonleveraged, U.S. dollars/other currency, etc.) suggest only about 2,000 different funds, with probably 8,000 different share classes.

†For example, McCarthy (2000) notes that from the TASS+ database, which, at the time of the analysis (August 2000), claimed to track over 2,600 funds, only 662 funds met the basic two criteria of $10 million assets under management and a current audited financial statement.

‡Some institutions new to the game will be going the do-it-yourself route. Whether the non-U.S. institution in Budapest has a competitive advantage to a U.S. fund of funds manager with respect to seeing 200 to 300 managers a year lies probably in the eyes of the beholder. The Budapest travel office industry will surely vote for the former. Note that most hedge funds are domiciled in the United States (where there is a concentration around the New York area).

trum of hedge funds than may otherwise be available due to high minimum investment requirements.

## Providers of Capacity

The notion that fund of funds managers are gatekeepers of capacity is not entirely uncontroversial. An established fund of funds manager is quick to spot talent and can secure a certain capacity in a new fund, even when the fund closes for new money. Many hedge fund managers are only soft-closed; they officially announce they are closed but are still open for high-quality investors.

**Most Swords Are Double-Edged**  The term "high-quality investor" is obviously subjective. However, hedge fund managers prefer sophisticated long-term investors who understand the merits and risks of the strategy. This reduces the risk that the investor will pull out of the fund at the worst possible moment. In other words, a hedge fund manager might prefer a professionally managed pension fund over a fund of funds. Although the fund of funds manager might understand the merits of the strategy, this might not necessarily be true for the investors in the fund of funds. In this respect, the capacity argument for fund of funds managers is a double-edged sword.

The capacity argument has been diminishing over time because the allocation from institutional investors into funds of funds has been increasing relative to hot (short-term) money. In other words, a hedge fund manager will distinguish between a fund of funds marketed to retail investors or a fund of funds where the client base is institutional or sophisticated or both.

Every investment decision can be broken down to balancing the advantages and disadvantages. The following section will discuss some of the disadvantages of investing in fund of funds. The main disadvantage is cost.

## DISADVANTAGES OF FUND OF FUNDS

### Double Fee Structure

**Paying the Farmer As Well As the Milkman**  With funds of funds, fees are charged twice. The individual hedge fund collects fees from the fund of funds manager and the fund of funds manager collects additional fees from the distributor or investor. The double fee structure is often seen as a negative aspect of investing in hedge funds. Some investors still regard the fee structure of a single hedge fund as excessive. However, fees are probably positively correlated with skill. An unskilled manager will not be in a position to demand high fees. Liang (1999), for example, finds that average hedge fund returns are positively correlated with incentive fees, fund assets, and the lockup period.

The double fee argument does not relate fees to the value added by the fund of funds manager. If a random selection of hedge funds yields the same gross risk-adjusted returns as the fund of funds approach, then we would have to question the double fee structure. However, we doubt that the hedge fund industry is efficient. Most likely it is quite the opposite. Information is still scarce and costly. Institutions have just begun to think about hedge funds on a grander scale.

In theory, an active fee should be paid on active management and a passive (lower) fee for passive management. The main reason for passive management having lower fees is that the costs of getting exposure to efficient markets such as the U.S. or U.K. stock market have continuously been falling. In other words, an active fee should be charged on exposure that is not available through indexation or other passive investment strategies. Put differently, excess returns attributed to skill (alpha) are scarce and costly while market exposure (beta) is not. Figure 10.4 is an indication why so many traditional long-only management houses are launching hedge fund products.* Fees, literally, went through the roof. Not only is the hedge fund business a high-margin business, but revenues from the newly launched asset management firm also are countercyclical to revenues from the traditional long-only business: When markets go up, so does fee income as the value of the underlying assets increases. When markets fall, fee income from traditional money management falls.† By launching a hedge fund product the asset manager can counter balance the decline in fees. In falling markets, absolute return products come into fashion. Hence, the fall in fees from the traditional business can be balanced through rising demand for hedge fund products.

---

*On a separate note: Some passive asset managers are moving up the slope in Figure 10.4. It is difficult to make a living by charging customers one or two basis points for managing money. This is probably the reason why the passive asset management industry in the United States is somewhat oligopolistic; that is, a few large players together have most of the market share. Only the lowest-cost producers survive the competition. There are essentially three ways to survive with a low-margin product: reduce costs further (mass production), sell more (economies of scale), or increase fees. The first route is hardly possible for index funds (some charge zero fees and make a couple of basis points through securities lending). The second route is what has happened in the United States and the United Kingdom and will most likely happen in continental Europe, where currently most banks offer a low-margin exchange-traded funds (ETF) program (which is unlikely to be sustainable). The third route is also being taken. By introducing some overlay strategy the passive manager is able to add an "active" element to the passive core ("enhanced indexing," "smart indexing," etc.) and sell it at a higher price.
†Revenues actually suffer a double whammy: First, revenues fall as a result of a falling base. Second, the (higher-margin) retail business suffers from redemptions, which normally coincide with a falling market.

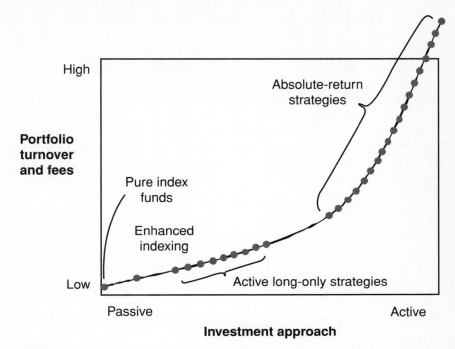

**FIGURE 10.4** Portfolio Turnover and Fees in Relation to Investment Approach

There is normally no passive alternative in inefficient markets. The high fees of hedge funds and the double layer of fees of the fund of funds manager have to be put in context with the value added on an after-fee basis. Exposure to price-efficient markets is most efficiently accessed through passive vehicles such as index funds or total return swaps or any other variant. Exposure to price and informationally inefficient markets do not normally have a passive alternative.

## Lack of Transparency

Some investors find it unnerving not to know what they are investing in when investing in a hedge fund, since transparency is lower compared with traditional managers. Note that there are different types of transparency. The two main types of transparency are with respect to risk of the positions held by the fund and transparency with respect to the investment process. Some refer to the lack of transparency as the "black-box syndrome." One pension fund manager was quoted in asking the (rhetorical) question:

*So you suggest we invest in a venture which is not regulated, its positions and investment philosophy are not transparent, is illiquid and is run by a bunch of 30-year-olds?*[1]

Figure 10.5 shows the results of a survey by Barra Strategic Consulting Group (BSCG) in the United States. The survey is based on over 70 interviews with both investors currently investing in hedge funds and those who do not, including senior executives of corporate and public pension plans, endowments and foundations, insurers, institutional investment consultants, intermediaries, prime brokerage operations, and hedge funds as well as fund of hedge fund managers. According to the survey, the lack of transparency was the primary investor concern.

In some cases, transparency is diminished still further when investing in funds of funds because not all fund of funds managers disclose the names of the funds they invest in. However, quite often fund of funds managers have greater knowledge of the positions of hedge fund managers they invest in than any other investor would have. Hedge fund managers might be more willing

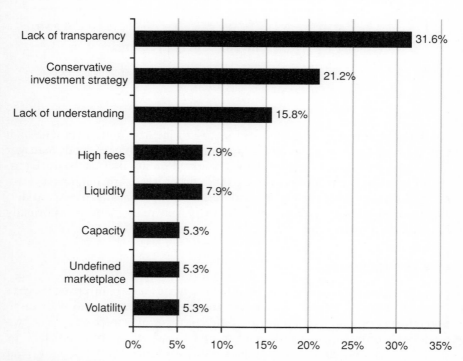

**FIGURE 10.5**   Primary Investor Concerns about Investing in Hedge Funds
*Source:* Barra Strategic Consulting Group (2001).

to disclose information to market participants who do not trade in the same markets and securities as they do.

The Alternative Investment Management Association (AIMA) commissioned Capital Market Risk Advisors, Inc. (CMRA) to conduct a survey on the issues of risk management and transparency due for release during 2002. The survey was conducted among institutional investors, fund of funds managers, and hedge fund managers. The survey was not available when this book went to press. However, AIMA announced some findings with respect to transparency:[2]

- First, 86 percent of investors indicate that transparency is an issue in selecting hedge funds and funds of funds.
- While 69 percent of investors are satisfied with the information they receive from their hedge funds and funds of funds, 29 percent of investors have had requests for information turned down by the hedge funds and funds of funds in which they invest.
- Disclosing detailed position level information is deemed to compromise the performance of a hedge fund "significantly" or "materially" by only 24 percent of funds of funds and 36 percent of hedge funds.
- Only 7 percent of funds of funds and 4 percent of individual hedge funds indicated that potential investors had declined to invest based on lack of transparency, but 64 percent of investors claim they have declined to invest.

Here is an attempt to challenge this disadvantage: How many hedge funds does the reader know by name? Hedge funds are not like stocks with respect to brand recognition. Every investor, or every person for that matter, has knowledge of companies because they affect our daily lives. Hedge funds, in most cases, do not. The industry itself is opaque to most investors. Even an investor who can name 20 different hedge funds still only knows a fraction of the industry. Fund of funds managers specialize and operate in a field where knowledge is attainable only at high cost. Allowing a blindfolded chimpanzee to throw darts at a list of 2,000 managers is unlikely to produce satisfactory results.

Asset management firms that specialize in alternative investment strategies in general or hedge funds in particular are not usually household names. This is a disadvantage for two reasons: unfamiliarity and information cost.

**Unfamiliarity** In the most general sense, everything else being equal, something unfamiliar has more subjective risk than something familiar; that is, uncertainty is perceived as higher. Unfamiliarity is not a very scientific and sophisticated way of expressing risk. Note, however, that LTCM was, without a shadow of a doubt, the most scientific and sophisticated risk manager

with honors and high-flying reputations in both academia as well as Wall Street. The point is that it is probably healthy to practice some degree of conservatism to anything new, even if we cannot model it econometrically. Some people call the lack of conservatism in combination with hubris the "Titanic effect." Or as Warren Buffett puts it: "Risk comes from not knowing what you're doing."

The unfamiliarity aspect is a disadvantage for some fund of funds manager when they pitch for institutional mandates and face competition from traditional asset management firms. Wall Street wisdom describes this as the "IBM effect": "No one ever got sacked for investing in IBM." In John Maynard Keynes' view this means "worldly wisdom teaches us that it is better for reputation to fail conventionally than to succeed unconventionally." The point is that an administrator at an institution might prefer an established brand over a no-name, irrespective of the objective superiority of the latter over the former. If IBM falls in price it's okay because everyone else is losing money as well.*

Swensen (2000) points out that investment success stems from contrarian impulses nearly by definition. However, he also makes notice of the extraordinary challenges within an institutional framework: "In an institutional environment with staff and committees and boards, nearly insurmountable obstacles exist. Creating a decision-making framework that encourages unconventional thinking constitutes a critical goal for fund fiduciaries."[3] As John Maynard Keynes put it: "The real difficulty in changing any enterprise lies not in developing new ideas, but in escaping from the old ones." According to a survey by Barra Strategic Consulting Group (2001), over 75 percent of the surveyed plans without current allocations to hedge funds are not even considering future allocations. This is an indication that either there are "insurmountable obstacles" or the risk of not investing with IBM is too large (disadvantageous risk/reward trade-off).

Many fund of funds managers are not well known to the decision maker in an institutional setup. However, today there is a core of asset management firms that have a track record of five years or longer. Given that the hedge fund industry is newer than the traditional long-only industry, investors are familiar with the large asset management institutions but unfamiliar with the newer alternative asset management firms.

Going forward we will probably witness combinations of traditional asset management firms with niche alternative asset management firms in general and funds of hedge funds in particular. That way the traditional asset

---

*Note that moving with the crowd (index hugging, peer-group orientation, etc.) is not irrational behavior. A risk-averse plan sponsor or trustee may conclude that the potential costs of failing with an unusual portfolio or investment process exceed the potential benefits of unconventional success.

manager can market a product where demand is increasing and margins are high, while the fund of funds manager gets distribution power.

**Cost**   Due diligence is costly. The cost of information in the hedge fund industry is high. The main reason is the persistent opaqueness of the industry. An institutional investor will have to go through a lengthy due diligence process before the fiduciaries and plan sponsors are prepared to invest the OPM (other people's money) they were entrusted to manage. The decision-making process for noninstitutional investors is faster and less rigid (i.e., cheaper) than it is for fiduciaries.

## Institutionalization

The lack of transparency in the hedge fund industry is not unrelated to the institutionalization process that has started around the year 2000, essentially when equity markets started declining. Anson (2001b) argues that "institutionalization" means three things: transparency, an investment process, and relative returns. He rightly points out that institutions face a dilemma because the flexibility with respect to institutionalization was what made hedge funds so attractive in the first place.

Anson argues that institutional investors "should be willing to accept economic risk but not process risk." This is a point of view that is not shared by all professionals in the investment community. Process risk is by definition idiosyncratic, as Anson also points out. However, if institutional investors should not bear process risk the logical consequence is that they should not be investing in companies. Hedge funds, like listed companies, are organizations where the owners try to make a profit by putting their competitive advantage to work.

The first segmentation of financial risk is normally between systematic risks and nonsystematic risks (idiosyncratic risks). The idiosyncratic risks (of which process risk is a part) can be neutralized through diversification. The systematic risk cannot be immunized through diversification (but can be hedged if need be). In other words, process risk is inherent in any type of investment in organizations irrespective of what the nature of business is. The logic of Anson (2001b) is as follows:

> *Process risk is not fundamental risk. It is an idiosyncratic risk of the hedge fund manager's structure and operations. Generally, it is not a risk that institutions wish to bear. Nor is it a risk to be compensated. Furthermore, how would an institution, or the financial markets for that matter, go about pricing the process risk of a hedge fund manager? It can't be quantified, and it can't be calibrated. Therefore, there is no way to tell whether an institutional investor is being properly compensated for risk.*

This is a strange point of view. Replace the term "hedge fund manager" with "Cisco," "Microsoft," or any other company. It is true that the investor does not get compensated for holding only Cisco or Microsoft in his or her portfolio. This is the whole point about diversification: Investors should not be exposed to idiosyncratic risk; they should diversify. Entrepreneurs, in contrast, *should* be exposed to idiosyncratic risk, primarily to focus their minds and straighten their incentives.

It is very unlikely that Mark Anson is alone with this point of view. A more likely scenario is that the views expressed represent the consensus and any opposing view does not. The Barra Strategic Consulting Group (2001) survey found that 75 percent of the surveyed pension plans without current allocations to hedge funds are not even considering future allocations. The survey states what was referred to earlier as the IBM effect—that there remains a significant reluctance to invest in hedge funds, despite interest in other alternative investments like private equity. The "fear factor" is explained by pension fund directors feeling a large amount of professional risk in possibly being associated with "the next LTCM".* This nonfinancial risk is not enough to balance the modest diversification benefits of a small allocation to hedge funds.

## Limited Liquidity

**Liquidity on a Single Hedge Fund Level**   Some investors might find comfort in the fact that most hedge fund managers have a large portion of their net wealth tied to the fund, and thus the same long redemption periods as the investor. A more pragmatic argument for low liquidity is the fact that hedge funds exploit inefficiencies and therefore are by definition operating in markets that are less liquid than the bluest of blue chips. In other words, exploiting inefficiencies by its nature involves some degree of illiquidity. The main

---

*In the United Kingdom there is the somewhat related "Nick Leeson effect." Fear is still in the bones of some pension fund trustees with respect to derivatives after Mr. Leeson brought down one of the oldest remnants of the British empire: Barings Bank. The failure of Barings Bank is probably the most often cited derivatives disaster. While the futures market had been the instrument used by Nick Leeson to play the zero-sum game (someone made a lot of money being short the Nikkei futures Mr. Leeson was buying), it is very unlikely that the futures contracts traveled into the famous "88888" account on their own. The losses can be attributed to a complete lack of internal control, lack of understanding by senior management of how futures worked, failure of management to properly reconcile their trading positions, and fraud. In other words, the failure is pure idiosyncratic risk, which investors should immunize themselves against through diversification.

reason for a hedge fund to have a lock-up period however is the benefit of a stable capital structure. There are many opportunities to exploit in periods of market distress. As Kenneth Griffith from Citadel puts it:

> *If you're Avis, and the lights suddenly go off at Hertz, you had better be in a position to make a lot of money.*[4]

**Liquidity on a Fund of Hedge Funds Level**   Limited liquidity in a fund of funds is certainly a disadvantage, especially when compared with single hedge funds offering superior liquidity or traditional investments offering daily withdrawal/redemption terms. Limited liquidity comes with a cost, and this cost ought to be compensated with proper returns for the investor. Earlier we examined the issue of liquidity of fund of funds managers in relation to performance. Skillful fund of funds managers should not only be able to construct portfolios that outperform, but also be able to target a liquidity horizon that is optimal both for hedge fund investments as well as the needs of the investors in the fund of funds.

Some funds of funds nonetheless offer opportunities for withdrawal on a weekly or daily basis, though mainly with penalties attached. A fund of funds manager who aggressively provides liquidity free of charge should be viewed with suspicion. Nonmarketable securities are by definition illiquid. The suspicion is based on two assumptions:

1. A fund of funds manager could be investing in hedge funds that are trading only in liquid markets. These funds are traditionally directional and their performance more volatile. One could view this as negative because market inefficiencies are by definition to be found in smaller, less liquid, and less efficient markets. Long-term investing in hedge funds, therefore, is to some extent about picking up a liquidity premium.
2. Beggars can't be choosers. It is very unlikely that the most talented managers in the alternative investment arena make compromises, at least not at this stage in the cycle. We assume these managers can resist the temptation of being part of a retail product that offers high-frequency (e.g., daily or weekly) liquidity (and real-time position level transparency).

## No Learning-by-Doing Effect

A further disadvantage of investing in a fund of funds instead of investing in hedge funds directly is a lack of knowledge transfer. One could argue that, at the most general level, investing involves a learning-by-doing effect. Mark McCormack's classic *What They Don't Teach You at Harvard Business School* could have easily been addressed to investment management as opposed to marketing sport celebrities. Success in investment management is to some extent a function of experience.*

This argument has two sides to it. Many institutions use funds of funds to get acquainted with the asset class, for example by investing some of the allocation with the fund of funds manager and, at the same time, investing with the hedge fund manager directly. This implies that the fund of funds manager is part fund manager and part adviser. The investor, therefore, benefits from the experience of the fund of funds manager in the field of alternative investments.

## CONCLUSION

The hedge fund industry is inefficient as information on managers is not available to all market participants at the same time and at the same price. This means a fund of funds manager with a competitive advantage should be able to add value through manager selection. However, fees for active management should be reciprocally related to market efficiency. As markets become efficient, fees go down.

The hedge fund industry is heterogeneous. This means different hedge fund strategies have different *expected* returns, volatilities, and correlation characteristics. Unlike with equities, portfolio volatility can be reduced to below 5 percent through portfolio construction. In portfolio construction it is expected return, volatility, and correlation that matter (although historical numbers are so much more practical to use). A fund of funds manager is probably more likely to estimate return, volatility, and correlation, and is therefore in a position to construct more efficient portfolios.

The main disadvantage of investing in funds of funds is the double fee structure. Fund of funds managers charge a fee on top of the fee structure of the hedge fund manager. However, investors should weigh the double fee structure with the value added of the fund of funds manager. Given that the hedge funds industry is still opaque and information gathering not necessarily

---

*The counterargument to this notion is that from 1995 until March 2000 inexperienced investors loading up on Internet stocks were outperforming the establishment, which, to a large extent, thought that the market was overpriced. Most seasoned investment veterans probably agreed with Alan Greenspan and Robert Shiller that the market was characterized by "irrational exuberance." That was in December 1996, many years before the peak. Some equity long/short managers went out of business because they had put on the no-brainer trade too early (i.e., sold technology stocks and bought value stocks in 1998 or 1999) and could not finance themselves through to March 2000 when markets reversed and the trade became profitable.

an efficient process, there are market participants with a competitive advantage and those with a competitive disadvantage. A well-established fund of funds with proper infrastructure and experienced investment professionals where the partners have their interests aligned with those of their investors does add value.

At one stage in the future, fund of funds margins could contract. One of the newer developments in the hedge fund industry in the 2000–2002 period was single-strategy hedge funds converting into multistrategy managers, as briefly mentioned in Chapter 5. A multistrategy hedge fund is a hedge fund involved in more than just one strategy. A multistrategy hedge fund is some sort of hybrid between a single-strategy hedge fund and a fund of funds. Being invested in more than one strategy means diversifying the source of return. One could argue that funds of funds also diversify the source of return as do multistrategy hedge funds. However, the latter do it for only one layer of fees.

# CHAPTER 11

# The Alpha in Funds of Hedge Funds

*As an investor, as long as you understand something better than
others, you have an edge.*

—George Soros

## INTRODUCTION

In an industry that lacks perfect competition (e.g., non-negligible barriers to
entry, unequal dissemination of information, etc.) there are bound to be some
market players with an edge over the competition. In this chapter we try to
first define and then isolate the factors that differentiate the top-quartile organizations from all the rest.

## PORTFOLIO MANDATE AND INVESTMENT PROCESS

### Portfolio Mandate

Different fund of funds managers have different objectives. Different portfolio designs will serve different purposes. Given the breadth of the hedge fund
industry it is likely that fund of funds managers might specialize in a certain
investment style. Some fund of funds managers have a bias toward nondirectional absolute return strategies, whereas other managers have an implicit or
explicit bias toward directional hedge fund managers and strategies. The dif-

ference between directional and nondirectional is probably the most general classification of the strategies in the hedge fund industry.

## Investment Process

Once the fund of funds manager has set up the business and knows what objectives are to be met, the actual investment process begins. At the most general level there are two variables and two processes. The two variables are the hedge fund managers (i.e., portfolio constituents) and the apportionment of capital to these constituents (i.e., allocation). The two processes are a selection and a monitoring process. An important aspect is that these two variables and processes are dynamically interrelated.

Figure 11.1 shows one way the investment process of the fund of funds manager can be graphically illustrated. It is important to note that the fund of funds manager adds value on both levels: manager as well as portfolio level.

As discussed in Chapter 10, the market inefficiency, which essentially justifies a fee for an active manager, lies within the opaqueness of the informa-

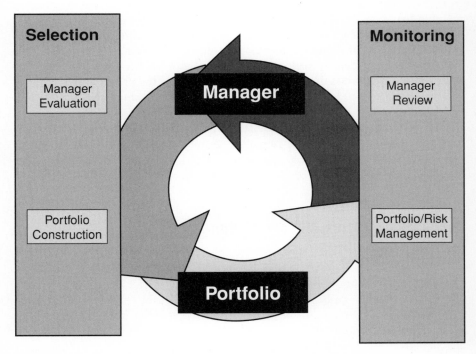

**FIGURE 11.1** Dynamic Investment Process of Fund of Funds Manager
*Source:* UBS Warburg (2001).

tion flow in the hedge fund industry. It is the manager level where the greatest barriers to entry are for new managers selecting and managing hedge funds. However, a fund of funds manager also adds value on the portfolio level (asset allocation). The portfolio construction is not just about entering some historical return, volatility, and correlation figures into an optimizer. Portfolios are constructed by entering *estimates* of return, volatility, and correlation figures into an optimizer and, at the same time, matching investors' objectives with the portfolio. It is hard to imagine that all market participants are in the position to obtain estimates for future strategy characteristics equally well. For arguing that fund of funds managers do not add value (as some investors do) one has to believe that the rules of the game change in an unpredictable fashion. This, however, is not the case. Changing the portfolio based on changes in the subindustry is a judgmental call. Some will do a better job than others. For example: In 2000 there was huge inflow into risk arbitrage as there is a certain amount of hot money that buys the current darlings of the market. In addition, the global economies were heading into recession. The question at the time was not whether there will be recession but whether it will be U-shaped or V-shaped. Nevertheless, the future prospects for risk arbitrage were changing. On the one hand the merger frenzy of the late 1990s bull market was coming to an end. On the other hand large flows swamped the subcategory and, as a result, narrowed spreads of announced deals. In other words, historical time series were not extremely valuable in a portfolio construction or management process. And the question is: Who else is in the position to see tidal waves and regime shifts early on in the process, other than a team of experienced fund of funds managers who do nothing else but manage hedge fund money?

The following section discusses the aspects with respect to the selection and monitoring process of the single hedge fund manager—the portfolio constituents. After that we look into issues of risk management and portfolio construction—the asset allocation of a portfolio of hedge funds.

## MANAGER SELECTION AND MONITORING

### Manager Evaluation

Manager identification and evaluation is probably the key to success. Investing in hedge funds is essentially a people and relationship business. By allocating funds to a manager or a group of managers, the investor expects to participate in the skill of the manager or managers and not necessarily in a particular investment strategy or a mechanical process. Allocating funds to a convertible arbitrage manager, for example, does not necessarily imply participation in the classic trade of buying the bond and managing the delta through selling the stock. The expectation is to participate in inefficiencies and opportunities in the convertible bond (CB) market where a skilled and experienced manager has a competitive advantage over the less skilled, that is, the rest of the market.*

Manager evaluation is not only the most important step but also the most cumbersome. Commercial databases on hedge funds are a starting point but are incomplete. The difficulty and effort of collecting information probably puts in place significant barriers to enter the fund of funds business in a serious entrepreneurial and institutional investor compliant fashion. Put differently, this means that fund of funds managers with an operating history of a couple of years might have a competitive advantage over those fund of funds managers who entered the industry recently. It should be patently obvious that a fund of funds dealing with a limited opportunity set because of a lack of focus on manager identification also faces limits on its performance potential.

Due diligence is the single most important aspect of the investment process for an investor investing in a hedge fund directly or a fund of hedge funds. Due diligence includes quantitative excellence as well as qualitative judgment. Quantitative analysis of (imperfect) data is incomplete. Qualitative judgment is at least as important as quantitative analysis. This view is probably the consensus in the alternative asset management industry. Due diligence includes a thorough analysis of the fund as a business and a validation of manager information, and covers operational infrastructure, financial and legal documentation, affiliates, investment terms, investor base, reference checks, and so on. Along with many others, Martino (1999) argues that "the due diligence process is an art, not a science" and also stresses the point of prudence and integrity in a loosely regulated market where the hedge fund structure provides a manager with a great deal of freedom. As Warren Buffett puts it:

---

*With respect to capacity of a strategy, the consensus view is that inefficiencies disappear if more capital chases the same inefficiency. This is probably true. However, what is often overlooked is that a flood of new capital creates new inefficiencies itself. A good example is risk arbitrage. A lot of capital went into risk arbitrage after the stunning M&A year of 2000. The fresh capital was to some extent coming from less experienced risk arbitrage managers or long/short equity managers feeling lucky (after making money on the Mannesmann/Vodafone deal). This caused spreads of announced deals to narrow much more quickly. For experienced risk arbitrage managers this opened up opportunities to "Chinese" a deal (buy acquirer and sell target) as opposed putting the trade on the other way around. This is one of the reasons why manager selection is key and passively putting on risk arbitrage trades is a questionable proposition.

*In evaluating people, you look for three qualities: integrity, intelligence, and energy. And if you don't have the first, the other two will kill you.*[1]

The due diligence done by the fund of funds manager is part of the value proposition. Chances are that the fund of funds manager adds more value by avoiding the losers than by picking winners. Whether a fund of funds manager is able to pick the best manager is, by definition, uncertain. As most bottom-up equity fund managers will claim to have superior stock picking skill, most fund of funds managers will equally claim to have superior hedge fund picking skill.* However, an investor can assess the due diligence capabilities of the fund of funds manager in advance by assessing the level of experience of the fund of funds managers in the field of absolute return strategies. This is the reason why most fund of funds managers will list the fund managers' number of years in the industry in the marketing prospectus.

There is no definitive guide to manager evaluation. Here is an incomplete list of some factors:

■ Intangibles: integrity, lifestyle, and attitude.
■ Strategy: identifiable opportunity sets, embedded market risks, definition of investment process, market knowledge in defined strategy.
■ Experience: portfolio management ability, risk assessment and management ability, strategy implementation, experience of different market conditions, understanding of the impact of market flows, overall trading savvy.
■ Assets: size (critical mass versus manageable amount), ability to manage growth, quality of investors.
■ Operation: back office infrastructure and reliability; fee structure; decision and execution process; quality, stability, compensation, and turnover of staff.

## Manager Review

Manager review is a dynamic and iterative process. The due diligence process never ends. As mentioned before, this is probably the consensus view among investors and hedge fund professionals.

What is amazing is that the value added of a fund of funds manager is often put in doubt (or the extra layer of fees determined as excessive and/or un-

---

*This is slightly unfair, because the hedge fund picker is operating in an opaque and inefficient market whereas a stock picker in, say, U.S. large caps is operating in a transparent and price-efficient market. The opportunity to add value is, by definition, larger in an inefficient market than in an efficient market. The value propositions of the two, therefore, are diametrically opposed.

necessary). This is a paradox: On the one hand, investors agree that seeing hundreds of hedge fund managers on a regular basis is important, yet on the other hand they postulate that fund of funds managers do not add value on an after-fee basis. Who else is in the position of doing the due diligence other than experienced and prudent investment professionals who are in the loop of the information flow? The industry itself is opaque; information does not flow efficiently, and so scarce resources must be expended to find and analyze the information. We doubt that the information advantage of a top-quartile fund of funds manager over a less informed investor will deteriorate anytime soon.*

## PORTFOLIO SELECTION AND MONITORING

### Portfolio Construction

Most portfolio construction will probably blend bottom-up (manager selection) and top-down (asset allocation) approaches. Different fund of funds managers will have different biases. These biases can be in terms of geographical focus, investment style, or strategy. Some managers put more weight on their personal network in the industry, while others have a more econometrical approach to portfolio construction. There are many wrong ways of approaching portfolio construction. There are many potential conflicts of interest which have to be addressed. However, there is no single right way of constructing a portfolio of hedge funds. Portfolios constructed in mean-variance space are a starting point but imperfect due to liquidity issues and the higher moment risk characteristics of some absolute return strategies.

As outlined earlier, the mandate and purpose of the portfolio determine the first step. For example, a fund of funds manager who believes that market timing in efficient capital markets does not work is tempted to ignore commodity trading adviser (CTA) funds from the start, despite their potentially attractive diversification features.†

---

*In addition, there are some doubts whether professionals with hedge fund experience will find employment in a large private or public institution competitively challenging and financially rewarding. This will continue to give fund of funds managers a competitive advantage over those market (less experienced) participants who pick hedge funds themselves.

†Caglayan and Edwards (2001) examined the returns of CTAs and hedge funds in bull and bear markets. They found that CTAs have higher returns in bear markets than hedge funds, and generally have an inverse correlation with stock returns in bear markets. Hedge funds typically exhibit a higher positive correlation with stock returns in bear markets than in bull markets. The authors also found that three hedge fund styles—market-neutral, event-driven, and global macro—provide fairly good downside protection, with more attractive returns over all markets than commodity funds.

The following section examines some aspects of hedge fund portfolio construction, (i.e., asset allocation). In the absence of perfect foresight, historical data was used. Table 11.1 shows the historical returns, volatility, and correlation of a selection of hedge fund strategies.

■ Fixed income arbitrage has the lowest off-diagonal average correlation of 0.15 from the selection in Table 11.1. This is intuitive, as fixed income arbitrageurs (most often) trade in spreads not related to the equity market.
■ Equity market-neutral has lower volatility, lower correlation, and lower returns than long/short equity (equity hedge). Off-diagonal average correlation with other hedge fund strategies in Table 11.1 was 0.16.
■ Equity nonhedge and emerging markets have higher volatility, equal correlation, and lower returns than equity hedge. This means these strategies add little value in terms of efficiency improvement in mean-variance space.

Table 11.2 shows three hedge fund portfolios along with four equity indexes and one global government bond index. The three hedge fund portfolios were optimized for lowest volatility, 5 percent volatility, and highest return, and were rebalanced monthly. Again historical data was used as a proxy for expectations. Calculations were based on monthly U.S. dollar total returns between January 1990 and December 2001.

■ The minimum risk portfolio* underperformed the maximum return portfolio in the years from 1990 to 1999 and outperformed in 2000 and

---

*The terms minimum risk portfolio, minimum volatility portfolio, and minimum variance portfolio were used interchangeably to describe the portfolio with the lowest possible expected volatility in mean-variance space. The terms could be misleading as, in the real world, risk is not equal to volatility and variance.

**Table 11.1**   Return, Volatility, and Correlation for a Selection of Hedge Fund Strategies

| Strategy | Return | Volatility | Equity Market-Neutral | Convertible Arbitrage | Fixed Income Arbitrage | Risk Arbitrage | Distressed Securities | Macro | Equity Hedge | Equity Non-hedge | Emerging Markets |
|---|---|---|---|---|---|---|---|---|---|---|---|
| Equity market-neutral | 11.1% | 3.3% | 1 | | | | | | | | |
| Convertible arbitrage | 11.9 | 3.4 | 0.14 | 1 | | | | | | | |
| Fixed income arbitrage | 8.6 | 4.8 | 0.06 | 0.14 | 1 | | | | | | |
| Risk arbitrage | 12.2 | 4.6 | 0.14 | 0.45 | −0.01 | 1 | | | | | |
| Distressed securities | 15.2 | 6.4 | 0.16 | 0.59 | 0.37 | 0.50 | 1 | | | | |
| Macro | 17.8 | 8.9 | 0.21 | 0.40 | 0.12 | 0.28 | 0.46 | 1 | | | |
| Equity hedge | 20.3 | 9.3 | 0.31 | 0.47 | 0.08 | 0.43 | 0.58 | 0.60 | 1 | | |
| Equity nonhedge | 17.3 | 14.9 | 0.16 | 0.47 | 0.12 | 0.49 | 0.63 | 0.58 | 0.89 | 1 | |
| Emerging markets | 14.3 | 16.3 | 0.06 | 0.45 | 0.29 | 0.43 | 0.66 | 0.61 | 0.64 | 0.70 | 1 |
| | | | | | | | | | | | |
| Off-diagonal correlation | | | 0.16 | 0.39 | 0.15 | 0.34 | 0.50 | 0.41 | 0.50 | 0.51 | 0.48 |

*Note:* Calculations are based on monthly U.S. dollar total returns January 1990 to December 2001. The off-diagonal correlation measures the average correlation of one subject with all subjects in the correlation matrix except itself (correlation of 1).
*Source:* Hedge Fund Research, author's own calculations.

**Table 11.2** Mean-Variance Optimal Hedge Fund Portfolios versus Selected Traditional Indexes

| | Skill-Based | | | Market-Based | | | | |
|---|---|---|---|---|---|---|---|---|
| | Minimum Risk Portfolio | 5%- Volatility Portfolio | Maximum Return Portfolio | MSCI World | S&P 500 | MSCI EAFE | MSCI Europe | JPM Global Government Bonds |
| Return (%) | 11.60 | 15.64 | 20.36 | 6.99 | 12.85 | 2.70 | 9.15 | 6.59 |
| Volatility (%) | 2.43 | 5.00 | 9.24 | 14.66 | 14.57 | 17.06 | 15.26 | 5.90 |
| Sharpe ratio (5%) | 2.72 | 2.13 | 1.66 | 0.14 | 0.54 | <0 | 0.27 | 0.27 |
| Worst month (%) | −2.93 | −5.93 | −7.96 | −14.30 | −15.64 | −14.97 | −13.42 | −3.35 |
| Worst month (date) | Aug. 1998 | Aug. 1998 | Aug. 1998 | Aug. 1998 | Aug. 1998 | Sep. 1990 | Aug. 1998 | Feb. 1999 |
| Worst 12 months (%) | 0.91 | −0.66 | −4.88 | −32.67 | −30.96 | −33.23 | −29.42 | −6.37 |
| Worst 12 months (date, 12m to) | Jan. 1995 | Jan. 1995 | Mar. 2001 | Sep. 2001 | Sep. 2001 | Sep. 2001 | Sep. 2001 | Jan. 2000 |
| Skew | −1.28 | −0.28 | −0.05 | −0.56 | −0.65 | −0.26 | −0.62 | 0.15 |
| Excess kurtosis | 5.21 | 2.12 | 1.28 | 0.65 | 1.16 | 0.48 | 0.68 | 0.00 |
| Correlation MSCI World (all) | 0.41 | 0.59 | 0.59 | 1.00 | 0.84 | 0.94 | 0.87 | 0.29 |
| Correlation JPM Global Gvt. Bonds | 0.04 | 0.06 | 0.07 | 0.29 | 0.15 | 0.35 | 0.33 | 1.00 |
| Negative months (%) | 8.8 | 20.4 | 25.5 | 39.6 | 35.4 | 43.1 | 37.5 | 41.0 |
| Average monthly return (%) | 0.95 | 1.31 | 1.63 | 0.56 | 1.01 | 0.22 | 0.73 | 0.53 |
| Average positive monthly return (%) | 1.09 | 1.91 | 2.77 | 3.27 | 3.32 | 3.11 | 3.05 | 0.91 |
| Average negative monthly return (%) | −0.56 | −1.02 | −1.70 | −3.57 | −2.53 | −4.19 | −2.81 | −0.04 |

*Source:* Hedge Fund Research, Datastream, UBS Warburg (2001).

2001. The underperformance ranged from 79 basis points in 1994 to 3,250 basis points in 1999. The outperformance in 2000 and 2001 was 435 basis points and 735 basis points, respectively.

■ The three hedge fund portfolios have much higher Sharpe ratios than the market-based strategies. If risk were equal with volatility of returns and, therefore, the Sharpe ratio a measure for risk-adjusted returns, the hedge fund portfolios would be superior by a wide margin.

■ The worst monthly drawdown in the 12-year period was August 1998 except for bonds and the MSCI EAFE index. This implies that in a stress-test scenario, correlation moves toward 1 for all portfolios. However, the worst monthly loss for the hedge fund portfolios is a fraction of the equity indexes.

■ The worst 12-month drawdown for the equity indexes ended in September 2001. It is worth pointing out that the worst drawdowns for the three hedge fund portfolios occur at different times than those from equities despite the maximum return portfolio having a strong long bias. The maximum return portfolio has its worst 12-month drawdown ending in March 2001 (after the Internet bubble had burst) and the minimum risk portfolio in January 1995 (after a dismal 1994).

■ Excess kurtosis is highest for the minimum risk portfolio, which constitutes only strategies based on a spread (arbitrage strategies). In the rare event of all the spreads blowing up at the same time, these strategies are prone to outliers on the left-hand side of the return distribution. In other words, spread risk has a nonsystematic component (for example deal risk in risk arbitrage) and a systematic component. Nonsystematic spread risk can by immunized through diversification. The systematic portion of the exposure to spreads is similar to continuously being short index put options.*

■ The excess kurtosis of the maximum return portfolio (100 percent in equity hedge) is similar to that of the S&P 500. Our previously raised concerns regarding the practicability of the Sharpe ratio as measure for risk-adjusted returns is less material for the maximum return portfolio than it is for the minimum risk portfolio. The Sharpe ratio of 1.66 for the maximum return portfolio can be (at least to some extent) compared with the Sharpe ratio of 0.54 of the S&P 500. In the past a diversified portfolio of long/short manager was the superior investment when compared with equities even when compared to the S&P 500, the strongest-performing index in the developed economies. However, past returns are, unfortunately, no guarantee for future returns.

Figure 11.2 shows the three skill-based portfolios just discussed. The portfolios in between have been added in 1 percent volatility increments. The graph shows the optimal allocation (vertical left-hand axis) with respect to portfolio volatility (horizontal axis). The dark line measures the expected return of the respective portfolio (right-hand scale). All efficient allocations have zero weight in equity nonhedge (long/short with long bias) and emerging markets absolute return strategies. The weights floated between 0 percent and 100 percent; that is, short positions were constrained. Calculations were based on monthly U.S. dollar total returns from January 1990 to December 2001.

The hedge fund portfolio will be biased toward directional or nondirectional depending on the fund of funds manager's objectives. The bias will be either toward the left-hand or right-hand side of Figure 11.2.†

---

*Being continuously short index put options is not a bad investment strategy per se, despite causing one of the major hedge fund industry blowups (Victor Niederhoffer). Selling insurance premium is the business of insurance companies who collect a premium in most market conditions but experience large cash outflows in difficult but rare market conditions. The cash flow distribution of a reinsurance company will have a positive mean but also have negative outliers on the left-hand side—caused, for example, by the 1906 earthquake in San Francisco or 9/11 more recently.

†Fung and Hsieh (2001a) point out that the "spread risk" inherent in a long/short portfolio, for example, often overwhelms the market-directional component of the portfolio's exposure. The authors make reference to the former Tiger fund favoring value stocks on the long side and being negative on growth stocks, which led to the dissolution of the fund in February 2000. The authors also note the destiny of George Soros' Quantum group of funds, which experienced substantial losses in a period when the Wilshire 5000 index showed positive returns. Volatility of returns can substantially underestimate the risk of a dynamic trading strategy.

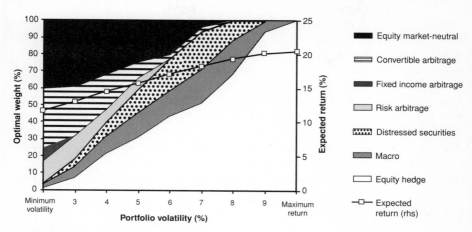

**FIGURE 11.2** Mean-Variance Optimal Hedge Fund Portfolios
*Source:* Hedge Fund Research, Datastream, UBS Warburg (2001).

If low portfolio volatility (stable positive returns) is the main objective, the hedge fund portfolio will include high Sharpe ratio strategies such as market-neutral, convertible arbitrage, and risk arbitrage. These are all spread-based strategies. Traditionally, these portfolios were designed for wealthy individuals who wanted to grow their wealth steadily with little downside volatility. Institutional investors use low-volatility hedge fund exposure to diversify exposure to equities and bonds (traditional assets). As outlined in Chapter 5, Schneeweis and Spurgin (2000) call these strategies "risk reducers."

The maximum return portfolio consists of 100 percent in long/short equity (equity hedge). These portfolios have a long bias; that is, correlation with equities is higher than portfolios constructed with arbitrage strategies. The assumption is that these portfolios will not yield positive returns in a bear market (i.e., not diversify portfolios of traditional risks) as well as hedge funds portfolios with nondirectional exposure. In the past these portfolios had more appeal to investors seeking high equitylike returns as opposed to diversification opportunities and stable income. Schneeweis and Spurgin (2000) call these strategies "return enhancers." The superiority of long/short equity strategies in the high-return spectrum in mean-variance space is one of the reasons why absolute return investment styles are as much a new paradigm as they are a bubble, as some market observers argue.

In UBS Warburg (2001) the same graph (Figure 11.2) was shown with data until May 2001 instead of December 2001. What has changed in mean-variance space since then? The first observation is that the allocation to distressed securities has increased whereas the allocation to risk arbitrage has decreased in the efficient portfolios. This is rather interesting because some (or most) fund of funds managers have been reducing exposure to risk arbitrage in favor of distressed securities, and so have event-driven multistrategy funds. However, it is unlikely that all market participants made the move at the same time. When this was written it was obvious that the prospect of risk arbitrage was not that great with M&A activity collapsing (or having collapsed in 2001) and spreads at a low. This means that some fund of funds managers who do active asset allocation (not all of them do) have an advantage if they can move early. It seems obvious that someone who has experienced the various absolute return strategies going through cycles will have a competitive advantage relative to those who are new to the game.

Figure 11.3 compares the mean-variance optimized hedge fund portfolios from Figure 11.2 with traditional asset classes. Figure 11.3 or a similar graph is probably the most often shown graph at any hedge fund conference. Some speakers even go as far as to describe the horizontal axis as "risk" instead of standard deviation of returns or volatility (which is fine in mean variance space but could be misleading in absolute return space, i.e., in the real world). Volatility (variance of returns) is only part of the risk in

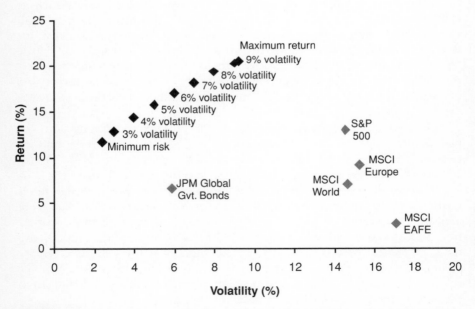

**FIGURE 11.3** Mean-Variance Optimized Hedge Fund Portfolios versus Traditional Indexes
*Source:* Hedge Fund Research, Datastream, UBS Warburg (2001).

investment management in general and in hedge funds in particular. The jacket of this book shows an iceberg where it is known that only a tiny part of the mass is above the surface, visible to the human eye. The risk of hedge fund investing is sort of similar. Volatility is the easily assessable part. Understanding the fundamentals of the other risk and interrelationships of related risks is what this book is all about. Even if we make the available data much worse than it really is, in mean variance space hedge funds are still far superior to any traditional asset class either in isolation or in combination with one another. Figure 11.4 indicates that even when we subtract 300 basis points from the historical returns to account for survivorship or any other bias, little changes when compared with traditional asset classes. Survivorship bias is a problem with any fund data. However, it is unlikely to be a rational reason for not investing in hedge funds. In Figure 11.4, in addition to reducing returns, volatility was also doubled (to account for non-normality of returns, the unfamiliarity aspect, and limited liquidity and transparency).

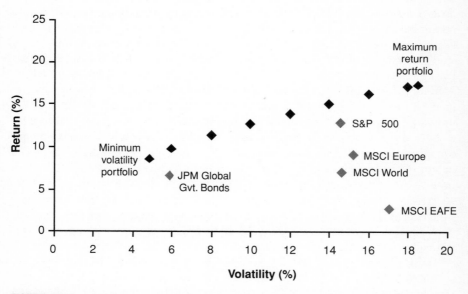

**FIGURE 11.4** Return versus Volatility (Hedge Fund Return Minus 300 Basis Points and Volatility Doubled)
*Note:* Calculations are based on monthly U.S. dollar total returns January 1990 to December 2001. 300 basis points were subtracted from historical returns to account for any imperfection in the data and volatility was doubled, potentially to account for imperfections in calculating standard deviations of nonmarketable financial instruments.
*Source:* Hedge Fund Research, Datastream, UBS Warburg (2001).

Mean-variance efficiency remained intact, even when subtracting 300 basis points for any upward bias from returns and doubling the volatility. Note that Fung and Hsieh (1999b) suggest that using a mean-variance criterion to rank hedge funds and mutual funds will produce rankings that are nearly correct. This means that the imperfect assumption of normally distributed returns (which does not hold for some nondirectional hedge fund strategies) does not make conclusions from mean-variance optimizations obsolete.

## Portfolio/Risk Management

The second monitoring process, next to reviewing the manager, is monitoring the portfolio or managing the risk of the portfolio on an ongoing basis. The preceding analysis is ex post. The key to success of any portfolio construction exercise is to estimate return, volatility, and correlation, the three input variables of the mean-variance optimization process, and to combine the variables to construct a mean-variance efficient portfolio. Outlining their investment policy, Yale Endowment (2001), for example, consider this to be as much art as science. It is therefore obvious that different fund of funds managers will have different portfolios, as their estimates for the future differ. Some might be more reliant on the past, and others might try to "call the market," that is, try to pick the strategy that will perform best over the next 12-to-24-month period.

The picking of strategies and the resultant portfolio rebalancing is probably not entirely independent of the fund of funds managers' marketing effort. A fund of funds involved in marketing to retail investors, for example, has an incentive to bias the portfolio constituents toward the current darlings of the industry. This would have meant having large allocations in convertible arbitrage and risk arbitrage in the beginning of 2001. This would also have meant no allocation to hedge funds operating in emerging markets and global macro. Convertible arbitrage and risk arbitrage performed well in 2000.* In other words, there are fund of funds managers who are opportunistic with respect to portfolio construction and rebalancing and those who accept less variance in their strategy allocations. However, there are some reservations with respect to timing strategies. In addition, short-term trading of hedge funds is counterintuitive due to limited liquidity and expensive to execute.

Risk management is not the same as risk measurement. The measurement of portfolio risk is to a large extent a quantitative process. However, risk management is judgmental. LTCM partners were the greatest risk measurers. However, they exercised poor judgment and were, according to Jorion

---

*Risk arbitrage did not perform that well in 2001, primarily due to fewer mergers and difficulties surrounding some larger deals (General Electric/Honeywell and, to a lesser extent, Hewlett Packard/Compaq).

(2000), inferior risk managers. Any investor investing in a fund of funds will probably find it easier to assess whether the fund of funds manager can measure risk. This can be achieved by examining the models, the data, and the skill and experience of the fund of funds management operation. These input parameters are more objective. The judgment to take action based on the changing risk parameters and investment landscape is more subjective.* Whether a fund of funds manager takes action according to its objectives is uncertain. One layer of comfort from the investors' perspective is when the fund of funds manager is also a principal. This is not a guarantee of prudently executed and continuous risk management. However, at least it should align the interests of the investor with those of the manager.

## DO FUND OF FUND MANAGERS ADD VALUE?

There is considerable debate as to whether fund of funds managers add value. The experienced fund of funds managers are likely to do so. The hedge funds industry is still opaque and increasingly flooded by greenhorns. Experience certainly trades at a premium. A more appropriate question, therefore, would be: How sustainable is the alpha of fund of funds managers?

At the most general level a fund of hedge funds manager should:

- Understand all hedge fund strategies.
- Understand all instruments used by hedge funds.
- Emphasize qualitative aspects relative to quantitative variables.
- Be in the information loop and have extensive proprietary data.
- Be of highest integrity, as there is little regulation or reputational risk of large corporates to assist investors.
- Have one's interests aligned with those of investors.

---

*There is a growing amount of research suggesting that hedge fund strategies are simply a function of some asset class factors, traded dynamically and resulting in nonlinear causality. The conclusion is often that hedge fund strategies are passively replicable once one has figured out what these factors are. This is a misunderstanding. A convertible arbitrage manager, for example, is not hired to systematically pull a lever, to buy bonds and sell stock short on every new convertible bond issue. A convertible manager is hired to find and exploit market inefficiencies and investment opportunities within the CB market. Pricing the CB is objective (risk measurement); trading the bond over its life is subjective (risk management). The observation that in the past a large part of the performance can be attributed to cheap issuance might or might not be a good indication for the future. The misconception is derived from ignoring the fact that the risk management of the hedge fund manager is active (as opposed to passive) as well as to a large extent subjective (as opposed to objective).

## Investment Philosophy of Fund of Funds Manager

As mentioned earlier, the hedge fund industry is heterogeneous when compared with the traditional long-only asset management industry. This heterogeneity allows one to pursue different strategies. The two extreme choices are to (1) minimize portfolio volatility or (2) maximize expected return. The former aims to capture stable returns in the region of 3 to 5 percentage points above the risk-free rate. The latter expects high absolute returns in the low 20s. Most funds of funds will opt for a blend of the two extremes with a bias toward either directional or nondirectional strategies.

Among important considerations is whether the fund of funds manager believes in market timing. Many investment professionals in a risk management discipline or professionals with a bias to academia have developed an aversion to market risk, which they perceive as being exposed to chance.* Those investors will find attraction in strategies where the manager's alpha is isolated from beta and the manager will have some reservations with respect to market timing.† The other extreme will be biased toward timing the market. These managers will include more opportunistic, directional strategies. Note that the goal of the first hedge fund (Alfred Jones) was to reduce exposure to chance (market risk) and increase exposure to skill (stock selection). Note also that the hedge fund boom of the early 1970s ended because funds were long and leveraged; the industry shrank dramatically after departing from its origins.‡

A fund of funds manager might also elaborate the demand structure of its clientele. Retail investors are probably more likely to be in get-rich mode and high-net-worth private investors in stay-rich mode, while institutional investors might seek diversifiers to their equity stake. Fund of funds managers

---

*Behaviorists argue that we have a hard time discerning probabilities of events and cannot distinguish a long-shot prediction from something that is likely to occur by pure chance. See for example Kahneman and Riepe (1998). Or as Warren Waver, author of the book *Lady Luck*, observed, "The best way to lose your shirt is to think that you have discovered a pattern in a game of chance." From Sherden (1998), p. 121.

†Peter Lynch was quoted as saying, "I don't believe in predicting markets," and that market timers "can't predict markets with any useful consistency, any more than the gizzard squeezers could tell the Roman emperors when the Huns would attack." From Sherden (1998), p. 106.

‡As already mentioned in Chapter 1, the difference between the 1970s and 2000–? bear market with respect to long/short managers was that the managers were leveraged long in the former and deleveraged and in cash (or even net short) in the latter bear market.

targeting a specific client type have an incentive to structure a fund of funds that matches what their clients demand.

One of the first decisions a fund of funds manager either implicitly or explicitly will take, therefore, is focus on the left- or right-hand side of Figure 11.2. Strategies on the right-hand side include market timing; strategies on the left do not, or do so to a much lesser extent. The more sophisticated fund of funds managers will blend either directional with nondirectional or nondirectional with directional strategies. The diversification benefits due to low correlation is, putting it simply, too great not to be utilized in constructing a portfolio of hedge funds.

Most hedge fund managers will aim for absolute returns and low volatility when compared with the traditional asset classes such as equities and bonds. Low volatility means managing total risk as opposed to active risk as in the case of long-only managers. Capital preservation or the protection of wealth is also the goal of most fund of hedge funds managers. Again, managing total risk is the name of the game. Not only is the return target defined in absolute levels, but the long-term risk target is also defined in absolute terms.*

## Risk Management Experience

The ability to identify and understand risk characteristics is one of the most important issues when investing in hedge funds. A fund of funds manager will have to demonstrate the skill as well as experience in the field of the most complex financial instruments and trading strategies. This expertise will allow the fund of funds manager to assess potential drawdowns for each manager in each strategy irrespective of his historical track record. This assessment will allow the fund of funds manager to get a feel for the risk of the overall fund when 25 percent, 50 percent, or even 100 percent of managers experience an extreme drawdown at the same time.

## Motivation and Other Intangibles

One of the intangibles of allocating funds to any money manager is motivation.† This is probably true for selecting a fund of funds manager in the tradi-

---

*However, the absolute return target is viewed relative to the risk-free rate. A 10 percent absolute return target is normally understood to be above LIBOR. Otherwise a 10 percent target in the United States would somewhat have a different feel to it than a 10 percent return target in Brazil.

†One approach to deal with factors difficult to model, such as intangibles, is to ignore them or build model assumptions into the model which allows exclusion. This might be an option in the controlled laboratory environment of the econometrician but could have disastrous consequences to the investor.

tional asset management arena as well as in alternative fund management. A highly motivated manager is more likely to go the extra mile in terms of negotiating fees, capacity, liquidity, and transparency than a less motivated manager. However, how do we measure motivation?

**Incentives**   One question a hedge fund manager is often asked by evaluators is how much of his or her own money is in the fund. The general perception is that a manager with 20 years of savings in the fund is, everything else held equal, superior to a manager who puts only last year's bonus at risk. The argument is that interests between manager and investor are aligned when both have their funds tied together. The alignment of interests is obviously also relevant between fund of funds manager and investor. Some fund of funds managers might be closer to a principal and investing alongside investors. Others might be closer to consultancy, that is, in the role of an agent with its own challenges regarding conflicts of interest.

However, the net amount invested by the manager is not necessarily a good indication of motivation. It does not account for potential optionlike characteristics that are observed in incentive schemes. For example, a 28-year-old investment professional with three years' experience might set up a hedge fund, initially investing his full net wealth of $1 million along with investors. In this case, applying the logic outlined earlier, this manager would be highly motivated to do well. However, we would argue that this is not necessarily the case. He has little to lose. If the venture does not work out he will go back to his Wall Street job having lost his savings of three years plus six months of work. He does not "have a lot of skin in the game." Such an incentive is similar to, as suggested by Anson (2001a), a free or cheap call option: unlimited upside profit potential with limited measurable downside risk.

The other extreme is the 20-year hedge fund veteran who might have 90 percent of $1 billion net wealth in his own funds. This structure might also have odd incentive characteristics when combined with hubris. For example, the prestige of winning a certain trade might weigh more strongly than the risk of a huge loss. However, a huge loss would not have an effect on the lifestyle of the manager. It may or may not affect self-confidence, but not the manager's personal economics.

A manager fading away is just another example of reversion to the mean. A manager who has compiled an excellent historical record gradually turns into just another manager, with higher risk than before, and lower return. Maybe he has lost his competitive edge, his hunger for success. Maybe his historical record was just a fluke, not really a symptom of genuine investment skill but a result of randomness. Or maybe the inefficiency he is an expert at exploiting has disappeared as others have copied his style. In any case, what looked like an exceptional investment opportunity turns into a disappointment.[2]

For many years the hedge fund industry had something like a natural hedge as managers had all their savings at risk. This "hedge" is becoming less prevalent. In Peltz (2001) retired hedge fund manager Michael Steinhardt (Steinhardt Partners) is quoted arguing that times have changed. In the old days things were different.

> *Steinhardt says the distinguishing characteristics were the manager investing his assets solely in his own fund, having a long track record, and being successful in a variety of economic climates. The manager was intense, intellectually superior, and motivated by performance—not growth of assets under management.*[3]

A point can be made that motivation is probably highest in the middle of the two extremes. This could be true for a single hedge fund as well as a fund of funds manager. A manager with full commitment of tangibles as well as intangibles is probably highly motivated for the venture to work. This, obviously, is no guarantee of success. However, if tangibles as well as intangibles are at risk, the incentive should not include any optionlike features and secure a realistic assessment of opportunities and risks.

Intuitively one would assume that a high-water mark, for example, could also create odd optionlike incentive features. For example, a large loss means that that the fund would have to perform well over the next couple of years without receiving an incentive fee. This could potentially damage a business as key staff leaves to create their own funds. It also creates an optionlike incentive to "bet the bank," as survival is at stake. Current research is not conclusive.

Fung and Hsieh (1997b) suggest that reputation costs have a mitigating effect on the gambling incentives implied by the manager contract. Results by Brown, Goetzmann, and Park (1999) confirm the hypothesis of Fung and Hsieh (1997b). Brown, Goetzmann, and Park (1999) investigated whether hedge fund and CTA return variance depends on whether the manager is doing well or poorly. Results show that managers whose performance is relatively poor increase the volatility of their funds, whereas managers whose performance is favorable decrease volatility. This is consistent with adverse incentives created by the existence of performance-based fee arrangements. A corollary of this theory is that managers whose performance contract is out of the money should increase volatility the most. The data does not support this further implication—managers whose return is negative do not substantially increase volatility. In some years of the sample, the authors found that they even decrease the volatility of their fund's return. Thus, while the data fit with certain conjectures derived from theory about investment manager compensation, they appear to contradict others.

**Conflicts of Interest**   Differences between principal goals and agent actions cause conflicts of interest. The agent is normally in a fees-only relationship with the principal and therefore the set of incentives might not be fully aligned. For example, the agent has a conflict of interest in recommending investments where the kickback is low. It lies in human nature to have a bias toward the fund where incentives are high. This, however, might not be in the interest of the principal.

Aligning the incentives of the manager with those of the investor reduces the principal/agent conflict and may lead to greater care in the management of funds. One could argue that the principal/agent conflict is to some extent relaxed when the manager is a principal.

There are other areas of potential conflict of interest—for example, an operator of a fund of funds in parallel with its prime brokerage or capital introduction franchise. The temptation of the fund of funds operator to favor clients would be a conflict of interest relative to the investors. Such a fund of funds operator should not survive the scrutiny of a sound due diligence process.

There are differences between fund of funds managers. Comparing the different fee structures on a like-for-like basis is not straightforward. The main difference is transparency. Some show all fees to the fund of funds investors, while others do not. Some fund of funds managers show a relatively low flat fee but receive kickbacks from the individual hedge fund managers. Others have performance-related fees on top of a flat fee. In any case, caveat emptor. The buyer will have to gain transparency and judge whether there is the potential for conflicts of interest.

**On Prudence, Trust, and Integrity**   Other intangibles important to investing in hedge funds include trust and integrity. An interesting observation, one could argue, is that intangibles such as prudence, trust, and integrity are not a big issue in most of the classic textbooks of economics and finance. However, many fund of funds managers regard these intangibles elementary in their decision-making process.

Some investment professionals are of the view that orthodox economics took a wrong turn at some stage in its evolution, treating economic agents as androids such as Data from *Star Trek* instead of more socially adept beings such as Deanna Troi. In other words, they believe that the so-called economic man (homo economicus), or the attempt to explain social phenomena with tools from the natural sciences, is an extreme deviation from reality. Just having witnessed the bursting of the Internet bubble, they are probably not entirely without a point. The practical implication is that there are far more inefficiencies in capital markets than the random walk or efficient market hypothesis wants us to believe.*

---

*See appendix to Chapter 4 for a brief discussion on EMH and the proverbial "free lunch."

The ultimate hoax of scientific mystification, confused thinking, and mis-use of scientific concepts was conducted by Sokal and Bricmont (1998). They submitted a parody of the type of work that has proliferated in the 1990s to an academic journal ("Transgressing the Boundaries: Toward a Transforma-tive Hermeneutics of Quantum Gravity"), to see whether the journal would publish it.* The article was accepted and published. The hoax was that the content was complete nonsense. The conclusion from the (uncontrolled) ex-periment was that one easily could contribute to contemporary (academic) thinking as long as it was in the right format. Why is this relevant in absolute return space?

The relevance for investors is that it is difficult to see when the current paradigm has run its course or does not any longer apply to a materially changed market environment. We have earlier questioned Lo's (2001) asser-tions regarding risk management. Andrew Lo is one of the most respected aca-demics in finance of our time. However, this is part of the problem. Andrew Lo represents the intellectual establishment in finance, whereas anyone who devi-ates in methodology does not. This is why Lo (2001) will have more disciples (lemmings) agreeing when he claims that "risk management is not central to hedge funds" and "risk management and transparency are essential" to the typical institutional investor. The establishment will probably also agree with Anson (2001b) with respect to institutionalization, that is, that full trans-parency, well-defined investment process, and relative returns are essential for institutional investors.† These notions are certainly true under the doctrine of the paradigm of relative returns. However, does the paradigm of relative re-turns encompass all information and knowledge on dealing with uncertainty, human behavior, and history of financial markets? It seems doubtful.

## MANAGER SELECTION AND ACCESS

### Talent Search and Identification

One could argue that the search for talent or skill is the single most important issue in the whole investment process of investing in AIS in general and hedge funds in particular.

---

*From the conclusion: "the $\pi$ of Euclid and the $G$ of Newton, formerly thought to be constant and universal, are now perceived in their ineluctable historicity; and the puta-tive observer becomes fatally decentered, disconnected from any epistemic link to a space-time point that can no longer be defined by geometry alone."

†The author of this book disagrees with the relative returns part of Anson (2001b). Otherwise this book would have been called *Relative Returns—The Risk and Oppor-tunities of Enhanced Indexing*.

One aspect of manager selection is reputation. Reputation is probably the closest thing to brand recognition in the world of intangibles. We even came across the notion that the talent of a manager is negatively correlated with the number of sales staff in a hedge fund. Although we would not go as far as that (it would be politically incorrect to do so), there is a huge difference in a few of the successful launches and the many me-too products.

A fund of funds manager has to be inside the information loop of high-caliber investment management personnel on the sell as well as the buy side of the investment business. This will enable him or her to spot talent early in the evaluation process. Some fund of funds managers identify and track skilled investment professionals before they announce that they are launching a hedge fund. In other words, a fund of funds manager who has superior information on key staff in the main investment centers will have a competitive advantage.

## Due Diligence and Track Record

Most investors are familiar with the statement "past performance is no guide to future performance." Every disclaimer in financial services carries this warning. Relying on past performance is tantamount to driving down a twisty mountain road while looking only in the rearview mirror.* However, many investors seem to focus on track record when evaluating investment in the hedge fund industry. Quantitative analysis has its limitations when evaluating and selecting hedge fund managers. At best it should be used to support in-depth qualitative research and rigorous due diligence. Quantitative analysis is more relevant for risk monitoring than it is for manager selection.

The advantage of quantitative research is its relatively low cost and easy access. Anyone can buy a database for a couple of thousand U.S. dollars and screen for top-quartile performers. However, many top performers in the hedge fund industry do not appear in commercially available databases.

A proprietary database that includes qualitative information is important. The qualitative information can be scored and used in a ranking process to compare different managers within a strategy. A ranking process also allows elaborating on the strengths and weaknesses of each manager. The weakness of one manager can then be balanced through the strength of another manager in the portfolio construction process. This option is not available to the fund of funds manager who does not have qualitative information.

Given the importance of qualitative research and due diligence, an in-

---

*The most extreme form of hindsight bias is probably that U.S. pension funds should be 100 percent invested in equities as opposed to their current 60/40 mix. See, for example, Thaler and Williamson (1994) or Swank et al. (2002).

vestor evaluating a fund of funds manager will want to assess whether the manager is equipped to manage the laborious task of due diligence on an increasing number of funds. One could argue that the job of the fund of funds manager used to be to pick one outstanding manager per quarter from 10 new managers. Today this task is probably more like picking one or two managers out of approximately 100 new funds per quarter, while, at the same time, avoiding the one or two managers who should not be bidding for business. Manager selection has become more difficult as well as labor-intensive over time.

## RISK AND PERFORMANCE MONITORING

### Transparency

Transparency is among the hottest topics discussed at fund of funds conferences and in the minds of institutional involvement in hedge funds. A hedge fund manager has an incentive not to reveal the fund's positions for two main reasons. First, the market can trade against the manager if the position is in an illiquid security or spread and the position is revealed to the market. Inefficiencies are found in illiquid markets, not liquid markets. The period of autumn 1998 was a showcase example of the market trading against LTCM once the company was in distress and positions were revealed to the market.* Second, most managers believe they have an edge relative to the market. They are making money by doing something the market does not know or by doing it better than the market does. This competitive advantage or edge is their whole value proposition and justification for being in business. It is only rational that they protect what they believe is most valuable.†

There are additional reasons why a hedge fund manager might not want to reveal positions to a prospective or existing investor. A rude cynic might argue that most investors would not understand the real-time or daily positions of an arbitrage fund in any case. The information given to the investor would

---

*To a disciplined absolute return manager with a healthy capital structure a period of distress is full of opportunities, as a period of distress is characterized by excess volatility and market inefficiencies. Hedge fund managers will want their funding intact and secured in such a period.
†This point is open to debate. We took the view that someone investing in a hedge fund invests in the skill of the manager and not in a mechanical investment process. However, there have been cases of zero transparency, black-box investment strategies where nothing is revealed to the investor or the prospect. These funds normally do not—one would expect—survive the first screen of an institutional setup of a fund of funds manager.

give transparency but would, in the cynic's view, cause more harm than good. However, as mentioned before, a fund of funds manager having full access to a manager's positions but not understanding the underlying strategies and instruments has a competitive disadvantage relative to the fund of funds manager who does.

In *Sound Practices for Hedge Fund Managers* (2000) the authors* recommend that investors should receive periodic performance and other information about their hedge fund investments. According to the report, hedge fund managers should also consider whether investors should receive interim updates on other matters in response to significant events. Hedge fund managers should negotiate with counterparts to determine the extent of financial and risk information that should be provided to them based on the nature of their relationship in order to increase the stability of financing and trading relationships. They should also work with regulators and counterparts to develop a consensus approach to public disclosure. Agreements and other safeguards should be established to protect against the unauthorized use of proprietary information furnished to outside parties.

## Manager Risk Factors

One of the most important factors in terms of risk is that risk is not synonymous with volatility.† This is especially true when investing in nonmarketable securities or ventures. When managing the risk of a manager, Jaeger (2000) distinguishes between portfolio market and non-market-related factors as well as operational factors. These factors also apply for someone investing with a fund of funds manager. (See Table 11.3.)

A fund of funds manager needs the sophistication and the operational setup to assess and weigh all of these factors. Note that there are some strange

---

*Caxton Corporation, Kingdon Capital Management, Moore Capital Management, Soros Fund Management, and Tudor Investment Corporation.
†Rahl (2000) elegantly uses the term "iceberg risk" in connection with the lessons learned from LTCM. The visible tip of the iceberg (for example, the volatility of returns) is not necessarily a clear indication of the full risk. A long/short equity manager, for example, normally has lower beta risk. This means volatility of returns is lower. However, the manager is also exposed to "spread risk." Spread risk is not necessarily captured be measuring the standard deviation of returns. Returns from beta are fairly normally distributed. Returns from taking spread risk are not normally distributed. The returns from spread risk are leptokurtic—narrowly distributed around the mean with (usually) negative outliers (when spreads blow up). Favoring one form of distribution over the other is subjective depending on personal preference or tolerance of risk. However, what is not subjective is the fact that the combination of different return distributions driven by different factors reduces portfolio volatility.

**Table 11.3** Manager Risk Factors

| Portfolio Factors: Non-market-Related | Portfolio Factors: Market-Related | Organizational Factors |
|---|---|---|
| • Leverage | • Directional factors: long bias, short bias, neutral, etc. | • Length of record |
| • Concentration | | • Assets under management: rate of growth, nature of client base |
| • Illiquidity | • Technical factors: volatility | |
| • Trading behavior | • Spread-related factors: sector tilts, style tilts, credit spreads | • Ownership/compensation structure |
| | | • Risk monitoring/control systems |

*Source:* Author's own illustration, adapted from Jaeger (2000).

policies with hedge fund as well as fund of hedge funds selection (e.g., "no-leverage managers only" or "five-year track record required"). It will be interesting to see whether these simplifications and generalizations pay off. From today's perspective, it seems unlikely.

In *Sound Practices for Hedge Fund Managers* (2000) the authors distinguish between three categories of risk that are quantifiable—market risk, credit risk, and liquidity risk—and on the less quantifiable operational risk. Market risk relates to losses that could be incurred due to changes in market factors (prices, volatilities, and correlations). Credit risk relates to losses that could be incurred due to declines in the creditworthiness of entities in which the fund invests or with which the fund deals as a counterpart. Liquidity risk relates to losses that could be incurred when declines in liquidity in the market reduce the value of the investments or reduce the ability of the fund to fund its investments.

The authors of the report recommend that while current market practice is to treat the risks separately, it is crucial for hedge fund managers to recognize and evaluate the overlap that exists between and among market, credit, and liquidity risks. This overlap is illustrated in Figure 11.5 (recognizing that the relative sizes of the circles will be different for different strategies).[4]

Consequently, any risk-monitoring activity should monitor three interrelated variants of market, liquidity, and credit risks in combination:

1. Market risk—including asset liquidity and the credit risk associated with investments.
2. Funding liquidity risk.
3. Counterpart credit risk.

In this framework, the risk sometimes referred to as "sovereign risk" would be included as credit risk if the potential loss is related to the financial solvency of the sovereign, or as market risk, if the potential loss is related to policy decisions made by the sovereign that change the market value of posi-

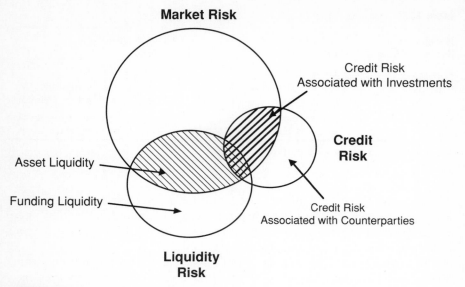

**FIGURE 11.5**   Risk Monitoring Function
*Source:* Sound Practices for Hedge Fund Managers (2000).

tions (e.g., currency controls). The term "event risk" is broader and could incorporate aspects of credit risk and operational risk, as well as some elements of market risk.

As mentioned in Chapter 2, funding liquidity is critical to a hedge fund manager's ability to continue trading in times of stress. Funding liquidity analysis should take into account the investment strategies employed, the terms governing the rights of investors to redeem their interests, and the liquidity of assets. All things being equal, the longer the expected period necessary to liquidate assets, the greater the potential funding requirements. Adequate funding liquidity gives a hedge fund manager the ability to continue a trading strategy without being forced to liquidate assets when losses arise.

The reason for highlighting this is to show the complexity of the task. If we are in a hedge fund bubble, as some market observers are suggesting, it is because shortcuts are being taken. Only a team of dedicated and experienced full-time financial professionals are equipped to implement and monitor these risk variables. The use of leverage adds a further layer of complexity.

## Leverage

One of the consistently hot topics in the hedge funds arena is the use and misuse of leverage. However, leverage is not a concept that can be uniquely defined, nor is it an independently useful measure of risk. Nevertheless, leverage is important to investors, counterparts, and fund managers because of the impact it can have on the three major quantifiable sources of risk: market risk, credit risk, and liquidity risk. A fund of funds manager must, therefore, have the ability to monitor accounting-based and risk-based leverage.

The variety of leverage measures used in banking and finance is evidence that leverage is not a uniquely defined concept:

> *These measures may be accounting-based (also referred to as "asset-based") or risk-based. The accounting-based measures attempt to capture the traditional notion of leverage as "investing borrowed funds." Using borrowed money (or its equivalent) enables an investor to increase the assets controlled for a given level of equity capital. Accounting-based measures of leverage relate some measure of asset value to equity. Both returns and risk, relative to equity, are magnified through the use of traditional, accounting-based leverage. The risk-based measures of leverage capture another aspect associated with leverage, namely, the risk of insolvency due to changes in the value of the portfolio. The risk-based measures relate a measure of a Fund's market risk to its equity (or liquidity). Although useful in this capacity, . . . risk-based leverage measures do not convey any information about the role borrowed money plays in the risk of insolvency.*[5]

No single measure captures all of the elements that market participants, regulators, or market observers attribute to the concept of leverage. Indeed, the authors of *Sound Practices for Hedge Fund Managers* show examples in which a risk-reducing transaction increases some leverage measures while decreasing others. This leads to the observation that leverage is not an independently useful concept, but must be evaluated in the context of the quantifiable exposures of market, credit, and liquidity.

While continuing to track and use accounting-based measures of leverage, the authors of *Sound Practices for Hedge Fund Managers* recommend that hedge fund managers focus their attention on measures of leverage that relate the riskiness of the portfolio to the capacity of the fund to absorb that risk. These measures must include elements of market risk (including the credit risk associated with the assets in the portfolio) and funding liquidity risk. Hedge fund managers should focus on such measures because traditional accounting-based leverage by itself does not necessarily convey risk of insolvency.

> *To say that one Fund is levered 2-to-1 while another is unlevered does not necessarily mean that the levered Fund is more risky or more likely to encounter liquidity problems. If the levered Fund is invested in government*

*securities while the unlevered Fund is invested in equities, accounting-based leverage would lead to erroneous conclusions about the riskiness of the two Funds. In this sense, accounting-based measures of leverage are arguably deficient since they convey the least information about the nature and risk of the assets in a portfolio.*[6]

The authors of the report argue that managers and investors alike must recognize that leverage is important, not in and of itself, but because of the impact it can have on market, credit, and liquidity risk. In other words, leverage influences the rapidity of changes in the value of the portfolio due to changes in market, credit, or liquidity risk factors.

*Consequently, the most relevant measures of leverage are "risk-based" measures that relate the riskiness of a portfolio to the ability of the Fund to absorb that risk. Recognizing the impact that leverage can have on a portfolio's exposure to market risk, credit risk, and liquidity risk, Hedge Fund Managers should assess the degree to which a Hedge Fund is able to modify its risk-based leverage in periods of stress or increased market risk. Hedge Fund Managers also should track traditional, accounting-based measures of leverage, which can provide insights into the source of risk-based leverage and how that leverage could be adjusted.*[7]

## Risk of Style Drift

A further ongoing risk factor to be monitored by the fund of funds manager is style drift. Style drift is the risk to investors that hedge fund managers drift away from their areas of expertise where they have an edge into fields where they have a competitive disadvantage. Historical examples have been fixed income arbitrageurs investing in nondomestic equity markets or equity managers investing in Russian debt.

There are probably two types of style drift: a short-term opportunistic style drift as well as a continuous departure from a manager's area of expertise. A permanent shift will force reassessment of the investment. One could argue that a short-term opportunistic drift into a related area is probably not as negative for the investor as a permanent shift. The short-term shift is both a risk to the investor as well as entrepreneurial expansion through exploiting economies of scale—an opportunity. A convertible arbitrage manager, for example, has a competitive advantage in areas of analyzing changes in credit and volatilities. There are, potentially, related trading opportunities by exploiting inefficiencies left behind by less informed investors.

Over the years, as mentioned earlier, there has been an increasing tendency for hedge fund managers to employ multiple strategies. The value of creating a more stable stream of returns over different market cycles has attracted hedge funds to adopt a multistrategy approach. By investing in a manager attempting to achieve absolute returns, one automatically invests in the skill of the manager, not in an asset class or mechanical execution of an investment technique, strategy, or process. This implies a higher degree of flexibility for the manager. The hedge fund manager is not restricted to replicate a benchmark but has a mandate to exploit investment opportunities or market inefficiencies. The basic question is how far a hedge fund manager should be allowed to drift away from his or her initial core area of expertise.

Restrictions work in both ways. On the one hand restrictions reduce risk; on the other they limit the set of opportunities to add value. Every market changes over time. Change, and its derivative, uncertainty, are the most certain variables in any social science. Market inefficiencies, for example, have a tendency to disappear as they become known to the market and attract capital. If manager restrictions were too tight, the manager would not be able to exploit inefficiencies in a neighboring or related market as they appear, thereby missing out on first-mover advantage.

**Handcuffs and Opportunism—A Trade-Off**   The belief that a high degree of freedom is good is based on the assumption that a large portion of the value added in the hedge fund industry is attributable to flexibility and not purely to skill. Long-only managers for example are measured with the information ratio. The ex ante information ratio* is defined as the expected level of annual residual return per unit of annual residual risk.[8] Grinold and Kahn (2000a) found an approximation to the information ratio that is called the *fundamental law of active management.*[9] The law is based on two attributes of a strategy, breadth and skill. The breadth of a strategy is the number of independent investment decisions that are made each year. The skill, represented in the information coefficient, measures the quality of those investment decisions. The information coefficient is the correlation of each forecast with the actual outcome. The information ratio is approximated by multiplying the information coefficient with the square root of breath.[†] If one of the two variables (skill or breadth) is zero, the product of the equation is also zero. A skilled manager stripped of all opportunities to add value has

---

*Ex post information ratio is calculated by dividing the manager's excess return over the benchmark with the tracking error.
†This means that the information coefficient can be negative where breadth cannot, i.e., a manager can have negative skill but the opportunity set can be zero but not negative.

an expected information ratio of zero and cannot add value. If ex-ante value added of an asset manager is defined as skill times the square root of breadth, then handcuffing an active manager (i.e., reducing breadth) has its limitations.

A high degree of freedom causes many challenges in terms of monitoring risk on an ongoing basis. In addition, investors construct portfolios of hedge fund strategies according to their own risk tolerances and return preferences. A high degree of flexibility means that the investor's portfolio of different hedge fund managers could occasionally experience a higher degree of overlap. This would result in higher volatility and higher correlation of the hedge fund portfolio.

One important aspect that aligns the interests of the investor with those of the manager is the fact that many hedge fund managers have large portions of their net wealth tied to their funds. Often hedge fund managers view their funds as the safest place for their wealth to compound. An aversion to market risk exposure was the main reason why hedge funds started back in 1949 in the first place.* To some extent, this alignment of interests is a hedge against managers leaving their areas of competence and risking their own and his investors' equity. However, human nature does not always work that way. There are no guarantees for a prudent assessment of new opportunities. Judgment is omnipresent in pure active management (hedge fund investing). The degree of tolerable style drift will remain in the eye of the beholder.

## Legal and Compliance

A fund of funds manager's legal/compliance personnel must have the authority and resources to operate independently and effectively. This function should seek to actively manage the legal risks presented by the hedge fund manager's trading, focusing on the documentation governing trading relationships and individual transactions. A fund of funds manager will have to ensure that the hedge fund managers pursue a consistent and methodical approach to documenting transactions so that the legal consequences of periods of market stress or performance declines may be more clearly anticipated and managed. The legal aspect should allow risk monitoring with useful input in the evaluation of a hedge fund's projected liquidity in stressed environments, including inputs derived from the fund's transaction documentation (e.g., terms regarding termination, collateral, and margining).

---

*Chapter 1 made the point that the investment philosophy of absolute return managers could be as old as investing and business itself.

## Data and Information

Generally speaking, data on hedge fund performance in general is poor and information is difficult and costly to obtain. Hedge fund data suffers from various biases, of which survivorship bias is the most often quoted deficiency. The hedge fund industry is still opaque. This means information flow is not efficient and transparent.

The lack of transparency, the poor quality of available data, and the high cost of information are risks to some investors, particularly those investors who are not in the information loop. However, information and high-quality data are among the competitive advantages of the fund of hedge funds manager.

## CONCLUSION

An active long-only strategy stems from a time when markets were less efficient than today and there were few or no alternative ways of getting exposure to a market. It also stems from a time when there were fewer investment style opportunities and the degree of complexity and flexibility in financial instruments was lower. There is reason to believe that the market is migrating to the view that it does not make much sense to attempt to get an informational advantage in an informationally efficient market. If this is the case, flows to specialists adopting an active approach in markets where there is no passive alternative might continue to grow. Given that fund of hedge funds managers operate in a market as inefficient and opaque as the hedge fund industry, they likely have a strong value proposition. However, economic logic suggests that over time the costs of active management (fees) are correlated with the set of exploitable opportunities and, therefore, inversely related to efficiency improvements of the marketplace—in the long term, that is.

# PART four

# Going Forward

# CHAPTER 12

# Game of Risk or Risky Game?

*Chance favors only the prepared mind.*

—Louis Pasteur*

*Risk, to state the obvious, is inherent in all business and financial activity.*

—Alan Greenspan

## BUBBLE OR NEW PARADIGM IN ASSET MANAGEMENT?

To some, hedge fund investing is a bubble; to others absolute return strategies embody a new paradigm in asset management. Reality is probably somewhere in between. On the one hand, expectations of high positive absolute returns from hedge funds when equity markets fall are probably upward biased. On the other hand, the focus on positive absolute returns and the definition of risk as *total risk* (as opposed to *active risk*) might be in the process of replacing the relative return approach.

---

*From inaugural lecture, University of Lille, 1954. Pasteur, father of bacteriology, formulated the fundamental tenets of the germ theory of fermentation and of diseases, which led to his pasteurization process of sterilization. He is also known for his pioneer work with vaccines, notably against anthrax and rabies.

## Bubble Theory

Some market observers view the increasing allocation to hedge funds as a bubble. More and more authors, experts, and analysts expect the hedge fund bubble to burst at any time.*

A bubble exists when investment horizons expand, expectations sky-rocket, and everyone does the same thing at the same time. In other words, bubbles occur when the consensus view with respect to expected returns increases and investors cuddle in the comfort of the consensus view and deemphasize sound research, due diligence, and logical economic reasoning. The South Sea bubble, tulip mania, and the Internet bubble were good examples of this pattern. In all cases, expectations slowly diverged from fundamentals. The bubble bursts when expectations converge with reality.

In "Bubbles and Fads in Asset Prices" Camerer (1989) distinguishes among three types of bubbles: *growing bubbles*, *fads*, and *information bubbles*.

> *Growing bubbles are typically constant terms that arise in solutions to difference equations that govern equilibrium prices. Such bubbles can occur even when market participants act rationally and have rational expectations.*[†1]

Tulip mania is an example of a growing bubble. The second category is fads. "Fads are mean-reverting deviations from intrinsic value caused by social or psychological forces like those that cause fashions in political beliefs or consumption goods (Shiller, 1984), or like Keynes's "animal spirits."[2] Camerer (1989) categorizes the South Sea bubble as a fad because prices were driven by unrealistic beliefs about the prospects of English companies given exclu-

---

*See, for example, "Hedge Funds—The Latest Bubble?" *The Economist*, September 1, 2001; "SEC's Paul Roye Issues a Warning About a Hedge Fund 'Craze,' " Bloomberg News, July 23, 2001; "The $500 Billion Hedge Fund Folly," *Forbes*, June 8, 2001; "The Hedge Fund Bubble," *Financial Times*, July 9, 2001; "Hedge Funds May Become the Next Investment Bubble," Bloomberg News, May 30, 2001. Not all articles are equal in terms of substance and quality of content (assuming the author is in a position to judge).

†Camerer (1989) stresses that "growing bubbles are consistent with rational expectations, and hence with the hypothesis that markets are informationally efficient, because current prices reflect the discounted price of the future bubble. Market participants cannot make excess profits by knowing prices will be too high next period, because the price is too high this period also. Indeed, because expected profits from the bubble are zero, risk-neutral market participants have no strong incentive to participate in it. Risk-averse investors, therefore, will not participate in the bubble."

sive rights to do business in those regions.\* Camerer calls the third type information bubbles. "Information bubbles occur when prices depart from intrinsic values based on all available information, because information is not perfectly aggregated by market prices (e.g., Friedman and Aoki, 1986), or because agents have different beliefs about how the economy works."[3] An example of an information bubble (or mini-bubble) is the observation that asset prices are much more volatile during regular trading hours than during after-hours trading. The ratio of per-hour trading-hour volatility to per-hour weekend volatility is about 70 to 1. Of course, more news is announced during trading hour, but the difference between trading-hour and non-trading-hour volatilities seems too large to be explained purely by the difference in the amount of news.

**New Wine in Old Wineskins?**   One of the main arguments for institutional investors investing in hedge funds is portfolio diversification. This, in essence, means reducing the expected volatility of portfolio returns without compromising expected returns or increasing expected returns while keeping volatility unchanged. Adding asset classes with expected returns that have low correlation with traditional asset classes increases the efficiency of the portfolio.[†] To some this might seem like new wine in old wineskins. A few decades ago, investing in emerging markets was marketed as a new asset class with low correlation to assets in the developed world. Experiences in the 1990s have aligned the hype with reality. The obvious question is whether investing in hedge funds will suffer a similar fate. It is possible that diversification benefits are currently overestimated. Only a small segment of the hedge fund universe has low correlation with equities.

**Short-Termism—a Red Herring?**   Every evolving industry goes through times of rapid change and innovation. Increased specialization seems to be one of the perpetual variables in the field of investment management. In the early stages of the asset management industry, a single manager managed a balanced portfolio. (In the Preface this was called the first paradigm of asset

---

\*Camerer (1989) also mentions other examples such as Atlantic City casinos that opened and crashed because expectations were too optimistic, or—quoting Arrow (1982)—"prices of high-technology stocks which soar when investors mistake scientific breakthroughs for financial breakthroughs." The latter has a very contemporary feel to it although it refers to the technology bubble in the 1960s when every stock soared whose name ended with "ionics" (like "com" in the 1990s).

†Note that hedge funds are also viewed as asset managers employing an alternative investment strategy within a traditional asset class as opposed to being treated as an asset class of there own. For example: A long/short portfolio is a different way of managing equity risk than is a long-only portfolio.

management.) Then equities and bonds were separated. Then equities were split into value and growth, or active and passive, or domestic and international, or developed and nondeveloped markets. The increased acceptance and current institutionalization of hedge funds could be viewed as a further specialization of the asset management industry between skill-based and market-based strategies.* However, not all of the recent developments are positive. Any investment that is fashionable has a tendency to attract short-term investors. Short-term investors have a tendency to buy last year's winners and have a less disciplined and rigorous investment process. This could have a negative impact on the industry if there is a sudden and unexpected mismatch between expectations and reality.

Currently, a gap is potentially opening between expectations and reality. Given the strong inflow of assets to hedge funds, some market observers are asking whether the inflows into hedge funds are decoupling from realistic expectations, that is, whether there is a pattern of a bubble in progress. Is the accelerating allocation of funds in the hedge fund industry a bubble?

If it is a bubble, it probably would not be comparable with the bursting of the Internet bubble, where losses were in the region of 80 to 100 percent; around $4.8 trillion of value was destroyed on the Nasdaq alone between the peak and the end of 2001. The first step could be an increase in dispersion of hedge fund returns. This is already happening. This is, to some extent, a function of the increase in the number of hedge funds and funds of funds. The increase of the number of hedge funds and funds of funds, however, is part of the problem. The increase in supply in response to increased demand is resulting in an absolute reduction of quality. Consequently, the dispersion between top- and low-quartile hedge funds or funds of funds widens.

In addition, the hedge fund industry as a whole has a long equity bias. The absolute returns of the 1990s are unlikely to be matched in the 2000s when equity markets compound at 0 to 5 percent in the 2000s instead of 10 to 20 percent as in the 1990s. In addition, volatility has been relatively high over the past five years. Lower volatility would mean fewer exploitable inefficiencies and therefore fewer investment opportunities. Lower hedge fund performance in the 2000s, therefore, could potentially also realign expectations with reality. This realignment could happen gradually or instantaneously. A number of catalysts could be found for an instantaneous correction (a crash). These catalysts might include market dislocation, regulatory change, corporate governance breakdown, or any other extreme event. However, these events are, by definition, not foreseeable. A gradual realignment of expecta-

---

*The performance of skill-based strategies is attributable to the manager's skill (alpha). The performance of market-based strategies is attributable to the return of the market (primarily beta) or other systematic risk factors.

tions with reality is therefore a more likely scenario than a bubble bursting à la the Internet.

Private equity has recently experienced such a realignment of expectations. Since the Internet bubble has burst, exit strategies have become much more difficult. Many late 1990s vintages have single-digit IRRs (internal rates of return) to date. The vintages of 1999 and 2000 (peak of the dot-com frenzy for venture capital funds) could turn out to become what 1998 was for hedge funds. High demand led to a dispersion of performance. Today the consensus view is that private equity yields high risk-adjusted returns only if one invests with the first- or second-quartile managers. Just being long the asset class is not enough.

This could happen to the hedge fund industry—not a collapse as in Internet shares but a realignment of expectations with reality. In the long term, such an adjustment is desirable. An adjustment could strengthen the business case for fund of funds managers. If the alpha in the hedge fund universe can be unlocked only through market participants with a competitive advantage, but not by simply being long or through random selection, then the case for funds of funds is strengthened.

## What Is a New Paradigm?

The opposite view of the current trend of hedge fund investing being a fad ending in the bubble bursting is the view that absolute return strategies involving risk management techniques and where risk is defined as total risk is a new paradigm in asset management.

Paradigm shifts happen when there are anomalies—disparate odd results that cannot be explained away by inadequate methodology alone. When sufficient anomalies occur, street-smart individuals, one could argue, must begin to consider that the paradigm under which they are doing their work is no longer of use or is actually dysfunctional. Thomas Kuhn (1962) observed that individuals who break through by inventing a new paradigm are "almost always . . . either very young or very new to the field whose paradigm they change." Further, "These are the men who, being little committed by prior practice to the traditional rules of normal science, are particularly likely to see that those rules no longer define a playable game and to conceive another set that can replace them."

The investment management industry is a continuum and subject to change. Two changes in recent years are particularly worth pointing out. First, the perception of risk has changed. Market participants have begun to examine and analyze the downside tail of the return distribution more closely. This is a departure from being satisfied with mere statistical variance of returns as a measure for risk. Second, portfolio management is mutating into risk management. Long-held methodologies and investment styles are gradually being replaced with more scientific approaches and tools to manage money, assets, and risk.

**Perception of Risk**   Since 1987, the far left-hand side of the return distribution has been getting more attention. The October 1987 crash was probably the main catalyst for investors to start observing and modeling the far left-hand side of the return distribution more carefully. Figure 12.1 shows the distribution of returns of the S&P 500 index on a daily return basis. Note that vertical axis has been capped to make outliers visible. The chart is based on daily log returns from January 1969 to July 16, 2002. Since 1969 there have been three occasions when the daily S&P 500 returns were larger than seven standard deviations from the mean. A normal distribution based on historical returns suggests about one log return four standard deviations on either side of the mean over the 33-year period.

Outliers have a great influence on the risk of the venture, in this case investing in equities. These outliers are, by definition, not foreseeable. As Bernstein (1999) points out: Any argument to the contrary must derive from a model with an R-squared of 1.00. However, there is no such thing. Decision making with respect to the future will always involve uncertainty regardless of the approach used (fundamental economics, technical analysis, market psychology, astrology, etc.). What we know for sure about equity markets and

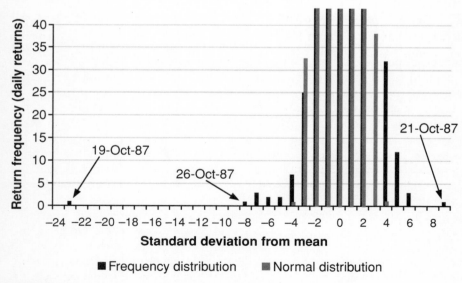

**FIGURE 12.1**   Frequency Distribution Based on Daily S&P 500 Returns
*Source:* Datastream.

their volatility is uncertainty itself. There will always be uncertainty. Or as John Maynard Keynes has put it: "It would be foolish, in forming our expectations, to attach great weight to matters which are very uncertain."

**Risk Management**   The above statement is not as fatuous as it may sound. It raises the question of what a money manager should focus on in the long term: expected return or risk. Looking at the world from the view of a risk manager it is obvious: risk. A risk manager would argue that one cannot manage expected return, but one can manage risk. Return is the by-product of taking risk. Banks today do not manage portfolios; they manage risk. Their long-term investment strategy is to define the risk they want to be exposed to and manage that exposure accordingly. This implies that banks have an absolute return focus as opposed to a relative return focus. Potentially, asset management could be in the process of moving in the direction of banks and hedge funds—that is, defining risk in absolute terms rather than relative terms (*total* risk as opposed to *active* risk). One could also argue that the asset management industry is moving back to an absolute return orientation and that the obsession with market benchmarks was only a brief blip in the industry's evolution, driven perhaps by an increasing involvement of consultants and trustees.

**Is the Asset Manager's Business Model Changing?**   Contrast the two business models in Table 12.1.

The main difference between hedge funds and traditional long-only manager is the absolute return objective. Hedge funds, like banks, define their return objective in absolute terms, not relative to a market or peer-group benchmark. In addition, risk is understood as the probability of absolute losses, that is, destruction of value (total risk). A long-only manager, also referred to as a relative return manager, measures success and failure relative to a benchmark. Risk is defined as active risk. A point can be made that this approach stems

**Table 12.1**   Two Different Business Models in Asset Management

|  | Relative Return Model (Market-Based) | Absolute Return Model (Skill-Based) |
|---|---|---|
| **Return objective** This means: | Relative to benchmark Capture asset class premium | Absolute, positive return Add value |
| **Risk management** This means: | Active risk Capture asset class premium | Total risk Avoid destroying value |

from a time where capturing the asset class premium (exposure to beta) was scarce. Given the huge diversity of indexed funds and derivatives, this is not the case anymore—at least not in information-efficient markets such as large-cap equity markets in the developed economies.

One could argue that anything that survived the wars, turbulence, crises, and market volatility of the 1990s has a high probability of sustainability. What might disappear is the term "hedge fund." It is, to some extent, a misnomer.* Not all hedge funds are hedged. However, the first hedge fund managers did not want their professional destiny and wealth to be dependent on chance (i.e., market risk).† That is why they hedged market risk in the first place. Their goal was to hedge their exposure to chance and volatility and to ensure that performance was attributable to skill (stock picking in the case of the Alfred Jones model).

In addition, the term "hedge fund" is also, to some extent, contaminated. It suffers from a similar fate as "derivatives" due to a mixture of myth, misrepresentation, negative press, and high-profile casualties in the 1990s. (See also the appendix to Chapter 2 on the press coverage of hedge funds.) The reputation of derivatives has improved because parts of the writing guild have found a new product to demonize: hedge funds. When Nick Leeson brought down Barings Bank in 1995, derivatives were blamed. Only mildly was it implied that some mismanagement by the London-based board could have partially been responsible. When rogue trader John Rusnak lost around $750 million for Allied Irish Bank in 2002, derivatives were involved but not blamed for the losses. In other words, there is a light at the end of the tunnel with respect to the press coverage on hedge funds improving one day.

Hedge funds are already in the process of being institutionalized. The traditional asset management industry has already started to offer what can best be described as absolute return strategies. The main characteristic of absolute return strategies is that there is no benchmark or the only benchmark is cash. The more successful ventures have proven to be highly profitable for the newly launched asset management firm. The separation between skill-based and market-based strategies in the asset management industry has already begun.

---

*A. W. Jones regarded the term "hedge fund" as grammatical barbarity: "My original expression, and the proper one, was 'hedged fund.' I still regard 'hedge fund,' which makes a noun serve for an adjective, with distaste." From Brooks (1998), p. 142.

†This is based on the assumption that market timing is about as difficult as long-term weather forecasting. Both, weather as well as an economic system, are complex, and their futures, therefore, are best described through a probability distribution. Apologies to all those readers who know at what level the S&P 500 is going to trade in 12 months' time.

Putting it crudely: Skill-based strategies are active while market-based strategies are passive approaches to money management. Institutional investing in skill-based strategies will continue to gain momentum due to two trends. First, the focus on absolute returns and the fact that failure is defined as destroying value causes some strategies utilized by hedge funds to perform significantly better than traditional strategies in falling capital markets. With investors accepting the fact that returns are not normally distributed (i.e., have fat tails) and the fact that negative utility from falling markets is higher than positive utility from rising markets, an increasing number of institutional as well as private investors are expected to acknowledge the benefits from investing in skill-based strategies.

Second, trying to beat an informationally efficient market, in what Charles Ellis (1998) calls the loser's game, might prove too mundane a strategy in the competitive environment of institutional asset management. A move away from traditional views and strategies should enlarge the scope for alternative views and strategies. This could result in a departure from simple capital markets indices to more tailored benchmarks that take into account idiosyncratic asset and liability characteristics as well as asymmetrical utility functions. This could flatten any hurdles in the path of investing in what today are referred to as hedge funds.

A market benchmark changes the incentives of the manager to become diametrically opposed to those of the investor. Today, a majority of investors see the disadvantages of limiting alpha generation by constraining a manager with a benchmark. Introducing a benchmark caused a lemming like effect with indexation and what some refer to as closet indexation. Closet indexation or hugging the benchmark means that most positions in an active portfolio are held to track the benchmark—often referred to as dead weight. Dead weight in a portfolio results from securities owned into which the manager has no insight. The proportion of the portfolio that is held to control residual volatility (volatility relative to the benchmark) is the proportion that will add no value.

Hedge funds carry less dead weight and therefore manage invested capital more efficiently. In a hedge fund, in general, only positions about which the manager has conviction will be held or sold short. Portfolio volatility, higher-moment, and residual risks are controlled with risk management instruments or other hedging techniques, most of which require less capital than holding dead weight positions in the cash market. Consequently, a higher proportion of the hedge fund manager's capital is invested in positions about which the manager has convictions. Hedge fund managers, therefore, should be able to provide higher alphas, since relative outperformance against a benchmark is not the primary objective.

Absolute return strategies are unlikely to replace relative return strategies, just as top gun fighter pilots have not replaced pilots of commercial aircraft.

One can view benchmarking as protection against unskilled managers. A relative return manager might be more suitable than an absolute return manager if an investor has little time, inclination, or ability to distinguish skill from luck from a portfolio manager. Benchmarking means that the manager cannot make investments that go horribly wrong—either by lack of skill or by bad luck. The dispersion of returns is small with relative return managers (and a function of the tracking error constraint given by the sponsor) and high with absolute return managers. By defining a market benchmark and a tracking error band, the plan sponsor gives the manager a risk budget in which he or she is expected to operate.

Indexation and its modified variants (smart indexation, enhanced indexation, etc.) have many followers. One of the main advantages of indexation is its lower cost and subsequently superior net performance. Total fees are generally lower with passive investments. However, if 80 percent of an active manager's positions are dead weight, then the portfolio is essentially 80 percent passive and 20 percent active. This means that a 50 basis point fee of funds under management is actually 250 basis points of the active portion. Hedge funds typically charge higher fees than long-only managers. However, the difference is not as extreme once the dead weight is taken into consideration. In other words, indexation (index funds, total return swaps) are the most cost-efficient form of getting exposure to a market. The ex ante alpha is zero. Investing in hedge funds is, in theory, about getting (and paying for) alpha without getting beta (market exposure) that can be obtained elsewhere more cost efficiently. In other words, long-only asset management with a benchmark is a hybrid of the two extreme forms of asset management.

Some take these arguments a step further. David Swensen (2000) argues:

> *If markets present no mispricings for active managers to exploit, good results stem from luck, not skill. Over time, managers in efficient markets gravitate toward closet indexing, structuring portfolios with only modest deviations from the market, ensuring both mediocrity and survival.*
>
> *In contrast, active managers in less efficient markets exhibit greater variability in returns. In fact, many private markets lack benchmarks for managers to hug, eliminating the problem of closet indexing. Inefficiencies in pricing allow managers with great skill to achieve great success, while unskilled managers post commensurately poor results.*

Alpha-generating strategies are normally skill-based strategies. If the flexibility of the manager is reduced to zero, the ex ante alpha is zero as a result. However, as with every other industry, the asset management as well as the hedge fund industry will most likely transform (or converge) over time. A possible future scenario is that those asset managers with a competitive advantage will be offering skill-based strategies. One of the pillars supporting this belief is that a competitive advantage, to some extent, is determinable in advance whereas the path of a market is not. Under the paradigm of absolute returns, a firm with prudent, intelligent, experienced, and hardworking managers will have an advantage over a firm with lazy, indifferent, unsophisticated, smooth-talking, ignorant rednecks. However, if both follow a long-only strategy in an information-efficient market, the latter can outperform the former due to luck.

Figure 12.2 classifies the most active and most passive investment styles into a two-dimensional grid, where the vertical axis is the level of fees and the horizontal axis the performance attribution. Absolute-return strategies are in quadrant I: fees are high and performance is, in theory and to some extent practice, determined by the manager's skill. The other

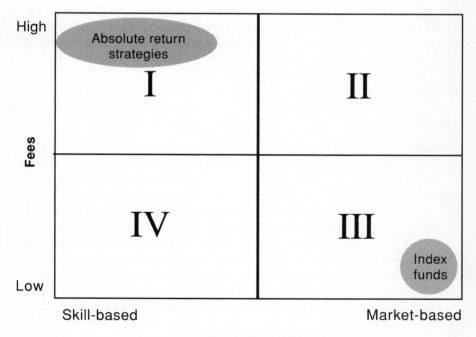

**FIGURE 12.2** Classification of Business Models
*Source:* UBS Warburg (2001).

extreme is quadrant III, where margins are low and performance is attributed to the market.

Not only is there a trend for specialist strategies in quadrant I, but there also is a trend for passive forms of investing (quadrant III). Greenwich Associates estimates that 38 percent of institutionally held assets in the United States are indexed. Watson Wyatt estimates that the degree of indexation is 25 percent for the United Kingdom, 20 percent for Switzerland, and 18 percent in the Netherlands, with the rest of the world in the process of closing the gap to the United States.

The reason for the increase in passive investment alternatives is primarily cost and, ultimately, performance. In price-efficient markets, passive strategies are cost-efficient. A cost-efficient investment vehicle is, ceteris paribus, superior to a cost-inefficient alternative. Passive strategies have become available outside the United States only in the past couple of years as the liquidity in equities outside the United States has increased. Increasing liquidity reduces the cost of execution and therefore increases the number of alternatives to get market exposure.

Strategies in quadrant II might be facing tough times ahead. Offering a passive product and charging customers an active fee has little survival probability. Those strategies stem from a time when there was no passive (i.e., cost-efficient) alternative. Today even retail investors can participate in developed markets on a cost-efficient basis through ETFs or market-replicating delta-one investment vehicles. A point could be made that asset managers currently in quadrant II will have to migrate into either quadrant I or III. Remaining in quadrant II might not be a sustainable option. No one inhabits quadrant IV and probably never will, as alpha will always trade at a premium.

In some parts of the world, migration is already happening through the core-satellite approach, where the core is passive and active satellites are added. These satellites are mandates given to managers operating in areas where the market is less price-efficient and there is no cost-efficient passive alternative. The day when a majority of investors agrees that focus on absolute returns and increased specialization leads to superior long-term performance and the heterogeneity of the satellites reduces portfolio risk through diversification will be the day when the absolute return paradigm has replaced the relative return paradigm.

According to Bill Gates, "We always overestimate the change that will occur in the next two years and underestimate the change that will occur in the next 10." Whether hedge funds are a bubble or new paradigm in asset management is open to debate. However, it is difficult to imagine that what today is referred to as a hedge fund—searching for investment opportunities while managing total risk—is a short-term phenomenon.

## ASSESSING AN UNCERTAIN FUTURE

There are many axioms regarding equity investing:

■ Equities will outperform bonds in the long term.
■ Young savers should have a large portion of their savings in equities because, in the long term, equities deliver superior performance.
■ Hedge funds are more risky than equities.

Reevaluation of these axioms can benefit thoughtful investors.

Equities as an asset class had a phenomenal two decades in the United States and Europe throughout the 1980s and 1990s. There is the possibility that this bull market caused an upward bias in return expectations and/or downward bias in risk perception. The average U.K. pension fund, for example, still has an allocation of 70 to 80 percent in equities. This is a huge social bet. If the future is identical to the past 20 years, the bet will pay off handsomely. If the future is different from the past two decades, the bet will not pay off and, as always, the man on the street (i.e., the pensioner) will have to bear the consequences.

Figure 12.3 shows the 25-year annual real price return (adjusted for inflation but excluding dividends) for the U.K. stock market from 1708 to July 16, 2002.*

Had a long-only immortal invested in the U.K. stock market in 1693 (data series starts in 1693) he or she would have lost 70 percent within three years. Recovery was not until the South Sea bubble of 1720. After the South Sea bubble burst, the immortal would have waited until 1961 to see the equity investments recovered on a nominal basis. The immortal investor's nominal annual return would have been around 1.44 percent (assuming dividends were taxed and the balance spent). When adjusted for inflation the return shrinks to below zero. The compound annual rate of return (CARR) was –0.082 percent. Figure 12.3 shows that there were many 25-year periods where the annualized real return was below zero. Equities might or might not outperform bonds in the long term. In absolute return space, it certainly matters whether the long-term investor buys at the peak or a low and whether dividends are reinvested or not.

Had an unlucky immortal bought at the market peak in June of 1720, he

---

*One could argue that we are not comparing like for like because the index constituents in 1708 were not exactly the same as in 2002. The index is an unweighted arithmetic average of Bank of England and East Indies stock from 1664 to August 1711, and of Bank of England, East Indies, and South Sea stock from September 1711 to January 1811. The FTSE All-Share Index was officially established in April 1962 and had 715 member constituents as of July 2002.

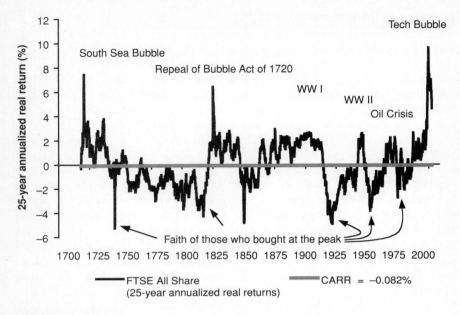

**FIGURE 12.3** 25-Year Annual Return for U.K. Stock Market
*Source:* Global Financial Data.

or she would still not have recovered from the losses in real terms (assuming dividends were not reinvested). As a matter of fact, that investor would currently stand at around 22.3 percent of the 1720 peak in real terms. The FTSE All-Share index stood at 1,961.4 on July 16, 2002. In nominal terms the estimated equivalent to the index stood at 104.4 in June 1720. The nominal annualized rate of return from the peak to today was 1.05 percent. However, in today's money the index was at 10,154 at the 1720 peak. This results in a real annualized rate of return of –0.58 percent. In other words, the unlucky immortal would have lost money had he or she not invested some of the dividends, in absolute return space, that is. Figure 12.3 is the reason why fighting inflation is important. It is also the reason why some equity brokerage houses normally do not display a great sense of history.

This analysis, obviously, fails to be conclusive on various fronts. One is that it suffers from a period bias; it shows only the most recent 300 years. An immortal, being able to make long-term comparisons, would surely find the past 300 years more investor friendly than the previous centuries.* In the thir-

---

*A counterargument to this is that the twentieth century saw both the most extreme deflation (1930s) and the most extreme inflation (1970s) in any period. See Ineichen (2000a).

teenth century, for example, Mongol conqueror Genghis Khan did not exactly contribute to an investor-friendly environment conquering most of the Chin empire of north China; subduing Turkistan, Transoxania, and Afghanistan; and raiding Persia and eastern Europe. The fourteenth century was the century of the Hundred Years' War and the Black Death. However, the fifteenth century opened new investment alternatives to the long-term investor. A new emerging market was discovered in 1492.

Comparing today's capital markets with markets 300 years ago is, admittedly, stretching it.* However, Figure 12.3 gives some long-term perspective with respect to the past two decades being phenomenal for equity investors in some parts of the world. Figure 12.4 gives a long-term perspective for the U.S. stock market—the most successful emerging market in the history of capital markets. The line measures the index level as a percentage of the previous all-time high. The longest five gaps were marked.

Probably the most extreme example of survivorship bias in capital markets today is the notion that equities outperform bonds in the long term, that

---

*On the other hand, as John Kenneth Galbraith put it: "There can be few fields of human endeavor in which history counts for so little as in the world of finance." From Warwick (2000).

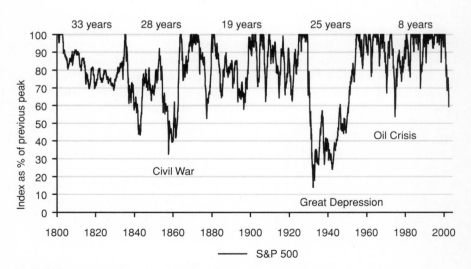

**FIGURE 12.4** Underwater Perspective of U.S. Stock Market
*Source:* Global Financial Data.

is, the widely touted equity risk premium puzzle. The term "equity risk premium puzzle" refers to the puzzling high historical average returns of U.S. stocks relative to bonds. Mehra and Prescott (1985) show that standard general equilibrium models cannot explain the size of the risk premium on U.S. equities, which averaged 6 percent over the period 1889–1978. The view that stocks outperform bonds could be because most analysis is based on a surviving stock market, the U.S. stock market. However, the standard error of such an analysis is high. Unfortunately, one cannot test the equity premium by rerunning U.S. market history to see what would have happened along other sample paths.

However, one can look at other stock markets. Jorion and Goetzmann (1999) did exactly that. They examined the twentieth century returns of 39 stock markets around the world, including several with experiences vastly different from the U.S. stock market, such as Russia (disappeared in 1917) and Germany and Japan (experienced discontinuities). The authors reported that the U.S. market was the best-performing market of all 39 markets. Note that the share of global equity market capitalization of the United States, Japan, and the United Kingdom in 2000 was 46 percent, 13 percent, and 8 percent respectively. This compares with 22 percent, 4 percent, and 12 percent 100 years earlier.[4] Imperial Russia and Argentina did not do as well over this 100-year period.

Arnott and Bernstein (2002b) argue that in 1926 U.S. stock investors should have been expecting a 1.4 percent premium of equities over bonds and not the 5 percent they actually earned over the next 75 years. The market exceeded objective expectations as a consequence of four accidents, one of which is the aforementioned survivor bias:* Since 1926, the United States has fought no wars on its own soil, nor has it experienced revolution. Four of the 15 largest stock markets in the world in 1900 suffered a total loss of capital at some point in the past century. The markets were China, Russia, Argentina, and Egypt. Two others came close—Germany (twice) and Japan. The authors conclude that U.S. investors in early 1926 would *not* have considered the likelihood to be zero, nor should today's true long-term investor. Some of the axioms supporting the case for equities as long-term investments, therefore, are founded on some debatable assumptions and long-term return expectations are probably too high.

Another line of argument is valuation. One could argue that valuations after nearly 20 years of asset inflation are stretched. In December 1996 Alan Greenspan used the term "irrational exuberance," which sent (brief) shock

---

*The other three historical accidents were: 1. Decoupling yields from real yields; 2. Rising valuation multiples; and 3. Regulatory reform. From Arnott and Bernstein (2002b), p. 67.

waves through the stock market when he indicated publicly that valuations might be stretched. Note that the S&P 500 index was around 750 in December 1996, compared with around 1,500 in March 2000 and 900 in July 2002. Figure 12.5 shows that the bull market was primarily a function of expanding valuations, that is, investors' current assessment of future earnings.

However, this assessment could have had a positive bias explained by factors other than rational expectations.* Viewing the historically unique market

---

*Gustave Le Bon, author of *The Crowd*, explains social excesses with what he calls the *law of the mental unity of the crowds*. As mentioned earlier, a bull market requires incremental buyers. Whether the incremental buyers are driven by a sound economic outlook or the length of skirts in this year's summer collection does not really matter. It is the belief in higher prices that triggers the action of the incremental buyer. As Le Bon (1982) puts it: "A crowd is at the mercy of all external exciting causes, and reflects their incessant variations. It is the slave of the impulses which it receives. . . . This very fact that crowds possess in common ordinary qualities explains why they can never accomplish acts demanding a high degree of intelligence." Or as Winston Churchill, not necessarily demonstrating an act of political correctness, put it: "The best argument against democracy is a five-minute conversation with the average voter."

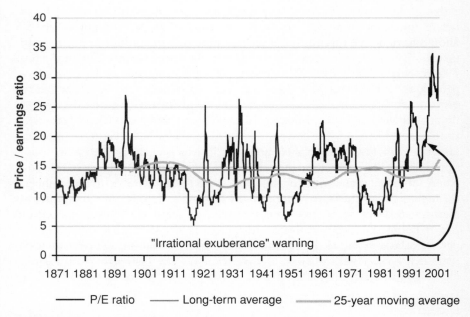

**FIGURE 12.5** Price/Earnings Ratio for U.S. Stock Market
*Source:* Based on P/E data from Robert Shiller (http://aida.econ.yale.edu/~shiller/data.htm).

valuation from a different perspective, Barr Rosenberg, in a presentation to the AXA Investment Managers Client Conference, noted that the market capitalization of the 500 largest companies in the San Francisco Bay area was $3.5 trillion. By comparison, he pointed out that the market capitalization of all of Asia (excluding Japan), a region of 3.2 billion people, including China and India, was $2.2 trillion.[5]

An interesting showcase on equity valuation was shown in the study mentioned earlier by Robert Arnott and Peter Bernstein (2002a,b). They argue that the 8 percent real return for U.S. stocks and the 5 percent risk premium for stocks relative to government bonds has never been a realistic expectation except from major market bottoms. They also analyzed S&P 500 data from 1802 to date. However, their methodology differed to most of the literature on long-term returns from stock prices. Most analysis in literature is based on total returns, that is, is based on the assumption that dividends and any other cash flows to the investor is reinvested in the index. However, this is not a realistic assumption.

Arnott and Bernstein (2002a) show that $100 invested in 1802 grows to $700 million in the 199 years to 2001 when dividends are reinvested. Some of the growth is due to inflation. When the analysis is adjusted for inflation the $100 in 1802 grow into "only" $33 million. However, and this is quite interesting, if we assume that dividends are spent then the $100 grow to $1,884, net of inflation.* The authors stress the point that the difference between $700 million and $1,884 is rather large and that the analysis has not even adjusted for taxes. In short, over 90 percent of the return on stocks over the past 199 years has come from (1) inflation, (2) the dividends that the stocks have paid, and (3) the rising valuation levels since 1982, rather than from growth in the underlying fundamentals or real dividends or earnings. As the authors point out: Most long-run forecasts of earnings or dividend growth ignore the simple fact that aggregate earnings and dividends in the economy cannot sustainably grow faster than the economy itself. Much of the growth in the economy comes from innovation and entrepreneurial capitalism.

Another characteristic of bubbles is that they are partially financed through debt, as illustrated conceptually in Figure 12.6. Higher prices give an incentive to lever up, increasing the asset price inflation. Needless to say, the 1990s bubble created enormous imbalances in the U.S. economy, notably a private sector financial deficit and a wide current account deficit. However, there is the view that the honeymoon period is over. The move from high inflation to low inflation has been made. That brought down nominal yields on

---

*Arnott and Bernstein also stress that the growth to $1,884 occurred in the bull market from 1982 to 2001. In the 180 years from 1802 to 1982, the real value of the $100 portfolio had grown to $300.

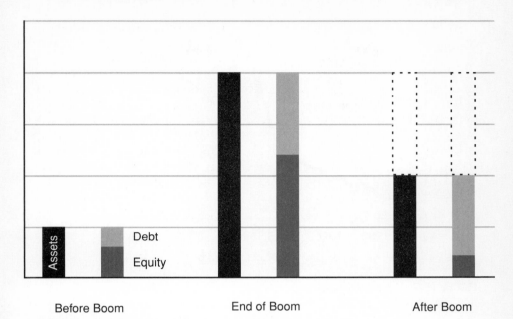

**FIGURE 12.6** Change of Balance Sheet from Boom to Bust
*Source:* Adapted from Zulauf (2002a).

financial assets and caused asset prices to rise. However, from here any kind of price change would not be good for equities. A return to inflation would push up yields and would further put pressure on share prices; a move to deflation (as in Japan) would put pressure on corporate profits. Assuming no upward rating of shares, future equity returns will equal the current dividend yield plus dividend growth. The further assumption that dividends move in line with gross domestic product (GDP), suggests that total annual equity returns could be in the single digits for a while.

Bubbles have burst before. Figure 12.6 shows the mechanics of such bubbles. Asset price inflation leads to boom and bust. Whether Figure 12.6 shows the balance sheet of a corporate investor or the balance sheet of a pension fund where "debt" represents liabilities to the pension beneficiaries is not relevant.

Figure 12.7 compares the Japanese equity experience from the 1980s with the U.S. equity experience from the 1990s (data is July 16, 2002, inclusive). Alan Greenspan's two remarks from December 1996 (irrational exuberance) and July 2002 (infectious greed) were added. The Nikkei index is shown with a different y-axis and without the time axis showing. The time series has been moved forward so the peak of the time series of the S&P 500 in-

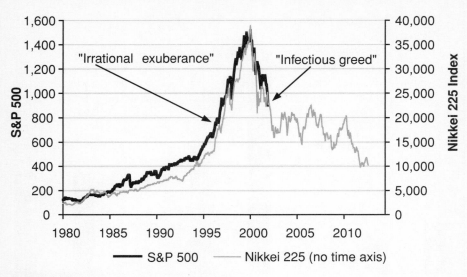

**FIGURE 12.7** S&P 500 versus Nikkei 225
*Source:* Datastream.

dex (August 2000) matches the peak of the Nikkei 225 index time series (December 1989). This chart is for illustration only. Never would we dare to imply that the S&P 500 could go to 400. After all, "this time it's different."*

Robert Shiller (2000) discusses speculative bubbles in connection with Ponzi schemes.

> *In a Ponzi scheme, the manager of the scheme promises to make large profits for investors by investing their money. But little or no investment of contributors' funds in any real assets is actually made. Instead, the manager pays off the initial investors with the proceeds of a sale to a second round of investors, and the second round with the proceeds from a sale to a third, and so on. . . .*
>
> *As part of their strategy, successful Ponzi schemes present to investors a plausible story about how great profits can be made. Charles Ponzi told investors that he was able to make money for them by exploit-*

---

*Recommending momentum (as opposed to reversal) is much more commercial. However, one can make the point that the law of gravity never changes. As Jim Rogers (2000) puts it: "In the laws of economics, in the laws of history, in the laws of politics, and in the laws of society, it's never different this time. The law of gravity isn't ever suspended for someone's convenience, and these laws are just as rigorous, though more subtle and complex. If they weren't universal, we wouldn't call them laws."

*ing an arbitrage profit opportunity involving international postage reply coupons.** . . .*

*Speculative feedback loops that are in effect naturally occurring Ponzi schemes do arise from time to time without the contrivance of a fraudulent manager. . . . When prices go up a number of times, investors are rewarded sequentially by price movements in these markets, just as they are in Ponzi schemes.*

While not claiming that with the stock market there is necessarily dishonest behavior, Shiller implies that there is an incentive of "telling stories that suggest that the market will go up further. There is no reason for these stories to be fraudulent; they need only emphasize the positive news and give less emphasis to the negative."[†] Shiller makes the point:

*The extension from Ponzi schemes to naturally occurring speculative bubbles appears so natural that one must conclude, if there is to be debate about speculative bubbles, that the burden of proof is on skeptics to provide evidence as to why Ponzi-like speculative bubbles **cannot** occur."*[6]

One often-heard fallacy is that the stock market is correlated with the economy. This is true only in the very long run, as, for example, Arnott and Bernstein (2002a,b) stress. However, emphasis should be on *long run*. Figure 12.8 compares the Dow Jones Industrial Average with U.S. nominal GDP at year-end 1964, 1981, and 2001 (i.e., the movement in between these three dates is not shown).

At a hedge funds conference, James Jundt (2002) made the point (quoting Warren Buffett) that equity can trade for quite long periods unsynchronized with economic growth due to swings in valuation, that is, due to mood swings from fear and greed and changing risk appetite. From year-end 1964 to 1981 the Dow Jones Industrial Average index gained less than a point, increasing from 874.1 to 875.0 index points. U.S. nominal GDP increased from

---

*Potentially there is a parallel between hedge funds and Ponzi schemes. The quest for alpha is a negative-sum game. If a small group of investors captures a large piece of alpha from the mistakes of the large group of investors, common sense suggests that the large group learns and adopts the strategies of the smaller group. The alpha, therefore, is spread over an increasing amount of investors as the small group increases. Early adopters, therefore, share an economic rent. The parallel ends here: Ponzi schemes in most jurisdictions are illegal. Exploiting market inefficiencies is not.

†We have discussed this bias in Chapters 2 and 8. Some of the beneficiaries of this "good information" bias are short sellers (or any other active manager who can sell short and can make an absolute profit if market prices are inflated relative to fair value).

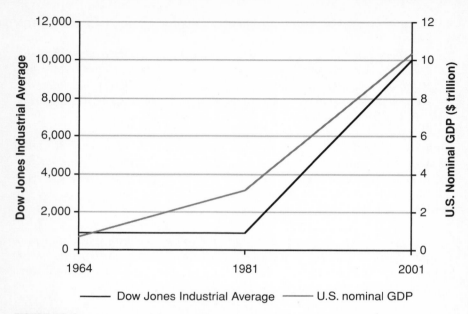

**FIGURE 12.8** U.S. Nominal Gross Domestic Product versus DJ Industrial Average

$664 billion to $3.1 trillion. This results in an increase of annual nominal GDP of 372 percent or 9.5 percent nominal and 3.4 percent real growth. In the 20-year period from December 1981 to 2001 the Dow Jones Industrial Average increased 11.4-fold from 875 to 10,021. This means nominal annual growth of 13.0 percent. U.S. nominal GDP increased from $3.1 trillion to $10.4 trillion. This results in a nominal annual growth rate of 6.2 percent (3.2 percent in real terms).

Over the long term the stock market should grow at the same rate as does the economy. Assuming the U.S. economy grows at 3 percent per year with no inflation (i.e., real growth is equal to nominal growth), U.S. nominal GDP will stand at $18.8 trillion in December 2021. For the Dow Jones Industrial Average to have the same growth between 1964 and 2021, the close of the index on Friday, December 31, 2021, should be 24,687. This index level implies an annual growth rate from the close of 2001 to 2021 of 4.61 percent. This growth rate would balance the below-average zero growth rate between 1964 and 1981 and the above-average 13 percent growth rate between 1981 and 2001. Note that actuarial growth rates for pension funds in some countries of the developed world are still around 8 to 10 percent.

Figure 12.9 shows the performance of the S&P 500, Nasdaq Composite, and FTSE All-Share from January 2000 to July 16, 2002. A potential path to loss recovery has been added whereby an annual growth rate of 5 percent was

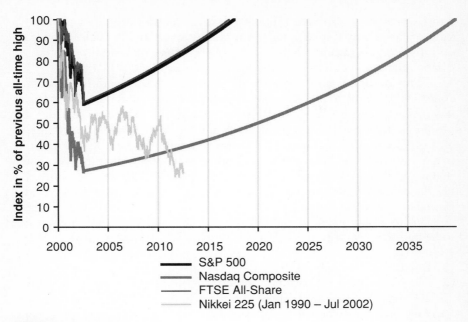

**FIGURE 12.9** Loss Recovery
*Source:* Datastream.

assumed. The 5 percent is an assumption and could be either 5 percent real or 8 percent nominal with 3 percent inflation or other combinations including or excluding dividends. The Nikkei 225 index was added for comparison purposes. The January 1990 to July 2002 period has been brought forward by 10 years starting at January 2000 to show alternative paths of "recovery." Note that Figure 12.9 is not the marketing way of showing how equities recover. The normal way is showing annual returns in bar charts. For example, showing the FTSE All-Share losing 31.4 percent and 55.3 percent in 1974 and 1975 and subsequently rising by a staggering 136.3 percent in 1976 implies to the enumerate reader high future profits. What it does not show is that after losing 31.4 percent and 55.3 percent and then recovering 136.3 percent, the wealth is still only at 72.5 percent from the initial investment of 100 percent in nominal terms. (In real terms, the wealth stood at 43.1 percent at the end of 1976.) Had an investor invested in the beginning of 1974, he or she would have recovered losses during 1979 in nominal terms and during 1990 in real terms (assuming dividends were taxed or spent and not reinvested).

Chapter 11 mentioned that issues such as trust, prudence, and integrity are not an issue in major finance textbooks although they are essential in day-to-day business life. Shiller (2000) notes that textbooks promote a view of financial markets as working rationally and efficiently, but do not provide arguments as to why feedback loops supporting speculative bubbles cannot occur. If such a positive bias exists, there is an inherent potential for disappointment in equity markets today.

Throughout this book we made the point that diversification is a laudable concept and not defining risk as total risk might not be the pinnacle of investment wisdom. Figure 12.9 underlines the notion that risk has to be defined in absolute return space. Investment opportunities have to be evaluated against an absolute yardstick. Long-only investing might yield satisfactory results, but—and this is the main point—it might not. Going forward, it is unlikely that active management will be considered being fully exposed to chance. Under the proposed paradigm of absolute returns, investors should request performance to depend on skill, not hope.

Due to an unfortunate lack of foresight, the author is not in the position to be bullish or bearish on stock markets. Three points can be made:

1. Equity is a very risky asset class.*
2. The observation that equities outperform bonds in the long term is probably true, but certainly depends on the definition of "long term."
3. Any investor (whether institutional or private) who faces uncertainty with respect to the investment horizon should define return target and risk target in absolute return space and should be managing money and assets in a volatility-reducing manner.

What is the irony?

The irony is that equities, or rather equity long-only managers, are considered less risky than hedge funds; that is, allocation to managers who do not replicate an asset class but focus on absolute returns while controlling portfolio volatility. This is ironic. The reason is that it is a fallacy which, unfortunately, might cause a lot of harm to investors and savers who buy into it. Subjective risk in equities is nonexistent or is very low. Full transparency exists. There are hardly any airports left where one *cannot* see the recent moves of major equity indexes. Any administrator or client adviser has very little career risk when recommending equities because the consensus view favors equities over all other asset classes in the long term. Even articles in peer-refereed financial journals suggest 100 percent equities for long-term investors based on historical returns. In Western societies equities have reached cult status. U.K. pension funds, to mention the most extreme form

---

*Or as Warren Buffett puts it: "Unless you can watch your stock holdings decline by 50 percent without becoming panic-stricken, you should not be in the stock market." From Hagstrom (1994), p. 53.

of portfolio concentration, have 70 to 80 percent in equities and until recently felt quite comfortable as everyone else had the same position. However, the number of glossy equity offering brochures could be negatively correlated with 20-year returns to the investor. Back in 1982, there were none or hardly any. Only as the momentum train (i.e., disinflation process of the 1990s) was in full swing did the consensus really start making equity long-only investing a cult.

In countries such as Germany and Italy the equity cult only started as recently as the mid-1990s. This might prove rather unfortunate. Having lived in a bond culture for most of the post–World War II period, some continental European pension funds have announced that they finally bought into the case for equities and will increase their minuscule allocations over the next years. As mentioned earlier, asset price inflation is fueled by marginal buyers—new investors or fresh money moving into the system driving prices higher. If the marginal buyer dies or changes his or her mind, a deflationary process starts, as illustrated in Figure 12.6. Since debt (liabilities) remain unchanged, net assets deflate. It is like with musical chairs: In the end there is always someone without a chair.

## CLOSING REMARKS

At the beginning of this book we made the point that the business of investing started with an absolute return focus. An absolute return focus, unlike the relative return focus, tries to balance profit opportunity with the risk of damaging the financial status quo. It is very unlikely that this investment philosophy is a short-term phenomenon as some market observers suggest. Much more likely is that the absolute return approach is the third paradigm in asset management that is currently in the process of replacing the second paradigm, the relative return approach.

Investors and capital markets in the developed economies might or might not have entered a new political and financial regime. However, uncertainty is here to stay. Uncertainty is probably the only certainty in the game of risk. The only certainty about the future is to expect the unexpected—which by definition is unpredictable. Portfolio diversification therefore is a laudable concept. Portfolio concentration, on the other hand, might soon turn out to be viewed as a bad idea. A good piece of advice is not to become victim to what Milton Friedman calls "the tyranny of the status quo."

Societies around the globe have some tough challenges ahead: demand for political regime shift from within (antiglobalization zealots and other juvenile moralists) and from outside (religious fanaticism); increasing current liabilities from demographic shifts (rising longevity, low real interest rates); increasing debt levels caused by myopic, interventionist, and short-term policies of post-Soviet Marxists (i.e., social democrats); continuous run to the Bastille by adolescent Rousseauists after every corporate failure, and so on. Given this kind of uncertainty, not defining risk in absolute terms seems ludicrous.

Hedge fund manager and *Barron's* Roundtable pundit Felix Zulauf (2002b) argues we (Western financial markets) are in a structural bear market lasting 5 to 10 years. This might or might not be true. He observes that most structural bear markets eventually hit a low where stocks trade at book value. In the case of the S&P 500 this is at an index level of around 220. If this book does not change the way investors think about risk, a decline in the S&P 500 index to 220 certainly will.

# notes

## Chapter 1     Introducing Absolute Returns

1. From Persaud (2001), p. 11.
2. From Hagstrom (1994), p. 73.
3. From Caldwell and Kirkpatrick (1995).
4. From Caldwell and Kirkpatrick (1995).
5. *Financial Times* (2002c).
6. From *Financial Times* (2002c).
7. From Caldwell and Kirkpatrick (1995).
8. From Caldwell and Kirkpatrick (1995).
9. From Caldwell (1995), p. 9.
10. Caldwell (1995), p. 10.
11. Caldwell (1995), p. 11.
12. From Hagstrom (1994), p. 3, quoting from Train (1981), p. 11.
13. From Hagstrom (1994), p. 4, quoting from Train (1981), p. 12.
14. Letter from Tiger Management LLC to limited partners dated March 30, 2000.
15. Soros (1987), p. 15.
16. Soros (1987), p. 15.
17. From Smith and Walter (1997), p. 10.
18. Bloomberg News (1998).
19. From Elden (2001), p. 47.
20. From Elden (2001), p. 48.
21. Rohrer (1986).
22. From Elden (2001), p. 49.
23. *Financial Times* (2002d).
24. From Board of Governors of the Federal Reserve System, Flow of Funds Accounts of the United States, December 7, 2001.
25. Bloomberg (2002b) quoting Eighth Annual Hennessee Hedge Fund Manager Survey.
26. Wall Street Journal Online (2002).
27. *EuroHedge*, July 31, 2000, from www.hedgeworld.com.

## Chapter 2 Myths and Misconceptions

This chapter draws on material from UBS Warburg (2000) and Ineichen (2001a).
1. Wace (2000).
2. See Jorion (2000).
3. From Jorion (2000).
4. From AIMR (1999).
5. Swensen (2000), p. 5.
6. Swensen (2000), p. 267.
7. From Schneeweis (1998b).
8. According to Lowenstein (2000).
9. Quote found in Cassidy (1997), p. 107.
10. *Financial Times* (2002a), p. 17.
11. From SEC (1999).
12. From Staley (1997), p. 6.
13. Bloomberg News (1999).
14. Bloomberg News (2002c).
15. From Chandler (1998).
16. From *Financial Times* (2002b), p. 29.
17. This notion is based on work done by De Ruiter (2001).

## Chapter 3 Difference between Long-Only and Absolute Return Funds

This chapter draws on material from UBS Warburg (2000).
1. According to Campbell, Lo, and MacKinlay (1997), p. 291.
2. See Shiller (1997).
3. See Fung and Hsieh (1997a).
4. From Edwards (1999).
5. From Edwards (1999).
6. From Edwards (1999).
7. Bloomberg News (2002a).
8. Bloomberg News (2002a).
9. See Soros (1995), p. 8.
10. From Peltz (2001), p. 51.

## Chapter 4 Advantages and Disadvantages of Investing in Hedge Funds

Chapter 4 draws on material from UBS Warburg (2000).
1. From Schwed (1995).
2. From Yale Endowment (2001), p. 6, from www.yale.org.

3. From Yale Endowment (2001), p. 12.
4. For a discussion on the subject see Coleman and Siegel (2000).
5. From Chandler (1998).
6. President's Working Group on Financial Markets (1999).
7. From HBS (1999).
8. From Jorion (2000).
9. Jorion (2000).
10. Niederhoffer (1997), p. ix.
11. Niederhoffer (1997), p. viii.
12. From Lo and MacKinlay (1999), p. 3.
13. From Lo and MacKinlay (1999), p. 4.
14. From Lo and MacKinlay (1999), p. 7.
15. Von Mises (1996).
16. Von Mises (1996), p. 57.
17. Von Mises (1996), p. 56.
18. Soros (1995), p. 72.
19. As mentioned in Bacon (2000).
20. Soros (1987), p. 9.
21. Soros (1987), p. 20.
22. Soros (1987), p. 14.
23. Soros (1987), p. 21.
24. Soros (1987), p. 29.
25. Soros (1994).
26. Olsen (1998).
27. Olsen (1998).
28. Leong et al. (2002).
29. From Leong et al. (2002).

## Chapter 6   Relative-Value and Market-Neutral Strategies

Chapter 6 draws on material from UBS Warburg (2000).
1. Lawrence Summers after 1987 crash, quote from Lowenstein (2000), p. 75.
2. From Weinstein (1931).
3. Lo and MacKinlay (1999), p. 16.
4. From Chandler (1998), p. 49.
5. Pension & Endowment Forum (2000), p. 23.
6. White (1996).
7. From Jorion (2000).
8. Shefrin (2000), p. 42, quoting from *Wall Street Journal*, January 11, 1999.
9. From Warburg Dillon Read (1998).

## Chapter 7    Event-Driven Strategies

Chapter 7 draws on material from UBS Warburg (2000).
1. From Endlich (1999).
2. From Endlich (1999), p. 109.
3. From Pension & Endowment Forum (2000), p. 28.
4. From Hagstrom (1994) quoting Berkshire Hathaway Annual Report 1988.
5. From Endlich (1999).
6. From Smith and Walter (1997), p. 5.
7. From Smith and Walter (1997), p. 6.
8. From Cottier (1997).
9. From Nicholas (1999).

## Chapter 8    Opportunistic Absolute Return Strategies

Chapter 8 draws on material from UBS Warburg (2000), UBS Warburg (2001), and Ineichen (2002c); the Appendix draws on material from UBS Warburg (2001) and Ineichen (2002c).
1. From Cottier (1997).
2. From Rogers (2000), p. 122.
3. From www.streetstories.com/James_Rogers.htm.
4. From Nicholas (1999).
5. From *Institutional Investor* (2000).
6. From Staley (1997), p. 20.
7. From Staley (1997), p. 4.
8. See Fama and French (1995) and Lakonishok, Shleifer, and Vishny (1994).
9. From Staley (1997), p. 26.
10. Bloomberg News (2002b) quoting the Eighth Annual Hennessee Hedge Fund Manager Survey.
11. From Fung and Hsieh (2000a).

## Chapter 9    Industry Overview

The first part of Chapter 9 draws on material in UBS Warburg (2001) and Ineichen (2002a).

## Chapter 10    Advantages and Disadvantages of Investing in Funds of Hedge Funds

This chapter draws on material from UBS Warburg (2001) and Ineichen (2002a).

1. From UBS Warburg (2001).
2. From AIMA (2002).
3. From Swensen (2000), p. 325.
4. *Institutional Investor* magazine, September 2001, p. 67.

## Chapter 11    The Alpha in Funds of Hedge Funds

This chapter draws on material from UBS Warburg (2001) and Ineichen (2002b).

1. Hagstrom (1994), p. 172, quoting Jim Rasmussen, "Buffett Talks Strategy with Students," *Omaha World-Herald*, January 2, 1994, p. 26.
2. From Jaeger (2000), p. 75.
3. From Peltz (2001), p. 30.
4. *Sound Practices for Hedge Fund Managers* (2000), p. 16.
5. *Sound Practices for Hedge Fund Managers* (2000), p. 50.
6. *Sound Practices for Hedge Fund Managers* (2000), p. 50.
7. *Sound Practices for Hedge Fund Managers* (2000), p. 22.
8. Grinold and Kahn (2000a), p. 113.
9. Grinold and Kahn (2000a), p. 148.

## Chapter 12    Game of Risk or Risky Game?

The first section of Chapter 12 (Bubble or New Paradigm in Asset Management?) draws on material in UBS Warburg (2001) and Ineichen (2001b).

1. From Camerer (1989).
2. From Camerer (1989).
3. From Camerer (1989).
4. From Dimson et al. (2002).
5. From Evensky (2001).
6. Shiller (2000), p. 67. Emphasis from Shiller.

Ackermann, C. (1998) "The Impact of Regulatory Restrictions on Fund Performance: A Comparative Study of Hedge Funds and Mutual Funds." FMA Presentation, October 1998.

Agarwal, Vikas, and Narayan Y. Naik. (2000a) "Multi-Period Performance Persistence Analysis of Hedge Fund." *Journal of Financial and Quantitative Analysis*, Vol. 35, No. 2.

Agarwal, Vikas, and Narayan Y. Naik. (2000b) "Performance Evaluation of Hedge Funds with Option-Based and Buy-and-Hold Strategies." FA Working Paper No. 300, August.

Agarwal, Vikas, and Narayan Y. Naik. (2000c) "On Taking the 'Alternative' Route: The Risks, Rewards, and Performance Persistence of Hedge Funds." *Journal of Alternative Investments*, Vol. 2, No. 4 (Spring), pp. 6–23.

AIMA. (2002) "Hedge Fund Risk Transparency." *AIMA Newsletter*, No. 50 (February).

AIMR. (1999) *Standards of Practice Handbook*, 8th edition. Charlottesville: AIMR.

Allais, Maurice. (1953) "Le comportement de l'homme rationnel devant le risque: Critique des Postulats et Axiomes de l'Ecole Americaine." *Econometrica*, Vol. 21, pp. 503–546.

Amin, Gaurav S., and Harry M. Kat. (2001) "Hedge Fund Performance 1990–2000—Do the Money Machines Really Add Value?" ISMA Working Paper, Forthcoming in *Journal of Financial and Quantitative Analysis* (July).

Amin, Gaurav S., and Harry M. Kat. (2002a) "Portfolios of Hedge Funds: What Investors Really Invest In." ISMA Working Paper (January 11).

Amin, Gaurav S., and Harry M. Kat. (2002b) "Who Should Buy Hedge Funds? The Effects of Including Hedge Funds in Portfolios of Stocks and Bonds." ISMA Working Paper (March 6).

Anson, Mark J.P. (2001a) "Hedge Fund Incentive Fees and the 'Free Option.'" *Journal of Alternative Investments*, Vol. 4, No. 2 (Fall), pp. 43–48.

Anson, Mark J.P. (2001b) "Should Hedge Funds Be Institutionalized?" *Journal of Investing*, Vol. 10, No. 3 (Fall), pp. 69–74.

Arnott, Robert D., and David J. Leinweber. (1994) "Long-Short Strategies Reassessed." *Financial Analysts Journal*, Vol. 50, No.5 (September/October), pp. 76–78.

Arnott, Robert D., and Peter L. Bernstein. (2002a) "What's 'Normal' Equity Return?" *Investments & Pensions Europe (IPE)* (January), p. 57.

Arnott, Robert D., and Peter L. Bernstein. (2002b) "What Risk Premium Is Normal?" *Financial Analysts Journal*, Vol. 58, No. 2 (March/April), pp. 64–85.

Arrow, Kenneth. (1982) "Risk Perception in Psychology and Economics," *Economic Inquiry*, Vol. 20, pp. 1–9.

Asquith, Paul, and Lisa Meulbroek. (1996) "An Empirical Investigation of Short Interest." Harvard University Working Paper.

Bacon, Louis Moore. (2000) Keynote speech at the 2000 Hedge Fund Symposium (EIM/EuroHedge/SFI), "Can Institutions Afford to Ignore Hedge Funds?" April 27, London.

Barra Strategic Consulting Group. (2001) "Fund of Hedge Funds—Rethinking Resource Requirements." (September), Survey.

Bekier, Matthias. (1996) *Marketing Hedge Funds—A Key Strategic Variable in Defining Possible Roles of an Emerging Investment Force*. Bern: Peter Lang AG, European Academic Publishers.

Benartzi, Shlomo, and Richard H. Thaler. (1995) "Myopic Loss Aversion and the Equity Premium Puzzle." *Quarterly Journal of Economics*, 110 (1), pp. 73–92.

Benartzi, Shlomo, and Richard H. Thaler. (1999) "Risk Aversion or Myopia? Choices in Repeated Gambles and Retirement Investments." *Management Science*, Vol. 45, pp. 364–381.

Bernstein, Peter L. (1992) *Capital Ideas—The Improbable Origins of Modern Wall Street*. New York: Free Press.

Bernstein, Peter L. (1995) "Risk as a History of Ideas." *Financial Analysts Journal*, Vol. 51, No. 1 (January/February), pp. 7–11.

Bernstein, Peter L. (1996) *Against the Gods: The Remarkable Story of Risk*. New York: John Wiley & Sons.

Bernstein, Peter L. (1999) "Wimps and Consequences." *Journal of Portfolio Management*, Vol. 26, No. 1 (Fall), p. 1.

Bierman, Harold, Jr. (1998) "Why Not 100% Equities?" Comment, *Journal of Portfolio Management*, Vol. 24, No. 2 (Fall), pp. 70–73.

Bird, Ron, and John McKinnon. (2001) "Changes in the Behaviour of Earnings Surprise: International Evidence and Implications." *Journal of Investing*, Vol. 10, No. 3 (Fall), pp. 19–32.

Black, Fischer, and Myron Scholes. (1973) "The Pricing of Options and Corporate Liabilities." *Journal of Political Economy*, Vol. 81, pp. 637–654.

Bloomberg News. (1998) "Warren Buffett Invested $270 Million in Bond Hedge Fund in July," by Katherine Burton (October 15).

Bloomberg News. (1999) "Singapore Welcomes Hedge Funds in Finance Center Bid" (January 4).

Bloomberg News. (2002a) "Hedge Funds Seek SEC Permission to Advertise Their Offerings" (February 28).

Bloomberg News. (2002b) "Hennessee Releases 8th Annual Hennessee Hedge Fund Manager Survey" (March 7).

Bloomberg News. (2002c) "H.K. Woos Hedge Funds, 4 Years After Attack on Dollar" (March 8).

Bogle, John C. (1991) "Investing in the 1990s: Remembrance of Things Past, and Things Yet to Come." *Journal of Portfolio Management*, Vol. 17, No. 3 (Spring), pp. 5–14.

Bogle, John C. (1998) "The Implication of Style Analysis for Mutual Fund Performance Evaluation." *Journal of Portfolio Management*, Vol. 24, No. 4 (Summer), pp. 34–42.

Brinson, Gary P., L. Randolph Hood, and Gilbert L. Beebower. (1986) "Determinants of Portfolio Performance." *Financial Analysts Journal*, Vol. 42, No. 4 (July/August), pp. 39–44.

Brooks, Chris, and Harry M. Kat. (2001) "The Statistical Properties of Hedge Fund Returns and Their Implications for Investors." ISMA Working Paper (October).

Brooks, John. (1998) *The Go-Go Years—The Drama and Crashing Finale of Wall Street's Bullish 60s*. First published 1973. New York: John Wiley & Sons.

Brown, Stephen J., and William N. Goetzmann. (2001) "'Hedge Funds with Style." National Bureau of Economic Research Working Paper (March).

Brown, Stephen J., William N. Goetzmann, and James Park. (1999) "Conditions for Survival: Changing Risk and the Performance of Hedge Fund Managers and CTAs." Working Paper (June). Early draft of Brown, Goetzmann, and Park (2001).

Brown, Stephen J., William N. Goetzmann, and James M. Park. (2000) "Hedge Funds and the Asian Currency Crisis." *Journal of Portfolio Management*, Vol. 26, No. 4 (Summer), pp. 95–101.

Brown, Stephen J., William N. Goetzmann, and James M. Park. (2001) "Careers and Survival: Competition and Risk in the Hedge Fund and CTA Industry." *Journal of Finance*, Vol. 56, No. 5, pp. 1869–1886.

Brown, Stephen J., William N. Goetzmann, and Roger G. Ibbotson. (1999) "Offshore Hedge Funds: Survival and Performance, 1989–1995." *Journal of Business*, Vol. 72, No. 1 (January), pp. 91–117.

Brown, Stephen J., William N. Goetzmann, Roger G. Ibbotson, and Stephen A. Ross. (1992) "Survivorship Bias in Performance Studies." *Review of Financial Studies*, Vol. 5, No. 4 (Winter), pp. 553–580.

Brunel, Jean L.P. (2002) "Absolute Return Strategies Revisited." *Journal of Wealth Management*, Vol. 4, No. 4 (Spring), pp. 63–75.

Brush, John S. (1997) "Comparisons and Combinations of Long and Long-

Short Strategies." *Financial Analysts Journal*, Vol. 53, No. 3 (May/June), pp. 81–89.

Caglayan, Mustafa Onur, and Franklin R. Edwards. (2001) "Hedge Fund and Commodity Fund Investment Styles in Bull and Bear Markets." *Journal of Portfolio Management*, Vol. 27, No. 4 (Summer), pp. 97–108.

Caldwell, Ted. (1995) "Introduction: The Model for Superior Performance." In Jess Lederman and Robert A. Klein, eds., *Hedge Funds*. New York: McGraw-Hill.

Caldwell, Ted, and Tom Kirkpatrick. (1995) "A Primer on Hedge Funds." Courtesy of Lookout Mountain Capital, Inc.

Camerer, Colin. (1989) "Bubbles and Fads in Asset Markets: A Review of Theory and Evidence." *Journal of Economic Surveys*, Vol. 3, pp. 3–38.

Campbell, John Y., Andrew W. Lo, and A. Craig MacKinlay. (1997) *The Econometrics of Financial Markets*. Princeton: Princeton University Press.

Capaul, Carlo, Ian Rowley, and William F. Sharpe. (1993) "International Value and Growth Stock Returns." *Financial Analysts Journal*, Vol. 49, No. 1 (January/February), pp. 10–23.

Cassidy, Donald L. (1997) *It's When You Sell That Counts*. New York: McGraw-Hill.

Chandler, Beverly. (1998) *Investing with the Hedge Fund Giants—Profit Whether Markets Rise or Fall*. London: Financial Times Pitman Publishing.

Chen, Hsiu-Lang, Narasimhan Jegadeesh, and Russ Wermers. (2000) "The Value of Active Mutual Fund Management: An Examination of the Stockholdings and Trades of Fund Managers." *Journal of Financial and Quantitative Analysis*, Vol. 35, No. 3 (September), pp. 343-368.

Clayman, Michelle. (1987) "In Search of Excellence: The Investor's Viewpoint." *Financial Analysts Journal*, Vol. 43, No. 3 (May–June), pp. 54–64.

Clayman, Michelle. (1994) "Excellence Revisited." *Financial Analysts Journal*, Vol. 50, No. 3 (May/June), pp. 61–65.

Clements, J. (1997) "Market Exuberance Isn't Too Rational? Sometimes, Investors Just Do It for Fun." *Wall Street Journal*, 15 July, C1.

Coleman, Thomas S., and Laurence B. Siegel. (2000) "Compensating Fund Managers for Risk-Adjusted Performance." Ford Foundation Working Paper, www.aima.org.

Cottier, Phillip. (1997) *Hedge Funds and Managed Futures—Performance, Risks, Strategies and Use in Investment Portfolios*. Bern: Verlag Paul Haupt.

Cowles, Alfred, 3rd. (1933) "Can Stock Market Forecasters Forecast?" *Econometrica*, Vol. 1 (July), pp. 309–324.

Crerend, William J. (1995) "Institutional Investment in Hedge Funds." In Jess Lederman and Robert A. Klein, eds., *Hedge Funds*. New York: McGraw-Hill.

Daniel, Kent, Mark Grinblatt, Sheridan Titman, and Russ Wermers. (1997) "Measuring Mutual Fund Performance with Characteristic-Based Benchmarks." *Journal of Finance*, Vol. 52, No. 3, pp. 1035–1058.

De Ruiter, Hans. (2001) "Assessing the Role and Risk of Hedge Funds within a Pension Fund Portfolio." Speech at hedge funds conference, Development Institute International, Geneva, December 12.

Dechow, Patricia M., Amy P. Hutton, Lisa Meulbroek, and Richard G. Sloan. (2001) "Short-Sellers, Fundamental Analysis, and Stock Returns." *Journal of Financial Economics*, Vol. 61, No. 1 (July), pp. 77–106.

Diamond, Douglas W., and Robert Verrechia. (1987) "Constraints on Short-Selling and Asset Price Adjustment to Private Information." *Journal of Financial Economics*, Vol. 18, June, pp. 277–311.

Dimson, Elroy, Paul Marsh, and Mike Staunton. (2002) *Triumph of the Optimists—101 Years of Global Investment Returns*. Princeton, NJ: Princeton University Press.

Dreman, David. (1997) *Contrarian Investment Strategies: The Next Generation*. New York: Simon & Schuster.

Edwards, Franklin R. (1999) "Do Hedge Funds Have a Future?" *Journal of Alternative Investments*, Vol. 2, No. 2 (Fall), pp. 63–68.

Edwards, Franklin R., and Mustafa Onur Caglayan. (2001) "Hedge Fund Performance and Manager Skill." *Journal of Futures Markets*, Vol. 21, No. 11, pp. 1003-1028.

Eichengreen, Barry, and Donald Mathieson. (1998) "Hedge Funds and Financial Market Dynamics." Occasional Paper No. 166. Washington, DC: International Monetary Fund (May).

Eichengreen, Barry, and Donald Mathieson. (1999) "Hedge Funds: What Do We Really Know?" Economic Issues No. 19, IMF (September). http://www.imf.org/external/pubs/ft/issues/issues19/#1.

Elden, Richard. (2001) "The Evolution of the Hedge Fund Industry." *Journal of Global Financial Markets*, Vol. 2, No. 4 (Winter), pp. 47–54.

Ellis, Charles D. (1993) *Investment Policy—How to Win the Loser's Game*. 2nd Edition. Homewood, IL: Business One Irwin.

Ellis, Charles D. (1998) *Winning the Loser's Game: Timeless Strategies for Successful Investing*. 3rd edition. New York: McGraw-Hill.

Ellis, Charles D., with James R. Vertin. (2001) *Wall Street People—True Stories of Today's Masters and Moguls*. New York: John Wiley & Sons.

Elton, E., M. Gruber, and C. Blake. (1996) "The Persistence of Risk-Adjusted Mutual Fund Performance." *Journal of Business*, Vol. 69, No. 2 (April), pp. 133–157.

Endlich, Lisa. (1999) *Goldman Sachs—The Culture of Success*. New York: Touchstone.

Estenne, Luc. (2000) "Risk Management Issues for the Family Office." In Virginia Reynolds Parker, ed., *Managing Hedge Fund Risk—From the Seat of the Practitioner*. London: Risk Books.

Evensky, Harold. (2001) "Heading for Disaster." *Financial Advisor* (April).

Fama, Eugene F. (1970) "Efficient Capital Markets: A Review of Theory and Empirical Work." *Journal of Finance*, Vol. 25, pp. 383–417.

Fama, Eugene F. (1998) "Market Efficiency, Long-Term Returns, and Behavioral Finance." *Journal of Financial Economics*, Vol. 49, No. 3, pp. 283–306.

Fama, Eugene, and Kenneth French. (1995) "Size and Book-to-Market Factors in Earnings and Stock Returns." *Journal of Finance*, Vol. 50, pp. 131–155.

*Financial Times*. (2002a) "The Dangers of Hedge Funds." *Personal View* column, by Hans Eichel (February 7).

*Financial Times*. (2002b) "Spotting the Dangers in Risk Management." *Global Investor*, by Vincent Boland (March 11).

*Financial Times*. (2002c) "Hesitation Is Honey for Wall Street Bear," *Global Investor*, by Alison Beard (March 26).

*Financial Times*. (2002d) "Equity Investments by Pension Funds Projected to Surge," by Paul Taylor (March 4). Article makes reference to study titled "Pension Reform and Global Equity Markets," by Birinyi Associates.

Fischel, Daniel R. (1995) *Payback: The Conspiracy to Destroy Michael Milken and His Financial Revolution*. New York: HarperCollins.

Frauenfelder, Eduard. (1987) *Optionen in Wertpapieren und Waren*, 2nd edition. Bern: Verlag Paul Haupt.

Freeman, John D. (1997) "Investment Deadweight and the Advantages of Long-Short Portfolio Managment." *VBA Journal* (September), pp. 11–14.

Friedman, Daniel, and Masanao Aoki. (1986) "Asset Price Bubbles from Poorly Aggregated Information: A Parametric Example." *Economic Letters*, 21, pp. 49–52.

Friedman, Milton, and Leonard Jimmy Savage. (1948) "The Utility Analysis of Choices Involving Risk." *Journal of Political Economy*, 56, pp. 279–304.

Fung, William, and David A. Hsieh. (1997a) "Empirical Characteristics of Dynamic Trading Strategies: The Case of Hedge Funds." *Review of Financial Studies*, Vol. 10, No. 2, pp. 275–302.

Fung, William, and David A. Hsieh. (1997b) "Survivorship Bias and Investment Style in the Returns of CTAs." *Journal of Portfolio Management*, Vol. 24, No. 1 (Fall), pp. 30–41.

Fung, William, and David A. Hsieh. (1999a) "A Primer on Hedge Funds." *Journal of Empirical Finance*, Vol. 6, No. 3 (September), pp. 309–331.

Fung, William, and David A. Hsieh. (1999b) "Is Mean-Variance Analysis Applicable to Hedge Funds?" *Economic Letters*, 62, pp. 53–58.

Fung, William, and David A. Hsieh. (2000a) "Measuring the Market Impact of Hedge Funds." *Journal of Empirical Finance*, Vol. 7, No. 1 (May), pp. 1–36.

Fung, William, and David A. Hsieh. (2000b) "Performance Characteristics of Hedge Funds and Commodity Funds: Natural versus Spurious Biases." *Journal of Financial and Quantitative Analysis*, Vol. 35, pp. 291–307.

Fung, William, and David A. Hsieh. (2001a) "Asset-Based Hedge Fund Styles and Portfolio Diversification." Working Paper. *Financial Analysts Journal* (August).

Fung, William, and David A. Hsieh. (2001b) "The Risk in Hedge Fund Strategies: Theory and Evidence from Trend Followers." *Review of Financial Studies*, Vol. 14, No. 2 (Summer), pp. 313–341.

Fung, William, and David A. Hsieh. (2002) "Hedge-Fund Benchmarks: Information Content and Biases." *Financial Analysts Journal*, Vol. 58, No. 1 (January/February), pp. 22–34.

Gastineau, Gary L. (1988) *The Options Manual*. 3rd edition. New York: McGraw-Hill.

Glassman, James K. (2002) "Faulty Analysis." *Opinion, Wall Street Journal*, (April 12) A18.

Goetzmann, William N., Jonathan Ingersoll Jr., and Stephen A. Ross. (2001) "High-Water Marks and Hedge Fund Management Contracts." Yale ICF Working Paper No. 00-34 (April 18).

Goldman, Sachs & Co., and Financial Risk Management Ltd. (1999) "The Hedge Fund Industry and Absolute Return Funds." *Journal of Alternative Investments*, Vol. 1, No. 4 (Spring), pp. 11–27.

Goldman, Sachs & Co., and Frank Russell Company. (2001) *Alternative Investing by Tax-Exempt Organizations 2001—A Survey of Organizations in North America, Europe, Australia and Japan*.

Golin/Harris Ludgate. (2001) *The Future Role of Hedge Funds in European Institutional Asset Management 2001*. Survey.

Grinblatt, Mark, and Sheridan Titman. (1989) "Mutual Fund Performance: An Analysis of Quarterly Portfolio Holdings." *Journal of Business*, 62, pp. 393–416.

Grinold, Richard C. (1989) "The Fundamental Law of Active Management." *Journal of Portfolio Management*, Vol. 15, No. 3 (Spring), pp. 30–37.

Grinold, Richard C., and Ronald N. Kahn. (2000a) *Active Portfolio Management—A Quantitative Approach for Producing Superior Returns and Controlling Risk*, 2nd edition. New York: McGraw-Hill.

Grinold, Richard C., and Ronald N. Kahn. (2000b) "The Efficiency Gains of Long-Short Investing." *Financial Analysts Journal*, Vol. 56, No. 6 (November/December), pp. 40–53. Article is based on Chapter 15 in Grinold and Kahn (2000a).

Grossman, S. (1976) "On the Efficiency of Competitive Stock Markets Where Trades Have Diverse Information." *Journal of Finance*, Vol. 31, pp. 573–585.

Hagstrom, Robert G., Jr. (1994) *The Warren Buffett Way: Investment Strategies of the World's Greatest Investor*. New York: John Wiley & Sons.

Harcourt Investment Consulting AG. (2002) "New Trends and Developments in the Hedge Fund Industry." Presented by Dr. Philipp Cottier, Hedge Fund Middle East 2002 conference, Terrapinn, Dubai, February 6.

HBS. (1999) *Long-Term Capital Management, L.P. (A) Boston:* Harvard Business School, 9-200-007 (November. 5).

Ikenberry, David L., Richard L. Shockley, and Kent L. Womack. (1998) "Why Active Fund Managers Often Underperform the S&P 500: The Impact of Size and Skewness." *Journal of Private Portfolio Management*, Vol. 1, No. 1 (Spring), pp. 13–26.

Indocam/Watson Wyatt. (2000) "Alternative Investment Review Relating to the Continental European Marketplace." (May). Survey.

Ineichen, Alexander M. (2000a) "Twentieth Century Volatility—A Review of Stock Market Volatility in the Twentieth Century." *Journal of Portfolio Management*, Vol. 27, No. 1 (Fall), pp. 93–101

Ineichen, Alexander M. (2000b) "The Risks of Hedge Funds." In Virginia Reynolds Parker, ed., *Managing Hedge Fund Risk—From the Seat of the Practitioner*. London: Risk Books.

Ineichen, Alexander M. (2001a) "The Myths of Hedge Funds—Are Hedge Funds Fireflies Ahead of the Storm?" *Journal of Global Financial Markets*, Vol. 2, No. 4 (Winter), pp. 34–46.

Ineichen, Alexander M. (2001b) "Hedge Funds: Bubble or New Paradigm?" *Journal of Global Financial Markets*, Vol. 2, No. 4 (Winter), pp. 55–63.

Ineichen, Alexander M. (2002a) "Fund of Hedge Funds: Industry Overview—Advantages and Disadvantages of Investing in Fund of Hedge Funds." *Journal of Wealth Management*, Vol. 4, No. 4 (Spring), pp. 47–62.

Ineichen, Alexander M. (2002b) "The Alpha in Fund of Hedge Funds." *Journal of Wealth Management*, Vol. 5, No. 1 (Summer), pp. 8–25.

Ineichen, Alexander M. (2002c) "Who's Long? Market-Neutral versus Long/Short Equity." *Journal of Alternative Investments*, Vol. 4, No. 4 (Spring), pp. 62–69.

*Institutional Investor* (2000), Europe edition (July 15).

Jacobs, Bruce I. (1998) "Controlled Risk Strategies." in *Alternative Investing*, ICFA Continuing Education, AIMR (August), No. 5, pp. 70–81.

Jacobs, Bruce I., and Kenneth N. Levy. (1995) "More on Long-Short Strategies." *Financial Analysts Journal*, Vol. 51, No. 2 (March/April), pp. 88–90.

Jacobs, Bruce I., and Kenneth N. Levy. (1996) "20 Myths about Long-Short." *Financial Analysts Journal*, Vol. 52, No. 5 (September/October), pp. 81–85.

Jacobs, Bruce I., and Kenneth N. Levy. (1997) "The Long and Short on Long-Short." *Journal of Investing*, Vol. 6, No. 1 (Spring), pp. 73–86.

Jacobs, Bruce I., and Kenneth N. Levy. (1998) "On the Optimality of Long-Short Strategies." *Financial Analysts Journal*, Vol. 54, No. 2 (March/April), pp. 40–51.

Jaeger, Robert A. (2000) "Fund of Funds Risk: Defining It, Measuring It and Managing it." In Virginia Reynolds Parker. ed., *Managing Hedge Fund Risk—From the Seat of the Practitioner*. London: Risk Books.

Jegadeesh, Narasimhan, and Sheridan Titman. (1993) "Returns to Buying Winners and Selling Losers: Implications for Stock Market Efficiency." *Journal of Finance*, Vol. 48 (March), pp. 65–91.

Jorion, Philippe. (2000) "Risk Management Lessons from Long-Term Capital Management." *European Financial Management*, 6 (September) pp. 277–300.

Jorion, Philippe, and William N. Goetzmann. (1999) "Global Stock Markets in the Twentieth Century." *Journal of Finance*, Vol. 54, No. 3 (June), pp. 953–980.

Jundt, James R. (2002) "Management von Hedge Funds—Praxiserfahrungen." Speech at Euroforum conference "Alternative Investments," Frankfurt, February 27.

Kahneman, Daniel, and Amos Tversky. (1979) "Prospect Theory: An Analysis of Decision under Risk." *Econometrica*, Vol. 47, pp. 263–291.

Kahneman, Daniel, and Mark W. Riepe. (1998) "Aspects of Investor Psychology—Beliefs, Preferences, and Biases Investment Advisors Should Know About." *Journal of Portfolio Management*, Vol. 24, No. 4 (Summer), pp. 52–65.

Kao, Duen-Li. (2002) "Battle for Alphas: Hedge Funds versus Long-Only Portfolios." *Financial Analysts Journal*, Vol. 58, No. 2 (March/April), pp. 16–36.

Keynes, John Maynard. (1936) *The General Theory of Employment, Interest, and Money*. New York: Harcourt, Brace & World.

Kritzman, Mark P. (2000) Puzzles of Finance—Six Practical Problems and Their Remarkable Solutions. New York: John Wiley & Sons.

Kuhn, Thomas. (1962) *The Structure of Scientific Revolutions*. Chicago: University of Chicago Press.

Lakonishok, Josef, Andrei Shleifer, and Robert W. Vishny. (1994) "Contrarian Investment, Extrapolation, and Risk." *Journal of Finance*, Vol. 49, pp. 1541–1578.

Lamm, R. McFall, Jr. (1999) "Portfolios of Alternative Assets: Why Not 100% Hedge Funds?" *Journal of Investing*, Vol. 8, No. 4 (Winter), pp. 87–97.

Le Bon, Gustave. (1982) "The Crowd—A Study of the Popular Mind," 2nd Edition. Atlanta: Cherokee Publishing Company. First published 1896, New York: Macmillan.

Leong, Clint Tan Chee, Michael J. Seiler, and Mark Lane. (2002) "Explaining Apparent Stock Market Anomalies: Irrational Exuberance or Archetypal Human Psychology." *Journal of Wealth Management*, Vol. 4, No. 4 (Spring), pp. 8–23.

Lewis, Michael. (1989) *Liar's Poker—Rising through the Wreckage on Wall Street*. New York: Penguin Books.

Liang, Bing. (1999) "On the Performance of Hedge Funds." *Financial Analysts Journal*, Vol. 55, No. 4 (July/August), pp. 72–85.

Lo, Andrew W. (2001) "Risk Management for Hedge Funds: Introduction and Overview." *Financial Analysts Journal*, Vol. 57, No. 6 (November/December), pp. 16–33.

Lo, Andrew W., and A. Craig MacKinlay. (1999) *A Non-random Walk Down Wall Street*. Princeton: Princeton University Press.

Lowenstein, R. (2000) *When Genius Failed—The Rise and Fall of Long-Term Capital Management*. New York: Random House.

Ludgate Communications. (2000) "The Future Role of Hedge Funds in European Institutional Asset Management" (March). Survey.

Malkiel, Burton G. (1995) "Returns from Investing in Equity Mutual Funds, 1971 to 1991." *Journal of Finance*, Vol. 50, No. 2 (June), pp. 549–572.

Martino, Roxanne M. (1999) "The Due Diligence Process." In Ronald A. Lake, ed., *Evaluating and Implementing Hedge Fund Strategies*, 2nd edition. London: Euromoney Books.

McCarthy, Charles. (2000) "Index Links." *Risk & Reward* (Winter).

McCarthy, David, and Richard Spurgin. (1998a) "A Comparison of Return Patterns in Traditional and Alternative Investments." In Sohail Jaffer, ed., *Alternative Investment Strategies*. London: Euromoney Books.

McCarthy, David, and Richard Spurgin. (1998b) "A Review of Hedge Fund Performance Benchmarks." *Journal of Alternative Investment*, Vol. 1, No. 1 (Summer), pp. 18–28.

McCormack, Mark. (1984) *What They Don't Teach You at Harvard Business School*. Glasgow: William Collins.

Mehra, Raj, and Edward C. Prescott. (1985) "The Equity Premium: A Puzzle." *Journal of Monetary Economics*, Vol. 15, No. 2, pp. 145–161.

Michaud, Richard. (1989) "The Markowitz Optimization Enigma: Is Optimized Optimal?" *Financial Analysts Journal*, Vol. 45, No. 1 (January/February), pp. 31–42.

Michaud, Richard. (1993) "Are Long-Short Equity Strategies Superior?" *Fi-*

*nancial Analysts Journal*, Vol. 49, No. 6 (November/December), pp. 44–49.

Michaud, Richard. (1994) "Reply to Arnott and Leinweber." Comment, *Financial Analysts Journal*, Vol. 50, No. 5 (September/October), pp. 78–80.

Miller, Edward M. (1987) "Bounded Efficient Markets: A New Wrinkle to the EMH." *Journal of Portfolio Management*, Vol. 13, No. 4 (Summer), pp. 4–13.

Miller, William P., II. (2000) "Fund of Funds: Risk Management Issues for Endowments and Foundations." In Virginia Reynolds Parker, ed., *Managing Hedge Fund Risk—From the Seat of the Practitioner*. London: Risk Books.

Mitchell, Mark, and Todd Pulvino. (2001) "Characteristics of Risk and Return in Risk Arbitrage." *Journal of Finance*, Vol. 56, No. 6 (June), pp. 2135–2175.

Moller, Thomas W. (2001) "Portable Alpha: Managed Futures as a Source of Excess Return." *Journal of Alternative Investments*, Vol. 4, No. 3 (Winter), pp. 59–68.

Moore, Keith M. (1999) *Risk Arbitrage—An Investor's Guide*. New York: John Wiley & Sons.

Morgan Stanley Dean Witter. (2001) "Hedge Funds—Strategy and Portfolio Insights." *Morgan Stanley Quantitative Strategies* (December).

Neill, Humphrey B. (2001) *The Art of Contrary Thinking—It Pays to Be Contrary!* 5th and enlarged edition. Caldwell: Caxton Press. First published 1954.

Nicholas, Joseph G. (1999) *Investing in Hedge Funds—Strategies for the New Marketplace*. Princeton: Bloomberg Press.

Nicholas, Joseph G. (2000) *Market-Neutral Investing—Long/Short Hedge Fund Strategies*. Princeton: Bloomberg Press.

Niederhoffer, Victor. (1997) *The Education of a Speculator*. New York: John Wiley & Sons.

Norton, L. P. (1996) "The Outliers: Refusing to Run with the Herd Can Be Dangerous, But It Can Pay Off." *Barron's* (May 20).

Olsen, R. (1998) "Behavioral Finance and Its Implications for Stock Price Volatility." *Financial Analysts Journal*, Vol. 54, No. 2 (March/April), pp. 10–18.

Park, James, Stephen J. Brown, and William N. Goetzmann. (1999) "Performance Benchmarks and Survivorship Bias for Hedge Funds and Commodity Trading Advisors." *Hedge Fund News* (August).

Peltz, Lois. (1995) "Track Record Length: The Ins and Outs of Hedge Fund Size." In Jess Lederman and Robert A. Klein, eds., *Hedge Funds*. New York: McGraw-Hill.

Peltz, Lois. (2001) *The New Investment Superstars—13 Great Investors and Their Strategies for Superior Returns*. New York: John Wiley & Sons.

Pension & Endowment Forum. (2000) *Hedge Funds Revisited*. Goldman, Sachs & Co. and Financial Risk Management Ltd.

Persaud, Avinash. (2001) "Liquidity Black Holes." State Street Working Paper (December.)

Peters, T. J., and R. H. Waterman. (1982) *In Search of Excellence: Lessons from America's Best Run Corporations*. New York: HarperCollins.

President's Working Group on Financial Markets. (1999) *Hedge Funds, Leverage, and the Lessons of Long-Term Capital Management*. Washington, D.C. Report.

Rahl, Leslie. (2000) "Risk Budgeting: The Next Step of the Risk Management Journey—A Veteran's Perspective." In Leslie Rahl, ed., *Risk Budgeting—A New Approach to Investing*. London: Risk Books.

Reuters. (2002) "Woman Unite to Cut into Hedge Funds' Male Ticket," by Svea Herbst-Bayliss (February 6).

Rogers, Jim. (2000) *Investment Biker—Around the World with Jim Rogers*. Chichester: John Wiley & Sons. First published 1994 by Beeland Interest, Inc.

Rohrer, Julie. (1986) "The Red-Hot World of Julian Robertson." *Institutional Investor* (May), pp. 86–92.

Samuelson, Paul A. (1965a) "Proof That Properly Anticipated Prices Fluctuate Randomly." *Industrial Management Review* 6 (Spring), pp. 41–49.

Samuelson, Paul A. (1965b) "Rational Theory of Warrant Price." *Industrial Management Review* 6 (Spring), pp. 13–39.

Samuelson, William, and Richard Zeckhauser. (1988) "Status-Quo Bias in Decision Making." *Journal of Risk and Uncertainty*, Vol. 1, pp. 7–59.

Savage, Leonard J. (1954) "The Sure-Thing Principle." The Foundations of Statistics. New York: John Wiley & Sons.

Schneeweis, Thomas. (1998a) "Dealing with Myths of Managed Futures." *Journal of Alternative Investments*, Vol. 1, No. 1 (Summer), pp. 9–17.

Schneeweis, Thomas. (1998b) "Dealing with Myths of Hedge Fund Investment." *Journal of Alternative Investments*, Vol. 1, No. 3 (Winter), pp. 11–15.

Schneeweis, Thomas. (1998c) "Evidence of Superior Performance Persistence in Hedge Funds: An Empirical Comment." *Journal of Alternative Investments*, Vol. 1, No. 2 (Fall), pp. 76–79.

Schneeweis, Thomas, and George Martin. (2001) "The Benefits of Hedge Funds: Asset Allocation for the Institutional Investor." *Journal of Alternative Investments*, Vol. 4, No. 3 (Winter), pp. 7–26.

Schneeweis, Thomas, and Joseph F. Pescatore. (1999) "Alternative Asset Returns: Theoretical Bases and Empirical Evidence." In *The Handbook of Alternative Investment Strategies*. New York: Institutional Investor Inc.

Schneeweis, Thomas, and Richard Spurgin. (1998) "Multifactor Analysis of Hedge Fund, Managed Futures, and Mutual Funds Return and Risk

Characteristics." *Journal of Alternative Investments*, Vol. 1, No. 2 (Fall), pp. 1–24.

Schneeweis, Thomas, and Richard Spurgin. (1999) "Alpha, Alpha . . . Who's Got the Alpha?" *Journal of Alternative Investments*, Vol. 2, No. 3 (Winter), pp. 83–87.

Schneeweis, Thomas, and Richard Spurgin. (2000) "Hedge Funds: Portfolio Risk Diversifiers, Return Enhancers or Both?" CISDM Working Paper (July 31).

Schwed, Fred, Jr. (1995) *Where Are the Customers' Yachts? or, A Good Hard Look at Wall Street*. New York: John Wiley & Sons. Originally published in 1940 by Simon & Schuster.

Scott, James, Mark Stumpp, and Peter Xu. (1999) "Behavioral Bias, Valuation, and Active Management." *Financial Analysts Journal*, Vol. 55, No. 4 (July/August), pp. 49–57.

Securities and Exchange Commission. (1999) *SEC Concept Release: Short Sales*. No. 34-42037. www.sec.gov/rules/concept/34-42037.htm#P39_7779s.

Sharpe, William. (1992) "Asset Allocation: Management Style and Performance Measurement." *Journal of Portfolio Management*, Vol. 18, No. 2 (Winter), pp. 7–19.

Shefrin, Hersh. (2000) *Beyond Greed and Fear*. Boston: Harvard Business School Press.

Sherden, William A. (1998) *The Fortune Sellers—The Big Business of Buying and Selling Predictions*. New York: John Wiley & Sons.

Shiller, Robert J. (1981) "Do Stock Prices Move Too Much to Be Justified by Subsequent Movements in Dividends?" *American Economic Review*, Vol. 71, No. 3, pp. 421–436.

Shiller, Robert J. (1984) "Stock Prices and Social Dynamics." *Brookings Papers on Economic Activity* 2, pp. 457–498.

Shiller, Robert J. (1989) *Market Volatility*. Cambridge, MA: MIT Press.

Shiller, Robert J. (1990) "Market Volatility and Investor Behavior." *American Economic Review*, Vol. 80, No. 2, pp. 58–62.

Shiller, Robert J. (1997) "Human Behavior and the Efficiency of the Financial System." NBER Working Paper (September 27).

Shiller, Robert J. (2000) *Irrational Exuberance*. Princeton: Princeton University Press.

Singer, Brian, Renato Staub, and Kevin Terhaar. (2001) "The Appropriate Policy Allocation for Alternative Investments." UBS Global Asset Management Working Paper (June).

Smith, Roy C., and Ingo Walter. (1997) *Street Smarts—Linking Professional Conduct with Shareholder Value in the Securities Industry*. Boston: Harvard Business School Press.

Sokal, Alan, and Jean Bricmont. (1998) *Fashionable Nonsense—Postmodern Intellectuals' Abuse of Science*. New York: Picador USA.

Soros, George. (1987) *The Alchemy of Finance: Reading the Mind of the Market*. New York: John Wiley & Sons.

Soros, George. (1994) "The Theory of Reflexivity." MIT Department of Economics World Economy Laboratory Conference, Washington D.C., April 26.

Soros, George, with Byron Wien and Krisztina Koenen. (1995) *Soros on Soros—Staying Ahead of the Curve*. New York: John Wiley & Sons.

*Sound Practices for Hedge Fund Managers* (2000), report by Caxton Corporation et al. (February).

Staley, Kathryn F. (1997) *The Art of Short Selling*. New York: John Wiley & Sons.

Standard & Poor's. (2002) "Record Defaults in 2001 the Result of Poor Credit Quality and a Weak Economy." Special Report, *Ratings Performance 2001* (February).

Swank, Peter B., Michael A. Rosen, and James W. Goebel. (2002) "The Next Step: 100% Equity Allocation for Pension Plans." *Journal of Investing*, Vol. 11, No. 1 (Spring), pp. 37–44.

Swensen, David F. (2000) *Pioneering Portfolio Management—An Unconventional Approach to Institutional Investment*. New York: Free Press.

Taleb, Nassim Nicholas. (2001) *Fooled by Randomness: The Hidden Role of Chance in the Markets and in Life*. New York: Textere.

Thaler, Richard H., and J. Peter Williamson. (1994) "College and University Endowment Funds: Why Not 100% Equities?" *Journal of Portfolio Management*, Vol. 21, No. 1 (Fall), pp. 27–37.

Thorp, Edward O., and Sheen T. Kassouf. (1967) *Beat the Market*. New York: Random House.

Train, John. (1981) *The Money Masters*. New York: Penguin Books.

Tremont Advisors. (2002) "The TASS Asset Flow Report—Third Quarter 2001."

Tremont Partners Inc. and TASS Investment Research. (1999) "The Case for Hedge Funds."

Tversky, Amos. (1995) "The Psychology of Decision Making." *Behavioral Finance and Decision Theory in Investment Management*, AIMR, No. 7.

Tversky, Amos, and Daniel Kahneman. (1974) "Judgement under Uncertainty: Heuristics and Biases." *Science*, 185.

Tversky, Amos, and Daniel Kahneman. (1992) "Advances in Prospect Theory: Cumulative Representation of Uncertainty." *Journal of Risk and Uncertainty*, Vol. 5, pp. 297–323.

UBS Warburg. (2000) "In Search of Alpha—Investing in Hedge Funds." *UBS Warburg Global Equity Research* (October). Extracts reprinted with permission.

UBS Warburg. (2001) "The Search for Alpha Continues—Do Fund of Hedge

Funds Managers Add Value?" *UBS Warburg Global Equity Research* (September). Extracts reprinted with permission.

Von Mises, Ludwig. (1996) *Human Action—A Treatise on Economics*, 4th edition. San Francisco: Fox & Wilkes. First published 1949 by Yale University.

Wace, Ian. (2000) "Hedge Funds in Europe." Speech at the 2000 Hedge Fund Symposium (EIM/EuroHedge/SFI), "Can Institutions Afford to Ignore Hedge Funds?" April 27, London.

*Wall Street Journal*. (2002) "Buying and Selling." *Review & Outlook*, April 12, A18.

Wall Street Journal Online. (2002) "Europe Hedge Fund Growth Slows to 40% in '01." (February 25).

Warburg Dillon Read. (1998) "The Reality of Hedge Funds." Warburg Dillon Read Equity Derivative and Quantitative Research, October 30.

Warwick, Ben. (2000) *Searching for Alpha—The Quest for Exceptional Investment Performance*. New York: John Wiley & Sons.

Weinstein, Meyer H. (1931) *Arbitrage in Securities*, New York: Harper & Brothers.

White, David A. (1995) "Investing in Hedge Funds: Investment Policy Implications." In Jess Lederman and Robert A. Klein, eds., *Hedge Funds*. New York: McGraw-Hill.

White, David A. (1996) "Introduction to Market-Neutral Investing." In Jess Lederman and Robert A. Klein, eds., *Market Neutral*. New York: McGraw-Hill.

Yale Endowment. (2001) Endowment Update, Fiscal Year 2001.

Zulauf, Felix W. (2002a) "Management von Hedge Funds—Praxisbericht." Speech at Euroforum conference "Alternative Investments," Frankfurt, February 27.

Zulauf, Felix W. (2002b) "Swiss Seer Ends His Silence, but with No Welcome Tidings." Interview in *International Herald Tribune* (March 2).

**A**lexander Ineichen, Managing Director, is Head of Equity Derivatives Research for UBS Warburg in London. He started his financial career in origination of risk management products at Swiss Bank Corporation (which today is UBS Warburg, the investment banking arm of UBS AG) in 1988 and has been in equity derivatives research since 1991. In his current role he oversees research on equity derivatives and indexes, a research product on capital flows and hedge funds.

Mr. Ineichen is the author of "In Search of Alpha—Investing in Hedge Funds" (October 2000), which has been the most often printed research publication in the documented history of UBS Warburg, and the author of "The Search for Alpha Continues—Do Fund of Hedge Funds Add Value?" (September 2001), the second most often printed research note at UBS Warburg. Mr. Ineichen has published research on equity derivatives and hedge funds in (peer-refereed) journals such as the *Journal of Portfolio Management*, *Journal of Alternative Investments*, *Derivatives Quarterly*, *Journal of Wealth Management*, and *Journal of Global Financial Markets*. In addition, he has written several book chapters as well as articles in financial magazines.

Mr. Ineichen holds a federal diploma in economics and business administration from the School of Economics and Business Administration (SEBA) in Switzerland and is a Chartered Financial Analyst (CFA). He is in the Index Advisory Committee of STOXX, and is a member of the Association for Investment Management and Research (AIMR) and the United Kingdom Society of Investment Professionals (UKSIP). He is married and has two children and lives in London, United Kingdom.